THE POLICE FUNCTION

SIXTH EDITION

by

FRANK W. MILLER
James Carr Professor Emeritus of Criminal Jurisprudence,
Washington University

ROBERT O. DAWSON
Bryant Smith Chair in Law,
University of Texas

GEORGE E. DIX
A. W. Walker Centennial Chair in Law,
University of Texas

RAYMOND I. PARNAS
Professor of Law Emeritus,
University of California, Davis

NEW YORK, NEW YORK
FOUNDATION PRESS
2000

Reprinted from
Miller, Dawson, Dix and Parnas'
Cases and Materials on Criminal Justice Administration
(Fifth Edition)
Pages 1–601

*TEXT IS PRINTED ON 10% POST
CONSUMER RECYCLED PAPER*

PREFACE

These materials are a complete extract of the Introduction and Chapters 1 through 10 of Miller, Dawson, Dix, and Parnas, Criminal Justice Administration (Fifth Edition, 2000).

The focus of these materials is upon the police role in the modern criminal justice process and the difficult legal issues that are raised by modern policing methods. Criminal defendants' right to have certain evidence excluded from trial where a violation of the defendants' rights occurred in the gathering of evidence, of course, is a consideration that runs throughout the materials.

In each chapter we have endeavored to present legal issues in the context in which they are raised in the criminal justice process. This, we hope, enables the student to gain some appreciation of the extent to which the legal system deals realistically with police practices and of the impact, if any, of various legal norms on police activities.

Footnotes retained from material reprinted have been renumbered. Footnotes added by the editors have been identified by number. Footnotes and textual citations to authority have been deleted from principal opinions without specific indication of the omissions. Editors' footnotes are indicated by letters. We have noted omitted opinions in principal cases only when, in our view, the existence of such opinions is useful in understanding the procedural or precedential significance of the opinion reprinted.

FRANK W. MILLER
ROBERT O. DAWSON
GEORGE E. DIX
RAYMOND I. PARNAS

March, 2000

*

SUMMARY OF CONTENTS

TABLE OF CONTENTS

*

TABLE OF CASES

Principal cases are in bold type. Non-principal cases are in roman type. References are to Pages.

xix TABLE OF CASES

THE POLICE FUNCTION

*

Analysis

NATIONAL ADVISORY COMMISSION ON CRIMINAL JUSTICE STANDARDS AND GOALS, COURTS 11–15 (1973)

* * *

ARREST

The first formal contact of an accused with the criminal justice system is likely to be an arrest by a police officer. In most cases, the arrest will be made upon the police officer's own evaluation that there is sufficient basis for believing that a crime had been committed by the accused. However, the arrest may be made pursuant to a warrant; in this case, the police officer or some other person will have submitted the evidence against the accused to a judicial officer, who determines whether the evidence is sufficient to justify an arrest. In some situations, the accused may have no formal contact with the law until he has been indicted by a grand jury. Following such an indictment, a court order may be issued authorizing police officers to take the accused into custody. But these are exceptional situations. Ordinarily, the arrest is made without any court order and the court's contact with the accused comes only after the arrest.

* * *

INITIAL JUDICIAL APPEARANCE

In all jurisdictions, a police officer or other person making an arrest must bring the arrested person before a judge within a short period of time. It is at this initial appearance that most accused have their first contact with the courts. This initial appearance is usually before a lower court—a justice of the peace or a magistrate. * * * Often by the time of the initial appearance, the prosecution will have prepared a formal document called a complaint, which charges the defendant with a specific crime.

At the initial appearance, several things may occur. First, the defendant will be informed of the charges against him, usually by means of the complaint. Second, he will be informed of his rights, including his constitutional privilege against self-incrimination. Third, if the case is one in which the accused will be provided with an attorney at State expense, the mechanical process of assigning the attorney at least may begin at this stage. Fourth, unless the defendant is convicted of an offense at this point, arrangements may be made concerning the release of the defendant before further proceedings. This may take the traditional form of setting bail, that is, establishment of an amount of security the defendant himself or a professional bondsman whom he may hire must deposit with the court (or assume the obligation to pay) to assure that the defendant does appear for later proceedings. Pre-trial release, in some jurisdictions, also may take the form of being released on one's own recognizance, that is, release simply upon the defendant's promise to appear at a later time. * * *

In addition to these matters collateral to the issue of guilt, it is at the initial appearance that judicial inquiry into the merits of the case begins. If the charge is one the lower court has authority to try, the defendant may be asked how he pleads. If he pleads guilty, he may be convicted at this point. If he pleads not guilty, a trial date may be set and trial held later in this court.

However, if the charge is more serious, the court must give the defendant the opportunity for a judicial evaluation to determine whether there is enough evidence to justify putting him to trial in the higher court. In this type of case, the judge at the initial appearance ordinarily will ask the defendant whether he wants a preliminary hearing. If the defendant does, the matter generally is continued, or postponed to give both the prosecution and the defense time to prepare their cases.

The matter will be taken up again later in the lower court at the preliminary hearing. At this proceeding, the prosecutor introduces evidence to try to prove the defendant's guilt. He need not convince the court of the defendant's guilt beyond a reasonable doubt, but need only establish that there is enough evidence from which an average person (juror) could conclude that the defendant was guilty of the crime charged. If this evidence is produced, the court may find that the prosecution has established probable cause to believe the defendant guilty.

At this preliminary hearing the defendant may cross-examine witnesses produced by the prosecution and present evidence himself. If the court finds at the end of the preliminary hearing that probable cause does not exist, it dismisses the complaint. This does not ordinarily prevent the prosecution from bringing another charge, however. If the court finds that probable cause does exist, it orders that the defendant be bound over to the next step in the prosecution. As a practical matter, the preliminary hearing also serves the function of giving the defendant and his attorney a look at the case the prosecution will produce at trial. It gives a defense attorney the opportunity to cross-examine witnesses he later will have to confront. This informal previewing function may be more valuable to defendants than the theoretical function of the preliminary hearing.

FILING OF FORMAL CRIMINAL CHARGE

Generally, it is following the decision of the lower court to bind over a defendant that the formal criminal charge is made in the court that would try the case if it goes to formal trial. If no grand jury action is to be taken, this is a simple step consisting of the prosecutor's filing a document called an information. But in many jurisdictions the involvement of the grand jury makes the process more complex. There, the decision at the preliminary hearing simply is to bind the defendant over for consideration by the grand jury. In these areas, the prosecutor then must go before the grand jury and again present his evidence. Only if the grand jury determines that there is probable cause does it act. Its action—consisting of issuing a document called an indictment—constitutes the formal charging of the defendant. If it does not find probable cause, it takes no action and the prosecution is dismissed.

In some jurisdictions, it is not necessary to have both a grand jury inquiry and a preliminary hearing. In most Federal jurisdictions, for example, if a defendant has been indicted by a grand jury he no longer has a right to a preliminary hearing, on the theory that he is entitled to only one determination as to whether probable cause exists.

Although the defendant is entitled to participate in the preliminary hearing, he has no right to take part in a grand jury inquiry. Traditionally, he has not been able to ascertain what went on in front of the grand jury, although increasingly the law has given him the right, after the fact, to know.

Following the formal charge—whether it has been by indictment or information—any of a variety of matters that require resolution may arise. The defendant's competency to stand trial may be in issue. This requires the court to resolve the question of whether the defendant is too ill mentally or otherwise impaired to participate meaningfully in his trial. If he is sufficiently impaired, trial must be postponed until he regains his competency.

The defendant also may challenge the validity of the indictment or information or the means by which they were issued. For example, he may assert that those acts with which he is charged do not constitute a crime under the laws of the jurisdiction. Or, if he was indicted by a grand jury, he may assert that the grand jury was selected in a manner not consistent with State or Federal law and, therefore, that the indictment is invalid.

A defendant also may—and in some jurisdictions must—raise, before trial, challenges to the admissibility of certain evidence, especially evidence seized by police officers in a search or statements obtained from him by interrogation. In view of the rapid growth of legal doctrine governing the admissibility of statements of defendants and evidence obtained by police search and seizure, resolution of the issues raised by defendants' challenges to the admissibility of such evidence may be more complex and time-consuming than anything involved in determining guilt or innocence.

* * *

ARRAIGNMENT

In view of the potential complexity of pretrial matters, much of the significant activity in a criminal prosecution already may have occurred at the time the defendant makes his first formal appearance before the court that is to try him. This first appearance—the arraignment—is the point at which he is asked to plead to the charge. He need not plead, in which case a plea of not guilty automatically is entered for him. If he pleads guilty, the law requires that certain precautions be taken to assure that this plea is made validly. Generally, the trial judge accepting the plea first must inquire of the defendant whether he understands the charge against him and the penalties that may be imposed. The judge also must assure himself that there is some reasonable basis in the facts of the case for the plea. This may involve requiring the prosecution to present some of its evidence to assure the court that there is evidence tending to establish guilt.

TRIAL

Unless the defendant enters a guilty plea, the full adversary process is put into motion. The prosecution now must establish to a jury or a judge the guilt of the defendant beyond a reasonable doubt. If the defendant elects to have the case tried by a jury, much effort is expended on the selection of a jury. Prospective jurors are questioned to ascertain whether they might be biased and what their views on numerous matters might be. Both sides have the right to have a potential juror rejected on the ground that he may be biased. In addition, both have the right to reject a limited number of potential jurors without having to state any reason. When the jury has been selected and convened, both sides may make opening statements explaining what they intend to prove or disprove.

The prosecution presents its evidence first, and the defendant has the option of making no case and relying upon the prosecution's inability to establish guilt beyond a reasonable doubt. He also has the option of presenting evidence tending to disprove the prosecution's case or tending to prove additional facts constituting a defense under applicable law. Throughout, however, the burden remains upon the prosecution. Procedurally, this is effectuated by defense motions to dismiss, which often are made after the prosecution's case has been presented and after all of the evidence is in. These motions in effect assert that the prosecution's case is so weak that no reasonable jury could conclude beyond a reasonable doubt that the defendant was guilty. If the judge grants the motion, he is in effect determining that no jury could reasonably return a verdict of guilty. This not only results in a dismissal of the prosecution but also prevents the prosecution from bringing another charge for the same crime.

After the evidence is in and defense motions are disposed of, the jury is instructed on the applicable law. Often both defense and prosecution lawyers submit instructions which they ask the court to read to the jury, and the court chooses from those and others it composes itself. It is in the formulation of these instructions that many issues regarding the definition of the applicable law arise and must be resolved. After—or sometimes before—the instructions are read, both sides present formal arguments to the jury. The jury then retires for its deliberations.

Generally, the jury may return only one of two verdicts: guilty or not guilty. A verdict of not guilty may be misleading; it may mean not that the jury believed that the defendant was not guilty but rather that the jury determined that the prosecution had not established guilt by the criterion—beyond a reasonable doubt—the law imposes. If the insanity defense has been raised, the jury may be told it should specify if insanity is the reason for acquittal; otherwise, there is no need for explanation. If a guilty verdict is returned, the court formally enters a judgment of conviction unless there is a legally sufficient reason for not doing so.

The defendant may attack his conviction, usually by making a motion to set aside the verdict and order a new trial. In his attack, he may argue that evidence was improperly admitted during the trial, that the evidence was so weak that no reasonable jury could have found that it established guilt beyond a reasonable doubt, or that there is newly discovered evidence which, had it been available at the time of trial, would have changed the result. If the court grants a motion raising one of these arguments, the effect generally is not to acquit the defendant but merely to require the holding of a new trial.

SENTENCING

Sentencing then follows. (If the court has accepted a plea of guilty, this step follows acceptance of the plea.) In an increasing number of jurisdictions, an investigation called the presentence report is conducted by professional probation officers. This involves investigation of the offense, the offender and his background, and any other matters of potential value to the sentencing judge. Following submission of the report to the court, the defendant is given the opportunity to comment upon the appropriateness of sentencing. In some jurisdictions, this has developed into a more extensive court hearing on sentencing issues, with the defendant given the opportunity to present evidence as well as argument for leniency. Sentencing itself generally is the responsibility of the judge, although in some jurisdictions juries retain that authority.

APPEAL

Following the conclusion of the proceeding in the trial court, the matter shifts to the appellate courts. In some jurisdictions, a defendant who is convicted of a minor offense in a lower court has the right to a new trial (trial de novo) in a higher court. But in most situations—and in all cases involving serious offenses—the right to appeal is limited to the right to have an appellate court examine the record of the trial proceedings for error. If error is found, the appellate court either may take definitive action—such as ordering that the prosecution be dismissed—or it may set aside the conviction and remand the case for a new trial. The latter gives the prosecution the opportunity to obtain a valid conviction. Generally, a time limit is placed upon the period during which an appeal may be taken.

COLLATERAL ATTACK

Even if no appeal is taken or the conviction is upheld, the courts' participation in the criminal justice process is not necessarily ended. To some extent, a convicted defendant who has either exhausted his appeal rights or declined to exercise them within the appropriate time limits can seek further relief by means of collateral attack upon the conviction. This method involves a procedure collateral to the standard process of conviction and appeal.

Traditionally this relief was sought by applying for a writ of habeas corpus on the ground that the conviction under which the applicant was held was invalid. Many jurisdictions have found this vehicle too cumbersome for modern problems and have developed special procedures for collateral attacks. * * *

A general view of The Criminal Justice System

This chart seeks to present a simple yet comprehensive view of the movement of cases through the criminal justice system. Procedures in individual jurisdictions may vary from the pattern shown here. The differing weights of line indicate the relative volumes of cases disposed of at various points in the system, but this is only suggestive since no nationwide data of this sort exists.

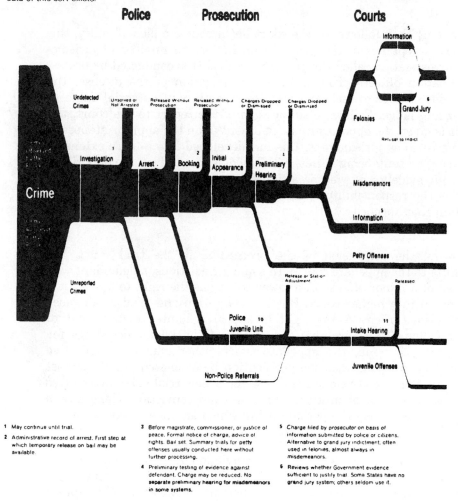

1 May continue until trial.

2 Administrative record of arrest. First step at which temporary release on bail may be available.

3 Before magistrate, commissioner, or justice of peace. Formal notice of charge, advice of rights. Bail set. Summary trials for petty offenses usually conducted here without further processing.

4 Preliminary testing of evidence against defendant. Charge may be reduced. No separate preliminary hearing for misdemeanors in some systems.

5 Charge filed by prosecutor on basis of information submitted by police or citizens. Alternative to grand jury indictment, often used in felonies, almost always in misdemeanors.

6 Reviews whether Government evidence sufficient to justify trial. Some States have no grand jury system; others seldom use it.

Source: The President's Commission on Law Enforcement and Administration of Justice, The Challenge of Crime in a Free Society (1967).

Corrections

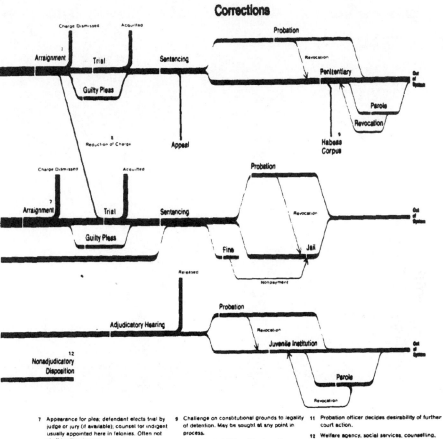

7 Appearance for plea; defendant elects trial by judge or jury (if available); counsel for indigent usually appointed here in felonies. Often not at all in other cases.

8 Charge may be reduced at any time prior to trial in return for plea of guilty or for other reasons.

9 Challenge on constitutional grounds to legality of detention. May be sought at any point in process.

10 Police often hold informal hearings, dismiss or adjust many cases without further processing.

11 Probation officer decides desirability of further court action.

12 Welfare agency, social services, counselling, medical care, etc., for cases where adjudicatory handling not needed.

*

PART ONE

INVESTIGATION OF CRIME

EDITORS' INTRODUCTION: FEDERAL AND STATE
CONSTITUTIONAL PROVISIONS AFFECTING LAW ENFORCEMENT
CONDUCT

Law enforcement conduct, and the admissibility of evidence developed by such conduct, is affected by law emanating from numerous sources other than the United States Constitution. Nevertheless, because of the United States Supreme Court's "constitutionalization" of criminal procedure, several provisions of the federal document—applicable to the states by virtue of the Fourteenth Amendment—have taken on immense significance for law enforcement activity. Much of the material in Part One of this book is devoted to exploring the content of these provisions.

United States Constitution

Amendment IV

The right of the people to be secure in their persons, houses, papers, and effects, against unreasonable searches and seizures, shall not be violated, and no Warrants shall issue, but upon probable cause, supported by Oath or affirmation, and particularly describing the place to be searched, and the persons or things to be seized.

Amendment V

No person * * * shall be compelled in any criminal case to be a witness against himself, nor be deprived of life, liberty, or property, without due process of law * * *.

Amendment VI

In all criminal prosecutions, the accused shall enjoy the right * * * to have the Assistance of Counsel for his defense.

Amendment XIV, Section 1

No State shall * * * deprive any person of life, liberty, or property, without due process of law; nor deny to any person within its jurisdiction the equal protection of the laws.

———

State constitutions usually have provisions analogous and sometimes identical to those provisions. Article 1 of the Utah constitution, for example, contains the following provisions:

Section 12. Right of accused persons

In criminal prosecutions the accused shall have the right to appear and defend in person and by counsel * * *. The accused shall not be compelled to give evidence against himself.

Section 14. Unreasonable searches forbidden—Issuance of warrant

The right of the people to be secure in their persons, houses, papers and effects against unreasonable searches and seizures shall not be violated; and no warrant shall issue but upon probable cause supported by oath or affirmation, particularly describing the place to be searched and the person or thing to be seized.

Other state provisions differ more significantly from their federal counterparts. Article 1, Section 4 of the Washington Constitution, for example, provides:

No person shall be disturbed in his private affairs, or his home invaded, without authority of law.

The state constitutional convention that proposed the Washington provision had been presented with language identical to that used in the Fourth Amendment to the United States Constitution but rejected it in favor of that finally used. See State v. Ringer, 100 Wn.2d 686, 690, 674 P.2d 1240, 1243 (1983).

Obviously, a state cannot—by constitutional provision or otherwise—deprive its citizens of rights which they have by virtue of the United States Constitution. But it is equally obvious that states can—by constitutional provision or otherwise—give their citizens more protection than those citizens are afforded by the federal Constitution. Even if a state constitutional provision is phrased similarly or identically to an analogous federal constitutional provision, the state courts need not construe the state provision as having the same content as the United States Supreme Court has given to the federal provision. State judicial willingness to "independently" construe state constitutional provisions has become widely labeled "new federalism." See, e.g., Wilkes, The New Federalism in Criminal Procedure: State Court Evasion of the Burger Court, 62 Ky.L.J. 421 (1974). The state tribunals may, of course, construe state provisions as conferring no more rights upon citizens, suspects or defendants than the Supreme Court construes the federal provisions as providing, and in fact many state courts do so.

When a state court properly construes a state provision more expansively than the Supreme Court has construed its federal counterpart is a difficult question. The Pennsylvania Supreme Court suggested it would look at four factors: 1) the text of the state constitutional provision; 2) the history of the provision, including state case law. 3) related case-law from other states; and 4) policy considerations unique to the state. Commonwealth v. Edmunds, 526 Pa. 374, 390, 586 A.2d 887, 895 (1991). In State v. Carter, 596 N.W.2d 654, 657 (Minn.1999), the Minnesota Supreme Court reviewed its "new federalism" case law. That case law, it concluded, reflects "we interpreted the Minnesota Constitution as according greater protection than the Supreme Court's interpretation of the Fourth Amendment because we viewed the Supreme Court's decisions as "radical" or "sharp" departures from precedent."

Some state courts have construed state provisions as conferring more rights upon suspects and defendants than their federal counterparts because the state tribunals concluded that the Supreme Court case law reflects inappropriate evaluation of relevant policy considerations. In State v. Mendez, 137 Wash.2d 208, 970 P.2d 722 (1999), for example, the Washington Supreme Court held that during a traffic stop the Washington constitution limits a police officer's authority to order passengers out of the vehicle. Such action is permitted only if the officer has an objective rationale for doing so based specifically on safety concerns regarding officers, vehicle occupants or other persons. As is discussed in Chapter 4, the Supreme Court has held that the Fourth Amendment requires no justification for such action by an officer. The Washington court explained its holding as based primarily upon its longstanding position that the Washington constitutional search and seizure provision recognizes greater privacy in automobiles in general and for passengers in particular than the Supreme Court has read into the Fourth Amendment.

In any case, State courts are in general agreement that a party seeking to have state courts construe state provisions as more protective of suspects and defendants than their federal counterparts must persuade the state courts of the propriety and wisdom of the proposed constructions.

> [A]   [state] court should not "cavalierly construe [the state] constitution more expansively than the United States Supreme Court has construed the federal constitution." Minnesota courts will not apply more stringent state standards, absent a compelling reason to do so.

State v. Martin, 595 N.W.2d 214, 217 (Minn.App.1999) review denied. California courts apply a "general rule of deference—that the California Constitution should only be interpreted more broadly when there are cogent reasons, independent state interests requiring additional protection, or strong countervailing policies justifying an independent reliance on a broader construction of the California Constitution." Iraheta v. Superior Court, 70 Cal.App.4th 1500, 1507, 83 Cal.Rptr.2d 471, 476 (1999) review denied. "When the issue of broader state constitutional protections arises," the Washington Supreme Court has explained, "the party seeking that broader protection must discuss reasons for reading the state provision differently from its federal counterpart." State v. Bustamante–Davila, 983 P.2d 590, 597 (Wash.1999).

These materials emphasize the federal constitutional provisions and their construction. But full treatment of these issues in state litigation cannot ignore "new federalism" and state law arguments independent of federal constitutional ones.

CHAPTER 1

THE EXCLUSIONARY SANCTION

Analysis

EDITORS' INTRODUCTION: EXCLUSIONARY RULES

The most dramatic development in American criminal procedure has been its "constitutionalization." To a significant extent, the requirements imposed by local statutes, case law and court rules have been eclipsed by the development of federal constitutional requirements. Constitutionalization of certain evidence matters by federal constitutional exclusionary requirements has been particularly important.

The major federal constitutional requirements affecting law enforcement conduct and the admissibility in a criminal trial of evidence obtained by law enforcement efforts are set out in the Editors' Introduction to Part One of these materials. These are, of course, binding on the states because of the Fourteenth Amendment. This chapter considers the enforcement of these provisions and other legal requirements by rules excluding evidence obtained in violation of their terms. The substance of these provisions is considered throughout much of the remainder of Part One; the basic contours of the Fourth and Fifth Amendments are addressed in Chapter 2.

Requirements that evidence offered by the prosecution at a criminal trial be rejected because of impropriety in the process of gathering it are often referred to as "exclusionary rules." In one sense, any legal rule resulting in evidence being held inadmissible is "exclusionary." But in common legal usage, the phrase "exclusionary rule" has come to mean a legal requirement mandating exclusion of evidence because of the illegal manner in which it was obtained. Exclusion is usually imposed without regard to whether the illegality affects the reliability of the evidence. The traditional requirement that out-of-court confessions given by defendants be "voluntary" (discussed in Chapter 7) is an exclusionary rule under this definition. But in its original form, the prohibition against the use of involuntary confessions appears to have been based more upon a perception that coercion rendered confessions unreliable than upon the desirability of responding to illegality in the interrogation process by holding the fruits of that illegality inadmissible.

Discussions are often conducted in terms of what is assumed to be "the exclusionary rule," as if only one doctrine or legal requirement is involved. This is simply not the case. "[T]he exclusionary rule" usually describes the requirement—announced in Mapp v. Ohio, reprinted in this chapter—that evidence obtained in violation of the Fourth Amendment be excluded from state criminal trials. But *Mapp* is not the only legal requirement mandating exclusion of evidence because of impropriety in the manner in which it was obtained. Other federal constitutional provisions also require exclusion of evidence obtained in violation of their requirements. Moreover, the exclusionary requirements attaching to the various federal constitutional provisions are not necessarily the same. As is developed later in these materials, for example, the extent to which evidence derived from a violation must be excluded may differ significantly depending upon whether the underlying violation is of the Fourth Amendment's requirements or, instead, of judicially-developed rules based upon the Fifth Amendment.

Evidence obtained by conduct violating state legal requirements but not a federal constitutional provision may be inadmissible as a matter of state law. If state law imposes such a requirement, the details of that requirement—as, for example, the number and scope of exceptions sometime permitting the use of illegally seized evidence—may not be the same as the details of the Fourth Amendment federal constitutional exclusionary rule.

Conceptually, then, it is best to regard exclusionary requirements as consisting of a number of potentially quite different exclusionary demands imposed by various legal requirements. There could be as many exclusionary rules as there are legal requirements that might be violated in the obtaining of evidence.

The Fourth Amendment exclusionary rule announced in Mapp v. Ohio has generated the most controversy. Consequently, these materials emphasize that holding and its development. Showings that evidence was obtained in violation of other legal requirements present distinguishable although related exclusionary rule issues.

Exclusionary rule concerns are presented throughout Part One of these materials. Chapters 2 through 6 address a variety of issues concerning law enforcement authority to make searches and seizures. Action taken beyond this authority may invoke exclusionary sanctions. While exclusionary rule considerations are less pervasive in the material addressed in Chapters 7 through 10, they are nevertheless present and important. Chapter 1 limits itself to the exclusionary sanction and its procedural aspects: When, if ever, is it appropriate? If it applies, when does it require the exclusion of challenged evidence? What exceptions to the general rule of exclusion do and should exist?

A.   ADOPTION OF THE FEDERAL CONSTITUTIONAL EXCLUSIONARY SANCTION

Exclusion of evidence resulting from improper law enforcement conduct was not a notion original with the United States Supreme Court. The Vermont court, for example, embraced an exclusionary rule as a matter of state law in State v. Slamon, 50 A. 1097 (Vt.1901). Nevertheless, the Supreme Court's adoption of this sanction for violation of federal constitutional rights is largely responsible for the pervasive impact exclusionary rules have on modern criminal procedure.

The Court's position in the case law culminating in the case reprinted in this part, Mapp v. Ohio, reflects both a break from evidence law tradition and the Court's prior position. In Adams v. New York, 192 U.S. 585, 24 S.Ct. 372, 48 L.Ed. 575 (1904), the Court rejected a state defendant's complaint regarding the use in his trial of evidence seized in violation of the Fourth Amendment. Where such evidence shows the accused's guilt, the Court explained, "the weight of authority as well as reason limits the inquiry to the competency of the proffered testimony, and the courts do not stop to inquire as to the means by which the evidence was obtained." This traditional position—that the manner in which otherwise competent evidence was obtained does not affect its admissibility—was supported by two major consideration: the need to have all available relevant evidence bearing on the important issues posed in criminal litigation, and the inconvenience, disruption, and other costs involved in making the complex and collateral inquiries determining whether challenged evidence was in fact improperly obtained. See generally, McCormick on Evidence § 164 (Fifth edition, J. Strong ed. 1999).

A major issue posed by *Mapp* is the role history should play in construction of those federal constitutional provisions applicable to law enforcement conduct. Some members of the Supreme Court believe many aspects of the Fourth Amendment's contents should be determined or informed by the "intent" or contemplation of the framers as reflected in then-current law. Thus in Wyoming v. Houghton, 526 U.S. 295, ___, 119 S.Ct. 1297, 1300, 143 L.Ed.2d 408, 414 (1999), reprinted in part in Chapter 5, Justice Scalia—writing for the Court—explained that "[i]n determining whether a particular governmental action violates [the Fourth Amendment], we inquire first whether the action was regarded as an unlawful search or seizure under the common law when the amendment was framed." Only if that inquiry provides no answer, he continued, is the Court to balance competing policy considerations in assessing the action's reasonableness. Should the Court have taken a similar approach in *Mapp*, and inquired whether under the common law in effect when the Fourth Amendment was framed a defendant such as *Mapp* was entitled to have excluded evidence improperly obtained?

The major argument against the approach applied by Justice Scalia in *Houghton* is its failure to take into account the vast difference between the common law context and modern criminal justice. In another decision relying heavily upon the common law position, the Supreme Court cautioned against excessive reliance upon this source:

> The significance accorded to [common law] authority * * * must be kept in perspective, for our decisions in this area have not "simply frozen into constitutional law those enforcement practices that existed at the time of the Fourth Amendment's passage." The common-law rules governing searches and arrests evolved in a society far simpler than ours is today. Crime has changed, as have the means of law enforcement, and it would therefore be naive to assume that those actions a constable could take in an English or American village three centuries ago should necessarily govern what we, as a society, now regard as proper. Instead, the Amendment's prohibition against "unreasonable searches and seizures" must be interpreted "in light of contemporary norms and conditions."

Steagald v. United States, 451 U.S. 204, 218 n. 10, 101 S.Ct. 1642, 1651 n. 10, 68 L.Ed.2d 38, 48 n. 10 (1981).

Mapp v. Ohio

Supreme Court of the United States, 1961.
367 U.S. 643, 81 S.Ct. 1684, 6 L.Ed.2d 1081.

■ MR. JUSTICE CLARK delivered the opinion of the Court.

Appellant stands convicted of knowingly having had in her possession and under her control certain lewd and lascivious books, pictures, and photographs * * * though "based primarily upon the introduction in evidence of lewd and lascivious books and pictures unlawfully seized during an unlawful search of defendant's home * * *." * * *

On May 23, 1957, three Cleveland police officers arrived at appellant's residence in that city pursuant to information that "a person [was] hiding out in the home, who was wanted for questioning in connection with a recent bombing, and that there was a large amount of policy paraphernalia being hidden in the home." * * * [B]ut appellant, after telephoning her attorney, refused to admit them without a search warrant. * * *

The officers again sought entrance some three hours later when four or more additional officers arrived on the scene. When Miss Mapp did not come to the door immediately, at least one of the several doors to the house was forcibly opened and the policemen gained admittance. Meanwhile Miss Mapp's attorney arrived, but the officers, having secured their own entry, and continuing in their defiance of the law, would permit him neither to see Miss Mapp nor to enter the house. It appears that Miss Mapp was halfway down the stairs from the upper floor to the front door when the officers, in this highhanded manner, broke into the hall. She demanded to see the search warrant. A paper, claimed to be a warrant, was held up by one of the officers. She grabbed the "warrant" and placed it in her bosom. A struggle ensued in which the officers recovered the piece of paper and as a result of which they handcuffed appellant because she had been "belligerent" in resisting their official rescue of the "warrant" from her person.

* * * The obscene materials for possession of which she was ultimately convicted were discovered in the course of [a] widespread search.

At the trial no search warrant was produced by the prosecution, nor was the failure to produce one explained or accounted for. * * * The Ohio Supreme Court believed a "reasonable argument" could be made that the conviction should be reversed "because the 'methods' employed to obtain the [evidence] were such as to 'offend "a sense of justice," ' " but the court found determinative the fact that the evidence had not been taken 'from defendant's person by the use of brutal or offensive physical force against defendant.' "

* * *

The State says that even if the search were made without authority, or otherwise unreasonably, it is not prevented from using the unconstitutionally seized evidence at trial, citing Wolf v. People of the State of Colorado, 1949, 338 U.S. 25, at page 33, 69 S.Ct. 1359 * * *, in which this Court did indeed hold "that in a prosecution in a State court for a State crime the Fourteenth Amendment does not forbid the admission of evidence obtained by an unreasonable search and seizure." On this appeal * * * it is urged once again that we review that holding.

I.

Seventy-five years ago, in Boyd v. United States, 1886, 116 U.S. 616, 630, 6 S.Ct. 524, 532, 29 L.Ed. 746, considering the Fourth and Fifth Amendments as running "almost into each other" on the facts before it, this Court held that the doctrines of those Amendments

"apply to all invasions on the part of the government and its employes of the sanctity of a man's home and the privacies of life. It is not the breaking of his doors, and the rummaging of his drawers, that constitutes the essence of the offence; but it is the invasion of his indefeasible right of personal security, personal liberty and private property * * * . Breaking into a house and opening boxes and drawers are circumstances of aggravation; but any forcible and compulsory extortion of a man's own testimony or of his private papers to be used as evidence to convict him of crime or to forfeit his goods, is within the condemnation * * * [of those Amendments]."

* * *

Less than 30 years after *Boyd*, this Court, in Weeks v. United States, 1914, [232 U.S. 383, 393, 34 S.Ct. 341, 344, 58 L.Ed.2d 652,] * * * [s]pecifically dealing with the use of * * * evidence unconstitutionally seized, * * * concluded:

"If letters and private documents can thus be seized and held and used in evidence against a citizen accused of an offense, the protection of the Fourth Amendment declaring his right to be secure against such searches and seizures is of no value, and, so far as those thus placed are concerned, might as well be stricken from the Constitution. The efforts of the courts and their officials to bring the guilty to punishment, praiseworthy as they are, are not to be aided by the sacrifice of those great principles established by years of endeavor and suffering which have resulted in their embodiment in the fundamental law of the land."

* * * Thus, in the year 1914, in the *Weeks* case, this Court "for the first time" held that "in a federal prosecution the Fourth Amendment barred the use of evidence secured through an illegal search and seizure."

* * * There are in the cases of this Court some passing references to the *Weeks* rule as being one of evidence. But the plain and unequivocal language of *Weeks* * * * to the effect that the *Weeks* rule is of constitutional origin, remains entirely undisturbed. * * *

II.

In 1949, 35 years after *Weeks* was announced, this Court, in Wolf v. People of the State of Colorado, supra, again for the first time, discussed the effect of the Fourth Amendment upon the States through the operation of the Due Process Clause of the Fourteenth Amendment. It said:

"[W]e have no hesitation in saying that were a State affirmatively to sanction such police incursion into privacy it would run counter to the guaranty of the Fourteenth Amendment." * * *

Nevertheless, after declaring that the "security of one's privacy against arbitrary intrusion by the police" is "implicit in 'the concept of ordered liberty' and as such enforceable against the States through the Due Process Clause," * * * and announcing that it "stoutly adhere[d]" to the *Weeks* decision, the Court decided that the *Weeks* exclusionary rule would not then be imposed upon the States as "an essential ingredient of the right." * * * The Court's reasons for not considering essential to the right to privacy, as a curb imposed upon the States by the Due Process Clause, that which decades before had been posited as part and parcel of the Fourth Amendment's limitation upon federal encroachment of individual privacy, were bottomed on factual considerations.

While they are not basically relevant to a decision that the exclusionary rule is an essential ingredient of the Fourth Amendment as the right it embodies is vouchsafed against the States by the Due Process Clause, we will consider the current validity of the factual grounds upon which *Wolf* was based.

The Court in *Wolf* * * * stated that "[t]he contrariety of views of the States" on the adoption of the exclusionary rule of *Weeks* was "particularly impressive" * * * ; and, in this connection that it could not "brush aside the experience of States which deem the incidence of such conduct by the police too slight to call for a deterrent remedy * * * by overriding the [States'] relevant rules of evidence." * * * While in 1949, prior to the *Wolf* case, almost two-thirds of the States were opposed to the use of the exclusionary rule, now, despite the *Wolf* case, more than half of those since passing upon it, by their own legislative or judicial decision, have wholly or partly adopted or adhered to the *Weeks* rule. * * * Significantly, among those now following the rule is California, which, according to its highest court, was "compelled to reach that conclusion because other remedies have completely failed to secure compliance with the constitutional provisions * * *." People v. Cahan, 1955, 44 Cal.2d 434, 445, 282 P.2d 905, 911. In connection with this California case, we note that the second basis elaborated in *Wolf* in support of its failure to enforce the exclusionary doctrine against the States was that "other means of protection" have been afforded "the right to privacy." The experience of California that such other remedies have been worthless and futile is buttressed by the experience of other States. The obvious futility of relegating the Fourth Amendment to the protection of other remedies has, moreover, been recognized by this Court since *Wolf*.

* * *

It, therefore, plainly appears that the factual considerations supporting the failure of the *Wolf* Court to include the *Weeks* exclusionary rule when it recognized the enforceability of the right to privacy against the States in 1949, while not basically relevant to the constitutional consideration, could not, in any analysis, now be deemed controlling.

III.

Some five years after *Wolf*, in answer to a plea made here Term after Term that we overturn its doctrine on applicability of the *Weeks* exclusionary rule, this Court indicated that such should not be done until the States had "adequate opportunity to adopt or reject the [*Weeks*] rule." Irvine v. People of State of California, [1954, 347 U.S. 128, 134, 74 S.Ct. 381, 384, 98 L.Ed. 561] * * *. Today we once again examine *Wolf's* constitutional documentation of the right to privacy free from unreasonable state intrusion, and, after its dozen years on our books, are led by it to close the only courtroom door remaining open to evidence secured by official lawlessness in flagrant abuse of that basic right, reserved to all persons as a specific guarantee against that very same unlawful conduct. We hold that all evidence obtained by searches and seizures in violation of the Constitution is, by that same authority, inadmissible in a state court.

IV.

Since the Fourth Amendment's right of privacy has been declared enforceable against the States through the Due Process Clause of the Fourteenth, it is enforceable against them by the same sanction of exclusion as is used against the Federal Government. Were it otherwise, then just as without the *Weeks* rule the assurance against unreasonable federal searches and seizures would be "a form of words", valueless and undeserving of mention in a perpetual charter of inestimable human liberties, so too, without that rule the freedom from state invasions of privacy would be so ephemeral and so neatly severed from its conceptual nexus with the freedom from all brutish means of coercing evidence as not to merit this Court's high regard as a freedom "implicit in 'the concept of ordered liberty.' " * * * In short, the admission of the new constitutional right by *Wolf* could not consistently tolerate denial of its most important constitutional privilege, namely, the exclusion of the evidence which an accused had been forced to give by reason of the unlawful seizure. To hold otherwise is to grant the right but in reality to withhold its privilege and enjoyment. Only last year the Court itself recognized that the purpose of the exclusionary rule "is to deter—to compel respect for the constitutional guaranty in the only effectively available way—by removing the incentive to disregard it." Elkins v. United States [1960, 364 U.S. 206, 217, 80 S.Ct. 1437, 1444, 4 L.Ed.2d 1669].

* * *

V.

Moreover, our holding that the exclusionary rule is an essential part of both the Fourth and Fourteenth Amendments is not only the logical dictate of prior cases, but it also makes very good sense. There is no war between the Constitution and common sense. Presently, a federal prosecutor may make no use of evidence illegally seized, but a State's attorney across the street may, although he supposedly is operating under the enforceable prohibitions of the same Amendment. Thus the State, by admitting evidence unlawfully seized, served to encourage disobedience to the Federal Constitution which it is bound to uphold. * * *

Federal-state cooperation in the solution of crime under constitutional standards will be promoted, if only by recognition of their now mutual obligation to respect the same fundamental criteria in their approaches. "However much in a particular case insistence upon such rules may appear as a technicality that inures to the benefit of a guilty person, the history of the criminal law proves that tolerance of shortcut methods in law enforcement impairs its enduring effectiveness." Miller v. United States, 1958, 357 U.S. 301, 313, 78 S.Ct. 1190, 1197, 2 L.Ed.2d 1332. Denying shortcuts to only one of two cooperating law enforcement agencies tends naturally to breed legitimate suspicion of "working arrangements" whose results are equally tainted. * * *

There are those who say, as did Justice (then Judge) Cardozo, that under our constitutional exclusionary doctrine "[t]he criminal is to go free because the constable has blundered." People v. Defore, [1926, 242 N.Y. 13, 21, 150 N.E. 585, 587]. In some cases this will undoubtedly be the result. But, as was said in *Elkins*, "there is another consideration—the imperative of judicial integrity." * * * The criminal goes free, if he must, but it is the law that sets him free. Nothing can destroy a government more quickly than its failure to observe its own laws, or worse, its disregard of the charter of its own existence. As Mr. Justice Brandeis, dissenting, said in Olmstead v. United States, 1928, 277 U.S. 438, 485, 48 S.Ct. 564, 575, 72 L.Ed. 944: "Our government is the potent, the omnipresent teacher. For good or for ill, it teaches the whole people by its example. * * * If the government becomes a lawbreaker, it breeds contempt for law; it invites every man to become a law unto himself; it invites anarchy." Nor can it lightly be assumed that, as a practical matter, adoption of the exclusionary rule fetters law enforcement. Only last year this Court expressly considered that contention and found that "pragmatic evidence of a sort" to the contrary was not wanting. Elkins v. United States, supra. The Court noted that

> "The federal courts themselves have operated under the exclusionary rule of *Weeks* for almost half a century; yet it has not been

suggested either that the Federal Bureau of Investigation has thereby been rendered ineffective, or that the administration of criminal justice in the federal courts has thereby been disrupted. Moreover, the experience of the states is impressive * * * . The movement towards the rule of exclusion has been halting but seemingly inexorable." * * *

The ignoble shortcut to conviction left open to the State tends to destroy the entire system of constitutional restraints on which the liberties of the people rest. Having once recognized that the right to privacy embodied in the Fourth Amendment is enforceable against the States, and that the right to be secure against rude invasions of privacy by state officers is, therefore, constitutional in origin, we can no longer permit that right to remain an empty promise. Because it is enforceable in the same manner and to like effect as other basic rights secured by the Due Process Clause, we can no longer permit it to be revocable at the whim of any police officer who, in the name of law enforcement itself, chooses to suspend its enjoyment. Our decision, founded on reason and truth, gives to the individual no more than that which the Constitution guarantees him, to the police officer no less than that to which honest law enforcement is entitled, and, to the courts, that judicial integrity so necessary in the true administration of justice.

The judgment of the Supreme Court of Ohio is reversed and the cause remanded for further proceedings not inconsistent with this opinion.

Reversed and remanded.

[The concurring opinions of JUSTICES BLACK and DOUGLAS and the dissenting opinion of JUSTICE HARLAN, joined by JUSTICES FRANKFURTER and WHITTAKER, are omitted.]

NOTES

1. **Exclusionary Sanctions for Fifth and Sixth Amendment Violations.** Following *Mapp,* the Supreme Court virtually without discussion assumed the federal constitution requires exclusion of evidence obtained in violation of the defendant's Fifth Amendment privilege against compelled self-incrimination, Miranda v. Arizona, 384 U.S. 436, 86 S.Ct. 1602, 16 L.Ed.2d 694 (1966), the Sixth Amendment right to counsel, Brewer v. Williams, 430 U.S. 387, 97 S.Ct. 1232, 51 L.Ed.2d 424 (1977), and the Sixth Amendment right to counsel during certain pretrial identification procedures, Gilbert v. California, 388 U.S. 263, 87 S.Ct. 1951, 18 L.Ed.2d 1178 (1967).

2. **Judicial Integrity.** In post-*Mapp* case law, the Supreme Court refined its view as to the policy considerations supporting the Fourth Amendment exclusionary rule developed in that case. *Mapp,* for example, relied in part upon what it called "judicial integrity." This has clearly become considerably less significant. Fifteen years after *Mapp* the Court commented:

Judicial integrity clearly does not mean that the courts must never admit evidence obtained in violation of the Fourth Amendment. * * *

The primary meaning of "judicial integrity" in the context of evidentiary rules is that the courts must not commit or encourage violations of the Constitution. In the Fourth Amendment area, however, * * * the violation is complete by the time the evidence is presented to the court. The focus therefore must be on the question whether the admission of the evidence encourages violations of Fourth Amendment rights. * * * [T]his inquiry is essentially the same as the inquiry into whether exclusion would serve a deterrent purpose.

United States v. Janis, 428 U.S. 433, 458 n. 35, 96 S.Ct. 3021, 3034 n. 35, 49 L.Ed.2d 1046, 1063 n. 35 (1976).

3. **Remedial Function.** Is the *Mapp* exclusionary requirement supportable on the ground it provides an appropriate remedy for the wrong done to the person unreasonably searched or seized? The Court has stated:

Post-*Mapp* decisions have established that the [exclusionary] rule is not a personal constitutional right. It is not calculated to redress the injury to the privacy of the victim of the search or seizure, for any "[r]eparation comes too late." Linkletter v. Walker, 381 U.S. 618, 637, 85 S.Ct. 1731, 14 L.Ed.2d 601 (1965). * * *

Stone v. Powell, 428 U.S. 465, 484–86, 96 S.Ct. 3037, 3047, 49 L.Ed.2d 1067, 1082–83 (1976).

4. **Systemic Prevention.** Most discussions of the exclusionary sanction assumes it works by consciously deterring particular officers from engaging in conduct they know will violate suspects' Fourth Amendment rights. But the sanction may prevent violations in other ways. In Stone v. Powell, 428 U.S. 465, 96 S.Ct. 3037, 49 L.Ed.2d 1067 (1976), the Court commented:

[W]e have assumed that the immediate effect of exclusion will be to discourage law enforcement officials from violating the Fourth Amendment by removing the incentive to disregard it. More importantly, over the long term, this demonstration that our society attaches serious consequences to violation of constitutional rights is thought to encourage those who formulate law enforcement policies, and the officers who implement them, to incorporate Fourth Amendment ideals into their value system.

428 U.S. at 492, 96 S.Ct. at 3051, 49 L.Ed.2d 1086–87. Even if exclusion of evidence does not cause law enforcement officials and officers to incorporate Fourth Amendment ideals into their internal value system, it may cause them to encourage compliance with the provision's requirements by the development of specific and practical guidelines and training programs. Some commentators refer to these processes by which exclusion might affect law enforcement behavior as "systemic deterrence." See Christopher Slobogin, Why Liberals Should Chuck the Exclusionary Rule, 1999 Ill.L.Rev. 363, 393 (1999).

5. **Other Uses of Unconstitutionally Obtained Evidence.** In determining whether a federal constitutional exclusionary rule should be expanded beyond a prohibition against using unconstitutionally obtained evidence at trial to prove the defendant's guilt, the Court has utilized a balancing analysis. That analysis asks how much the functions of the rule would be increased by the additional exclusion of evidence that would result from the potential expansion. Addressing this generally involves primarily a consideration of the incremental deterrence that would be accomplished. The Court then weighs against this incremental deterrence the costs of so expanding the rule, and inquires whether the incremental deterrence is worth the cost. See United States v. Calandra, 414 U.S. 338, 349–52, 94 S.Ct. 613, 620–22, 38 L.Ed.2d 561, 572–73 (1974).

In Pennsylvania Board of Probation and Parole v. Scott, 524 U.S. 357, 118 S.Ct. 2014, 141 L.Ed.2d 344 (1998), for example, the Court addressed whether evidence obtained in violation of the Fourth Amendment could be used at a parole violation hearing to prove a convicted and paroled defendant violated the conditions of parole. By a 5-to-4 vote, it held such evidence could be so used. Justice Thomas' opinion first stressed the cost of exclusion:

Because the exclusionary rule precludes consideration of reliable, probative evidence, it imposes significant costs: it undeniably detracts from the truthfinding process and allows many who would otherwise be incarcerated to escape the consequences of their actions . . * * * [O]ur cases have repeatedly emphasized that the rule's "costly toll" upon truth-seeking and law enforcement objectives presents a high obstacle for those urging application of the rule.

524 U.S. at ___, 118 S.Ct. at 2020, 141 L.Ed.2d at 352. These costs are particularly high in the parole context, the Court continued, because states give up the right to continue incarceration of convicted persons on the condition they abide by the terms and conditions of parole release. Therefore, states have an "overwhelming interest" in enforcing these terms and limits, and this interest would be frustrated by application of the exclusionary rule. Further, application of the exclusionary rule would compel the states to transform parole revocation proceedings from "a 'productive and discretionary' effort to promote the best interests of both parolees and society into trial-like proceedings less attuned to the interests of the parolee."

The deterrent effect of applying the exclusionary rule to parole revocation would not, the *Scott* majority added, outweigh these costs. Officers will often be unaware that suspects are parolees, and thus "the remote possibility that the subject is a parolee and that the evidence may be admitted at a parole revocation proceeding surely has little, if any, effect on the officer's incentives."

The state court held the Fourth Amendment exclusionary rule should apply to parole revocation proceedings but only upon proof officers who engaged in the challenged search or seizure were aware of the suspect's status as a parolee. Rejecting this view, *Scott* first indicated this "piecemeal approach" would add to exclusionary rule procedure an undesirable need to inquire into officers' knowledge of parolees' status. Even in these cases, it added, deterrence would be minimal. Police officers aware of a suspect's parolee status will be deterred by the inadmissibility of illegally-seized evidence at criminal trials. Parole officers' relationship with parolees "is more supervisory than adversarial." This means "the harsh deterrent of exclusion [from parole revocation proceedings] is unwarranted," because adequate deterrence can be achieved by "other deterrents as departmental training and discipline and the threat of damages actions."

For these reasons, the *Scott* majority declined "to extend the operation of the exclusionary rule beyond the criminal trial context" as urged by Scott.

Four members of the Court disagreed:

[T]he majority does not see that in the investigation of criminal conduct by someone known to be on parole, Fourth Amendment standards will have very little deterrent sanction unless evidence offered for parole revocation is subject to suppression for unconstitutional conduct. * * * [P]arole revocation will frequently be pursued instead of prosecution as the course of choice * * *. * * * [W]ithout a suppression remedy in revocation proceedings, there will often be no influence capable of deterring Fourth Amendment violations when parole revocation is a possible response to new crime. Suppression in the revocation proceeding cannot be looked upon, then, as furnishing merely incremental or marginal deterrence over and above the effect of exclusion in criminal prosecution. Instead, it will commonly provide the only deterrence to unconstitutional conduct when the incarceration of parolees is sought, and the reasons that support the suppression remedy in prosecution therefore support it in parole revocation.

524 U.S. at ___, 118 S.Ct. at 2027, 141 L.Ed.2d at 361–62 (Souter, J., dissenting).

In *Calandra*, using a similar analysis, the Court held the Fourth Amendment exclusionary rule does not apply before a grand jury. Thus a suspect questioned by a grand jury has no right to avoid questions based on information obtained in violation of his Fourth Amendment rights. Any increase in deterrence resulting from extending the exclusionary rule to grand juries would be "speculative and undoubtedly minimal," the Court reasoned, and applying the exclusionary demand in this area might delay and impede grand jury investigations. 414 U.S. at 351–52, 94 S.Ct. at 621–22, 38 L.Ed.2d 572–73.

The same approach used in *Calandra* and *Scott* was used in Stone v. Powell, 428 U.S. 465, 96 S.Ct. 3037, 49 L.Ed.2d 1067 (1976), to determine whether state criminal defendants who had unsuccessfully sought suppression of evidence in their state trials on Fourth Amendment grounds could seek reconsideration of the matters in federal habeas corpus proceedings. Unless such state defendants were denied in the state trial an opportunity for full and fair litigation of their Fourth Amendment claims, the Court held, the *Mapp* exclusionary requirement did not entitle them to seek federal habeas corpus relief. If permitting state defendants to seek such relief in federal court would increase the deterrent effect of the exclusionary requirement—a matter on which the Court expressed doubt—this increased deterrence would be outweighed by the costs of so expanding the rule.

Much the same approach has been taken in the Court's consideration of proposed exceptions to the general requirements of exclusion. Exceptions in general, and the "good faith" exception in particular, are addressed in Part C of this chapter.

6. **Actual Effect of Exclusion of Evidence.** Do exclusionary requirements affect law enforcement conduct? If so, how do they do so? What costs are paid for these requirements? These are matters that in theory should be subject to empirical study. Engaging in such study, however, is difficult because there are few opportunities to compare police actions subject to exclusionary sanctions and similar actions not so limited.

Many efforts to conduct such research on the effectiveness of the federal constitutional rules were reviewed in T. Perrin, H. Caldwell, C. Chase, and R. Fagan, It It's Broken, Fix It: Moving Beyond the Exclusionary Rule, 83 Iowa L.Rev. 669, 678–710 (1998). Some involved analysis of statistics regarding arrests, convictions, and suppression motions, others were conducted by direct observation of police officers, and a number undertook to survey police officers and others regarding their knowledge and attitudes. Perrin and his colleagues concluded the research is subject to methodological criticism but in general fails to support the promise that *Mapp* would "dramatically and beneficially impact[ ] police practices." They elaborated:

> The most that can be said is that *Mapp* has probably made officers more aware of the Fourth Amendment, and has increased the number of warrants they obtain, although it is less certain that it has actually affected their performance of their other duties. One costly effect of the exclusionary rule that emerges from the studies in that it has encouraged police officers to falsify their reports and their testimony.
>
> The studies show that *Mapp* has significantly increased the number of suppression motions filed * * *. The filing of these motions has driven up the cost of processing cases, and it beyond dispute that a number of apparently guilty defendants go free as a result of the rule.

83 Iowa L.Rev. at 710–11.

In 1984, the Supreme Court noted the developing research and commented on some interpretations of the leading study of the costs of *Mapp*:

> Researchers have only recently begun to study extensively the effects of the exclusionary rule on the disposition of felony arrests. One study suggests that

the rule results in the nonprosecution or nonconviction of between 0.6% and 2.35% of individuals arrested for felonies. Davies, A Hard Look at What We Know (and Still Need to Learn) About the "Costs" of the Exclusionary Rule: The NIJ Study and Other Studies of "Lost" Arrests, 1983 A.B.F.Res.J. 611, 621. The estimates are higher for particular crimes the prosecution of which depends heavily on physical evidence. Thus, the cumulative loss due to nonprosecution or nonconviction of individuals arrested on felony drug charges is probably in the range of 2.8% to 7.1%. Davies' analysis of California data suggests that screening by police and prosecutors results in the release because of illegal searches or seizures of as many as 1.4% of all felony arrestees, that 0.9% of felony arrestees are released, because of illegal searches or seizures, at the preliminary hearing or after trial, and that roughly 0.5% of all felony arrestees benefit from reversals on appeal because of illegal searches. * * *

Many * * * researchers have concluded that the impact of the exclusionary rule is insubstantial, but the small percentages with which they deal mask a large absolute number of felons who are released because the cases against them were based in part on illegal searches or seizures. * * *

United States v. Leon, 468 U.S 897, 908 n. 6, 104 S.Ct. 3405, 3412 n. 6, 82 L.Ed.2d 677,–688 n. 6 (1984).

Christopher Slobogin, Why Liberals Should Chuck the Exclusionary Rule, 1999 Ill.L.Rev. 363, 369, 394 (1999), agreeing generally with Perrin, Caldwell, Chase, and Fagan, observed "we do not know how much the [exclusionary] rule deters, * * * [and, given the limitations of empirical inquiry, w]e probably never will." With regard to "systemic" deterrence or prevention, he concluded that "the systemic deterrent effect of the exclusionary rule is just not powerful enough to overcome a police culture that is unsympathetic to rules that restrict investigative powers."

7. **Nonconstitutional Illegality.** When evidence is obtained in violation of a nonconstitutional legal requirement—such as a federal or state statute—whether exclusion is possible or required presents a more difficult question. Clearly, there is no federal or state constitutional right to have evidence excluded because of a statutory violation. A few states have statutory provisions or court rules requiring exclusion in many such situations. E.g., Vernon's Ann.Tex.Code Crim.Pro. art. 38.23 (evidence obtained in violation of "any provisions of the Constitution or laws of the State of Texas" must be excluded); Alaska Evid.R. 412 (evidence "illegally obtained" is not to be used in a criminal prosecution). Sometimes statutory requirements explicitly direct exclusion.

Courts differ in their willingness to find unexpressed legislative "intentions" that violations of statutes are to result in exclusion of evidence. The Supreme Court has held without explanation that violation of a federal statute requiring prior announcement before entering premises to execute a warrant required exclusion. Miller v. United States, 357 U.S. 301, 78 S.Ct. 1190, 2 L.Ed.2d 1332 (1958). In addition, the Supreme Court has held it has a "supervisory power" giving it authority to sometimes require exclusion of evidence obtained in violation of nonconstitutional legal requirements. McNabb v. United States, 318 U.S. 332, 63 S.Ct. 608, 87 L.Ed. 819 (1943). State courts may have a similar power. See People v. Dyla, 142 A.D.2d 423, 536 N.Y.S.2d 799 (1988). The Supreme Court has in recent cases been unwilling to exercise its supervisory power to create or develop "new" exclusionary requirements. See United States v. Payner, 447 U.S. 727, 100 S.Ct. 2439, 65 L.Ed.2d 468 (1980); United States v. Caceres, 440 U.S. 741, 99 S.Ct. 1465, 59 L.Ed.2d 733 (1979).

B.   SCOPE OF EXCLUSIONARY SANCTIONS: STANDING, FRUIT OF THE POISONOUS TREE, INDEPENDENT SOURCE AND ATTENUATION OF THE TAINT

EDITORS' INTRODUCTORY NOTE: EXCLUSIONARY SANCTION ISSUES, REQUIREMENTS AND EXCEPTIONS

Determinations that law enforcement officers engaged in activity during the preparation of the prosecution's case and that this activity violated the Fourth Amendment or some other legal requirement that triggers an exclusionary sanction does not complete inquiry into the admissibility of evidence obtained by the officers. In fact, the Supreme Court's post-*Mapp* case law has greatly increased the complexity of two subissues needing consideration: (1) what evidence is rendered inadmissible by demonstrated law enforcement misconduct; and (2) what persons are able to invoke the exclusionary remedy?

In considering the issues presented by these cases, it may be useful to first identify those matters a defendant seeking exclusion of evidence must establish to make a basic case for exclusion. These might usefully be distinguished from "exceptions" to the requirement of exclusion triggered by the making of such a basic case. The distinction may be useful in litigation because it may determine which party has the burden of persuasion. Although the Supreme Court has never comprehensively addressed the allocation of the burden[s] of persuasion in litigation under the federal constitutional exclusionary sanction, there is widespread agreement that a defendant seeking to have evidence suppressed must prove (1) illegality sufficient to trigger the exclusionary sanction; (2) the defendant's right to invoke that sanction ("standing"); and (3) that the challenged evidence was obtained as a factual result of the illegality or, as courts often put the matter, that the evidence was "fruit of the poisonous tree." There is also widespread agreement that if the prosecution responds by relying on an "exception" to the general requirement of exclusion, the prosecution bears the burden of persuasion regarding the exception.

Whatever the allocation of the burden[s] of persuasion, those burdens are not high. In general, the Court announced in United States v. Matlock, 415 U.S. 164, 178 n. 14, 94 S.Ct. 988, 996 n. 14, 39 L.Ed.2d 242, 253 n. 14 (1974), the controlling burden of proof at suppression hearings should impose no greater burden than proof by a preponderance of the evidence.

The principal case in this part is an early one, but the opinion demonstrates the interrelationship among the issues presented by many instances of exclusionary sanction litigation. The propriety of the arrests of the defendants was in dispute. Four members of the Supreme Court, in a dissenting opinion by Justice Clark, took the position that neither arrest was constitutionally impermissible. For present purposes, assume the arrests were constitutionally unreasonable and consider what effect those arrests have upon the admissibility of the various evidence offered by the prosecution against each of the defendants.

Wong Sun v. United States

Supreme Court of the United States, 1963.
371 U.S. 471, 83 S.Ct. 407, 9 L.Ed.2d 441.

■ MR. JUSTICE BRENNAN delivered the opinion of the Court.

The petitioners were tried without a jury in the District Court for the Northern District of California under a two-count indictment for violation of the Federal Narcotics Laws * * *. They were acquitted under the first count which charged a conspiracy, but convicted under the second count which charged the substantive offense of fraudulent and knowing transportation and concealment of illegally imported heroin. The Court of Appeals for the Ninth Circuit, one judge dissenting, affirmed the convictions. We granted certiorari. * * *.

About 2 a. m. on the morning of June 4, 1959, federal narcotics agents in San Francisco, after having had one Hom Way under surveillance for six weeks, arrested him and found heroin in his possession. Hom Way, who had not before been an informant, stated after his arrest that he had bought an ounce of heroin the night before from one known to him only as "Blackie Toy," proprietor of a laundry on Leavenworth Street.

About 6 a. m. that morning six or seven federal agents went to a laundry at 1733 Leavenworth Street. The sign above the door of this establishment said "Oye's Laundry." It was operated by the petitioner James Wah Toy. There is, however, nothing in the record which identifies James Wah Toy and "Blackie Toy" as the same person. The other federal officers remained nearby out of sight while Agent Alton Wong, who was of Chinese ancestry, rang the bell. When petitioner Toy appeared and opened the door, Agent Wong told him that he was calling for laundry and dry cleaning. Toy replied that he didn't open until 8 o'clock and told the agent to come back at that time. Toy started to close the door. Agent Wong thereupon took his badge from his pocket and said, "I am a federal narcotics agent." Toy immediately "slammed the door and started running" down the hallway through the laundry to his living quarters at the back where his wife and child were sleeping in a bedroom. Agent Wong and the other federal officers broke open the door and followed Toy down the hallway to the living quarters and into the bedroom. Toy reached into a nightstand drawer. Agent Wong thereupon drew his pistol, pulled Toy's hand out of the drawer, placed him under arrest and handcuffed him. There was nothing in the drawer and a search of the premises uncovered no narcotics.

One of the agents said to Toy " * * * [Hom Way] says he got narcotics from you." Toy responded, "No, I haven't been selling any narcotics at all. However, I do know somebody who has." When asked who that was, Toy said, "I only know him as Johnny. I don't know his last name." However, Toy described a house on Eleventh Avenue where he said Johnny lived; he also described a bedroom in the house where he said "Johnny kept about a piece"[1] of heroin, and where he and Johnny had smoked some of the drug the night before. The agents left immediately for Eleventh Avenue and

---

1. A "piece" is approximately one ounce.

located the house. They entered and found one Johnny Yee in the bedroom. After a discussion with the agents, Yee took from a bureau drawer several tubes containing in all just less than one ounce of heroin, and surrendered them. Within the hour Yee and Toy were taken to the Office of the Bureau of Narcotics. Yee there stated that the heroin had been brought to him some four days earlier by petitioner Toy and another Chinese known to him only as "Sea Dog."

Toy was questioned as to the identity of "Sea Dog" and said that "Sea Dog" was Wong Sun. Some agents, including Agent Alton Wong, took Toy to Wong Sun's neighborhood where Toy pointed out a multifamily dwelling where he said Wong Sun lived. Agent Wong rang a downstairs door bell and a buzzer sounded, opening the door. The officer identified himself as a narcotics agent to a woman on the landing and asked "for Mr. Wong." The woman was the wife of petitioner Wong Sun. She said that Wong Sun was "in the back room sleeping." Alton Wong and some six other officers climbed the stairs and entered the apartment. One of the officers went into the back room and brought petitioner Wong Sun from the bedroom in handcuffs. A thorough search of the apartment followed, but no narcotics were discovered.

Petitioner Toy and Johnny Yee were arraigned before a United States Commissioner on June 4 on a complaint * * *. Later that day, each was released on his own recognizance. Petitioner Wong Sun was arraigned on a similar complaint filed the next day and was also released on his own recognizance. Within a few days, both petitioners and Yee were interrogated at the office of the Narcotics Bureau by Agent William Wong, also of Chinese ancestry. The agent advised each of the three of his right to withhold information which might be used against him, and stated to each that he was entitled to the advice of counsel, though it does not appear that any attorney was present during the questioning of any of the three. The officer also explained to each that no promises or offers of immunity or leniency were being or could be made.

The agent interrogated each of the three separately. After each had been interrogated the agent prepared a statement in English from rough notes. The agent read petitioner Toy's statement to him in English and interpreted certain portions of it for him in Chinese. Toy also read the statement in English aloud to the agent, said there were corrections to be made, and made the corrections in his own hand. Toy would not sign the statement, however; in the agent's words "he wanted to know first if the other persons involved in the case had signed theirs." Wong Sun had considerable difficulty understanding the statement in English and the agent restated its substance in Chinese. Wong Sun refused to sign the statement although he admitted the accuracy of its contents.

Hom Way did not testify at petitioners' trial. The Government offered Johnny Yee as its principal witness but excused him after he invoked the privilege against self-incrimination and flatly repudiated the statement he had given to Agent William Wong. That statement was not offered in evidence nor was any testimony elicited from him identifying either petitioner as the source of the heroin in his possession, or otherwise tending to support the charges against the petitioners.

The statute expressly provides that proof of the accused's possession of the drug will support a conviction under the statute unless the accused satisfactorily explains the possession. The Government's evidence tending to prove the petitioners' possession (the petitioners offered no exculpatory testimony) consisted of four items which the trial court admitted over timely objections that they were inadmissible as "fruits" of unlawful arrests or of attendant searches: (1) the statements made orally by petitioner Toy in his bedroom at the time of his arrest; (2) the heroin surrendered to the agents by Johnny Yee; (3) petitioner Toy's pretrial unsigned statement; and (4) petitioner Wong Sun's similar statement. The dispute below and here has centered around the correctness of the rulings of the trial judge allowing these items in evidence.

The Court of Appeals held that the arrests of both petitioners were illegal because not based on " 'probable cause' within the meaning of the Fourth Amendment" * * * [but] nevertheless [also] held that the four items of proof were not the "fruits" of the illegal arrests and that they were therefore properly admitted in evidence.

The Court of Appeals rejected [an] additional [contention] of the petitioners. [This] was that there was insufficient evidence to corroborate the petitioners' unsigned admissions of possession of narcotics. The court held that the narcotics in evidence surrendered by Johnny Yee, together with Toy's statements in his bedroom at the time of arrest corroborated petitioners' admissions. * * *

We believe that significant differences between the cases of the two petitioners require separate discussion of each. We shall first consider the case of petitioner Toy.

I.

The Court of Appeals found there was [not] probable cause for Toy's arrest. Giving due weight to that finding, we think it is amply justified by the facts clearly shown on this record. * * *

II.

It is conceded that Toy's declarations in his bedroom are to be excluded if they are held to be "fruits" of the agents' unlawful action.

In order to make effective the fundamental constitutional guarantees of sanctity of the home and inviolability of the person, this Court held nearly half a century ago that evidence seized during an unlawful search could not constitute proof against the victim of the search. The exclusionary prohibition extends as well to the indirect as the direct products of such invasions. Silverthorne Lumber Co. v. United States, 251 U.S. 385, 40 S.Ct. 182, 64 L.Ed. 319. Mr. Justice Holmes, speaking for the Court in that case, in holding that the Government might not make use of information obtained during an unlawful search to subpoena from the victims the very documents illegally viewed, expressed succinctly the policy of the broad exclusionary rule:

"The essence of a provision forbidding the acquisition of evidence in a certain way is that not merely evidence so acquired shall not be held before the Court but that it shall not be used at all. Of course this does not mean that the facts thus obtained become sacred and inaccessible. If knowledge of them is gained from an independent source they may be proved like any others, but the knowledge gained by the Government's own wrong cannot be used by it in the way proposed."

The exclusionary rule has traditionally barred from trial physical, tangible materials obtained either during or as a direct result of an unlawful invasion. It follows from our holding in Silverman v. United States, 365 U.S. 505, 81 S.Ct. 679, 5 L.Ed.2d 734, that the Fourth Amendment may protect against the overhearing of verbal statements as well as against the more traditional seizure of "papers and effects." Similarly, testimony as to matters observed during an unlawful invasion has been excluded in order to enforce the basic constitutional policies. Thus, verbal evidence which derives so immediately from an unlawful entry and an unauthorized arrest as the officers' action in the present case is no less the "fruit" of official illegality than the more common tangible fruits of the unwarranted intrusion. Nor do the policies underlying the exclusionary rule invite any logical distinction between physical and verbal evidence. * * * [T]he danger in relaxing the exclusionary rules in the case of verbal evidence would seem too great to warrant introducing such a distinction.

The Government argues that Toy's statements to the officers in his bedroom, although closely consequent upon the invasion which we hold unlawful, were nevertheless admissible because they resulted from "an intervening independent act of a free will." This contention, however, takes insufficient account of the circumstances. Six or seven officers had broken the door and followed on Toy's heels into the bedroom where his wife and child were sleeping. He had been almost immediately handcuffed and arrested. Under such circumstances it is unreasonable to infer that Toy's response was sufficiently an act of free will to purge the primary taint of the unlawful invasion.

* * *

III.

We now consider whether the exclusion of Toy's declarations requires also the exclusion of the narcotics taken from Yee, to which those declarations led the police. The prosecutor candidly told the trial court that "we wouldn't have found those drugs except that Mr. Toy helped us to." Hence this is not the case envisioned by this Court where the exclusionary rule has no application because the Government learned of the evidence "from an independent source," Silverthorne Lumber Co. v. United States, 251 U.S. 385, 392, 40 S.Ct. 182, 183, 64 L.Ed. 319; nor is this a case in which the connection between the lawless conduct of the police and the discovery of the challenged evidence has "become so attenuated as to dissipate the taint." Nardone v. United States, 308 U.S. 338, 341, 60 S.Ct. 266, 268, 84 L.Ed. 307. We need not hold that all evidence is "fruit of the poisonous tree" simply because it would not have come to light but for the illegal actions of the police. Rather, the more apt question in such a case is "whether, granting establishment of the primary illegality, the evidence to which instant objection is made has been come at by exploitation of that illegality or instead by means sufficiently distinguishable to be purged of the primary taint." Maguire, Evidence of Guilt, 221 (1959). We think it clear that the narcotics were "come at by the exploitation of that illegality" and hence that they may not be used against Toy.

IV.

It remains only to consider Toy's unsigned statement. We need not decide whether, in light of the fact that Toy was free on his own recognizance when he made the statement, that statement was a fruit of the illegal arrest. Since we have concluded that his declarations in the bedroom and the narcotics surrendered by Yee should not have been admitted in evidence against him, the only proofs remaining to sustain his conviction are his and Wong Sun's unsigned statements. Without scrutinizing the contents of Toy's ambiguous recitals, we conclude that no reference to Toy in Wong Sun's statement constitutes admissible evidence corroborating any admission by Toy. We arrive at this conclusion upon two clear lines of decisions which converge to require it. One line of our decisions establishes that criminal confessions and admissions of guilt require extrinsic corroboration; the other line of precedents holds that an out-of-court declaration made after arrest may not be used at trial against one of the declarant's partners in crime.

It is a settled principle of the administration of criminal justice in the federal courts that a conviction must rest upon firmer ground than the uncorroborated admission or confession of the accused. We observed in Smith v. United States, 348 U.S. 147, 153, 75 S.Ct. 194, 197, 99 L.Ed. 192, that the requirement of corroboration is rooted in "a long history of judicial experience with confessions and in the realization that sound law enforcement requires police investigations which extend beyond the words of the accused." * * * Wong Sun's unsigned confession does not furnish competent corroborative evidence. The second governing principle, likewise well settled in our decisions, is that an out-of-court declaration made after arrest may not be used at trial against one of the declarant's partners in crime. While such a statement is "admissible against the others where it is in furtherance of the criminal undertaking * * * all such responsibility is at an end when the conspiracy ends." Fiswick v. United States, 329 U.S. 211, 217, 67 S.Ct. 224, 227, 91 L.Ed. 196. * * *

V.

We turn now to the case of the other petitioner, Wong Sun. We have no occasion to disagree with the finding of the Court of Appeals that his arrest, also, was without probable cause or reasonable grounds. At all events no evidentiary consequences turn upon that question. For Wong Sun's unsigned confession was not the fruit of that arrest, and was therefore properly admitted at trial. On the evidence that Wong Sun had been released on his own recognizance after a lawful arraignment, and had returned voluntarily several days later to make the statement, we hold that the connection between the arrest and the statement had "become so attenuated as to dissipate the taint." * * *

We must then consider the admissibility of the narcotics surrendered by Yee. Our holding, supra, that this ounce of heroin was inadmissible against Toy does not compel a like result with respect to Wong Sun. The exclusion of the narcotics as to Toy was required solely by their tainted relationship to information unlawfully obtained from Toy, and not by any official impropriety connected with their surrender by Yee. The seizure of this heroin invaded no right of privacy of person or premises which would entitle Wong Sun to object to its use at his trial.

However, for the reasons that Wong Sun's statement was incompetent to corroborate Toy's admissions contained in Toy's own statement, any references to Wong Sun in Toy's statement were incompetent to corroborate Wong Sun's admissions. Thus, the only competent source of corroboration for Wong Sun's statement was the heroin itself. We cannot be certain, however, on this state of the record, that the trial judge may not also have considered the contents of Toy's statement as a source of corroboration. Petitioners raised as one ground of objection to the introduction of the statements the claim that each statement, "even if it were a purported admission or confession or declaration against interest of a defendant * * * would not be binding upon the other defendant." The trial judge, in allowing the statements in, apparently overruled all of petitioners' objections, including this one. Thus we presume that he considered all portions of both statements as bearing upon the guilt of both petitioners.

We intimate no view one way or the other as to whether the trial judge might have found in the narcotics alone sufficient evidence to corroborate Wong Sun's admissions that he delivered heroin to Yee and smoked heroin at Yee's house around the date in question. But because he might, as the factfinder, have found insufficient corroboration from the narcotics alone, we cannot be sure that the scales were not tipped in favor of conviction by reliance upon the inadmissible Toy statement. * * * We therefore hold that petitioner Wong Sun is also entitled to a new trial.

The judgment of the Court of Appeals is reversed and the case is remanded to the District Court for further proceedings consistent with this opinion.

It is so ordered.

Judgment of Court of Appeals reversed and case remanded to the District Court.

[The concurring opinion of JUSTICE DOUGLAS and the dissenting opinion of JUSTICE CLARK, joined by JUSTICES HARLAN, STEWART and WHITE, are omitted.]

NOTES

1.   The requirement that a confession be corroborated is discussed in Chapter 7.

2.   **"Standing" Or the "Personal Nature" of Federal Constitutional Rights.** The doctrine which precluded Wong Sun from successfully objecting to the introduction of the heroin on the same grounds as were successful for Toy has traditionally been described as a requirement of "standing." Application of the

requirement to specific search situations is explored further in Part B(3) of Chapter 2.

In Rakas v. Illinois, 439 U.S. 128, 99 S.Ct. 421, 58 L.Ed.2d 387 (1978) (reprinted in part in Chapter 2), however, the Supreme Court appeared to "dispens[e] with the rubric of standing." Cases containing standing discussions, it explained, simply applied the principle that Fourth Amendment rights are personal in nature. Whether particular defendants can challenge particular law enforcement conduct should be discussed in those terms:

> Analyzed in these terms, the question is whether the challenged search or seizure violated the Fourth Amendment rights of a criminal defendant who seeks to exclude the evidence obtained during it. That inquiry in turn requires a determination of whether the disputed search and seizure has infringed an interest of the defendant which the Fourth Amendment was designed to protect. * * * [T]his aspect of the analysis belongs more properly under the heading of substantive Fourth Amendment doctrine rather than under the heading of standing * * *.

439 U.S. at 140, 99 S.Ct. at 429, 58 L.Ed.2d at 399. The majority emphasized the abandonment of standing rubric would not change either the basic inquiry or the outcome of cases. But the shift, it explained, should focus concern on "the extent of a particular defendant's rights under the Fourth Amendment, rather than on any theoretically separate, but invariably intertwined concept of standing." Further, this approach should result in particular decisions resting on "sounder logical footing."

Earlier, the Court had defended the requirement of "standing" on its merits:

> Fourth Amendment rights are personal rights which, like some other constitutional rights, may not be vicariously asserted. * * * There is no necessity to exclude evidence against one defendant in order to protect the rights of another. No rights of the victim of an illegal search are at stake when the evidence is offered against some other party. The victim can and very probably will object for himself when and if it becomes important for him to do so. * * * [None of our cases] hold that anything which deters illegal searches is thereby commanded by the Fourth Amendment. The deterrent values of preventing the incrimination of those whose rights the police have violated have been considered sufficient to justify the suppression of probative evidence even though the case against the defendant is weakened or destroyed. We adhere to that judgment. But we are not convinced that the additional benefits of extending the exclusionary rule to other defendants would justify further encroachment upon the public interest in prosecuting those accused of crime and having them acquitted or convicted on the basis of all the evidence which exposes the truth.

Alderman v. United States, 394 U.S. 165, 174–75, 89 S.Ct. 961, 966–97, 22 L.Ed.2d 176, 187 (1969).

In *Rakas*, the Court rejected a proposal that it permit any criminal defendant at whom a search was "directed" to challenge the admissibility of evidence obtained as a result of that search. It explained it was unwilling to increase the amount of reliable evidence that would be rendered unavailable by the exclusionary rule. It also quoted with approval Justice Harlan's argument in *Alderman* that such a "target" rule would involve excessive administrative costs in the form of lengthy hearings to determine whether or not particular defendants were the "targets" of particular police action.

3. **Fruit of the Poisonous Tree.** In holding Toy's bedroom statements inadmissible, *Wong Sun* applied what is often called the "fruit of the poisonous tree" rule. Once a defendant establishes a violation of his constitutional rights, he is

entitled to suppression of all "fruit of [that] poisonous tree." Nardone v. United States, 308 U.S. 338, 341, 60 S.Ct. 266, 268, 84 L.Ed. 307, 312 (1939). This position is sometimes stated as the "derivative evidence" rule—all evidence derived from a violation of the defendant's rights must be suppressed. The "core rationale" for this rule, the Court has explained, is "that this admittedly drastic and socially costly course is needed to deter police from violations" of the protections involved. Nix v. Williams, 467 U.S. 431, 442–43, 104 S.Ct. 2501, 2508, 81 L.Ed.2d 377, 386–87 (1984).

The "fruits" rule is not applied in some situations where police illegality consists of a violation of *Miranda* requirements. Admissibility of evidence obtained as a result of a *Miranda* violation is developed in subsection B(4) of Chapter 7.

A defendant seeking to invoke the "fruits" doctrine must establish that the challenged evidence was obtained by police as a factual result of a violation of his rights. Murray v. United States, 487 U.S. 533, 108 S.Ct. 2529, 101 L.Ed.2d 472 (1988). Obviously, evidence obtained by law enforcement officers *before* they violated a defendant's rights is not the "fruit" of the violation and hence is not subject to challenge. See Waller v. Georgia, 467 U.S. 39, 104 S.Ct. 2210, 81 L.Ed.2d 31 (1984).

Murray illustrates the difficulty sometimes involved in showing the required factual causation. Federal officers conducting a drug investigation observed several suspicious vehicles enter and leave a warehouse in South Boston. About 2:30 p.m. and without a search warrant, the officers went to the warehouse, forced open the door, and entered. While inside, they observed burlap-wrapped bales. They then, without seizing or disturbing those bales, left the warehouse. Later, the officers applied for a search warrant for the warehouse. The application relied upon other information possessed by the officers at the time of their first entry and did not mention they had already entered the structure. The warrant issued about 10:45 p.m. Pursuant to that warrant, the officers entered the warehouse and seized 270 bales of marijuana—including the bales observed during the earlier entry—as well as other incriminating items. Murray and Carter were charged with conspiracy to possess and distribute the marijuana. Before trial, they moved to suppress the evidence obtained from the warehouse on the ground it was the "fruit" of the officers' first and unreasonable warrantless entry of the warehouse. The Court of Appeals held that this motion should have been granted. By a 4–3 vote, with two justices not participating, the Supreme Court vacated and remanded. Knowledge that the marijuana was in the warehouse, Justice Scalia wrote for the majority, was obtained in the first and presumably-unreasonable search of the warehouse. But such knowledge as well as the marijuana itself were acquired in the second and reasonable search pursuant to the warrant. If the search pursuant to the warrant was "genuinely independent" of the first search, the evidence would be admissible. This "independent source" rule, he explained, is based on the need to limit exclusion of evidence to those situations in which rejecting it is necessary to deter improper police activity. Deterrence is adequately accomplished by placing the police in the position they would have occupied had the illegal search not occurred. It does not require placing them in a *worse* position. Excluding evidence having an independent source would be to unjustifiably place the police in such a worse position; they would be deprived of evidence that they in fact obtained independently of their improper conduct.

But this doctrine requires that the manner in which the evidence was obtained be "genuinely independent" of the illegal search. "This would not have been the case," Justice Scalia explained, "if the agents' decision to seek the warrant was prompted by what they had seen during the initial entry, or if information obtained during that entry was presented to the Magistrate and affected his decision to issue the warrant." The lower courts determined the officers had not revealed to the magistrate issuing the search warrant any information from the illegal entry. But no finding was made as to whether or not the officers would have sought a warrant for the warehouse if they had not earlier entered it. The matter was therefore remanded to the District Court for a determination as to whether the search pursuant to the warrant was an independent source of the challenged evidence in the sense that the opinion defined independent source.

4. **Limits on Fruits Doctrine.** In one search situation, the Supreme Court has refused to apply the general rule that all evidence obtained as a factual result of conduct violating Fourth Amendment standards must be suppressed. In New York v. Harris, 495 U.S. 14, 110 S.Ct. 1640, 109 L.Ed.2d 13 (1990), officers had probable cause to believe Harris committed a homicide but obtained no warrant. They nevertheless entered his home and placed him under arrest. This warrantless entry violated the Fourth Amendment; the warrant requirement in this context is considered in Chapter 4. Harris was warned of his rights and admitted the killing. He was taken to the stationhouse, warned again, and signed a written incriminating statement. Later, ignoring Harris's expressed desire to remain silent, police videotaped an interview with him. The trial court suppressed the oral statement made at his home and the videotaped statement, but admitted the written statement despite the earlier violation of his Fourth Amendment rights.

The Supreme Court held admission of the statement this was proper, applying what the dissenters characterized as a "newly-fashioned *per se* rule." No need existed to inquire whether the taint of the improper entry became attenuated, Justice White reasoned for the majority, because that analysis is necessary only if the challenged evidence is the product or fruit of the Fourth Amendment violation. The illegality of the officers' entry and Harris's arrest in his home, he continued, did not render unlawful Harris's continued custody once he was removed from the house:

> Harris's statement taken at the police station was not the product of being in unlawful custody. Neither was it the fruit of having been arrested in the home rather than someplace else. * * * [T]he police had a justification to question Harris prior to his arrest; therefore, his subsequent statement was not an exploitation of the illegal entry into Harris' home.

495 U.S. at 19, 110 S.Ct. at 1644, 109 L.Ed.2d at 21. Therefore:

> [W]here the police have probable cause to arrest a suspect, the exclusionary rule does not bar the State's use of a statement made by the defendant outside of his home, even though the statement is taken after an arrest made in the home in violation of [the Fourth Amendment].

495 U.S. at 21, 110 S.Ct. at 1644–45, 109 L.Ed.2d at 22.

Its decision, the Court explained further, implemented the principle that penalties, including exclusion of evidence, must bear some relation to the purposes of the legal requirement violated. The underlying rule requiring a warrant for arrests in the home was designed to protect the physical integrity of the home. "[I]t was not intended to grant criminal suspects, like Harris, protection for statements made outside their premises where the police have probable cause to arrest the suspects for committing a crime." Once incriminating evidence gathered from arresting the suspect in his home, the purpose of the rule is vindicated. Moreover, the threat of suppression of such evidence retains the principal incentive for officers to comply with the warrant requirement. Suppression of statements obtained after the suspect is removed would provide only "minimal" incremental deterrence.

5. **Independent Source.** Justice Holmes's discussion in *Silverthorne Lumber Co.*, quoted in *Wong Sun*, referred to evidence gained from "an independent source." If evidence is obtained by police after they violated a defendant's rights,

but not as a consequence of that violation, the evidence is often said to have such an independent source and, as a result, is admissible despite officers' intrusion upon the defendant's rights.

If the prosecution argues challenged evidence is admissible under the independent source doctrine, which side has the burden of persuasion? This may depend upon how the doctrine is conceptualized. If it is an exception to the general rule that all evidence proved fruit of a poisonous tree must be suppressed, the prosecution would most likely have the burden of establishing its applicability. Independent source may, on the other hand, be simply a label for a conclusion that a defendant has failed to establish that the challenged evidence was obtained as a factual result of the official misconduct. A defendant probably has the burden of establishing that challenged evidence was obtained as a factual result of unreasonable law enforcement conduct. Thus independent source would seem to be only a theory on which the prosecution argue that the defendant has failed to meet his burden of persuasion regarding the necessary causal link.

In general, the Supreme Court has not made clear either the nature of independent source or the placement of the burden of persuasion. It has, however,addressed the situation in which a defendant establishes a lineup was conducted in violation of his Sixth Amendment right to counsel, and a witness identified him at that lineup. The prosecution can escape suppression of the witness's in-court identification testimony only if it establishes—by clear and convincing evidence— the in-court testimony of that witness's in-court identification testimony would be based on a source independent of the tainted lineup. United States v. Wade, 388 U.S. 218, 240, 87 S.Ct. 1926, 1939, 18 L.Ed.2d 1149, 1165 (1967) (reprinted in Chapter 10). This holding may rest upon a perception that independent source, as applied in lineup situations, involves such an unusually difficult and speculative inquiry that error can be avoided only by placing the burden of persuasion on the prosecution. Cf., Nix v. Williams. 467 U.S. 431, 444 n. 5, 104 S.Ct. 2501, 2509 n. 5, 81 L.Ed.2d 377, 388 n. 5 (1984). In other situations, the burden of proof may remain on the defendant to show the challenged evidence was discovered as a factual result of the illegality, although only by a preponderance of the evidence.

6. **Defendant's Presence as "Fruit."** The Supreme Court recognized one qualification to the general rule that "fruit of the poisonous tree" must be excluded: the defendant's physical presence for trial and punishment is never the excludable "fruit" of improper law enforcement conduct. Illegal police activity, the Court made clear, affects only the admissibility of evidence; it does not affect the jurisdiction of the trial court or otherwise serve as a basis for dismissing the prosecution. Ker v. Illinois, 119 U.S. 436, 7 S.Ct. 225, 30 L.Ed.2d 421 (1886). In United States v. Blue, 384 U.S. 251, 86 S.Ct. 1416, 16 L.Ed.2d 510 (1966), the Court explained its adherence to this approach despite *Mapp* and the "constitutionalization" of the exclusionary rule:

> So drastic a step [as barring the prosecution altogether] might advance marginally some of the ends served by the exclusionary rules, but it would also increase to an intolerable degree interference with the public interest in having the guilty brought to book.

384 U.S. at 225, 86 S.Ct. at 1419, 16 L.Ed.2d at 515.

7. **Attenuation of the Taint.** As the principal case makes clear, the "fruit of the poisonous tree" doctrine is subject to the qualification that "fruit" of a violation of the defendant's rights becomes admissible if the prosecution establishes the "taint" of the constitutional violation was "attenuated" when the challenged evidence was obtained. Determining whether attenuation has occurred is sometimes difficult. The issue has arisen in a number of post—*Wong Sun* Supreme Court cases, many involving defendants' claims that their confessions were excludable

fruit of an earlier improper arrest or detention. Perhaps the leading case is Brown v. Illinois, 422 U.S. 590, 95 S.Ct. 2254, 45 L.Ed.2d 416 (1975), in which the Court held compliance with Miranda v. Arizona, 384 U.S. 436, 86 S.Ct. 1602, 16 L.Ed.2d 694 (1966) (reprinted in Chapter 7), would not alone attenuate the taint. Moreover, a finding that the statement was "voluntary," while a "threshold requirement" for a finding of attenuation of taint, does not resolve the matter. Taylor v. Alabama, 457 U.S. 687, 690, 102 S.Ct. 2664, 2667, 73 L.Ed.2d 314, 319 (1982). Instead, events intervening between the unlawful detention and the making of the statement determine whether the statement was a sufficient act of free will to purge the taint. In *Brown,* the Court explained:

> No single fact is dispositive. * * * The *Miranda* warnings are an important factor, to be sure, in determining whether the confession is obtained by exploitation of an illegal arrest. But they are not the only factor to be considered. The temporal proximity of the arrest and the confession, the presence of intervening circumstances, and, particularly, the purpose and flagrancy of the official misconduct are all relevant.

422 U.S. at 603–04, 95 S.Ct. at 2261–62, 45 L.Ed.2d at 427.

Application of this approach was illustrated in Rawlings v. Kentucky, 448 U.S. 98, 100 S.Ct. 2556, 65 L.Ed.2d 633 (1980). Six officers arrived at a residence with a warrant for the arrest of one Marquess. Two of the occupants and four guests, including Rawlings and Cox, were present. During the search for Marquess, the officers smelled marihuana smoke and observed marihuana seeds. Two officers left to obtain a search warrant and four officers remained. The officers who remained on the scene permitted any occupant who would submit to a body search to leave; two did. About 45 minutes later, the two officers returned with a search warrant. The warrant and the *Miranda* rights were read to the remaining occupants. One officer then approached Cox and ordered her to empty her purse. 1,800 tablets of LSD and a variety of other controlled substances were among the contents. After pouring these items on a table, Cox turned to Rawlings and told him "to take what was his." Rawlings immediately claimed ownership of the controlled substances. At Rawlings's trial for trafficking in and possession of the controlled substances, his claim of ownership was admitted over his objection that it was the fruit of an illegal detention.

The Supreme Court upheld the admission of the statement. Assuming without deciding that the detention was invalid, the Court held the statement not tainted by this detention. Several factors were relevant. First, that the *Miranda* warnings were given was "important" but not "dispositive." Second, the atmosphere during the period of detention was "congenial." This outweighed the short 45 minute period between the detention and the making of the statement which under more "strict" conditions would not be long enough to purge the taint of the detention. Third, the discovery of the drugs in Cox's purse and Rawlings's apparent desire to assume responsibility for them was a "circumstance" which "intervened between the initial detention and the challenged statements." Fourth, the police misconduct "[did] not rise to the level of conscious or flagrant misconduct." Finally, the statement was "voluntary," i.e., it was an act of free will unaffected by any illegality in the detention.

In regard to the motive for the illegal detention, contrast *Taylor* in which the Court found no attenuation of taint. The detention in that case was characterized as "an investigatory arrest without probable cause" followed by the involuntary transportation of the defendant to the station "for interrogation in the hope that something would turn up."

8. **Testimony of Witness as Excludable Fruit.** When, if ever, should the fruits of the poisonous tree doctrine include testimony of a witness whose identity

was discovered in violation of a defendant's constitutional rights? In United States v. Ceccolini, 435 U.S. 268, 98 S.Ct. 1054, 55 L.Ed.2d 268 (1978), Biro, a local police officer, entered Ceccolini's place of business to talk with Lois Hennessey, a friend and an employee of the shop. During the course of the conversation he noticed an envelope with money sticking out of it lying on the drawer of the cash register behind the counter. Biro picked up the envelope and, upon examining its contents, discovered it contained not only money but policy (gambling) slips. He placed the envelope back on the register and, without telling his friend what he had seen, asked her to whom the envelope belonged. She replied the envelope belonged to Ceccolini and that he had instructed her to give it to someone. The officer related what he had observed and been told to local police detectives who, in turn, gave the information to an FBI agent. Ceccolini had already been the subject of an FBI gambling investigation. An agent interviewed Ms. Hennessey at her home and she agreed to provide information about the envelope to the agent. Ceccolini was subpoenaed before a grand jury, where he denied any knowledge of a policy operation run from his shop. Ms. Hennessey testified about the envelope and the grand jury indicted Ceccolini for committing perjury in his grand jury testimony. The District Court and the Court of Appeals concluded that Biro's examination of the envelope was an unreasonable search and that the trial testimony of the store employee was a fruit of that illegality. The Supreme Court disagreed. Writing for the Court, Justice Rehnquist concluded that although there was a causal connection between the initial illegality and the employee's testimony, the taint had been dissipated:

> [W]e hold that the Court of Appeals erred in holding that the degree of attenuation was not sufficient to dissipate the connection between the illegality and the testimony. The evidence indicates overwhelmingly that the testimony given by the witness was an act of her own free will in no way coerced or even induced by official authority as a result of Biro's discovery of the policy slips. Nor were the slips themselves used in questioning Hennessey. Substantial periods of time elapsed between the time of the illegal search and the initial contact with the witness, on the one hand, and between the latter and the testimony at trial on the other. While the particular knowledge to which Hennessey testified at trial can be logically traced back to Biro's discovery of the policy slips both the identity of Hennessey and her relationship with the respondent was well known to those investigating the case. There is in addition, not the slightest evidence to suggest that Biro entered the shop or picked up the envelope with the intent of finding tangible evidence bearing on an illicit gambling operation, much less any suggestion that he entered the shop and searched with the intent of finding a willing and knowledgeable witness to testify against respondent. Application of the exclusionary rule in this situation could not have the slightest deterrent effect on the behavior of an officer such as Biro. The cost of permanently silencing Hennessey is too great for an even-handed system of law enforcement to bear in order to secure such a speculative and very likely negligible deterrent effect.
>
> Obviously no mathematical weight can be assigned to any of the factors which we have discussed, but just as obviously they all point to the conclusion that the exclusionary rule should be invoked with much greater reluctance where the claim is based on a causal relationship between a constitutional violation and the discovery of a live witness than when a similar claim is advanced to support suppression of an inanimate object.

435 U.S. at 279–80, 98 S.Ct. at 1062, 55 L.Ed.2d at 279. Justices Marshall and Brennan dissented.

C.   EXCEPTIONS TO EXCLUSIONARY REQUIREMENTS

EDITORS' INTRODUCTION: EXCLUSIONARY SANCTION
EXCEPTIONS

The federal constitutional requirement that evidence obtained as a result of a violation of a defendant's Fourth, Fifth, or Sixth Amendment rights be excluded from evidence is subject to exceptions.

Attenuation of Taint and Independent Source

Several of these have already been addressed. The last part of this chapter considered the attenuation of taint doctrine rendering certain evidence admissible.

As the last part similarly developed, the independent source doctrine also renders challenged evidence admissible at the behest of the prosecution. There is some question, however, whether independent source is properly conceptualized as an exception to the general requirement of exclusion. It may be a description of certain situations in which defendants failed to carry the burden of proving challenged evidence was obtained as factual results of the law enforcement conduct.

Impeachment of Testifying Defendant

Generally, the exceptions permit the use of evidence prove the defendant's guilt. One, however, allows use of evidence only for the limited purpose of impeaching the credibility of a testifying defendant.

Evidence obtained in violation of a defendant's Fourth Amendment rights can be used, if the defendant takes the witness stand at trial, to impeach the defendant's credibility. Harris v. New York, 401 U.S. 222, 91 S.Ct. 643, 28 L.Ed.2d 1 (1971). It may even be used to contradict answers given by a testifying defendant on cross-examination, as long as the testimony is in response to questions "plainly within the scope of the defendant's direct examination." United States v. Havens, 446 U.S. 620, 627, 100 S.Ct. 1912, 1916, 64 L.Ed.2d 559, 566 (1980). The exception applies to other federal constitutional exclusionary requirements. See Michigan v. Harvey, 494 U.S. 344, 350–53, 110 S.Ct. 1176, 1180–81, 108 L.Ed.2d 293, 302–04 (1990) (evidence obtained in violation of the defendant's Sixth Amendment right to counsel could be used to impeach).

In support of the impeachment exception, the Court has stressed the great need for such evidence, as it limits defendants' ability to give possibly perjurious testimony. It has characterized the possibility that the exception will encourage impermissible law enforcement conduct as purely "speculative." Thus:

> Assuming that the exclusionary rule has a deterrent effect on proscribed police conduct, sufficient deterrence flows when the evidence in question is made unavailable to the prosecution in its case in chief.

Harris v. New York, 401 U.S. at 225, 91 S.Ct. at 645, 28 L.Ed.2d at 4, "reaffirmed" in United States v. Havens, supra, 446 U.S. at 627, 100 S.Ct.

at 1916–17, 64 L.Ed.2d at 566. Dissenters argued impeachment exception "will seriously undermine the achievement of [the exclusionary rule's deterrent] objective," and is inconsistent with the exclusionary rule's objective of preserving the courts from the taint of aiding and abetting the law-breaking police officer. Harris v. New York, 401 U.S. at 232, 91 S.Ct. at 649, 28 L.Ed.2d at 8–9 (Brennan, J., dissenting).

In *Harris*, the Court made clear the exception would apply only if "the trustworthiness of the evidence satisfies legal standards." A confession obtained in a manner rendering it involuntary therefore cannot be used to impeach the defendant if he testifies at trial. Mincey v. Arizona, 437 U.S. 385, 402, 98 S.Ct. 2408, 2418, 57 L.Ed.2d 290, 306 (1978).

The Supreme Court—by a close 5-to-4 vote—refused to expand the *Harris* impeachment exception into a broader rule permitting the use of unconstitutionally obtained evidence to rebut *any* evidence offered by the defense. James v. Illinois, 493 U.S. 307, 110 S.Ct. 648, 107 L.Ed.2d 676 (1990). The balancing approach used in *Harris*, the *James* majority reasoned, did not support this narrowing of the exclusionary sanction. Permitting such rebuttal use of unconstitutionally obtained evidence, the Court acknowledged, might deter some perjurious testimony. It would also, however, discourage defendants from producing even legitimate defenses. Non-defendant witnesses cannot be "controlled" by defense counsel as effectively as defendant witnesses, so calling such witnesses might often result in accidentally rendering improperly obtained evidence admissible. Defendants would with some frequency, then, refrain from presenting defense witnesses. Moreover, once law enforcement officers learned of the expanded exception they would have significant incentive to proceed in violation of suspects' rights because the more extensive use that could be made of the fruits of their action would make such activity worthwhile. Thus expansion of the exception would significantly weaken the exclusionary sanction's deterrent effect.

* * *

The principal case that follows develops what is often—but perhaps improperly—called the "good faith" exception. One other exception is considered in the notes after the decision.

United States v. Leon

Supreme Court of the United States, 1984.
468 U.S. 897, 104 S.Ct. 3405, 82 L.Ed.2d 677.

■ JUSTICE WHITE delivered the opinion of the Court.

This case presents the question whether the Fourth Amendment exclusionary rule should be modified so as not to bar the use in the prosecution's case-in-chief of evidence obtained by officers acting in reasonable reliance on a search warrant issued by a detached and neutral magistrate but ultimately found to be unsupported by probable cause.
* * *

I

In August 1981, a confidential informant of unproven reliability informed an officer of the Burbank Police Department that two persons known to him as "Armando" and "Patsy" were selling large quantities of cocaine and methaqualone from their residence at 620 Price Drive in Burbank, Cal. The informant also indicated that he had witnessed a sale of methaqualone by "Patsy" at the residence approximately five months earlier and had observed at that time a shoebox containing a large amount of cash that belonged to "Patsy." He further declared that "Armando" and "Patsy" generally kept only small quantities of drugs at their residence and stored the remainder at another location in Burbank.

On the basis of this information, the Burbank police initiated an extensive investigation focusing first on the Price Drive residence and later on two other residences as well. Cars parked at the Price Drive residence were determined to belong to respondents Armando Sanchez, who had previously been arrested for possession of marihuana, and Patsy Stewart, who had no criminal record. During the course of the investigation, officers observed an automobile belonging to respondent Ricardo Del Castillo, who had previously been arrested for possession of 50 pounds of marihuana, arrive at the Price Drive residence. The driver of that car entered the house, exited shortly thereafter carrying a small paper sack, and drove away. A check of Del Castillo's probation records led the officers to respondent Alberto Leon, whose telephone number Del Castillo had listed as his employer's. Leon had been arrested in 1980 on drug charges, and a companion had informed the police at that time that Leon was heavily involved in the importation of drugs into this country. Before the current investigation began, the Burbank officers had learned that an informant had told a Glendale police officer that Leon stored a large quantity of methaqualone at his residence in Glendale. During the course of this investigation, the Burbank officers learned that Leon was living at 716 South Sunset Canyon in Burbank.

Subsequently, the officers observed several persons, at least one of whom had prior drug involvement, arriving at the Price Drive residence and leaving with small packages; observed a variety of other material activity at the two residences as well as at a condominium at 7902 Via Magdalena; and witnessed a variety of relevant activity involving respondents' automobiles. The officers also observed respondents Sanchez and Stewart board separate flights for Miami. The pair later returned to Los Angeles together, consented to a search of their luggage that revealed only a small amount of marihuana, and left the airport. Based on these and other observations summarized in the affidavit, Officer Cyril Rombach of the Burbank Police Department, an experienced and well-trained narcotics investigator, prepared an application for a warrant to search 620 Price Drive, 716 South Sunset Canyon, 7902 Via Magdalena, and automobiles registered to each of the respondents for an extensive list of items believed to be related to respondents' drug-trafficking activities. Officer Rombach's extensive application was reviewed by several Deputy District Attorneys.

A facially valid search warrant was issued in September 1981 by a state superior court judge. The ensuing searches produced large quantities of drugs at the Via Magdalena and Sunset Canyon addresses and a small quantity at the Price Drive residence. Other evidence was discovered at each of the residences and in Stewart's and Del Castillo's automobiles. Respondents were indicted by a grand jury in the District Court for the Central District of California and charged with conspiracy to possess and distribute cocaine and a variety of substantive counts.

The respondents then filed motions to suppress the evidence seized pursuant to the warrant. The District Court held an evidentiary hearing and, while recognizing that the case was a close one, granted the motions to suppress in part. It concluded that the affidavit was insufficient to establish probable cause, but did not suppress all of the evidence as to all of the respondents because none of the respondents had standing to challenge all of the searches. In response to a request from the Government, the court made clear that Officer Rombach had acted in good faith, but it rejected the Government's suggestion that the Fourth Amendment exclusionary rule should not apply where evidence is seized in reasonable, good-faith reliance on a search warrant.

[A] divided panel of the Court of Appeals for the Ninth Circuit affirmed. * * *

The Government's petition for certiorari expressly declined to seek review of the lower courts' determinations that the search warrant was unsupported by probable cause and presented only the question "[w]hether the Fourth Amendment exclusionary rule should be modified so as not to bar the admission of evidence seized in reasonable, good-faith reliance on a search warrant that is subsequently held to be defective." We granted certiorari to consider the propriety of such a modification. * * *

We have concluded that, in the Fourth Amendment context, the exclusionary rule can be modified somewhat without jeopardizing its ability to perform its intended functions. Accordingly, we reverse the judgment of the Court of Appeals.

II

Language in opinions of this Court and of individual Justices has sometimes implied that the exclusionary rule is a necessary corollary of the Fourth Amendment. * * * These implications need not detain us long. The * * * Fourth Amendment "has never been interpreted to proscribe the introduction of illegally seized evidence in all proceedings or against all persons."

A

The Fourth Amendment contains no provision expressly precluding the use of evidence obtained in violation of its commands * * *. The [exclusionary] rule * * * operates as "a judicially created remedy designed to safeguard Fourth Amendment rights generally through its deterrent effect, rather than a personal constitutional right of the person aggrieved."

Whether the exclusionary sanction is appropriately imposed in a particular case, our decisions make clear, is "an issue separate from the question whether the Fourth Amendment rights of the party seeking to invoke the rule were violated by police conduct." Only the former question is currently before us, and it must be resolved by weighing the costs and benefits of preventing the use in the prosecution's case-in-chief of inherently trustworthy tangible evidence obtained in reliance on a search warrant issued by a detached and neutral magistrate that ultimately is found to be defective.

The substantial social costs exacted by the exclusionary rule for the vindication of Fourth Amendment rights have long been a source of concern. "Our cases have consistently recognized that unbending application of the exclusionary sanction to enforce ideals of governmental rectitude would impede unacceptably the truth-finding functions of judge and jury." United States v. Payner, 447 U.S. 727, 734, 100 S.Ct. 2439, 2445, 65 L.Ed.2d 468 (1980). An objectionable collateral consequence of this interference with the criminal justice system's truth-finding function is that some guilty defendants may go free or receive reduced sentences as a result of favorable plea bargains. Particularly when law enforcement officers have acted in objective good faith or their transgressions have been minor, the magnitude of the benefit conferred on such guilty defendants offends basic concepts of the criminal justice system. Indiscriminate application of the exclusionary rule, therefore, may well "generat[e] disrespect for the law and the administration of justice." Accordingly, "[a]s with any remedial device, the application of the rule has been restricted to those areas where its remedial objectives are thought most efficaciously served."

B

Close attention to those remedial objectives has characterized our recent decisions concerning the scope of the Fourth Amendment exclusionary rule. * * * [T]he balancing approach that has evolved in various contexts—including criminal trials—"forcefully suggest[s] that the exclusionary rule be more generally modified to permit the introduction of evidence obtained in the reasonable good-faith belief that a search or seizure was in accord with the Fourth Amendment."

* * *

As yet, we have not recognized any form of good-faith exception to the Fourth Amendment exclusionary rule. But the balancing approach that has evolved during the years of experience with the rule provides strong support for the modification currently urged upon us. As we discuss below, our evaluation of the costs and benefits of suppressing reliable physical evidence seized by officers reasonably relying on a warrant issued by a detached and neutral magistrate leads to the conclusion that such evidence should be admissible in the prosecution's case-in-chief.

III

A

Because a search warrant "provides the detached scrutiny of a neutral magistrate, which is a more reliable safeguard against improper searches than the hurried judgment of a law enforcement officer 'engaged in the often competitive enterprise of ferreting out crime,'" we have expressed a strong preference for warrants and declared that "in a doubtful or marginal case a search under a warrant may be sustainable where without one it would fail." Reasonable minds frequently may differ on the question whether a particular affidavit establishes probable cause, and we have thus concluded that the preference for warrants is most appropriately effectuated by according "great deference" to a magistrate's determination.

[Seldom], however, has the Court set forth a rationale for suppressing evidence obtained pursuant to a search warrant; * * * it has [frequently] simply excluded such evidence without considering whether Fourth Amendment interests will be advanced. To the extent that proponents of exclusion rely on its behavioral effects on judges and magistrates in these areas, their reliance is misplaced. First, the exclusionary rule is designed to deter police misconduct rather than to punish the errors of judges and magistrates. Second, there exists no evidence suggesting that judges and magistrates are inclined to ignore or subvert the Fourth Amendment or that lawlessness among these actors requires application of the extreme sanction of exclusion.[2]

Third, and most important, we discern no basis, and are offered none, for believing that exclusion of evidence seized pursuant to a warrant will have a significant deterrent effect on the issuing judge or magistrate. Many of the factors that indicate that the exclusionary rule cannot provide an effective "special" or "general" deterrent for individual offending law enforcement officers apply as well to judges or magistrates. And, to the extent that the rule is thought to operate as a "systemic" deterrent on a wider audience, it clearly can have no such effect on individuals empowered to issue search warrants. Judges and magistrates are not adjuncts to the law enforcement team; as neutral judicial officers, they have no stake in the outcome of particular criminal prosecutions. The threat of exclusion thus cannot be expected significantly to deter them. Imposition of the exclusionary sanction is not necessary meaningfully to inform judicial officers of their errors, and we cannot conclude that admitting evidence obtained pursuant to a warrant while at the same time declaring that the warrant was somehow defective will in any way reduce judicial officers' professional incentives to comply with the Fourth Amendment, encourage them to repeat their mistakes, or lead to the granting of all colorable warrant requests.[3]

B

If exclusion of evidence obtained pursuant to a subsequently invalidated warrant is to have any deterrent effect, therefore, it must alter the

---

2. Although there are assertions that some magistrates become rubber stamps for the police and others may be unable effectively to screen police, * * * we are not convinced that this is a problem of major proportions. * * *

3. Limiting the application of the exclusionary sanction may well increase the care with which magistrates scrutinize warrant applications. We doubt that magistrates are more desirous of avoiding the exclusion of evidence obtained pursuant to warrants they have issued than of avoiding invasions of privacy.

Federal magistrates, moreover, are subject to the direct supervision of district courts. They may be removed for "incompetency, misconduct, neglect of duty, or physical or mental disability." 28 U.S.C. § 631(i). If a magistrate serves merely as a "rubber stamp" for the police or is unable to exercise mature judgment, closer supervision or removal provides a more effective remedy than the exclusionary rule.

behavior of individual law enforcement officers or the policies of their departments. One could argue that applying the exclusionary rule in cases where the police failed to demonstrate probable cause in the warrant application deters future inadequate presentations or "magistrate shopping" and thus promotes the ends of the Fourth Amendment. Suppressing evidence obtained pursuant to a technically defective warrant supported by probable cause also might encourage officers to scrutinize more closely the form of the warrant and to point out suspected judicial errors. We find such arguments speculative and conclude that suppression of evidence obtained pursuant to a warrant should be ordered only on a case-by-case basis and only in those unusual cases in which exclusion will further the purposes of the exclusionary rule.

We have frequently questioned whether the exclusionary rule can have any deterrent effect when the offending officers acted in the objectively reasonable belief that their conduct did not violate the Fourth Amendment. * * *[4]

This is particularly true, we believe, when an officer acting with objective good faith has obtained a search warrant from a judge or magistrate and acted within its scope. In most such cases, there is no police illegality and thus nothing to deter. It is the magistrate's responsibility to determine whether the officer's allegations establish probable cause and, if so, to issue a warrant comporting in form with the requirements of the Fourth Amendment. In the ordinary case, an officer cannot be expected to question the magistrate's probable-cause determination or his judgment that the form of the warrant is technically sufficient. "[O]nce the warrant issues, there is literally nothing more the policeman can do in seeking to comply with the law." Penalizing the officer for the magistrate's error, rather than his own, cannot logically contribute to the deterrence of Fourth Amendment violations.[5]

C

We conclude that the marginal or nonexistent benefits produced by suppressing evidence obtained in objectively reasonable reliance on a subse-

---

4. We emphasize that the standard of reasonableness we adopt is an objective one. Many objections to a good-faith exception assume that the exception will turn on the subjective good faith of individual officers. * * * The objective standard we adopt, moreover, requires officers to have a reasonable knowledge of what the law prohibits.

5. [Considerations relating to the integrity of the courts do not support exclusion in these situations.] Our cases establish that the question whether the use of illegally obtained evidence in judicial proceedings represents judicial participation in a Fourth Amendment violation and offends the integrity of the courts

"is essentially the same as the inquiry into whether exclusion would serve a deterrent purpose. * * * The analysis

showing that exclusion in this case has no demonstrated deterrent effect and is unlikely to have any significant such effect shows, by the same reasoning, that the admission of the evidence is unlikely to encourage violations of the Fourth Amendment." United States v. Janis, [428 U.S. 433, 459, n. 35, 96 S.Ct. 3021, 3034, n. 35, 49 L.Ed.2d 1046 (1976)].

Absent unusual circumstances, when a Fourth Amendment violation has occurred because the police have reasonably relied on a warrant issued by a detached and neutral magistrate but ultimately found to be defective, "the integrity of the courts is not implicated." Illinois v. Gates, [462 U.S. 213 245, n. 14, 103 S.Ct. 2317, 2343, n. 14, 76 L.Ed.2d 527 (1983)] (White, J., concurring in the judgment).

quently invalidated search warrant cannot justify the substantial costs of exclusion. We do not suggest, however, that exclusion is always inappropriate in cases where an officer has obtained a warrant and abided by its terms. * * * [T]he officer's reliance on the magistrate's probable-cause determination and on the technical sufficiency of the warrant he issues must be objectively reasonable,[6] and it is clear that in some circumstances the officer[7] will have no reasonable grounds for believing that the warrant was properly issued.

Suppression therefore remains an appropriate remedy if the magistrate or judge in issuing a warrant was misled by information in an affidavit that the affiant knew was false or would have known was false except for his reckless disregard of the truth. Franks v. Delaware, 438 U.S. 154, 98 S.Ct. 2674, 57 L.Ed.2d 667 (1978). The exception we recognize today will also not apply in cases where the issuing magistrate wholly abandoned his judicial role in the manner condemned in Lo–Ji Sales, Inc. v. New York, 442 U.S. 319, 99 S.Ct. 2319, 60 L.Ed.2d 920 (1979); in such circumstances, no reasonably well-trained officer should rely on the warrant. Nor would an officer manifest objective good faith in relying on a warrant based on an affidavit "so lacking in indicia of probable cause as to render official belief in its existence entirely unreasonable." Brown v. Illinois, [422 U.S. 590, 610–611, 95 S.Ct. 2254, 2265, 45 L.Ed.2d 416 (1975)] (Powell, J., concurring in part). Finally, depending on the circumstances of the particular case, a warrant may be so facially deficient—i.e., in failing to particularize the place to be searched or the things to be seized—that the executing officers cannot reasonably presume it to be valid.

In so limiting the suppression remedy, we leave untouched the probable-cause standard and the various requirements for a valid warrant. Other objections to the modification of the Fourth Amendment exclusionary rule we consider to be insubstantial. The good-faith exception for searches conducted pursuant to warrants is not intended to signal our unwillingness strictly to enforce the requirements of the Fourth Amendment, and we do not believe that it will have this effect. As we have already suggested, the good-faith exception, turning as it does on objective reasonableness, should not be difficult to apply in practice. When officers have acted pursuant to a

---

6. [W]e * * * eschew inquiries into the subjective beliefs of law enforcement officers who seize evidence pursuant to a subsequently invalidated warrant. * * * [W]e believe that "sending state and federal courts on an expedition into the minds of police officers would produce a grave and fruitless misallocation of judicial resources." Massachusetts v. Painten, 389 U.S. 560, 565, 88 S.Ct. 660, 663, 19 L.Ed.2d 770 (1968) (WHITE, J., dissenting). Accordingly, our good-faith inquiry is confined to the objectively ascertainable question whether a reasonably well trained officer would have known that the search was illegal despite the magistrate's authorization. In making this determination, all of the circumstances—including whether the warrant application had previously been rejected by a different magistrate—may be considered.

7. References to "officer" throughout this opinion should not be read too narrowly. It is necessary to consider the objective reasonableness, not only of the officers who eventually executed a warrant, but also of the officers who originally obtained it or who provided information material to the probable-cause determination. Nothing in our opinion suggests, for example, that an officer could obtain a warrant on the basis of a "bare bones" affidavit and then rely on colleagues who are ignorant of the circumstances under which the warrant was obtained to conduct the search.

warrant, the prosecution should ordinarily be able to establish objective good faith without a substantial expenditure of judicial time.

Nor are we persuaded that application of a good-faith exception to searches conducted pursuant to warrants will preclude review of the constitutionality of the search or seizure, deny needed guidance from the courts, or freeze Fourth Amendment law in its present state. There is no need for courts to adopt the inflexible practice of always deciding whether the officers' conduct manifested objective good faith before turning to the question whether the Fourth Amendment has been violated. * * *

If the resolution of a particular Fourth Amendment question is necessary to guide future action by law enforcement officers and magistrates, nothing will prevent reviewing courts from deciding that question before turning to the good-faith issue. Indeed, it frequently will be difficult to determine whether the officers acted reasonably without resolving the Fourth Amendment issue. Even if the Fourth Amendment question is not one of broad import, reviewing courts could decide in particular cases that magistrates under their supervision need to be informed of their errors and so evaluate the officers' good faith only after finding a violation. In other circumstances, those courts could reject suppression motions posing no important Fourth Amendment questions by turning immediately to a consideration of the officers' good faith. We have no reason to believe that our Fourth Amendment jurisprudence would suffer by allowing reviewing courts to exercise an informed discretion in making this choice.

IV

When the principles we have enunciated today are applied to the facts of this case, it is apparent that the judgment of the Court of Appeals cannot stand. * * *

In the absence of an allegation that the magistrate abandoned his detached and neutral role, suppression is appropriate only if the officers were dishonest or reckless in preparing their affidavit or could not have harbored an objectively reasonable belief in the existence of probable cause. * * * Officer Rombach's application for a warrant clearly was supported by much more than a "bare bones" affidavit. The affidavit related the results of an extensive investigation and, as the opinions of the divided panel of the Court of Appeals make clear, provided evidence sufficient to create disagreement among thoughtful and competent judges as to the existence of probable cause. Under these circumstances, the officers' reliance on the magistrate's determination of probable cause was objectively reasonable, and application of the extreme sanction of exclusion is inappropriate.

Accordingly, the judgment of the Court of Appeals is reversed.

[The concurring opinion of JUSTICE BLACKMUN is omitted.]

■ JUSTICE BRENNAN, with whom JUSTICE MARSHALL joins, dissenting.

* * * I have witnessed the Court's gradual but determined strangulation of the [exclusionary] rule. It now appears that the Court's victory over the Fourth Amendment is complete. * * *

I

* * *

At bottom, the Court's decision turns on the proposition that the exclusionary rule is merely a " 'judicially created remedy designed to safeguard Fourth Amendment rights generally through its deterrent effect, rather than a personal constitutional right.' " * * * This reading of the Amendment implies that its proscriptions are directed solely at those government agents who may actually invade an individual's constitutionally protected privacy. The courts are not subject to any direct constitutional duty to exclude illegally obtained evidence, because the question of the admissibility of such evidence is not addressed by the Amendment. * * *

Such a reading appears plausible, because * * * the Fourth Amendment makes no express provision for the exclusion of evidence secured in violation of its commands. A short answer to this claim, of course, is that many of the Constitution's most vital imperatives are stated in general terms and the task of giving meaning to these precepts is therefore left to subsequent judicial decision-making in the context of concrete cases. * * *

[T]he Court's decisions over the past decade have made plain that the entire enterprise of attempting to assess the benefits and costs of the exclusionary rule in various contexts is virtually an impossible task for the judiciary to perform honestly or accurately. Although the Court's language in those cases suggests that some specific empirical basis may support its analyses, the reality is that the Court's opinions represent inherently unstable compounds of intuition, hunches, and occasional pieces of partial and often inconclusive data. * * * Rather than seeking to give effect to the liberties secured by the Fourth Amendment through guesswork about deterrence, the Court should restore to its proper place the principle framed 70 years ago in *Weeks* that an individual whose privacy has been invaded in violation of the Fourth Amendment has a right grounded in that Amendment to prevent the government from subsequently making use of any evidence so obtained.

* * *

III

Even if I were to accept the Court's general approach to the exclusionary rule, I could not agree with today's result. * * * [S]uch a result cannot be justified even on the Court's own terms.

At the outset, the Court suggests that society has been asked to pay a high price—in terms either of setting guilty persons free or of impeding the proper functioning of trials—as a result of excluding relevant physical evidence in cases where the police, in conducting searches and seizing evidence, have made only an "objectively reasonable" mistake concerning the constitutionality of their actions. But what evidence is there to support such a claim?

Significantly, the Court points to none, and, indeed, * * * recent studies have demonstrated that the "costs" of the exclusionary rule—

calculated in terms of dropped prosecutions and lost convictions—are quite low. * * *

What then supports the Court's insistence that this evidence be admitted? Apparently, the Court's only answer is that even though the costs of exclusion are not very substantial, the potential deterrent effect in these circumstances is so marginal that exclusion cannot be justified. * * *

The flaw in the Court's argument, however, is that its logic captures only one comparatively minor element of the generally acknowledged deterrent purposes of the exclusionary rule. To be sure, the rule operates to some extent to deter future misconduct by individual officers who have had evidence suppressed in their own cases. But what the Court overlooks is that the deterrence rationale for the rule is not designed to be, nor should it be thought of as, a form of "punishment" of individual police officers for their failures to obey the restraints imposed by the Fourth Amendment. Instead, the chief deterrent function of the rule is its tendency to promote institutional compliance with Fourth Amendment requirements on the part of law enforcement agencies generally. Thus, as the Court has previously recognized, "over the long term, [the] demonstration [provided by the exclusionary rule] that our society attaches serious consequences to violation of constitutional rights is thought to encourage those who formulate law enforcement policies, and the officers who implement them, to incorporate Fourth Amendment ideals into their value system." It is only through such an institution-wide mechanism that information concerning Fourth Amendment standards can be effectively communicated to rank and file officers.

If the overall educational effect of the exclusionary rule is considered, application of the rule to even those situations in which individual police officers have acted on the basis of a reasonable but mistaken belief that their conduct was authorized can still be expected to have a considerable long-term deterrent effect. If evidence is consistently excluded in these circumstances, police departments will surely be prompted to instruct their officers to devote greater care and attention to providing sufficient information to establish probable cause when applying for a warrant, and to review with some attention the form of the warrant that they have been issued, rather than automatically assuming that whatever document the magistrate has signed will necessarily comport with Fourth Amendment requirements.

After today's decision, however, that institutional incentive will be lost. Indeed, the Court's "reasonable mistake" exception to the exclusionary rule will tend to put a premium on police ignorance of the law. Armed with the assurance provided by today's decision that evidence will always be admissible whenever an officer has "reasonably" relied upon a warrant, police departments will be encouraged to train officers that if a warrant has simply been signed, it is reasonable, without more, to rely on it. Since in close cases there will no longer be any incentive to err on the side of constitutional behavior, police would have every reason to adopt a "let's-wait-until-it's-decided" approach in situations in which there is a question about a warrant's validity or the basis for its issuance. * * *

Although the Court brushes these concerns aside, a host of grave consequences can be expected to result from its decision to carve this new exception out of the exclusionary rule. A chief consequence of today's decision will be to convey a clear and unambiguous message to magistrates that their decisions to issue warrants are now insulated from subsequent judicial review. Creation of this new exception for good faith reliance upon a warrant implicitly tells magistrates that they need not take much care in reviewing warrant applications, since their mistakes will from now on have virtually no consequence: If their decision to issue a warrant was correct, the evidence will be admitted; if their decision was incorrect but the police relied in good faith on the warrant, the evidence will also be admitted. Inevitably, the care and attention devoted to such an inconsequential chore will dwindle. Although the Court is correct to note that magistrates do not share the same stake in the outcome of a criminal case as the police, they nevertheless need to appreciate that their role is of some moment in order to continue performing the important task of carefully reviewing warrant applications. Today's decision effectively removes that incentive.

Moreover, the good faith exception will encourage police to provide only the bare minimum of information in future warrant applications. The police will now know that if they can secure a warrant, so long as the circumstances of its issuance are not "entirely unreasonable," all police conduct pursuant to that warrant will be protected from further judicial review. The clear incentive that operated in the past to establish probable cause adequately because reviewing courts would examine the magistrate's judgment carefully, has now been so completely vitiated that the police need only show that it was not "entirely unreasonable" under the circumstances of a particular case for them to believe that the warrant they were issued was valid. The long-run effect unquestionably will be to undermine the integrity of the warrant process.

* * *

IV

[T]he relaxation of Fourth Amendment standards seems a tempting, costless means of meeting the public's demand for better law enforcement. In the long run, however, we as a society pay a heavy price for such expediency, because as Justice Jackson observed, the rights guaranteed in the Fourth Amendment "are not mere second-class rights but belong in the catalog of indispensable freedoms." Brinegar v. United States, 338 U.S. 160, 180, 69 S.Ct. 1302, 1313, 93 L.Ed. 1879 (1949) (dissenting opinion). Once lost, such rights are difficult to recover. There is hope, however, that in time this or some later Court will restore these precious freedoms to their rightful place as a primary protection for our citizens against over-reaching officialdom.

I dissent.

■ JUSTICE STEVENS, * * * dissenting.

* * * It is probable, though admittedly not certain, that the Court of Appeals would now conclude that the warrant * * * satisfied the Fourth Amendment if it were given the opportunity to reconsider the issue in the light of [Illinois v.] Gates [462 U.S. 213, 103 S.Ct. 2317, 76 L.Ed.2d 527 (1983), reprinted in Chapter 3]. * * * Yet if the Court's assumption is correct—if there was no probable cause—it must follow that it was "unreasonable" for the authorities to make unheralded entries into and searches of private dwellings and automobiles. The Court's conclusion that such searches undertaken without probable cause can nevertheless be "reasonable" is totally without support in our Fourth Amendment jurisprudence.

[I]f * * * there is no probable cause here, then by definition—as a matter of constitutional law—the officers' conduct was unreasonable. * * *

The majority's contrary conclusion rests on the notion that it might be reasonable for a police officer to rely on a magistrate's finding. Until today that has plainly not been the law; it has been well-settled that even when a magistrate issues a warrant there is no guarantee that the ensuing search and seizure is constitutionally reasonable. * * *

The notion that a police officer's reliance on a magistrate's warrant is automatically appropriate is one the Framers of the Fourth Amendment would have vehemently rejected. The precise problem that the Amendment was intended to address was *the unreasonable issuance of warrants.* * * * The fact that colonial officers had magisterial authorization for their conduct when they engaged in general searches surely did not make their conduct "reasonable." The Court's view that it is consistent with our Constitution to adopt a rule that it is presumptively reasonable to rely on a defective warrant is the product of constitutional amnesia.

* * * I would vacate the judgment * * * and remand the case to the Court of Appeals for reconsideration in light of *Gates.* * * *

NOTES

1.   In Massachusetts v. Sheppard, 468 U.S. 981, 104 S.Ct. 3424, 82 L.Ed.2d 737 (1984), a companion case to *Leon,* evidence at issue was also obtained during a search pursuant to a warrant. In *Sheppard,* the judge issuing the warrant incorrectly assured the officer he had modified the warrant form to incorporate by reference a list of items for which the warrant authorized police to search. Although the warrant may have been inadequate for failure to specify the items for which the officers could search, see Part 3 of Chapter 3, the officer reasonably believed it was valid. Thus the evidence was admissible under *Leon.*

2.   **Warrantless Activity Authorized by Invalid Statute.** The "good faith" exception was extended to warrantless searches made pursuant to an invalid statute in Illinois v. Krull, 480 U.S. 340, 107 S.Ct. 1160, 94 L.Ed.2d 364 (1987). A Chicago police officer made a warrantless inspection of a junkyard, believing that the Illinois statute authorizing such inspections was valid. But the statute authorizing inspections of this sort was later held invalid. Nevertheless, the Supreme Court held, the evidence was admissible because of the officer's reliance on the statute. *Krull,* therefore, extended *Leon* to at least certain searches conducted without warrants. *Leon's* analysis, Justice Blackmun explained for the *Krull* majority, indicated a *Leon*-like exception covering the facts before it should be recognized:

> The application of the exclusionary rule to suppress evidence obtained by an officer acting in objectively reasonable reliance on a statute would have as little deterrent effect on the officer's actions as would the exclusion of evidence when an officer acts in objectively reasonable reliance on a warrant. Unless a statute

is clearly unconstitutional, an officer cannot be expected to question the judgment of the legislature that passed the law. * * *

Any difference between our holding in *Leon* and our holding in the instant case * * * must rest on a difference between the effect of the exclusion of evidence on judicial officers and the effect of the exclusion on legislators. * * * We noted in *Leon* as an initial matter that the exclusionary rule was aimed at deterring police misconduct. Thus, legislators, like judicial officers, are not the focus of the rule. * * *

There is no evidence suggesting that Congress or state legislatures have enacted a significant number of statutes permitting warrantless administrative searches violative of the Fourth Amendment. * * * Thus, we are given no basis for believing that legislators are inclined to subvert their oaths and the Fourth Amendment and that "lawlessness among these actors requires application of the extreme sanction of exclusion." * * * There is nothing to indicate that applying the exclusionary rule to evidence seized pursuant to [an invalid] statute prior to the declaration of its invalidity will act as a significant, additional deterrent. Moreover, to the extent that application of the exclusionary rule could provide some incremental deterrent, that possible benefit must be weighed against the "substantial social costs exacted by the exclusionary rule." When we indulge in such weighing, we are convinced that applying the exclusionary rule in this context is unjustified.

480 U.S. at 351–53, 107 S.Ct. at 1168–69, 94 L.Ed.2d at 376–77. But, the Court continued, the *Krull* exception is subject to certain constraints:

A statute cannot support objectively reasonable reliance if, in passing the statute, the legislature wholly abandoned its responsibility to enact constitutional laws. Nor can a law enforcement officer be said to have acted in good-faith reliance upon a statute if its provisions are such that a reasonable officer should have known that the statute was unconstitutional. As we emphasized in *Leon,* the standard of reasonableness we adopt is an objective one; the standard does not turn on the subjective good faith of individual officers.

480 U.S. at 355, 107 S.Ct. at 1170, 94 L.Ed.2d at 378–79.

Turning to the case before it, the majority concluded any such defects as existed in the Illinois statute were not so obvious that an objectively reasonable police officer would have realized the statute was unconstitutional. The officer "relied, in objective good faith, on a statute that appeared legitimately to allow a warrantless administrative search of [Krull's] business," and the evidentiary products of his actions were therefore admissible against Krull. The majority assumed the officer acted within the scope of the statute, but indicated this could be explored on remand:

At this juncture, we decline the State's invitation to recognize an exception for an officer who erroneously but in good faith believes he is acting within the scope of a statute. * * * [S]uch a ruling * * * does not follow inexorably from today's decision. As our opinion makes clear, the question whether the exclusionary rule is applicable in a particular context depends significantly upon the actors who are making the relevant decision that the rule is designed to influence. The answer to this question might well be different when police officers act outside the scope of a statute, albeit in good faith. In that context, the relevant actors are not legislators or magistrates, but police officers who concededly are "engaged in the often competitive enterprise of ferreting out crime."

480 U.S. at 360 n. 17, 107 S.Ct. at 1172 n. 17, 94 L.Ed.2d at 382 n. 17. Justice O'Connor, joined by Justices Brennan, Marshall and Stevens, dissented.

3. **Mistaken Perception that Valid Warrant Exists.** Does the *Leon* good faith exception apply if no valid warrant actually exists but an officer reasonably believes it does? The issue was presented in Arizona v. Evans, 514 U.S. 1, 115 S.Ct. 1185, 131 L.Ed.2d 34 (1995), in which Evans was stopped by a Phoenix police officer for a traffic offense. The officer entered Evans's name into a computer terminal located in the patrol car and he received a message in reply indicating there was an outstanding misdemeanor warrant for Evans's arrest. Based on his belief that such a warrant existed, the officer placed Evans under arrest and, in the process, discovered marijuana. In fact, an arrest warrant was issued for Evans but was quashed 17 days before his arrest. When Evans was prosecuted for possession of the marijuana, he sought suppression of the marijuana. Testimony at the hearing on his motion established the warrant had been for nonappearance on traffic tickets. When Evans appeared before a Justice of the Peace, the justice made a notation on the file to "quash warrant." Evidence also showed standard procedure in such a case was for a justice court clerk to telephone the sheriff's office and relay that the warrant had been quashed. The sheriff's office would then remove the warrant from its computer records. Evans's file did not contain the notation usually made when the clerk calls the sheriff's office and the sheriff's office had no record of a call from the clerk. The trial court made no findings regarding whether the court clerk or the sheriff's office erred but suppressed the marijuana. The Arizona Supreme Court upheld this action, indicating it attached no significance to whether the error was made by a court employee or law enforcement personnel.

The Supreme Court reversed. The Arizona Supreme Court's conclusion that suppression was required even if responsibility for the error rested with the clerk of the justice court "is contrary to the reasoning of [*Leon, Sheppard,* and *Krull*]." Chief Justice Rehnquist continued for the Court:

If court employees were responsible for the erroneous computer record, the exclusion of evidence at trial would not sufficiently deter future errors so as to warrant such a severe sanction. First, as we noted in *Leon,* the exclusionary rule was historically designed as a means of deterring police misconduct, not mistakes by court employees. Second, respondent offers no evidence that court employees are inclined to ignore or subvert the Fourth Amendment or that lawlessness among these actors requires application of the extreme sanction of exclusion. To the contrary, the Chief Clerk of the Justice Court testified at the suppression hearing that this type of error occurred once every three or four years.

Finally, and most important, there is no basis for believing that application of the exclusionary rule in these circumstances will have a significant effect on court employees responsible for informing the police that a warrant has been quashed. Because court clerks are not adjuncts to the law enforcement team engaged in the often competitive enterprise of ferreting out crime, they have no stake in the outcome of particular criminal prosecutions. The threat of exclusion of evidence could not be expected to deter such individuals from failing to inform police officials that a warrant had been quashed.

If it were indeed a court clerk who was responsible for the erroneous entry on the police computer, application of the exclusionary rule also could not be expected to alter the behavior of the arresting officer. As the trial court in this case stated: "I think the police officer [was] bound to arrest. I think he would [have been] derelict in his duty if he failed to arrest." The Chief Clerk of the Justice Court testified that this type of error occurred "on[c]e every three or four years." In fact, once the court clerks discovered the error, they immediately corrected it, and then proceeded to search their files to make sure that no similar mistakes had occurred. There is no indication that the arresting officer was not acting objectively reasonable when he relied upon the police computer record. Application of the *Leon* framework supports a categorical exception to the exclusionary rule for clerical errors of court employees.

514 U.S. at 14–16, 115 S.Ct. at 1193–94, 131 L.Ed.2d at 47. The Court explicitly refused to address whether it would apply a similar analysis to determine whether the evidence would be suppressed if "police personnel" were responsible for the error. It remanded the case to the Arizona Supreme Court for further proceedings not inconsistent with the Supreme Court's opinion.

Justice Stevens dissented on the merits of the basic issue:

Leon stands for the dubious but limited proposition that courts should not look behind the face of a warrant on which police have relied in good faith. The *Leon* Court's exemption of judges and magistrates from the deterrent ambit of the exclusionary rule rested, consistently with the emphasis on the warrant requirement, on those officials' constitutionally determined role in issuing warrants. Taken on its own terms, *Leon's* logic does not extend to the time after the warrant has issued; nor does it extend to court clerks and functionaries, some of whom work in the same building with police officers and may have more regular and direct contact with police than with judges or magistrates.

514 U.S. at 20, 115 S.Ct. at 1196, 131 L.Ed.2d at 50–51 (Stevens, J., dissenting). Justice Ginsburg, joined by Justice Stevens, dissented on the ground that the Arizona court's ruling should be regarded as based on state rather than federal constitutional law.

There have been no further substantive proceedings on remand in *Evans*. The Arizona Supreme Court remanded the case to the trial court for further proceedings. At an appearance before the trial court, the prosecution was informed that, since the original changes were dismissed to render the matter appealable under local procedure, there was no longer any case in which further proceedings could occur. The State refiled the case and the court issued a bench warrant for Evans. Arizona law enforcement agencies are apparently not vigorously searching for Evans given the minor nature of the offense, but the trial prosecutor indicated if Evans is rearrested the case will proceed. Interview with Kim N. Stuart, Deputy Maricopa County Attorney, February 7, 1997.

4. **Statutory "Good Faith" Proposals.** A number of efforts have been made to enact legislation providing for "good faith" exceptions to various exclusionary rules. On the federal level, numerous legislative proposals have been made; none have been enacted. A 1997 proposal for reform, the "Exclusionary Rule Reform Act of 1997," for example, was part of S.B. 3 (105th Congress, Jan. 21, 1997). It would have added the following to Title 18 of the United States Code:

Sec. 3510. Admissibility of evidence obtained by search or seizure

(a) EVIDENCE OBTAINED BY OBJECTIVELY REASONABLE SEARCH OR SEIZURE—

(1) IN GENERAL—Evidence that is obtained as a result of a search or seizure shall not be excluded in a proceeding in a court of the United States on the ground that the search or seizure was in violation of the fourth amendment to the Constitution of the United States, if the search or seizure was carried out in circumstances justifying an objectively reasonable belief that the search or seizure was in conformity with the fourth amendment.

(2) PRIMA FACIE EVIDENCE—The fact that evidence was obtained pursuant to and within the scope of a warrant constitutes prima facie

evidence of the existence of circumstances justifying an objectively reasonable belief that it was in conformity with the fourth amendment.

* * *

The proposal was not enacted. Identical language was introduced in the 1st Session of the 106th Congress. See S.B. 899 (April 28, 1999).

5. **Inevitable Discovery Exception.** Another exception to exclusionary sanctions attaching to violations of federal constitutional rights was recognized in Nix v. Williams, 467 U.S. 431, 104 S.Ct. 2501, 81 L.Ed.2d 377 (1984). Williams was convicted of the murder of a young girl. Following his first trial, the Supreme Court determined he was interrogated in violation of his Sixth and Fourteenth Amendments right to counsel and consequently the statements he made during this interrogation were improperly admitted into evidence at his trial. Brewer v. Williams, 430 U.S. 387, 97 S.Ct. 1232, 51 L.Ed.2d 424 (1977), discussed in Chapter 6(C). In addition, however, Williams revealed to the interrogating officers the location of the victim's body. Using this information, officers found the body. At Williams's second trial, the prosecution did not offer into evidence his incriminating statements nor did it show Williams directed police to the body. It did, however, offer evidence of the condition of the body as found, articles and photographs of clothing found on the body, and the results of medical and chemical tests performed on the body. In support of its offer of this evidence, the prosecution showed that, at the time of Williams' interrogation, a search for the body was underway and that 200 volunteers were involved. This search was called off when Williams began to cooperate with law enforcement officers. But, the state's witness testified, had the search not been called off it would have resulted in discovery of the body after three to five additional hours of searching. The trial judge admitted the evidence on the ground that the prosecution showed that, if Williams had not been improperly interrogated, the victim's body would nevertheless have been found and therefore evidence resulting from the body's discovery was admissible. Williams was again convicted and later sought invalidation of that conviction in federal habeas corpus litigation.

The Supreme Court found no violation of Williams's federal constitutional rights in the use of the evidence. All nine members of the Court agreed the exclusionary sanction attaching to the violation of Williams's Sixth and Fourteenth Amendments right to counsel is subject to an "ultimate or inevitable discovery" exception:

> [W]hen * * * the evidence in question would inevitably have been discovered without reference to the police error or misconduct, there is no nexus [between the error and the evidence] sufficient to provide a taint and the evidence is admissible.

467 U.S. at 448, 104 S.Ct. at 2511, 81 L.Ed.2d at 390. The rationale for this exception, Chief Justice Burger explained for the Court, is the same as that for the "independent source" rule discussed in Part B of this chapter. The need to deter unlawful police conduct is sufficiently met if police engaging in misconduct are put in the same position they would have been in had the misconduct not occurred. This need does not, however, justify putting law enforcement in a worse position than it would have been in had no misconduct taken place. Society's need for reliable evidence of offenders' guilt, on the other hand, strongly argues against any aspect of the exclusionary rules putting a law enforcement agency in a worse position than it would have been in had misconduct not taken place. Both the inevitable discovery exception and the independent source doctrine serve the purpose of assuring that misbehaving law enforcement agencies are not put in any worse position than they would have been in had they avoided the misbehavior. While the case involved the exclusionary penalty for a violation of the Sixth Amendment right to counsel, the

Court's discussion strongly suggests identical exceptions will be recognized with regard to other exclusionary rules, including that adopted in *Mapp* for violations of the Fourth Amendment.

All members of the Court agreed the inevitable discovery exception should not be qualified by requiring the prosecution, as a condition of invoking it, to show the officers acted without "bad faith." Such a condition, the Court reasoned, would in no way further the purpose of the inevitable discovery exception. The members of the Court split, however, on the appropriate burden of proof. Justice Brennan, joined by Justice Marshall, reasoned:

> The inevitable discovery exception necessarily implicates a hypothetical finding that differs in kind from the factual finding that precedes application of the independent source rule. To ensure that this hypothetical finding is narrowly confined to circumstances that are functionally equivalent to an independent source, and to protect fully the fundamental rights served by the exclusionary rule, I would require clear and convincing evidence before concluding that the government had met its burden of proof on this issue.

467 U.S. at 459, 104 S.Ct. at 2517, 81 L.Ed.2d at 397–98 (Brennan, J., dissenting). The Court, however, rejected Justice Brennan's characterization of the analysis and conclusion as to the appropriate burden of proof:

> [I]nevitable discovery involves no speculative elements but focuses on demonstrated historical facts capable of ready verification or impeachment and does not require a departure from the usual burden of proof [by a preponderance of the evidence] at suppression hearings.

467 U.S. at 444 n. 5, 104 S.Ct. at 2509 n. 5, 81 L.Ed.2d at 388 n. 5.

CHAPTER 2

CONSTITUTIONAL DOCTRINES RELATING TO LAW ENFORCEMENT CONDUCT

Analysis

Exclusionary sanctions of the sort considered in Chapter 1 come into operation only if there has been a violation of underlying legal requirements. In constitutional terms, challenges to law enforcement conduct usually rest on provisions guaranteeing protection from compelled self-incrimination, rights to privacy and freedom from unreasonable searches and seizures, rights to the assistance of counsel, and general rights to due process of law. Major federal provisions and illustrative state provisions are set out in the Editors' Introduction at the beginning of Part One of these materials.

This chapter develops the basic content of the major federal constitutional provisions. Part A provides an opportunity to compare several of these provisions as they apply to the extraction of a sample of a suspect's blood. Part B then focuses on the Fourth Amendment. The Fifth Amendment privilege against compelled self-incrimination applies primarily to law enforcement efforts to obtain confessions and other self-incriminating admissions; this is the subject of Chapter 7, and the Fifth Amendment privilege is considered at length in that chapter.

A.   SCOPE OF THE BASIC DOCTRINES

Before considering in detail the impact of the major doctrines, it is important to consider the framework for analyzing situations under these doctrines. The principal case in this section addresses the relevance of these doctrines to a single police activity—the extraction from a suspect of a sample of blood. It is important to distinguish two matters. First, what are the "threshold" issues determining whether the doctrine applies? Second, *if* the doctrine applies, what requirements does it impose upon law enforcement conduct?

Schmerber v. California

Supreme Court of the United States, 1966.
384 U.S. 757, 86 S.Ct. 1826, 16 L.Ed.2d 908.

■ MR. JUSTICE BRENNAN delivered the opinion of the Court.

Petitioner was convicted in Los Angeles Municipal Court of the criminal offense of driving an automobile while under the influence of intoxicating liquor. He had been arrested at a hospital while receiving treatment for injuries suffered in an accident involving the automobile that he had apparently been driving. At the direction of a police officer, a blood sample was then withdrawn from petitioner's body by a physician at the hospital. The chemical analysis of this sample revealed a percent by weight of alcohol in his blood at the time of the offense which indicated intoxication, and the report of this analysis was admitted in evidence at the trial. Petitioner objected to receipt of this evidence of the analysis on the ground that the blood had been withdrawn despite his refusal, on the advice of his counsel, to consent to the test. He contended that in that circumstance the withdrawal of the blood and the admission of the analysis in evidence denied him due process of law under the Fourteenth Amendment, as well as specific guarantees of the Bill of Rights secured against the States by that Amendment: his privilege against self-incrimination under the Fifth Amendment; * * * and his right not to be subjected to unreasonable searches and seizures in violation of the Fourth Amendment. The Appellate Department of the California Superior Court rejected these contentions and affirmed the conviction. In view of constitutional decisions since we last considered these issues in Breithaupt v. Abram, 352 U.S. 432, 77 S.Ct. 408, 1 L.Ed.2d 448 we granted certiorari. We affirm.

I.

The Due Process Clause Claim

[In Rochin v. California, 342 U.S. 165, 72 S.Ct. 205, 96 L.Ed. 183, officers lacking probable cause had entered Rochin's house through an open door. Forcing open the door to Rochin's second floor room, they found Rochin partly dressed and sitting on a bed, upon which his wife was lying. When they asked about two capsules which were on a night stand next to the bed, Rochin grabbed the capsules and swallowed them despite the efforts of the three officers to prevent this. Rochin was then taken to a hospital, where a doctor forced an emetic solution through a tube into his stomach, causing him to vomit. In the vomited matter were found the two capsules which were used in evidence in his later prosecution for possession of the morphine in the capsules. The Supreme Court held that the resulting conviction violated due process:

> This is conduct that shocks the conscience. Illegally breaking into the privacy of [Rochin], the struggle to open his mouth and remove what was there, the forcible extraction of his stomach contents—this course of proceeding by agents of government to obtain evidence is bound to offend even hardened sensibilities. They are methods too close to the rack and screw to permit of constitutional differentiation.

342 U.S. at 172, 72 S.Ct. at 209–10, 96 L.Ed. at 190. Petitioner argues that *Rochin* controls here. Editors.]

Breithaupt was also a case in which police officers caused blood to be withdrawn from the driver of an automobile involved in an accident, and in which there was ample justification for the officer's conclusion that the driver was under the influence of alcohol. There, as here, the extraction was made by a physician in a simple, medically acceptable manner in a hospital environment. There, however, the driver was unconscious at the time the blood was withdrawn and hence had no opportunity to object to the procedure. We affirmed the conviction there resulting from the use of the test in evidence, holding that under such circumstances the withdrawal did not offend "that 'sense of justice' of which we spoke in *Rochin*." *Breithaupt* thus requires the rejection of petitioner's due process argument, and nothing in the circumstances of this case or in supervening events persuades us that this aspect of *Breithaupt* should be overruled.

II.

The Privilege Against Self-incrimination Claim

Breithaupt summarily rejected an argument that the withdrawal of blood and the admission of the analysis report involved in that state case violated the Fifth Amendment privilege of any person not to "be compelled in any criminal case to be a witness against himself," citing Twining v. State of New Jersey, 211 U.S. 78, 29 S.Ct. 14, 53 L.Ed. 97. But that case, holding that the protections of the Fourteenth Amendment do not embrace this Fifth Amendment privilege, has been succeeded by Malloy v. Hogan, 378 U.S. 1, 8, 84 S.Ct. 1489, 1493, 12 L.Ed.2d 653. We there held that "[t]he Fourteenth Amendment secures against state invasion the same privilege that the Fifth Amendment guarantees against federal infringement—the right of a person to remain silent unless he chooses to speak in the unfettered exercise of his own will, and to suffer no penalty * * * for such silence." We therefore must now decide whether the withdrawal of the blood and admission in evidence of the analysis involved in this case violated petitioner's privilege. We hold that the privilege protects an accused only from being compelled to testify against himself, or otherwise provide the State with evidence of a testimonial or communicative nature,[1] and that the withdrawal of blood and use of the analysis in question in this case did not involve compulsion to these ends.

It could not be denied that in requiring petitioner to submit to the withdrawal and chemical analysis of his blood the State compelled him to submit to an attempt to discover evidence that might be used to prosecute him for a criminal offense. He submitted only after the police officer rejected his objection and directed the physician to proceed. The officer's direction to the physician to administer the test over petitioner's objection constituted compulsion for the purposes of the privilege. The critical question, then, is whether petitioner was thus compelled "to be a witness against himself."

If the scope of the privilege coincided with the complex of values it helps to protect, we might be obliged to conclude that the privilege was violated. In Miranda v. Arizona, 384 U.S. 436, at 460, 86 S.Ct. 1602, at 1620, 16 L.Ed.2d 694, at 715, the Court said of the interests protected by the privilege: "All these policies point to one overriding thought: the constitutional foundation underlying the privilege is the respect a government—state or federal—must accord to the dignity and integrity of its citizens. To maintain a 'fair state-individual balance,' to require the government 'to shoulder the entire load,' * * * to respect the inviolability of the human personality, our accusatory system of criminal justice demands that the government seeking to punish an individual produce the evidence against him by its own independent labors, rather than by the cruel, simple expedient of compelling it from his own mouth." The withdrawal of blood necessarily involves puncturing the skin for extraction, and the percent by weight of alcohol in that blood, as established by chemical analysis, is evidence of criminal guilt. Compelled submission fails on one view to respect the "inviolability of the human personality." Moreover, since it enables the State to rely on evidence forced from the accused, the compulsion violates at least one meaning of the requirement that the State procure the evidence against an accused "by its own independent labors."

As the passage in *Miranda* implicitly recognizes, however, the privilege has never been given the full scope which the values it helps to protect suggest. History and a long line of authorities in lower courts have consistently limited its protection to situations in which the State seeks to submerge those values by obtaining the evidence against an accused through "the cruel, simple expedient of compelling it from his own mouth. * * * In sum, the privilege is fulfilled only when the person is guaranteed

---

1. A dissent suggests that the report of the blood test was "testimonial" or "communicative," because the test was performed in order to obtain the testimony of others, communicating to the jury facts about petitioner's condition. Of course, all evidence received in court is "testimonial" or "communicative" if these words are thus used. But the Fifth Amendment relates only to acts on the part of the person to whom the privilege applies, and we use these words subject to the same limitations. A nod or headshake is as much a "testimonial" or "communicative" act in this sense as are spoken words. But the terms as we use them do not apply to evidence of acts noncommunicative in nature as to the person asserting the privilege, even though, as here, such acts are compelled to obtain the testimony of others.

the right 'to remain silent unless he chooses to speak in the unfettered exercise of his own will.' " The leading case in this Court is Holt v. United States, 218 U.S. 245, 31 S.Ct. 2, 54 L.Ed. 1021. There the question was whether evidence was admissible that the accused, prior to trial and over his protest, put on a blouse that fitted him. It was contended that compelling the accused to submit to the demand that he model the blouse violated the privilege. Mr. Justice Holmes, speaking for the Court, rejected the argument as "based upon an extravagant extension of the 5th Amendment," and went on to say: "[T]he prohibition of compelling a man in a criminal court to be witness against himself is a prohibition of the use of physical or moral compulsion to extort communications from him, not an exclusion of his body as evidence when it may be material. The objection in principle would forbid a jury to look at a prisoner and compare his features with a photograph in proof."

It is clear that the protection of the privilege reaches an accused's communications, whatever form they might take * * *. On the other hand, both federal and state courts have usually held that it offers no protection against compulsion to submit to fingerprinting, photographing, or measurements, to write or speak for identification, to appear in court, to stand, to assume a stance, to walk, or to make a particular gesture. The distinction which has emerged, often expressed in different ways, is that the privilege is a bar against compelling "communications" or "testimony," but that compulsion which makes a suspect or accused the source of "real or physical evidence" does not violate it.

Although we agree that this distinction is a helpful framework for analysis, we are not to be understood to agree with past applications in all instances. There will be many cases in which such a distinction is not readily drawn. Some tests seemingly directed to obtain "physical evidence," for example, lie detector tests measuring changes in body function during interrogation, may actually be directed to eliciting responses which are essentially testimonial. To compel a person to submit to testing in which an effort will be made to determine his guilt or innocence on the basis of physiological responses, whether willed or not, is to evoke the spirit and history of the Fifth Amendment. Such situations call to mind the principle that the protection of the privilege "is as broad as the mischief against which it seeks to guard." Counselman v. Hitchcock, 142 U.S. 547, 562, 12 S.Ct. 195, 198.

In the present case, however, no such problem of application is presented. Not even a shadow of testimonial compulsion upon or enforced communication by the accused was involved either in the extraction or in the chemical analysis. Petitioner's testimonial capacities were in no way implicated; indeed, his participation, except as a donor, was irrelevant to the results of the test, which depend on chemical analysis and on that alone.[2] Since the blood test evidence, although an incriminating product of

2. This conclusion would not necessarily govern had the State tried to show that the accused had incriminated himself when told that he would have to be tested. Such incriminating evidence may be an unavoidable by- product of the compulsion to take the test, especially for an individual who fears the extraction or opposes it on religious grounds. If it wishes to compel persons to submit to such attempts to discover evidence, the State compulsion, was neither petitioner's testimony nor evidence relating to some communicative act or writing by the petitioner, it was not inadmissible on privilege grounds.

* * *

IV.

The Search and Seizure Claim

* * *

The values protected by the Fourth Amendment * * * substantially overlap those the Fifth Amendment helps to protect. History and precedent have required that we today reject the claim that the Self–Incrimination Clause of the Fifth Amendment requires the human body in all circumstances to be held inviolate against state expeditions seeking evidence of crime. But if compulsory administration of a blood test does not implicate the Fifth Amendment, it plainly involves the broadly conceived reach of a search and seizure under the Fourth Amendment. That Amendment expressly provides that "[t]he right of the people to be secure in their *persons*, houses, papers, and effects, against unreasonable searches and seizures, shall not be violated * * * ." (Emphasis added.) It could not reasonably be argued, and indeed respondent does not argue, that the administration of the blood test in this case was free of the constraints of the Fourth Amendment. Such testing procedures plainly constitute searches of "persons," and depend antecedently upon seizures of "persons," within the meaning of that Amendment.

Because we are dealing with intrusions into the human body rather than with state interferences with property relationships or private papers—"houses, papers, and effects"—we write on a clean slate. Limitations on the kinds of property which may be seized under warrant, as distinct from the procedures for search and the permissible scope of search, are not instructive in this context. We begin with the assumption that once the privilege against self-incrimination has been found not to bar compelled intrusions into the body for blood to be analyzed for alcohol content, the Fourth Amendment's proper function is to constrain, not against all intrusions as such, but against intrusions which are not justified in the circumstances, or which are made in an improper manner. In other words, the questions we must decide in this case are whether the police were justified in requiring petitioner to submit to the blood test, and whether the means and procedures employed in taking his blood respected relevant Fourth Amendment standards of reasonableness.

In this case, as will often be true when charges of driving under the influence of alcohol are pressed, these questions arise in the context of an arrest made by an officer without a warrant. Here, there was plainly

may have to forego the advantage of any *testimonial* products of administering the test—products which would fall within the privilege. Indeed, there may be circumstances in which the pain, danger, or severity of an operation would almost inevitably cause a person to prefer confession to undergoing the "search," and nothing we say today should be taken as establishing the permissibility of compulsion in that case. But no such situation is presented in this case. * * *

probable cause for the officer to arrest petitioner and charge him with driving an automobile while under the influence of intoxicating liquor. The police officer who arrived at the scene shortly after the accident smelled liquor on petitioner's breath, and testified that petitioner's eyes were "bloodshot, watery, sort of a glassy appearance." The officer saw petitioner again at the hospital, within two hours of the accident. There he noticed similar symptoms of drunkenness. He thereupon informed petitioner "that he was under arrest and that he was entitled to the services of an attorney, and that he could remain silent, and that anything that he told me would be used against him in evidence."

While early cases suggest that there is an unrestricted "right on the part of the government always recognized under English and American law, to search the person of the accused when legally arrested, to discover and seize the fruits or evidences of crime," the mere fact of a lawful arrest does not end our inquiry. The suggestion of these cases apparently rests on two factors—first, there may be more immediate danger of concealed weapons or of destruction of evidence under the direct control of the accused; second, once a search of the arrested person for weapons is permitted, it would be both impractical and unnecessary to enforcement of the Fourth Amendment's purpose to attempt to confine the search to those objects alone. Whatever the validity of these considerations in general, they have little applicability with respect to searches involving intrusions beyond the body's surface. The interests in human dignity and privacy which the Fourth Amendment protects forbid any such intrusions on the mere chance that desired evidence might be obtained. In the absence of a clear indication that in fact such evidence will be found, these fundamental human interests require law officers to suffer the risk that such evidence may disappear unless there is an immediate search.

Although the facts which established probable cause to arrest in this case also suggested the required relevance and likely success of a test of petitioner's blood for alcohol, the question remains whether the arresting officer was permitted to draw these inferences himself, or was required instead to procure a warrant before proceeding with the test. Search warrants are ordinarily required for searches of dwellings, and absent an emergency, no less could be required where intrusions into the human body are concerned. The requirement that a warrant be obtained is a requirement that inferences to support the search "be drawn by a neutral and detached magistrate instead of being judged by the officer engaged in the often competitive enterprise of ferreting out crime." The importance of informed, detached and deliberate determinations of the issue whether or not to invade another's body in search of evidence of guilt is indisputable and great.

The officer in the present case, however, might reasonably have believed that he was confronted with an emergency, in which the delay necessary to obtain a warrant, under the circumstances, threatened "the destruction of evidence." We are told that the percentage of alcohol in the blood begins to diminish shortly after drinking stops, as the body functions to eliminate it from the system. Particularly in a case such as this, where time had to be taken to bring the accused to a hospital and to investigate the scene of the accident, there was no time to seek out a magistrate and secure a warrant. Given these special facts, we conclude that the attempt to secure evidence of blood-alcohol content in this case was an appropriate incident to petitioner's arrest.

Similarly, we are satisfied that the test chosen to measure petitioner's blood-alcohol level was a reasonable one. Extraction of blood samples for testing is a highly effective means of determining the degree to which a person is under the influence of alcohol. Such tests are a commonplace in these days of periodic physical examinations and experience with them teaches that the quantity of blood extracted is minimal, and that for most people the procedure involves virtually no risk, trauma, or pain. Petitioner is not one of the few who on grounds of fear, concern for health, or religious scruple might prefer some other means of testing, such as the "breathalyzer" test petitioner refused. * * * We need not decide whether such wishes would have to be respected.

Finally, the record shows that the test was performed in a reasonable manner. Petitioner's blood was taken by a physician in a hospital environment according to accepted medical practices. We are thus not presented with the serious questions which would arise if a search involving use of a medical technique, even of the most rudimentary sort, were made by other than medical personnel or in other than a medical environment—for example, if it were administered by police in the privacy of the stationhouse. To tolerate searches under these conditions might be to invite an unjustified element of personal risk of infection and pain.

We thus conclude that the present record shows no violation of petitioner's right under the Fourth and Fourteenth Amendments to be free of unreasonable searches and seizures. It bears repeating, however, that we reach this judgment only on the facts of the present record. The integrity of an individual's person is a cherished value of our society. That we today hold that the Constitution does not forbid the States minor intrusions into an individual's body under stringently limited conditions in no way indicates that it permits more substantial intrusions, or intrusions under other conditions.

Affirmed.

NOTES

1. **Providing Voice Samples as Nontestimonial Activity.** In United States v. Wade, 388 U.S. 218, 87 S.Ct. 1926, 18 L.Ed.2d 1149 (1967), the Court held that police did not violate the Fifth Amendment by requiring Wade to say at a lineup the words uttered by a robber—"put the money in the bag." Wade was required, the Court reasoned, only to use his voice in demonstrating its physical characteristics. See also, United States v. Dionisio, 410 U.S. 1, 93 S.Ct. 764, 35 L.Ed.2d 67 (1973) (Fifth Amendment not implicated by subpoena directing suspect to appear at prosecutor's office and read into a recording device from a transcript); United States v. Mara, 410 U.S. 19, 93 S.Ct. 774, 35 L.Ed.2d 99 (1973) (Fifth Amendment not implicated by compulsion to prepare and provide exemplar of handwriting or printing).

2. **Testimonial Aspects of Field Sobriety Tests.** The Court discussed the Fifth Amendment requirement that a compelled act be "testimonial" and the rationale for this demand in Pennsylvania v. Muniz, 496 U.S. 582, 110 S.Ct. 2638, 110 L.Ed.2d 528 (1990), involving the processing—and videotaping—of a suspect arrested for driving while intoxicated. Requiring the arrestee to speak to demonstrate the slurred nature of his speech, all justices agreed, did not involve compelled testimonial activity. "Requiring a suspect to reveal the physical manner in which he articulates words, like requiring him to reveal the physical properties of the sound produced by his voice ... does not, without more, compel him to provide a 'testimonial' response for purposes of the privilege." Having him perform sobriety tests (the "horizontal gaze nystagus" test, the "walk and turn" test and the "one leg stand" test), eight of the justices also held, did not implicate the Fifth Amendment. But asking him the date of his sixth birthday (apparently to determine if he could calculate that from his date of birth), a 5 to 4 majority concluded, did demand testimonial activity. It rejected the argument, accepted by the four dissenters, that this question simply sought a demonstration of the physiological functioning of the suspect's brain, and thus was no different from requiring him to demonstrate his ability to articulate words. Justice Brennan explained for the majority:

> We recently explained in Doe v. United States, 487 U.S. 201, 108 S.Ct. 2341, 101 L.Ed.2d 184 (1988), that "in order to be testimonial, an accused's communication must itself, explicitly or implicitly, relate a factual assertion or disclose information." We reached this conclusion after addressing our reasoning in *Schmerber,* supra, and its progeny:
>
>> The Court accordingly held that the privilege was not implicated in [the line of cases beginning with *Schmerber*] because the suspect was not required "to disclose any knowledge he might have," or "to speak his guilt." *Wade,* 388 U.S., at 222–223, 87 S.Ct. at 1929–1930. It is the "extortion of information from the accused," the attempt to force him "to disclose the contents of his own mind," that implicates the Self–Incrimination Clause * * * "Unless some attempt is made to secure a communication—written, oral or otherwise—upon which reliance is to be placed as involving (the accused's) consciousness of the facts and the operations of his mind in expressing it, the demand made upon him is not a testimonial one." 8 Wigmore § 2265, p. 386.

487 U.S., at 210–211, 108 S.Ct. at 2348.

> After canvassing the purposes of the privilege recognized in prior cases, we concluded that "[t]hese policies are served when the privilege is asserted to spare the accused from having to reveal, directly or indirectly, his knowledge of facts relating him to the offense or from having to share his thoughts and beliefs with the Government."
>
> This definition of testimonial evidence reflects an awareness of the historical abuses against which the privilege against self-incrimination was aimed. "Historically, the privilege was intended to prevent the use of legal compulsion to extract from the accused a sworn communication of facts which would incriminate him. Such was the process of the ecclesiastical courts and the Star Chamber—the inquisitorial method of putting the accused upon his oath and compelling him to answer questions designed to uncover uncharged offenses, without evidence from another source. The major thrust of the policies undergirding the privilege is to prevent such compulsion." At its core, the privilege reflects our fierce "unwillingness to subject those suspected of crime to the cruel trilemma of self-accusation, perjury or contempt," that defined the operation of the Star Chamber, wherein suspects were forced to choose between

revealing incriminating private thoughts and forsaking their oath by committing perjury. See United States v. Nobles, 422 U.S. 225, 233, 95 S.Ct. 2160, 2167, 45 L.Ed.2d 141 (1975) ("The Fifth Amendment privilege against compulsory self-incrimination ... protects 'a private inner sanctum of individual feeling and thought and proscribes state intrusion to extract self-condemnation' ").

We need not explore the outer boundaries of what is "testimonial" today, for our decision flows from the concept's core meaning. Because the privilege was designed primarily to prevent "a recurrence of the Inquisition and the Star Chamber, even if not in their stark brutality," it is evident that a suspect is "compelled ... to be a witness against himself" at least whenever he must face the modern-day analog of the historic trilemma—either during a criminal trial where a sworn witness faces the identical three choices, or during custodial interrogation where ... the choices are analogous and hence raise similar concerns. Whatever else it may include, therefore, the definition of "testimonial" evidence ... must encompass all responses to questions that, if asked of a sworn suspect during a criminal trial, could place the suspect in the "cruel trilemma." This conclusion is consistent with our recognition in *Doe* that "[t]he vast majority of verbal statements thus will be testimonial" because "[t]here are very few instances in which a verbal statement, either oral or written, will not convey information or assert facts." Whenever a suspect is asked for a response requiring him to communicate an express or implied assertion of fact or belief, the suspect confronts the "trilemma" of truth, falsity, or silence and hence the response (whether based on truth or falsity) contains a testimonial component.

496 U.S. at 594–97, 110 S.Ct. at 2646–48, 110 L.Ed.2d at 547–49.

Turning to the facts of the case, it continued:

When [the officer] asked Muniz if he knew the date of his sixth birthday and Muniz, for whatever reason, could not remember or calculate that date, he was confronted with the trilemma. By hypothesis the inherently coercive environment created by the custodial interrogation precluded the option of remaining silent. Muniz was left with the choice of incriminating himself by admitting that he did not then know the date of his sixth birthday, or answering untruthfully by reporting a date that he did not then believe to be accurate (an incorrect guess would be incriminating as well as untruthful). The content of his truthful answer supported an inference that his mental faculties were impaired, because his assertion (he did not know the date of his sixth birthday) was different from the assertion (he knew the date was (correct date)) that the trier of fact might reasonably have expected a lucid person to provide. Hence, the incriminating inference of impaired mental faculties stemmed, not just from the fact that Muniz slurred his response, but also from a testimonial aspect of that response.

496 U.S. at 599, 110 S.Ct. at 2649, 110 L.Ed.2d at 550. The Court did not reach whether asking Muniz to count out loud while performing the physical sobriety tests involved "testimonial" activity. During one test, he counted accurately and thus his responses were not incriminating. During another, he failed to count and did not argue that his silence had any "independent incriminating significance."

3. **Compulsion Must be "Impermissible."** The Fifth Amendment is violated only if compulsion to engage in testimonial and self-incriminating activity is impermissible. Many states provide under "implied consent" statutes that, under certain circumstances, a person suspected of driving while intoxicated may be "requested" by an officer to provide a blood or breath sample but may not be forced to provide the sample if he refuses. Such a refusal is itself often admissible against

the suspect if he does not provide the requested sample. In South Dakota v. Neville, 459 U.S. 553, 103 S.Ct. 916, 74 L.Ed.2d 748 (1983), the Court held that whether or not such a refusal is "testimonial," the Fifth Amendment does not bar use of such evidence because no "impermissible compulsion" is imposed upon the suspect. *Schmerber,* the Court observed, clearly permits a State under certain circumstances to force a person to submit to a blood test:

> Given * * * that the offer of taking a blood-alcohol test is clearly legitimate, the action becomes no *less* legitimate when the State offers a second option of refusing the test, with the attendant penalties of making that choice.

459 U.S. at 563, 103 S.Ct. at 923, 74 L.Ed.2d at 759 (emphasis in original).

4. The application of the privilege against compelled self-incrimination to subpoenas requiring the production of documents is considered in Chapter 9. Fifth Amendment self-incrimination principles are examined more fully in the setting of police interrogation in Chapter 7.

5. **Requirement That Compelled Activity be "Incriminating."** The Fifth Amendment bars law enforcement officers compelling a person to engage in testimonial activity only when that activity is "incriminating." In Minnesota v. Murphy, 465 U.S. 420, 104 S.Ct. 1136, 79 L.Ed.2d 409 (1984), the Supreme Court, in dicta, indicated revocation of probation is not "incrimination" within the meaning of the privilege. Thus, probationers can apparently be compelled, without violation of the privilege, to answer questions that might result in revocation of probation but that pose "no realistic threat of incrimination in a separate criminal proceeding."

6. **Fourth Amendment Warrant Requirement.** *Schmerber's* Fourth Amendment analysis reflects the Court's controversial conclusion that the Fourth Amendment reasonableness requirement demands—as a general rule subject to exceptions—a search be conducted pursuant to a search warrant. The literal terms of the provision impose no such requirement, and in fact have little to offer concerning when a search warrant is necessary. Would the spirit and purpose of the Fourth Amendment be better served if the Court did not focus upon a need to fit a warrantless search into one of the exceptions to a general rule that a warrant is necessary? The Court might instead scrutinize each search for reasonableness under a more flexible standard.

7. **Fourth Amendment Probable Cause Requirement.** *Schmerber* appeared to recognize a general Fourth Amendment requirement that a search be based upon "probable cause" to believe that the search would result in discovery of something the officers had a right to seize. The meaning of probable cause is developed in part A(1) of Chapter 3, addressing the showing that must be made for issuance of a search warrant. Generally, however, probable cause means "a fair probability" that seizable material or items will be found in the location at issue. Thus as applied to the *Schmerber* situation, facts establishing probable cause would mean facts establishing a fair probability that seizable material—evidence that Schmerber was guilty of driving while intoxication—would be found if the search were conducted.

Is it clear that *Schmerber* required probable cause for the search at issue in the case—the insertion of a needle into the suspect's arm to seek blood believed to contain alcohol?

8. **Due Process Prohibition Against Conduct Shocking the Conscience.** *Schmerber* discussed the due process claim based on *Rochin* as an independent potential basis for excluding the evidence obtained from a blood withdrawal. Is the due process prohibition against law enforcement conduct that "shocks the conscience" still a viable independent basis for challenging the admissi-

bility of evidence? County of Sacramento v. Lewis, 523 U.S. 833, 118 S.Ct. 1708, 140 L.Ed.2d 1043 (1998), indicated yes and suggested the requirements for such an attack. In *Lewis*, the Court addressed the civil liability of officers' employing governmental entity for damages based on the Lewis's death, caused by a vehicle collision resulting from a high speed police chase. The plaintiff argued the officers' actions violated suspect Lewis's right to substantive due process. Discussing *Rochin*, the Court commented that the case "today would be treated under the Fourth Amendment, albeit with the same result." This is apparently because the officers' actions in *Rochin* would now constitute unreasonable searches and seizures and the resultant evidence would be inadmissible under *Mapp*.

The law enforcement action in *Lewis*, however, was held at most an *attempted* seizure, and thus not within the Fourth Amendment's prohibition against unreasonable seizures. Nevertheless, *Lewis* indicated a high speed chase could constitute an actionable violation of substantive due process under *Rochin* if the officers acted with "intent to harm [the] suspects physically or to worsen their legal plight * * *." In *Rochin*, it added, "it was not the ultimate purpose of the [officers] to harm the plaintiff, but they apparently acted with full appreciation of what the Court described as the brutality of their acts." This appreciation of the brutality of the conduct apparently sufficed to trigger substantive due process in *Rochin*.

B.   THE FOURTH AMENDMENT'S PROHIBITION AGAINST UNREASONABLE SEARCHES AND SEIZURES

Perhaps in part because of the limited applicability of the Fifth Amendment, the Fourth Amendment's prohibition against unreasonable searches and seizures has become the major federal constitutional vehicle for regulating police conduct in gathering evidence. Several threshold issues presented by efforts to invoke this prohibition are considered in this portion of the materials. The first two subsections consider when law enforcement conduct constitutes a "search" or a "seizure" so as to invoke the Fourth Amendment. The third subsection then addresses the effect of the requirement of standing and a narrow conception of what constitutes a search. But first the Introduction discusses the limitation of the Fourth Amendment to official conduct.

EDITORS' INTRODUCTION: PRIVATE PARTY SEARCHES AND SEIZURES

The Fourth Amendment's application is limited by the Supreme Court's position that it constrains only governmental action and does not apply to the conduct of a person acting purely in a private capacity. The leading case on private party searches is Burdeau v. McDowell, 256 U.S. 465, 41 S.Ct. 574, 65 L.Ed. 1048 (1921). The petitioner moved for return of private papers wrongfully taken from his office by private persons and turned over to the government. The Court disposed of his Fourth Amendment claim with the following comments:

> The Fourth Amendment gives protection against unlawful searches and seizures, and * * * its protection applies to governmental action. Its origin and history clearly show that it was intended as a restraint upon the activities of sovereign authority, and was not intended to be a limitation upon other than governmental agencies * * *.

In the present case the record clearly shows that no official of the federal government had anything to do with the wrongful seizure of the petitioner's property, or any knowledge thereof until several months after the property had been taken from him and was in the possession of the Cities Service Company. It is manifest that there was no invasion of the security afforded by the Fourth Amendment against unreasonable searches and seizure, as whatever wrong was done was the act of individuals in taking the property of another. A portion of the property so taken and held was turned over to the prosecuting officers of the federal government. We assume that petitioner has an unquestionable right of redress against those who illegally and wrongfully took his private property under the circumstances here disclosed, but with such remedies we are not now concerned.

256 U.S. at 475, 41 S.Ct. at 576, 65 L.Ed. at 1051.

The Court continued to apply this approach, although leaving open the possibility that involvement of governmental officers in stimulating or conducting a search by a private person might render that search within the scope of the Fourth Amendment. See United States v. Jacobsen, 466 U.S. 109, 113, 104 S.Ct. 1652, 1656, 80 L.Ed.2d 85, 94 (1984); Walter v. United States, 447 U.S. 649, 100 S.Ct. 2395, 65 L.Ed.2d 410 (1980). In Coolidge v. New Hampshire, 403 U.S. 443, 91 S.Ct. 2022, 29 L.Ed.2d 564 (1971), for example, the murder suspect's wife was interviewed at the couple's home while he was in custody. In response to officers' inquiries concerning guns owned by her husband and the clothing he wore the day of the crime, she—apparently on her own initiative—obtained guns and clothing and offered them to the officers. Rejecting Coolidge's argument that this was a search despite Burdeau v. McDowell, the Court explained:

The question presented here is whether the conduct of the police officers at the Coolidge house was such as to make her actions their actions for purposes of the Fourth and Fourteenth Amendment and their attendant exclusionary rules. The test * * * is whether Mrs. Coolidge, in light of all the circumstances of the case, must be regarded as having acted as an "instrument" or agent of the state when she produced her husband's belongings. * * * Mrs. Coolidge described her own motive as that of clearing her husband, and that she believed that she had nothing to hide. * * * The two officers who questioned her behaved, as her own testimony shows, with perfect courtesy. There is not the slightest implication of an attempt of their part to coerce or dominate her, or, for that matter, to direct her actions by the more subtle techniques of suggestion that are available to officials in circumstances like these.

403 U.S. at 487–89, 91 S.Ct. at 2048–50, 29 L.Ed.2d at 595–96.

1. POLICE ACTIVITY CONSTITUTING A "SEARCH"

EDITORS' INTRODUCTION: THE *KATZ* CRITERION FOR IDENTIFYING SEARCHES AND THE REASONABLENESS OF SEARCHES

Whether law enforcement conduct constitutes a search for purposes of the Fourth Amendment is often determined by application of a standard derived from Katz v. United States, 389 U.S. 347, 88 S.Ct. 507, 19 L.Ed.2d 576 (1967). Whether conduct constituting a search is reasonable is generally determined by whether it is based on probable cause and is either supported by a warrant or within an exception to the general requirement of a warrant.

Katz and the Reasonable Expectation of Privacy Test

Prior to *Katz,* Fourth Amendment case law defining searches focused to some extent upon whether police had intruded in some physical sense into a protected area. In Silverman v. United States, 365 U.S. 505, 81 S.Ct. 679, 5 L.Ed.2d 734 (1961), for example, the Court held that officers engaged in a search when they used a "spike mike" to overhear conversations in an adjacent row house. The discussion suggested that this result was based on the showing officers inserted the microphone into a wall of the suspects house until it touched a heating duct. Thus the police conducted "an unauthorized physical penetration into the premises."

In *Katz,* federal officers attached an electronic listening and recording device to the outside of a public telephone booth that they anticipated Katz would use. Katz did use the booth, and the officers were able to overhear his end of the conversation. Finding the officers engaged in a "search," the Court stressed this conclusion did not turn upon whether the phone booth was a protected area. Instead it explained:

> What a person knowingly exposes to the public, even in his own home or office, is not a subject of Fourth Amendment protection. * * * But what he seeks to preserve as private, even in an area accessible to the public, may be constitutionally protected.

389 U.S. at 351, 88 S.Ct. at 511, 19 L.Ed.2d at 582. Later cases, however, often cite and use language from a concurring opinion by Justice Harlan:

> My understanding of the rule [determining the protection provided by the Fourth Amendment] is that there is a twofold requirement, first that a person have exhibited an actual (subjective) expectation of privacy and, second, that the expectation be one that society is prepared to recognize as "reasonable."

389 U.S. at 361, 88 S.Ct. at 516, 19 L.Ed.2d at 587–88 (Harlan, J., concurring). Thus a search was conducted in *Katz* because when Katz used the telephone booth, he subjectively believed his conversation would be private between him and the other party and that belief was objectively reasonable.

"Plain View" Observations

The definition of law enforcement activity constituting a search is closely related to one use of the term, "plain view." As the Supreme Court noted in Horton v. California, 496 U.S. 128, 133 n. 4, 110 S.Ct. 2301, 2306 n. 4, 110 L.Ed.2d 112, 121 n. 4 (1990), the term sometimes describes a situation in which an officer has merely observed an item "left in plain view." In these situations, characterization of the facts as presenting plain view—what might be best termed a "plain view observation"—means the observation was not a search. This is because the location of the item in plain view means the owner had no reasonable expectation of privacy in information obtainable by looking at the item. As *Horton* (reprinted later in this chapter) makes clear, this use of the term plain view must be distinguished from its use in describing or justifying a *seizure* of an item. This use generally reflects a conclusion that an officer's action, although constituting a seizure, was nevertheless reasonable under the Fourth Amendment requirements applicable to seizures of items.

In the principal cases reprinted in the following two sections of this chapter, for example, the question is whether the officers engaged in unreasonable searches by either going on the land or observing a structure from an aircraft. Suppose Fourth Amendment law established the officers in the first case engaged in no searches by entering upon the land of the defendants. In that case, the officers' observations of the marijuana were plain view observations; neither getting to the place where the observations were made nor making the observation involved an intrusion upon a reasonable expectation of privacy harbored by the defendants. Had the officers also seized the marijuana, the case would present a much different question—the reasonableness of what was clearly a seizure. This seizure would probably have been defended by the prosecution as a reasonable— although warrantless—plain view seizure.

If, because of darkness, an officer cannot see what is in a parked car but shines his flashlight into the car and observes incriminating items, has the officer "searched" or has the offer merely exercised the right to engage in plain view observations? A plurality of the Court, with no disagreement from other justices, indicated that "the use of artificial means to illuminate a darkened area," like the use of "a marine glass or a field glass," does not constitute a search. Texas v. Brown, 460 U.S. 730, 740, 103 S.Ct. 1535, 1542, 75 L.Ed.2d 502, 512 (1983) (opinion of Rehnquist, J., announcing the judgment of the Court).

Law Enforcement Conduct Revealing Only Criminal Information

Law enforcement conduct may escape characterization as a search if it can reveal only information which, because of its criminal nature, permits no reasonable expectation of privacy.

In United States v. Jacobsen, 466 U.S. 109, 104 S.Ct. 1652, 80 L.Ed.2d 85 (1984), federal officers took small amounts of a suspicious substance found in plastic bags and subjected them to field tests to determine whether the substance was cocaine. This action was held not to involve a search, on the assumption that the tests could reveal nothing other than whether or not the substance was cocaine. Congress criminalized even private possession of cocaine; "thus governmental conduct that can reveal whether a substance is cocaine and no other arguably 'private' fact, compromises no legitimate privacy interest."

Searches Permissible on Less Than Probable Cause

Generally, law enforcement activity constituting a search is reasonable under the Fourth Amendment only if: (a) it is conducted pursuant to a search warrant; and (b) it is supported by probable cause to believe it will result in obtaining information that a crime has been committed or the identity of a person who has committed a crime. A number of exceptions to the requirement of a warrant have also been developed; these exceptions are addressed in Chapter 5. As Chapter 5 also demonstrates, the Supreme Court has sometimes been willing to hold law enforcement activity constituting a seizure reasonable on less than such probable cause. The Court has been reluctant, however, to characterize searches—at least of items rather than persons—as permissible on such a relaxed standard.

This reluctance was reflected in Arizona v. Hicks, 480 U.S. 321, 107 S.Ct. 1149, 94 L.Ed.2d 347 (1987). An officer, properly present in an apartment to look for someone who had shot through the floor into the apartment below, moved some suspicious stereo equipment slightly to permit him to see serial numbers on the items. This movement of the equipment was a search, because it enabled the officer to obtain information—the serial numbers—otherwise unavailable to them. Justice O'Connor, joined in dissent by the Chief Justice and Justice Powell, characterized the action as not a "full-blown search" but rather a "cursory inspection of an item in view." Since the action intruded upon privacy interests less than a full-blown search, it should be reasonable on less than is required for such a full-blown search. Specifically, Justice O'Connor argued that it should require not probable cause but only "reasonable suspicion." Reasonable suspicion is used in several contexts as the standard for determining the Fourth Amendment reasonableness of relatively-nonintrusive law enforcement activity; its content—as applied to certain nonarrest detentions of suspects—is addressed in Part C(1) of Chapter 4. Reasonable suspicion requires some objective basis for a belief that "seizable" items or information will be found by a search, but it clearly does not demand as firm a basis for this belief as is required for probable cause. Justice O'Connor explained specifically:

> [T]he balance of the governmental and privacy interests strongly supports a reasonable suspicion standard for the cursory examination of items in plain view. The additional intrusion caused by an inspection of an item in plain view for its serial number is minuscule. * * *
>
> Weighed against this * * * are rather major gains in law enforcement. The use of identification numbers in tracing stolen property is a powerful law enforcement tool. Serial numbers are far more helpful and accurate in detecting stolen property than simple police recollection of the evidence. Given the prevalence of mass produced goods in our national economy, a serial number is often the only sure method of detecting stolen property.

480 U.S. at 338–39, 107 S.Ct. at 1159–60 94 L.Ed.2d at 355 (O'Connor, J., dissenting). Justice Scalia's opinion for the Court, however, rejected this approach:

> [A] truly cursory inspection—one that involves merely looking at what is already exposed to view, without disturbing it—is not a "search" for Fourth Amendment purposes, and therefore does not even require reasonable suspicion. We are unwilling to send police and judges into a new thicket of Fourth Amendment law, to seek a creature of uncertain description that is neither a plain-view inspection nor yet a "full-blown search."

480 U.S. at 328–29, 107 S.Ct. at 1154, 94 L.Ed.2d at 356.

Electronic Surveillance as a Search

Katz itself established that mechanical interception of spoken words is sometimes a "search," and thus gave rise to the law dealing with wiretapping and electronic surveillance considered in Chapter 6. But in Smith v. Maryland, 442 U.S. 735, 99 S.Ct. 2577, 61 L.Ed.2d 220 (1979), the Court considered the use of a pen register. Installed at the telephone company's main office, this device records the numbers dialed from a given telephone but does not permit the overhearing of conversations. Under *Katz,* this recording of dialed numbers was not a search, the Court concluded, because telephone users cannot reasonably entertain an expectation of privacy in numbers dialed from telephones:

> All telephone users realize that they must "convey" phone numbers to the telephone company, since it is through telephone company switching equipment that their calls are completed. All subscribers realize, moreover, that the phone company has facilities for making permanent records of the numbers they dial, for they see a list of their long-distance (toll) calls on their monthly bills. * * * Although most people may be oblivious to a pen register's esoteric functions, they presumably have some awareness of one common use: to aid in the identification of persons making annoying or obscene calls.

442 U.S. at 742, 99 S.Ct. at 2581, 61 L.Ed.2d at 228.

Dog Sniffing as a Search

In United States v. Place, 462 U.S. 696, 103 S.Ct. 2637, 77 L.Ed.2d 110 (1983), the Court held that exposure of luggage, located in a public place, to "sniffing" by a drug detecting dog did not amount to a "search." The Court explained:

> A "canine sniff" by a well-trained dog * * * does not require opening the luggage. It does not expose noncontraband items that otherwise would remain hidden from public view, as does, for example, an officer's rummaging through the contents of the luggage. Thus, the manner in which information is obtained through this investigative technique is much less intrusive than a typical search. Moreover, the sniff discloses only the presence or absence of narcotics, a contraband item. Thus, despite the fact that the sniff tells the authorities something about the contents of the luggage, the information obtained is limited. This limited disclosure also ensures that the owner of the property is not subjected to the embarrassment and inconvenience entailed in less discriminate and more intrusive investigative methods.

462 U.S. at 707, 103 S.Ct. at 2644, 77 L.Ed.2d at 121.

Examination of Trash as a Search

Whether law enforcement examination of a suspect's trash constitutes a search was considered in California v. Greenwood, 486 U.S. 35, 108 S.Ct. 1625, 100 L.Ed.2d 30 (1988). Suspicious Greenwood might be involved in drug trafficking, a police officer asked the trash collector to pick up the plastic garbage bags from Greenwood's curb and turn them over to the officer rather than mixing them with other trash. Before going past Greenwood's curb, the garbage collector removed all previously-collected trash from his truck. He then collected the bags from Greenwood's curb and gave them to the officer, who found items indicating that Greenwood used narcotics. Police used this information was used to procure a search warrant for Greenwood's residence. Drugs were found during execution of that warrant. Greenwood and Dyanne Van Houten were arrested at the premises. After their release on bail, officers again inspected their trash and a search pursuant to another warrant disclosed additional drugs. The state courts held the officers' examinations of the trash constituted unreasonable searches under the Fourth Amendment. Reversing, a majority of the Supreme Court found no Fourth Amendment search in the officers' conduct:

[Respondents] assert * * * that they had, and exhibited, an expectation of privacy with respect to the trash that was searched by the police: The trash, which was placed on the street for collection at a fixed time, was contained in opaque plastic bags, which the garbage collector was expected to pick up, mingle with the trash of others, and deposit at the garbage dump. The trash was only temporarily on the street, and there was little likelihood that it would be inspected by anyone.

It may well be that respondents did not expect that the contents of their garbage bags would become known to the police or any other members of the public. An expectation of privacy does not give rise to Fourth Amendment protection, however, unless society is prepared to accept that expectation as objectively reasonable.

Here, we conclude that respondents exposed their garbage to the public sufficiently to defeat their claim to Fourth Amendment protection. It is common knowledge that plastic garbage bags left on or at the side of a public street are readily accessible to animals, children, scavengers, snoops, and other members of the public. Moreover, respondents placed their refuse at the curb for the express purpose of conveying it to a third party, the trash collector, who might himself have sorted through respondents' trash or permitted others, such as the police, to do so. Accordingly, having deposited their garbage "in an area particularly suited for public inspection, and, in a manner of speaking, public consumption, for the express purpose of having strangers take it," United States v. Reicherter, 647 F.2d 397, 399 (3d Cir.1981), respondents could have had no reasonable expectation of privacy in the inculpatory items that they discarded.

486 U.S. at 39–41, 108 S.Ct. at 1628–29, 100 L.Ed.2d at 36–37.

Justice Brennan, joined by Justice Marshall, dissented. He argued that a trash bag, like other containers, is a repository of personal effects and therefore associated with privacy expectations. Given the nature of trash and what it reveals about "sexual practices, health, and personal hygiene," a sealed trash bag often harbors evidence of private activities closely associated with the sanctity of the home and the privacies of life protected by the Fourth Amendment. He continued:

Had Greenwood flaunted his intimate activity by strewing his trash all over the curb for all to see, or had some nongovernmental intruder invaded his privacy and done the same, I could accept the Court's conclusion that an expectation of privacy would have been unreasonable. Similarly, had police searching the city dump run across incriminating evidence that, despite commingling with the trash of others, still retained its identity as Greenwood's, we would have a different case. * * *

The mere *possibility* that unwelcome meddlers *might* open and rummage through the containers does not negate the expectation of privacy in its contents any more than the possibility of a burglary negates an expectation of privacy in the home * * * .

Nor is it dispositive that "respondents placed their refuse at the curb * * *." In the first place, Greenwood can hardly be faulted for leaving trash on his curb when a county ordinance commanded him to do so * * *. More importantly, even the voluntary relinquishment of possession or control over an effect does not necessarily amount to a relinquishment of a privacy expectation in it. Were it otherwise, a letter or package would lose all Fourth Amendment protection when placed in a mail box * * *.

486 U.S. at 53–55, 108 S.Ct. at 1636–37, 100 L.Ed.2d at 45–46 (Brennan, J., dissenting).

* * *

The two following subsections consider application of the *Katz* standard to two particularly important areas: physical entry of private property and aerial and other surveillance. In each of the principal cases, the police failed to obtain a warrant; if their activity is a search, that search will almost certainly be unreasonable and the evidence unavailable to the prosecution. But on a more general level, characterizing such activity as a search does not mean the Fourth Amendment prohibits police from engaging in the conduct. Rather, the conduct becomes subject to the requirements of Fourth Amendment reasonableness. The Fourth Amendment should be construed as applicable to law enforcement conduct sufficiently intruding upon privacy concerns to justify its *regulation*—not its *prohibition*—by application of the Fourth Amendment's requirement of reasonableness. Does the Court properly follow this approach in the two principal cases?

a.   ENTRY ONTO "OPEN FIELDS"

When officers physically go on real property, do they engage in a search? To what extent does the answer to this question depend upon the efforts the person in possession or control of the property has taken to preserve from others what is or occurs on the property?

Oliver v. United States

Supreme Court of the United States, 1984.
466 U.S. 170, 104 S.Ct. 1735, 80 L.Ed.2d 214.

■ JUSTICE POWELL delivered the opinion of the Court.

The "open fields" doctrine, first enunciated by this Court in Hester v. United States, 265 U.S. 57, 44 S.Ct. 445, 68 L.Ed. 898 (1924), permits police officers to enter and search a field without a warrant. We granted certiorari in these cases to clarify confusion that has arisen as to the continued vitality of the doctrine.

I

No. 82–15. Acting on reports that marijuana was being raised on the farm of petitioner Oliver, two narcotics agents of the Kentucky State Police went to the farm to investigate.[3] Arriving at the farm, they drove past petitioner's house to a locked gate with a "No Trespassing" sign. A footpath led around one side of the gate. The agents walked around the gate and along the road for several hundred yards, passing a barn and a parked camper. At that point, someone standing in front of the camper shouted, "No hunting is allowed, come back here." The officers shouted back that they were Kentucky State Police officers, but found no one when they returned to the camper. The officers resumed their investigation of the farm and found a field of marijuana over a mile from petitioner's home.

Petitioner was arrested and indicted for "manufactur[ing]" a "controlled substance." After a pretrial hearing, the District Court suppressed evidence of the discovery of the marijuana fields. Applying Katz v. United States, 389 U.S. 347, 357, 88 S.Ct. 507, 514, 19 L.Ed.2d 576 (1967), the court found that petitioner had a reasonable expectation that the fields would remain private because petitioner "had done all that could be expected of him to assert his privacy in the area of farm that was searched." He had posted no trespassing signs at regular intervals and had locked the gate at the entrance to the center of the farm. Further, the court noted that the fields themselves are highly secluded: they are bounded on all sides by woods, fences and embankments and cannot be seen from any point of public access. The court concluded that this was not an "open" field that invited casual intrusion.

The Court of Appeals for the Sixth Circuit, sitting *en banc,* reversed the district court. The court concluded that *Katz,* upon which the District Court relied, had not impaired the vitality of the open fields doctrine of *Hester.* Rather, the open fields doctrine was entirely compatible with *Katz's* emphasis on privacy. The court reasoned that the "human relations that create the need for privacy do not ordinarily take place" in open fields, and that the property owner's common law right to exclude trespassers is insufficiently linked to privacy to warrant the Fourth Amendment's protection. We granted certiorari.

No. 82–1273. After receiving an anonymous tip that marijuana was being grown in the woods behind respondent Thornton's residence, two police officers entered the woods by a path between this residence and a neighboring house. They followed a footpath through the woods until they reached two marijuana patches fenced with chicken wire. Later, the officers determined that the patches were on the property of respondent, obtained a

---

3. It is conceded that the police did not have a warrant authorizing the search, that there was no probable cause for the search and that no exception to the warrant requirement is applicable.

warrant to search the property and seized the marijuana. On the basis of this evidence, respondent was arrested and indicted.

The trial court granted respondent's motion to suppress the fruits of the second search. The warrant for this search was premised on information that the police had obtained during their previous warrantless search, that the court found to be unreasonable. "No Trespassing" signs and the secluded location of the marijuana patches evinced a reasonable expectation of privacy. Therefore, the court held, the "open fields" doctrine did not apply.

The Maine Supreme Judicial Court affirmed. It agreed with the trial court that the correct question was whether the search "is a violation of privacy on which the individual justifiably relied," and that the search violated respondent's privacy. The court also agreed that the "open fields" doctrine did not justify the search. That doctrine applies, according to the court, only when officers are lawfully present on property and observe "open and patent" activity. In this case, the officers had trespassed upon defendant's property, and the respondent had made every effort to conceal his activity. We granted certiorari.

II

The rule announced in Hester v. United States was founded upon the explicit language of the Fourth Amendment. That Amendment indicates with some precision the places and things encompassed by its protections. As Justice Holmes explained for the Court in his characteristically laconic style: "[T]he special protection accorded by the Fourth Amendment to the people in their 'persons, houses, papers, and effects,' is not extended to the open fields. The distinction between the latter and the house is as old as the common law." Hester v. United States, 265 U.S., at 59, 44 S.Ct., at 446.

Nor are the open fields "effects" within the meaning of the Fourth Amendment. In this respect, it is suggestive that James Madison's proposed draft of what became the Fourth Amendment preserves "[t]he rights of the people to be secured in their persons, their houses, their papers, and their other property, from all unreasonable searches and seizures...." Although Congress' revisions of Madison's proposal broadened the scope of the Amendment in some respects, the term "effects" is less inclusive than "property" and cannot be said to encompass open fields.[4] We conclude, as did the Court in deciding Hester v. United States, that the government's intrusion upon the open fields is not one of those "unreasonable searches" proscribed by the text of the Fourth Amendment.

III

This interpretation of the Fourth Amendment's language is consistent with the understanding of the right to privacy expressed in our Fourth Amendment jurisprudence. Since Katz v. United States, 389 U.S. 347, 88 S.Ct. 507, 19 L.Ed.2d 576 (1967), the touchstone of Amendment analysis

---

4. The Framers would have understood the term "effects" to be limited to personal, rather than real, property. See generally, Doe v. Dring, 2 M. & S. 448, 454 (1814) (discussing prior cases); 2 Blackstone, Commentaries 16, 384–385.

has been the question whether a person has a "constitutionally protected reasonable expectation of privacy." 389 U.S., at 360, 88 S.Ct., at 516 (Harlan, J., concurring). The Amendment does not protect the merely subjective expectation of privacy, but only "those expectations that society is prepared to recognize as 'reasonable.'"

A

No single factor determines whether an individual legitimately may claim under the Fourth Amendment that a place should be free of government intrusion not authorized by warrant. In assessing the degree to which a search infringes upon individual privacy, the Court has given weight to such factors as the intention of the Framers of the Fourth Amendment, the uses to which the individual has put a location, and our societal understanding that certain areas deserve the most scrupulous protection from government invasion. These factors are equally relevant to determining whether the government's intrusion upon open fields without a warrant or probable cause violates reasonable expectations of privacy and is therefore a search proscribed by the Amendment.

In this light, the rule of Hester v. United States, supra, that we reaffirm today, may be understood as providing that an individual may not legitimately demand privacy for activities conducted out of doors in fields, except in the area immediately surrounding the home. This rule is true to the conception of the right to privacy embodied in the Fourth Amendment. The Amendment reflects the recognition of the Founders that certain enclaves should be free from arbitrary government interference. For example, the Court since the enactment of the Fourth Amendment has stressed "the overriding respect for the sanctity of the home that has been embedded in our traditions since the origins of the Republic."

In contrast, open fields do not provide the setting for those intimate activities that the Amendment is intended to shelter from government interference or surveillance. There is no societal interest in protecting the privacy of those activities, such as the cultivation of crops, that occur in open fields. Moreover, as a practical matter these lands usually are accessible to the public and the police in ways that a home, an office or commercial structure would not be. It is not generally true that fences or no trespassing signs effectively bar the public from viewing open fields in rural areas. And both petitioner Oliver and respondent Thornton concede that the public and police lawfully may survey lands from the air.[5] For these reasons, the asserted expectation of privacy in open fields is not an expectation that "society recognizes as reasonable."[6]

5. In practical terms, petitioner Oliver's and respondent Thornton's analysis merely would require law enforcement officers, in most situations, to use aerial surveillance to gather the information necessary to obtain a warrant or to justify warrantless entry onto the property. It is not easy to see how such a requirement would advance legitimate privacy interests.

6. The dissent conceives of open fields as bustling with private activity as diverse as lovers' trysts and worship services. But in most instances police will disturb no one when they enter upon open fields. These fields, by their very character as open and unoccupied, are unlikely to provide the setting for activities whose privacy is sought to be protected by the Fourth Amendment. One

The historical underpinnings of the "open fields" doctrine also demonstrate that the doctrine is consistent with respect for "reasonable expectations of privacy." As Justice Holmes, writing for the Court, observed in *Hester,* the common law distinguished "open fields" from the "curtilage," the land immediately surrounding and associated with the home. The distinction implies that only the curtilage, not the neighboring open fields, warrants the Fourth Amendment protections that attach to the home. At common law, the curtilage is the area to which extends the intimate activity associated with the "sanctity of a man's home and the privacies of life," and therefore has been considered part of home itself for Fourth Amendment purposes. Thus, courts have extended Fourth Amendment protection to the curtilage; and they have defined the curtilage, as did the common law, by reference to the factors that determine whether an individual reasonably may expect that an area immediately adjacent to the home will remain private. Conversely, the common law implies, as we reaffirm today, that no expectation of privacy legitimately attaches to open fields.[7]

We conclude, from the text of the Fourth Amendment and from the historical and contemporary understanding of its purposes, that an individual has no legitimate expectation that open fields will remain free from warrantless intrusion by government officers.

B

Petitioner Oliver and respondent Thornton contend, to the contrary, that the circumstances of a search sometimes may indicate that reasonable expectations of privacy were violated; and that courts therefore should analyze these circumstances on a case-by-case basis. The language of the Fourth Amendment itself answers their contention.

Nor would a case-by-case approach provide a workable accommodation between the needs of law enforcement and the interests protected by the Fourth Amendment. Under this approach, police officers would have to guess before every search whether landowners had erected fences sufficiently high, posted a sufficient number of warning signs, or located contraband in an area sufficiently secluded to establish a right of privacy. The lawfulness of a search would turn on "[a] highly sophisticated set of

need think only of the vast expanse of some western ranches or of the undeveloped woods of the Northwest to see the unreality of the dissent's conception. Further, the Fourth Amendment provides ample protection to activities in the open fields that might implicate an individual's privacy. An individual who enters a place defined to be "public" for Fourth Amendment analysis does not lose all claims to privacy or personal security. For example, the Fourth Amendment's protections against unreasonable arrest or unreasonable seizure of effects upon the person remain fully applicable.

7. Neither petitioner Oliver nor respondent Thornton has contended that the property searched was within the curtilage. Nor is it necessary in this case to consider the scope of the curtilage exception to the open fields doctrine or the degree of Fourth Amendment protection afforded the curtilage, as opposed to the home itself. It is clear, however, that the term "open fields" may include any unoccupied or undeveloped area outside of the curtilage. An open field need be neither "open" nor a "field" as those terms are used in common speech. For example, contrary to respondent Thornton's suggestion, a thickly wooded area nonetheless may be an open field as that term is used in construing the Fourth Amendment.

rules, qualified by all sorts of ifs, ands, and buts and requiring the drawing of subtle nuances and hairline distinctions. . . ." New York v. Belton, 453 U.S. 454, 458, 101 S.Ct. 2860, 2863, 69 L.Ed.2d 768 (1981) (quoting LaFave, "Case–By–Case Adjudication" versus "Standardized Procedures": The Robinson Dilemma, 1974 S.Ct.Rev. 127, 142). This Court repeatedly has acknowledged the difficulties created for courts, police and citizens by an *ad hoc,* case-by-case definition of Fourth Amendment standards to be applied in differing factual circumstances. The *ad hoc* approach not only makes it difficult for the policeman to discern the scope of his authority; it also creates a danger that constitutional rights will be arbitrarily and inequitably enforced.[8]

IV

In any event, while the factors that petitioner Oliver and respondent Thornton urge the courts to consider may be relevant to Fourth Amendment analysis in some contexts, these factors cannot be decisive on the question whether the search of an open field is subject to the Amendment. Initially, we reject the suggestion that steps taken to protect privacy establish that expectations of privacy in an open field are legitimate. It is true, of course, that petitioner Oliver and respondent Thornton, in order to conceal their criminal activities, planted the marijuana upon secluded land and erected fences and no trespassing signs around the property. And it may be that because of such precautions, few members of the public stumbled upon the marijuana crops seized by the police. Neither of these suppositions demonstrates, however, that the expectation of privacy was *legitimate* in the sense required by the Fourth Amendment. The test of legitimacy is not whether the individual chooses to conceal assertedly "private" activity. Rather, the correct inquiry is whether the government's intrusion infringes upon the personal and societal values protected by the Fourth Amendment. As we have explained, we find no basis for concluding that a police inspection of open fields accomplishes such an infringement.

Nor is the government's intrusion upon an open field a "search" in the constitutional sense because that intrusion is a trespass at common law. The existence of a property right is but one element in determining whether expectations of privacy are legitimate. * * *

The common law may guide consideration of what areas are protected by the Fourth Amendment by defining areas whose invasion by others is wrongful. The law of trespass, however, forbids intrusions upon land that the Fourth Amendment would not proscribe. For trespass law extends to instances where the exercise of the right to exclude vindicates no legitimate

---

8. The clarity of the open fields doctrine that we reaffirm today is not sacrificed, as the dissent suggests, by our recognition that the curtilage remains within the protections of the Fourth Amendment. Most of the many millions of acres that are "open fields" are not close to any structure and so not arguably within the curtilage. And, for most homes, the boundaries of the curtilage will be clearly marked; and the conception defining the curtilage—as the area around the home to which the activity of home life extends—is a familiar one easily understood from our daily experience. The occasional difficulties that courts might have in applying this, like other, legal concepts, do not argue for the unprecedented expansion of the Fourth Amendment advocated by the dissent.

privacy interest.[9] Thus, in the case of open fields, the general rights of property protected by the common law of trespass have little or no relevance to the applicability of the Fourth Amendment.

V

We conclude that the open fields doctrine, as enunciated in *Hester,* is consistent with the plain language of the Fourth Amendment and its historical purposes. Moreover, Justice Holmes' interpretation of the Amendment in *Hester* accords with the "reasonable expectation of privacy" analysis developed in subsequent decisions of this Court. We therefore affirm Oliver v. United States; Maine v. Thornton is reversed and remanded for further proceedings not inconsistent with this opinion.

It is so ordered.

■ JUSTICE WHITE, concurring in part and in the judgment.

I concur in the judgment and join Parts I and II of the Court's opinion. These parts dispose of the issue before us; there is no need to go further and deal with the expectation of privacy matter. However reasonable a landowner's expectations of privacy may be, those expectations cannot convert a field into a "house" or an "effect."

■ JUSTICE MARSHALL, with whom JUSTICE BRENNAN and JUSTICE STEVENS join, dissenting.

* * *

I

The first ground on which the Court rests its decision is that the Fourth Amendment "indicates with some precision the places and things encompassed by its protections," and that real property is not included in the list of protected spaces and possessions. This line of argument has several flaws. Most obviously, it is inconsistent with the results of many of our previous decisions, none of which the Court purports to overrule. For example, neither a public telephone booth nor a conversation conducted therein can fairly be described as a person, house, paper, or effect, yet we have held that the Fourth Amendment forbids the police without a warrant to eavesdrop on such a conversation. Katz v. United States, 389 U.S. 347, 88 S.Ct. 507, 19 L.Ed.2d 576 (1967). * * *

---

9. The law of trespass recognizes the interest in possession and control of one's property and for that reason permits exclusion of unwanted intruders. But it does not follow that the right to exclude conferred by trespass law embodies a privacy interest also protected by the Fourth Amendment. To the contrary, the common law of trespass furthers a range of interests that have nothing to do with privacy and that would not be served by applying the strictures of trespass law to public officers. Criminal laws against trespass are prophylactic: they protect against intruders who poach, steal livestock and crops or vandalize property. And the civil action of trespass serves the important function of authorizing an owner to defeat claims of prescription by asserting his own title. In any event, unlicensed use of property by others is presumptively unjustified, as anyone who wishes to use the property is free to bargain for the right to do so with the property owner. For these reasons, the law of trespass confers protections from intrusion by others far broader than those required by Fourth Amendment interests.

II

The second ground for the Court's decision is its contention that any interest a landowner might have in the privacy of his woods and fields is not one that "society is prepared to recognize as 'reasonable.'" The mode of analysis that underlies this assertion is certainly more consistent with our prior decisions than that discussed above. But the Court's conclusion cannot withstand scrutiny.

As the Court acknowledges, we have traditionally looked to a variety of factors in determining whether an expectation of privacy asserted in a physical space is "reasonable." Though those factors do not lend themselves to precise taxonomy, they may be roughly grouped into three categories. First, we consider whether the expectation at issue is rooted in entitlements defined by positive law. Second, we consider the nature of the uses to which spaces of the sort in question can be put. Third, we consider whether the person claiming a privacy interest manifested that interest to the public in a way that most people would understand and respect. When the expectations of privacy asserted by petitioner Oliver and respondent Thornton are examined through these lenses, it becomes clear that those expectations are entitled to constitutional protection.

A

We have frequently acknowledged that privacy interests are not coterminous with property rights. However, because "property rights reflect society's explicit recognition of a person's authority to act as he wishes in certain areas, [they] should be considered in determining whether an individual's expectations of privacy are reasonable." * * *

It is undisputed that Oliver and Thornton each owned the land into which the police intruded. That fact alone provides considerable support for their assertion of legitimate privacy interests in their woods and fields. But even more telling is the nature of the sanctions that Oliver and Thornton could invoke, under local law, for violation of their property rights. In Kentucky, a knowing entry upon fenced or otherwise enclosed land, or upon unenclosed land conspicuously posted with signs excluding the public, constitutes criminal trespass. The law in Maine is similar. * * * Thus, positive law not only recognizes the legitimacy of Oliver's and Thornton's insistence that strangers keep off their land, but subjects those who refuse to respect their wishes to the most severe of penalties—criminal liability. Under these circumstances, it is hard to credit the Court's assertion that Oliver's and Thornton's expectations of privacy were not of a sort that society is prepared to recognize as reasonable.

B

The uses to which a place is put are highly relevant to the assessment of a privacy interest asserted therein. If, in light of our shared sensibilities, those activities are of a kind in which people should be able to engage without fear of intrusion by private persons or government officials, we extend the protection of the Fourth Amendment to the space in question, even in the absence of any entitlement derived from positive law.

Privately-owned woods and fields that are not exposed to public view regularly are employed in a variety of ways that society acknowledges deserve privacy. Many landowners like to take solitary walks on their property, confident that they will not be confronted in their rambles by strangers or policemen. Others conduct agricultural businesses on their property. Some landowners use their secluded spaces to meet lovers, others to gather together with fellow worshippers, still others to engage in sustained creative endeavor. Private land is sometimes used as a refuge for wildlife, where flora and fauna are protected from human intervention of any kind. Our respect for the freedom of landowners to use their posted "open fields" in ways such as these partially explains the seriousness with which the positive law regards deliberate invasions of such spaces, and substantially reinforces the landowners' contention that their expectations of privacy are "reasonable."

C

Whether a person "took normal precautions to maintain his privacy" in a given space affects whether his interest is one protected by the Fourth Amendment. The reason why such precautions are relevant is that we do not insist that a person who has a right to exclude others exercise that right. A claim to privacy is therefore strengthened by the fact that the claimant somehow manifested to other people his desire that they keep their distance.

Certain spaces are so presumptively private that signals of this sort are unnecessary; a homeowner need not post a "do not enter" sign on his door in order to deny entrance to uninvited guests. Privacy interests in other spaces are more ambiguous, and the taking of precautions is consequently more important; placing a lock on one's footlocker strengthens one's claim that an examination of its contents is impermissible. Still other spaces are, by positive law and social convention, presumed accessible to members of the public *unless* the owner manifests his intention to exclude them.

Undeveloped land falls into the last-mentioned category. If a person has not marked the boundaries of his fields or woods in a way that informs passersby that they are not welcome, he cannot object if members of the public enter onto the property. There is no reason why he should have any greater rights as against government officials. Accordingly, we have held that an official may, without a warrant, enter private land from which the public is not excluded and make observations from that vantage point. Fairly read, the case on which the majority so heavily relies, Hester v. United States, 265 U.S. 57, 44 S.Ct. 445, 68 L.Ed. 898 (1924), affirms little more than the foregoing unremarkable proposition. From aught that appears in the opinion in that case, the defendants, fleeing from revenue agents who had observed them committing a crime, abandoned incriminating evidence on private land from which the public had not been excluded. Under such circumstances, it is not surprising that the Court was unpersuaded by the defendants' argument that the entry onto their fields by the agents violated the Fourth Amendment.

A very different case is presented when the owner of undeveloped land has taken precautions to exclude the public. As indicated above, a deliberate entry by a private citizen onto private property marked with "no trespassing" signs will expose him to criminal liability. I see no reason why a government official should not be obliged to respect such unequivocal and universally understood manifestations of a landowner's desire for privacy.

In sum, examination of the three principal criteria we have traditionally used for assessing the reasonableness of a person's expectation that a given space would remain private indicates that interests of the sort asserted by Oliver and Thornton are entitled to constitutional protection. An owner's right to insist that others stay off his posted land is firmly grounded in positive law. Many of the uses to which such land may be put deserve privacy. And, by marking the boundaries of the land with warnings that the public should not intrude, the owner has dispelled any ambiguity as to his desires.

The police in these cases proffered no justification for their invasions of Oliver's and Thornton's privacy interests; in neither case was the entry legitimated by a warrant or by one of the established exceptions to the warrant requirement. I conclude, therefore, that the searches of their land violated the Fourth Amendment, and the evidence obtained in the course of those searches should have been suppressed.

III

A clear, easily administrable rule emerges from the analysis set forth above: Private land marked in a fashion sufficient to render entry thereon a criminal trespass under the law of the state in which the land lies is protected by the Fourth Amendment's proscription of unreasonable searches and seizures. One of the advantages of the foregoing rule is that it draws upon a doctrine already familiar to both citizens and government officials. In each jurisdiction, a substantial body of statutory and case law defines the precautions a landowner must take in order to avail himself of the sanctions of the criminal law. The police know that body of law, because they are entrusted with responsibility for enforcing it against the public; it therefore would not be difficult for the police to abide by it themselves.

By contrast, the doctrine announced by the Court today is incapable of determinate application. Police officers, making warrantless entries upon private land, will be obliged in the future to make on-the-spot judgments as to how far the curtilage extends, and to stay outside that zone. In addition, we may expect to see a spate of litigation over the question of how much improvement is necessary to remove private land from the category of "unoccupied or undeveloped area" to which the "open fields exception" is now deemed applicable.

The Court's holding not only ill serves the need to make constitutional doctrine "workable for application by rank and file, trained police officers," it withdraws the shield of the Fourth Amendment from privacy interests that clearly deserve protection. * * *

I dissent.

NOTE: THE PROTECTED CURTILAGE

The role played by the concept of the "curtilage" in defining the scope of Fourth Amendment coverage was confirmed and the definition of curtilage fleshed out in United States v. Dunn, 480 U.S. 294, 107 S.Ct. 1134, 94 L.Ed.2d 326 (1987). Federal officers, suspecting Dunn of manufacturing controlled substances, went to his Texas ranch on the evening of November 5, 1980. The ranch's 198 acres were completely encircled by a "perimeter fence" and contained a number of internal fenced areas. About a half-mile from a public road, one internal fenced enclosure included the ranch house and a greenhouse. Approximately fifty yards from this fence were two barns. The larger of the two was enclosed by a wooden fence; locked waist-high gates prevented entry into the barn and a netting material was stretched from the ceiling of the barn to the top of the fence gates. The officers crossed over the perimeter fence, climbed a barbed wire fence and the fence surrounding the large barn front and approached the barn. They walked under the overhang and up to the locked gates. By shining a flashlight through the netting, they observed a drug laboratory. At no point did the officers physically enter the barn. Using the information obtained by looking into the barn, they obtained a search warrant and by executing the warrant they seized evidence of Dunn's manufacture of controlled substances. This evidence was held inadmissible by the intermediate federal court on the ground it was the product of a warrantless—and therefore unreasonable—search.

The Supreme Court reversed, concluding that under *Oliver* the officers did not engage in a search. Whether the officers' approach to the barn constituted a search, Justice White explained for the Court, depended upon whether the barn was within the protected curtilage. Turning to the meaning of that term, he continued:

> [W]e believe that curtilage questions should be resolved with particular reference to four factors: the proximity of the area claimed to be curtilage to the home, whether the area is included within an enclosure surrounding the home, the nature of the uses to which the area is put, and the steps taken by the resident to protect the area from observation by people passing by. We do not suggest that combining these factors produces a finely tuned formula that, when mechanically applied, yields a "correct" answer to all extent-of-curtilage questions. Rather, these factors are useful analytical tools only to the degree that, in any given case, they bear upon the centrally relevant consideration—whether the area in question is so intimately tied to the home itself that it should be placed under the home's "umbrella" of Fourth Amendment protection.

480 U.S. at 301, 107 S.Ct. at 1139–40, 94 L.Ed.2d at 334–35.

Applying this approach to the facts of *Dunn* led the Court "with little difficulty" to conclude the barn and the area immediately surrounding it lay outside the protected curtilage. First, the 50 yards separating the barn from the house—a "substantial distance"—rendered it "in isolation." Second, the fence surrounding the ranch house demarked "a specific area of land immediately adjacent to the house that is readily identifiable as part and parcel of the house," and the barn was not within it. Third, the officers had substantial information from surveillance and smells emanating from the barn indicating it was used for the manufacture of drugs. This information indicated "the use to which the barn was being put could not fairly be characterized as so associated with the activities and privacies of domestic life that the officers should have deemed the barn as part of [the] home." Finally, Dunn had done little to protect the barn area from observation by those "standing in the open fields." The fences were designed to corral livestock and did not bar observations.

The majority also rejected Dunn's argument that, regardless of whether the barn was within the curtilage of the ranch house, the officers' actions intruded upon a protected privacy interest related to the barn and his use of it. Assuming the barn protected from entry by the Fourth Amendment, the Court stressed it was situated on an "open field." The officers' progression up to the barn involved only entry onto "open fields" and did not constitute a "search," regardless of whether the objects they observed from this vantage point lay within an area that might be protected by the Fourth Amendment.

b. AERIAL AND OTHER OBSERVATIONS

When officers make observations by use of some aid such as an aircraft or a transmitter or "beeper," have the officers engaged in a search? The principal case reprinted here involves the use of a helicopter.

Florida v. Riley

Supreme Court of the United States, 1989.
488 U.S. 445, 109 S.Ct. 693, 102 L.Ed.2d 835.

■ JUSTICE WHITE announced the judgment of the Court and delivered an opinion, in which THE CHIEF JUSTICE, JUSTICE SCALIA and JUSTICE KENNEDY join.

On certification to it by a lower state court, the Florida Supreme Court addressed the following question: "Whether surveillance of the interior of a partially covered greenhouse in a residential backyard from the vantage point of a helicopter located 400 feet above the greenhouse constitutes a 'search' for which a warrant is required under the Fourth Amendment and Article I, Section 12 of the Florida Constitution." The court answered the question in the affirmative, and we granted the State's petition for certiorari challenging that conclusion.

Respondent Riley lived in a mobile home located on five acres of rural property. A greenhouse was located 10 to 20 feet behind the mobile home. Two sides of the greenhouse were enclosed. The other two sides were not enclosed but the contents of the greenhouse were obscured from view from surrounding property by trees, shrubs and the mobile home. The greenhouse was covered by corrugated roofing panels, some translucent and some opaque. At the time relevant to this case, two of the panels, amounting to approximately 10% of the roof area, were missing. A wire fence surrounded the mobile home and the greenhouse, and the property was posted with a "DO NOT ENTER" sign.

This case originated with an anonymous tip to the Pasco County Sheriff's office that marijuana was being grown on respondent's property. When an investigating officer discovered that he could not see the contents of the greenhouse from the road, he circled twice over respondent's property in a helicopter at the height of 400 feet. With his naked eye, he was able to see through the openings in the roof and one or more of the open sides of the greenhouse and to identify what he thought was marijuana growing in the structure. A warrant was obtained based on these observations, and the ensuing search revealed marijuana growing in the greenhouse. Respondent was charged with possession of marijuana under

Florida law. The trial court granted his motion to suppress; the Florida Court of Appeals reversed but certified the case to the Florida Supreme Court, which quashed the decision of the Court of Appeals and reinstated the trial court's suppression order.

We agree with the State's submission that our decision in California v. Ciraolo, 476 U.S. 207, 106 S.Ct. 1809, 90 L.Ed.2d 210 (1986), controls this case. There, acting on a tip, the police inspected the back yard of a particular house while flying in a fixed-wing aircraft at 1,000 feet. With the naked eye the officers saw what they concluded was marijuana growing in the yard. A search warrant was obtained on the strength of this airborne inspection, and marijuana plants were found. The trial court refused to suppress this evidence, but a state appellate court held that the inspection violated the Fourth and Fourteenth Amendments of the United States Constitution and that the warrant was therefore invalid. We in turn reversed, holding that the inspection was not a search subject to the Fourth Amendment. We recognized that the yard was within the curtilage of the house, that a fence shielded the yard from observation from the street and that the occupant had a subjective expectation of privacy. We held, however, that such an expectation was not reasonable and not one "that society is prepared to honor." Our reasoning was that the home and its curtilage are not necessarily protected from inspection that involves no physical invasion. " 'What a person knowingly exposes to the public, even in his own home or office, is not a subject of Fourth Amendment protection.' "Id., at 213, 106 S.Ct., at 1812, quoting Katz v. United States, 389 U.S. 347, 351, 88 S.Ct. 507, 511, 19 L.Ed.2d 576 (1967). As a general proposition, the police may see what may be seen "from a public vantage point where [they have] a right to be." Thus the police, like the public, would have been free to inspect the backyard garden from the street if their view had been unobstructed. They were likewise, free to inspect the yard from the vantage point of an aircraft flying in the navigable airspace as this plane was. "In an age where private and commercial flight in the public airways is routine, it is unreasonable for respondent to expect that his marijuana plants were constitutionally protected from being observed with the naked eye from an altitude of 1,000 feet. The Fourth Amendment simply does not require the police traveling in the public airways at this altitude to obtain a warrant in order to observe what is visible to the naked eye."

We arrive at the same conclusion in the present case. In this case, as in Ciraolo, the property surveyed was within the curtilage of respondent's home. Riley no doubt intended and expected that his greenhouse would not be open to public inspection, and the precautions he took protected against ground-level observation. Because the sides and roof of his greenhouse were left partially open, however, what was growing in the greenhouse was subject to viewing from the air. Under the holding in Ciraolo, Riley could not reasonably have expected the contents of his greenhouse to be immune from examination by an officer seated in a fixed-wing aircraft flying in navigable airspace at an altitude of 1,000 feet or, as the Florida Supreme Court seemed to recognize, at an altitude of 500 feet, the lower limit of the navigable airspace for such an aircraft. Here, the inspection was made from a helicopter, but as is the case with fixed-wing planes, "private and commercial flight [by helicopter] in the public airways is routine" in this country, and there is no indication that such flights are unheard of in Pasco County, Florida. Riley could not reasonably have expected that his greenhouse was protected from public or official observation from a helicopter had it been flying within the navigable airspace for fixed-wing aircraft.

Nor on the facts before us, does it make a difference for Fourth Amendment purposes that the helicopter was flying at 400 feet when the officer saw what was growing in the greenhouse through the partially open roof and sides of the structure. We would have a different case if flying at that altitude had been contrary to law or regulation. But helicopters are not bound by the lower limits of the navigable airspace allowed to other aircraft.[10] Any member of the public could legally have been flying over Riley's property in a helicopter at the altitude of 400 feet and could have observed Riley's greenhouse. The police officer did no more. This is not to say that an inspection of the curtilage of a house from an aircraft will always pass muster under the Fourth Amendment simply because the plane is within the navigable airspace specified by law. But it is of obvious importance that the helicopter in this case was not violating the law, and there is nothing in the record or before us to suggest that helicopters flying at 400 feet are sufficiently rare in this country to lend substance to respondent's claim that he reasonably anticipated that his greenhouse would not be subject to observation from that altitude. Neither is there any intimation here that the helicopter interfered with respondent's normal use of the greenhouse or of other parts of the curtilage. As far as this record reveals, no intimate details connected with the use of the home or curtilage were observed, and there was no undue noise, no wind, dust, or threat of injury. In these circumstances, there was no violation of the Fourth Amendment.

The judgment of the Florida Supreme Court is accordingly reversed.

SO ORDERED.

■ JUSTICE O'CONNOR, concurring in the judgment.

I concur in the judgment reversing the Supreme Court of Florida because I agree that police observation of the greenhouse in Riley's curtilage from a helicopter passing at an altitude of 400 feet did not violate an expectation of privacy "that society is prepared to recognize as 'reasonable.'" I write separately, however, to clarify the standard I believe follows from California v. Ciraolo, 476 U.S. 207, 106 S.Ct. 1809, 90 L.Ed.2d 210 (1986). In my view, the plurality's approach rests the scope of Fourth Amendment protection too heavily on compliance with FAA regulations whose purpose is to promote air safety not to protect "[t]he right of the people to be secure in their persons, houses, papers, and effects, against unreasonable searches and seizures." U.S. Const., Amdt. 4.

* * *

10. While Federal Aviation Administration regulations permit fixed wing aircraft to be operated at an altitude of 1,000 feet while flying over congested areas and at an altitude of 500 feet above the surface in other than congested areas, helicopters may be operated at less than the minimums for fixed wing aircraft "if the operation is conducted without hazard to persons or property on the surface. In addition, each person operating a helicopter shall comply with routes or altitudes specifically prescribed for helicopters by the [FAA] Administrator." 14 CFR § 91.79 (1988).

Ciraolo's expectation of privacy was unreasonable not because the airplane was operating where it had a "right to be," but because public air travel at 1,000 feet is a sufficiently routine part of modern life that it is unreasonable for persons on the ground to expect that their curtilage will not be observed from the air at that altitude. * * * Because the FAA has decided that helicopters can lawfully operate at virtually any altitude so long as they pose no safety hazard, it does not follow that the expectations of privacy "society is prepared to recognize as 'reasonable' "simply mirror the FAA's safety concerns.

* * *

In determining whether Riley had a reasonable expectation of privacy from aerial observation, the relevant inquiry after *Ciraolo* is not whether the helicopter was where it had a right to be under FAA regulations. Rather, consistent with *Katz,* we must ask whether the helicopter was in the public airways at an altitude at which members of the public travel with sufficient regularity that Riley's expectation of privacy from aerial observation was not "one that society is prepared to recognize as 'reasonable.' " *Katz,* supra, 389 U.S., at 361, 88 S.Ct., at 516. * * * [I]t is not conclusive to observe, as the plurality does, that "[a]ny member of the public could legally have been flying over Riley's property in a helicopter at the altitude of 400 feet and could have observed Riley's greenhouse." Nor is it conclusive that police helicopters may often fly at 400 feet. If the public rarely, if ever, travels overhead at such altitudes, the observation cannot be said to be from a vantage point generally used by the public and Riley cannot be said to have "knowingly expose[d]" his greenhouse to public view. However, if the public can generally be expected to travel over residential backyards at an altitude of 400 feet, Riley cannot reasonably expect his curtilage to be free from such aerial observation.

In my view, the defendant must bear the burden of proving that his expectation of privacy was a reasonable one, and thus that a "search" within the meaning of the Fourth Amendment even took place.

Because there is reason to believe that there is considerable public use of airspace at altitudes of 400 feet and above, and because Riley introduced no evidence to the contrary before the Florida courts, I conclude that Riley's expectation that his curtilage was protected from naked-eye aerial observation from that altitude was not a reasonable one. However, public use of altitudes lower than that—particularly public observations from helicopters circling over the curtilage of a home—may be sufficiently rare that police surveillance from such altitudes would violate reasonable expectations of privacy, despite compliance with FAA air safety regulations.

■ JUSTICE BRENNAN, with whom JUSTICE MARSHALL and JUSTICE STEVENS, join, dissenting.

* * *

The opinion for a plurality of the Court reads almost as if Katz v. United States, 389 U.S. 347, 88 S.Ct. 507, 19 L.Ed.2d 576 (1967), had never been decided. * * *

I agree, of course, that "[w]hat a person knowingly exposes to the public . . . is not a subject of Fourth Amendment protection." But I cannot agree that one "knowingly exposes [an area] to the public" solely because a helicopter may legally fly above it. Under the plurality's exceedingly grudging Fourth Amendment theory, the expectation of privacy is defeated if a single member of the public could conceivably position herself to see into the area in question without doing anything illegal. It is defeated whatever the difficulty a person would have in so positioning herself, and however infrequently anyone would in fact do so. In taking this view the plurality ignores the very essence of *Katz*. The reason why there is no reasonable expectation of privacy in an area that is exposed to the public is that little diminution in "the amount of privacy and freedom remaining to citizens" will result from police surveillance of something that any passerby readily sees. To pretend, as the plurality opinion does, that the same is true when the police use a helicopter to peer over high fences is, at best, disingenuous.
* * *

* * * The question before us must be not whether the police were where they had a right to be, but whether public observation of Riley's curtilage was so commonplace that Riley's expectation of privacy in his backyard could not be considered reasonable. While, as we held in *Ciraolo*, air traffic at elevations of 1000 feet or more may be so common that whatever could be seen with the naked eye from that elevation is unprotected by the Fourth Amendment, it is a large step from there to say that the Amendment offers no protection against low-level helicopter surveillance of enclosed curtilage areas. To take this step is error enough. That the plurality does so with little analysis beyond its determination that the police complied with FAA regulations is particularly unfortunate.

* * *

Equally disconcerting is the lack of any meaningful limit to the plurality's holding. It is worth reiterating that the FAA regulations the plurality relies on as establishing that the officer was where he had a right to be set no minimum flight altitude for helicopters. It is difficult, therefore, to see what, if any, helicopter surveillance would run afoul of the plurality's rule that there exists no reasonable expectation of privacy as long as the helicopter is where it has a right to be.

* * *

Perhaps the most remarkable passage in the plurality opinion is its suggestion that the case might be a different one had any "intimate details connected with the use of the home or curtilage [been] observed." What, one wonders, is meant by "intimate details"? If the police had observed Riley embracing his wife in the backyard greenhouse, would we then say that his reasonable expectation of privacy had been infringed? Where in the Fourth Amendment or in our cases is there any warrant for imposing a requirement that the activity observed must be "intimate" in order to be protected by the Constitution?

It is difficult to avoid the conclusion that the plurality has allowed its analysis of Riley's expectation of privacy to be colored by its distaste for the activity in which he was engaged. It is indeed easy to forget, especially in view of current concern over drug trafficking, that the scope of the Fourth Amendment's protection does not turn on whether the activity disclosed by a search is illegal or innocuous. But we dismiss this as a "drug case" only at the peril of our own liberties. * * *

I find little to disagree with in Justice O'CONNOR's concurrence, apart from its closing paragraphs. A majority of the Court thus agrees that the fundamental inquiry is not whether the police were where they had a right to be under FAA regulations, but rather whether Riley's expectation of privacy was rendered illusory by the extent of public observation of his backyard from aerial traffic at 400 feet.

What separates me from Justice O'CONNOR is essentially an empirical matter concerning the extent of public use of the airspace at that altitude, together with the question of how to resolve that issue. I do not think the constitutional claim should fail simply because "there is reason to believe" that there is "considerable" public flying this close to earth or because Riley "introduced no evidence to the contrary before the Florida courts." * * * I think we could take judicial notice that, while there may be an occasional privately owned helicopter that flies over populated areas at an altitude of 400 feet, such flights are a rarity and are almost entirely limited to approaching or leaving airports or to reporting traffic congestion near major roadways. * * *

If, however, we are to resolve the issue by considering whether the appropriate party carried its burden of proof, I again think that Riley must prevail. Because the State has greater access to information concerning customary flight patterns and because the coercive power of the State ought not be brought to bear in cases in which it is unclear whether the prosecution is a product of an unconstitutional, warrantless search, the burden of proof properly rests with the State and not with the individual defendant. The State quite clearly has not carried this burden.

* * *

* * * I respectfully dissent.

■ JUSTICE BLACKMUN, dissenting.

The question before the Court is whether the helicopter surveillance over Riley's property constituted a "search" within the meaning of the Fourth Amendment. Like Justice Brennan, Justice Marshall, Justice Stevens, and Justice O'Connor, I believe that answering this question depends upon whether Riley has a "reasonable expectation of privacy" that no such surveillance would occur, and does not depend upon the fact that the helicopter was flying at a lawful altitude under FAA regulations. A majority of this Court thus agrees to at least this much.

The inquiry then becomes how to determine whether Riley's expectation was a reasonable one. Both Justice Brennan, and the two Justices who have joined him, and Justice O'Connor believe that the reasonableness of Riley's expectation depends, in large measure, on the frequency of nonpolice helicopter flights at an altitude of 400 feet. Again, I agree.

How is this factual issue to be decided? Justice Brennan suggests that we may resolve it ourselves without any evidence in the record on this point. I am wary of this approach. While I, too, suspect that for most American communities it is a rare event when nonpolice helicopters fly over one's curtilage at an altitude of 400 feet, I am not convinced that we should establish a *per se* rule for the entire Nation based on judicial suspicion alone.

But we need not abandon our judicial intuition entirely. * * * [I]t is appropriate for us to take into account our estimation of the frequency of nonpolice helicopter flights. * * * [B]ecause I believe that private helicopters rarely fly over curtilages at an altitude of 400 feet, I would impose upon the prosecution the burden of proving contrary facts necessary to show that Riley lacked a reasonable expectation of privacy. * * *

In this case, the prosecution did not meet this burden of proof, as Justice Brennan notes. This failure should compel a finding that a Fourth Amendment search occurred. But because our prior cases gave the parties little guidance on the burden of proof issue, I would remand this case to allow the prosecution an opportunity to meet this burden.

The order of this Court, however, is not to remand the case in this manner. Rather, because Justice O'Connor would impose the burden of proof on Riley and because she would not allow Riley an opportunity to meet this burden, she joins the plurality's view that no Fourth Amendment search occurred. The judgment of the Court, therefore, is to reverse outright on the Fourth Amendment issue. Accordingly, for the reasons set forth above, I respectfully dissent.

NOTES

1. On remand, the Florida Supreme Court concluded, "A majority of the United States Supreme Court agreed that the record below lacked evidentiary development concerning the reasonableness of Riley's expectation of privacy." Therefore, the Florida tribunal directed the case remanded to the trial court "for further proceedings consistent with the opinion of the United States Supreme Court in this cause." Riley v. State, 549 So.2d 673, 674 (Fla.1989). Counsel for Riley construed this as meaning they were entitled to an evidentiary hearing at which to develop further whether helicopter flights in the area of Riley's home were insufficient in number and/or nature that he had a reasonable expectation his greenhouse would not be observed from the vantage provided by such a flight. The trial judge, however, refused to hold such a hearing. Counsel for Riley sought relief from the state appellate courts in action generating no published opinions. When these efforts proved unsuccessful, Riley pleaded guilty and received a sentence of four years probation. Interviews with Craig Vallente and Keith Hammond, Feb. 7, 12, 1997.

2. **Use of Camera in Aerial Surveillance.** In Dow Chemical Company v. United States, 476 U.S. 227, 106 S.Ct. 1819, 90 L.Ed.2d 226 (1986), investigators for the Environmental Protection Agency (EPA) used an airplane equipped with a precision aerial mapping camera to photograph Dow's Midland, Michigan plant from altitudes of 12,000, 3,000 and 1,200 feet. The plant was a 2,000 acre facility surrounded by a fence. Precautions were not taken to conceal all of the manufacturing equipment in the plant from aerial view. Nevertheless, its desire to protect trade secret information caused Dow to remain concerned about aerial photography. Low-flying planes were identified when possible and efforts made to obtain possession of

any photographs taken. A majority of the Court concluded the EPA's actions did not constitute a search for Fourth Amendment purposes:

> Admittedly, Dow's enclosed plant complex, like the area in *Oliver*, does not fall precisely within the "open fields" doctrine. The area at issue here can perhaps be seen as falling somewhere between "open fields" and curtilage, but lacking some of the critical characteristics of both. Dow's inner manufacturing areas are elaborately secured to ensure they are not open or exposed to the public from the ground. Any actual physical entry by EPA into any enclosed area would raise significantly different questions * * *. The narrow issue raised by [Dow] * * * concerns aerial observation of a 2,000 acre outdoor manufacturing facility without physical entry.

> * * *

> It may well be, as the Government concedes, that surveillance of private property by using highly sophisticated surveillance equipment not generally available to the public, such as satellite technology, might be constitutionally proscribed absent a warrant. But the photographs here are not so revealing of intimate details as to raise constitutional concerns. Although they undoubtedly give EPA more detailed information than naked-eye views, they remain limited to an outline of the facility's buildings and equipment. The mere fact that human vision is enhanced somewhat, at least to the degree here, does not give rise to constitutional problems.

476 U.S. at 236–38, 106 S.Ct. at 1826, 90 L.Ed.2d at 236–38.

3. **Surveillance by "Beeper."** Law enforcement's use of "beepers" to conduct surveillance raises issue akin to those presented by aerial surveillance. The Supreme Court addressed these issues in two decisions.

In United States v. Knotts, 460 U.S. 276, 103 S.Ct. 1081, 75 L.Ed.2d 55 (1983), the defendants were under suspicion because of reports they were purchasing chemicals which could be used in the manufacture of illicit drugs. With the consent of the seller, federal agents placed a "beeper" inside a five gallon container of chloroform that was to be sold to one of the defendants, Petschen. This beeper emitted signals that could be picked up by a radio receiver. Petschen, as he drove off with the container, was followed by means of both visual surveillance and a monitor which received signals from the beeper. The surveillance ended after Petschen took evasive maneuvers. About one hour later, a monitoring device in a helicopter located the beeper at a cabin owned by defendant Knotts. On the basis of this and other information obtained during three days of intermittent visual surveillance of the cabin, a search warrant for the cabin was obtained. The resulting search disclosed a fully operable drug laboratory; the container of chloroform containing the beeper was found under a barrel outside the cabin. The Court held the monitoring activities by the officers did not invade any legitimate expectation of privacy and therefore did not constitute a "search" under *Katz:*

> The governmental surveillance conducted by means of the beeper in this case amounted principally to the following of an automobile on public streets and highways. * * *

> A person travelling in an automobile on public thoroughfares has no reasonable expectation of privacy in his movements from one place to another. When Petschen traveled over the public street he voluntarily conveyed to anyone who wanted to look the fact that he was travelling over particular roads in a particular direction, the fact of whatever stops he made, and the fact of his final destination when he exited from public roads onto private property.

> Respondent Knotts, as the owner of the cabin and surrounding premises to which Petschen drove, undoubtedly had the traditional expectation of privacy within a dwelling place insofar as the cabin was concerned * * *. But no such

expectation of privacy extended to the visual observation of Petschen's automobile arriving on his premises after leaving a public highway, nor to movements of objects such as the drum of chloroform outside the cabin in the "open fields." Hester v. United States, 265 U.S. 57, 44 S.Ct. 445, 68 L.Ed. 898 (1924).

Visual surveillance from public places along Petschen's route or adjoining Knotts' premises would have sufficed to reveal all of these facts to the police. The fact that the officers in this case relied not only on visual surveillance, but on the use of the beeper to signal the presence of Petschen's automobile to the police receiver, does not alter the situation. Nothing in the Fourth Amendment prohibited the police from augmenting the sensory faculties bestowed upon them at birth with such enhancement as science and technology afforded them in this case.

460 U.S. at 281–82, 103 S.Ct. at 1085–86, 75 L.Ed.2d at 62–63. After noting the failure of the visual surveillance, the majority acknowledged the use of the beeper enabled officers to ascertain the destination of the chloroform when they would not have been able to do so by reliance solely by sight. "But scientific enhancement of this sort raises no constitutional issues," the Court commented, "which visual surveillance would not also raise." It also noted the record contained no indication the beeper was used to reveal information concerning the movement of the drum inside the cabin or any other movement of it that would not have been visible to the naked eye from outside the cabin. All members of the Court joined in the result.

The Court noted that the warrantless installation of the beeper had not been challenged and the propriety of this action by the officers was therefore not addressed. Justice Brennan, joined by Justice Marshall, commented that a challenge to the installation of the beeper would have made the case more difficult.

In United States v. Karo, 468 U.S. 705, 104 S.Ct. 3296, 82 L.Ed.2d 530 (1984), the Court returned to beeper issues. A beeper was installed in a can of ether sold to the defendants; this beeper was then used to determine the can was inside a specific house. A majority of the Court held that no Fourth Amendment interest of the defendants was infringed by installation of the beeper. At the time the device was placed in the can, it reasoned, the defendants had neither title to nor possession of the can. Therefore, installing the beeper in the can intruded upon no expectation of privacy.

But the Court found the use of the beeper once installed constituted a search because it enabled the officers to obtain information they could not have obtained by observation from outside the curtilage of the house:

> The beeper tells the agent that a particular article is actually located at a particular time in the private residence and is in the possession of the person or persons whose residence is being surveilled. Even if visual surveillance has revealed that the article to which the beeper is attached has entered the house, the later monitoring not only verifies the officers' observations but also establishes that the article remains on the premises.

468 U.S. at 715, 104 S.Ct. at 3303, 82 L.Ed.2d at 541. The *Karo* beeper, unlike the *Knotts'* beeper, revealed the article to which it was attached was inside the house, a fact that could not have been determined by visual observation of the premises.

2. DEFINITION AND REASONABLENESS OF ACTIVITY CONSTITUTING A "SEIZURE" OF PROPERTY

EDITORS' INTRODUCTION: SEIZURES OF ITEMS UNDER FOURTH AMENDMENT LAW

The Fourth Amendment's application to "seizures" of property was reaffirmed in Soldal v. Cook County, Illinois, 506 U.S. 56, 113 S.Ct. 538,

121 L.Ed.2d 450 (1992), a civil case. Soldal's trailer home was removed from its location in a mobile home park by the park owners, acting illegally under state law but with the active protection of local police. He sued for civil damages under 42 U.S.C.A. § 1983, claiming a conspiracy to unreasonably seize and remove his trailer. The district court granted summary judgment for the defendants; the Court of Appeals affirmed, reasoning the defendants had not seized Soldal's trailer within the meaning of the Fourth Amendment.

A unanimous Supreme Court reversed. The Court of Appeals, Justice White explained, construed the Fourth Amendment as not covering "technical" seizures infringing upon neither privacy nor liberty interests. Therefore, in its view, no seizure occurred since the officers had not invaded Soldal's privacy by entering or rummaging through the house or his liberty by detaining him. *Katz* and its progeny make clear, Justice White responded for the Court, property rights "are not the sole measure of Fourth Amendment violations." That case law did not, however, signal abandonment of the previously recognized protection for property under the Amendment. "[O]ur cases unmistakably hold," he emphasized, "that the [Fourth] Amendment protects property as well as privacy."

The Court of Appeals reasoned that the "plain view" seizure cases— such as the principal case reprinted after this Introduction—reflect that the Fourth Amendment protects against seizures resulting from "searches" but not seizures generally. This reading of the "plain view" cases was faulty, Justice White explained:

> [A]n officer who happens to come across an individual's property in a public area could seize it only if Fourth Amendment standards are satisfied—for example, if the items are evidence of a crime or contraband.

506 U.S. at 68, 113 S.Ct. at 547, 121 L.Ed.2d at 463.

Soldal's complaint, the Court concluded, alleged not simply a " 'garden-variety' landlord-tenant or commercial dispute" below Fourth Amendment recognition. Rather, it alleged a situation plainly implicating the interests protected by the Fourth Amendment and thus constituted a seizure within the meaning of that provision.

A person as well as an item may, of course, be seized. Seizures of persons raise quite different issues, and this topic is addressed in Chapter 4.

Definition of "Seizures." Whether police activity concerning places or items constitutes a "seizure" turns not upon whether that activity intrudes upon privacy interests but rather whether it constitutes a meaningful interference with the suspect's possessory interests. United States v. Jacobsen, 466 U.S. 109, 113, 104 S.Ct. 1652, 1656, 80 L.Ed.2d 85, 94 (1984). In United States v. Karo, 468 U.S. 705, 104 S.Ct. 3296, 82 L.Ed.2d 530 (1984), the defense urged that a seizure occurred when Karo took possession of a can of ether which, unbeknownst to him, contained a beeping device placed there by federal officers. Rejecting this, the Court explained:

> Although the can may have contained an unknown and unwanted foreign object, it cannot be said that anyone's possessory interest was

interfered with in any meaningful way. At most, there was a technical trespass on the space occupied by the beeper.

468 U.S. at 712, 104 S.Ct. at 3302, 82 L.Ed.2d at 540.

Items Subject to Seizure. Officers are clearly entitled—if other requirements are met—to seize items which they have sufficient reason to believe are seizable. Seizable items include stolen property and other "fruits" of criminal conduct, instrumentalities used in the commission of crime, or contraband, i.e., items—such as drugs—the possession of which is prohibited by law. But seizure of items of "mere evidence"—items which are of concern or value to public officers only because they constitute evidence of the commission of a crime or of someone's guilt of a crime—was at one time barred by the Fourth Amendment. Gouled v. United States, 255 U.S. 298, 311, 41 S.Ct. 261, 265, 65 L.Ed. 647, 653 (1921). In Warden v. Hayden, 387 U.S. 294, 87 S.Ct. 1642, 18 L.Ed.2d 2d 782 (1967), the Supreme Court abandoned this rule, holding that the Fourth Amendment did not absolutely bar seizure of mere evidence. No significant objective of the Amendment is served by the distinction, the Court noted, and citizens can be adequately protected from improper searches whether the object of those searches is to find and seize mere evidence or items subject to seizure under traditional doctrines.

The traditional list of items subject to seizure—contraband, instrumentalities and fruits of crime, and evidence—may be incomplete. Law enforcement officers may sometimes have authority to assume possession of items not coming within these categories. For example, an officer who arrests a suspect in or near the suspect's automobile may, under some circumstances, have authority to seize the automobile to protect the suspect's interest or to protect the officer from later claims that by his actions he subjected the automobile to increased risk of vandalism or other harm.

Need for Probable Cause. Does a seizure require probable cause to believe the item seized one to which the officers are entitled to possession, i.e., probable cause to believe that the item is contraband, an instrument or fruit of a crime or evidence? The plurality discussion in Coolidge v. New Hampshire, 403 U.S. 443, 91 S.Ct. 2022, 29 L.Ed.2d 564 (1971), considered at length in the principal case, suggested a "plain view" seizure requires it be "immediately apparent" to the officer that the item is subject to seizure. Whether this meant probable cause is necessary was considered but not resolved in Texas v. Brown, 460 U.S. 730, 103 S.Ct. 1535, 75 L.Ed.2d 502 (1983). The Court returned to the question in Arizona v. Hicks, 480 U.S. 321, 107 S.Ct. 1149, 94 L.Ed.2d 347 (1987), and addressed specifically whether probable cause was necessary for the plain view seizure of an item which officers came upon during a reasonable warrantless search of an apartment:

> We now hold that probable cause is required. To say otherwise would cut the "plain view" doctrine loose from its theoretical and practical moorings. The theory of that doctrine consists of extending to nonpublic places such as the home * * * the police's longstanding authority to make warrantless seizures in public places of such objects as weapons and contraband. And the practical justification for that extension is the desirability of sparing police, whose viewing of the

object in the course of a lawful search is as legitimate as it would have been in a public place, the inconvenience and the risk—to themselves or to preservation of the evidence—of going to obtain a warrant. Dispensing with the need for a warrant is worlds apart from permitting a lesser standard of *cause* for the seizure than a warrant would require, i.e., the standard of probable cause. No reason is apparent why an object should routinely be seizable on lesser grounds, during an unrelated search and seizure, than would have been needed to obtain a warrant for the same object if it had been known to be on the premises.

480 U.S. at 326–27, 107 S.Ct. at 1153, 94 L.Ed.2d at 355.

Searches of Seized Items. If an item is "seized" under the Fourth Amendment and that seizure is "reasonable," what additional is necessary before officers may "search" the seized item?

In United States v. Chadwick, 433 U.S. 1, 97 S.Ct. 2476, 53 L.Ed.2d 538 (1977), officers observed two Amtrak rail passengers arrive in Boston, and suspected the large footlocker they brought contained contraband. A trained dog released near the footlocker signaled it contained a controlled substance. Chadwick met the two passengers and the footlocker was placed in the trunk of Chadwick's car, parked outside the rail station. While the trunk of the car was still open, officers arrested all three and seized the footlocker. The footlocker was taken to the federal building in Boston. An hour and a half after the arrests, the footlocker was opened and searched. It was locked with a padlock and a regular trunk lock; the evidence did not establish how the officers opened it. Marijuana was found inside. Assuming the officers validly seized the footlocker, the Court nevertheless held their search of it unreasonable because they obtained no warrant:

> Once law enforcement authorities have reduced luggage or other personal property not immediately associated with the person of [an] arrestee to their exclusive control, and there is no longer any danger that the arrestee might gain access to the property to seize a weapon or destroy evidence, a search of that property is no longer an incident of the arrest.
>
> Here the search was conducted more than an hour after federal agents had gained exclusive control of the footlocker and long after [the arrestees] were securely in custody; the search therefore cannot be viewed as incidental to the arrest or as justified by any other exigency. Even though on this record the issuance of a warrant by a judicial officer was reasonably predictable, a line must be drawn. In our view, where no exigency is shown to support the need for an immediate search, the Warrant Clause places the line at the point where the property to be searched comes under the exclusive dominion of police authority.

433 U.S. at 15, 97 S.Ct. at 2485–86, 53 L.Ed.2d at 551.

Chadwick has given rise to significant difficulties, especially with regard to "containers" found in automobiles. These issues are considered in Chapters 4 and 5.

* * *

Fourth Amendment discussion, culminating in the principal case, has focused upon when, if ever, the Fourth Amendment requires judicial authorization for a seizure, in the form of a warrant or a specific provision in a warrant authorizing seizure of the property.

Horton v. California

Supreme Court of the United States, 1990.
496 U.S. 128, 110 S.Ct. 2301, 110 L.Ed.2d 112.

Justice STEVENS delivered the opinion of the Court.

In this case we revisit an issue that was considered, but not conclusively resolved, in Coolidge v. New Hampshire, 403 U.S. 443, 91 S.Ct. 2022, 29 L.Ed.2d 564 (1971): Whether the warrantless seizure of evidence of crime in plain view is prohibited by the Fourth Amendment if the discovery of the evidence was not inadvertent. We conclude that even though inadvertence is a characteristic of most legitimate "plain view" seizures, it is not a necessary condition.

I

Petitioner was convicted of the armed robbery of Erwin Wallaker, the treasurer of the San Jose Coin Club. When Wallaker returned to his home after the Club's annual show, he entered his garage and was accosted by two masked men, one armed with a machine gun and the other with an electrical shocking device, sometimes referred to as a "stun gun." The two men shocked Wallaker, bound and handcuffed him, and robbed him of jewelry and cash. During the encounter sufficient conversation took place to enable Wallaker subsequently to identify petitioner's distinctive voice. His identification was partially corroborated by a witness who saw the robbers leaving the scene, and by evidence that petitioner had attended the coin show.

Sergeant LaRault, an experienced police officer, investigated the crime and determined that there was probable cause to search petitioner's home for the proceeds of the robbery and for the weapons used by the robbers. His affidavit for a search warrant referred to police reports that described the weapons as well as the proceeds, but the warrant issued by the Magistrate only authorized a search for the proceeds, including three specifically described rings.

Pursuant to the warrant, LaRault searched petitioner's residence, but he did not find the stolen property. During the course of the search, however, he discovered the weapons in plain view and seized them. Specifically, he seized an Uzi machine gun, a .38 caliber revolver, two stun guns, a handcuff key, a San Jose Coin Club advertising brochure, and a few items of clothing identified by the victim.[11] LaRault testified that while he was searching for the rings, he also was interested in finding other evidence

11. Although the officer viewed other handguns and rifles, he did not seize them because there was no probable cause to be-lieve they were associated with criminal activity.

connecting petitioner to the robbery. Thus, the seized evidence was not discovered "inadvertently."

The trial court refused to suppress the evidence found in petitioner's home and, after a jury trial, petitioner was found guilty and sentenced to prison. The California Court of Appeal affirmed. * * * The California Supreme Court denied petitioner's request for review.

* * *

II

* * *

The right to security in person and property protected by the Fourth Amendment may be invaded in quite different ways by searches and seizures. A search compromises the individual interest in privacy; a seizure deprives the individual of dominion over his or her person or property. The "plain view" doctrine is often considered an exception to the general rule that warrantless searches are presumptively unreasonable, but this characterization overlooks the important difference between searches and seizures.[12] If an article is already in plain view, neither its observation nor its seizure would involve any invasion of privacy. A seizure of the article, however, would obviously invade the owner's possessory interest. If "plain view" justifies an exception from an otherwise applicable warrant requirement, therefore, it must be an exception that is addressed to the concerns that are implicated by seizures rather than by searches.

The criteria that generally guide "plain view" seizures were set forth in Coolidge v. New Hampshire, 403 U.S. 443, 91 S.Ct. 2022, 29 L.Ed.2d 564 (1971). The Court held that the seizure of two automobiles parked in plain view on the defendant's driveway in the course of arresting the defendant violated the Fourth Amendment. Accordingly, particles of gun powder that had been subsequently found in vacuum sweepings from one of the cars could not be introduced in evidence against the defendant. The State endeavored to justify the seizure of the automobiles, and their subsequent search at the police station, on four different grounds, including the "plain view" doctrine. The scope of that doctrine as it had developed in earlier cases was fairly summarized in these three paragraphs from Justice Stewart's opinion:

> It is well established that under certain circumstances the police may seize evidence in plain view without a warrant. But it is important to keep in mind that, in the vast majority of cases, ANY evidence seized by the police will be in plain view, at least at the moment of seizure. The problem with the "plain view" doctrine has been to identify the circumstances in which plain view has legal significance rather than being simply the normal concomitant of any search, legal or illegal.

12. It is important to distinguish "plain view," as used in *Coolidge* to justify seizure of an object, from an officer's mere observation of an item left in plain view. Whereas the latter generally involves no Fourth Amendment search, the former generally does implicate the Amendment's limitations upon seizures of personal property.

An example of the applicability of the "plain view" doctrine is the situation in which the police have a warrant to search a given area for specified objects, and in the course of the search come across some other article of incriminating character. Where the initial intrusion that brings the police within plain view of such an article is supported, not by a warrant, but by one of the recognized exceptions to the warrant requirement, the seizure is also legitimate. Thus the police may inadvertently come across evidence while in "hot pursuit" of a fleeing suspect. And an object that comes into view during a search incident to arrest that is appropriately limited in scope under existing law may be seized without a warrant. Finally, the "plain view" doctrine has been applied where a police officer is not searching for evidence against the accused, but nonetheless inadvertently comes across an incriminating object.

What the "plain view" cases have in common is that the police officer in each of them had a prior justification for an intrusion in the course of which he came inadvertently across a piece of evidence incriminating the accused. The doctrine serves to supplement the prior justification—whether it be a warrant for another object, hot pursuit, search incident to lawful arrest, or some other legitimate reason for being present unconnected with a search directed against the accused—and permits the warrantless seizure. Of course, the extension of the original justification is legitimate only where it is immediately apparent to the police that they have evidence before them; the "plain view" doctrine may not be used to extend a general exploratory search from one object to another until something incriminating at last emerges.

Justice Stewart then described the two limitations on the doctrine that he found implicit in its rationale: First, "that plain view ALONE is never enough to justify the warrantless seizure of evidence,"; and second, "that the discovery of evidence in plain view must be inadvertent."

Justice Stewart's analysis of the "plain view" doctrine did not command a majority and a plurality of the Court has since made clear that the discussion is "not a binding precedent." Texas v. Brown, [460 U.S. 730, 737, 103 S.Ct. 1535, 1541, 75 L.Ed.2d 502 (1983)] (opinion of REHN-QUIST, J.). Justice Harlan, who concurred in the Court's judgment and in its response to the dissenting opinions, did not join the plurality's discussion of the "plain view" doctrine. The decision nonetheless is a binding precedent. Before discussing the second limitation, which is implicated in this case, it is therefore necessary to explain why the first adequately supports the Court's judgment.

It is, of course, an essential predicate to any valid warrantless seizure of incriminating evidence that the officer did not violate the Fourth Amendment in arriving at the place from which the evidence could be plainly viewed. There are, moreover, two additional conditions that must be satisfied to justify the warrantless seizure. First, not only must the item be in plain view, its incriminating character must also be "immediately apparent." Thus, in *Coolidge,* the cars were obviously in plain view, but their probative value remained uncertain until after the interiors were swept and examined microscopically. Second, not only must the officer be lawfully located in a place from which the object can be plainly seen, but he or she must also have a lawful right of access to the object itself. As the Solicitor General has suggested, Justice Harlan's vote in *Coolidge* may have rested on the fact that the seizure of the cars was accomplished by means of a warrantless trespass on the defendant's property.

In all events, we are satisfied that the absence of inadvertence was not essential to the Court's rejection of the State's "plain view" argument in *Coolidge*.

III

Justice Stewart concluded that the inadvertence requirement was necessary to avoid a violation of the express constitutional requirement that a valid warrant must particularly describe the things to be seized. He explained:

> The rationale of the exception to the warrant requirement, as just stated, is that a plain-view seizure will not turn an initially valid (and therefore limited) search into a "general" one, while the inconvenience of procuring a warrant to cover an inadvertent discovery is great. But where the discovery is anticipated, where the police know in advance the location of the evidence and intend to seize it, the situation is altogether different. The requirement of a warrant to seize imposes no inconvenience whatever, or at least none which is constitutionally cognizable in a legal system that regards warrantless searches as "per se unreasonable" in the absence of "exigent circumstances."

> If the initial intrusion is bottomed upon a warrant that fails to mention a particular object, though the police know its location and intend to seize it, then there is a violation of the express constitutional requirement of "Warrants . . . particularly describing . . . [the] things to be seized."

We find two flaws in this reasoning. First, evenhanded law enforcement is best achieved by the application of objective standards of conduct, rather than standards that depend upon the subjective state of mind of the officer. The fact that an officer is interested in an item of evidence and fully expects to find it in the course of a search should not invalidate its seizure if the search is confined in area and duration by the terms of a warrant or a valid exception to the warrant requirement. If the officer has knowledge approaching certainty that the item will be found, we see no reason why he or she would deliberately omit a particular description of the item to be seized from the application for a search warrant. Specification of the additional item could only permit the officer to expand the scope of the search. On the other hand, if he or she has a valid warrant to search for one item and merely a suspicion concerning the second, whether or not it amounts to probable cause, we fail to see why that suspicion should immunize the second item from seizure if it is found during a lawful search for the first. * * *

Second, the suggestion that the inadvertence requirement is necessary to prevent the police from conducting general searches, or from converting specific warrants into general warrants, is not persuasive because that interest is already served by the requirements that no warrant issue unless it "particularly describ[es] the place to be searched and the persons or things to be seized," and that a warrantless search be circumscribed by the exigencies which justify its initiation. Scrupulous adherence to these requirements serves the interests in limiting the area and duration of the search that the inadvertence requirement inadequately protects. Once those commands have been satisfied and the officer has a lawful right of access, however, no additional Fourth Amendment interest is furthered by requiring that the discovery of evidence be inadvertent. If the scope of the search exceeds that permitted by the terms of a validly issued warrant or the character of the relevant exception from the warrant requirement, the subsequent seizure is unconstitutional without more. * * *

In this case, the scope of the search was not enlarged in the slightest by the omission of any reference to the weapons in the warrant. Indeed, if the three rings and other items named in the warrant had been found at the outset—or if petitioner had them in his possession and had responded to the warrant by producing them immediately—no search for weapons could have taken place. * * * Justice White's dissenting opinion in *Coolidge* is instructive:

> Police with a warrant for a rifle may search only places where rifles might be and must terminate the search once the rifle is found; the inadvertence rule will in no way reduce the number of places into which they may lawfully look.

As we have already suggested, by hypothesis the seizure of an object in plain view does not involve an intrusion on privacy.[13] If the interest in privacy has been invaded, the violation must have occurred before the object came into plain view and there is no need for an inadvertence limitation on seizures to condemn it. The prohibition against general searches and general warrants serves primarily as a protection against unjustified intrusions on privacy. But reliance on privacy concerns that support that prohibition is misplaced when the inquiry concerns the scope of an exception that merely authorizes an officer with a lawful right of access to an item to seize it without a warrant.

In this case the items seized from petitioner's home were discovered during a lawful search authorized by a valid warrant. When they were discovered, it was immediately apparent to the officer that they constituted incriminating evidence. He had probable cause, not only to obtain a warrant to search for the stolen property, but also to believe that the weapons and handguns had been used in the crime he was investigating. The search was authorized by the warrant, the seizure was authorized by the "plain view" doctrine. The judgment is affirmed.

It is so ordered.

---

13. Even if the item is a container, its seizure does not compromise the interest in preserving the privacy of its contents because it may only be opened pursuant to either a search warrant, see * * * United States v. Chadwick, 433 U.S. 1, 97 S.Ct. 2476, 53 L.Ed.2d 538 (1977) * * *, or one of the well-delineated exceptions to the warrant requirement.

■ JUSTICE BRENNAN, with whom JUSTICE MARSHALL joins, dissenting.

* * *

The Fourth Amendment * * * protects two distinct interests. The prohibition against unreasonable searches and the requirement that a warrant "particularly describ[e] the place to be searched" protect an interest in privacy. The prohibition against unreasonable seizures and the requirement that a warrant "particularly describ[e] ...the ...things to be seized" protect a possessory interest in property. The Fourth Amendment, by its terms, declares the privacy and possessory interests to be equally important. As this Court recently stated, "Although the interest protected by the Fourth Amendment injunction against unreasonable searches is quite different from that protected by its injunction against unreasonable seizures, neither the one nor the other is of inferior worth or necessarily requires only lesser protection." Arizona v. Hicks, 480 U.S. 321, 328, 107 S.Ct. 1149, 1154, 94 L.Ed.2d 347 (1987) (citation omitted).

The Amendment protects these equally important interests in precisely the same manner: by requiring a neutral and detached magistrate to evaluate, before the search or seizure, the government's showing of probable cause and its particular description of the place to be searched and the items to be seized. Accordingly, just as a warrantless search is per se unreasonable absent exigent circumstances, so too a seizure of personal property is "per se unreasonable within the meaning of the Fourth Amendment unless it is accomplished pursuant to a judicial warrant issued upon probable cause and particularly describing the items to be seized." * * *

The plain view doctrine is an exception to the general rule that a seizure of personal property must be authorized by a warrant. As Justice Stewart explained in *Coolidge,* we accept a warrantless seizure when an officer is lawfully in a location and inadvertently sees evidence of a crime because of "the inconvenience of procuring a warrant" to seize this newly discovered piece of evidence. But "where the discovery is anticipated, where the police know in advance the location of the evidence and intend to seize it," the argument that procuring a warrant would be "inconvenient" loses much, if not all, of its force. Barring an exigency, there is no reason why the police officers could not have obtained a warrant to seize this evidence before entering the premises. The rationale behind the inadvertent discovery requirement is simply that we will not excuse officers from the general requirement of a warrant to seize if the officers know the location of evidence, have probable cause to seize it, intend to seize it, and yet do not bother to obtain a warrant particularly describing that evidence. To do so would violate "the express constitutional requirement of 'Warrants ...particularly describing ...[the] things to be seized,' and would 'fly in the face of the basic rule that no amount of probable cause can justify a warrantless seizure.' "

* * *

The Court posits two "flaws" in Justice Stewart's reasoning that it believes demonstrate the inappropriateness of the inadvertent discovery requirement. But these flaws are illusory. First, the majority explains that it can see no reason why an officer who "has knowledge approaching certainty" that an item will be found in a particular location "would deliberately omit a particular description of the item to be seized from the application for a search warrant." * * * [T]here are[, however,] a number of instances in which a law enforcement officer might deliberately choose to omit certain items from a warrant application even though he has probable cause to seize them, knows they are on the premises, and intends to seize them when they are discovered in plain view. For example, the warrant application process can often be time-consuming, especially when the police attempt to seize a large number of items. An officer interested in conducting a search as soon as possible might decide to save time by listing only one or two hard-to-find items, such as the stolen rings in this case, confident that he will find in plain view all of the other evidence he is looking for before he discovers the listed items. Because rings could be located almost anywhere inside or outside a house, it is unlikely that a warrant to search for and seize the rings would restrict the scope of the search. An officer might rationally find the risk of immediately discovering the items listed in the warrant—thereby forcing him to conclude the search immediately—outweighed by the time saved in the application process.

The majority also contends that, once an officer is lawfully in a house and the scope of his search is adequately circumscribed by a warrant, "no additional Fourth Amendment interest is furthered by requiring that the discovery of evidence be inadvertent." * * * The majority is correct, but it has asked the wrong question. It is true that the inadvertent discovery requirement furthers no privacy interests. The requirement in no way reduces the scope of a search or the number of places into which officers may look. But it does protect possessory interests. The inadvertent discovery requirement is essential if we are to take seriously the Fourth Amendment's protection of possessory interests as well as privacy interests. The Court today eliminates a rule designed to further possessory interests on the ground that it fails to further privacy interests. I cannot countenance such constitutional legerdemain.

* * *

* * * I respectfully dissent.

NOTE

If officers "secure" premises, as for example pending application for a search warrant, by preventing the owner or residents from entering, have they "seized" those premises? The Court has not resolved this issue. See Segura v. United States, 468 U.S. 796, 104 S.Ct. 3380, 82 L.Ed.2d 599 (1984).

3.   APPLYING THE "STANDING" REQUIREMENT

As *Wong Sun* and the material in Part B of Chapter 1 make clear, the Supreme Court has traditionally limited defendants to claims that evidence was obtained in violation of their own federal constitutional rights. Application of this requirement has presented the greatest difficulty in search and seizure cases. Once a court determines officers' activity constituted a "search," a "seizure," or both, it is often faced with a further and

sometimes difficult determination as to whose Fourth Amendment interests were infringed upon by the searches and seizures that occurred. These
determinations are the subject of the principal case in this subsection.

Rakas v. Illinois

Supreme Court of the United States, 1978.
439 U.S. 128, 99 S.Ct. 421, 58 L.Ed.2d 387.

■ MR. JUSTICE REHNQUIST delivered the opinion of the Court.

Petitioners were convicted of armed robbery in the Circuit Court of
Kankakee County, Ill., and their convictions were affirmed on appeal. At
their trial, the prosecution offered into evidence a sawed-off rifle and rifle
shells that had been seized by police during a search of an automobile in
which petitioners had been passengers. Neither petitioner is the owner of
the automobile and neither has ever asserted that he owned the rifle or
shells seized. The Illinois Appellate Court held that petitioners lacked
standing to object to the allegedly unlawful search and seizure and denied
their motion to suppress the evidence. We granted certiorari in light of the
obvious importance of the issues raised to the administration of criminal
justice, and now affirm.

I.

Because we are not here concerned with the issue of probable cause, a
brief description of the events leading to the search of the automobile will
suffice. A police officer on a routine patrol received a radio call notifying
him of a robbery of a clothing store in Bourbonnais, Ill., and describing the
getaway car. Shortly thereafter, the officer spotted an automobile which he
thought might be the getaway car. After following the car for some time
and after the arrival of assistance, he and several other officers stopped the
vehicle. The occupants of the automobile, petitioners and two female
companions, were ordered out of the car and after the occupants had left
the car, two officers searched the interior of the vehicle. They discovered a
box of rifle shells in the glove compartment, which had been locked, and a
sawed-off rifle under the front passenger seat. After discovering the rifle
and the shells, the officer took petitioners to the station and placed them
under arrest.

Before trial petitioners moved to suppress the rifle and shells seized
from the car on the ground that the search violated the Fourth and
Fourteenth Amendments. They conceded that they did not own the automobile and were simply passengers; the owner of the car had been the
driver of the vehicle at the time of the search. Nor did they assert that they
owned the rifle or the shells seized. The prosecutor challenged petitioners'
standing to object to the lawfulness of the search of the car because neither
the car, the shells nor the rifle belonged to them. The trial court agreed
that petitioners lacked standing and denied the motion to suppress the
evidence. In view of this holding, the court did not determine whether there
was probable cause for the search and seizure. On appeal after petitioners'
conviction, the Appellate Court of Illinois, Third Judicial District, affirmed
the trial court's denial of petitioners' motion to suppress because it held

that "without a proprietary or other similar interest in an automobile, a mere passenger therein lacks standing to challenge the legality of the search of the vehicle." * * * The Illinois Supreme Court denied petitioners leave to appeal.

II.

* * *

[The Court first rejected petitioners' argument that the traditional standing requirement should be relaxed or broadened. After adhering to its traditional position, the Court further commented, that "the type of standing requirement * * * reaffirmed today is more properly subsumed under substantive Fourth Amendment doctrine." This aspect of the decision is discussed in part B of Chapter 1. Editors.]

Analyzed in these terms, the question is whether the challenged search or seizure violated the Fourth Amendment rights of a criminal defendant who seeks to exclude the evidence obtained during it. That inquiry in turn requires a determination of whether the disputed search and seizure has infringed an interest of the defendant which the Fourth Amendment was designed to protect. We are under no illusion that by dispensing with the rubric of standing * * * we have rendered any simpler the determination of whether the proponent of a motion to suppress is entitled to contest the legality of a search and seizure. But by frankly recognizing that this aspect of the analysis belongs more properly under the heading of substantive Fourth Amendment doctrine than under the heading of standing, we think the decision of this issue will rest on sounder logical footing.

C.

Here petitioners, who were passengers occupying a car which they neither owned nor leased, seek to analogize their position to that of the defendant in Jones v. United States, 362 U.S. 257, 80 S.Ct. 725, 4 L.Ed.2d 697 (1960). In *Jones*, petitioner was present at the time of the search of an apartment which was owned by a friend. The friend had given Jones permission to use the apartment and a key to it, with which Jones had admitted himself on the day of the search. He had a suit and shirt at the apartment and had slept there "maybe a night," but his home was elsewhere. At the time of the search, Jones was the only occupant of the apartment because the lessee was away for a period of several days. Under these circumstances, this Court stated that while one wrongfully on the premises could not move to suppress evidence obtained as a result of searching them, "anyone legitimately on premises where a search occurs may challenge its legality." Petitioners argue that their occupancy of the automobile in question was comparable to that of Jones in the apartment and that they therefore have standing to contest the legality of the search— or as we have rephrased the inquiry, that they, like Jones, had their Fourth Amendment rights violated by the search.

We do not question the conclusion in *Jones* that the defendant in that case suffered a violation of his personal Fourth Amendment rights if the search in question was unlawful. Nonetheless, we believe that the phrase "legitimately on premises" coined in *Jones* creates too broad a gauge for measurement of Fourth Amendment rights. For example, applied literally, this statement would permit a casual visitor who has never seen, or been permitted to visit the basement of another's house to object to a search of the basement if the visitor happened to be in the kitchen of the house at the time of the search. Likewise, a casual visitor who walks into a house one minute before a search of the house commences and leaves one minute after the search ends would be able to contest the legality of the search. The first visitor would have absolutely no interest or legitimate expectation of privacy in the basement, the second would have none in the house, and it advances no purpose served by the Fourth Amendment to permit either of them to object to the lawfulness of the search.

We think that *Jones* on its facts merely stands for the unremarkable proposition that a person can have a legally sufficient interest in a place other than his own home so that the Fourth Amendment protects him from unreasonable governmental intrusion into that place. In defining the scope of that interest, we adhere to the view expressed in *Jones* and echoed in later cases that arcane distinctions developed in property and tort law between guests, licensees, invitees, and the like, ought not to control. But the *Jones* statement that a person need only be "legitimately on premises" in order to challenge the validity of the search of a dwelling place cannot be taken in its full sweep beyond the facts of that case.

* * *

Our BROTHER WHITE in dissent expresses the view that by rejecting the phrase "legitimately on [the] premises" as the appropriate measure of Fourth Amendment rights, we are abandoning a thoroughly workable, "bright line" test in favor of a less certain analysis of whether the facts of a particular case give rise to a legitimate expectation of privacy. If "legitimately on premises" were the successful litmus test of Fourth Amendment rights that he assumes it is, his approach would have at least the merit of easy application, whatever it lacked in fidelity to the history and purposes of the Fourth Amendment. But a reading of lower court cases that have applied the phrase "legitimately on premises," and of the dissent itself, reveals that this expression is not a shorthand summary for a bright line rule which somehow encapsulates the "core" of the Fourth Amendment's protections.

The dissent itself shows that the facile consistency it is striving for is illusory. The dissenters concede that "there comes a point when use of an area is shared with so many that one simply cannot reasonably expect seclusion." But surely the "point" referred to is not one demarcating a line which is black on one side and white on another; it is inevitably a point which separates one shade of gray from another. We are likewise told by the dissent that a person "legitimately on *private* premises * * *, though his privacy is *not absolute*, is entitled to expect that he is sharing it only with those persons and that governmental officials will intrude only with *consent* or by complying with the Fourth Amendment." (emphasis added). This single sentence describing the contours of the supposedly easily applied rule virtually abounds with unanswered questions: What are "private" premises? Indeed, what are the "premises?" It may be easy to describe the "premises" when one is confronted with a one-room apartment, but what of the case of a 10–room house, or of a house with an attached garage that is searched? Also, if one's privacy is not absolute, how is it bounded? If he risks governmental intrusion "with consent," who may give that consent?

Again, we are told by the dissent that the Fourth Amendment assures that "*some* expectations of privacy are justified and will be protected from official intrusion." (emphasis added). But we are not told which of many possible expectations of privacy are embraced within this sentence. And our dissenting Brethren concede that "perhaps the Constitution provides some degree less protection for the personal freedom from unreasonable governmental intrusion when one does not have a possessory interest in the invaded private place." But how much "less" protection is available when one does not have such a possessory interest?

* * *

D.

Judged by the foregoing analysis, petitioners' claims must fail. They asserted neither a property nor a possessory interest in the automobile, nor an interest in the property seized. And as we have previously indicated, the fact that they were "legitimately on [the] premises" in the sense that they were in the car with the permission of its owner is not determinative of whether they had a legitimate expectation of privacy in the particular areas of the automobile searched. It is unnecessary for us to decide here whether the same expectations of privacy are warranted in a car as would be justified in a dwelling place in analogous circumstances. We have on numerous occasions pointed out that cars are not to be treated identically with houses or apartments for Fourth Amendment purposes. But here petitioners' claim is one which would fail even in an analogous situation in a dwelling place since they made no showing that they had any legitimate expectation of privacy in the glove compartment or area under the seat of the car in which they were merely passengers. Like the trunk of an automobile, these are areas in which a passenger *qua* passenger simply would not normally have a legitimate expectation of privacy.

Jones v. United States, 362 U.S. 257, 80 S.Ct. 725, 4 L.Ed.2d 697 (1960), involved significantly different factual circumstances. Jones not only had permission to use the apartment of his friend, but had a key to the apartment with which he admitted himself on the day of the search and kept possessions in the apartment. Except with respect to his friend, Jones had complete dominion and control over the apartment and could exclude others from it. * * *

IV.

The Illinois courts were therefore correct in concluding that it was unnecessary to decide whether the search of the car might have violated the rights secured to someone else by the Fourth and Fourteenth Amendments to the United States Constitution. Since it did not violate any rights of these petitioners, their judgment of conviction is

Affirmed.

■ MR. JUSTICE WHITE, with whom MR. JUSTICE BRENNAN, MR. JUSTICE MARSHALL, and MR. JUSTICE STEVENS, join, dissenting.

The Court today holds that the Fourth Amendment protects property, not people, and specifically that a legitimate occupant of an automobile may not invoke the exclusionary rule and challenge a search of that vehicle unless he happens to own or have a possessory interest in it. * * * If the Court is troubled by the practical impact of the exclusionary rule, it should face the issue of that rule's continued validity squarely instead of distorting other doctrines in an attempt to reach what are perceived as the correct results in specific cases.

* * *

[M]any of our opinions have assumed that a mere passenger in an automobile is entitled to protection against unreasonable searches occurring in his presence. In decisions upholding the validity of automobile searches, we have gone directly to the merits even though some of the petitioners did not own or possess the vehicles in question. * * * The Court's silence on this issue in light of its actions can only mean that, until now, we, like most lower courts, had assumed that *Jones* foreclosed the answer now supplied by the majority. That assumption was perfectly understandable, since all private premises would seem to be the same for the purposes of the analysis set out in *Jones*.

* * * My Brethren in the majority assertedly do not deny that automobiles warrant at least some protection from official interference with privacy. Thus, the next step is to decide who is entitled, vis à vis the State, to enjoy that privacy. The answer to that question must be found by determining "whether petitioner had an interest in connection with the searched premises that gave rise to 'a reasonable expectation [on his part] of freedom from governmental intrusion' upon those premises." Combs v. United States, 408 U.S. 224, 227, 92 S.Ct. 2284, 2286, 33 L.Ed.2d 308 (1972), quoting Mancusi v. DeForte, 392 U.S. 364, 368, 88 S.Ct. 2120, 2123, 20 L.Ed.2d 1154 (1968) (bracketed material in original).

Not only does *Combs* supply the relevant inquiry, it also directs us to the proper answer. We recognized there that *Jones* had held that one of those protected interests is created by legitimate presence on the searched premises, even absent any possessory interest. This makes unquestionable sense. We have concluded on numerous occasions that the entitlement to an expectation of privacy does not hinge on ownership * * *.

* * *

[O]ne consistent theme in our decisions under the Fourth Amendment has been, until now, that "the Amendment does not shield only those who have title to the searched premises." Mancusi v. DeForte, 392 U.S. 364, 367, 88 S.Ct. 2120, 2123, 20 L.Ed.2d 1154 (1968). Though there comes a point when use of an area is shared with so many that one simply cannot reasonably expect seclusion, short of that limit a person legitimately on private premises knows the others allowed there and, though his privacy is not absolute, is entitled to expect that he is sharing it only with those persons and that governmental officials will intrude only with consent or by complying with the Fourth Amendment.

It is true that the Court asserts that it is not limiting the Fourth Amendment bar against unreasonable searches to the protection of property rights, but in reality it is doing exactly that.[14] Petitioners were in a private place with the permission of the owner, but the Court states that that is not sufficient to establish entitlement to a legitimate expectation of privacy. But if that is not sufficient, what would be? We are not told, and it is hard to imagine anything short of a property interest that would satisfy the majority. Insofar as the Court's rationale is concerned, no passenger in an automobile, without an ownership or possessory interest and regardless of his relationship to the owner, may claim Fourth Amendment protection against illegal stops and searches of the automobile in which he is rightfully present. The Court approves the result in *Jones*, but it fails to give any explanation why the facts in *Jones* differ, in a fashion material to the Fourth Amendment, from the facts here.[15] More importantly, how is the Court able to avoid answering the question why presence in a private place with the owner's permission is insufficient? * * *

* * *

* * * If the owner of the car had not only invited petitioners to join her but had said to them, "I give you a temporary possessory interest in my vehicle so that you will share the right to privacy that the Supreme Court says that I own," then apparently the majority would reverse. But people seldom say such things, though they may mean their invitation to encompass them if only they had thought of the problem. If the nonowner were the spouse or child of the owner, would the Court recognize a sufficient interest? If so, would distant relatives somehow have more of an expectation of privacy than close friends? What if the nonowner were driving with the owner's permission? Would nonowning drivers have more of an expectation of privacy than mere passengers? What about a passenger in a taxicab? * * *

* * * The *Jones* rule is relatively easily applied by police and courts; the rule announced today will not provide law enforcement officials with a bright line between the protected and the unprotected. Only rarely will

---

14. The Court's reliance on property law concepts is additionally shown by its suggestion that visitors could "contest the lawfulness of the seizure of evidence or the search if their own property were seized during the search." What difference should that property interest make to constitutional protection against unreasonable searches, which is concerned with privacy? Contrary to the Court's suggestion, a legitimate passenger in a car expects to enjoy the privacy of the vehicle whether or not he happens to carry some item along for the ride. We have never before limited our concern for a person's privacy to those situations in which he is in possession of personal property. Even a person living in a barren room without possessions is entitled to expect that the police will not intrude without cause.

15. Jones had permission to use the apartment, had slept in it one night, had a key, had left a suit and a shirt there, and was the only occupant at the time of the search. Petitioners here had permission to be in the car and were occupying it at the time of the search. Thus the only distinguishing fact is that Jones could exclude others from the apartment by using his friend's key. But petitioners and their friend the owner had excluded others by entering the automobile and shutting the doors. Petitioners did not need a key because the owner was present. * * *

police know whether one private party has or has not been granted a sufficient possessory or other interest by another private party. Surely in this case the officers had no such knowledge. The Court's rule will ensnare defendants and police in needless litigation over factors that should not be determinative of Fourth Amendment rights.

More importantly, the ruling today undercuts the force of the exclusionary rule in the one area in which its use is most certainly justified—the deterrence of bad-faith violations of the Fourth Amendment. This decision invites police to engage in patently unreasonable searches every time an automobile contains more than one occupant. Should something be found, only the owner of the vehicle, or of the item, will have standing to seek suppression, and the evidence will presumably be usable against the other occupants. The danger of such bad faith is especially high in cases such as this one where the officers are only after the passengers and can usually infer accurately that the driver is the owner. The suppression remedy for those owners in whose vehicles something is found and who are charged with crime is small consolation for all those owners *and* occupants whose privacy will be needlessly invaded by officers following mistaken hunches not rising to the level of probable cause but operated on in the knowledge that someone in a crowded car will probably be unprotected if contraband or incriminating evidence happens to be found. After this decision, police will have little to lose by unreasonably searching vehicles occupied by more than one person.

* * *

NOTES

1. **Privacy in Premises.** Whether a search of premises violates the privacy rights of persons on the premises is, as the Court noted in *Rakas*, potentially a different question than that resolved in *Rakas*. The premises issue was addressed in two post-*Rakas* decisions.

In Minnesota v. Olson, 495 U.S. 91, 110 S.Ct. 1684, 109 L.Ed.2d 85 (1990), Olson was arrested in a duplex unit used as a residence by Luanne and Julie Bergstrom. Olson, with permission of the Bergstroms, spent the previous night in the duplex (sleeping on the floor) and had a change of clothes with him. At issue was whether Olson could contest the reasonableness of police entry of the duplex. The Supreme Court held that he could: "Olson's status as an overnight guest is alone enough to show that he had an expectation of privacy in the home that society is prepared to recognize as reasonable." Jones v. United States, distinguished in *Rakas,* was controlling, Justice White explained, despite the State's argument that Olson, unlike Jones, was never left alone in the unit and was never given a key to it.

> That the guest has a host who has ultimate control of the house is not inconsistent with the guest having a legitimate expectation of privacy. * * * [H]osts will more likely than not respect the privacy interests of their guests, who are entitled to a legitimate expectation of privacy despite the fact that they have no legal interest in the premises and do not have the legal authority to determine who may or may not enter the household.

495 U.S. at 99, 110 S.Ct. at 1689, 109 L.Ed.2d at 95. Chief Justice Rehnquist and Justice Blackmun dissented without opinion.

Olson was developed in Minnesota v. Carter, 525 U.S. 83, 119 S.Ct. 469, 142 L.Ed.2d 373 (1998). The question was whether Carter and Johns had a privacy interest in an apartment located in Eagan, Minnesota, and leased by Kimberly Thompson. Carter and Johns lived in Chicago and came to the apartment for the sole purpose of packaging cocaine for resale. They had never been in the apartment before and were in it for about 2 and 1/2 hours. In return for the brief use of the apartment, Carter and Johns gave Thompson one-eighth of an ounce of the cocaine. At issue in the case was whether Carter and Johns could challenge the admissibility of certain evidence on the ground it was the result of an observation of the packaging process in the apartment that Carter and Johns contended was an unreasonable search. The Court held Carter and Johns had no protected privacy interest in the premises and thus could not challenge any search that might have been involved in the observation:

> The [Fourth] Amendment protects persons against unreasonable searches of "their persons [and] houses" and thus indicates that the Fourth Amendment is a personal right that must be invoked by an individual. See Katz v. United States, 389 U.S. 347, 351, 88 S.Ct. 507, 19 L.Ed.2d 576 (1967). But the extent to which the Fourth Amendment protects people may depend upon where those people are. * * *

> The text of the Amendment suggests that its protections extend only to people in "their" houses. But we have held that in some circumstances a person may have a legitimate expectation of privacy in the house of someone else. In Minnesota v. Olson, 495 U.S. 91, 110 S.Ct. 1684, 109 L.Ed.2d 85 (1990), for example, we decided that an overnight guest in a house had the sort of expectation of privacy that the Fourth Amendment protects. * * *

> Respondents here were obviously not overnight guests, but were essentially present for a business transaction and were only in the home a matter of hours. There is no suggestion that they had a previous relationship with Thompson, or that there was any other purpose to their visit. Nor was there anything similar to the overnight guest relationship in *Olson* to suggest a degree of acceptance into the household. While the apartment was a dwelling place for Thompson, it was for these respondents simply a place to do business.

> Property used for commercial purposes is treated differently for Fourth Amendment purposes than residential property. "An expectation of privacy in commercial premises, however, is different from, and indeed less than, a similar expectation in an individual's home." New York v. Burger, 482 U.S. 691, 700, 107 S.Ct. 2636, 96 L.Ed.2d 601 (1987). And while it was a "home" in which respondents were present, it was not their home. Similarly, the Court has held that in some circumstances a worker can claim Fourth Amendment protection over his own workplace. See, e.g., O'Connor v. Ortega, 480 U.S. 709, 107 S.Ct. 1492, 94 L.Ed.2d 714 (1987). But there is no indication that respondents in this case had nearly as significant a connection to Thompson's apartment as the worker in O'Connor had to his own private office.

> If we regard the overnight guest in Minnesota v. Olson as typifying those who may claim the protection of the Fourth Amendment in the home of another, and one merely "legitimately on the premises" as typifying those who may not do so, the present case is obviously somewhere in between. But the purely commercial nature of the transaction engaged in here, the relatively short period of time on the premises, and the lack of any previous connection between respondents and the householder, all lead us to conclude that respondents' situation is closer to that of one simply permitted on the premises. We therefore hold that any search which may have occurred did not violate their Fourth Amendment rights.

525 U.S. at 88–91, 119 S.Ct. at 470–74, 142 L.Ed.2d at 379–81. Four members of the Court disagreed. They reasoned that "when a homeowner or lessor personally invites a guest into her home to share in a common endeavor, whether it be for conversation, to engage in leisure activities, or for business purposes licit or illicit, that guest should share his host's shelter against unreasonable searches and seizures." 525 U.S. at 106, 119 S.Ct. at 481–82, 142 L.Ed.2d at 390, 392 (Ginsburg, J., dissenting,), 525 U.S. at 103, 119 S.Ct. at 480, 142 L.Ed.2d at 388 (Breyer, J., concurring in the judgment) (agreeing with Justice Ginsburg that the respondents can claim Fourth Amendment protection but concluding further that the challenged observation did not violate that protection).

2. **Use of a Place for Storage.** Suppose Rakas had testified he owned the rifle and shells and the owner of the automobile permitted him to use the car a repository for his property. Would he have established a protected privacy interest in at least that portion of the car the owner permitted him to use for storage of his property?

The issue was presented in Rawlings v. Kentucky, 448 U.S. 98, 100 S.Ct. 2556, 65 L.Ed.2d 633 (1980). Rawlings, the petitioner before the Supreme Court, Vannessa Cox and several others were detained by Bowling Green officers while other officers applied for a search warrant. One officer approached Cox and directed her to empty the contents of her purse onto a nearby coffee table. She complied. The contents of her purse included a jar containing 1,800 tablets of LSD and other controlled substances. She turned to Rawlings—standing next to her—and told him "to take what was his." Rawlings claimed ownership of the controlled substances. At his trial for possession of and trafficking in those substances, could he challenge the officer's search of Cox's purse? The Court described the testimony explaining the situation as follows:

> Petitioner testified that he had flown into Bowling Green about a week before his arrest to look for a job and perhaps to attend the local university. He brought with him at that time the drugs later found in Cox's purse. Initially, petitioner stayed in the house where the arrest took place as the guest of Michael Swank, who shared the house with Marquess and Saddler. While at a party at that house, he met Cox and spent at least two nights of the next week on a couch at Cox's house.
>
> On the morning of petitioner's arrest, Cox had dropped him off at Swank's house where he waited for her to return from class. At that time, he was carrying the drugs in a green bank bag. When Cox returned to the house to meet him, petitioner dumped the contents of the bank bag into Cox's purse. Although there is dispute over the discussion that took place, petitioner testified that he "asked her if she would carry this for me, and she said, 'yes'...." Petitioner then left the room to use the bathroom and, by the time he returned, discovered that the police had arrived * * *.

During Rawlings' testimony, the following exchange took place:

> Q: Did you feel that Vanessa Cox's purse would be free from the intrusion of the officers as you sat there [waiting for the warrant?] When you put the pills in her purse, did you feel that they would be free from governmental intrusion?
>
> A: No, sir.

The state court, emphasizing Rawlings' admission he did not believe Cox's purse would be free from governmental intrusion, held Rawlings failed to show that the search of the purse violated his reasonable expectation of privacy.

The Supreme Court affirmed. It explained:

We believe that the record in this case supports [the state court's] conclusion. Petitioner, of course, bears the burden of proving * * * that he had a legitimate expectation of privacy in [the] purse. At the time petitioner dumped thousands of dollars worth of illegal drugs into Cox's purse, he had known her for only a few days. According to Cox's uncontested testimony, petitioner had never sought or received access to her purse prior to that sudden bailment. Nor did petitioner have any right to exclude other persons from access to Cox's purse. In fact, Cox testified that Bob Stallons, a longtime acquaintance and frequent companion of Cox's, had free access to her purse and on the very morning of the arrest had rummaged through its contents in search of a hairbrush. Moreover, even assuming that petitioner's version of the bailment is correct and that Cox did consent to the transfer of possession, the precipitous nature of the transaction hardly supports a reasonable inference that petitioner took normal precautions to maintain his privacy. * * * [T]he record also contains a frank admission by petitioner that he had no subjective expectation that Cox's purse would remain free from governmental intrusion * * *.

Petitioner contends nevertheless that, because he claimed ownership of the drugs in Cox's purse, he should be entitled to challenge the search regardless of his expectation of privacy. We disagree. While petitioner's ownership of the drugs is undoubtedly one fact to be considered in this case, *Rakas* emphatically rejected the notion that "arcane" concepts of property law ought to control the ability to claim the protections of the Fourth Amendment. * * *

In sum, we find no reason to overturn the lower court's conclusion that petitioner had no legitimate expectation of privacy in Cox's purse at the time of the search.

448 U.S. at 104–06, 100 S.Ct. at 2561–62, 65 L.Ed.2d at 641–42.

CHAPTER 3

ISSUANCE AND EXECUTION OF ARREST AND SEARCH WARRANTS

Analysis

EDITORS' INTRODUCTION: WARRANTS, THEIR USE, AND BASIC FOURTH AMENDMENT REQUIREMENTS

A warrant is a court order authorizing a law enforcement officer to arrest an identified person or search a specified place for and to seize specific items, or for both arrest and search. It also typically commands the officer executing the warrant to bring the person or items seized to the issuing magistrate. For obvious reasons, a judge, or sometimes a clerk, issues a warrant *ex parte*, that is, without notice to the person whose arrest is sought or whose property will be searched. The warrant is issued upon presentation of information believed justifying the arrest or search. When an arrest warrant is sought, that information is presented in a document usually called a complaint. When a search warrant is desired, the document of application is ordinarily called simply an affidavit. The warrant may be executed by any law enforcement officer in the jurisdiction of the issuing

115

judge; the executing officers are not necessarily the same persons supplying the information upon which issuance was based.

Warrants play an important role in the theory of Fourth Amendment law. The Fourth Amendment itself concludes with the admonition that "no Warrants shall issue, but upon probable cause supported by Oath or affirmation, and particularly describing the place to be searched, and the persons or things to be seized." The Supreme Court has made clear that Fourth Amendment law should encourage law enforcement officers to use arrest and search warrants. Use of warrants is preferred because the warrant process interposes a decision by an impartial official—called a magistrate when performing warrant issuance functions—between the desires of the police to apprehend violators and citizens' privacy and liberty. Whether grounds exist for an arrest or search—whether probable cause exists—is determined by a person with no vested interest in finding that such grounds do exist. This is preferable to litigating the matters in response to a defendant's motion to suppress evidence because the warrant process can prevent unreasonable searches and arrests rather than respond to an after-the-fact demonstration that an unreasonable search or arrest occurred.

The warrant process regulates but does not bar those police actions to which it applies. This point was made by Justice Jackson in language that has been repeated numerous times in Supreme Court opinions:

> The point of the Fourth Amendment, which often is not grasped by zealous officers, is not that it denies law enforcement the support of the usual inferences which reasonable men draw from evidence. Its protection consists in requiring that those inferences be drawn by a neutral and detached magistrate instead of being judged by the officer engaged in the often competitive enterprise of ferreting out crime.

Johnson v. United States, 333 U.S. 10, 13–14, 68 S.Ct. 367, 369, 92 L.Ed. 436, 440 (1948). Warrants involve the judiciary in the investigative process before action is taken by law enforcement. This should often prevent violation of the Fourth Amendment right to be free from unreasonable searches and seizures, which is obviously preferable to efforts after-the-fact to remedy violations that have taken place. Furthermore, use of the warrant process to prevent improper law enforcement actions avoids the difficult task of litigating after-the-fact whether a violation occurred and of then selecting an appropriate remedy if a violation is found. Finally, when an arrest or search warrant has been issued, it gives specific instructions to law enforcement officers as to what they may and may not do in execution of the warrant. It also subjects further investigative effort to supervision of the judiciary by requiring a report of action taken under the warrant in the form of a return (and inventory of items seized) on a search warrant or, with respect to an arrest warrant, the presentation of the arrestee before the court.

In fact, arrest warrants are far less significant than search warrants. This is in part because Fourth Amendment law requires an arrest warrant be used only in very limited situations; the limited Fourth Amendment need for an arrest warrant is addressed in Chapter 4. Fourth Amendment theory generally requires that an arrest warrant be issued and drafted under the same rules applicable to search warrants. Because an arrest warrant is seldom needed, however, courts only rarely reach the validity of arrest warrants.

Use of Search Warrants in Actual Practice

The extent to which the warrant process actually functions in the manner intended by Fourth Amendment theory has been the subject of much speculation. An extensive empirical study of search warrant practices was, however, conducted by the National Center for State Courts. The results are reported in Van Duizend, Sutton and Cater, The Search Warrant Process: Preconceptions, Perceptions, and Practices (National Center for State Courts, undated). Probably the most important part of the study consisted of examining 844 search warrant cases and resulting prosecutions in seven different cities. In addition, interviews with police, judges, prosecutors and defense lawyers were conducted in these seven cities and direct observations of the warrant issuing process were undertaken in one location.

The study confirmed that officers seek search warrants in relatively few investigations and that they conduct the vast majority of searches without warrants. Id., at 20–21. In regard to search warrants issued, an average (or "mean") of 38% involved drug offenses and 29% concerned property crimes. But an average of 21% were used in investigations of violent offenses. Id., at 33. An average of 40% of the warrants were issued in part upon the basis of information received from a confidential informant—that is, an unidentified informant. Id., at 40.

Many of the judges issuing warrants perceived themselves as performing a role independent of law enforcement, but a few saw their role as "assisting the police." Id., at 64. Often, officers were able, by "judge shopping," to avoid submitting a request for a warrant to a judge known as particularly demanding. Because of difficulty in locating rejected applications, the study could not address how often warrant applications were rejected. But the authors suggested the rate of "outright rejection" was probably "extremely low." Id., at 32. On the other hand, warrant applications were often reviewed and screened by a superior police official or a prosecutor. While this review apparently led to few "screening outs," the process sometimes resulted in the officer being requested to add further information to the application. Id., at 24–25. Similarly, judicial officers who did not reject applications with some frequency required additional information from applying officers. The judge's review was seldom lengthy. Of the warrant proceedings directly observed, 65% lasted 2.5 minutes or less. Only 11% lasted longer than five minutes. Id., at 31.

In all of the cities studied, searches conducted pursuant to those warrants actually served resulted in the discovery of something which the officers thought worth seizing in at least 90% of the cases. In an average of over one third of the cases, officers seized items not specifically identified in the warrant. Id. at 52.

Motions to suppress evidence were filed in a significant number of the prosecutions arising out of the searches. But they were seldom granted. Of 347 warrant-related prosecutions studied, motions to suppress evidence were granted in only 17. In at least 12 of these 17, convictions were nevertheless obtained.

Interviewed police officers often complained of the delay involved in applying for and getting a search warrant and of the resulting loss of "good cases." But the study found little relationship between the delay and the actual loss of cases. Id., at 96.

In regard to "bottom lines," the study concluded the search warrant requirement has several beneficial effects. First, it requires officers to "at least contemplate" the requirement of probable cause before a search, and this reflection induces a higher standard of care than they would otherwise use. Second, it produces "a multi-layered review that reduces the likelihood that a search will occur in the absence of probable cause." Finally, it provides a clear and tangible record permitting a more objective later evaluation of the search. On the other hand, the study concluded "it was clear in many cases that the review process was largely perfunctory," and that there was "infrequent but significant" evidence of efforts undermining "and sometimes entirely defeat[ing]" the integrity of the review process. But "the most striking and significant—and perhaps the most troubling— discovery," the report concluded, was the infrequency with which the search warrant process was invoked. It is perceived as "burdensome, time-consuming, intimidating, frustrating, and confusing." Many easier methods of obtaining incriminating evidence or of developing a case against a suspect exist. "It is not surprising * * *," the report concluded, "that many officers tend to regard the warrant option as a last resort." Id., at 148–49.

Does the study suggest reason to rethink the central role of warrants in the theory of Fourth Amendment law? Or, to the extent that there are deficiencies in warrant practice, should efforts be focused upon making practice more closely correspond with theory?

The Foundation Requirement—A Neutral and Detached Magistrate

As a basic foundation requirement for an effective search or arrest warrant, the Supreme Court has mandated the issuing person be an individual sufficiently likely to perform the tasks the Fourth Amendment requires—a critical and independent evaluation of the sufficiently of the information offered to justify the warrant

Generally, courts assume the person issuing a warrant must be a "judicial officer" or a "magistrate." In Shadwick v. Tampa, 407 U.S. 345, 92 S.Ct. 2119, 32 L.Ed.2d 783 (1972), however, the Court noted that the constitutional validity of a warrant "does not turn on the labeling of the issuing party." It explained:

> [A]n issuing magistrate must meet two tests. He must be neutral and detached, and he must be capable of determining whether probable cause exists for the requested arrest or search.

407 U.S. at 350, 92 S.Ct. at 2123, 32 L.Ed.2d at 788. In Shadwick itself, the Court held misdemeanor arrest warrants for violations of city ordinance could be issued by clerks of a municipal court, rather than by the judge of the court. No showing had been made, it emphasized, that these clerks

were affiliated with prosecutors or police or that they were partial in any sense. Nor had any demonstration been made that the clerks were incapable of determining probable cause. It was not considering, the Court stressed, whether "someone completely outside the sphere of the judicial branch" could issue warrants. Nor did *Shadwick* address whether court clerks could issue arrest warrants for more serious offenses or search warrants.

Where those issuing warrants were subject to some institutional risk of bias in favor of those applying for warrants, the Court held the resulting warrants unreasonable. An attorney general actively involved in an investigation, then, could not issue a search warrant for that investigation. Coolidge v. New Hampshire, 403 U.S. 443, 450, 91 S.Ct. 2022, 2029, 29 L.Ed.2d 564, 573 (1971). A justice of the peace paid $5.00 for each search warrant issued but nothing for a search warrant application denied was held to have a direct, personal, and substantial pecuniary interest favoring the issuance of warrants. Consequently, a search under a warrant issued by such a judicial officer was unreasonable. Connally v. Georgia, 429 U.S. 245, 97 S.Ct. 546, 50 L.Ed.2d 444 (1977).

Further, the conduct of a judicial officer in the specific case may show the officer lacked the Fourth Amendment capacity to issue an effective warrant. Thus in In Lo–Ji Sales, Inc. v. New York, 442 U.S. 319, 99 S.Ct. 2319, 60 L.Ed.2d 920 (1979), upon a showing two obscene films had been purchased by a police officer at a bookstore, a Town Justice issued a search warrant for other copies of the films. In addition, the warrant authorized the officers to seize the "following" items "that the Court independently [on examination] has determined to be" obscene. No items were listed. But the Justice accompanied the officers to the bookstore and there examined numerous items. Those he found obscene he included in the warrant. The Court held that this violated the Fourth Amendment:

> The Town Justice did not manifest that neutrality and detachment demanded of a judicial officer when presented with a warrant application for a search and seizure. We need not question the subjective belief of the Town Justice in the propriety of his actions, but the objective facts of record manifest an erosion of whatever neutral and detached posture existed at the outset. He allowed himself to become a member, if not the leader, of the search party which was essentially a police operation.

442 U.S. at 326–27, 99 S.Ct. at 2324, 60 L.Ed.2d at 928–29. It continued:

> We do not suggest, of course, that a "neutral and detached magistrate" loses his character as such merely because he leaves his regular office in order to make himself readily available to law enforcement officers who may wish to seek the issuance of warrants by him. * * * But * * * [in] this case * * * the Town Justice undertook not merely to issue a warrant, but to participate with the police and prosecutors in its execution.

442 U.S. at 328 n. 6, 99 S.Ct. 2325 n. 6, 60 L.Ed.2d at 930 n. 6.

* * *

This chapter addresses separately several major aspects of Fourth Amendment "warrant law." First, it considers the requirement that the warrant be issued on a showing of probable cause and several related issues. Second, it addresses limitations on the manner of gaining entry to execute the warrant and some related limits on execution of warrants. Finally, it turns to the terms of the warrant and their role in the warrant's execution.

A.   THE SHOWING OF PROBABLE CAUSE

The essence of the warrant process is the judicial scrutiny of the information submitted as justification for the warrant's issuance. Effective scrutiny requires, of course, the information presented be sufficient and adequately detailed. The information required to support a warrant's issuance is considered in the first subsection. A defendant's later ability to challenge the accuracy of this information is addressed in the next subsection.

1.   THE INITIAL SHOWING BEFORE THE MAGISTRATE

EDITORS' INTRODUCTION: THE "PROBABLE CAUSE" SHOWING

The specific terms of the Fourth Amendment prohibit the issuance of a warrant except "upon probable cause supported by Oath or affirmation." A warrant application often is accompanied by a written and sworn affidavit setting out the facts which the applying officers believe constitute the required probable cause. In many cases, then, the issuing magistrate's function consists largely of reviewing the affidavit to determine if the alleged information rises to this level.

There is probably no federal constitutional requirement that all or even any of the information submitted to the magistrate be written. Statutes and court rules sometimes authorize a warrant's issuance in whole or in part upon oral information. Rule 41(c)(1) of the Federal Rules of Criminal Procedure requires, as a general rule, a search warrant issue on the basis of a sworn affidavit. But it further provides:

> Before ruling on a request for a warrant the federal magistrate * * * may require the affiant to appear personally and may examine under oath the affiant and any witnesses he may produce, provided that such proceedings shall be taken down by a court reporter or recording equipment and made part of the affidavit.

If a magistrate requires such additional information beyond the affidavit, it is quite likely any warrant issued will be based in part upon that additional and oral information. Generally, however, magistrates do not demand further facts. Therefore, the magistrate's task is usually one of reviewing the affidavit "on its face"—probably assuming the correctness of the facts alleged—to determine if those facts establish probable cause. Insofar as this is the process, no critical consideration of whether the facts alleged are correct occurs until and if the defendant later challenges the accuracy of the "face" of the affidavit. The next subsection considers defendants' ability to make such challenges.

Rule 41(c)(2) authorizes a search warrant's issuance "upon sworn oral testimony communicated by telephone or other appropriate means" if "circumstances make it reasonable to dispense with a written affidavit." Where application for a warrant is made by telephone, the applicant prepares a "duplicate original" warrant and reads it to the magistrate. The magistrate then signs the original warrant (which is before the magistrate) and authorizes the applicant to sign the magistrate's name to the duplicate original. If a voice recording device is available, the magistrate records the telephone call, has the recording transcribed, certifies the accuracy of the recording, and files a copy with the court. If no such device is available, a stenographic or longhand verbatim record is made, and a copy signed by the magistrate is filed. Fed.R.Crim.P. 41(D). Interestingly, the rule provides that absent a "finding of bad faith," evidence obtained pursuant to a warrant is not subject to a motion to suppress on the ground the circumstances did not justify dispensing with a written affidavit. Fed.R.Crim.P. 41(G).

The Supreme Court decisions addressing the sufficiency of warrant affidavits involve situations in which the information submitted for a warrant consists in part of information from persons other than the affiant. The leading—or at least the seminal—case is Aguilar v. Texas, 378 U.S. 108, 84 S.Ct. 1509, 12 L.Ed.2d 723 (1964). Two police officers submitted to a Justice of the Peace an application for a search warrant for Aguilar's home. In support, they provided an affidavit which stated:

> Affiants have received reliable information from a credible person and do believe that heroin, marijuana, barbiturates and other narcotics and narcotics paraphernalia are being kept at the above described premises for the purpose of sale and use contrary to the provisions of the law.

The justice issued the warrant; the officers executed it and found drugs. These drugs were admitted into evidence at Aguilar's trial. Finding constitutional error, the Supreme Court reasoned the guiding principles must be that the magistrate must decide for himself whether probable cause exists and not accept without question the officers' "mere conclusion." These principles require an affidavit permitting the magistrate to perform these tasks. Further:

> Although an affidavit may be based on hearsay information and need not reflect the direct personal observations of the affiant, the magistrate must be informed of some of the underlying circumstances from which the informant concluded that the narcotics were where he claimed they were, and some of the underlying circumstances from which the officer concluded that the informant, whose identity need not be disclosed, was "credible" or his information "reliable." Otherwise, "the inferences from the facts which lead to the complaint" will be drawn not "by a neutral and detached magistrate," as the Constitution requires, but instead, by a police officer * * *, or, as in this case, by an unidentified informant.

378 U.S. at 114–15, 84 S.Ct. at 1514, 12 L.Ed.2d at 729.

This approach was developed further in Spinelli v. United States, 393 U.S. 410, 89 S.Ct. 584, 21 L.Ed.2d 637 (1969). Evidence of gambling activities was obtained in a search pursuant to a warrant of an apartment located in St. Louis. The affidavit on which the warrant was issued recited in part:

> The Federal Bureau of Investigation has been informed by a confidential reliable informant that William Spinelli is operating a handbook and accepting wagers and disseminating wagering information by means of the telephones which have been assigned the numbers WYdown 4–0029 and WYdown 4–0136.

In addition, the affidavit recited that telephone company records disclosed the phones to which those numbers were assigned were located in a specific apartment under the name of Grace B. Hagen. Further, the affidavit stated federal agents conducting surveillance had observed Spinelli enter the apartment once, and on several other occasions they observed him in the parking lot of the apartment building or in its vicinity. Holding the warrant invalid, a majority of the Court noted that the tip met neither prong of *Aguilar*. It then suggested a tip was not sufficient under *Aguilar* might nevertheless establish probable cause for either of two reasons. First, the tip might describe the suspect's criminal activity in sufficient detail that a magistrate could infer from this detail that the informant had gained the information in a reliable way. Second, other reliable information might sufficiently corroborate parts of the information in the tip to justify a magistrate in concluding that the tip's ultimate and incriminating assertions could be relied upon. Neither method "cured" the *Spinelli* affidavit, however. The detailed information in the tip concerning the telephones was a "meager report" that "could easily have been obtained from an offhand remark heard at a neighborhood bar." The corroborating evidence gathered by the federal agents "at most * * * indicated that Spinelli could have used the telephones specified by the informant for some purpose."

As the principal case in this subsection makes clear, the *Aguilar–Spinelli* approach has not survived further consideration.

Illinois v. Gates

Supreme Court of the United States, 1983.
462 U.S. 213, 103 S.Ct. 2317, 76 L.Ed.2d 527.

■ JUSTICE REHNQUIST delivered the opinion of the Court.

Respondents Lance and Susan Gates were indicted for violation of state drug laws after police officers, executing a search warrant, discovered marijuana and other contraband in their automobile and home. Prior to trial the Gates moved to suppress evidence seized during this search. The Illinois Supreme Court affirmed the decisions of lower state courts granting the motion. It held that the affidavit submitted in support of the State's application for a warrant to search the Gates' property was inadequate under this Court's decisions in Aguilar v. Texas, 378 U.S. 108, 84 S.Ct.

1509, 12 L.Ed.2d 723 (1964) and Spinelli v. United States, 393 U.S. 410, 89 S.Ct. 584, 21 L.Ed.2d 637 (1969).

* * *

II

* * * A chronological statement of events usefully introduces the issues at stake. Bloomingdale, Ill., is a suburb of Chicago located in DuPage County. On May 3, 1978, the Bloomingdale Police Department received by mail an anonymous handwritten letter which read as follows:

"This letter is to inform you that you have a couple in your town who strictly make their living on selling drugs. They are Sue and Lance Gates, they live on Greenway, off Bloomingdale Rd. in the condominiums. Most of their buys are done in Florida. Sue his wife drives their car to Florida, where she leaves it to be loaded up with drugs, then Lance flys down and drives it back. Sue flys back after she drops the car off in Florida. May 3 she is driving down there again and Lance will be flying down in a few days to drive it back. At the time Lance drives the car back he has the trunk loaded with over $100,000.00 in drugs. Presently they have over $100,000.00 worth of drugs in their basement.

They brag about the fact they never have to work, and make their entire living on pushers.

I guarantee if you watch them carefully you will make a big catch. They are friends with some big drugs dealers, who visit their house often.

Lance & Susan Gates

Greenway

in Condominiums"

The letter was referred by the Chief of Police of the Bloomingdale Police Department to Detective Mader, who decided to pursue the tip. Mader learned, from the office of the Illinois Secretary of State, that an Illinois driver's license had been issued to one Lance Gates, residing at a stated address in Bloomingdale. He contacted a confidential informant, whose examination of certain financial records revealed a more recent address for the Gates, and he also learned from a police officer assigned to O'Hare Airport that "L. Gates" had made a reservation on Eastern Airlines flight 245 to West Palm Beach, Fla., scheduled to depart from Chicago on May 5 at 4:15 p.m.

Mader then made arrangements with an agent of the Drug Enforcement Administration for surveillance of the May 5 Eastern Airlines flight. The agent later reported to Mader that Gates had boarded the flight, and that federal agents in Florida had observed him arrive in West Palm Beach and take a taxi to the nearby Holiday Inn. They also reported that Gates went to a room registered to one Susan Gates and that, at 7:00 a.m. the next morning, Gates and an unidentified woman left the motel in a Mercury bearing Illinois license plates and drove northbound on an interstate frequently used by travelers to the Chicago area. In addition, the DEA agent informed Mader that the license plate number on the Mercury was registered to a Hornet station wagon owned by Gates. The agent also advised Mader that the driving time between West Palm Beach and Bloomingdale was approximately 22 to 24 hours.

Mader signed an affidavit setting forth the foregoing facts, and submitted it to a judge of the Circuit Court of DuPage County, together with a copy of the anonymous letter. The judge of that court thereupon issued a search warrant for the Gates' residence and for their automobile. The judge, in deciding to issue the warrant, could have determined that the *modus operandi* of the Gates had been substantially corroborated. As the anonymous letter predicted, Lance Gates had flown from Chicago to West Palm Beach late in the afternoon of May 5th, had checked into a hotel room registered in the name of his wife, and, at 7:00 a.m. the following morning, had headed north, accompanied by an unidentified woman, out of West Palm Beach on an interstate highway used by travelers from South Florida to Chicago in an automobile bearing a license plate issued to him.

At 5:15 a.m. on May 7th, only 36 hours after he had flown out of Chicago, Lance Gates, and his wife, returned to their home in Bloomingdale, driving the car in which they had left West Palm Beach some 22 hours earlier. The Bloomingdale police were awaiting them, searched the trunk of the Mercury, and uncovered approximately 350 pounds of marijuana. A search of the Gates' home revealed marijuana, weapons, and other contraband. The Illinois Circuit Court ordered suppression of all these items, on the ground that the affidavit submitted to the Circuit Judge failed to support the necessary determination of probable cause to believe that the Gates' automobile and home contained the contraband in question. This decision was affirmed in turn by the Illinois Appellate Court and by a divided vote of the Supreme Court of Illinois.

The Illinois Supreme Court concluded—and we are inclined to agree—that, standing alone, the anonymous letter sent to the Bloomingdale Police Department would not provide the basis for a magistrate's determination that there was probable cause to believe contraband would be found in the Gates' car and home. The letter provides virtually nothing from which one might conclude that its author is either honest or his information reliable; likewise, the letter gives absolutely no indication of the basis for the writer's predictions regarding the Gates' criminal activities. Something more was required, then, before a magistrate could conclude that there was probable cause to believe that contraband would be found in the Gates' home and car.

The Illinois Supreme Court also properly recognized that Detective Mader's affidavit might be capable of supplementing the anonymous letter with information sufficient to permit a determination of probable cause. In holding that the affidavit in fact did not contain sufficient additional information to sustain a determination of probable cause, the Illinois court applied a "two-pronged test," derived from our decision in Spinelli v. United States, 393 U.S. 410, 89 S.Ct. 584, 21 L.Ed.2d 637 (1969). The Illinois Supreme Court, like some others, apparently understood *Spinelli* as requiring that the anonymous letter satisfy each of two independent requirements before it could be relied on. According to this view, the letter, as supplemented by Mader's affidavit, first had to adequately reveal the "basis of knowledge" of the letter writer—the particular means by which he came by the information given in his report. Second, it had to provide facts sufficiently establishing either the "veracity" of the affiant's informant, or, alternatively, the "reliability" of the informant's report in this particular case.

The Illinois court * * * found that the test had not been satisfied. First, the "veracity" prong was not satisfied because, "there was simply no basis [for] * * * conclud[ing] that the anonymous person [who wrote the letter to the Bloomingdale Police Department] was credible." The court indicated that corroboration by police of details contained in the letter might never satisfy the "veracity" prong, and in any event, could not do so if, as in the present case, only "innocent" details are corroborated. In addition, the letter gave no indication of the basis of its writer's knowledge of the Gates' activities. The Illinois court understood *Spinelli* as permitting the detail contained in a tip to be used to infer that the informant had a reliable basis for his statements, but it thought that the anonymous letter failed to provide sufficient detail to permit such an inference. Thus, it concluded that no showing of probable cause had been made.

We agree with the Illinois Supreme Court that an informant's "veracity," "reliability" and "basis of knowledge" are all highly relevant in determining the value of his report. We do not agree, however, that these elements should be understood as entirely separate and independent requirements to be rigidly exacted in every case, which the opinion of the Supreme Court of Illinois would imply. Rather, as detailed below, they should be understood simply as closely intertwined issues that may usefully illuminate the common-sense, practical question whether there is "probable cause" to believe that contraband or evidence is located in a particular place.

III

This totality of the circumstances approach is far more consistent with our prior treatment of probable cause than is any rigid demand that specific "tests" be satisfied by every informant's tip. Perhaps the central teaching of our decisions bearing on the probable cause standard is that it is a "practical, nontechnical conception." * * * [P]robable cause is a fluid concept—turning on the assessment of probabilities in particular factual contexts—not readily, or even usefully, reduced to a neat set of legal rules. Informants' tips doubtless come in many shapes and sizes from many different types of persons. * * * Rigid legal rules are ill-suited to an area of such diversity. * * *

Moreover, the "two-pronged test" directs analysis into two largely independent channels—the informant's "veracity" or "reliability" and his "basis of knowledge." There are persuasive arguments against according these two elements such independent status. Instead, they are better understood as relevant considerations in the totality of circumstances analysis that traditionally has guided probable cause determinations: a deficiency in one may be compensated for, in determining the overall reliability of a tip, by a strong showing as to the other, or by some other indicia of reliability. * * * Unlike a totality of circumstances analysis, which permits a balanced assessment of the relative weights of all the various indicia of reliability (and unreliability) attending an informant's tip, the "two-pronged test" has encouraged an excessively technical dissection of informants' tips, with undue attention being focused on isolated issues that cannot sensibly be divorced from the other facts presented to the magistrate.

* * *

We * * * have recognized that affidavits "are normally drafted by nonlawyers in the midst and haste of a criminal investigation. Technical requirements of elaborate specificity once exacted under common law pleading have no proper place in this area." Likewise, search and arrest warrants long have been issued by persons who are neither lawyers nor judges, and who certainly do not remain abreast of each judicial refinement of the nature of "probable cause." The rigorous inquiry into the *Spinelli* prongs and the complex superstructure of evidentiary and analytical rules that some have seen implicit in our *Spinelli* decision, cannot be reconciled with the fact that many warrants are—quite properly—issued on the basis of nontechnical, commonsense judgments of laymen applying a standard less demanding than those used in more formal legal proceedings. Likewise, given the informal, often hurried context in which it must be applied, the "built-in subtleties," of the "two-pronged test" are particularly unlikely to assist magistrates in determining probable cause.

Similarly, we have repeatedly said that after-the-fact scrutiny by courts of the sufficiency of an affidavit should not take the form of *de novo* review. A magistrate's "determination of probable cause should be paid great deference by reviewing courts."

If the affidavits submitted by police officers are subjected to the type of scrutiny some courts have deemed appropriate, police might well resort to warrantless searches, with the hope of relying on consent or some other exception to the warrant clause that might develop at the time of the search. * * * Reflecting this preference for the warrant process, the traditional standard for review of an issuing magistrate's probable cause determination has been that so long as the magistrate had a "substantial basis for ... conclud[ing]" that a search would uncover evidence of wrongdoing, the Fourth Amendment requires no more. Jones v. United States, 362 U.S. 257, 271, 80 S.Ct. 725, 736, 4 L.Ed.2d 697 (1960). We think reaffirmation of this standard better serves the purpose of encouraging recourse to the warrant procedure and is more consistent with our traditional deference to the probable cause determinations of magistrates than is the "two-pronged test."

Finally, the direction taken by decisions following *Spinelli* poorly serves "the most basic function of any government": "to provide for the security of the individual and of his property." The strictures that inevitably accompany the "two-pronged test" cannot avoid seriously impeding the task of law enforcement. If, as the Illinois Supreme Court apparently thought, that test must be rigorously applied in every case, anonymous tips seldom would be of greatly diminished value in police work. Ordinary citizens, like ordinary witnesses, generally do not provide extensive recitations of the basis of their everyday observations. Likewise, as the Illinois Supreme Court observed in this case, the veracity of persons supplying anonymous tips is by hypothesis largely unknown, and unknowable. As a result, anonymous tips seldom could survive a rigorous application of either of the *Spinelli* prongs. Yet, such tips, particularly when supplemented by independent police investigation, frequently contribute to the solution of otherwise "perfect crimes." While a conscientious assessment of the basis for crediting such tips is required by the Fourth Amendment, a standard that leaves virtually no place for anonymous citizen informants is not.

For all these reasons, we conclude that it is wiser to abandon the "two-pronged test" established by our decisions in *Aguilar* and *Spinelli*.[1] In its place we reaffirm the totality of the circumstances analysis that traditionally has informed probable cause determinations. The task of the issuing magistrate is simply to make a practical, common-sense decision whether, given all the circumstances set forth in the affidavit before him, including the "veracity" and "basis of knowledge" of persons supplying hearsay information, there is a fair probability that contraband or evidence of a crime will be found in a particular place. And the duty of a reviewing court is simply to ensure that the magistrate had a "substantial basis for * * * conclud[ing]" that probable cause existed. We are convinced that this flexible, easily applied standard will better achieve the accommodation of public and private interests that the Fourth Amendment requires than does the approach that has developed from *Aguilar* and *Spinelli*.

Our earlier cases illustrate the limits beyond which a magistrate may not venture in issuing a warrant. A sworn statement of an affiant that "he has cause to suspect and does believe that" liquor illegally brought into the United States is located on certain premises will not do. Nathanson v. United States, 290 U.S. 41, 54 S.Ct. 11, 78 L.Ed. 159 (1933). An affidavit must provide the magistrate with a substantial basis for determining the existence of probable cause, and the wholly conclusory statement at issue in *Nathanson* failed to meet this requirement. An officer's statement that "affiants have received reliable information from a credible person and believe" that heroin is stored in a home, is likewise inadequate. Aguilar v. Texas, 378 U.S. 108, 84 S.Ct. 1509, 12 L.Ed.2d 723 (1964). As in *Nathanson,* this is a mere conclusory statement that gives the magistrate virtually no basis at all for making a judgment regarding probable cause. Sufficient information must be presented to the magistrate to allow that official to determine probable cause; his action cannot be a mere ratification of the bare conclusions of others. In order to ensure that such an abdication of the magistrate's duty does not occur, courts must continue to conscientiously review the sufficiency of affidavits on which warrants are issued. But when

---

1. * * *

Whether the allegations submitted to the magistrate in *Spinelli* would, under the view we now take, have supported a finding of probable cause, we think it would not be profitable to decide. There are so many variables in the probable cause equation that one determination will seldom be a useful "prece-

dent" for another. Suffice it to say that while we in no way abandon *Spinelli's* concern for the trustworthiness of informers and for the principle that it is the magistrate who must ultimately make a finding of probable cause, we reject the rigid categorization suggested by some of its language.

we move beyond the "bare bones" affidavits present in cases such as *Nathanson* and *Aguilar,* this area simply does not lend itself to a prescribed set of rules, like that which had developed from *Spinelli.* Instead, the flexible, commonsense standard * * * better serves the purposes of the Fourth Amendment's probable cause requirement.

* * *

IV

Our decisions applying the totality of circumstances analysis outlined above have consistently recognized the value of corroboration of details of an informant's tip by independent police work. * * *

Our decision in Draper v. United States, 358 U.S. 307, 79 S.Ct. 329, 3 L.Ed.2d 327 (1959), however, is the classic case on the value of corroborative efforts of police officials. There, an informant named Hereford reported that Draper would arrive in Denver on a train from Chicago on one of two days, and that he would be carrying a quantity of heroin. The informant also supplied a fairly detailed physical description of Draper, and predicted that he would be wearing a light colored raincoat, brown slacks and black shoes, and would be walking "real fast." Hereford gave no indication of the basis for his information.

On one of the stated dates police officers observed a man matching this description exit a train arriving from Chicago; his attire and luggage matched Hereford's report and he was walking rapidly. We explained in *Draper* that, by this point in his investigation, the arresting officer "had personally verified every facet of the information given him by Hereford except whether petitioner had accomplished his mission and had the three ounces of heroin on his person or in his bag. And surely, with every other bit of Hereford's information being thus personally verified, [the officer] had 'reasonable grounds' to believe that the remaining unverified bit of Hereford's information—that Draper would have the heroin with him—was likewise true."

The showing of probable cause in the present case was fully as compelling as that in *Draper.* Even standing alone, the facts obtained through the independent investigation of Mader and the DEA at least suggested that the Gates were involved in drug trafficking. In addition to being a popular vacation site, Florida is well-known as a source of narcotics and other illegal drugs. Lance Gates' flight to Palm Beach, his brief, overnight stay in a motel, and apparent immediate return north to Chicago in the family car, conveniently awaiting him in West Palm Beach, is as suggestive of a prearranged drug run, as it is of an ordinary vacation trip.

In addition, the magistrate could rely on the anonymous letter, which had been corroborated in major part by Mader's efforts—just as had occurred in *Draper.* The Supreme Court of Illinois reasoned that *Draper* involved an informant who had given reliable information on previous occasions, while the honesty and reliability of the anonymous informant in this case were unknown to the Bloomingdale police. While this distinction might be an apt one at the time the police department received the anonymous letter, it became far less significant after Mader's independent investigative work occurred. The corroboration of the letter's predictions that the Gates' car would be in Florida, that Lance Gates would fly to Florida in the next day or so, and that he would drive the car north toward Bloomingdale all indicated, albeit not with certainty, that the informant's other assertions also were true. "Because an informant is right about some things, he is more probably right about other facts,"—including the claim regarding the Gates' illegal activity. This may well not be the type of "reliability" or "veracity" necessary to satisfy some views of the "veracity prong" of *Spinelli,* but we think it suffices for the practical, commonsense judgment called for in making a probable cause determination. It is enough, for purposes of assessing probable cause, that "corroboration through other sources of information reduced the chances of a reckless or prevaricating tale," thus providing "a substantial basis for crediting the hearsay."

Finally, the anonymous letter contained a range of details relating not just to easily obtained facts and conditions existing at the time of the tip, but to future actions of third parties ordinarily not easily predicted. The letter writer's accurate information as to the travel plans of each of the Gates was of a character likely obtained only from the Gates themselves, or from someone familiar with their not entirely ordinary travel plans. If the informant had access to accurate information of this type a magistrate could properly conclude that it was not unlikely that he also had access to reliable information of the Gates' alleged illegal activities.[2] Of course, the Gates' travel plans might have been learned from a talkative neighbor or travel agent; under the "two-pronged test" developed from *Spinelli,* the character of the details in the anonymous letter might well not permit a sufficiently clear inference regarding the letter writer's "basis of knowledge." But, as discussed previously, probable cause does not demand the certainty we associate with formal trials. It is enough that there was a fair probability that the writer of the anonymous letter had obtained his entire

2. The dissent seizes on one inaccuracy in the anonymous informant's letter—its statement that Sue Gates would fly from Florida to Illinois, when in fact she drove—and argues that the probative value of the entire tip was undermined by this allegedly "material mistake." We have never required that informants used by the police be infallible, and can see no reason to impose such a requirement in this case. Probable cause, particularly when police have obtained a warrant, simply does not require the perfection the dissent finds necessary.

Likewise, there is no force to the dissent's argument that the Gates' action in leaving their home unguarded undercut the informant's claim that drugs were hidden there. Indeed, the line-by-line scrutiny that the dissent applies to the anonymous letter is akin to that we find inappropriate in reviewing magistrate's decisions. The dissent apparently attributes to the magistrate who issued the warrant in this case the rather implausible notion that persons dealing in drugs always stay at home, apparently out of fear that to leave might risk intrusion by criminals. If accurate, one could not help sympathizing with the self-imposed isolation of people so situated. In reality, however, it is scarcely likely that the magistrate ever thought that the anonymous tip "kept one spouse" at home, much less that he relied on the theory advanced by the dissent. The letter simply says that Sue would fly from Florida to Illinois, without indicating whether the Gates made the bitter choice of leaving the drugs in their house, or those in their car, unguarded. The magistrate's determination that there might be drugs or evidence of criminal activity in the Gates' home was well-supported by the less speculative theory, noted in text, that if the informant could predict with considerable accuracy the somewhat unusual travel plans of the Gates, he probably also had a reliable basis for his statements that the Gates kept a large quantity of drugs in their home and frequently were visited by other drug traffickers there.

story either from the Gates or someone they trusted. And corroboration of major portions of the letter's predictions provides just this probability. It is apparent, therefore, that the judge issuing the warrant had a "substantial basis for ... conclud[ing]" that probable cause to search the Gates' home and car existed. The judgment of the Supreme Court of Illinois therefore must be

Reversed.

■ JUSTICE BRENNAN, with whom JUSTICE MARSHALL joins, dissenting.

Although I join Justice Stevens' dissenting opinion and agree with him that the warrant is invalid even under the Court's newly announced "totality of the circumstances" test, I write separately to dissent from the Court's unjustified and ill-advised rejection of the two-prong test for evaluating the validity of a warrant based on hearsay announced in Aguilar v. Texas, 378 U.S. 108, 84 S.Ct. 1509, 12 L.Ed.2d 723 (1964), and refined in Spinelli v. United States, 393 U.S. 410, 89 S.Ct. 584, 21 L.Ed.2d 637 (1969).

* * *

Although the rules drawn from the [*Aguilar–Spinelli* line of cases] are cast in procedural terms, they advance an important underlying substantive value: Findings of probable cause, and attendant intrusions, should not be authorized unless there is some assurance that the information on which they are based has been obtained in a reliable way by an honest or credible person. As applied to police officers, the rules focus on the way in which the information was acquired. As applied to informants, the rules focus both on the honesty or credibility of the informant and on the reliability of the way in which the information was acquired. Insofar as it is more complicated, an evaluation of affidavits based on hearsay involves a more difficult inquiry. This suggests a need to structure the inquiry in an effort to insure greater accuracy. The standards announced in *Aguilar,* as refined by *Spinelli,* fulfill that need. The standards inform the police of what information they have to provide and magistrates of what information they should demand. The standards also inform magistrates of the subsidiary findings they must make in order to arrive at an ultimate finding of probable cause. *Spinelli,* properly understood, directs the magistrate's attention to the possibility that the presence of self-verifying detail might satisfy *Aguilar's* basis of knowledge prong and that corroboration of the details of a tip might satisfy *Aguilar's* veracity prong. By requiring police to provide certain crucial information to magistrates and by structuring magistrates' probable cause inquiries, *Aguilar* and *Spinelli* assure the magistrate's role as an independent arbiter of probable cause, insure greater accuracy in probable cause determinations, and advance the substantive value identified above.

* * *

■ JUSTICE STEVENS, with whom JUSTICE BRENNAN joins, dissenting.

The fact that Lance and Sue Gates made a 22hour nonstop drive from West Palm Beach, Florida, to Bloomingdale, Illinois, only a few hours after Lance had flown to Florida provided persuasive evidence that they were engaged in illicit activity. That fact, however, was not known to the magistrate when he issued the warrant to search their home.

What the magistrate did know at that time was that the anonymous informant had not been completely accurate in his or her predictions. The informant had indicated that "Sue drives their car to Florida *where she leaves it to be loaded up with drugs.... Sue flies back after she drops the car off in Florida.*" (emphasis added). Yet Detective Mader's affidavit reported that she "left the West Palm Beach area driving the Mercury northbound."

The discrepancy between the informant's predictions and the facts known to Detective Mader is significant for three reasons. First, it cast doubt on the informant's hypothesis that the Gates already had "over $100,000 worth of drugs in their basement." The informant had predicted an itinerary that always kept one spouse in Bloomingdale, suggesting that the Gates did not want to leave their home unguarded because something valuable was hidden within. That inference obviously could not be drawn when it was known that the pair was actually together over a thousand miles from home.

Second, the discrepancy made the Gates' conduct seem substantially less unusual than the informant had predicted it would be. It would have been odd if, as predicted, Sue had driven down to Florida on Wednesday, left the car, and flown right back to Illinois. But the mere facts that Sue was in West Palm Beach with the car, that she was joined by her husband at the Holiday Inn on Friday, and that the couple drove north together the next morning are neither unusual nor probative of criminal activity.

Third, the fact that the anonymous letter contained a material mistake undermines the reasonableness of relying on it as a basis for making a forcible entry into a private home.

Of course, the activities in this case did not stop when the magistrate issued the warrant. The Gates drove all night to Bloomingdale, the officers searched the car and found 400 pounds of marijuana, and then they searched the house. However, none of these subsequent events may be considered in evaluating the warrant, and the search of the house was legal only if the warrant was valid. I cannot accept the Court's casual conclusion that, *before the Gates arrived in Bloomingdale,* there was probable cause to justify a valid entry and search of a private home. No one knows who the informant in this case was, or what motivated him or her to write the note. Given that the note's predictions were faulty in one significant respect, and were corroborated by nothing except ordinary innocent activity, I must surmise that the Court's evaluation of the warrant's validity has been colored by subsequent events.

* * *

NOTE: ASSERTIONS OF LAW ENFORCEMENT "KNOWLEDGE"

In *Spinelli,* the affidavit recited the suspect "is known to this affiant and to federal law enforcement agents and local law enforcement agents as a bookmaker, an associate of bookmakers, a gambler, and an associate of gamblers." In considering whether the affidavit supported the magistrate's determination that probable cause existed, the Court commented that his allegation "is but a bald and unilluminating assertion of suspicion that is entitled to no weight in appraising the magistrate's decision."

In United States v. Harris, 403 U.S. 573, 91 S.Ct. 2075, 29 L.Ed.2d 723 (1971), the affidavit recited that the suspect "has had a reputation with me for over four years as being a trafficker of nontax-paid distilled spirits * * *." There was no opinion of the Court; the judgment of the Court was announced in an opinion by the Chief Justice. In a portion of that opinion joined by two other members of the Court, he considered the significance of this allegation in the warrant affidavit:

> We cannot conclude that a policeman's knowledge of a suspect's reputation—something that policemen frequently know * * *—is not a "practical consideration of everyday life" upon which an officer (or a magistrate) may properly rely in assessing the reliability of an informant's tip. To the extent that *Spinelli* prohibits the use of such probative information, it has no support in our prior cases, logic, or experience and we decline to apply it to preclude a magistrate from relying on a law enforcement officer's knowledge of a suspect's reputation.

403 U.S. at 583, 91 S.Ct. at 2081–82, 29 L.Ed.2d at 733 (opinion of Burger, C.J., announcing the judgment of the Court).

2. CHALLENGING FACTUAL STATEMENTS IN THE AFFIDAVIT

Prior to the principal case in this subsection, many courts took the position that whether there was probable cause for issuance of an arrest or search warrant could be determined only from the face of the affidavit or complaint. The facts alleged were to be accepted as true and the sole question for debate was whether they established probable cause. To some extent, this position—barring defendants from attacking the "face" of a warrant affidavit—was based on the perception that the appropriate inquiry was whether the magistrate had probable cause to issue the warrant. If the magistrate had probable cause, no significance was attached to the fact the officer who applied for the warrant may not have had probable cause justifying a request for a warrant.

The principal case in this subsection requires defendants, to some extent, be permitted to challenge the accuracy of the facts in a warrant affidavit. Consider separately (although not necessarily in this order) what facts a defendant must establish to prevail on a challenge of this sort and what a defendant must do in order to have a factual hearing where he can establish those facts.

Franks v. Delaware

Supreme Court of the United States, 1978.
438 U.S. 154, 98 S.Ct. 2674, 57 L.Ed.2d 667.

■ MR. JUSTICE BLACKMUN delivered the opinion of the Court.

This case presents an important and longstanding issue of Fourth Amendment law. Does a defendant in a criminal proceeding ever have the right, under the Fourth and Fourteenth Amendments, subsequent to the *ex parte* issuance of a search warrant, to challenge the truthfulness of factual statements made in an affidavit supporting the warrant?

In the present case the Supreme Court of Delaware held, as a matter of first impression for it, that a defendant under *no* circumstances may so challenge the veracity of a sworn statement used by police to procure a search warrant. We reverse, and we hold that, where the defendant makes a substantial preliminary showing that a false statement knowingly and intentionally, or with reckless disregard for the truth, was included by the affiant in the warrant affidavit, and if the allegedly false statement is necessary to the finding of probable cause, the Fourth Amendment requires that a hearing be held at the defendant's request. In the event that at that hearing the allegation of perjury or reckless disregard is established by the defendant by a preponderance of the evidence, and, with the affidavit's false material set to one side, the affidavit's remaining content is insufficient to establish probable cause, the search warrant must be voided and the fruits of the search excluded to the same extent as if probable cause was lacking on the face of the affidavit.

I.

The controversy over the veracity of the search warrant affidavit in this case arose in connection with petitioner Jerome Franks' state conviction for rape, kidnapping, and burglary. On Friday, March 5, 1976, Mrs. Cynthia Bailey told police in Dover, Delaware, that she had been confronted in her home earlier that morning by a man with a knife, and that he had sexually assaulted her. She described her assailant's age, race, height, build, and facial hair, and gave a detailed description of his clothing as consisting of a white thermal undershirt, black pants with a silver or gold buckle, a brown leather three-quarter length coat, and a dark knit cap that he wore pulled down around his eyes.

That same day, petitioner Franks coincidentally was taken into custody for an assault involving a 15-year-old girl, Brenda B. _____, six days earlier. After his formal arrest, and while awaiting a bail hearing in Family Court, petitioner allegedly stated to Robert McClements, the youth officer accompanying him, that he was surprised the bail hearing was "about Brenda B. _____. I know her. I thought you said Bailey. I don't know her." At the time of this statement, the police allegedly had not yet recited to petitioner his rights under Miranda v. Arizona, 384 U.S. 436, 86 S.Ct. 1602, 16 L.Ed.2d 694 (1966).

On the following Monday, March 8, officer McClements happened to mention the courthouse incident to a detective, Ronald R. Brooks, who was working on the Bailey case. On March 9, detective Brooks and detective Larry D. Gray submitted a sworn affidavit to a justice of the peace in Dover, in support of a warrant to search petitioner's apartment.[3] In paragraph 8 of the affidavit's "probable cause page" mention was made of petitioner's statement to McClements. In paragraph 10, it was noted that the description of the assailant given to the police by Mrs. Bailey included the abovementioned clothing. Finally, the affidavit also described the

---

3. The affidavit is reproduced as Appendix A of this opinion.

attempt made by police to confirm that petitioner's typical outfit matched that of the assailant. Paragraph 15 recited: "On Tuesday, 3/9/76, your affiant contacted Mr. James Williams and Mr. Wesley Lucas of the Delaware Youth Center where Jerome Franks is employed and did have personal conversation with both these people." Paragraphs 16 and 17 respectively stated: "Mr. James Williams revealed to your affiant that the normal dress of Jerome Franks does consist of a white knit thermal undershirt and a brown leather jacket," and "Mr. Wesley Lucas revealed to your affiant that in addition to the thermal undershirt and jacket, Jerome Franks often wears a large green knit hat."

The warrant was issued on the basis of this affidavit. Pursuant to the warrant, police searched petitioner's apartment and found a white thermal undershirt, a knit hat, dark pants, and a leather jacket, and, on petitioner's kitchen table, a single-blade knife. All these ultimately were introduced in evidence at trial.

Prior to the trial, however, petitioner's counsel filed a written motion to suppress the clothing and the knife found in the search; this motion alleged that the warrant on its face did not show probable cause and that the search and seizure were in violation of the Fourth and Fourteenth Amendments. At the hearing on the motion to suppress, defense counsel orally amended the challenge to include an attack on the veracity of the warrant affidavit; he also specifically requested the right to call as witnesses detective Brooks, Wesley Lucas of the Youth Center, and James D. Morrison, formerly of the Youth Center.[4] Counsel asserted that Lucas and Morrison would testify that neither had been personally interviewed by the warrant affiants, and that, although they might have talked to another police officer, any information given by them to that officer was "somewhat different" from what was recited in the affidavit. Defense counsel charged that the misstatements were included in the affidavit not inadvertently, but in "bad faith." * * *

In rebuttal, the State's attorney argued in detail (a) that [Delaware law] contemplated that any challenge to a search warrant was to be limited to questions of sufficiency based on the face of the affidavit; [and] (b) that, purportedly, a majority of the States whose practice was not dictated by statute observed such a rule * * *. * * * The State objected to petitioner's "going behind [the warrant affidavit] in any way," and argued that the court must decide petitioner's motion "on the four corners" of the affidavit.

The trial court sustained the State's objection to petitioner's proposed evidence. The motion to suppress was denied, and the clothing and knife were admitted as evidence at the ensuing trial. Petitioner was convicted

---

4. The references in paragraphs 15 and 16 of the warrant affidavit's probable cause page to "James Williams" appear to have been intended as references to James D. Morrison, who was petitioner's supervisor at the Youth Center. This misapprehension on the part of the State continued until shortly before trial. Eleven days prior to trial, the prosecution requested the clerk of the Kent County Superior Court to summon "James Williams, Delaware Youth Center," for petitioner's trial. In his return on the summons, Record Document No. 15, the Kent County sheriff stated that he "[s]erved the within summons upon * * * James Williams (Morrison)." The summons actually delivered was made out in the name of James Morrison.

[and] sentenced to two consecutive terms of 25 years each and an additional consecutive life sentence.

On appeal, the Supreme Court of Delaware affirmed. It agreed with what it deemed to be the "majority rule" that no attack upon the veracity of a warrant affidavit could be made:

> "We agree with the majority rule for two reasons. First, it is the function of the issuing magistrate to determine the reliability of information and credibility of affiants in deciding whether the requirement of probable cause has been met. There has been no need demonstrated for interfering with this function. Second, neither the probable cause nor suppression hearings are adjudications of guilt or innocence; the matters asserted by defendant are more properly considered in a trial on the merits."

Because of this resolution, the Delaware Supreme Court noted that there was no need to consider petitioner's "other contentions, relating to the evidence that would have been introduced for impeachment purposes."

Franks' petition for certiorari presented only the issue whether the trial court had erred in refusing to consider his allegation of misrepresentation in the warrant affidavit. Because of the importance of the question, and because of the conflict among both state and federal courts, we granted certiorari.

II.

* * *

Respondent * * * suggests that any error here was harmless. Assuming, *arguendo*, respondent says, that petitioner's Fourth Amendment claim was valid, and that the warrant should have been tested for veracity and the evidence excluded, it is still clear beyond a reasonable doubt that the evidence complained of did not contribute to petitioner's conviction. This contention falls of its own weight. The sole issue at trial was that of consent. Petitioner admitted that he had engaged in sexual relations with Mrs. Bailey on the day in question. She testified that she had not consented to this, and that petitioner, upon first encountering her in the house, had threatened her with a knife to force her to submit. Petitioner claimed that she had given full consent and that no knife had been present. To corroborate its contention that consent was lacking, the State introduced in evidence a stainless steel wooden-handled kitchen knife found by the detectives on the kitchen table in petitioner's apartment four days after the alleged rape. Defense counsel objected to its admission, arguing that Mrs. Bailey had not given any detailed description of the knife alleged to be involved in the incident and had claimed to have seen the knife only in "pitch blackness." The State obtained its admission, however, as a knife that matched the description contained in the search warrant, and Mrs. Bailey testified that the knife allegedly used was, like the knife in evidence, single-edged and not a pocket knife, and that the knife in evidence was the same length and thickness as the knife used in the crime. The State carefully elicited from detective Brooks the fact that this was the only knife found in petitioner's apartment. Although respondent argues that the knife was presented to the jury as "merely exemplary of the generic class of weapon testimonially described by the victim," the State at trial clearly meant to suggest that this was the knife that had been used against Mrs. Bailey. Had the warrant been quashed, and the knife excluded from the trial as evidence, we cannot say with any assurance that the jury would have reached the same decision on the issue of consent, particularly since there was other countervailing evidence on that issue.

* * *

III.

Whether the Fourth and Fourteenth Amendments, and the derivative exclusionary rule made applicable to the States under Mapp v. Ohio, 367 U.S. 643, 81 S.Ct. 1684, 6 L.Ed.2d 1081 (1961), ever mandate that a defendant be permitted to attack the veracity of a warrant affidavit after the warrant has been issued and executed, is a question that encounters conflicting values. The bulwark of Fourth Amendment protection, of course, is the Warrant Clause, requiring that, absent certain exceptions, police obtain a warrant from a neutral and disinterested magistrate before embarking upon a search. In deciding today, that, in certain circumstances, a challenge to a warrant's veracity must be permitted, we derive our ground from language of the Warrant Clause itself, which surely takes the affiant's good faith as its premise: "[N]o warrants shall issue, but upon probable cause, supported by Oath or affirmation * * * ." Judge Frankel, in United States v. Halsey, 257 F.Supp. 1002, 1005 (S.D.N.Y.1966), aff'd, Docket No. 31369 (CA2, June 12, 1967) (unreported), put the matter simply: "[W]hen the Fourth Amendment demands a factual showing sufficient to comprise 'probable cause,' the obvious assumption is that there will be a *truthful* showing" (emphasis in original). This does not mean "truthful" in the sense that every fact recited in the warrant affidavit is necessarily correct, for probable cause may be founded upon hearsay and upon information received from informants, as well as upon information within the affiant's own knowledge that sometimes must be garnered hastily. But surely it is to be "truthful" in the sense that the information put forth is believed or appropriately accepted by the affiant as true. It is established law that a warrant affidavit must set forth particular facts and circumstances underlying the existence of probable cause, so as to allow the magistrate to make an independent evaluation of the matter. If an informant's tip is the source of information, the affidavit must recite "some of the underlying circumstances from which the informant concluded" that relevant evidence might be discovered, and "some of the underlying circumstances from which the officer concluded that the informant, whose identity need not be disclosed, * * * was 'credible' or his information 'reliable.' " Because it is the magistrate who must determine independently whether there is probable cause, it would be an unthinkable imposition upon his authority if a warrant affidavit, revealed after the fact to contain a deliberately or recklessly false statement, were to stand beyond impeachment.

In saying this, however, one must give cognizance to competing values that lead us to impose limitations. They perhaps can best be addressed by noting the arguments of respondent and others against allowing veracity challenges. The arguments are several:

First, respondent argues that the exclusionary rule is not a personal constitutional right, but only a judicially created remedy extended where its benefit as a deterrent promises to outweigh the societal cost of its use. * * * Respondent argues that applying the exclusionary rule to another situation—the deterrence of deliberate or reckless untruthfulness in a warrant affidavit—is not justified * * * [because] interfering with a criminal conviction in order to deter official misconduct is a burden too great to impose on society.

Second, respondent argues that a citizen's privacy interests are adequately protected by a requirement that applicants for a warrant submit a sworn affidavit and by the magistrate's independent determination of sufficiency based on the face of the affidavit. Applying the exclusionary rule to attacks upon veracity would weed out a minimal number of perjurious government statements, says respondent, but would overlap unnecessarily with existing penalties against perjury, including criminal prosecutions, departmental discipline for misconduct, contempt of court, and civil actions.

Third, it is argued that the magistrate already is equipped to conduct a fairly vigorous inquiry into the accuracy of the factual affidavit supporting a warrant application. He may question the affiant, or summon other persons to give testimony at the warrant proceeding. The incremental gain from a post-search adversary proceeding, it is said, would not be great.

Fourth, it is argued that it would unwisely diminish the solemnity and moment of the magistrate's proceeding to make his inquiry into probable cause reviewable in regard to veracity. The less final, and less deference paid to, the magistrate's determination of veracity, the less initiative will he use in that task. Denigration of the magistrate's function would be imprudent insofar as his scrutiny is the last bulwark preventing any particular invasion of privacy before it happens.

Fifth, it is argued that permitting a post-search evidentiary hearing on issues of veracity would confuse the pressing issue of guilt or innocence with the collateral question as to whether there had been official misconduct in the drafting of the affidavit. The weight of criminal dockets, and the need to prevent diversion of attention from the main issue of guilt or innocence, militate against such an added burden on the trial courts. And if such hearings were conducted routinely, it is said, they would be misused by defendants as a convenient source of discovery. Defendants might even use the hearings in an attempt to force revelation of the identity of informants.

Sixth and finally, it is argued that a post-search veracity challenge is inappropriate because the accuracy of an affidavit in large part is beyond the control of the affiant. An affidavit may properly be based on hearsay, on fleeting observations, and on tips received from unnamed informants whose identity often will be properly protected from revelation under McCray v. Illinois, 386 U.S. 300, 87 S.Ct. 1056, 18 L.Ed.2d 62 (1967).

None of these considerations is trivial. Indeed, because of them, the rule announced today has a limited scope, both in regard to when exclusion of the seized evidence is mandated, and when a hearing on allegations of misstatements must be accorded. But neither do the considerations cited by respondent and others have a fully controlling weight; we conclude that they are insufficient to justify an *absolute* ban on post-search impeachment of veracity. On this side of the balance, also, there are pressing considerations:

First, a flat ban on impeachment of veracity could denude the probable cause requirement of all real meaning. The requirement that a warrant not issue "but upon probable cause, supported by Oath or affirmation," would be reduced to a nullity if a police officer was able to use deliberately falsified allegations to demonstrate probable cause, and, having misled the magistrate, then was able to remain confident that the ploy was worthwhile. It is this specter of intentional falsification that, we think, has evoked such widespread opposition to the flat nonimpeachment rule * * *. On occasion, of course, an instance of deliberate falsity will be exposed and confirmed without a special inquiry either at trial, or at a hearing on the sufficiency of the affidavit. A flat nonimpeachment rule would bar reexamination of the warrant even in these cases.

Second, the hearing before the magistrate not always will suffice to discourage lawless or reckless misconduct. The pre-search proceeding is necessarily *ex parte*, since the subject of the search cannot be tipped off to the application for a warrant lest he destroy or remove evidence. The usual reliance of our legal system on adversary proceedings itself should be an indication that an *ex parte* inquiry is likely to be less vigorous. The magistrate has no acquaintance with the information that may contradict the good faith and reasonable basis of the affiant's allegations. The pre-search proceeding will frequently be marked by haste, because of the understandable desire to act before the evidence disappears; this urgency will not always permit the magistrate to make an extended independent examination of the affiant or other witnesses.

Third, the alternative sanctions of a perjury prosecution, administrative discipline, contempt, or a civil suit are not likely to fill the gap. Mapp v. Ohio, supra, implicitly rejected the adequacy of these alternatives. * * *

Fourth, allowing an evidentiary hearing, after a suitable preliminary proffer of material falsity, would not diminish the importance and solemnity of the warrant-issuing process. It is the *ex parte* nature of the initial hearing, rather than the magistrate's capacity, that is the reason for the review. A magistrate's determination is presently subject to review before trial as to *sufficiency* without any undue interference with the dignity of the magistrate's function. Our reluctance today to extend the rule of exclusion beyond instances of deliberate misstatements, and those of reckless disregard, leaves a broad field where the magistrate is the sole protection of a citizen's Fourth Amendment rights, namely, in instances where police have been merely negligent in checking or recording the facts relevant to a probable cause determination.

Fifth, the claim that a post-search hearing will confuse the issue of the defendant's guilt with the issue of the State's possible misbehavior is footless. The hearing will not be in the presence of the jury. An issue extraneous to guilt already is examined in any probable cause determination or review of probable cause. Nor, if a sensible threshold showing is required and sensible substantive requirements for suppression are maintained, need there be any new large-scale commitment of judicial resources; many claims will wash out at an early stage, and the more substantial ones in any event would require judicial resources for vindication if the suggested alternative sanctions were truly to be effective. The requirement of a substantial preliminary showing should suffice to prevent the misuse of a veracity hearing for purposes of discovery or obstruction. And because we are faced today with only the question of the integrity of the affiant's representations as to his own activities, we need not decide, and we in no way predetermine, the difficult question whether a reviewing court must ever require the revelation of the identity of an informant once a substantial preliminary showing of falsity has been made. McCray v. Illinois, the Court's earlier disquisition in this area, concluded only that the Due Process Clause of the Fourteenth Amendment did not require the State to expose an informant's identity routinely, upon a defendant's mere demand, when there was ample evidence in the probable cause hearing to show that the informant was reliable and his information credible.

Sixth and finally, as to the argument that the exclusionary rule should not be extended to a "new" area, we cannot regard any such extension really to be at issue here. Despite the deep skepticism of Members of this Court as to the wisdom of extending the exclusionary rule to collateral areas, such as civil or grand jury proceedings, the Court has not questioned, in the absence of a more efficacious sanction, the continued application of the rule to suppress evidence from the State's case where a Fourth Amendment violation has been substantial and deliberate. We see no principled basis for distinguishing between the question of the sufficiency of an affidavit, which also is subject to a post-search reexamination, and the question of its integrity.

IV.

In sum, and to repeat with some embellishment what we stated at the beginning of this opinion: There is, of course, a presumption of validity with respect to the affidavit supporting the search warrant. To mandate an evidentiary hearing, the challenger's attack must be more than conclusory and must be supported by more than a mere desire to cross-examine. There must be allegations of deliberate falsehood or of reckless disregard for the truth, and those allegations must be accompanied by an offer of proof. They should point out specifically the portion of the warrant affidavit that is claimed to be false; and they should be accompanied by a statement of supporting reasons. Affidavits or sworn or otherwise reliable statements of witnesses should be furnished, or their absence satisfactorily explained. Allegations of negligence or innocent mistake are insufficient. The deliberate falsity or reckless disregard whose impeachment is permitted today is only that of the affiant, not of any nongovernmental informant. Finally, if these requirements are met, and if, when material that is the subject of the alleged falsity or reckless disregard is set to one side, there remains sufficient content in the warrant affidavit to support a finding of probable cause, no hearing is required. On the other hand, if the remaining content is insufficient, the defendant is entitled, under the Fourth Amendment, to his hearing. Whether he will prevail at that hearing is, of course, another issue.

Because of Delaware's absolute rule, its courts did not have occasion to consider the proffer put forward by petitioner Franks. Since the framing of suitable rules to govern proffers is a matter properly left to the States, we decline ourselves to pass on petitioner's proffer. The judgment of the Supreme Court of Delaware is reversed, and the case is remanded for further proceedings not inconsistent with this opinion.

It is so ordered.

APPENDIX A TO OPINION OF THE COURT

J.P.Court #7

IN THE MATTER OF: Jerome Franks, B/M, DOB: 10/9/54 and 222 S. Governors Ave., Apt. #3, Dover, Delaware. A two room apartment located on the South side, second floor, of a white block building on the west side of S. Governors Avenue, between Loockerman Street and North Street, in the City of Dover. The ground floor of this building houses Wayman's Barber Shop.

STATE OF DELAWARE

ss:

COUNTY OF KENT

Be it remembered that on this 9th day of March A.D. 1976 before me John Green, personally appeared Det. Ronald R. Brooks and Det. Larry Gray of the Dover Police Department who being by me duly sworn depose and say:

That they have reason to believe and do believe that in the 222 S. Governors Avenue, Apartment #3, Dover, Delaware. A two room apartment located on the South side second floor of a white block building on the west side of S. Governors Avenue between Loockerman Street and North Street in the City of Dover. The ground floor of this building houses Wayman's Barber Shop the occupant of which is Jerome Franks. There has been and/or there is now located and/or concealed certain property in said house, place, conveyance and/or on the person or persons of the occupants thereof, consisting of property, papers, articles, or things which are the instruments of criminal offense, and/or obtained in the commission of a crime, and/or designated to be used in the commission of a crime, and not reasonably calculated to be used for any other purpose and/or the possession of which is unlawful, papers, articles, or things which are of an evidentiary nature pertaining to the commission of a crime or crimes specified therein and in particular, a white knit thermal undershirt; a brown ¾ length leather jacket with a tie-belt; a pair of black mens pants; a dark colored knit hat; a long thin bladed knife or other instruments or items relating to the crime.

Articles, or things were, are, or will be possessed and/or used in violation of Title 11, Sub-Chapter D, Section 763, Delaware Code in that [See attached probable cause page].

Wherefore, affiants pray that a search warrant may be issued authorizing a search of the aforesaid 222 S. Governors Avenue, Apartment #3, Dover, Delaware. A two room apartment located on the south side second floor of a white block building on the west side of S. Governors Avenue between Loockerman St. and North Street, in the City of Dover in the manner provided by law.

/s/ Det. Ronald R. Brooks

Affiant

/s/ Det. Larry D. Gray

Affiant

Sworn to (or affirmed) and subscribed before me this 9th day of March A.D. 1976.

/s/ John [illegible] Green

Judge Ct 7

The facts tending to establish probable cause for the issuance of this search warrant are:

1. On Saturday, 2/28/76, Brenda L. B. _____, W/F/15, reported to the Dover Police Department that she had been kidnapped and raped.

2. An investigation of this complaint was conducted by Det. Boyce Failing of the Dover Police Department.

3. Investigation of the aforementioned complaint revealed that Brenda B. _____, while under the influence of drugs, was taken to 222 S. Governors Avenue, Apartment 3, Dover, Delaware.

4. Investigation of the aforementioned complaint revealed that 222 S. Governors Avenue, Apartment #3, Dover, Delaware, is the residence of Jerome Franks, B/M DOB: 10/9/54.

5. Investigation of the aforementioned complaint revealed that on Saturday, 2/29/76, Jerome Franks did have sexual contact with Brenda B. _____ without her consent.

6. On Thursday, 3/4/76 at the Dover Police Department, Brenda B. _____, revealed to Det. Boyce Failing that Jerome Franks was the person who committed the Sexual Assault against her.

7. On Friday, 3/5/76, Jerome Franks was placed under arrest by Cpl. Robert McClements of the Dover Police Department, and charged with Sexual Misconduct.

8. On 3/5/76 at Family Court in Dover, Delaware, Jerome Franks did, after being arrested on the charge of Sexual Misconduct, make a statement of Cpl. Robert McClements, that he thought the charge was concerning Cynthia Bailey not Brenda B. _____.

9.   On Friday, 3/5/76, Cynthia C. Bailey, W/F/21 of 132 North Street, Dover, Delaware, did report to Dover Police Department that she had been raped at her residence during the night.

10.   Investigation conducted by your affiant on Friday, 3/5/76, revealed the perpetrator of the crime to be an unknown black male, approximately 57, 150 lbs., dark complexion, wearing white thermal undershirt, black pants with a belt having a silver or gold buckle, a brown leather ¾ length coat with a tie belt in the front, and a dark knit cap pulled around the eyes.

11.   Your affiant can state, that during the commission of this crime, Cynthia Bailey was forced at knife point and with the threat of death to engage in sexual intercourse with the perpetrator of the crime.

12.   Your affiant can state that entry was gained to the residence of Cynthia Bailey through a window located on the east side of the residence.

13.   Your affiant can state that the residence of Jerome Franks is within a very short distance and direct sight of the residence of Cynthia Bailey.

14.   Your affiant can state that the description given by Cynthia Bailey of the unknown black male does coincide with the description of Jerome Franks.

15.   On Tuesday, 3/9/76, your affiant contacted Mr. James Williams and Mr. Wesley Lucas of the Delaware Youth Center where Jerome Franks is employed and did have personal conversation with both these people.

16.   On Tuesday, 3/9/76, Mr. James Williams revealed to your affiant that the normal dress of Jerome Franks does consist of a white knit thermal undershirt and a brown leather jacket.

17.   On Tuesday, 3/9/76, Mr. Wesley Lucas revealed to your affiant that in addition to the thermal undershirt and jacket, Jerome Franks often wears a dark green knit hat.

18.   Your affiant can state that a check of official records reveals that in 1971 Jerome Franks was arrested for the crime of rape and subsequently convicted with Assault with intent to Rape.

NOTES

1.   On remand in *Franks*, the Delaware Supreme Court held that even if paragraphs 15 through 17 were set aside in their entirety, the remaining allegations were sufficient to establish probable cause. Consequently, Franks' proffer of evidence to contradict the facts alleged in the affidavit was insufficient and the trial judge erred in failing to hold an evidentiary hearing. The conviction was, therefore, again upheld by that court. Franks v. State, 398 A.2d 783 (Del.1979).

2.   **Availability of Informant's Identity.** A defendant's ability to determine whether there is any viable basis for attacking a warrant under *Franks* may depend

upon his ability to determine the identity of the informant whose information was relied upon in the showing of probable cause. But does the Fourth Amendment ever give a defendant a right to that information in order to determine whether a *Franks* challenge is possible?

Defendants' right under the Fourth Amendment to the identity of an informant whose information was used to support law enforcement action challenged on Fourth Amendment grounds was addressed in McCray v. Illinois, 386 U.S. 300, 87 L.Ed.2d 1056, 18 L.Ed.2d 62 (1967), noted several times in the principal case. McCray complained of the trial court's refusal to require officers to disclose the name of the informant on whose tip they made a warrantless arrest of McCray. Roviaro v. United States, 353 U.S. 53, 77 S.Ct. 623, 1 L.Ed.2d 639 (1957), *McCray* suggested, held that federal procedural law and perhaps due process require the disclosure of an informant's identity when the facts show the informant may have information bearing on the accused's guilt or innocence. This obligation to disclose an informant's identity did not apply, the Court continued, to situations such as McCray's, where defendants sought similar information only to challenge the evidence's admissibility on Fourth Amendment exclusionary rule grounds. Thus the trial court's refusal to require disclosure to McCray did not violate his Fourth Amendment rights.

The Court left unclear whether *McCray* simply held that on the facts of the case the defendant failed to make a persuasive enough case for his need for the informant's identity or, rather, that no defendant could ever establish a right to disclosure of an informant's identity for purposes of litigating a Fourth Amendment right to exclusion of evidence. *McCray's* discussion leaves open the possibility that some defendants may, under some quite limited circumstances, have a Fourth Amendment right to disclosure of this information. Perhaps such a right exists only if the trial judge hears all other evidence and determines a reliable resolution of the Fourth Amendment issue is difficult or impossible without further information that might become available if the defendant is permitted to know and perhaps interview the informant.

In at least some warrant situations, it is arguable the *Franks* right to challenge the accuracy of a search warrant affidavit is of no significance unless the defendant has the right to find out the identity of the informant and to inquire of that informant whether the affidavit accurately states what he told officers. Despite *McCray*, then, *Franks* suggests defendants sometimes may have a Fourth Amendment right to an informant's identity to determine whether, on the facts of the case, *Franks* permits a challenge to the affidavit's accuracy and the warrant's validity.

Whatever the constitutional demands, local statutes and court rules sometimes give defendants some right to informants' identities to investigate the validity of possible challenges to evidence's admissibility. The Model Code of Pre-Arraignment Procedure would require disclosure of the identity of an informant where the information relied upon to establish probable cause includes a report of information from that informant unless the judge finds "that the issue of [probable] cause can be fairly determined without such disclosure." Model Code of Pre-Arraignment Procedure § 290.4 (Official Draft, 1975). Disclosure would not be required, however, if (a) the evidence at issue was seized under a search warrant; or (b) the prosecution produced "substantial corroboration of the informant's existence and reliability" consisting of testimony of someone other than the person to whom the informant gave his information. For purposes of deciding whether a "fair" determination can be made without disclosure, the judge is authorized to require the prosecution, *in camera,* to disclose the informant's identity or to produce the informant for questioning by the judge. Is this approach inconsistent with *Roviaro* and *McCray*? Perhaps *McCray* can be read as a case in which the trial judge implicitly found on the facts before him that a "fair" determination of whether the officers had probable cause could be made without requiring disclosure.

B. ENTERING THE PREMISES AND OTHER LIMITS ON EXECUTION OF WARRANTS

EDITORS' INTRODUCTION: ANNOUNCEMENT DEMANDS AND OTHER REQUIREMENTS FOR EXECUTION OF WARRANTS

Officers' executions of warrants—especially search warrants—are often affected by numerous statutory and perhaps court rule requirements. Those requirements govern matters such as the time of day or night the warrant may be executed, the need to serve the warrant upon, or present it to, those on the premises when the officers arrive, and the making of a "return" to the issuing magistrate indicating the warrant has been executed and, perhaps, in the case of a search warrant specifying the items seized during the search.

These requirements raise two related: First, to what if any extent do the Fourth Amendment or similar state constitutional provisions embody some version of these requirements? Second, what if any is the effect of violating these requirements upon the admissibility of evidence obtained during execution of the warrants.

Announcement Requirements

The most controversial of these execution requirements has been that demanding that before entering premises to execute a warrant, or at least before certain kinds of entry, officers announce their identity and purpose and perhaps comply with other requirements related to entry. Often the issue is posed negatively: when are so-called "no-knock" entries—those involving no such announcement—permitted?

Statutes in many jurisdictions address the matter. A federal statute, 18 U.S.C.A. § 3109, for example, provides:

> The officer may break open any outer or inner door or window of a house, or any part of a house, or anything therein, to execute a search warrant, if, after notice of his authority and purpose, he is refused admittance or when necessary to liberate himself or a person aiding him in the execution of a warrant.

In Miller v. United States, 357 U.S. 301, 78 S.Ct. 1190, 2 L.Ed.2d 1332 (1958), and Sabbath v. United States, 391 U.S. 585, 88 S.Ct. 1755, 20 L.Ed.2d 828 (1968), the Supreme Court held the "validity" of an entry made to effect an arrest without a warrant must comply with criteria identical to those set out in the statute, apparently as a matter of nonconstitutional law applicable to arrests made by federal officers. Evidence obtained in a search related to an entry violating these provisions cannot be used in a federal criminal trial.

Whether the Fourth Amendment ever requires announcement prior to entry remained uncertain until the Supreme Court addressed the issue in Wilson v. Arkansas, 514 U.S. 927, 115 S.Ct. 1914, 131 L.Ed.2d 976 (1995).

Holding that the Arkansas court below erred in concluding the Fourth Amendment imposed no "knock and announce" requirement for execution of a search warrant, Justice Thomas's *Wilson* opinion for the Court reviewed the common law authority requiring announcement and continued:

> Our own cases have acknowledged that the common-law principle of announcement is "embedded in Anglo-American law," but we have never squarely held that this principle is an element of the reasonableness inquiry under the Fourth Amendment. We now so hold. Given the longstanding common-law endorsement of the practice of announcement, we have little doubt that the Framers of the Fourth Amendment thought that the method of an officer's entry into a dwelling was among the factors to be considered in assessing the reasonableness of a search or seizure. Contrary to the decision below, we hold that in some circumstances an officer's unannounced entry into a home might be unreasonable under the Fourth Amendment.

> This is not to say, of course, that every entry must be preceded by an announcement. The Fourth Amendment's flexible requirement of reasonableness should not be read to mandate a rigid rule of announcement that ignores countervailing law enforcement interests. * * * [T]he common-law principle of announcement was never stated as an inflexible rule requiring announcement under all circumstances.

> Indeed, at the time of the framing, the common-law admonition that an officer "ought to signify the cause of his coming," had not been extended conclusively to the context of felony arrests. The common-law principle gradually was applied to cases involving felonies, but at the same time the courts continued to recognize that under certain circumstances the presumption in favor of announcement necessarily would give way to contrary considerations.

> Thus, because the common-law rule was justified in part by the belief that announcement generally would avoid "the destruction or breaking of any house ... by which great damage and inconvenience might ensue," courts acknowledged that the presumption in favor of announcement would yield under circumstances presenting a threat of physical violence. See, e.g., Read v. Case, 4 Conn. 166, 170 (1822) (plaintiff who "had resolved ... to resist even to the shedding of blood ... was not within the reason and spirit of the rule requiring notice"); Mahomed v. The Queen, 4 Moore 239, 247, 13 Eng. Rep. 293, 296 (P.C. 1843) ("While he was firing pistols at them, were they to knock at the door, and to ask him to be pleased to open it for them? The law in its wisdom only requires this ceremony to be observed when it possibly may be attended with some advantage, and may render the breaking open of the outer door unnecessary"). Similarly, courts held that an officer may dispense with announcement in cases where a prisoner escapes from him and retreats to his dwelling. See, e.g., ibid.; Allen v. Martin, 10 Wend. 300, 304 (N.Y.Sup.Ct.1833). Proof of "demand and refusal" was deemed unnecessary in such cases because it would be a "senseless ceremony" to require an officer in pursuit of a recently escaped arrestee to make an announcement prior to breaking the door

to retake him. Finally, courts have indicated that unannounced entry may be justified where police officers have reason to believe that evidence would likely be destroyed if advance notice were given.

We need not attempt a comprehensive catalog of the relevant countervailing factors here. For now, we leave to the lower courts the task of determining the circumstances under which an unannounced entry is reasonable under the Fourth Amendment. We simply hold that although a search or seizure of a dwelling might be constitutionally defective if police officers enter without prior announcement, law enforcement interests may also establish the reasonableness of an unannounced entry.

514 U.S. at 934–36, 115 S.Ct. at 1918–19, 131 L.Ed.2d at 982–84.

Wilson made clear the Fourth Amendment sometimes requires announcement, but it did not address the effect of officers' failure to announce and the admissibility of evidence obtained in the post-entry search. To the contrary, the Court commented:

Respondent * * * ask[s] us to affirm the denial of petitioner's suppression motion on an alternative ground: that exclusion is not a constitutionally compelled remedy where the unreasonableness of a search stems from the failure of announcement. Analogizing to the "independent source" doctrine * * *, and the "inevitable discovery" rule * * *, respondent * * * argue[s] that any evidence seized after an unreasonable, unannounced entry is causally disconnected from the constitutional violation and that exclusion goes beyond the goal of precluding any benefit to the government flowing from the constitutional violation. Because this remedial issue was not addressed by the court below and is not within the narrow question on which we granted certiorari, we decline to address these arguments.

514 U.S. at 937 n. 4, 115 S.Ct. at 1919 n. 4, 131 L.Ed.2d at 984 n. 4.

In *Miller* and *Sabbath*, the Court assumed entry of premises to make an arrest, if made in violation of the federal statute, rendered the arrest "unlawful," and evidence that would otherwise be admissible as seized in a search incident to the defendant's arrest must be suppressed. Perhaps the Fourth Amendment requirement recognized in *Wilson* will not have the same effect on subsequently obtained evidence as the statutory requirement applied in *Miller* and *Sabbath*. Or, perhaps exclusionary sanction developments since *Miller* and *Sabbath* have reduced the effect of an improper no-knock entry on the admissibility of evidence obtained by searching the premises.

The details of *Wilson's* Fourth Amendment announcement requirement are explored in the principal case reprinted in this subsection.

Return of the Warrant and Inventories of Seized Items

Despite *Wilson's* "constitutionalization" of the announcement requirement, the Supreme Court made clear not all traditional procedural requirements for the execution of warrants are imposed as a matter of Fourth Amendment law.

Statutes or court rules often require search warrants be in some sense returned to the issuing magistrate and persons on the searched premises be provided with an inventory of items seized. Fed.R.Crim.P. 41(d), for example, provides in part:

> (d) Execution and Return with Inventory. The officer taking property under the warrant shall give to the person from whom or from whose premises the property was taken a copy of the warrant and a receipt for the property taken or shall leave the copy and receipt at the place from which the property was taken. The return shall be made promptly and shall be accompanied by a written inventory of any property taken. * * *

Are there circumstances in which failure to observe these requirements means the Fourth Amendment is violated? If so, does this demand the exclusion of evidence obtained in the search?

In Cady v. Dombrowski, 413 U.S. 433, 93 S.Ct. 2523, 37 L.Ed.2d 706 (1973), the officers failed to list all items seized on the inventory filed with the court issuing the search warrant. The Court rejected the argument that this failure required the exclusion of the unlisted items:

> As these items were constitutionally seized, we do not deem it constitutionally significant that they were not listed in the return of the warrant. The ramification of that "defect," if such it was, is purely a question of state law.

93 U.S. at 449, 93 S.Ct. at 2532, 37 L.Ed.2d at 719.

Due process—but not Fourth Amendment—requirements were at issue in City of West Covina v. Perkins, 525 U.S. 234, 119 S.Ct. 678, 142 L.Ed.2d 636 (1999). Officers executing a search warrant searched Perkins' home and seized certain personal property. The officers left a notice giving their names, identifying their employing department (the West Covina Police Department) and a telephone number at which they could be contacted. In addition, they attached an inventory of property seized, but the notice did not specify the number of the warrant because it was under seal to preserve the integrity of an ongoing investigation. After unsuccessful efforts to secure return of his property, Perkins and his family members sued the officers and West Covina, arguing the process by which the property was taken and retained violated their federal constitutional rights. The federal district court granted summary judgment for the defendants, but the Court of Appeals reversed on the ground the officers failed to give constitutionally-required notice regarding state law procedures for seeking the return of seized property.

The Supreme Court reversed:

> When the police seize property for a criminal investigation, * * * due process does not require them to provide the owner with notice of state law remedies.
>
> A primary purpose of the notice required by the Due Process Clause is to ensure that the opportunity for a hearing is meaningful. It follows that when law enforcement agents seize property pursuant to warrant, due process requires them to take reasonable steps to give

notice that the property has been taken so the owner can pursue available remedies for its return. Individualized notice that the officers have taken the property is necessary in a case such as the one before us because the property owner would have no other reasonable means of ascertaining who was responsible for his loss.

No similar rationale justifies requiring individualized notice of state-law remedies which, like those at issue here, are established by published, generally available state statutes and case law. Once the property owner is informed that his property has been seized, he can turn to these public sources to learn about the remedial procedures available to him. The City need not take other steps to inform him of his options. * * *

Respondents urge that * * * we should, at least, affirm the Court of Appeals' judgment on the narrower ground that the notice provided respondents was inadequate because it did not provide them with the factual information—specifically, the search warrant number—they needed to invoke their judicial remedies. The District Court, however, made an explicit factual finding that respondents failed to establish that they needed the search warrant number to file a court motion seeking return of their property * * *. This finding undermines the factual predicate for respondents' alternative argument, and we need not discuss it further.

525 U.S. at ___, 119 S.Ct. at 681–83, 142 L.Ed.2d at 642–44. *Perkins* seemed to assume some notice is constitutionally demanded. Would failure to provide such notice serve as a basis for challenging the admissibility of the evidence seized?

Richards v. Wisconsin

Supreme Court of the United States, 1997.
520 U.S. 385, 117 S.Ct. 1416, 137 Ed.2d 615.

■ JUSTICE STEVENS delivered the opinion of the Court.

* * *

In this case, the Wisconsin Supreme Court concluded that police officers are never required to knock and announce their presence when executing a search warrant in a felony drug investigation. In so doing, it reaffirmed a pre-[Wilson v. Arkansas, 514 U.S. 927, 115 S.Ct. 1914, 131 L.Ed.2d 976 (1995)] holding and concluded that *Wilson* did not preclude this *per se* rule. * * *

I

On December 31, 1991, police officers in Madison, Wisconsin obtained a warrant to search Steiney Richards' hotel room for drugs and related paraphernalia. The search warrant was the culmination of an investigation that had uncovered substantial evidence that Richards was one of several individuals dealing drugs out of hotel rooms in Madison. The police requested a warrant that would have given advance authorization for a "no-knock" entry into the hotel room, but the magistrate explicitly deleted those portions of the warrant.

The officers arrived at the hotel room at 3:40 a.m. Officer Pharo, dressed as a maintenance man, led the team. With him were several plainclothes officers and at least one man in uniform. Officer Pharo knocked on Richards' door and, responding to the query from inside the room, stated that he was a maintenance man. With the chain still on the door, Richards cracked it open. Although there is some dispute as to what occurred next, Richards acknowledges that when he opened the door he saw the man in uniform standing behind Officer Pharo. He quickly slammed the door closed and, after waiting two or three seconds, the officers began kicking and ramming the door to gain entry to the locked room. At trial, the officers testified that they identified themselves as police while they were kicking the door in. When they finally did break into the room, the officers caught Richards trying to escape through the window. They also found cash and cocaine hidden in plastic bags above the bathroom ceiling tiles.

Richards sought to have the evidence from his hotel room suppressed on the ground that the officers had failed to knock and announce their presence prior to forcing entry into the room. The trial court denied the motion, concluding that the officers could gather from Richards' strange behavior when they first sought entry that he knew they were police officers and that he might try to destroy evidence or to escape. The judge emphasized that the easily disposable nature of the drugs the police were searching for further justified their decision to identify themselves as they crossed the threshold instead of announcing their presence before seeking entry. Richards appealed the decision to the Wisconsin Supreme Court and that court affirmed.

The Wisconsin Supreme Court did not delve into the events underlying Richards' arrest in any detail, but accepted the following facts: "[O]n December 31, 1991, police executed a search warrant for the motel room of the defendant seeking evidence of the felonious crime of Possession with Intent to Deliver a Controlled Substance * * *. They did not knock and announce prior to their entry. Drugs were seized."

Assuming these facts, the court proceeded to consider whether our decision in *Wilson* required the court to abandon its decision in State v. Stevens, 181 Wis.2d 410, 511 N.W.2d 591 (1994), cert. denied, 515 U.S. 1102, 115 S.Ct. 2245, 132 L.Ed.2d 254 (1995), which held that "when the police have a search warrant, supported by probable cause, to search a residence for evidence of delivery of drugs or evidence of possession with intent to deliver drugs, they necessarily have reasonable cause to believe exigent circumstances exist" to justify a no-knock entry. The court concluded that nothing in *Wilson's* acknowledgment that the knock-and-announce rule was an element of the Fourth Amendment "reasonableness" requirement would prohibit application of a *per se* exception to that rule in a category of cases.

In reaching this conclusion, the Wisconsin court found it reasonable— after considering criminal conduct surveys, newspaper articles, and other judicial opinions—to assume that all felony drug crimes will involve "an extremely high risk of serious if not deadly injury to the police as well as the potential for the disposal of drugs by the occupants prior to entry by the police." Notwithstanding its acknowledgment that in "some cases, police officers will undoubtedly decide that their safety, the safety of others, and the effective execution of the warrant dictate that they knock and announce," the court concluded that exigent circumstances justifying a no-knock entry are always present in felony drug cases. Further, the court reasoned that the violation of privacy that occurs when officers who have a search warrant forcibly enter a residence without first announcing their presence is minimal, given that the residents would ultimately be without authority to refuse the police entry. The principal intrusion on individual privacy interests in such a situation, the court concluded, comes from the issuance of the search warrant, not the manner in which it is executed. Accordingly, the court determined that police in Wisconsin do not need specific information about dangerousness, or the possible destruction of drugs in a particular case, in order to dispense with the knock-and-announce requirement in felony drug cases.

* * *

II

We recognized in *Wilson* that the knock-and-announce requirement could give way "under circumstances presenting a threat of physical violence," or "where police officers have reason to believe that evidence would likely be destroyed if advance notice were given." It is indisputable that felony drug investigations may frequently involve both of these circumstances. The question we must resolve is whether this fact justifies dispensing with case-by-case evaluation of the manner in which a search was executed.

The Wisconsin court explained its blanket exception as necessitated by the special circumstances of today's drug culture, and the State asserted at oral argument that the blanket exception was reasonable in "felony drug cases because of the convergence in a violent and dangerous form of commerce of weapons and the destruction of drugs." But creating exceptions to the knock-and-announce rule based on the "culture" surrounding a general category of criminal behavior presents at least two serious concerns.

First, the exception contains considerable overgeneralization. For example, while drug investigation frequently does pose special risks to officer safety and the preservation of evidence, not every drug investigation will pose these risks to a substantial degree. For example, a search could be conducted at a time when the only individuals present in a residence have no connection with the drug activity and thus will be unlikely to threaten officers or destroy evidence. Or the police could know that the drugs being searched for were of a type or in a location that made them impossible to destroy quickly. In those situations, the asserted governmental interests in preserving evidence and maintaining safety may not outweigh the individual privacy interests intruded upon by a no-knock entry.[5] Wisconsin's blanket rule impermissibly insulates these cases from judicial review.

5. The State asserts that the intrusion on individual interests effectuated by a no-knock entry is minimal because the execution of the warrant itself constitutes the primary

A second difficulty with permitting a criminal-category exception to the knock-and-announce requirement is that the reasons for creating an exception in one category can, relatively easily, be applied to others. Armed bank robbers, for example, are, by definition, likely to have weapons, and the fruits of their crime may be destroyed without too much difficulty. If a *per se* exception were allowed for each category of criminal investigation that included a considerable—albeit hypothetical—risk of danger to officers or destruction of evidence, the knock-and-announce element of the Fourth Amendment's reasonableness requirement would be meaningless.

Thus, the fact that felony drug investigations may frequently present circumstances warranting a no-knock entry cannot remove from the neutral scrutiny of a reviewing court the reasonableness of the police decision not to knock and announce in a particular case. Instead, in each case, it is the duty of a court confronted with the question to determine whether the facts and circumstances of the particular entry justified dispensing with the knock-and-announce requirement.

In order to justify a "no-knock" entry, the police must have a reasonable suspicion that knocking and announcing their presence, under the particular circumstances, would be dangerous or futile, or that it would inhibit the effective investigation of the crime by, for example, allowing the destruction of evidence. This standard—as opposed to a probable cause requirement—strikes the appropriate balance between the legitimate law enforcement concerns at issue in the execution of search warrants and the individual privacy interests affected by no-nock entries. This showing is not high, but the police should be required to make it whenever the reasonableness of a no-knock entry is challenged.

III

Although we reject the Wisconsin court's blanket exception to the knock-and-announce requirement, we conclude that the officers' no-knock entry into Richards' hotel room did not violate the Fourth Amendment. We agree with the trial court * * *, that the circumstances in this case show that the officers had a reasonable suspicion that Richards might destroy evidence if given further opportunity to do so.

The judge who heard testimony at Richards' suppression hearing concluded that it was reasonable for the officers executing the warrant to

intrusion on individual privacy and that the individual privacy interest cannot outweigh the generalized governmental interest in effective and safe law enforcement. While it is true that a no-knock entry is less intrusive than, for example, a warrantless search, the individual interests implicated by an unannounced, forcible entry should not be unduly minimized. As we observed in [*Wilson*], the common law recognized that individuals should have an opportunity to themselves comply with the law and to avoid the destruction of property occasioned by a forcible entry. These interests are not inconsequential.

Additionally, when police enter a residence without announcing their presence, the residents are not given any opportunity to prepare themselves for such an entry. The State pointed out at oral argument that, in Wisconsin, most search warrants are executed during the late night and early morning hours. The brief interlude between announcement and entry with a warrant may be the opportunity that an individual has to pull on clothes or get out of bed.

believe that Richards knew, after opening the door to his hotel room the first time, that the men seeking entry to his room were the police. Once the officers reasonably believed that Richards knew who they were, the court concluded, it was reasonable for them to force entry immediately given the disposable nature of the drugs.

In arguing that the officers' entry was unreasonable, Richards places great emphasis on the fact that the magistrate who signed the search warrant for his hotel room deleted the portions of the proposed warrant that would have given the officers permission to execute a no-knock entry. But this fact does not alter the reasonableness of the officers' decision, which must be evaluated as of the time they entered the hotel room. At the time the officers obtained the warrant, they did not have evidence sufficient, in the judgment of the magistrate, to justify a no-knock warrant. Of course, the magistrate could not have anticipated in every particular the circumstances that would confront the officers when they arrived at Richards' hotel room. These actual circumstances—petitioner's apparent recognition of the officers combined with the easily disposable nature of the drugs—justified the officers' ultimate decision to enter without first announcing their presence and authority.

* * *

Accordingly, although we reject the blanket exception to the knock-and-announce requirement for felony drug investigations, the judgment of the Wisconsin Supreme Court is affirmed.

It is so ordered.

NOTES AND QUESTIONS

1. **Entries Requiring Announcement.** What entries require announcement? In Sabbath v. United States 391 U.S. 585, 88 S.Ct. 1755, 20 L.Ed.2d 828 (1968), discussed in the Introductory Note to this part of the present chapter, the entry at issue was made by officers who knocked on the door of the premises and, upon receiving no answer after a few seconds passed, opened the unlocked door and entered. Sabbath argued that the entry violated 18 U.S.C. § 3109, reprinted in the Introductory Note. The Government argued in response that "the use of 'force' is an indispensable element of the statute," and since no force was used on the facts, the entry was not subject to the statute. Rejecting the Government's contention, the Court explained:

> Considering the purposes of § 3109, it would indeed be a "grudging application" to hold, as the Government urges, that the use of "force" is an indispensable element of the statute. To be sure, the statute uses the phrase "break open" and that connotes some use of force. But linguistic analysis seldom is adequate when a statute is designed to incorporate fundamental values and the ongoing development of the common law. * * * [Lower courts have] held that § 3109 applies to entries effected by the use of a passkey, which requires no more force than does the turning of a doorknob. An unannounced intrusion into a dwelling—what § 3109 basically proscribes—is no less an unannounced intrusion whether officers break down a door, force open a chain lock on a partially open door, open a locked door by use of a passkey, or, as here, open a closed but unlocked door. The protection afforded by, and the values inherent in, § 3109 must be "governed by something more than the

fortuitous circumstance of an unlocked door." Keiningham v. United States, 109 U.S.App.D.C. 272, 276, 287 F.2d 126, 130 (1960).

391 U.S. at 589–90, 88 S.Ct. at 1758, 20 L.Ed.2d at 833–34. "We do not deal here with entries obtained by ruse," the Court added, "which have been viewed as involving no 'breaking.' "

Will the Court take the same approach in construing the Fourth Amendment requirement as it took in *Sabbath* with the federal statutory requirement? If *Sabbath* applies the common law position and *Wilson* finds the basic common law requirement embodied in the Fourth Amendment, perhaps that Fourth Amendment requirement applies to those situations *Sabbath* indicated were covered by the federal statute.

2. **Service of the Warrant.** Statutory provisions often require some sort of service of the warrant. For example, Fed.R.Crim.P. 41(d), reprinted in the Editors' Introduction, requires an officer taking property under a search warrant "shall give to the person from whom or from whose premises the property was taken a copy of the warrant * * * or shall leave the copy * * * at the place from which the property was taken." Courts often take the position that violations of these requirements affect the admissibility of evidence obtained only if the violation was "substantial" or intentional or if the complaining defendant was in some sense prejudiced. See Moya v. State, 335 Ark. 193, 205, 981 S.W.2d 521, 527 (1998).

The federal provision, however, was taken with unusual seriousness in United States v. Gantt, 179 F.3d 782 (9th Cir.1999). Federal agents executing a search warrant showed Gantt, the occupant of the premises, "the face of the warrant" but not the incorporated attachment specifying the items for which the agents were authorized to search. The court rejected the Government's contention that Rule 41(d) is complied with if officers leave a copy of the warrant at the scene, even if— as in *Gantt*—the person is arrested and thus has no opportunity to examine that copy. Rule 41(d), the court reasoned, implements important policies flowing from the Fourth Amendment warrant requirement:

> If the warrant is not disclosed until after the completion of the search then * * * [t]he individual [searched] loses the opportunity to point out to the agents that certain items are beyond the scope of the warrant or even that the agents have targeted the wrong residence. Most importantly, until the search is completed, the individual cannot be certain that the officers are acting under valid judicial authority.

179 F.3d at 879. The court found unconvincing the Government's argument that enabling those on the premises to challenge whether the agents exceeded the authority of the warrant would encourage violent confrontation between officers and those searched. Given the nature and importance of the underlying purposes of the Rule 41(d) requirement, the court concluded, those executing a search warrant "should utilize the disfavored alternative of leaving behind a copy of the warrant only when necessary."

The officers' violation of Rule 41(b), *Gantt* further reasoned, required exclusion even if it was only a "technical" or "non-fundamental" violation of the rule. Such a violation should lead to exclusion of the resulting evidence only upon proof that it was a deliberate disregard of the rule or the defendant was prejudiced. Gantt asked to see the warrant; the agents nevertheless failed to show her the full warrant with the attachment and the Government provided no explanation or justification for this failure to comply with her request. Thus, the court concluded, the violation was deliberate. Prejudice, in this context, requires proof the search might not have occurred or would not have been as abrasive had the rule been followed. *Gantt* determined that Gantt had also shown prejudice as so defined:

> Had Gantt been provided a copy of the warrant the search would have been less abrasive. She would not have been in doubt as to the authority of the agents, and she might also have been able to point out to the agents that many of the items seized were beyond the scope of the warrant.

179 F.3d at 791.

3. **Destruction of Property in Entering.** The relationship between no-knock entry under *Wilson* and *Richards* and destruction of property was addressed in United States v. Ramirez, 523 U.S. 65, 118 S.Ct. 992, 140 L.Ed.2d 191 (1998). Officers with a search warrant made an unannounced entry into Ramirez's home to locate and arrest Shelby, a violent escaped prison inmate. The officers believed there were weapons in the garage. As they entered, the officers broke a window in the garage and pointed a gun through it to dissuade any occupants from rushing to those weapons. The lower courts held that an unannounced entry involving destruction of property requires a higher degree of exigency than other such entries and that this heightened standard had not been met. The Supreme Court rejected this approach:

> Neither [*Wilson* nor *Richards*] explicitly addressed the question whether the lawfulness of a no-knock entry depends on whether property is damaged in the course of the entry. It is obvious from their holdings, however, that it does not. Under *Richards*, a no-knock entry is justified if police have a "reasonable suspicion" that knocking and announcing would be dangerous, futile, or destructive to the purposes of the investigation. Whether such a "reasonable suspicion" exists depends in no way on whether police must destroy property in order to enter.
>
> This is not to say that the Fourth Amendment speaks not at all to the manner of executing a search warrant. The general touchstone of reasonableness which governs Fourth Amendment analysis governs the method of execution of the warrant. Excessive or unnecessary destruction of property in the course of a search may violate the Fourth Amendment, even though the entry itself is lawful and the fruits of the search not subject to suppression.

523 U.S. at 70–71, 118 S.Ct. at 996, 140 L.Ed.2d at 198. Given what the officers knew about Shelby, it continued, they had reasonable suspicion that announcement might be dangerous required by *Richards* for no-knock entry. The Court then concluded:

> As for the manner in which the entry was accomplished, the police here broke a single window in respondent's garage. They did so because they wished to discourage Shelby, or any other occupant of the house, from rushing to the weapons that the informant had told them respondent might have kept there. Their conduct was clearly reasonable and we conclude that there was no Fourth Amendment violation.

523 U.S. at 71–72, 118 S.Ct. at 997, 140 L.Ed.2d at 198. Since it found no Fourth Amendment violation, the Court added, it was not required to decide whether unreasonable damage to property in the course of an entry to execute a search warrant would require suppression of evidence found in a search conducted after that entry.

4. **Magistrate's Authorization for No–Knock Entry.** What is the constitutionally necessary role of the magistrate issuing a warrant in determining the propriety of no-knock entry? In *Richards*, the police officers applying for the search warrant requested a warrant authorizing no-knock entry and submitted to the magistrate a "proposed" warrant containing such authorization. The magistrate, however, explicitly deleted this authorization from the warrant before issuing it. In arguing that the no-knock entry was unreasonable, Richards emphasized the

magistrate's judgment that such entry was not justified. The Court, however, found this of little or no significance:

> [The magistrate's denial of permission to make a no-knock entry] does not alter the reasonableness of the officers' decision, which must be evaluated as of the time they entered the hotel room. At the time the officers obtained the warrant, they did not have evidence sufficient, in the judgment of the magistrate, to justify a no-knock warrant. Of course, the magistrate could not have anticipated in every particular the circumstances that would confront the officers when they arrived at Richards' hotel room. These actual circumstances * * * justified the officers' ultimate decision to enter without first announcing their presence and authority.

520 U.S. at 395–96, 117 S.Ct. at 1422, 137 L.Ed.2d at 625. Commenting more generally, the Court added:

> A number of States give magistrate judges the authority to issue "no-knock" warrants if the officers demonstrate ahead of time a reasonable suspicion that entry without prior announcement will be appropriate in a particular context.
>
> The practice of allowing magistrates to issue no-knock warrants seems entirely reasonable when sufficient cause to do so can be demonstrated ahead of time. But, as the facts of this case demonstrate, a magistrate's decision not to authorize a no-knock entry should not be interpreted to remove the officers' authority to exercise independent judgment concerning the wisdom of a no-knock entry at the time the warrant is being executed.

520 U.S. at 396 n. 7, 117 S.Ct. at 1422 n. 7, 137 L.Ed.2d at 625 n. 7.

5. **Delay in Execution of a Warrant.** Statutory provisions and court rules often direct that search warrants be executed within specified times of their issuance, and permit the magistrate issuing a warrant to further limit the time for execution. Federal Rule of Criminal Procedure 41(c), for example, mandates that a search warrant "shall command the officer to search, within a specified period of time not to exceed 10 days, the person or place named for the property or person specified."

What is the effect of execution of a warrant beyond such time limits? In Sgro v. United States, 287 U.S. 206, 53 S.Ct. 138, 77 L.Ed.2d 260 (1932), the Supreme Court considered the admissibility of evidence obtained pursuant to a federal search warrant. The warrant was subject to a since-repealed statute directing such warrants be executed within ten days and specifically adding, "[A]fter the expiration of this time the warrant, unless executed, is void." Officers did not execute the warrant within ten days of its initial issuance, but took it back to the issuing magistrate who changed the date on it and "thus reissued [it]." It was executed soon thereafter. An issuing magistrate has no authority to simply and summarily redate a warrant, the Court held, and that was what was done in the case. Thus the redating of the warrant was ineffective. The Court then assumed without discussion execution of the warrant after the expiration of the ten day period required suppression of the evidence obtained.

Does *Sgro* mean the Fourth Amendment somehow incorporates legislatively-mandated timing requirements? Perhaps the language of the statute convinced the Court that Congress intended any evidence obtained by executing a warrant beyond the ten day period be inadmissible—not as a matter of federal constitutional law but as a matter of legislative mandate.

Search warrants may become subject to challenge due to passage of time within generally permissible time periods for execution, such as the ten day window provided for in the federal rule. In United States v. Williams, 10 F.3d 590 (8th

Cir.1993), for example, a warrant for an apartment issued on October 22, 1992, for an apartment. It was based on information from an informant that on that same day the informant saw a kilogram of cocaine, in its original packaging from Colombia, and $25,000.00 in currency inside the apartment. After the warrant was issued, the officer learned from the informant the kilo of cocaine was distributed; the officer therefore did not execute the warrant immediately. On October 29, however, the officer had the informant telephone Williams. The informant learned Williams received another shipment of cocaine. Consequently, the officer executed the warrant at 1:15 a.m. on October 30. Williams contended that the delay in executing the warrant, although within the ten day rule, nevertheless was unreasonable and rendered the search constitutionally unreasonable. By the time of the search, he reasoned, the information on which the warrant was issued was "stale" and failed to establish probable cause to believe that at the time the warrant was executed cocaine was on the premises. "Whether the period of delay between issuance and execution of a warrant is reasonable," the court explained in rejecting this contention, "necessarily depends upon the facts and circumstances of each case." Specifically, a court must consider the nature of the criminal activity involved and the kind of property sought to determine whether the passage of the time so increased the likelihood that the property sought was no longer on the premises. At some point, this likelihood is high enough to destroy the probable cause originally existing. On the facts of *Williams*, the court concluded, the eight day delay did not have this effect:

> [T]he continuing and ongoing nature of cocaine trafficking supports the continued existence of probable cause. It is reasonable for law enforcement officers to conclude that large-scale drug operations continued at the same location for a period of time.

10 F.3d at 595. "[T]he better practice," the court nevertheless acknowledged, would have been for the officer to have obtained a new warrant based on the information obtained on the 29th.

6. **Nighttime Execution.** What if any limits are there upon the time of day or night officers may execute a search warrant, and what are the effects of violating these requirements? Statutes and court rules often require nighttime execution of a warrant be authorized by the issuing magistrate. These provisions sometimes explicitly require any such authorization be supported by information made available to the issuing magistrate. Federal Rule of Criminal Procedure 41(c)(1), for example, provides that "the warrant shall be served in the daytime, unless the issuing authority, by appropriate provision in the warrant, and for reasonable cause shown, authorizes its execution at times other than daytime."

These provisions are construed and applied with varying degrees of vigor. In State v. Richardson, 80 Hawai'i 1, 904 P.2d 886 (1995), the court construed the Hawai'i rule on the assumption that at least a nighttime search of a family-occupied residence might have federal or state constitutional implications. It acknowledged, however, that some courts have indicated to the contrary. Given the importance of limitation on nighttime execution of warrants, the court concluded, judges issuing warrants for nighttime execution must have facts presented to them demonstrating the existence of circumstances justifying a nighttime search before issuing such a warrant. Turning to what might justify a nighttime search, the court explained that one justification might be "reasonable necessity." Such necessity would usually be based upon apprehension that evidence within the place would be removed, hidden or destroyed before morning. It continued:

> [A] nighttime search warrant * * * may also be properly authorized when a nighttime search will not violate the policies that underlie the nighttime search prohibition.

One policy underlying the nighttime search prohibition is protection of the greater expectation of privacy that individuals possess in their homes at night. * * *

In addition * * * "ordinarily a nighttime search would pose a heightened safety risk since people may tend to overreact to an entry by force in the dead of night. Darkness may exacerbate the reaction or heighten the confusion inherent in a search[.]" [State v. Rowe, 806 P.2d 730, 734 n. 5 (Utah App. 1991)]. Thus, the rule against nighttime searches also functions "to avoid the possibility of terror and gunplay which may arise from forcible nighttime entries[.]" [State v. Brock, 294 Or. 15, 19, 653 P.2d 543, 545 (1982).].

Under some circumstances, nighttime searches will not encroach upon either the special privacy interests or the public safety concerns that underlie the nighttime search prohibition. * * *

In the instant case, the affidavit in support of the warrant indicated that sales of crystal methamphetamine were taking place until at least 2:00 a.m., thereby implying that the occupants of the home would neither be asleep nor surprised by a knock at the door until a later hour. * * * Thus, we hold that the authorization for a search until 2:00 a.m. that was given in the instant case was justified because such a search would not conflict with the policies underlying the ordinary prohibition against nighttime searches.

80 Hawai'i at 7–8, 904 P.2d at 892.

In Gooding v. United States, 416 U.S. 430, 94 S.Ct. 1780, 40 L.Ed.2d 250 (1974), the United States Supreme Court took a quite different approach to 21 U.S.C.A. § 879(a), governing execution of certain search warrants for drugs. The statute provides:

A search warrant relating to offenses involving controlled substances may be served at any time of the day or night if the judge or United States magistrate issuing the warrant is satisfied that there is probable cause to believe that grounds exist for the warrant and for its service at this time.

Relying on the legislative history of this statute, the Court held that the statute requires for nighttime execution of a warrant only a showing that the contraband is likely to be on the premises at that time. It does *not* require any showing that nighttime execution is necessary, justified in any sense, or even preferable to daytime execution. Although the majority did not explicitly address whether the Fourth Amendment requires a specific justification for nighttime execution of a search warrant, the Court's failure to mention any such possibility suggests it was not receptive to the argument that any special showing is constitutionally required.

If a warrant is executed in violation of nonconstitutional limits on nighttime searches, exclusion of the resulting evidence may not be required. In State v. Moore, 2 Neb.App. 206, 508 N.W.2d 305 (1993) review overruled, for example, the court held that if the search warrant at issue had been issued in violation of state rule requirements, suppression was required only upon "a showing that there was prejudice in the sense that the search might not have occurred, that the search would not have been so abusive if the rule had been followed, or that there was evidence that the rule was deliberately and intentionally disregarded." Turning to the contention that the evidence before it showed prejudice, the court responded:

[W]e do not find that the search would not have occurred or would not have been so abusive if the search had been during the daytime. There was probable cause for the issuance of a warrant. The warrant was executed at about 9 p.m., not in the middle of the night, but at a time of the year when it is dark before 8 p.m. Moore has not shown that she was prejudiced by the execution of the warrant at approximately 9 p.m. * * *

2 Neb.App. at 212, 508 N.W.2d at 309. Other courts, however, find exclusion required—sometimes with little or no discussion. See State v. Fitch, 255 Neb. 108, 582 N.W.2d 342 (1998), holding that since the affidavit for a search warrant contained no factual basis supporting a nighttime search, issuance of the search warrant authorizing a search "at any time" was "error" and evidence obtained by 10:00 p.m. execution of that warrant had to be suppressed.

C. PARTICULARITY DEMANDED OF WARRANTS AND RELATED LIMITS ON EXECUTION OF WARRANTS

The Fourth Amendment reasonableness of a search or arrest pursuant to a warrant may be affected by the manner in which that search or arrest is carried out as well as by the procedure followed in issuing the warrant. Some, although not all, Fourth Amendment requirements affecting the execution of warrants flow from limits imposed by the terms of the warrants themselves; this is particularly true with regard to search warrants. It is therefore useful to consider together the Fourth Amendment requirements governing what the warrant itself must specify and the often-related requirements applicable to the manner in which officers execute warrants.

In connection with the material in this section, reconsider Horton v. California, 496 U.S. 128, 110 S.Ct. 2301, 110 L.Ed.2d 112 (1990), reprinted in part B(2) of Chapter 2, concerning the right of officers executing a search warrant to seize undescribed items found in "plain view" during the course of the search.

EDITORS' INTRODUCTION: PARTICULARITY AND ITS EFFECT ON EXECUTION OF THE WARRANT

The terms of the Fourth Amendment provide in part that "no Warrants shall issue, but * * * particularly describing the place to be searched, and the persons or things to be seized." Compared to the probable cause requirement for warrant issuance, however, the mandate of particularity in the warrant has received relatively little attention from the Supreme Court. It is clear, however, the particularity requirement is related to the execution of the warrant and is designed to limit the officers' activity under the warrant. Without a warrant describing with precision the place to be searched and the things to be seized, the Court has observed, "officers are free to determine for themselves the extent of their search and the precise objects to be seized." Trupiano v. United States, 334 U.S. 699, 710, 68 S.Ct. 1229, 1235, 92 L.Ed. 1663, 1672 (1948).

The Place to Be Searched. Until the case reprinted in this section, the Supreme Court seldom addressed the requirement that the place to be searched be described with precision. In United States v. Karo, 468 U.S. 705, 104 S.Ct. 3296, 82 L.Ed.2d 530 (1984), however, the Court indirectly considered the scope of this Fourth Amendment demand. The discussion makes clear that the Court regards the precision requirements as having sufficient flexibility to accommodate use of warrants for law enforcement activity other than traditional searches of premises easily described.

In *Karo*, the Government concealed an electronic beeping device in a can of chemicals which was then transferred to Karo; law enforcement officers used the device to trace Karo's movements in his car. Karo contended that the Government's concealment of the device in the car was a search. In response, the Government urged that if this was a search, no valid warrant could be obtained for it because the Government would not be able to describe the "place to be searched" with adequate precision. In fact, it suggested, the very purpose of the use of the beeper was to determine the place to be searched, i.e., the place to which the can of chemicals would be taken. The Court rejected the Government's argument:

> [I]t will still be possible to describe the object into which the beeper is to be placed, the circumstances that led agents to wish to install the beeper, and the length of time for which beeper surveillance is requested. In our view, this information will suffice to permit issuance of a warrant authorizing beeper installation and surveillance.

468 U.S. at 718, 104 S.Ct. at 3305, 82 L.Ed.2d at 543.

Things to Be Seized. As to the purpose of the mandate that "things to be seized" be described with precision in a search warrant, the Court offered:

> The requirement * * * makes general searches under [warrants] impossible and prevents the seizure of one thing under a warrant describing another. As to what is to be taken, nothing is left to the discretion of the officer executing the warrant.

Marron v. United States, 275 U.S. 192, 196, 48 S.Ct. 74, 76, 72 L.Ed. 231, 237 (1927). The Court's comment that officers executing warrants have no discretion as to what is to be seized is, to some extent, incorrect. Under the "plain view seizure rule" (considered in Part B(2) of Chapter 2), officers may sometimes seize items not described in the search warrant if they have probable cause to believe the items are subject to seizure and they come upon the items while searching within the terms of the warrant.

But, as *Marron* suggests, the description of things to be seized may limit the officers' authority to search within the described premises. This is illustrated by Stanley v. Georgia, 394 U.S. 557, 89 S.Ct. 1243, 22 L.Ed.2d 542 (1969). Officers searched Stanley's residence under a warrant authorizing them to search the premises for, and to seize, numerous categories of items related to bookmaking. While searching desk drawers in a bedroom, they discovered three reels of eight millimeter film. Using Stanley's projector and screen, they viewed the films. This screening convinced the officers—apparently with good cause—the films were obscene and, therefore, they seized them. At Stanley's trial for possession of the films, the films were admitted into evidence over his objection. A majority of the Supreme Court reversed Stanley's conviction on other grounds and did not reach the propriety of the officers' actions. Justice Stewart, however, concurred on the ground the officers, by examining the film as they did, had gone beyond their authority to search under the warrant. Consequently, he reasoned, the films had been improperly seized:

> To condone what happened here is to invite a governmental official to use a seemingly precise and legal warrant only as a ticket to get into a man's home, and, once inside, to launch forth upon unconfined searches and indiscriminate seizures as if armed with all the unbridled and illegal power of a general warrant.

394 U.S. at 572, 89 S.Ct. at 1251–52, 22 L.Ed.2d at 553. Under this approach, when did the officers' conduct become improper? Did the warrant authorize them to look into closed desk drawers? Almost certainly so, since the bookmaking items might well have been located there. But did it authorize them to examine the film in such a manner as was necessary to determine its contents? to screen the film as they did? Perhaps this turns upon whether the officers could reasonably have anticipated that this action—examining the film—would enable them to locate and seize those items which the warrant specified.

If the specificity of description of the things to be searched for and seized in a search warrant limits the officers' right to search the premises, this may explain the requirement of specificity. Only a specific warrant can limit the officers to a search of no greater scope or intensity than is necessary to locate the items which the officers have reason to believe are in the premises.

The Court addressed the required specificity in regard to "things." In Stanford v. Texas, 379 U.S. 476, 85 S.Ct. 506, 13 L.Ed.2d 431 (1965), a search warrant was issued listing various materials believed related to the operation of the Communist Party in Texas. The Court invalidated the resulting conviction on the ground the warrant offended the requirement of particularity:

> We need not decide in the present case whether the description of the things to be seized would have been too generalized to pass constitutional muster, had the things been weapons, narcotics or "cases of whiskey." * * * The point is that it was not any contraband of that kind which was ordered to be seized, but literary material—"books, records, pamphlets, cards, receipts, lists, memoranda, pictures, recordings and other written instruments concerning the Communist Party of Texas and the operation of the Communist Party in Texas." The indiscriminate sweep of that language is constitutionally intolerable. To hold otherwise would be false to the terms of the Fourth Amendment, false to its meaning, and false to its history.

379 U.S. at 486, 85 S.Ct. at 512, 13 L.Ed.2d at 437–38.

In Andresen v. Maryland, 427 U.S. 463, 96 S.Ct. 2737, 49 L.Ed.2d 627 (1976), on the other hand, the warrant listed numerous documents believed related to the fraudulent transfer of a specifically described piece of realty. It concluded with authorization to seize "other fruits, instrumentalities and evidence of crime at this [time] unknown." The Court construed this as limited to other evidence relating to the crime committed by transfer of the identified lot. As so construed, it concluded, the warrant did not authorize the officers to conduct a search for evidence of other crimes and, therefore, was sufficiently precise. Andresen did not argue it was constitutionally necessary for the warrant to describe the evidence of the crime more specifically. But he did contend the list of the specified documents constituted a prohibited "general warrant." The Court responded:

> We disagree. Under investigation was a complex real estate scheme whose existence could be proved only by piecing together many bits of evidence. * * * The complexity of an illegal scheme may not be used as a shield to avoid detection when the State has demonstrated probable cause to believe that a crime has been committed and probable cause to believe that evidence of this crime is in the suspect's possession. * * *

427 U.S. at 482 n. 10, 96 S.Ct. at 2749 n. 10, 49 L.Ed.2d at 642–43 n. 10. Apparently, this means that the complexity of a crime under investigation sometimes causes difficulty in predicting in advance of a search what documents would constitute evidence of its commission. *Andresen* seems to hold that this justifies some relaxation of the specificity requirement. The things sought in *Stanford* (or the things that might have been seized under the warrant in that case) were more likely protected by the First Amendment than the items sought in *Andresen*. This may help explain the demand for greater specificity on the facts of *Stanford*.

Persons to Be Seized. The terms of the Fourth Amendment also require that at least certain warrants describe "persons * * * to be seized" with particularity. Presumably, this requirement applies to arrest warrants. When is a person described with sufficient particularity? Is a name sufficient? A name and a date of birth? A physical description without a name? In Visor v. State, 660 S.W.2d 816 (Tex.Crim.App.1983), the arrest warrant described the person to be arrested as an "unknown black female." Holding this aspect of the warrant ineffective, the court observed that to uphold it "would be to approve a general warrant prohibited by the federal constitution."

* * *

The principal case in this section addresses the criterion for determining whether a warrant is sufficiently precise for Fourth Amendment purposes. In addition, however, it considers the demands upon officers who in the process of executing a warrant discover the warrant is not as precise—at least "as applied"—as they previously thought.

Maryland v. Garrison

Supreme Court of the United States, 1987.
480 U.S. 79, 107 S.Ct. 1013, 94 L.Ed.2d 72.

■ JUSTICE STEVENS delivered the opinion of the Court.

Baltimore police officers obtained and executed a warrant to search the person of Lawrence McWebb and "the premises known as 2036 Park Avenue third floor apartment." When the police applied for the warrant and when they conducted the search pursuant to the warrant, they reasonably believed that there was only one apartment on the premises described in the warrant. In fact, the third floor was divided into two apartments, one occupied by McWebb and one by respondent. Before the officers executing the warrant became aware that they were in a separate apartment occupied by respondent, they had discovered the contraband that provided the basis for respondent's conviction for violating Maryland's Controlled Substances Act. The question presented is whether the seizure of that contraband was prohibited by the Fourth Amendment.

The trial court denied respondent's motion to suppress the evidence seized from his apartment, and the Maryland Special Court of Appeals affirmed. The Court of Appeals of Maryland reversed and remanded with instructions to remand the case for a new trial.

There is no question that the warrant was valid and was supported by probable cause. The trial court found, and the two appellate courts did not dispute, that after making a reasonable investigation, including a verification of information obtained from a reliable informant, an exterior examination of the three-story building at 2036 Park Avenue, and an inquiry of the utility company, the officer who obtained the warrant reasonably concluded that there was only one apartment on the third floor and that it was occupied by McWebb. When six Baltimore police officers executed the warrant, they fortuitously encountered McWebb in front of the building and used his key to gain admittance to the first floor hallway and to the locked door at the top of the stairs to the third floor. As they entered the vestibule on the third floor, they encountered respondent, who was standing in the hallway area. The police could see into the interior of both McWebb's apartment to the left and respondent's to the right, for the doors to both were open. Only after respondent's apartment had been entered and heroin, cash, and drug paraphernalia had been found did any of the officers realize that the third floor contained two apartments. As soon as they became aware of that fact, the search was discontinued. All of the officers reasonably believed that they were searching McWebb's apartment. No further search of respondent's apartment was made.

The matter on which there is a difference of opinion concerns the proper interpretation of the warrant. A literal reading of its plain language, as well as the language used in the application for the warrant, indicates that it was intended to authorize a search of the entire third floor.[6] [T]he Court of Appeals[, however,] concluded that the warrant [authorized a search of McWebb's apartment only and thus] did not authorize the search of respondent's apartment and the police had no justification for making a warrantless entry into his premises.

* * *

In our view, the case presents two separate constitutional issues, one concerning the validity of the warrant and the other concerning the

---

6.   The warrant states:

"Affidavit having been made before me by Detective Albert Marcus, Baltimore Police Department, Narcotic Unit, that he has reason to believe that on the person of Lawrence Meril McWebb . . . (and) that on the premises known as 2036 Park Avenue third floor apartment, described as a three story brick dwelling with the numerals 2–0–3–6 affixed to the front of same in the City of Baltimore, there is now being concealed certain property. . . .

You are therefor commanded, with the necessary and proper assistants, to search forthwith the person/premises hereinabove described for the property specified, executing this warrant and making the search. . . ."

reasonableness of the manner in which it was executed. We shall discuss the questions separately.

I

The Warrant Clause of the Fourth Amendment categorically prohibits the issuance of any warrant except one "particularly describing the place to be searched and the persons or things to be seized." The manifest purpose of this particularity requirement was to prevent general searches. By limiting the authorization to search to the specific areas and things for which there is probable cause to search, the requirement ensures that the search will be carefully tailored to its justifications, and will not take on the character of the wide-ranging exploratory searches the Framers intended to prohibit. Thus, the scope of a lawful search is "defined by the object of the search and the places in which there is probable cause to believe that it may be found. Just as probable cause to believe that a stolen lawnmower may be found in a garage will not support a warrant to search an upstairs bedroom, probable cause to believe that undocumented aliens are being transported in a van will not justify a warrantless search of a suitcase."

In this case there is no claim that the "persons or things to be seized" were inadequately described or that there was no probable cause to believe that those things might be found in "the place to be searched" as it was described in the warrant. With the benefit of hindsight, however, we now know that the description of that place was broader than appropriate because it was based on the mistaken belief that there was only one apartment on the third floor of the building at 2036 Park Avenue. The question is whether that factual mistake invalidated a warrant that undoubtedly would have been valid if it had reflected a completely accurate understanding of the building's floor plan. Plainly, if the officers had known, or even if they should have known, that there were two separate dwelling units on the third floor of 2036 Park Avenue, they would have been obligated to exclude respondent's apartment from the scope of the requested warrant. But we must judge the constitutionality of their conduct in light of the information available to them at the time they acted. Those items of evidence that emerge after the warrant is issued have no bearing on whether or not a warrant was validly issued. Just as the discovery of contraband cannot validate a warrant invalid when issued, so is it equally clear that the discovery of facts demonstrating that a valid warrant was unnecessarily broad does not retroactively invalidate the warrant. The validity of the warrant must be assessed on the basis of the information that the officers disclosed, or had a duty to discover and to disclose, to the issuing magistrate.[7] On the basis of that information, we

---

7. Arguments can certainly be made that the police in this case should have been able to ascertain that there was more than one apartment on the third floor of this building. It contained seven separate dwelling units and it was surely possible that two of them might be on the third floor. But the record also establishes that Officer Marcus made specific inquiries to determine the iden-

tity of the occupants of the third floor premises. The officer went to 2036 Park Avenue and found that it matched the description given by the informant: a three-story brick dwelling with the numerals 2-0-3-6 affixed to the front of the premises. The officer "made a check with the Baltimore Gas and Electric Company and discovered that the premises of 2036 Park Ave. third floor was in agree with the conclusion of all three Maryland courts that the warrant, insofar as it authorized a search that turned out to be ambiguous in scope, was valid when it issued.

II

The question whether the execution of the warrant violated respondent's constitutional right to be secure in his home is somewhat less clear. We have no difficulty concluding that the officers' entry into the third-floor common area was legal; they carried a warrant for those premises, and they were accompanied by McWebb, who provided the key that they used to open the door giving access to the thirdfloor common area. If the officers had known, or should have known, that the third floor contained two apartments before they entered the living quarters on the third floor, and thus had been aware of the error in the warrant, they would have been obligated to limit their search to McWebb's apartment. Moreover, as the officers recognized, they were required to discontinue the search of respondent's apartment as soon as they discovered that there were two separate units on the third floor and therefore were put on notice of the risk that they might be in a unit erroneously included within the terms of the warrant. The officers' conduct and the limits of the search were based on the information available as the search proceeded. While the purposes justifying a police search strictly limit the permissible extent of the search, the Court has also recognized the need to allow some latitude for honest mistakes that are made by officers in the dangerous and difficult process of making arrests and executing search warrants.

In Hill v. California, 401 U.S. 797, 91 S.Ct. 1106, 28 L.Ed.2d 484 (1971), we considered the validity of the arrest of a man named Miller based on the mistaken belief that he was Hill. The police had probable cause to arrest Hill and they in good faith believed that Miller was Hill when they found him in Hill's apartment. As we explained:

> "The upshot was that the officers in good faith believed Miller was Hill and arrested him. They were quite wrong as it turned out, and subjective good-faith belief would not in itself justify either the arrest or the subsequent search. But sufficient probability, not certainty, is the touchstone of reasonableness under the Fourth Amendment and on the record before us the officers' mistake was understandable and the arrest a reasonable response to the situation facing them at the time."

While *Hill* involved an arrest without a warrant, its underlying rationale that an officer's reasonable misidentification of a person does not invalidate a valid arrest is equally applicable to an officer's reasonable

the name of Lawrence McWebb." Officer Marcus testified at the suppression hearing that he inquired of the Baltimore Gas and Electric Company in whose name the third floor apartment was listed: "I asked if there is a front or rear or middle room. They told me, one third floor was only listed to Lawrence McWebb." The officer also discovered from a check with the Baltimore police department that the police records of Lawrence McWebb matched the address and physical description given by the informant. The Maryland courts that are presumptively familiar with local conditions were unanimous in concluding that the officer reasonably believed McWebb was the only tenant on that floor. Because the evidence supports their conclusion, we accept that conclusion for the purpose of our decision.

failure to appreciate that a valid warrant describes too broadly the premises to be searched. Under the reasoning in *Hill,* the validity of the search of respondent's apartment pursuant to a warrant authorizing the search of the entire third floor depends on whether the officers' failure to realize the overbreadth of the warrant was objectively understandable and reasonable. Here it unquestionably was. The objective facts available to the officers at the time suggested no distinction between McWebb's apartment and the third-floor premises.[8]

For that reason, the officers properly responded to the command contained in a valid warrant even if the warrant is interpreted as authorizing a search limited to McWebb's apartment rather than the entire third floor. Prior to the officers' discovery of the factual mistake, they perceived McWebb's apartment and the third-floor premises as one and the same; therefore their execution of the warrant reasonably included the entire third floor.[9] Under either interpretation of the warrant, the officers' conduct was consistent with a reasonable effort to ascertain and identify the place intended to be searched within the meaning of the Fourth Amendment.

The judgment of the Court of Appeals is reversed, and the case is remanded for further proceedings not inconsistent with this opinion.

It is so ordered.

■ JUSTICE BLACKMUN, with whom JUSTICE BRENNAN and JUSTICE MARSHALL join, dissenting.

* * *

I

* * *

* * * The words of the warrant were plain and distinctive: the warrant directed the officers to seize marijuana and drug paraphernalia on the person of McWebb and in McWebb's apartment, i.e., "on the premises known as 2036 Park Avenue third floor apartment." * * * Accordingly, * * * the warrant was limited in its description to the third floor apartment of McWebb, then the search of an additional apartment—respondent's—was warrantless and is presumed unreasonable "in the absence of some one of a number of well defined 'exigent circumstances.' " Because the State has not advanced any such exception to the warrant requirement,

---

8. Nothing McWebb did or said after he was detained outside 2036 Park Avenue would have suggested to the police that there were two apartments on the third floor. McWebb provided the key that opened the doors on the first floor and on the third floor. The police could reasonably have believed that McWebb was admitting them to an undivided apartment on the third floor. When the officers entered the foyer on the third floor, neither McWebb nor Garrison informed them that they lived in separate apartments.

9. We expressly distinguish the facts of this case from a situation in which the police know there are two apartments on a certain floor of a building, and have probable cause to believe that drugs are being sold out of that floor, but do not know in which of the two apartments the illegal transactions are taking place. A search pursuant to a warrant authorizing a search of the entire floor under those circumstances would present quite different issues from the ones before us in this case.

the evidence obtained as a result of this search should have been excluded.[10]

II

[T]he Court * * * analyzes the police conduct here in terms of "mistake." * * * [But even if] there is no Fourth Amendment violation where the officers' mistake is reasonable, it is questionable whether that standard was met in this case. The "place" at issue here is a small multiple-occupancy building. Such forms of habitation are now common in this country, particularly in neighborhoods with changing populations and of declining affluence. Accordingly, any analysis of the "reasonableness" of the officers' behavior here must be done with this context in mind.

The efforts of Detective Marcus, the officer who procured the search warrant, do not meet a standard of reasonableness, particularly considering that the detective knew the search concerned a unit in a multiple-occupancy building. Upon learning from his informant that McWebb was selling marijuana in his third floor apartment, Marcus inspected the outside of the building. He did not approach it, however, to gather information about the configuration of the apartments. Had he done so, he would have discovered, as did another officer on the day of executing the warrant, that there were seven separate mailboxes and bells on the porch outside the main entrance to the house. Although there is some dispute over whether names were affixed near these boxes and bells, their existence alone puts a reasonable observer on notice that the three-story structure (with, possibly, a basement) had seven individual units. The detective, therefore, should have been aware that further investigation was necessary to eliminate the possibility of more than one unit's being located on the third floor. Moreover, when Detective Marcus' informant told him that he had purchased drugs in McWebb's apartment, it appears that the detective never thought to ask the informant whether McWebb's apartment was the only one on the third floor. These efforts, which would have placed a slight burden upon the detective, are necessary in order to render reasonable the officer's behavior in seeking the warrant.

Moreover, even if one believed that Marcus' efforts in providing information for issuance of the warrant were reasonable, I doubt whether the officers' execution of the warrant could meet such a standard. * * *

In my view, * * * the "objective facts" should have made the officers aware that there were two different apartments on the third floor well

---

10. If the officers were confused about the residence of respondent when they encountered him in the third floor vestibule * * *, they might have been justified in detaining him temporarily as an occupant of McWebb's apartment. The officers asserted that, upon entering the vestibule, they observed marijuana lying upon a dresser in respondent's bedroom, the door to respondent's apartment being open. Although it is not entirely clear that the drug could have been seized immediately under the "plain view" exception to the warrant requirement, for this would depend upon whether the officers' "access to the object has some prior Fourth Amendment justification," the officers probably would have had probable cause to obtain a search warrant and conceivably could have impounded respondent's apartment while seeking the warrant. Nothing, however, justified the full-scale search of respondent's apartment in which the officers engaged.

before they discovered the incriminating evidence in respondent's apartment. Before McWebb happened to drive up while the search party was preparing to execute the warrant, one of the officers, Detective Shea, somewhat disguised as a construction worker, was already on the porch of the row house and was seeking to gain access to the locked first-floor door that permitted entrance into the building. From this vantage point he had time to observe the seven mailboxes and bells; indeed, he rang all seven bells, apparently in an effort to summon some resident to open the front door to the search party. A reasonable officer in Detective Shea's position, already aware that this was a multiunit building and now armed with further knowledge of the number of units in the structure, would have conducted at that time more investigation to specify the exact location of McWebb's apartment before proceeding further. For example, he might have questioned another resident of the building.

It is surprising, moreover, that the Court places so much emphasis on the failure of McWebb to volunteer information about the exact location of his apartment. * * * [I]t would * * * have been reasonable for the officers, aware of the problem, from Detective Shea's discovery, in the specificity of their warrant, to ask McWebb whether his apartment was the only one on the third floor. As it is, the officers made several requests of and questioned McWebb, * * * and yet failed to ask him the question, obvious in the circumstances, concerning the exact location of his apartment.

Moreover, a reasonable officer would have realized the mistake in the warrant during the moments following the officers' entrance to the third floor. The officers gained access to the vestibule separating McWebb's and respondent's apartments through a locked door for which McWebb supplied the key. There, in the open doorway to his apartment, they encountered respondent, clad in pajamas and wearing a halfbody cast as a result of a recent spinal operation. Although the facts concerning what next occurred are somewhat in dispute, it appears that respondent, together with McWebb and the passenger from McWebb's car, were shepherded into McWebb's apartment across the vestibule from his own. Once again, the officers were curiously silent. The informant had not led the officers to believe that anyone other than McWebb lived in the third-floor apartment; the search party had McWebb, the person targeted by the search warrant, in custody when it gained access to the vestibule; yet when they met respondent on the third floor, they simply asked him who he was but never where he lived. Had they done so, it is likely that they would have discovered the mistake in the warrant before they began their search.

Finally and most importantly, even if the officers had learned nothing from respondent, they should have realized the error in the warrant from their initial security sweep. Once on the third floor, the officers first fanned out through the rooms to conduct a preliminary check for other occupants who might pose a danger to them. * * * [T]he two apartments were almost a mirror image of each other—each had a bathroom, a kitchen, a living room, and a bedroom. Given the somewhat symmetrical layout of the apartments, it is difficult to imagine that, in the initial security sweep, a reasonable officer would not have discerned that two apartments were on the third floor, realized his mistake, and then confined the ensuing search to McWebb's residence.

Accordingly, even if a reasonable error on the part of police officers prevents a Fourth Amendment violation, the mistakes here, both with respect to obtaining and executing the warrant, are not reasonable and could easily have been avoided.

I respectfully dissent.

NOTES

1. **Search of Persons on Premises.** The extent to which a search warrant does and can authorize officers to search persons on the premises to be searched pursuant to a warrant was addressed in Ybarra v. Illinois, 444 U.S. 85, 100 S.Ct. 338, 62 L.Ed.2d 238 (1979). In support of the warrant application, officers recounted an informant's tip that he had observed tinfoil packets on the person of "Greg," bartender at the Aurora Tap Tavern, and behind the bar. He also previously observed such packets in the same places. The informant knew from experience that such tinfoil packets are a common method of packaging heroin. In addition, Greg told the informant that he would have heroin for sale on March 1. A warrant was obtained authorizing the search of "the Aurora Tap Tavern" and "the person of 'Greg,' the bartender," for controlled substances. An Illinois statute purported to authorize officers executing a search warrant to detain and search "any person in the place at the time" either to protect themselves from attack or to prevent disposal or concealment of items described in the warrant. Ill.Rev.Stat., ch. 38, section 108–9. When, on March 1, the warrant was executed, Ybarra was one of about a dozen persons in the bar. He was first "frisked" and then more thoroughly searched. Drugs were found. Addressing the officers' right under the warrant to search Ybarra, the Court first indicated the warrant did not authorize such a search given the specific authorization to search the person of "Greg:"

> Had the issuing judge intended that the warrant would or could authorize a search of every person found within the tavern, he would hardly have specifically authorized the search of "Greg" alone. "Greg" was an employee of the tavern, and the complaint upon which the search warrant was issued gave every indication that he would be present at the tavern on March 1.

444 U.S. at 90 n. 2, 100 S.Ct. at 342 n. 2, 62 L.Ed.2d at 245 n. 2. It then suggested the warrant *could not* constitutionally be read as authorizing such a search. The officers' probable cause, the Court stressed, did not extend to Ybarra and others like him. Moreover:

> The Fourth Amendment directs that "no Warrants shall issue, but upon probable cause . . . and particularly describing the place to be searched, and the persons or things to be seized." Thus, "open-ended" or "general" warrants are constitutionally prohibited. It follows that a warrant to search a place cannot normally be construed to authorize a search of each individual in that place. The warrant for the Aurora Tap Tavern provided no basis for departing from this general rule. Consequently, we need not consider situations where the warrant itself authorizes the search of unnamed persons in a place and is supported by probable cause to believe that persons who will be in the place at the time of the search will be in possession of illegal drugs.

444 U.S. at 92 n. 4, 100 S.Ct. at 342 n. 4, 62 L.Ed.2d at 246 n. 4.

Finally, the prosecution asked that the Court recognize a "new" exception to the warrant requirement:

to permit evidence searches of persons who, at the commencement of the search, are on "compact" premises subject to a search warrant, at least where the police have a "reasonable belief" that such persons "are connected with" drug trafficking and "may be concealing or carrying away the contraband."

Rejecting this request, the Court explained the "long-prevailing" standard of probable cause embodies the appropriate compromise between citizens' interests and law enforcement; the Court was unprepared to deviate from that standard in this situation.

The State also defended the first frisk of Ybarra as a permissible weapons search under Terry v. Ohio, 392 U.S. 1, 88 S.Ct. 1868, 20 L.Ed.2d 889 (1968). This aspect of the case is discussed in Chapter 4.

2. **Detention of Persons "Associated With" Premises.** In some situations, a warrant may authorize the detention of persons associated with the searched premises. Should the limitations on searching persons present when a search warrant is executed apply to the occupants of a private residence being searched?

In Michigan v. Summers, 452 U.S. 692, 101 S.Ct. 2587, 69 L.Ed.2d 340 (1981), law officers were approaching Summers' home to execute a search warrant for contraband when they observed him leave the residence. They detained him while the home was searched. When the search revealed narcotics, they arrested Summers, whom they knew owned the premises, and searched his person, finding still more narcotics. He was prosecuted for possession of the drugs found on his person. The state argued the authority to search premises granted by the warrant implicitly included the authority to search persons on those premises, just as that authority included authorization to search furniture and containers in which the particular things described might be concealed. But the Court, in an opinion authored by Justice Stevens, did not rule on that contention because it found the search warrant implicitly authorized the temporary detention of Summers while the search was conducted and that the discovery of the contraband in respondent's home gave the police authority to arrest him for its possession. The search of his person was justified as a search incident to his lawful arrest. Justices Stewart, Brennan and Marshall dissented.

3. **Permitting News Media Coverage.** What if any Fourth Amendment significance arises from officers' permitting media members to accompany them when executing a warrant?

In Wilson v. Layne, 526 U.S. 603, 119 S.Ct. 1692, 143 L.Ed.2d 818 (1999), federal marshals with an arrest warrant for Dominic Wilson entered a residence in Rockville, Maryland listed on a computer as Wilson's home. In fact, this was the residence of Wilson's parents, Charles and Geraldine Wilson. The marshals were accompanied by a reporter and a photographer from the Washington Post, invited by the marshals to accompany them as part of a ride-along program. The Supreme Court described the events:

> At around 6:45 a.m., the officers, with media representatives in tow, entered the dwelling * * *. Petitioners Charles and Geraldine Wilson were still in bed when they heard the officers enter the home. Petitioner Charles Wilson, dressed only in a pair of briefs, ran into the living room to investigate. Discovering at least five men in street clothes with guns in his living room, he angrily demanded that they state their business, and repeatedly cursed the officers. Believing him to be an angry Dominic Wilson, the officers quickly subdued him on the floor. Geraldine Wilson next entered the living room to investigate, wearing only a nightgown. She observed her husband being restrained by the armed officers.

When their protective sweep was completed, the officers learned that Dominic Wilson was not in the house, and they departed. During the time that the officers were in the home, the Washington Post photographer took numerous pictures. The print reporter was also apparently in the living room observing the confrontation between the police and Charles Wilson. At no time, however, were the reporters involved in the execution of the arrest warrant. The Washington Post never published its photographs of the incident.

The Wilsons sued the marshals for money damages, contending the marshals' actions violated their Fourth Amendment rights. The federal District Court denied the defendant marshals' motion for summary judgment. On review, the Supreme Court first considered whether the marshals' actions violated the Wilsons' Fourth Amendment rights:

[T]he officers had * * * a[n arrest] warrant, and they were undoubtedly entitled to enter the Wilson home in order to execute the arrest warrant for Dominic Wilson. But it does not necessarily follow that they were entitled to bring a newspaper reporter and a photographer with them. In Horton v. California, 496 U.S. 128, 140, 110 S.Ct. 2301, 110 L.Ed.2d 112 (1990), we held "[i]f the scope of the search exceeds that permitted by the terms of a validly issued warrant or the character of the relevant exception from the warrant requirement, the subsequent seizure is unconstitutional without more." While this does not mean that every police action while inside a home must be explicitly authorized by the text of the warrant, the Fourth Amendment does require that police actions in execution of a warrant be related to the objectives of the authorized intrusion.

Certainly the presence of reporters inside the home was not related to the objectives of the authorized intrusion. Respondents concede that the reporters did not engage in the execution of the warrant, and did not assist the police in their task. The reporters therefore were not present for any reason related to the justification for police entry into the home the apprehension of Dominic Wilson.

* * *

[I]t is a violation of the Fourth Amendment for police to bring members of the media or other third parties into a home during the execution of a warrant when the presence of the third parties in the home was not in aid of the execution of the warrant.

526 U.S. at ___, 119 S.Ct. at 1697–99, 143 L.Ed.2d at 828–30. It added:

Even though such actions might violate the Fourth Amendment, if the police are lawfully present, the violation of the Fourth Amendment is the presence of the media and not the presence of the police in the home. We have no occasion here to decide whether the exclusionary rule would apply to any evidence discovered or developed by the media representatives.

526 U.S. at ___ n. 2, 119 S.Ct. at 1699 n. 2, 143 L.Ed.2d at 830 n. 2.

CHAPTER 4

Detentions of Persons and Related Searches

Analysis

EDITORS' INTRODUCTION: DETENTIONS, SEIZURES AND THEIR CHARACTERIZATION

This chapter addresses law enforcement detentions of persons suspected of crime—"seizures" of the person in the language of the Fourth Amendment—and related searches. An lawful detention may, in theory at least, create civil or possibly even criminal liability on the part of the officer. In most circumstances, however, the legality of an arrest or other detention is of practical significance only if it is accompanied by or leads to a search yielding incriminating evidence. Should such evidence be offered against the suspect at trial and challenged, its admissibility is often affected by the validity of the detention.

At one time, all detentions were regarded as indistinguishable from one another and characterized as arrests. This is no longer the case. Case law, much of it involving the Fourth Amendment requirement that "seizures" of the person be "reasonable," distinguishes a variety of detentions. Given the different requirements that have developed for different detentions and the variation in the searches that can be made in relation to different types of detentions, how a detention is characterized is often important. See generally, LaFave, "Seizures" Typology: Classifying Detentions of the Person To Resolve Warrant, Grounds, and Search Issues, 17 U.Mich.J.L.Reform 417 (1984).

This chapter begins with the problem of determining whether any detention at all has occurred. It then considers detentions or seizures constituting "arrests," the benchmark of Fourth Amendment analysis in this area. After this, it addresses field detentions for investigation—so-called *"Terry"* stops—and the right to make weapon searches where no arrest has occurred. Next, the chapter considers certain non-arrest detentions of persons in automobiles. The following section deals with traffic stops, detentions arguably different from both arrests and field detentions. Finally, attention turns to roadblock stops and the "pretext" issue—whether an otherwise proper arrest or detention can be challenged on the basis of the officer's subjective "intent" or on the basis of what a reasonable officer would do in the situation.

A. DETERMINING WHETHER A PERSON IS DETAINED OR SEIZED

EDITORS' INTRODUCTION: DEFINING "SEIZURES" OF THE PERSON

Whether confrontations between police officers and suspects involve "seizures" as that term is used in the Fourth Amendment has long presented a difficult problem. Until the principal case, the Supreme Court's case law appeared to indicate that whether a seizure occurred depended upon how a reasonable person would react to the officer's actions.

In 1984, the Court indicated that "police questioning, by itself" is unlikely to result in a seizure. Only if an officer, "by means of physical force or show of authority," restrains a person's liberty has the person been seized. An officer seizes a person by approaching him and posing questions, therefore, only if "the circumstances of the encounter are so intimidating as to demonstrate that a reasonable person would have believed he was not free to leave if he [did not respond]." Immigration and Naturalization Service v. Delgado, 466 U.S. 210, 216, 104 S.Ct. 1758, 1762, 80 L.Ed.2d 247, 255 (1984).

The standard was applied in Michigan v. Chesternut, 486 U.S. 567, 108 S.Ct. 1975, 100 L.Ed.2d 565 (1988). Four Detroit officers were engaged in routine patrol in a marked police cruiser. As the cruiser came to an intersection, one officer saw a car pull over to the curb and an occupant alight. This person approached Chesternut, standing alone on the corner. Chesternut saw the cruiser as it approached; he immediately turned and ran. The cruiser caught up with him and drove alongside him for a short distance. During this time, the officers observed Chesternut pull several packets from his pocket and discard them. Chesternut then stopped and one officer examined the discarded packets. Concluding that the packets contained codeine, the officers placed Chesternut under arrest. A search revealed other drugs, including heroin. After Chesternut was charged with drug offenses, a magistrate held he had been unlawfully seized before he discarded the codeine. This holding was affirmed on appeal in reliance upon state court holdings that any police pursuit was a seizure. Since the officers did not have reasonable suspicion when their pursuit of Chesternut began, the state courts reasoned, their seizure of him was unreasonable.

A unanimous Supreme Court reversed. Justice Blackmun, writing for the Court, rejected both the position that any pursuit is a seizure and the view that no seizure can occur until and if the officer actually apprehends the person. Instead, he indicated, the Court would continue to apply its traditional "contextual approach." Under this approach, "the police can be said to have seized an individual 'only if, in view of all of the circumstances surrounding the incident, a reasonable person would have believed that he was not free to leave.' "Applying this standard, the Court found no seizure occurred before Chesternut discarded the packets:

> [T]he police conduct involved here would not have communicated to the reasonable person an attempt to capture or otherwise intrude upon [the person's] freedom of movement. The record does not reflect that the police activated a siren or flashers; or that they commanded [Chesternut] to halt, or displayed any weapons; or that they operated the car in an aggressive manner to block [Chesternut's] course or otherwise control the direction or speed of his movement. While the very presence of a police car driving parallel to a running pedestrian could be somewhat intimidating, this kind of police presence does not, standing alone, constitute a seizure.

486 U.S. at 575, 108 S.Ct. at 1980, 100 L.Ed.2d at 573. Consequently, the prosecution was not required to establish the reasonableness of the officers' actions prior to Chesternut's discarding of the packets.

California v. Hodari D.

Supreme Court of the United States, 1991.
499 U.S. 621, 111 S.Ct. 1547, 113 L.Ed.2d 690.

■ JUSTICE SCALIA delivered the opinion of the Court.

Late one evening in April 1988, Officers Brian McColgin and Jerry Pertoso were on patrol in a high-crime area of Oakland, California. They were dressed in street clothes but wearing jackets with "Police" embossed on both front and back. Their unmarked car proceeded west on Foothill Boulevard, and turned south onto 63rd Avenue. As they rounded the corner, they saw four or five youths huddled around a small red car parked at the curb. When the youths saw the officers' car approaching they apparently panicked, and took flight. The respondent here, Hodari D., and one companion ran west through an alley; the others fled south. The red car also headed south, at a high rate of speed.

The officers were suspicious and gave chase. McColgin remained in the car and continued south on 63rd Avenue; Pertoso left the car, ran back north along 63rd, then west on Foothill Boulevard, and turned south on 62nd Avenue. Hodari, meanwhile, emerged from the alley onto 62nd and ran north. Looking behind as he ran, he did not turn and see Pertoso until the officer was almost upon him, whereupon he tossed away what appeared to be a small rock. A moment later, Pertoso tackled Hodari, handcuffed him, and radioed for assistance. Hodari was found to be carrying $130 in cash and a pager; and the rock he had discarded was found to be crack cocaine.

In the juvenile proceeding brought against him, Hodari moved to suppress the evidence relating to the cocaine. The court denied the motion without opinion. The California Court of Appeal reversed, holding that Hodari had been "seized" when he saw Officer Pertoso running towards him, that this seizure was unreasonable under the Fourth Amendment, and that the evidence of cocaine had to be suppressed as the fruit of that illegal seizure. The California Supreme Court denied the State's application for review. We granted certiorari.

As this case comes to us, the only issue presented is whether, at the time he dropped the drugs, Hodari had been "seized" within the meaning of the Fourth Amendment. If so, respondent argues, the drugs were the fruit of that seizure and the evidence concerning them was properly excluded. If not, the drugs were abandoned by Hodari and lawfully recovered by the police, and the evidence should have been admitted. * * *

We have long understood that the Fourth Amendment's protection against "unreasonable . . . seizures" includes seizure of the person. From the time of the founding to the present, the word "seizure" has meant a "taking possession," 2 N. Webster, An American Dictionary of the English Language 67 (1828). For most purposes at common law, the word connoted not merely grasping, or applying physical force to, the animate or inanimate object in question, but actually bringing it within physical control. * * * To constitute an arrest, however—the quintessential "seizure of the person" under our Fourth Amendment jurisprudence—the mere grasping or application of physical force with lawful authority, whether or not it succeeded in subduing the arrestee, was sufficient. See, e.g., Whithead v. Keyes, 85 Mass. 495, 501 (1862) ("[A]n officer effects an arrest of a person whom he has authority to arrest, by laying his hand on him for the purpose of arresting him, though he may not succeed in stopping and holding him"). * * *

To say that an arrest is effected by the slightest application of physical force, despite the arrestee's escape, is not to say that for Fourth Amendment purposes there is a continuing arrest during the period of fugitivity. If, for example, Pertoso had laid his hands upon Hodari to arrest him, but Hodari had broken away and had then cast away the cocaine, it would hardly be realistic to say that that disclosure had been made during the course of an arrest. The present case, however, is even one step further removed. It does not involve the application of any physical force; Hodari was untouched by Officer Pertoso at the time he discarded the cocaine. His defense relies instead upon the proposition that a seizure occurs "when the officer, by means of physical force *or show of authority*, has in some way restrained the liberty of a citizen." Terry v. Ohio, 392 U.S. 1, 19, n. 16, 88 S.Ct. 1868, 1879, n. 16, 20 L.Ed.2d 889 (1968) (emphasis added). Hodari contends (and we accept as true for purposes of this decision) that Pertoso's pursuit qualified as a "show of authority" calling upon Hodari to halt. The narrow question before us is whether, with respect to a show of authority as with respect to application of physical force, a seizure occurs even though the subject does not yield. We hold that it does not.

The language of the Fourth Amendment, of course, cannot sustain respondent's contention. The word "seizure" readily bears the meaning of a laying on of hands or application of physical force to restrain movement, even when it is ultimately unsuccessful. ("She seized the purse-snatcher, but he broke out of her grasp.") It does not remotely apply, however, to the prospect of a policeman yelling "Stop, in the name of the law!" at a fleeing form that continues to flee. That is no seizure. Nor can the result respondent wishes to achieve be produced—indirectly, as it were—by suggesting that Pertoso's uncomplied-with show of authority was a common-law arrest, and then appealing to the principle that all common-law arrests are seizures. An arrest requires either physical force (as described above) or, where that is absent, submission to the assertion of authority.

* * *

We do not think it desirable, even as a policy matter, to stretch the Fourth Amendment beyond its words and beyond the meaning of arrest, as respondent urges. Street pursuits always place the public at some risk, and compliance with police orders to stop should therefore be encouraged. Only a few of those orders, we must presume, will be without adequate basis, and since the addressee has no ready means of identifying the deficient ones it almost invariably is the responsible course to comply. Unlawful orders will not be deterred, moreover, by sanctioning through the exclusionary rule those of them that are not obeyed. Since policemen do not command "Stop!" expecting to be ignored, or give chase hoping to be outrun, it fully suffices to apply the deterrent to their genuine, successful seizures.

Respondent contends that his position is sustained by the so-called *Mendenhall* test, formulated by Justice Stewart's opinion in United States v. Mendenhall, 446 U.S. 544, 554, 100 S.Ct. 1870, 1877, 64 L.Ed.2d 497 (1980), and adopted by the Court in later cases: "[A] person has been 'seized' within the meaning of the Fourth Amendment only if, in view of all the circumstances surrounding the incident, a reasonable person would have believed that he was not free to leave." In seeking to rely upon that test here, respondent fails to read it carefully. It says that a person has been seized "only if," not that he has been seized "whenever"; it states a necessary, but not a sufficient, condition for seizure—or, more precisely, for seizure effected through a "show of authority." *Mendenhall* establishes that the test for existence of a "show of authority" is an objective one: not whether the citizen perceived that he was being ordered to restrict his movement, but whether the officer's words and actions would have conveyed that to a reasonable person. Application of this objective test was the basis for our decision in the other case principally relied upon by respondent, [Michigan v. Chesternut, 486 U.S. 567, 108 S.Ct. 1975, 100 L.Ed.2d 565 (1988)], where we concluded that the police cruiser's slow following of the defendant did not convey the message that he was not free to disregard the police and go about his business. We did not address in *Chesternut,* however, the question whether, if the *Mendenhall* test was met—if the message that the defendant was not free to leave had been conveyed—a Fourth Amendment seizure would have occurred.

Quite relevant to the present case, however, was our decision in Brower v. Inyo County, 489 U.S. 593, 596, 109 S.Ct. 1378, 1381, 103 L.Ed.2d 628 (1989). In that case, police cars with flashing lights had chased the decedent for 20 miles—surely an adequate "show of authority"—but he did not stop until his fatal crash into a police-erected blockade. The issue was whether his death could be held to be the consequence of an unreasonable seizure in violation of the Fourth Amendment. We did not even consider the possibility that a seizure could have occurred during the course of the chase because, as we explained, that "show of authority" did not produce his stop. * * *

In sum, assuming that Pertoso's pursuit in the present case constituted a "show of authority" enjoining Hodari to halt, since Hodari did not comply with that injunction he was not seized until he was tackled. The cocaine abandoned while he was running was in this case not the fruit of a seizure, and his motion to exclude evidence of it was properly denied. We reverse the decision of the California Court of Appeal, and remand for further proceedings not inconsistent with this opinion.

It is so ordered.

■ JUSTICE STEVENS, with whom JUSTICE MARSHALL joins, dissenting.

* * *

The first question * * * is whether the common law should define the scope of the outer boundaries of the constitutional protection against unreasonable seizures. Even if, contrary to settled precedent, traditional common-law analysis were controlling, it would still be necessary to decide whether the unlawful attempt to make an arrest should be considered a seizure within the meaning of the Fourth Amendment, and whether the exclusionary rule should apply to unlawful attempts.

* * *

Whatever else one may think of today's decision, it unquestionably represents a departure from earlier Fourth Amendment case law. * * *

Because the facts of this case are somewhat unusual, it is appropriate to note that the same issue would arise if the show of force took the form of a command to "freeze," a warning shot, or the sound of sirens accompanied by a patrol car's flashing lights. In any of these situations, there may be a significant time interval between the initiation of the officer's show of force and the complete submission by the citizen. At least on the facts of this case, the Court concludes that the timing of the seizure is governed by the citizen's reaction, rather than by the officer's conduct. One consequence of this conclusion is that the point at which the interaction between citizen and police officer becomes a seizure occurs, not when a reasonable citizen believes he or she is no longer free to go, but, rather, only after the officer exercises control over the citizen.

In my view, our interests in effective law enforcement and in personal liberty would be better served by adhering to a standard that "allows the police to determine in advance whether the conduct contemplated will implicate the Fourth Amendment." The range of possible responses to a police show of force, and the multitude of problems that may arise in determining whether, and at which moment, there has been "submission," can only create uncertainty and generate litigation.

* * *

It seems equally clear to me that the constitutionality of a police officer's show of force should be measured by the conditions that exist at the time of the officer's action. A search must be justified on the basis of the facts available at the time it is initiated; the subsequent discovery of evidence does not retroactively validate an unconstitutional search. The same approach should apply to seizures; the character of the citizen's response should not govern the constitutionality of the officer's conduct.

If an officer effects an arrest by touching a citizen, apparently the Court would accept the fact that a seizure occurred, even if the arrestee should thereafter break loose and flee. In such a case, the constitutionality of the seizure would be evaluated as of the time the officer acted. That category of seizures would then be analyzed in the same way as searches, namely, was the police action justified when it took place? It is anomalous, at best, to fashion a different rule for the subcategory of "show of force" arrests.

In cases within this new subcategory, there will be a period of time during which the citizen's liberty has been restrained, but he or she has not yet completely submitted to the show of force. A motorist pulled over by a highway patrol car cannot come to an immediate stop, even if the motorist intends to obey the patrol car's signal. If an officer decides to make the kind of random stop forbidden by Delaware v. Prouse, 440 U.S. 648, 99 S.Ct. 1391, 59 L.Ed.2d 660 (1979), and, after flashing his lights, but before the vehicle comes to a complete stop, sees that the license plate has expired, can he justify his action on the ground that the seizure became lawful after it was initiated but before it was completed? In an airport setting, may a drug enforcement agent now approach a group of passengers with his gun drawn, announce a "baggage search," and rely on the passengers' reactions to justify his investigative stops? The holding of today's majority fails to recognize the coercive and intimidating nature of such behavior and creates a rule that may allow such behavior to go unchecked.

The deterrent purposes of the exclusionary rule focus on the conduct of law enforcement officers and on discouraging improper behavior on their part, and not on the reaction of the citizen to the show of force. In the present case, if Officer Pertoso had succeeded in tackling respondent before he dropped the rock of cocaine, the rock unquestionably would have been excluded as the fruit of the officer's unlawful seizure. Instead, under the Court's logic-chopping analysis, the exclusionary rule has no application because an attempt to make an unconstitutional seizure is beyond the coverage of the Fourth Amendment, no matter how outrageous or unreasonable the officer's conduct may be.

It is too early to know the consequences of the Court's holding. If carried to its logical conclusion, it will encourage unlawful displays of force that will frighten countless innocent citizens into surrendering whatever privacy rights they may still have. * * *

I respectfully dissent.

NOTE: SEIZURE OF A STATIONARY SUSPECT

Whether a person approached while stationary has been seized presents a somewhat different question. Florida v. Bostick, 501 U.S. 429, 111 S.Ct. 2382, 115 L.Ed.2d 389 (1991), presented the issue in the context of "bus sweeps." Bostick was prosecuted for possession of cocaine found in his luggage; his motion to suppress the cocaine was overruled. The basic facts were as follows:

> Two officers, complete with badges, insignia and one of them holding a recognizable zipper pouch, containing a pistol, boarded a bus bound from Miami to Atlanta during a stopover in Fort Lauderdale. Eyeing the passengers, the officers admittedly without articulable suspicion, picked out the defendant passenger and asked to inspect his ticket and identification. The ticket, from Miami to Atlanta, matched the defendant's identification and both were immediately returned to him as unremarkable. However, the two police officers persisted and explained their presence as narcotics agents on the lookout for illegal drugs. In pursuit of that aim, they then requested the defendant's consent to search his luggage.

Although the testimony was conflicting, the trial court implicitly found the officers advised Bostick that he had a right to refuse the consent and that he nevertheless consented to a search of the bag in which the cocaine was found.

A majority of the Supreme Court construed the Florida Supreme Court's holding below as adopting a *per se* rule that officers who board buses during scheduled stops to question passengers and to seek consent for luggage searches necessarily seize the passengers confronted. If the officers lack reasonable suspicion, the seizure is unreasonable and taints the subsequently-given consent. In so adopting a *per se* rule, the Supreme Court held, the Florida tribunal erred. As in other situations, a seizure does not necessarily occur simply because an officer approaches a bus passenger and asks a few questions. Whether on the facts of *Bostick* a seizure took place, the Court observed, was in "some doubt," and it remanded the case for the state courts to address this under the correct legal standard. That standard, it continued, requires in the context presented the state courts not focus upon whether Bostick felt "free to leave":

When police attempt to question a person who is walking down the street or through an airport lobby, it makes sense to inquire whether a reasonable person would feel free to continue walking. But when the person is seated on a bus and has no desire to leave, the degree to which a reasonable person would feel that he or she could leave is not an accurate measure of the coercive effect of the encounter. * * * In such a situation, the appropriate inquiry is whether a reasonable person would feel free to decline the officers' requests or otherwise terminate the encounter. This formulation follows logically from prior cases and breaks no new ground. We have said before that the crucial test is whether, taking into account all of the circumstances surrounding the encounter, the police conduct would "have communicated to a reasonable person that he was not at liberty to ignore the police presence and go about his business." Where the encounter takes place is one factor, but it is not the only one. And * * * an individual may decline an officer's request without fearing prosecution. We have consistently held that a refusal to cooperate, without more, does not furnish the minimal level of objective justification needed for a detention or seizure.

501 U.S. at 435–37, 111 S.Ct. at 2387, 115 L.Ed.2d at 399–400.

B. ARRESTS AND ASSOCIATED SEARCHES

EDITORS' INTRODUCTION: ARRESTS AND THEIR VALIDITY

The right to search arising by virtue of effectuation of certain "arrests" is quite broad. It is at least broader than the right to search arising when other detentions are made. Among the reasons why it is important to identify those detentions constituting arrests, therefore, is that characterizing detentions will often determine officers' right to search because of those detentions.

Definition of Arrest. The increased complexity of the law relating to detentions makes the definition of arrest more difficult. In part, this is because the definition may be called into play to distinguish arrests from other detentions. One court—with these considerations in mind—offered:

> The classic definition of arrest consists of " ' ... the apprehending or restraining of one's person, in order to be forthcoming to answer an alleged or suspected crime.' " E. Fisher, *Laws of Arrest* 7 (1967) (quoting 4 W. Blackstone, *Commentaries* 288, 289). The necessary first step in determining whether there has been an arrest is to ask whether the individual was free to leave the presence of the police.

> A second element of arrest is the likelihood that the present confinement will be accompanied by future interference with the individual's freedom of movement. This element reflects the common law notion that an arrest is more than a present confinement. To be an arrest, confinement should simply be the initial action in criminal prosecution.

State v. Rupe, 101 Wn.2d 664, 683–84, 683 P.2d 571, 584 (1984). This definition suggest an arrest requires a certain intention on the part of the officer. Discussions of arrest sometimes speak of a necessity for an intent to effect an arrest. E.g., United States v. Chaffen, 587 F.2d 920, 923 (8th Cir.1978).

"Custodial" and Other Arrests. As the cases discussed in this section and elsewhere in these materials make clear, the Supreme Court's case law sometimes speaks in terms of "custodial" arrests. The Court has never developed precisely what is meant by this term. Perhaps, however, the Court intends to distinguish those arrests that will result in the release of the suspect in the field from those that will result in the suspect's being removed to some other location—a stationhouse or courtroom—for further "processing." The distinction between custodial arrests and other detentions is considered later in this chapter in the material on so-called "traffic stops."

"Formal" Arrests. The Supreme Court's cases also refer to "formal" arrests. Berkemer v. McCarty, 468 U.S. 420, 441, 104 S.Ct. 3138, 3151, 82 L.Ed.2d 317, 336 (1984); Rawlings v. Kentucky, 448 U.S. 98, 111, 100 S.Ct. 2556, 2564, 65 L.Ed.2d 633, 645 (1980). Again, however, the Court has not defined this term. It seems likely, however, the Court regards a "formal" arrest as a detention accompanied by the officer's expressed announcement to the detained person that the officer is making an arrest.

Some jurisdictions require such an announcement. In a number of jurisdictions, for example, an officer is directed to inform the person of the officer's authority and the reason or cause for the arrest. Exceptions are commonly provided for situations in which the suspect's flight or resistance make such action by the officer impractical. E.g., Mich.Code Crim.Pro. § 764.19; N.Y.—McKinney's Crim.Pro.L. § 00140.15(2). Nevertheless, lower courts have held that compliance with provisions such as these is not necessary to the making of a valid arrest under state law. E.g., Williams v. State, 278 Ark. 9, 12, 642 S.W.2d 887, 889 (1982). The Supreme Court has never indicated that the Fourth Amendment requires such an announcement. Nor has an announcement of this sort been required by the lower courts as a matter of federal constitutional law. As one federal court stated, "the determination of whether an arrest has occurred for Fourth Amendment purposes does not depend upon whether the officers announced that they were placing the suspects under arrest." United States v. Rose, 731 F.2d 1337, 1342 (8th Cir.1984).

Warrant Requirements—Arrests. Arrests may be made pursuant to arrest warrants, issued by magistrates on the basis of information found by those magistrates to constitute probable cause to believe the persons guilty of offenses. Rule 4 of the Federal Rules of Criminal Procedure, for example, authorizes issuance of an arrest warrant.

Such warrants are, however, seldom required as a matter of Fourth Amendment law. In United States v. Watson, 423 U.S. 411, 96 S.Ct. 820, 46 L.Ed.2d 598 (1976), the Supreme Court considered whether the Fourth Amendment requires—in the absence of exigent circumstances—that an arrest warrant be procured for an arrest in a public place. The Court noted long and widespread acceptance of the common law rule that a warrantless arrest for a felony was permissible, even if the felony was not committed in the presence of the officer, if the officer had probable cause to believe the suspect guilty. Congressional enactments authorizing such arrests reflected the understanding of that body that the Fourth Amendment did not require more. Thus, the Court concluded:

> Law enforcement officers may find it wise to seek arrest warrants where practicable to do so, and their judgments about probable cause may be more readily accepted where backed by a warrant issued by a magistrate. But we decline to transform this judicial preference into a constitutional rule when the judgment of the Nation and Congress has for so long been to authorize warrantless public arrests on probable cause rather than to encumber criminal prosecutions with endless litigation with respect to the existence of exigent circumstances, whether it was practicable to get a warrant, whether the suspect was about to flee, and the like.

423 U.S. at 423–24, 96 S.Ct. at 827–28, 46 L.Ed.2d at 609.

In regard to misdemeanors, the law is less clear. At common law, a warrantless arrest was permitted for a misdemeanor only if the offense was a breach of the peace and committed in the presence of the officer. See Commonwealth v. Reeves, 223 Pa.Super. 51, 52–53, 297 A.2d 142, 143 (1972). Many American jurisdictions, however, permit warrantless misdemeanor arrests in more circumstances. Warrantless arrests are, for example, often permitted for any misdemeanor committed in the presence of the officer. Sometimes state statutory authority or case law is broader. See State v. Martin, 275 S.C. 141, 268 S.E.2d 105 (1980), construing the South Carolina statutes as permitting an officer to make a warrantless arrest for a misdemeanor when the facts and circumstances observed by the officer give the officer probable cause to believe that a misdemeanor has been "freshly committed."

If a misdemeanor arrest is invalid *under state law* because an arrest warrant was not obtained, does the Fourth Amendment require suppression of evidence obtained in a search incident to that arrest? If not, does state law? Some courts—without much consideration—conclude evidence of this sort cannot be used. See Commonwealth v. Trefry, 249 Pa.Super. 117, 375 A.2d 786 (1977); Commonwealth v. Reeves, supra.

Does the Fourth Amendment impose some version of the traditional requirement of an arrest warrant for certain arrests? *Watson* relied heavily upon acceptance of the common law rule that felony arrests did not require warrants. Perhaps the widespread acceptance of the common law notion that some misdemeanor arrests demand warrants means a warrant requirement for such arrests is incorporated into the Fourth Amendment. The Supreme Court has never addressed the issue.

Warrant Requirements—Search for Person to be Arrested. When an arrest requires entry into premises to find the suspect and arrest him, it is clear the Fourth Amendment's warrant requirement comes into play. In Payton v. New York, 445 U.S. 573, 100 S.Ct. 1371, 63 L.Ed.2d 639 (1980), officers entered the suspects' residences seeking them for purposes of arrest. Such activity, the Court reasoned, breaches the entrance of an individual's home just as does a search for evidence. "Absent exigent circumstance," it concluded, "that threshold may not reasonably be crossed without a warrant." It then continued:

[W]e note the State's suggestion that only a search warrant based on probable cause to believe the suspect is at home at a given time can adequately protect the privacy interests at stake, and since such a warrant requirement is manifestly impractical, there need be no warrant of any kind. We find this ingenious argument unpersuasive. It is true that an arrest warrant requirement may afford less protection than a search warrant requirement, but it will suffice to interpose the magistrate's determination of probable cause between the zealous officer and the citizen. If there is sufficient evidence of a citizen's participation in a felony to persuade a judicial officer that his arrest is justified, it is constitutionally reasonable to require him to open his doors to the officers of the law. Thus, for Fourth Amendment purposes, an arrest warrant founded on probable cause implicitly carries with it the limited authority to enter a dwelling in which the suspect lives when there is reason to believe the suspect is within.

445 U.S. at 602–03, 100 S.Ct. at 1388, 63 L.Ed.2d at 660–61.

But when the premises entered are not those of the suspect, a different situation arises. In Steagald v. United States, 451 U.S. 204, 101 S.Ct. 1642, 68 L.Ed.2d 38 (1981), federal drug Enforcement Administration agents had a warrant for the arrest of Lyons. Two days after receiving a tip from an informant that Lyons could be found at a particular residence, they searched that residence. They did not find Lyons but discovered a substantial quantity of cocaine. This was admitted at Steagald's trial for possession of that substance. Finding constitutional error, the Supreme Court held the absence of a valid search warrant rendered the search of the premises for Lyons unreasonable:

[W]hile the [arrest] warrant * * * may have protected Lyons from an unreasonable seizure, it did absolutely nothing to protect [Steagald's] privacy interest in being free from an unreasonable invasion and search of his home. Instead, [Steagald's] only protection from an illegal entry and search was the agent's personal determination of probable cause. In the absence of exigent circumstances, we have consistently held that such judicially untested determinations are not reliable enough to justify an entry into a person's home to arrest him without a warrant, or a search of a home for objects in the absence of a search warrant. We see no reason to depart from this settled course when the search of a home is for a person rather than an object.

451 U.S. at 213–14, 101 S.Ct. at 1648, 68 L.Ed.2d at 46. In *Steagald*, Steagald and one Gaultney were apprehended standing outside the house; Gaultney's wife was inside when it was searched. Before the Supreme Court, the Government urged that Steagald had failed to demonstrate he had an expectation of privacy in the house. The Court, however, concluded the Government had effectively conceded in the lower courts that Steagald had a privacy interest in the premises and that it could therefore not challenge the matter before the Court. In future cases where a suspect is found during a search of a third party's premises, will the suspect be able to show a sufficient privacy interest in those premises to enable him to challenge the absence of the search warrant required by *Steagald*?

The warrant requirement here, just as the general search warrant requirement (see part A of Chapter 5), is subject to an emergency exception. The matter was addressed in Welsh v. Wisconsin, 466 U.S. 740, 104 S.Ct. 2091, 80 L.Ed.2d 732 (1984). Information from a witness led police officers to believe Welsh had, while intoxicated, driven his automobile off the highway into a field, abandoned it, and gone to his nearby residence. Police went to his residence, entered, and—upon finding Welsh lying naked in bed—placed him under arrest for driving a motor vehicle under the influence of an intoxicant. They took him to the station where he refused to submit to a breathalyzer test. Subsequently, authorities began proceedings to revoke his driver's license, based upon his refusal to submit to the breathalyzer test. Under Wisconsin law, if his arrest had been unlawful his refusal to submit to the breathalyzer test would have been reasonable and that refusal could not serve as the basis for revocation. The state courts ultimately rejected Welsh's argument that his arrest violated the Fourth Amendment, despite the officers' failure to obtain a warrant. The officers' actions were reasonable, they reasoned, in view of their "hot pursuit," the risk of harm to the public and Welsh himself, and the need for an immediate arrest and breath test before the alcohol in Welsh's blood disappeared from his system.

The Supreme Court reversed. Justice Brennan, writing for the Court, acknowledged that some "emergency conditions" would sometimes justify warrantless home arrests. But, he continued:

> [A]n important factor to be considered when determining whether any exigency exists is the gravity of the underlying offense for which the arrest is being made. * * * [A]pplication of the exigent-circumstances exception in the context of a home entry should rarely be sanctioned where there is probable cause to believe that only a minor offense, such as the kind at issue in this case, has been committed.

466 U.S. at 753, 104 S.Ct. at 2099, 80 L.Ed.2d at 745. Under Wisconsin law, first offense driving while intoxicated is a noncriminal civil forfeiture offense for which the maximum penalty was, at the time, a $200 fine. Turning to the facts of the case, the Court continued:

> [T]he claim of hot pursuit is unconvincing because there was no immediate or continuous pursuit of the petitioner from the scene of a crime. Moreover, because the petitioner had already arrived home and had abandoned his car at the scene of the accident, there was little remaining threat to the public safety. Hence, the only potential emergency claimed by the State was the need to ascertain the petitioner's blood-alcohol level.
>
> Even assuming, however, that the underlying facts would support a finding of this exigent circumstance, mere similarity to other cases involving the imminent destruction of evidence is not sufficient. [Wisconsin's classification of driving while intoxicated as a civil offense for which no imprisonment is possible] * * * is the best indication of the state's interest in precipitating an arrest, and is one that can easily be identified both by the courts and by officers faced with a decision to arrest. Given this expression of the state's interest, a warrantless home arrest cannot be upheld simply because evidence of the petitioner's

blood-alcohol level might have dissipated while the police obtained a warrant.

466 U.S. at 753–54, 104 S.Ct. at 2099–2100, 80 L.Ed.2d at 745–46.

In view of this conclusion, the Court found "no occasion to consider whether the Fourth Amendment might impose an absolute ban on warrantless home arrests for certain minor offenses."

The Supreme Court had earlier applied a "hot pursuit" sort of exception to the warrant requirement in this context. In United States v. Santana, 427 U.S. 38, 96 S.Ct. 2406, 49 L.Ed.2d 300 (1976), officers in an automobile pulled up in front of Santana's residence. She was standing in the door. When the officers shouted, "Police," displayed their badges and advanced, she "retreated" into the vestibule of her house. The officers—without a warrant—followed her into the vestibule and arrested her. No constitutional defect was found in the officers' actions. While she was in her doorway, the Court reasoned, Santana was in a "public place" and, under *Watson,* no warrant was required. Where the police follow in "true 'hot pursuit,' " a suspect may not, by retreating into a house, "defeat an arrest which has been set in motion in a public place * * *."

Entry to Arrest—Announcement Requirement. Where officers rely upon a search warrant as authority to enter premises and search those premises for a suspect they have grounds to arrest, the propriety of the officers' actions in gaining entry is undoubtedly governed by the rules relating to entry to execute a search warrant, discussed in Chapter 3. In other situations, however, must officers make some sort of preliminary announcements—as, for example, to their purpose—and perhaps also a request for admission before entering?

In Miller v. United States, 357 U.S. 301, 78 S.Ct. 1190, 2 L.Ed.2d 1332 (1958), the Government conceded that the validity of an entry to make an arrest without a warrant was to be tested by criteria identical to those which 18 U.S.C.A. § 3109 (set out in the Editors' Introduction to Part 3 of Chapter 3) imposes upon entry to execute a search warrant. Since the officers in *Miller* failed to give notice of their authority and purpose before breaking to enter to locate and arrest Miller, the entry, Miller's arrest, and the search incident to the arrest were held invalid and the evidence obtained in the search was inadmissible. The Court reached a similar result in Sabbath v. United States, 391 U.S. 585, 88 S.Ct. 1755, 20 L.Ed.2d 828 (1968). *Miller* and *Sabbath* may, of course, reflect only the Court's application of federal statutory law. However, the Supreme Court's Fourth Amendment case law concerning entry to execute a search warrant, covered in Part C of Chapter 3, suggests that entry to make an arrest is subject to similar requirements. Thus, *Miller* and *Sabbath* may reflect a constitutionally-required construction of the federal statute.

State law often imposes a notice requirement and frequently provides for exceptions. Under New York statutory law, for example, an officer must, before entering to effect an arrest, give "or make reasonable effort to give" notice of "his authority and purpose." Notice is not required if the officer has reasonable cause to believe giving the notice would result in the suspect escaping (or attempting to escape), the life or safety of anyone being endangered, or the destruction, damaging or secretion of material evidence. N.Y.—McKinney's Crim.Proc.L. §§ 120.80(4) (arrests under arrest warrants), 140.15(4) (warrantless arrests). See also, West's Ann.Cal.Penal Code § 844 (officer may "break open the door or window" to make an arrest "after having demanded admittance and explained the purpose for which admittance is desired").

Probable Cause Requirement—In General. Although the warrant requirement has relatively little application to the reasonableness of an arrest, the Fourth Amendment's requirement of probable cause has substantial significance:

> Whether [an] arrest was constitutionally valid depends * * * upon whether, at the moment the arrest was made, the officers had probable cause to make it—whether at that moment the facts and circumstances within their knowledge and of which they had reasonably trustworthy information were sufficient to warrant a prudent man in believing that the [suspect] had committed or was committing an offense.

Beck v. Ohio, 379 U.S. 89, 91, 85 S.Ct. 223, 225, 13 L.Ed.2d 142, 145 (1964).

A subaspect of the probable cause issue is the effect of an arrest under a law later determined invalid. In Michigan v. DeFillippo, 443 U.S. 31, 99 S.Ct. 2627, 61 L.Ed.2d 343 (1979), DeFillippo was arrested under a Detroit ordinance. A search incident to that arrest resulted in discovery of controlled substances and DeFillippo was prosecuted for possession of those substances. The state courts held the ordinance under which he was arrested was unconstitutionally vague and therefore the arrest and the incidental search were invalid. The Supreme Court reversed, holding the information indicating DeFillippo violated the ordinance rendered the arrest constitutionally permissible. As to the unconstitutionality of the ordinance, the Court continued:

> Police are charged to enforce laws until and unless they are declared unconstitutional. The enactment of a law forecloses speculation by enforcement officers concerning its constitutionality—with the possible exception of a law so grossly and flagrantly unconstitutional that any person of reasonable prudence would be bound to see its flaws. Society would be ill-served if its police officers took upon themselves to determine which laws are and which are not constitutionally entitled to enforcement.

443 U.S. at 37–38, 99 S.Ct. at 2632, 61 L.Ed.2d at 350.

Probable Cause—Cooperative Action and "Collective" Information. Given the complexity of many criminal offenses and the mobility of many suspects, investigations often involve more than one officer and, in fact, officers of several jurisdictions. Action by law enforcement officers may be taken upon request of other officers, perhaps ones of another jurisdiction. When one officer or agency makes an arrest upon the request of another officer or police agency, what information is to be considered in determining if probable cause exists?

In Whiteley v. Warden, 401 U.S. 560, 91 S.Ct. 1031, 28 L.Ed.2d 306 (1971), a Carbon County, Wyoming sheriff issued a message through a statewide law enforcement radio network describing a suspect and stating an arrest warrant had been issued for him. The information submitted in support of the warrant request was not set out in the message. In response to the message, officers in another Wyoming locality—Laramie—arrested and searched the suspect. During the suspect's prosecution, items found in the search were admitted into evidence over his objection. The State urged, with regard to the Laramie officers, the radio request constituted probable cause on which they could act regardless of the validity of the warrant on which the request was based. After concluding the warrant was invalid because it was issued without probable cause, the Court continued:

> We do not * * * question that the Laramie police were entitled to act on the strength of the radio bulletin. Certainly police officers called upon to aid other officers in executing arrest warrants are entitled to assume that the officers requesting aid offered the magistrate the information requisite to support an independent judicial assessment of probable cause. Where, however, the contrary turns out to be true, an otherwise illegal arrest cannot be insulated from challenge by the decision of the instigating officer to rely on fellow officers to make the arrest.

401 U.S. at 568, 91 S.Ct. at 1037, 28 L.Ed.2d at 313.

In United States v. Hensley, 469 U.S. 221, 105 S.Ct. 675, 83 L.Ed.2d 604 (1985), the Court developed the implications of this holding:

> *Whiteley* supports the proposition that, when evidence is uncovered during a search incident to an arrest in reliance merely on a flyer or bulletin, its admissibility turns on whether the officers who *issued* the flyer possessed probable cause to make the arrest. It does not turn on whether those relying on the flyer were themselves aware of the specific facts which led their colleagues to seek their assistance. In an era when criminal suspects are increasingly mobile and increasingly likely to flee across jurisdictional boundaries, this rule is a matter of common sense: it minimizes the volume of information concerning suspects that must be transmitted to other jurisdictions and enables police in one jurisdiction to act promptly in reliance on information from another jurisdiction.

469 U.S. at 231, 105 S.Ct. at 681, 83 L.Ed.2d at 613–14.

Excessive Force. Traditionally, the amount of force permissible to make an arrest has been a matter of nonconstitutional law. In Tennessee v. Garner, 471 U.S. 1, 105 S.Ct. 1694, 85 L.Ed.2d 1 (1985), however, the Supreme Court held excessive deadly force in making an otherwise proper arrest renders that arrest "unreasonable" under the Fourth Amendment. Such reasonableness, the Court explained, depends not simply upon whether there are grounds for arrest—that is, probable cause—"but also on how [the arrest] is carried out." In Graham v. Connor, 490 U.S. 386, 109 S.Ct. 1865, 104 L.Ed.2d 443 (1989), it held that nondeadly but excessive force could have the same effect.

Traditional law permitted officers to use deadly force whenever they reasonably believed that necessary to make the arrest of a person reasonably believed to have committed a felony. *Garner* defined acceptable deadly force for purposes of the Fourth Amendment rule more narrowly. Use of deadly force, the Court concluded, is unreasonable if used against a nondangerous suspect. Putting the holding affirmatively, it explained:

> Where the officer has probable cause to believe that the suspect poses a threat of serious physical harm, either to the officer or to others, it is not constitutionally unreasonable to prevent escape by using deadly force. Thus, if the suspect threatens the officer with a weapon or there is probable cause to believe that he has committed a crime involving the infliction or threatened infliction of serious physical harm, deadly force may be used if necessary to prevent escape, and if, where feasible, some warning has been given.

471 U.S. at 11–12, 105 S.Ct. at 1701, 85 L.Ed.2d at 10. On the facts of *Garner,* the Court held the officer's reasonable belief the suspect had committed nighttime burglary was *not* sufficient to justify the use of the fatal gunfire there at issue to stop the suspect.

In *Graham,* the Court explained whether nondeadly force was excessive under the Fourth Amendment

> requires careful attention to the facts and circumstances of each particular case, including the severity of the crime at issue, whether the suspect poses an immediate threat to the safety of officers or others, and whether he is actively resisting arrest or attempting to evade arrest by flight.

490 U.S. at 396, 109 S.Ct. at 1872, 104 L.Ed.2d at 454–55. Courts must consider the evidence "from the perspective of a reasonable officer on the scene," rather than with "the 20–20 vision of hindsight," and make allowances for officers' need to make split-second judgments in situations that are tense, uncertain, and rapidly evolving.

Both *Garner* and *Graham* were civil cases in which damages were sought under 42 U.S.C.A. § 1983 on the theory that the officers' use of force had made the arrests unreasonable. When, if ever, will force that is excessive under these cases render evidence inadmissible? Suppose, for example, in *Garner* the officer's gunfire had not killed Garner but had disabled him and thus enabled the officer to arrest him. Suppose further in a search incident to this arrest, items taken from the burglarized premises were found on Garner's person. Would these items be inadmissible because of the excessive force?

1. SEARCHES INCIDENT TO ARRESTS

EDITORS' INTRODUCTION: SEARCHES INCIDENT TO ARRESTS AND THOSE PART OF STATIONHOUSE PROCESSING

The occurrence of a valid arrest itself brings into play a right to make certain searches. This right to search because of an arrest is the subject of the present subsection.

This right to search a suspect incident to an arrest must be distinguished from what may be done as part of later processing of the suspect. The Supreme Court addressed authorities' right to search at the stationhouse in Illinois v. Lafayette, 462 U.S. 640, 103 S.Ct. 2605, 77 L.Ed.2d 65

(1983). LaFayette was arrested and handcuffed at a theater for disturbing the peace. He carried a "purse-type shoulder bag" with him to the police station. Upon arrival at the station, officers took him to the "booking room" and examined the bag's contents; they found amphetamines. These were admitted into evidence at LaFayette's prosecution for possession of a controlled substance. The Supreme Court found no constitutional error, reasoning "it is not 'unreasonable' for police, as part of the routine procedure incident to incarcerating an arrested person, to search any container or article in his possession, in accordance with established inventory procedures." Characterizing an inventory search as "not an independent legal consent but rather an incidental administrative step following arrest and preceding incarceration," the majority explained its holding:

> At the stationhouse, it is entirely proper for police to remove and list or inventory property found on the person or in the possession of an arrested person who is to be jailed. A range of governmental interests support such an inventory process. It is not unheard of for persons employed in police activities to steal property taken from arrested persons; similarly, arrested persons have been known to make false claims regarding what was taken from their possession at the stationhouse. A standardized procedure for making a list or inventory as soon as reasonable after reaching the stationhouse not only deters false claims but also inhibits theft or careless handling of articles taken from the arrested person. Arrested persons have also been known to injure themselves—or others—with belts, knives, drugs or other items on their persons while being detained. Dangerous instrumentalities—such as razor blades, bombs, or weapons—can be concealed in innocent-looking articles taken from the arrestee's possession. The bare recital of these mundane realities justifies reasonable measures by police to limit these risks—either while the items are in police possession or at the time they are returned to the arrestee upon his release. Examining all the items removed from the arrestee's person or possession and listing or inventorying them is an entirely reasonable administrative procedure. It is immaterial whether the police actually fear any particular package or container; the need to protect against such risks arises independent of a particular officer's subjective concerns. Finally, inspection of an arrestee's personal property may assist the police in ascertaining or verifying his identity.

462 U.S. at 646, 103 S.Ct. at 2609–10, 77 L.Ed.2d at 71. These interests, the Court noted, may sometimes be greater than those supporting a search immediately after arrest:

> Consequently, the scope of a stationhouse search will often vary from that made at the time of arrest. Police conduct that would be impractical or unreasonable—or embarrassingly intrusive—on the street can more readily—and privately—be performed at the station. For example, the interest supporting a search incident to arrest would hardly justify disrobing an arrestee on the street, but the practical necessities of routine jail administration may even justify taking a prisoner's

clothing from him before confining him, although that step would be rare.

462 U.S. at 645, 103 S.Ct. at 2609, 77 L.Ed.2d at 70–71. The majority noted that it was not addressing the circumstances in which a strip search of an arrestee "may or may not be appropriate."

The Illinois court had held the search of LaFayette's shoulder bag unreasonable because the State's interests could be served by less intrusive methods, such as placing the bag in a secured locker or sealing it in a plastic bag. Granting this might have been so, a majority of the Supreme Court rejected the position that the Fourth Amendment required the Illinois police to use such less intrusive methods:

> The reasonableness of any particular governmental activity does not necessarily or invariably turn on the existence of alternative "less intrusive" means. * * * We are hardly in a position to second-guess police departments as to what practical administrative method will best deter theft by and false claims against its employees and preserve the security of the stationhouse. * * *

> Even if less intrusive means existed of protecting some particular types of property, it would be unreasonable to expect police officers in the everyday course of business to make fine and subtle distinctions in deciding which containers or items may be searched and which must be sealed as a unit.

462 U.S. at 647–48, 103 S.Ct. at 2610, 77 L.Ed.2d at 72. But the Court apparently intended to limit inventory inspections to situations in which the suspect was to be more than "booked." It noted uncertainty in the record as to whether LaFayette was to be incarcerated after being booked for disturbing the peace. "That," it offered, "is an appropriate inquiry on remand."

Perhaps the most troublesome aspect of the right to search incident to arrests is defining the scope of the permissible search. This is the subject of the principal case that follows.

Chimel v. California

Supreme Court of the United States, 1969.
395 U.S. 752, 89 S.Ct. 2034, 23 L.Ed.2d 685.

■ Mr. Justice Stewart delivered the opinion of the Court.

This case raises basic questions concerning the permissible scope under the Fourth Amendment of a search incident to a lawful arrest.

The relevant facts are essentially undisputed. Late in the afternoon of September 13, 1965, three police officers arrived at the Santa Ana, California, home of the petitioner with a warrant authorizing his arrest for the burglary of a coin shop. The officers knocked on the door, identified themselves to the petitioner's wife, and asked if they might come inside. She ushered them into the house, where they waited 10 or 15 minutes until the petitioner returned home from work. When the petitioner entered the house, one of the officers handed him the arrest warrant and asked for permission to "look around." The petitioner objected, but was advised that "on the basis of the lawful arrest," the officers would nonetheless conduct a search. No search warrant had been issued.

Accompanied by the petitioner's wife, the officers then looked through the entire three-bedroom house, including the attic, the garage, and a small workshop. In some rooms the search was relatively cursory. In the master bedroom and sewing room, however, the officers directed the petitioner's wife to open drawers and "to physically move contents of the drawers from side to side so that [they] might view any items that would have come from [the] burglary." After completing the search, they seized numerous items— primarily coins, but also several medals, tokens, and a few other objects. The entire search took between 45 minutes and an hour.

At the petitioner's subsequent state trial on two charges of burglary, the items taken from his house were admitted into evidence against him, over his objection that they had been unconstitutionally seized. He was convicted, and the judgments of conviction were affirmed by both the California Court of Appeal, and the California Supreme Court. Both courts accepted the petitioner's contention that the arrest warrant was invalid because the supporting affidavit was set out in conclusory terms, but held that since the arresting officers had procured the warrant "in good faith," and since in any event they had had sufficient information to constitute probable cause for the petitioner's arrest, that arrest had been lawful. From this conclusion the appellate courts went on to hold that the search of the petitioner's home had been justified, despite the absence of a search warrant, on the ground that it had been incident to a valid arrest. * * *

Without deciding the question, we proceed on the hypothesis that the California courts were correct in holding that the arrest of the petitioner was valid under the Constitution. This brings us directly to the question whether the warrantless search of the petitioner's entire house can be constitutionally justified as incident to that arrest. The decisions of this Court bearing upon that question have been far from consistent * * *.

Approval of a warrantless search incident to a lawful arrest seems first to have been articulated by the Court in 1914 as dictum in Weeks v. United States, 232 U.S. 383, 34 S.Ct. 341, 58 L.Ed. 652. * * *

That statement made no reference to any right to search the *place* where an arrest occurs, but was limited to a right to search the "person." * * *

In 1950 * * * came United States v. Rabinowitz, 339 U.S. 56, 70 S.Ct. 430, 94 L.Ed. 653, the decision upon which California primarily relies in the case now before us. In *Rabinowitz*, federal authorities had been informed that the defendant was dealing in stamps bearing forged over-prints. On the basis of that information they secured a warrant for his arrest, which they executed at his one-room business office. At the time of the arrest, the officers "searched the desk, safe, and file cabinets in the office for about an hour and a half," and seized 573 stamps with forged overprints. The stamps were admitted into evidence at the defendant's trial, and this Court affirmed his conviction, rejecting the contention that the warrantless search had been unlawful. The Court held that the search in its entirety fell within the principle giving law enforcement authorities "[t]he right 'to search the place where the arrest is made in order to find and seize things connected with the crime * * *.' " * * *

Rabinowitz has come to stand for the proposition, *inter alia*, that a warrantless search "incident to a lawful arrest" may generally extend to the area that is considered to be in the "possession" or under the "control" of the person arrested. And it was on the basis of that proposition that the California courts upheld the search of the petitioner's entire house in this case. That doctrine, however, at least in the broad sense in which it was applied by the California courts in this case, can withstand neither historical nor rational analysis.

Even limited to its own facts, the *Rabinowitz* decision was * * * hardly founded on an unimpeachable line of authority. * * * Nor is the rationale by which the State seeks here to sustain the search of the petitioner's house supported by a reasoned view of the background and purpose of the Fourth Amendment.

* * *

Only last Term in Terry v. Ohio, 392 U.S. 1, 88 S.Ct. 1868, 20 L.Ed.2d 889, we emphasized that "the police must, whenever practicable, obtain advance judicial approval of searches and seizures through the warrant procedure," and that "[t]he scope of [a] search must be 'strictly tied to and justified by' the circumstances which rendered its initiation permissible." * * *

A similar analysis underlies the "search incident to arrest" principle, and marks its proper extent. When an arrest is made, it is reasonable for the arresting officer to search the person arrested in order to remove any weapons that the latter might seek to use in order to resist arrest or effect his escape. Otherwise, the officer's safety might well be endangered, and the arrest itself frustrated. In addition, it is entirely reasonable for the arresting officer to search for and seize any evidence on the arrestee's person in order to prevent its concealment or destruction. And the area into which an arrestee might reach in order to grab a weapon or evidentiary items must, of course, be governed by a like rule. A gun on a table or in a drawer in front of one who is arrested can be as dangerous to the arresting officer as one concealed in the clothing of the person arrested. There is ample justification, therefore, for a search of the arrestee's person and the area "within his immediate control" construing that phrase to mean the area from within which he might gain possession of a weapon or destructible evidence.

There is no comparable justification, however, for routinely searching any room other than that in which an arrest occurs—or, for that matter, for searching through all the desk drawers or other closed or concealed areas in that room itself. Such searches, in the absence of well-recognized exceptions, may be made only under the authority of a search warrant. The "adherence to judicial processes" mandated by the Fourth Amendment requires no less.

* * *

It is argued in the present case that it is "reasonable" to search a man's house when he is arrested in it. Under such an unconfined analysis, Fourth Amendment protection in this area would approach the evaporation point. It is not easy to explain why, for instance, it is less subjectively "reasonable" to search a man's house when he is arrested on his front lawn—or just down the street—than it is when he happens to be in the house at the time of arrest.

No consideration relevant to the Fourth Amendment suggests any point of rational limitation, once the search is allowed to go beyond the area from which the person arrested might obtain weapons or evidentiary items. The only reasoned distinction is one between a search of the person arrested and the area within his reach on the one hand and more extensive searches on the other.

The petitioner correctly points out that one result of decisions such as *Rabinowitz* * * * is to give law enforcement officials the opportunity to engage in searches not justified by probable cause, by the simple expedient of arranging to arrest suspects at home rather than elsewhere. We do not suggest that the petitioner is necessarily correct in his assertion that such a strategy was utilized here but the fact remains that had he been arrested earlier in the day, at his place of employment rather than at home, no search of his house could have been made without a search warrant.

* * *

Rabinowitz * * * [has] been the subject of critical commentary for many years, and [has] been relied upon less and less in our own decisions. It is time, for the reasons we have stated, to hold that * * * [it is] no longer to be followed.

Application of sound Fourth Amendment principles to the facts of this case produces a clear result. The search here went far beyond the petitioner's person and the area from within which he might have obtained either a weapon or something that could have been used as evidence against him. There was no constitutional justification, in the absence of a search warrant, for extending the search beyond that area. The scope of the search was, therefore, "unreasonable" under the Fourth and Fourteenth Amendments and the petitioner's conviction cannot stand.

Reversed.

■ Mr. Justice White, with whom Mr. Justice Black joins, dissenting.

* * * The Court has always held, and does not today deny, that when there is probable cause to search and it is "impracticable" for one reason or another to get a search warrant, then a warrantless search may be reasonable.

* * *

* * * An arrest itself may often create an emergency situation making it impracticable to obtain a warrant before embarking on a related search. Again assuming that there is probable cause to search premises at the spot where a suspect is arrested, it seems to me unreasonable to require the police to leave the scene in order to obtain a search warrant when they are

already legally there to make a valid arrest, and when there must almost always be a strong possibility that confederates of the arrested man will in the meanwhile remove the items for which the police have probable cause to search. This must so often be the case that it seems to me as unreasonable to require a warrant for a search of the premises as to require a warrant for search of the person and his very immediate surroundings.

* * *

NOTES

1. **Establishing the Arrest.** Is it important when—or whether—the formal arrest occurs? In Rawlings v. Kentucky, 448 U.S. 98, 100 S.Ct. 2556, 65 L.Ed.2d 633 (1980), Rawlings was present when officers searched his companion's purse; they found 1,800 tablets of LSD and a variety of other controlled substances. When the companion told Rawlings to "take what was his," he claimed ownership of all the substances. One of the officers searched Rawlings and found $4,500 in a shirt pocket and a knife in a sheath at his side. Rawlings was then placed under "formal arrest." Challenging the admissibility of the money and the knife, Rawlings argued the search could not be justified as incident to his arrest since the arrest did not occur until after the search. A majority of the Court experienced "no difficulty" in rejecting this claim:

> Once [Rawlings] admitted ownership of the sizable quantity of drugs found in [the] purse, the police clearly had probable cause to place [him] under arrest. Where the formal arrest followed quickly on the heels of the challenged search of [Rawlings'] person, we do not believe it particularly important that the search preceded the arrest rather than vice versa.

448 U.S. at 111, 100 S.Ct. at 2564, 65 L.Ed.2d at 645–46.

2. **Need for Case Specific Justification.** Do officers need reason to believe a particular search incident to an arrest would be fruitful? In United States v. Robinson, 414 U.S. 218, 94 S.Ct. 467, 38 L.Ed.2d 427 (1973), District of Columbia police officer Jenks stopped Robinson's automobile to arrest him on probable cause to believe Robinson was driving after revocation of his motor vehicle operator's license. Jenks then searched Robinson:

> Jenks felt an object in the left breast pocket of the heavy coat [Robinson] was wearing, but testified that he "couldn't tell what it was" and also that he "couldn't actually tell the size of it." Jenks then reached into the pocket and pulled out the object, which turned out to be a "crumpled up cigarette package." Jenks testified that at this point he still did not know what was in the package:
>
>> "As I felt the package I could feel objects in the package but I couldn't tell what they were * * *. I knew they weren't cigarettes."
>
> The officer then opened the cigarette pack and found 14 gelatin capsules of white powder which he thought to be, and which later analysis proved to be, heroin. Jenks then continued his search of [Robinson] to completion, feeling around his waist and trouser legs, and examining the remaining pockets. The heroin * * * was admitted into evidence at the trial which resulted in his conviction in the District Court.

The Supreme Court, reversing the Court of Appeals, held the search permissible:

> [O]ur * * * fundamental disagreement with the Court of Appeals arises from its suggestion that there must be litigated in each case the issue of whether or

not there was present one of the reasons supporting the authority for a search of the person incident to a lawful arrest. We do not think the long line of authorities of this Court * * *, nor what we can glean from the history of practice in this country and in England, requires such a case by case adjudication. A police officer's determination as to how and where to search the person of a suspect whom he has arrested is necessarily a quick *ad hoc* judgment which the Fourth Amendment does not require to be broken down in each instance into an analysis of each step in the search. The authority to search the person incident to a lawful custodial arrest, while based upon the need to disarm and to discover evidence, does not depend on what a court may later decide was the probability in a particular arrest situation that weapons or evidence would in fact be found upon the person of the suspect. A custodial arrest of a suspect based on probable cause is a reasonable intrusion under the Fourth Amendment; that intrusion being lawful, a search incident to the arrest requires no additional justification. It is the fact of the lawful arrest which establishes the authority to search, and we hold that in the case of a lawful custodial arrest a full search of the person is not only an exception to the warrant requirement of the Fourth Amendment, but is also a "reasonable" search under that Amendment.

414 U.S. at 235, 94 S.Ct. at 477, 38 L.Ed.2d at 440–41. Justices Marshall, Douglas and Brennan dissented.

3. **Moving and Accompanying the Suspect.** May an officer who has arrested a suspect in a public place accompany the suspect into his dwelling or into particular parts of the dwelling as an incident of the arrest? In Washington v. Chrisman, 455 U.S. 1, 102 S.Ct. 812, 70 L.Ed.2d 778 (1982), a campus police officer observed a student, Overdahl, exit a dormitory carrying a half-gallon bottle of gin. Overdahl appeared to be underage. The officer stopped him and asked for identification. He responded that his identification was in his dormitory room and asked whether the officer could wait until he retrieved it. The officer replied he would have to accompany Overdahl to his room, to which Overdahl responded, "O.K." Overdahl's roommate, Chrisman, was in the room when the officer and Overdahl arrived. The officer remained at the doorway while Overdahl entered the room to look for identification. While at the doorway, the officer observed what he believed to be marijuana seeds and a pipe on a desk about 8 to 10 feet away. He entered the room and confirmed his suspicions. After placing the roommates under arrest and obtaining their consent to a search of the room, the officer found additional drugs. Chrisman was prosecuted for possession of controlled substances. His conviction was overturned by the Washington Supreme Court on the ground that, although the officer could have accompanied Overdahl into the room after arresting him, he was not permitted under the Fourth Amendment to enter the room to seize evidence of crime without a warrant or exigent circumstances.

The Supreme Court reversed. The majority reasoned the Fourth Amendment permits the officer "to remain literally at [the arrestee's] elbow at all times":

[I]t is not "unreasonable" under the Fourth Amendment for a police officer, as a matter of routine, to monitor the movements of an arrested person, as his judgment dictates, following the arrest. The officer's need to ensure his own safety—as well as the integrity of the arrest—is compelling. Such surveillance is not an impermissible invasion of the privacy or personal liberty of an individual who has been arrested.

455 U.S. at 7, 102 S.Ct. at 817, 70 L.Ed.2d at 785. The majority also concluded that since the officer could have accompanied Overdahl into the dormitory room, his remaining in the doorway did not make his entry into the room after seeing contraband in plain view a Fourth Amendment violation.

4.   **Search for Dangerous Persons.** What action may officers take at the scene of an arrest to protect themselves from persons other than the individual arrested? In Maryland v. Buie, 494 U.S. 325, 334, 110 S.Ct. 1093, 1098, 108 L.Ed.2d 276, 286 (1990), the Court commented that officers making an arrest in a private residence could, "as an incident to the arrest * * *, as a precautionary matter and without probable cause or reasonable suspicion, look in closets and other spaces immediately adjoining the place of arrest from which an attack could be immediately launched."

A more intensive and extensive "protective sweep" of the premises—described by the Court as "a quick and limited search of a premises, incident to an arrest and conducted to protect the safety of officers or others"—requires "articulable facts which, taken together with the rational inferences from those facts, would warrant a reasonably prudent officer in believing that the area to be swept harbors an individual posing a danger to those on the arrest scene." The Court continued:

> We should emphasize that such a protective sweep, aimed at protecting the arresting officers, if justified by the circumstances, is nevertheless not a full search of the premises, but may extend only to a cursory inspection of those spaces where a person may be found. The sweep lasts no longer than is necessary to dispel the reasonable suspicion of danger and in any event no longer than it takes to complete the arrest and depart the premises.

494 U.S. at 335, 110 S.Ct. at 1099, 108 L.Ed.2d at 287.

2.   "INCIDENTAL" SEARCHES OF VEHICLES

Searches of vehicles have given rise to particularly difficult problems. The Supreme Court's approach to these problems has been colored by— among other matters—its perception that persons have a less significant privacy interest in their vehicles than in their residences. This is developed further in Part D of Chapter 5, considering the so-called "vehicle exception" to the requirement of a warrant; this exception permits warrantless searches of certain vehicles *if* the officers have probable cause to believe that the vehicles contain items the officers are entitled to seize. As the principal case in this subsection makes clear, however, officers may often search vehicles incident to the arrest of person in and perhaps around those vehicles, regardless of whether those searches would be reasonable under the vehicle exception.

Consider whether in the principal case the Supreme Court is true to the rationale and spirit of *Chimel.*

New York v. Belton

Supreme Court of the United States, 1981.
453 U.S. 454, 101 S.Ct. 2860, 69 L.Ed.2d 768.

■ JUSTICE STEWART delivered the opinion of the Court.

When the occupant of an automobile is subject to a lawful custodial arrest, does the constitutionally permissible scope of a search incident to his arrest include the passenger compartment of the automobile in which he was riding? That is the question at issue in the present case.

I.

On April 9, 1978, Trooper Douglas Nicot, a New York State policeman driving an unmarked car on the New York Thruway, was passed by another automobile travelling at an excessive rate of speed. Nicot gave chase, overtook the speeding vehicle, and ordered its driver to pull it over to the side of the road and stop. There were four men in the car, one of whom was Roger Belton, the respondent in this case. The policeman asked to see the driver's license and automobile registration, and discovered that none of the men owned the vehicle or was related to its owner. Meanwhile, the policeman had smelled burnt marihuana and had seen on the floor of the car an envelope marked "Supergold" that he associated with marihuana. He therefore directed the men to get out of the car, and placed them under arrest for the unlawful possession of marihuana. He patted down each of the men and "split them up into four separate areas of the Thruway at this time so they would not be in physical touching area of each other." He then picked up the envelope marked "Supergold" and found that it contained marihuana [and next] searched the passenger compartment of the car. On the back seat he found a black leather jacket belonging to Belton. He unzipped one of the pockets of the jacket and discovered cocaine. Placing the jacket in his automobile, he drove the four arrestees to a nearby police station.

Belton was subsequently indicted for criminal possession of a controlled substance. In the trial court he moved that the cocaine the trooper had seized from the jacket pocket be suppressed. The court denied the motion. * * *

The New York Court of Appeals reversed, holding that "[a] warrantless search of the zippered pockets of an unaccessible jacket may not be upheld as a search incident to a lawful arrest where there is no longer any danger that the arrestee or a confederate might gain access to the article." * * * We granted certiorari to consider the constitutionally permissible scope of a search in circumstances such as these.

II.

It is a first principle of Fourth Amendment jurisprudence that the police may not conduct a search unless they first convince a neutral magistrate that there is probable cause to do so. This Court has recognized, however, that "the exigencies of the situation" may sometimes make exemption from the warrant requirement "imperative." Specifically, the Court held in Chimel v. California, 395 U.S. 752, 89 S.Ct. 2034, 23 L.Ed.2d 685, that a lawful custodial arrest creates a situation which justifies the contemporaneous search without a warrant of the person arrested and of the immediately surrounding area. Such searches have long been considered valid because of the need "to remove any weapons that [the arrestee] might seek to use in order to resist arrest or effect his escape" and the need to prevent the concealment or destruction of evidence.

The Court's opinion in *Chimel* emphasized the principle that * * *, "The scope of [a] search must be 'strictly tied to and justified by' the circumstances which rendered its initiation permissible." Thus while the Court in *Chimel* found "ample justification" for a search of "the area from within which [an arrestee] might gain possession of a weapon or destructible evidence," the Court found "no comparable justification . . . for routinely searching any room other than that in which an arrest occurs—or, for that matter, for searching through all the desk drawers or other closed or concealed areas in that room itself."

Although the principle that limits a search incident to a lawful custodial arrest may be stated clearly enough, courts have discovered the principle difficult to apply in specific cases. Yet, as one commentator has pointed out, the protection of the Fourth and Fourteenth Amendments "can only be realized if the police are acting under a set of rules which, in most instances, makes it possible to reach a correct determination beforehand as to whether an invasion of privacy is justified in the interest of law enforcement." LaFave, "Case-by-Case Adjudication" versus "Standardized Procedures": The Robinson Dilemma, 1974 Sup.Ct.Rev. 127, 142. This is because

> "Fourth Amendment doctrine, given force and effect by the exclusionary rule, is primarily intended to regulate the police in their day-to-day activities and thus ought to be expressed in terms that are readily applicable by the police in the context of the law enforcement activities in which they are necessarily engaged. A highly sophisticated set of rules, qualified by all sorts of ifs, ands, and buts and requiring the drawing of subtle nuances and hairline distinctions, may be the sort of heady stuff upon which the facile minds of lawyers and judges eagerly feed, but they may be 'literally impossible of application by the officer in the field.' "

In short, "A single, familiar standard is essential to guide police officers, who have only limited time and expertise to reflect on and balance the social and individual interests involved in the specific circumstances they confront."

* * *

But no straightforward rule has emerged from the litigated cases respecting the question involved here—the question of the proper scope of a search of the interior of an automobile incident to a lawful custodial arrest of its occupants. * * *

When a person cannot know how a court will apply a settled principle to a recurring factual situation, that person cannot know the scope of his constitutional protection, nor can a policeman know the scope of his authority. While the *Chimel* case established that a search incident to an arrest may not stray beyond the area within the immediate control of the arrestee, courts have found no workable definition of "the area within the immediate control of the arrestee" when that area arguably includes the interior of an automobile and the arrestee is its recent occupant. Our reading of the cases suggests the generalization that articles inside the relatively narrow compass of the passenger compartment of an automobile are in fact generally, even if not inevitably, within "the area into which an arrestee might reach in order to grab a weapon or evidentiary item." In order to establish the workable rule this category of cases requires, we read *Chimel's* definition of the limits of the area that may be searched in light of that generalization. Accordingly, we hold that when a policeman has made a lawful custodial arrest of the occupant of an automobile, he may, as a contemporaneous incident of that arrest, search the passenger compartment of that automobile.[1]

It follows from this conclusion that the police may also examine the contents of any containers found within the passenger compartment, for if the passenger compartment is within reach of the arrestee, so also will containers in it be within his reach.[2] Such a container may, of course, be searched whether it is open or closed, since the justification for the search is not that the arrestee has no privacy interest in the container, but that the lawful custodial arrest justifies the infringement of any privacy interest the arrestee may have. Thus, while the Court in *Chimel* held that the police could not search all the drawers in an arrestee's house simply because the police had arrested him at home, the Court noted that drawers within an arrestee's reach could be searched because of the danger their contents might pose to the police.

It is true, of course, that these containers will sometimes be such that they could hold neither a weapon nor evidence of the criminal conduct for which the suspect was arrested. However, [a custodial arrest of a reasonably arrested suspect is a reasonable intrusion that requires no additional justification in terms of the facts of the specific case].

* * *

III.

It is not questioned that the respondent was the subject of a lawful custodial arrest on a charge of possessing marihuana. The search of the respondent's jacket followed immediately upon that arrest. The jacket was located inside the passenger compartment of the car in which the respondent had been a passenger just before he was arrested. The jacket was thus within the area which we have concluded was "within the arrestee's immediate control" within the meaning of the *Chimel* case.[3] The search of the jacket, therefore, was a search incident to a lawful custodial arrest, and it did not violate the Fourth and Fourteenth Amendments. Accordingly, the judgment is reversed.

It is so ordered.

■ Justice Brennan, with whom Justice Marshall joins, dissenting.

* * *

1. Our holding today does no more than determine the meaning of *Chimel's* principles in this particular and problematic content. It in no way alters the fundamental principles established in the *Chimel* case regarding the basic scope of searches incident to lawful custodial arrests.

2. "Container" here denotes any object capable of holding another object. It thus includes closed or open glove compartments, consoles, or other receptacles located any-

where within the passenger compartment, as well as luggage, boxes, bags, clothing, and the like. Our holding encompasses only the interior of the passenger compartment of an automobile and does not encompass the trunk.

3. Because of this disposition of the case, there is no need here to consider whether the search and seizure were permissible under the so-called "automobile exception."

The * * * new approach leaves open too many questions and, more important, it provides the police and the courts with too few tools with which to find the answers.

Thus, although the Court concludes that a warrantless search of a car may take place even though the suspect was arrested outside the car, it does not indicate how long after the suspect's arrest that search may validly be conducted. Would a warrantless search incident to arrest be valid if conducted five minutes after the suspect left his car? Thirty minutes? Three hours? Does it matter whether the suspect is standing in close proximity to the car when the search is conducted? Does it matter whether the police formed probable cause to arrest before or after the suspect left his car? And *why* is the rule announced today necessarily limited to searches of cars? What if a suspect is seen walking out of a house where the police, peering in from outside, had formed probable cause to believe a crime was being committed? Could the police then arrest that suspect and enter the house to conduct a search incident to arrest? Even assuming today's rule is limited to searches of the "interior" of cars—an assumption not demanded by logic—what is meant by "interior"? Does it include locked glove compartments, the interior of door panels, or the area under the floorboards? Are special rules necessary for station wagons and hatchbacks, where the luggage compartment may be reached through the interior, or taxicabs, where a glass panel might separate the driver's compartment from the rest of the car? Are the only containers that may be searched those that are large enough to be "capable of holding another object"? Or does the new rule apply to any container, even if it "could hold neither a weapon nor evidence of the criminal conduct for which the suspect was arrested"?

C. FIELD DETENTIONS FOR INVESTIGATION AND RELATED SEARCHES

EDITORS' INTRODUCTION: *TERRY* "STOPS" AND "FRISKS"

Prior to a trilogy of Supreme Court decisions in 1968, the Court's case law could have been read as holding that any seizure of a person challenged under the Fourth Amendment must be supported by at least the probable cause necessary to render reasonable an arrest. In 1968, however, the Court decided Terry v. Ohio, 392 U.S. 1, 88 S.Ct. 1868, 20 L.Ed.2d 889 (1968), and two companion cases, Sibron v. New York and Peters v. New York, 392 U.S. 40, 88 S.Ct. 1889, 20 L.Ed.2d 917 (1968). Those decisions, particularly *Terry*, established that the Fourth Amendment has sufficient flexibility to permit certain law enforcement conduct—often called "stop and frisk"—on less than probable cause.

Terry and its companion cases made clear Fourth Amendment analysis requires a distinction to be drawn between investigatory "stops"—seizures of suspects for purposes of questioning or other investigation— and "frisks"—searches to locate weapons to prevent suspects from harming investigating officers. The two subparts of this section address, first, so-called *Terry* stops and, second, weapon searches permissible in nonarrest situations. The impact of the *Terry* trilogy on Fourth Amendment law in general and the role of stop and frisk in law enforcement general policy, however, deserve preliminary discussion.

The Terry Trilogy: Fourth Amendment Flexibility

Terry noted the exclusionary sanction attaching to Fourth Amendment requirements may be less effective in preventing improper nonarrest field practices than deterring other unacceptable law enforcement conduct:

> [W]e approach the issues in this case mindful of the limitations of the judicial function in controlling the myriad daily situations in which policemen and citizens confront each other on the street. * * * Ever since its inception, the rule excluding evidence seized in violation of the Fourth Amendment has been recognized as a principal mode of discouraging lawless police conduct. * * * The exclusionary rule has its limitations, however, as a tool of judicial control. * * * [I]n some contexts the rule is ineffective as a deterrent. * * * Encounters are initiated by the police for a wide variety of purposes, some of which are wholly unrelated to a desire to prosecute for crime. Doubtless some police "field interrogation" conduct violates the Fourth Amendment. But a stern refusal by this Court to condone such activity does not necessarily render it responsive to the exclusionary rule. Regardless of how effective the rule may be where obtaining convictions is an important objective of the police, it is powerless to deter invasions of constitutionally guaranteed rights where the police either have no interest in prosecuting or are willing to forgo successful prosecution in the interest of serving some other goal.
>
> Proper adjudication of cases in which the exclusionary rule is invoked demands a constant awareness of these limitations. * * *

392 U.S. at 12–14, 88 S.Ct. at 1875–76, 20 L.Ed.2d at 900–02.

The Fourth Amendment reasonableness of law enforcement conduct, *Terry* continued, must be determined by balancing the extent to which particular kinds of police conduct further governmental interests, such as those in crime detection and prevention, against the nature and extent of the conduct's intrusion on Fourth Amendment interests. The first consideration, it noted, suggests "in dealing with the rapidly unfolding and often dangerous situations on city streets the police are in need of an escalating set of flexible responses, graduated in relation to the amount of information they possess." The safety of officers engaged in legitimate investigations, of course, is an especially important objective of this area's law.

Among the factors bearing on the second consideration, *Terry* suggested, is the risk that power to make nonarrest detentions will be abused and its use or abuse experienced as particularly oppressive by minorities. Nonarrest field practices may be particularly subject to abuse, the Court noted. Further, it cited reason to fear that officers' implementation of the right to make field stops and frisks may be influenced by the race of the suspects:

> The President's Commission on Law Enforcement and Administration of Justice found that "[I]n many communities, field interrogations

are a major source of friction between the police and minority groups." President's Commission on Law Enforcement and Administration of Justice, Task Force Report: The Police 183 (1967). It was reported that the friction caused by "[m]isuse of field interrogations" increases "as more police departments adopt 'aggressive patrol' in which officers are encouraged routinely to stop and question persons on the street who are unknown to them, who are suspicious, or whose purpose for being abroad is not readily evident." While the frequency with which "frisking" forms a part of field interrogation practice varies tremendously with the locale, the objective of the interrogation, and the particular officer, it cannot help but be a severely exacerbating factor in police-community tensions. This is particularly true in situations where the "stop and frisk" of youths or minority group members is "motivated by the officers' perceived need to maintain the power image of the beat officer, an aim sometimes accomplished by humiliating anyone who attempts to undermine police control of the streets."

392 U.S. at 15 n. 11, 88 S.Ct. at 1877 n. 11, 20 L.Ed.2d at 902 n. 11.

Much of the Court's discussion in *Terry* and its companion cases was very broad and obviously applied to fields stops for investigation as well as weapons searches. Nevertheless, the three 1968 cases actually decided only the constitutionality of police action, on less than probable cause, constituting weapons searches and seizures of suspects to the extent necessary to perform those protective searches.

Conducting the balancing analysis identified as necessary, the Court rejected Terry's argument that no search or seizure was reasonable unless supported by probable cause as developed in the law of arrest:

[Terry's] argument * * * assumes that the law of arrest has already worked out the balance between the particular interests involved here—the neutralization of danger to the policeman in the investigative circumstance and the sanctity of the individual. But this is not so. An arrest is a wholly different kind of intrusion upon individual freedom from a limited search for weapons, and the interests each is designed to serve are likewise quite different. An arrest is the initial stage of a criminal prosecution. It is intended to vindicate society's interest in having its laws obeyed, and it is inevitably accompanied by future interference with the individual's freedom of movement, whether or not trial or conviction ultimately follows. The protective search for weapons, on the other hand, constitutes a brief, though far from inconsiderable, intrusion upon the sanctity of the person. It does not follow that because an officer may lawfully arrest a person only when he is apprised of facts sufficient to warrant a belief that the person has committed or is committing a crime, the officer is equally unjustified, absent that kind of evidence, in making any intrusions short of an arrest. Moreover, a perfectly reasonable apprehension of danger may arise long before the officer is possessed of adequate information to justify taking a person into custody for the purpose of prosecuting him for a crime. [Terry's] reliance on cases which have worked out standards of reasonableness with regard to "seizures" constituting arrests and searches incident thereto is thus misplaced. It assumes that the interests sought to be vindicated and the invasions of personal security may be equated in the two cases, and thereby ignores a vital aspect of the analysis of the reasonableness of particular types of conduct under the Fourth Amendment.

Our evaluation of the proper balance that has to be struck in this type of case leads us to conclude that there must be a narrowly drawn authority to permit a reasonable search for weapons for the protection of the police officer, where he has reason to believe that he is dealing with an armed and dangerous individual, regardless of whether he has probable cause to arrest the individual for a crime.

392 U.S. at 26–27, 88 S.Ct. at 1882, 20 L.Ed.2d at 908–09. The precise contours of the right to search for weapons on less than probable cause is developed in more detail in the material that follows.

In *Terry* and its companion cases, the Court appeared satisfied to set out its general approach to resolving issues in this area and to decide only the narrow question of the propriety of a weapon search and any detention necessary to accomplish that search. "We * * * decide nothing today," it stressed, "concerning the constitutional propriety of an investigative 'seizure' upon less than probable cause for purposes of 'detention' and/or interrogation." *Terry*, 392 U.S. at 19 n. 16, 88 S.Ct. at 1879 n. 16, 20 L.Ed.2d at 95 n. 16. Nevertheless, its general approach strongly suggested that it would be receptive to the argument that such detentions are—at least under certain circumstances—constitutionally reasonable. In fact, the Court subsequently assumed that *Terry* established the permissibility of such stops. Consequently, nonarrest stops for investigation are widely referred to as *Terry* stops.

Statutory provisions in some jurisdictions authorize the sort of law enforcement activity discussed by the Supreme Court in the *Terry* trilogy. Probably the leading example is the New York statute, which provides:

140.50   Temporary questioning of persons in public places; search for weapons

1.   * * * [A] police officer may stop a person in a public place located within the geographical area of such officer's employment when he reasonably suspects that such person is committing, has committed or is about to commit either (a) a felony or (b) a misdemeanor defined in the penal law, and may demand of him his name, address and an explanation of his conduct.

* * *

3.   When upon stopping a person under circumstances prescribed in subdivision[ ] one * * * a police officer * * * reasonably suspects that he is in danger of physical injury, he may search such person for a deadly weapon or any instrument, article or substance readily capable of causing serious physical injury and of a sort not ordinarily carried in public places by law-abiding persons. If he finds such a weapon or instrument, or any other property possession of which he reasonably believes may constitute the commission of a crime, he may take it and keep it until the completion of the questioning, at which time he shall either return it, if lawfully possessed, or arrest such person.

Stop and Frisk in the Context of General Law Enforcement Philosophy

When New York's Attorney General undertook a comprehensive examination of stop and frisk practices in New York City, he began by putting the formal law in conceptual context. See The New York City Police Department's "Stop & Frisk" Practices: A Report to the People of the State of New York from the Office of the Attorney General (1999) ("New York Report"). Stop and frisk, he suggested, can only be fully understood if it is considered not simply as a specific law enforcement technique to prevent, investigate, detect, and solve crime but also as part of an overall crime-fighting philosophy.

Addressing stop and frisk as part of New York City's comprehensive law enforcement approach to crime, the report noted that New York police, like many other modern departments, embrace modern policing philosophies of "community policing" and "order maintenance"/"broken windows" theory.

> "Community policing" holds that effective crime-fighting is based on a "partnership" between police and the residents of the immediate community they serve. The goal of the partnership is to ensure that police "meet the demands" of law-abiding people within their jurisdiction.

New York Report at 47. Implementing community policing, the department discovered that rank-and-file community residents were more concerned about petty crime and disorder problem than the major crimes that had preoccupied police.

> The * * * impact was to increase police presence in the everyday life of the community. The cop on foot patrol—walking the neighborhood, interacting with its residents, learning the complex social dynamics of the area, and responding to low-level disorder complaints—is emblematic of the "community policing" model.

New York Report at 47. In addition, New York police adopted

> a second approach known as "order maintenance" theory (or simply, "broken windows"). Order maintenance theory rests on two fundamental premises * * *.

> The first premise holds that low-level disorder in the streets—graffiti, aggressive panhandling, public drunkenness and the like—makes people fearful and weakens neighborhood social controls. In this atmosphere, law-abiding civilians become more fearful and withdrawn from the daily life of the community, effectively ceding the street to the forces of greater disorder and more serious crime. As Kelling and Wilson [Broken Windows: The Police and Neighborhood Safety, Atlantic Monthly, March 1982] put it: "[I]f [one broken window] is left unrepaired, all the rest of the windows will soon be broken."

> Only by actively combating low-level disorder, can police and the neighborhood residents signal to the criminal element their resolve that "law breaking of any kind will not be tolerated"—and thus begin to restore standards of behavior which make serious crime untenable.

Second, as a tactical matter, order maintenance theory "advocate[s] close collaboration between police and citizens ... in the development of neighborhood standards" of conduct. Such standards are "to be enforced for the most part though non-arrest approaches—education, persuasion, counseling, and ordering"—so that arrest would only be resorted to when other approaches failed. In this sense, order maintenance theory and "community policing" connect and overlap to a substantial degree.

The results * * * seemed to confirm the order maintenance hypothesis. * * * [Police] discovered that persons arrested for turnstyle-jumping frequently were found to be "carrying weapons or [to] have outstanding warrants." As the progenitor of "broken windows" theory would later describe the key lesson of the * * * experience: "Restoring order reduces crime ... at least in part because restoring order puts police in contact with persons who carry weapons and who commit serious crime." [G.L. Kelling & C.M. Coles, Fixing Broken Windows: Restoring Order and Reducing Crime in Our communities (1996).]

* * *

[T]he role of "stop & frisk" in furthering the Department's goals of order maintenance, deterrence, crime prevention, and a direct attack on gun violence is clear. Given the Department's focus on apprehending violent criminals and preventing more serious crimes by aggressively enforcing laws aimed at low-level criminality, "stop & frisk" serves as an important wedge into the criminal element.

Order maintenance theory encourages officers to intervene in instances of low-level disorder, whether observed or suspected, with approaches which fall short of arrest. A "stop" intervention provides an occasion for the police to have context with persons presumably involved in low-level criminality—without having to effect a formal arrest, and under a lower-constitutional standard (i.e., "reasonable suspicion"). Indeed, because low-level "quality of life" and misdemeanor offenses are more likely to be committed in the open, as a theoretical matter, the "reasonable suspicion" standard may be more readily satisfied as to those sorts of crimes. To the extent that "stop" encounters create points of contact between police and low-level offenders, such contacts can lead to the apprehension of persons already wanted for more serious crimes, or who might be prepared to commit them in the near future.

* * *

Finally, as implemented by the NYPD, "stop & frisk" serves the Department's No. 1 strategic goal—"getting guns off the streets of New York." Notwithstanding its origin as a technique designed to assure officer safety, "stop & frisk" plainly has been used as a method to detect and seize illegal handguns. [During a study period], fully 34% of all documented "stop & frisk" encounters by NYPD officers citywide were for suspected weapons possession.

* * *

Thus, a model which values both proactive police interventions short of arrest and an aggressive approach to low-level disorder is well served by aggressive use of "stop & frisk." More to the point, "stop & frisk" has served as an important tactical resource in promoting the Department's specific strategic crime-fighting goals.

New York Report at 47–59. The specific conclusions of the report concerning stop and frisk practices in New York are discussed later in this subsection.

1. FIELD DETENTIONS

EDITORS' INTRODUCTION: REASONABLE SUSPICION

The Supreme Court's case law after *Terry* and its companion decisions clearly regards law enforcement as constitutionally permitted to seize and briefly detain persons for purposes of investigation on less than the probable cause required for an arrest. What factual basis is required for such action? Post-*Terry* decisions used somewhat different terminology to describe the required basis, but the Court appears to have settled on "reasonable suspicion" as the standard.

What is this required reasonable suspicion? In Alabama v. White, 496 U.S. 325, 110 S.Ct. 2412, 110 L.Ed.2d 301 (1990), the Court explained in general terms:

Reasonable suspicion is a less demanding standard than probable cause not only in the sense that reasonable suspicion can be established with information that is different in quantity or content than that required to establish probable cause, but also in the sense that reasonable suspicion can arise from information that is less reliable than that required to show probable cause. * * * Reasonable suspicion, like probable cause, is dependent upon both the content of information possessed by police and its degree of reliability. Both factors—quantity and quality—are considered in the "totality of the circumstances—the whole picture," that must be taken into account when evaluating whether there is reasonable suspicion. * * *

496 U.S. at 330, 110 S.Ct. at 2416, 110 L.Ed.2d at 309. The case reprinted in this section presents an interesting application of this standard. Several specific aspects of reasonable suspicion as the standard for nonarrest investigatory field detentions, however, merit preliminary consideration.

Reasonable Suspicion as Applied

What specific facts support valid nonarrest field detentions is obviously a difficult question. The Supreme Court has addressed the problem in a number of contexts.

Several cases involved informant tips. In Adams v. Williams, 407 U.S. 143, 92 S.Ct. 1921, 32 L.Ed.2d 612 (1972), an informant approached a police cruiser and informed the officer a person seated in a nearby vehicle was carrying narcotics and had a gun at his waist. The officer knew the informant and had received information from him in the past. On the other hand, this information involved claims of homosexual activity in a local railroad station and the followup investigation resulted in neither confirmation nor arrests. The officer located the person described by the informant and detained him. Upholding the detention, the Supreme Court rejected the proposition that the necessary reasonable cause must be based upon the officer's personal observation. While the tip may not have amounted to probable cause justifying an arrest, it did support the action taken:

> This is a stronger case than obtains in the case of an anonymous telephone tip. The informant here came forward personally to give information that was immediately verifiable at the scene. Indeed, * * * the informant might have been subject to immediate arrest for making a false complaint had [the] investigation proved the tip incorrect.

407 U.S. at 146–47, 92 S.Ct. at 1923, 32 L.Ed.2d at 617.

An anonymous tip was at issue in Alabama v. White, 496 U.S. 325, 110 S.Ct. 2412, 110 L.Ed.2d 301 (1990). The facts were as follows:

> On April 22, 1987, at approximately 3 p.m., Corporal B.H. Davis of the Montgomery Police Department received a telephone call from an anonymous person, stating that Vanessa White would be leaving 235–C Lynwood Terrace Apartments at a particular time in a brown Plymouth station wagon with the right taillight lens broken, that she would be going to Dobey's Motel, and that she would be in possession of about an ounce of cocaine inside a brown attache case. Corporal Davis and his partner, Corporal P.A. Reynolds, proceeded to the Lynwood Terrace Apartments. The officers saw a brown Plymouth station wagon with a broken right taillight in the parking lot in front of the 235 building. The officers observed [White] leave the 235 building, carrying nothing in her hands, and enter the station wagon. They followed the vehicle as it drove the most direct route to Dobey's Motel. When the vehicle reached the Mobile Highway, on which Dobey's Motel is located, Corporal Reynolds requested a patrol unit to stop the vehicle. The vehicle was stopped at approximately 4:18 p.m., just short of Dobey's Motel.

Relying heavily upon Illinois v. Gates, reprinted in Chapter 3, the Court held *Gates'* totality of the circumstances approach should be taken, with appropriate accommodation for the less demanding standard applicable in field stop situations. It declined to conclude that an anonymous caller's tip alone could never provide reasonable suspicion. Further, the range of detailed assertions in the tip before it suggested that it was reliable. Nevertheless, the Court—after acknowledging the case was a close one— finally concluded the tip lacked sufficient indicia of reliability to itself constitute reasonable suspicion. But the tip and the officers' corroboration of some information in it adequately supported suspicion White was engaged in criminal activity:

> What was important was the caller's ability to predict [White's] *future behavior,* because it demonstrated inside information—a special familiarity with [White's] affairs. The general public would have no way of knowing that [White] would shortly leave the building, get in the described car, and drive the most direct route to Dobey's Motel.

Because only a small number of people are generally privy to an individual's itinerary, it is reasonable for police to believe that a person with access to such information is likely to also have access to reliable information about that individual's illegal activities. When significant aspects of the caller's predictions were verified, there was reason to believe not only that the caller was honest but also that he was well informed, at least well enough to justify the stop.

496 U.S. at 332, 110 S.Ct. at 2417, 110 L.Ed.2d at 310 (emphasis in original).

The leading decision finding reasonable suspicion lacking is Brown v. Texas, 443 U.S. 47, 99 S.Ct. 2637, 61 L.Ed.2d 357 (1979). The Court described the facts as follows:

At 12:45 on the afternoon of December 9, 1977, officers Venegas and Soleto of the El Paso Police Department were cruising in a patrol car. They observed [Brown] and another man walking in opposite directions away from one another in an alley. Although the two men were a few feet apart when they were first seen, officer Venegas later testified that both officers believed the two had been together or were about to meet until the patrol car appeared.

The area had a high incidence of drug traffic. Brown was stopped because, as one officer testified, the situation "looked suspicious" and the officers had never seen Brown in the area before. The Supreme Court held the stop unreasonable:

Officer Venegas testified at [Brown's] trial that the situation in the alley "looked suspicious," but he was unable to point to any facts supporting that conclusion. There is no indication in the record that it was unusual for people to be in the alley. The fact that [Brown] was in a neighborhood frequented by drug users, standing alone, is not a basis for concluding that [Brown] himself was engaged in criminal conduct. * * * When pressed, Officer Venegas acknowledged that the only reason he stopped [Brown] was to ascertain his identity. The record suggests an understandable desire to assert a police presence; however that purpose does not negate Fourth Amendment guarantees.

443 U.S. at 52, 99 S.Ct. at 2641, 61 L.Ed.2d at 362–63.

Reasonable Suspicion, Airport Stops, and "Profiles"

Investigatory stops at airports have given rise to particular difficulties in determining whether reasonable suspicion was shown. Barebones testimony that a passenger meets a "drug carrier profile" does not constitute reasonable suspicion. Reid v. Georgia, 448 U.S. 438, 100 S.Ct. 2752, 65 L.Ed.2d 890 (1980) (per curiam). But passengers' evasive and objectively suspicious may meet the standard. Florida v. Rodriguez, 469 U.S. 1, 105 S.Ct. 308, 83 L.Ed.2d 165 (1984).

Airport stops—and the significance of profile testimony—were addressed at length in United States v. Sokolow, 490 U.S. 1, 109 S.Ct. 1581, 104 L.Ed.2d 1 (1989). In July of 1984, Andrew Sokolow and a female companion flew from Honolulu to Miami, a 20 hour flight. When they returned after a 48 hour stay in Miami, DEA officers stopped Sokolow for investigative purposes. The officers had the following information: Sokolow was about 25 years old. He paid $2,100 for the tickets with cash from a roll of $20 bills that appeared to contain about $4,000. He was wearing a black jumpsuit and gold jewelry and appeared nervous. His destination was Miami, a "source city for drugs." Neither Sokolow nor his companion checked their luggage. Sokolow gave the ticket agent a home telephone number. Although he gave his name to the agent as "Andrew Kray," the telephone number was listed to "Karl Herman." The agent, however, identified the voice on the answering machine tape at the number as that of the man who purchased the tickets. (Herman, it was later discovered, was Sokolow's roommate.) The majority acknowledged Sokolow's activity was itself "lawful" but held it established reasonable suspicion. It stressed the evidence that Sokolow was traveling under an alias, that he conducted a large-scale purchase in cash, and that his trip to a source city was surprisingly short for the expense involved. After concluding that the facts established reasonable suspicion, the majority noted that one of the agents had testified that Sokolow's behavior "had all the classic aspects of a drug courier." It then commented:

> We do not agree with [Sokolow] that our analysis is somehow changed by the agents' belief that his behavior was consistent with one of the DEA's "drug courier profiles." A court sitting to determine the existence of reasonable suspicion must require the agent to articulate the factors leading to that conclusion, but the fact that these factors may be set forth in a "profile" does not somehow detract from their evidentiary significance as seen by a trained agent.

490 U.S. at 10, 109 S.Ct. at 1587, 104 L.Ed.2d at 12. Justice Marshall, joined by Justice Brennan, dissented.

Possible Limits on Suspected Offenses

Are there any limits on the offenses for which field stops may be made? Stops might, for example, be permitted only on reasonable suspicion that the person is involved in relatively serious criminal behavior. In United States v. Hensley, 469 U.S. 221, 105 S.Ct. 675, 83 L.Ed.2d 604 (1985), discussed in detail later in this Introduction, the Court was careful to limit its approval of investigatory stops to those involving past *serious* offenses— those constituting felonies. "We need not and do not decide today," it commented, "whether *Terry* stops to investigate all past crimes, however serious, are permitted."

The nature of some offenses may suggest too high a risk that *Terry* stops to investigate them might be abused. In Adams v. Williams, 407 U.S. 143, 92 S.Ct. 1921, 32 L.Ed.2d 612 (1972), the officer's suspicion concerned the suspect's possible commission of crimes consisting of possessing items— possession of drugs and possession of a prohibited weapon. One of the judges in the Court of Appeals urged stops not be permitted for such possessory crimes. "There is too much danger," he reasoned, "that, instead of the stop being the object and the protective frisk an incident thereto, the reverse will be true." Williams v. Adams, 436 F.2d 30, 38 (2d Cir.1970) (Friendly, J., dissenting), reversed 441 F.2d 394 (2d Cir.1971) (en banc) (per curiam). Justice Brennan adopted this position in the Supreme Court.

407 U.S. at 151–53, 92 S.Ct. at 1926–27, 32 L.Ed.2d at 620 (Brennan, J., dissenting). The opinion of the Court, written by then-Justice Rehnquist, did not address the matter.

Reasonable Suspicion Concerning Past and Future Offenses

The Court has somewhat offhanded suggested *Terry* and later decisions settled the constitutionality of investigatory stops for past and future offenses as well as those being committed at the time of the stop. "Under the Fourth Amendment [] we have held," the Court commented in Berkemer v. McCarty, 468 U.S. 420, 439, 104 S.Ct. 3138, 3150, 82 L.Ed.2d 317, 334 (1984), "a policeman who lacks probable cause but whose 'observations lead him reasonably to suspect' that a particular person has committed, is committing, or is about to commit a crime, may detain that person briefly in order to 'investigate the circumstances that provoke suspicion.' "

Until United States v. Hensley, 469 U.S. 221, 105 S.Ct. 675, 83 L.Ed.2d 604 (1985), however, the cases decided by the Court—many of which were discussed earlier in this Introduction—all involved situations in which the suspected criminal activity was still in progress when the officers intervened. In *Hensley*, the Court acknowledged it had never actually held a nonarrest *Terry* stop constitutionally permissible on probable cause to believe the suspect had committed an offense in the past. Hensley had been stopped on reasonable suspicion that he had been involved in a robbery committed twelve days earlier. The Court treated the question whether stops for investigation are permissible for completed past offenses as a significant one, and addressed the matter at length. Application of the balancing analysis used to determine the reasonableness of nonarrest stops, it acknowledged, must be somewhat different in past crime situations:

> The factors in the balance may be somewhat different when a stop to investigate past criminal activity is involved rather than a stop to investigate ongoing criminal conduct. * * * [O]ne general interest present in the context of ongoing or imminent criminal activity is "that of effective crime prevention and detention." A stop to investigate an already completed crime does not necessarily promote the interest of crime prevention as directly as a stop to investigate suspected ongoing criminal activity. Similarly, the exigent circumstances which require a police officer to step in before a crime is committed or completed are not necessarily as pressing long afterwards. Public safety may be less threatened by a suspect in a past crime who now appears to be going about his lawful business than it is by a suspect who is currently in the process of violating the law. Finally, officers making a stop to investigate past crimes may have a wider range of opportunity to choose the time and circumstances of the stop.

469 U.S. at 228–29, 105 S.Ct. at 680, 83 L.Ed.2d at 612. Nevertheless, the Court concluded in some situations the law enforcement interests at stake outweigh the interests of individuals in being free of relatively nonintrusive *Terry* stops. Disclaiming a decision on whether its holding would apply to less serious crimes, the Court concluded that "if police have a reasonable suspicion, grounded in specific and articulable facts, that a person they

encounter was involved in or is wanted in connection with a completed felony, then a *Terry* stop may be made to investigate that suspicion."

Neither *Hensley* nor any other of the Court's decisions has actually passed on the reasonableness of an investigatory stop based on reasonable suspicion the person would commit a crime *in the future*. *Hensley* characterized *Terry* itself as a case in which "police stopped or seized a person because they suspected he was about to commit a crime." But *Terry* in fact passed only on the seizure of Terry to the extent necessary to conduct the weapons search. Arguably the Court was careful to avoid, at this early stage in the development of nonarrest detention law, any definitive decision on stops to investigate concern that a person will commit a future crime. In *Terry's* companion cases, the parties sought to have the Court pass on the constitutionality of New York's "stop-and-frisk" law, set out earlier in the Editors' Introduction to Part C of this chapter, which authorized an officer to stop a person "whom [the officer] reasonably suspects is committing, has committed or *is about to commit*" one of the specific offenses. In neither case, however, did the Court address the facial validity of the statute generally or, in particular, the authorization to stop those reasonably suspected of being "about to commit" an offense.

If officers are permitted by the Fourth Amendment to make investigatory stops regarding future offenses, whether *Terry's* facts justified such a stop arguably presented a quite difficult question. The Supreme Court acknowledged the reasonableness of detentions on less than probable cause only in the 1968 trilogy of decisions. It may have believed that the courts should have more opportunity to address investigatory stop situations before the Supreme Court resolved particularly difficult subquestions concerning the scope of the stop authority. The facts of *Terry* were as follows:

Officer McFadden testified that while he was patrolling in plain clothes in downtown Cleveland at approximately 2:30 in the afternoon of October 31, 1963, his attention was attracted by two men, Chilton and Terry, standing on the corner of Huron Road and Euclid Avenue. He had never seen the two men before, and he was unable to say precisely what first drew his eye to them. However, he testified that he had been a policeman for 39 years and a detective for 35 and that he had been assigned to patrol this vicinity of downtown Cleveland for shoplifters and pickpockets for 30 years. He explained that he had developed routine habits of observation over the years and that he would "stand and watch people or walk and watch people at many intervals of the day." He added: "Now, in this case when I looked over they didn't look right to me at the time."

His interest aroused, Officer McFadden took up a post of observation in the entrance to a store 300 to 400 feet away from the two men. "I get more purpose to watch them when I seen their movements,' " he testified. He saw one of the men leave the other one and walk southwest on Huron Road, past some stores. The man paused for a moment and looked in a store window, then walked on a short distance, turned around and walked back toward the corner, pausing once again to look in the same store window. He rejoined his companion at the corner, and the two conferred briefly. Then the second man went through the same series of motions, strolling down Huron Road, looking in the same window, walking on a short distance, turning back, peering in the store window again, and returning to confer with the first man at the corner. The two men repeated this ritual alternately between five and six times apiece—in all, roughly a dozen trips. At one point, while the two were standing together on the corner, a third man approached them and engaged them briefly in conversation. This man then left the two others and walked west on Euclid Avenue. Chilton and Terry resumed their measured pacing, peering and conferring. After this had gone on for 10 to 12 minutes, the two men walked off together, heading west on Euclid Avenue, following the path taken earlier by the third man. By this time Officer McFadden had become thoroughly suspicious. He testified that after observing their elaborately casual and oft-repeated reconnaissance of the store window on Huron Road, he suspected the two men of "casing a job, a stick-up," and that he considered it his duty as a police officer to investigate further. He added that he feared "they may have a gun." Thus, Officer McFadden followed Chilton and Terry and saw them stop in front of Zucker's store to talk to the same man who had conferred with them earlier on the street corner. Deciding that the situation was ripe for direct action, Officer McFadden approached the three men, identified himself as a police officer and asked for their names. At this point his knowledge was confined to what he had observed. He was not acquainted with any of the three men by name or by sight, and he had received no information concerning them from any other source. When the men "mumbled something" in response to his inquiries, Officer McFadden grabbed petitioner Terry, spun him around so that they were facing the other two, with Terry between McFadden and the others, and patted down the outside of his clothing. In the left breast pocket of Terry's overcoat Officer McFadden felt a pistol. He reached inside the overcoat pocket, but was unable to remove the gun. At this point, keeping Terry between himself and the others, the officer ordered all three men to enter Zucker's store. As they went in, he removed Terry's overcoat completely, removed a .38–caliber revolver from the pocket and ordered all three men to face the wall with their hands raised. Officer McFadden proceeded to pat down the outer clothing of Chilton and the third man, Katz. He discovered another revolver in the outer pocket of Chilton's overcoat, but no weapons were found on Katz. The officer testified that he only patted the men down to see whether they had weapons, and that he did not put his hands beneath the outer garments of either Terry or Chilton until he felt their guns. So far as appears from the record, he never placed his hands beneath Katz' outer garments. Officer McFadden seized Chilton's gun, asked the proprietor of the store to call a police wagon, and took all three men to the station, where Chilton and Terry were formally charged with carrying concealed weapons.

If McFadden seized Terry when he confronted him and his companions in front of Zucker's store and requested their names, was that stop constitutionally permissible? Finding McFadden could constitutionally search the trio for weapons, the Court explained:

[O]n the facts and circumstances Officer McFadden detailed before the trial judge a reasonably prudent man would have been warranted in believing petitioner was armed and thus presented a threat to the officer's safety while he was investigating his suspicious behavior. The actions of Terry and Chilton were consistent with McFadden's hypothesis that these men were contemplating a daylight robbery—which, it is reasonable to assume, would be likely to involve the use of weapons—and nothing in their conduct from the time he first noticed them until the time he confronted them and identified himself as a police officer gave him sufficient reason to negate that hypothesis. Although the trio had departed the original scene, there was nothing to indicate abandonment of an intent to commit a robbery at some point. Thus, when Officer McFadden approached the three men gathered before the display window at Zucker's store he had observed enough to make it quite reasonable to fear that they were armed * * *.

392 U.S. at 28, 88 S.Ct. at 1883, 20 L.Ed.2d at 910. The Court did not, however, reach whether McFadden could seize Terry to question him about any plans he might have had to commit robber.

Perhaps the difficulty of predicting whether suspects will commit future crimes means that stops on reasonable suspicion this will occur are unacceptable. Or, perhaps such stops are acceptable only if an officer has reasonable suspicion the suspect is—in the words of the New York statute—*about to* commit an offense. Arguably predictions concerning whether suspects will quite soon engage in criminal activity are more accurate than other predictions, and therefore only stops for relatively imminent future offenses are reasonable. If investigatory stops are permissible only upon reasonable suspicion that the suspect is about to commit an offense, could McFadden have reasonably suspected that Terry and his companions were *about to* commit the robbery McFadden reasonably suspected the three had in mind?

Stop and Frisk in Practice

The New York Attorney General made an effort to determine how New York City police actually used the authority to make *Terry* stops. The results were reported in New York City. The New York City Police Department's "Stop & Frisk" Practices: A Report to the People of the State of New York from the Office of the Attorney General (1999) ("New York Report").

Under New York departmental policies, an officer is required to file a "UF–250" report on each incident in which a person is stopped and (a) force is used to make the stop; (b) the person stopped is frisked or searched; (c) the person stopped is arrested; or (d) the person stopped refuses to identify himself. If an incident involves a stop but none of the factors mandating a report applies, the officer may file a report. The reports are to include the race of the person stopped and the facts which led the officer to make the stop. The study analyzed 174,919 reports of stops during 1998–1999; 72.5% of the reports reflected incidents in which a report was required, and the remaining 27.5% reflected incidents in which the officer chose to file a report.

The investigators looked at which the facts set out by the officers were sufficient to constitute reasonable suspicion. The results were as follows:

facts sufficient to constitute reasonable suspicion	61.1%
facts not sufficient to constitute reasonable suspicion	15.4%
report insufficient to permit determination	23.5%
	100%

New York Report at xiii-xiv. A form was put into the insufficient to determine category if the situation suggested that additional information "readily hypothesized" might justify the stop. Thus if a form said, "moving furniture/carrying 'out of place objects,'" the investigators assumed other information available but not reported might justify the stop and they treated it as insufficient to permit determination.

Overall, one out of nine stops resulted in an arrest. The study found this "unsurprising, given the purpose of a 'stop' and the lower level of suspicion required to justify a 'stop' as opposed to an arrest." New York Report at viii.

The study provided some support for concern that field stops are made in part on racial grounds. Overall, the results were as follows

	City Population	Stops
Blacks	25.6%	50.6%
Hispanics	23.7%	33.0%
Whites	43.4%	12.9%

The disparity was most pronounced in those precincts in which a majority of the population was white. New York Report at vii-viii.

Precincts in which minorities constituted the majority of the population tended to have more "stop & frisk" activity than precincts in which whites constituted the majority. Some, but not all, of this was accounted for by the higher crime rate in those precincts with a nonwhite majority.

Blacks were less likely to be stopped on suspicion of property crimes than whites or hispanics. But—controlling for other factors—blacks were 2.1 times more often than whites stopped on suspicion of committing a violent crime and 2.4 times more often on suspicion of carrying a weapon. Hispanics were stopped 1.7 times as often as whites on suspicion of committing a violent crime and 2.0 times as often on suspicion of carrying a weapon. New York Report at x-xi.

* * *

Questioning of suspects during a nonarrest detention raises special issues concerning the suspects' right to be free from compelled self-incrimination and related matters. These questioning issues are considered in Chapter 7.

Florida v. Royer

Supreme Court of the United States, 1983.
460 U.S. 491, 103 S.Ct. 1319, 75 L.Ed.2d 229.

■ JUSTICE WHITE announced the judgment of the Court and delivered an opinion in which JUSTICES MARSHALL, POWELL and STEVENS joined.

* * *

I

On January 3, 1978, Royer was observed at Miami International Airport by two plain-clothes detectives of the Dade County, Florida, Public Safety Department assigned to the County's Organized Crime Bureau, Narcotics Investigation Section. Detectives Johnson and Magdalena believed that Royer's appearance, mannerisms, luggage, and actions fit the so-called "drug courier profile." Royer, apparently unaware of the attention he had attracted, purchased a one-way ticket to New York City and checked his two suitcases, placing on each suitcase an identification tag bearing the name "Holt" and the destination, "LaGuardia". As Royer made his way to the concourse which led to the airline boarding area, the two detectives approached him, identified themselves as policemen working out of the sheriff's office, and asked if Royer had a "moment" to speak with them; Royer said "Yes."

Upon request, but without oral consent, Royer produced for the detectives his airline ticket and his driver's license. The airline ticket, like the baggage identification tags, bore the name "Holt," while the driver's license carried respondent's correct name, "Royer." When the detectives asked about the discrepancy, Royer explained that a friend had made the reservation in the name of "Holt." Royer became noticeably more nervous during this conversation, whereupon the detectives informed Royer that they were in fact narcotics investigators and that they had reason to suspect him of transporting narcotics.

The detectives did not return his airline ticket and identification but asked Royer to accompany them to a room, approximately forty feet away, adjacent to the concourse. Royer said nothing in response but went with the officers as he had been asked to do. The room was later described by Detective Johnson as a "large storage closet," located in the stewardesses' lounge and containing a small desk and two chairs. Without Royer's consent or agreement, Detective Johnson, using Royer's baggage check stubs, retrieved the "Holt" luggage from the airline and brought it to the room where respondent and Detective Magdalena were waiting. Royer was asked if he would consent to a search of the suitcases. Without orally responding to this request, Royer produced a key and unlocked one of the suitcases, which the detective then opened without seeking further assent from Royer. Drugs were found in that suitcase. According to Detective Johnson, Royer stated that he did not know the combination to the lock on the second suitcase. When asked if he objected to the detective opening the second suitcase, Royer said "no, go ahead," and did not object when the detective explained that the suitcase might have to be broken open. The suitcase was pried open by the officers and more marihuana was found.

Royer was then told that he was under arrest. Approximately fifteen minutes had elapsed from the time the detectives initially approached respondent until his arrest upon the discovery of the contraband.

Prior to his trial for felony possession of marihuana, Royer made a motion to suppress the evidence obtained in the search of the suitcases. The trial court found that Royer's consent to the search was "freely and voluntarily given," and that, regardless of the consent, the warrantless search was reasonable because "the officer doesn't have the time to run out and get a search warrant because the plane is going to take off." Following the denial of the motion to suppress, Royer * * * was convicted.

The District Court of Appeal, sitting en banc, reversed Royer's conviction. * * * We granted the State's petition for certiorari, and now affirm.

II

* * * The Florida Court of Appeal * * * concluded * * * that Royer had been seized when he gave his consent to search his luggage [and] also that the bounds of an investigative stop had been exceeded. In its view the "confinement" in this case went beyond the limited restraint of a *Terry* investigative stop, and Royer's consent was thus tainted by the illegality, a conclusion that required reversal in the absence of probable cause to arrest. The question before us is whether the record warrants that conclusion. We think that it does.

III

The State proffers three reasons for holding that when Royer consented to the search of his luggage, he was not being illegally detained. First, it is submitted that the entire encounter was consensual and hence Royer was not being held against his will at all. We find this submission untenable. Asking for and examining Royer's ticket and his driver's license were no doubt permissible in themselves, but when the officers identified themselves as narcotics agents, told Royer that he was suspected of transporting narcotics, and asked him to accompany them to the police room, while retaining his ticket and driver's license and without indicating in any way that he was free to depart, Royer was effectively seized for the purposes of the Fourth Amendment. These circumstances surely amount to a show of official authority such that "a reasonable person would have believed he was not free to leave." United States v. Mendenhall, 446 U.S. 544, 554, 100 S.Ct. 1870, 1877, 64 L.Ed.2d 497 (Opinion of Stewart, J.).

Second, the State submits that if Royer was seized, there existed reasonable, articulable suspicion to justify a temporary detention and that the limits of a *Terry*-type stop were never exceeded. We agree with the State that when the officers discovered that Royer was travelling under an assumed name, this fact, and the facts already known to the officers— paying cash for a one-way ticket, the mode of checking the two bags, and Royer's appearance and conduct in general—were adequate grounds for suspecting Royer of carrying drugs and for temporarily detaining him and his luggage while they attempted to verify or dispel their suspicions in a manner that did not exceed the limits of an investigative detention. We also agree that had Royer voluntarily consented to the search of his luggage while he was justifiably being detained on reasonable suspicion, the products of the search would be admissible against him. We have concluded, however, that at the time Royer produced the key to his suitcase, the detention to which he was then subjected was a more serious intrusion on his personal liberty than is allowable on mere suspicion of criminal activity.

By the time Royer was informed that the officers wished to examine his luggage, he had identified himself when approached by the officers and had attempted to explain the discrepancy between the name shown on his identification and the name under which he had purchased his ticket and identified his luggage. The officers were not satisfied, for they informed him they were narcotics agents and had reason to believe that he was carrying illegal drugs. They requested him to accompany them to the police room. Royer went with them. He found himself in a small room—a large closet—equipped with a desk and two chairs. He was alone with two police officers who again told him that they thought he was carrying narcotics. He also found that the officers, without his consent, had retrieved his checked luggage from the airlines. What had begun as a consensual inquiry in a public place had escalated into an investigatory procedure in a police interrogation room, where the police, unsatisfied with previous explanations, sought to confirm their suspicions. The officers had Royer's ticket, they had his identification, and they had seized his luggage. Royer was never informed that he was free to board his plane if he so chose, and he reasonably believed that he was being detained. At least as of that moment, any consensual aspects of the encounter had evaporated, and we cannot fault the Florida Court of Appeal for concluding that Terry v. Ohio and the cases following it did not justify the restraint to which Royer was then subjected. As a practical matter, Royer was under arrest. Consistent with this conclusion, the State conceded in the Florida courts that Royer would not have been free to leave the interrogation room had he asked to do so. Furthermore, the state's brief in this Court interprets the testimony of the officers at the suppression hearing as indicating that had Royer refused to consent to a search of his luggage, the officers would have held the luggage and sought a warrant to authorize the search.

We also think that the officers' conduct was more intrusive than necessary to effectuate an investigative detention otherwise authorized by the *Terry* line of cases. First, by returning his ticket and driver's license, and informing him that he was free to go if he so desired, the officers may have obviated any claim that the encounter was anything but a consensual matter from start to finish. Second, there are undoubtedly reasons of safety and security that would justify moving a suspect from one location to another during an investigatory detention, such as from an airport concourse to a more private area. There is no indication in this case that such reasons prompted the officers to transfer the site of the encounter from the concourse to the interrogation room. It appears, rather, that the primary interest of the officers was not in having an extended conversation with Royer but in the contents of his luggage, a matter which the officers did not pursue orally with Royer until after the encounter was relocated to the police room. The record does not reflect any facts which would support a finding that the legitimate law enforcement purposes which justified the detention in the first instance were furthered by removing Royer to the police room prior to the officer's attempt to gain his consent to a search of his luggage. As we have noted, had Royer consented to a search on the spot, the search could have been conducted with Royer present in the area where the bags were retrieved by Officer Johnson and any evidence recovered would have been admissible against him. If the search proved negative, Royer would have been free to go much earlier and with less likelihood of missing his flight, which in itself can be a very serious matter in a variety of circumstances.

Third, the State has not touched on the question whether it would have been feasible to investigate the contents of Royer's bags in a more expeditious way. The courts are not strangers to the use of trained dogs to detect the presence of controlled substances in luggage. There is no indication here that this means was not feasible and available. If it had been used, Royer and his luggage could have been momentarily detained while this investigative procedure was carried out. Indeed, it may be that no detention at all would have been necessary. A negative result would have freed Royer in short order; a positive result would have resulted in his justifiable arrest on probable cause.

We do not suggest that there is a litmus-paper test for distinguishing a consensual encounter from a seizure or for determining when a seizure exceeds the bounds of an investigative stop. Even in the discrete category of airport encounters, there will be endless variations in the facts and circumstances, so much variation that it is unlikely that the courts can reduce to a sentence or a paragraph a rule that will provide unarguable answers to the question whether there has been an unreasonable search or seizure in violation of the Fourth Amendment. Nevertheless, we must render judgment, and we think that the Florida Court of Appeal cannot be faulted in concluding that the limits of a *Terry*-stop had been exceeded.

IV

The State's third and final argument is that Royer was not being illegally held when he gave his consent because there was probable cause to arrest him at that time. Officer Johnson testified at the suppression hearing and the Florida Court of Appeal held that there was no probable cause to arrest until Royer's bags were opened, but the fact that the officers did not believe there was probable cause and proceeded on a consensual or *Terry*-stop rationale would not foreclose the State from justifying Royer's custody by proving probable cause and hence removing any barrier to relying on Royer's consent to search. We agree with the Florida Court of Appeal, however, that probable cause to arrest Royer did not exist at the time he consented to the search of his luggage. The facts are that a nervous young man with two American Tourister bags paid cash for an airline ticket to a "target city." These facts led to inquiry, which in turn revealed that the ticket had been bought under an assumed name. The proffered explanation did not satisfy the officers. We cannot agree with the State, if this is its position, that every nervous young man paying cash for a ticket to New York City under an assumed name and carrying two heavy American Tourister bags may be arrested and held to answer for a serious felony charge.

V

Because we affirm the Florida Court of Appeal's conclusion that Royer was being illegally detained when he consented to the search of his luggage, we agree that the consent was tainted by the illegality and was ineffective to justify the search. The judgment of the Florida Court of Appeal is accordingly

Affirmed.

■ JUSTICE BRENNAN, concurring in the result.

* * *

To the extent that the plurality endorses the legality of the officers' initial stop of Royer, it was wholly unnecessary to reach that question. For even assuming the legality of the initial stop, the plurality correctly holds, and I agree, that the officers' subsequent actions clearly exceeded the permissible bounds of a *Terry* "investigative" stop. * * *

In any event, I dissent from the plurality's view that the initial stop of Royer was legal. For plainly Royer was "seized" * * *. [The] facts clearly are not sufficient to provide the reasonable suspicion of criminal activity necessary to justify the * * * seizure * * *.

■ JUSTICE REHNQUIST, with whom THE CHIEF JUSTICE and JUSTICE O'CONNOR join, dissenting.

* * *

I think the articulable suspicion which concededly focused upon Royer [after the officers' initial conversation with him] justified the length and nature of his detention.

The reasonableness of the officers' activity in this case did not depend upon Royer's consent to the investigation. Nevertheless, the presence of consent further justifies the action taken. * * * [I]f Royer was legally approached in the first instance and consented to accompany the detectives to the room, it does not follow that his consent went up in smoke and he was "arrested" upon entering the room. * * * [L]ogical analysis would focus on whether the environment in the room rendered the subsequent consent to a search of the luggage involuntary.

[T]here is nothing in the record which would indicate that Royer's resistance was overborne by anything * * *.

NOTES

1. **Movement of the Suspect.** How much may officers who have made a proper nonarrest investigatory detention move the suspect? In Dunaway v. New York, 442 U.S. 200, 99 S.Ct. 2248, 60 L.Ed.2d 824 (1979), officers with information—but less than probable cause—connecting Dunaway with a robbery-murder had Dunaway "picked up" at a neighbor's home. They drove him to police headquarters, placed him in an interrogation room, warned him of his rights, and questioned him. Finding that the officers' actions were "in important respects indistinguishable from an arrest," the Court held the lack of probable cause rendered the detention invalid. The *Dunaway* holding that movement to the

stationhouse is prohibited was confirmed in Hayes v. Florida, 470 U.S. 811, 105 S.Ct. 1643, 84 L.Ed.2d 705 (1985).

2. **Stationhouse Detentions on Reasonable Suspicion.** In Davis v. Mississippi, 394 U.S. 721, 89 S.Ct. 1394, 22 L.Ed.2d 676 (1969), the Court had indicated in dictum that stationhouse detentions for fingerprinting might be permissible upon less than probable cause:

> It is arguable * * * that, because of the unique nature of the fingerprinting process, * * * detentions [for fingerprinting] might, under narrowly defined circumstances, be found to comply with the Fourth Amendment even though there is no probable cause in the traditional sense. Detention for fingerprinting may constitute a much less serious intrusion upon personal security than other types of police searches and detentions. Fingerprinting involves none of the probing into an individual's private life and thoughts that mark an interrogation or search. Nor can fingerprint detention be employed repeatedly to harass any individual, since the police need only one set of each person's prints. Furthermore, fingerprinting is an inherently more reliable and effective crimestopping tool than eyewitness identification or confessions and is not subject to such abuses as the improper lineup and the "third degree." Finally, because there is no danger of destruction of fingerprints, the limited detention need not come unexpectedly or at an inconvenient time. For this same reason, the general requirement that the authorization of a judicial officer be obtained in advance of detention would seem not to admit of any exception in the fingerprinting context.

394 U.S. at 727–28, 89 S.Ct. at 1397–98, 22 L.Ed.2d at 681. The court reaffirmed this suggestion in Hayes v. Florida, 470 U.S. 811, 817, 105 S.Ct. 1643, 1647, 84 L.Ed.2d 705, 711 (1985), noting a number of jurisdictions, in reliance on the *Davis* suggestion, had enacted provisions for judicial authorizations for fingerprinting detentions.

3. **Length of the Detention.** How long may a non-arrest investigatory detention last? The American Law Institute has proposed such detentions be limited to a "period as is reasonably necessary for the accomplishment of the purposes authorized * * * but in no case for more than twenty minutes * * *". Model Code of Pre-Arraignment Procedure § 110.2(1) (Official Draft 1975). In United States v. Place, 462 U.S. 696, 103 S.Ct. 2637, 77 L.Ed.2d 110 (1983), dealing with detention of luggage as discussed later in these Notes, the Court noted the Institute's proposal but declined "to adopt any outside time limitation for a permissible *Terry* stop:"

> We understand the desirability of providing law enforcement authorities with a clear rule to guide their conduct. Nevertheless, we question the wisdom of a rigid time limitation. Such a limit would undermine the equally important need to allow authorities to graduate their responses to the demands of any particular situation.

462 U.S. at 710 n. 10, 103 S.Ct. at 2646 n. 10, 77 L.Ed.2d at 122 n. 10. But it then continued:

> The [90–minute] length of the detention of [Place's] luggage alone precludes the conclusion that the seizure was reasonable in the absence of probable cause. Although we have recognized the reasonableness of seizures longer than * * * momentary ones * * *, the brevity of the invasion of the individual's Fourth Amendment interests is an important factor in determining whether the seizure is so minimally intrusive as to be justifiable on reasonable suspicion. Moreover, in assessing the effect of the length of the detention, we take into account whether the police diligently pursue their investigation. We note that here the New York agents knew the time of Place's scheduled arrival

at LaGuardia [Airport], had ample time to arrange for their additional investigation at that location, and thereby could have minimized the intrusion on [Place's] Fourth Amendment interests. * * * [W]e have never approved a seizure of the person for the prolonged 90–minute period involved here and cannot do so on the facts presented by this case.

462 U.S. at 709–10, 103 S.Ct. at 2645–46, 77 L.Ed.2d at 122.

The permissible length of investigatory detentions was again addressed in United States v. Sharpe, 470 U.S. 675, 105 S.Ct. 1568, 84 L.Ed.2d 605 (1985). Drug Enforcement Administration agent Cooke was patrolling a coastal road in North Carolina and observed a pickup truck (driven by Savage) and a Pontiac (driven by Sharpe) traveling "in tandem." After observing the pickup truck was heavily loaded, Cooke called for assistance. Highway patrol officer Thrasher, driving a marked patrol car, responded. Within approximately a minute of Thrasher's joining the "procession," the truck and the Pontiac turned off the highway onto a campground road and—despite the 35 mph speed limit—progressed at 55 to 60 mph until the road looped back onto the highway. The officers decided to stop the vehicles and Thrasher pulled aside the Pontiac (which was in the lead), turned on his flashing light, and motioned for the driver to pull over. As the Pontiac pulled over, the pickup truck "cut" between the Pontiac and the patrol car and continued down the highway. Thrasher pursued the truck and Cooke pulled over behind the Pontiac. Cooke obtained identification from Sharpe, the driver of the Pontiac. When he was unable to make radio contact with Thrasher, he called local police, directed them to "maintain the situation," and joined Thrasher.

Thrasher had stopped and secured identification from the driver of the truck, Savage. Savage explained that the truck belonged to a friend (and produced a bill of sale) and that he was taking the truck to have its shock absorbers repaired. Thrasher told Savage that the two would await the arrival of a DEA agent. Savage became nervous and asked for his identification; Thrasher told him that he was not free to leave. Cooke arrived at the scene about 15 minutes after the truck had been stopped. When Cooke stated that he believed the truck contained marihuana and twice asked for permission to search it, Savage twice refused. Cooke stepped on the rear of the truck, noting that it did not sink. He then put his nose against the rear window, reported that he could smell marihuana, and searched the vehicle. Bales of marihuana were found and Savage was placed under arrest. Cooke then returned to the Pontiac and arrested Sharpe; this was about 30 to 40 minutes from the time the Pontiac was stopped. At the trial of Sharpe and Savage for possession of the marihuana, the marihuana was admitted into evidence. On appeal, the Court of Appeals reversed, reasoning that the detentions of Sharpe and Savage were too long to be supported on less than probable cause and that these detentions tainted the discovery and seizure of the marihuana.

The Supreme Court reversed. Writing for the Court, Chief Justice Burger reaffirmed that the Fourth Amendment imposes no "hard-and-fast" time limit upon the duration of a *Terry* stop:

In assessing whether a detention is too long in duration to be justified as an investigative stop, we consider it appropriate to examine whether the police diligently pursued a means of investigation that was likely to confirm or dispel their suspicions quickly, during which time it was necessary to detain the defendant. A court making this assessment should take care to consider whether the police are acting in a swiftly developing situation, and in such cases the court should not indulge in unrealistic second-guessing. * * * The question is not simply whether some other alternative was available, but whether the police acted unreasonably in failing to recognize or pursue it.

470 U.S. at 686–87, 105 S.Ct. at 1575–76, 84 L.Ed.2d at 615–16.

On the facts before it, the Court concluded, Cooke pursued the investigation with regard to Savage in a diligent and reasonable manner. Most of the delay was attributable to Savage's actions in maneuvering around the Pontiac and Thrasher's patrol car, which required separate stops of the two vehicles. The Court assumed this was a conscious effort by Savage to elude the officers, but commented that Savage's actions would also justify the delay even if they were "innocent." To affirm the decision of the lower court with regard to Savage's 20 minute detention, the majority concluded, would be to "effectively establish a *per se* rule that a 20–minute detention is too long to be justified under the *Terry* doctrine." This, the Court indicated, it was unwilling to do. In regard to Sharpe's detention, the Court found no reason to consider the validity of its 30 to 40 minute duration. The challenged evidence was obtained by searching the truck and was not "fruit" of any improper detention of Sharpe as may have taken place.

4. **Investigatory "Detentions" of Items.** Some seizures of items as well as persons may be made upon less than probable cause. In United States v. Place, 462 U.S. 696, 103 S.Ct. 2637, 77 L.Ed.2d 110 (1983), Drug Enforcement Administration officers approached Place at New York's LaGuardia airport after he aroused suspicion while departing from Miami and upon arrival in New York. Discrepancies were noted concerning the addresses placed on his two pieces of luggage. At both Miami and New York, he volunteered to officers who approached him that he had recognized them as police officers. At New York, he falsely claimed that his baggage had been searched in Miami. He refused to consent to a search of the luggage at the New York airport. One of the agents then informed him that the officers would take the luggage to a federal judge and apply for a search warrant. He added that Place was free to accompany the officers (and the luggage). Place declined the invitation, but obtained a number at which the officers indicated they could be reached. The officers took the bags to another airport where, one hour and thirty minutes later, a trained narcotics detection dog reacted positively to the smaller bag but "ambiguously" to the larger one. As it was late on Friday, the agents retained the bags until Monday, when they obtained a search warrant. The smaller bag was found to contain cocaine. Applying the principles of *Terry,* the Supreme Court concluded certain seizures of personal luggage on the basis of "reasonable, articulable suspicion, premised on objective facts," would be reasonable under the Fourth Amendment. Balancing the relevant interests, the Court noted a substantial governmental interest in a brief seizure of luggage believed to contain drugs. On the other hand, some brief seizures of luggage intrude only minimally upon the owner's Fourth Amendment protected interests:

> In sum, we conclude that when an officer's observations lead him reasonably to believe that a traveler is carrying luggage that contains narcotics, the principles of *Terry* and its progeny would permit the officer to detain the luggage briefly to investigate the circumstances that aroused his suspicion, provided that the investigative detention is properly limited in scope.

462 U.S. at 706, 103 S.Ct. at 2644, 77 L.Ed.2d at 120. But—as discussed earlier in these Notes—the Court further concluded the length of the detention before it exceeded what was permissible on less than probable cause.

2.   WEAPON SEARCHES

EDITORS' INTRODUCTION: SEARCHING FOR WEAPONS ON LESS THAN PROBABLE CAUSE

In *Terry*, the Supreme Court held Officer McFadden's search of Terry for weapons was, at its inception, reasonable despite McFadden's lack of probable cause to believe Terry in possession of a weapon. The Court's reasoning was set out in the last subsection. Subsequent decisions have confirmed *Terry* established the reasonableness of such a search on less than probable cause:

> *Terry* * * * held that "[w]hen an officer is justified in believing that the individual whose suspicious behavior he is investigating at close range is armed and presently dangerous to the officer or others," the officer may conduct a patdown search "to determine whether the person is in fact carrying a weapon" * * * [A] protective search [is] permitted without a warrant and on the basis of reasonable suspicion less than probable cause * * *.

Minnesota v. Dickerson, 508 U.S. 366, 373, 113 S.Ct. 2130, 2136, 124 L.Ed.2d 334, 344 (1993).

Terry made clear the Fourth Amendment limits not only when such a search may be conducted but the manner in which it may be made. After concluding that McFadden's search of Terry was reasonable at its inception, the Court in *Terry* turned to whether McFadden's search was reasonable in Fourth Amendment terms "as conducted." It explained:

> The manner in which the seizure and search were conducted is, of course, as vital a part of the inquiry as whether they were warranted at all. * * *
>
> We need not develop at length in this case * * * the limitations which the Fourth Amendment places upon a protective seizure and search for weapons. * * * Suffice it to note that such a search, unlike a search without a warrant incident to a lawful arrest, is not justified by any need to prevent the disappearance or destruction of evidence of crime. The sole justification of the search in the present situation is the protection of the police officer and others nearby, and it must therefore be confined in scope to an intrusion reasonably designed to discover guns, knives, clubs, or other hidden instruments for the assault of the police officer.
>
> The scope of the search in this case presents no serious problem in light of these standards. Officer McFadden patted down the outer clothing of petitioner and his two companions. He did not place his hands in their pockets or under the outer surface of their garments until he had felt weapons, and then he merely reached for and removed the guns. * * * Officer McFadden confined his search strictly to what was minimally necessary to learn whether the men were armed and to disarm them once he discovered the weapons. He did not conduct a general exploratory search for whatever evidence of criminal activity he might find.

392 U.S. at 28–30, 88 S.Ct. at 1883–84, 20 L.Ed.2d at 910–11.

In Sibron v. New York, 392 U.S. 40, 88 S.Ct. 1889, 20 L.Ed.2d 917 (1968), a companion case to *Terry*, the Court further developed limits on weapons searches. The Court stated *Sibron's* facts as follows:

> Sibron * * * was convicted of the unlawful possession of heroin. He moved before trial to suppress the heroin seized from his person by the arresting officer, Brooklyn Patrolman Anthony Martin. * * * At

the hearing on the motion to suppress, Officer Martin testified that while he was patrolling his beat in uniform on March 9, 1965, he observed Sibron "continually from the hours of 4:00 P.M. to 12:00, midnight * * * in the vicinity of 742 Broadway." He stated that during this period of time he saw Sibron in conversation with six or eight persons whom he (Patrolman Martin) knew from past experience to be narcotics addicts. The officer testified that he did not overhear any of these conversations, and that he did not see anything pass between Sibron and any of the others. Late in the evening Sibron entered a restaurant. Patrolman Martin saw Sibron speak with three more known addicts inside the restaurant. Once again, nothing was overheard and nothing was seen to pass between Sibron and the addicts. Sibron sat down and ordered pie and coffee, and, as he was eating Patrolman Martin approached him and told him to come outside. Once outside, the officer said to Sibron, "You know what I am after." According to the officer, Sibron "mumbled something and reached into his pocket." Simultaneously, Patrolman Martin thrust his hand into the same pocket, discovering several glassine envelopes, which, it turned out, contained heroin.

    * * * Patrolman Martin * * * [never] seriously suggest[ed] that he was in fear of bodily harm and that he searched Sibron in self-protection to find weapons.

The Court concluded Officer Martin lacked probable cause to arrest until after the heroin was seized. It then turned to the reasonableness of the officer's conduct under *Terry*. As to whether the officer was entitled under *Terry* to frisk Sibron, the Court observed:

> The suspect's mere act of talking with a number of known addicts over an eight-hour period no more gives rise to reasonable fear of life or limb on the part of the police officer than it justifies an arrest for committing a crime. Nor did Patrolman Martin urge that when Sibron put his hand in his pocket, he feared that he was going for a weapon and acted in self-defense. His opening statement to Sibron—"You know what I am after"—made it abundantly clear that he sought narcotics, and his testimony at the hearing left no doubt that he thought there were narcotics in Sibron's pocket.

392 U.S. at 64, 88 S.Ct. at 1903, 20 L.Ed.2d at 935. Finally, the Court concluded even if the officer had been authorized to frisk Sibron, the officer's actions did went beyond a self-protective search and constituted a search for evidence:

> [W]ith no attempt at an initial limited exploration for arms, Patrolman Martin thrust his hand into Sibron's pocket and took from him envelopes of heroin. His testimony shows that he was looking for narcotics, and he found them. The search was not reasonably limited in scope to the accomplishment of the only goal which might conceivably have justified its inception—the protection of the officer by disarming a potentially dangerous man.

392 U.S. at 65, 88 S.Ct. at 1904, 20 L.Ed.2d at 936.

Minnesota v. Dickerson

Supreme Court of the United States, 1993.
508 U.S. 366, 113 S.Ct. 2130, 124 L.Ed.2d 334.

■ JUSTICE WHITE delivered the opinion of the Court.

In this case, we consider whether the Fourth Amendment permits the seizure of contraband detected through a police officer's sense of touch during a protective pat-down search.

I

On the evening of November 9, 1989, two Minneapolis police officers were patrolling an area on the city's north side in a marked squad car. At about 8:15 p.m., one of the officers observed respondent leaving a 12–unit apartment building on Morgan Avenue North. The officer, having previously responded to complaints of drug sales in the building's hallways and having executed several search warrants on the premises, considered the building to be a notorious "crack house." According to testimony credited by the trial court, respondent began walking toward the police but, upon spotting the squad car and making eye contact with one of the officers, abruptly halted and began walking in the opposite direction. His suspicion aroused, this officer watched as respondent turned and entered an alley on the other side of the apartment building. Based upon respondent's seemingly evasive actions and the fact that he had just left a building known for cocaine traffic, the officers decided to stop respondent and investigate further.

The officers pulled their squad car into the alley and ordered respondent to stop and submit to a patdown search. The search revealed no weapons, but the officer conducting the search did take an interest in a small lump in respondent's nylon jacket. The officer later testified: "[A]s I pat-searched the front of his body, I felt a lump, a small lump, in the front pocket. I examined it with my fingers and it slid and it felt to be a lump of crack cocaine in cellophane." The officer then reached into respondent's pocket and retrieved a small plastic bag containing one fifth of one gram of crack cocaine. Respondent was arrested and charged in Hennepin County District Court with possession of a controlled substance.

Before trial, respondent moved to suppress the cocaine. The trial court first concluded that the officers were justified under Terry v. Ohio, 392 U.S. 1, 88 S.Ct. 1868, 20 L.Ed.2d 889 (1968), in stopping respondent to investigate whether he might be engaged in criminal activity. The court further found that the officers were justified in frisking respondent to ensure that he was not carrying a weapon. Finally, analogizing to the "plain-view" doctrine, under which officers may make a warrantless seizure of contraband found in plain view during a lawful search for other items, the trial court ruled that the officers' seizure of the cocaine did not violate the Fourth Amendment:

"To this Court there is no distinction as to which sensory perception the officer uses to conclude that the material is contraband. An experienced officer may rely upon his sense of smell in DWI stops or in recognizing the smell of burning marijuana in an automobile. The sound of a shotgun being racked would clearly support certain reactions by an officer. The sense of touch, grounded in experience and training, is as reliable as perceptions drawn from other senses. 'Plain feel,' therefore, is no different than plain view and will equally support the seizure here."

His suppression motion having failed, respondent proceeded to trial and was found guilty.

On appeal, the Minnesota Supreme Court affirmed [the intermediate court's reversal of the conviction]. * * * [T]he State Supreme Court held that both the stop[a] and the frisk[b] of respondent were valid under *Terry,* but found the seizure of the cocaine to be unconstitutional. The court expressly refused "to extend the plain view doctrine to the sense of touch" on the grounds that "the sense of touch is inherently less immediate and less reliable than the sense of sight" and that "the sense of touch is far more intrusive into the personal privacy that is at the core of the [F]ourth [A]mendment." The court thus appeared to adopt a categorical rule barring the seizure of any contraband detected by an officer through the sense of touch during a patdown search for weapons. The court further noted that "[e]ven if we recognized a 'plain feel' exception, the search in this case would not qualify" because "[t]he pat search of the defendant went far beyond what is permissible under *Terry.*" As the State Supreme Court read the record, the officer conducting the search ascertained that the lump in respondent's jacket was contraband only after probing and investigating what he certainly knew was not a weapon.

We granted certiorari to resolve a conflict among the state and federal courts over whether contraband detected through the sense of touch during a patdown search may be admitted into evidence. We now affirm.

II

A

* * *

Terry * * * held that "[w]hen an officer is justified in believing that the individual whose suspicious behavior he is investigating at close range is armed and presently dangerous to the officer or to others," the officer may conduct a patdown search "to determine whether the person is in fact carrying a weapon." * * * [A] protective search * * * must be strictly "limited to that which is necessary for the discovery of weapons which might be used to harm the officer or others nearby." If the protective search goes beyond what is necessary to determine if the suspect is armed,

a. The Minnesota court explained that "the defendant's suspicious behavior, the history of drug activity in the immediate vicinity and [the officer's] personal experience in seizing guns from the building the defendant left justified a pat search." State v. Dickerson, 481 N.W.2d 840, 843 (Minn.1992).

b. The Minnesota court explained that Dickerson's "evasive conduct after eye contact with police, combined with his departure from a building with a history of drug activity, justified police in reasonably suspecting criminal activity [and] therefore * * * the stop was valid." State v. Dickerson, 481 N.W.2d 840, 843 (Minn.1992).

it is no longer valid under *Terry* and its fruits will be suppressed. Sibron v. New York, 392 U.S. 40, 65–66, 88 S.Ct. 1889, 1904, 20 L.Ed.2d 917 (1968).

These principles were settled 25 years ago when, on the same day, the Court announced its decisions in *Terry* and *Sibron*. The question presented today is whether police officers may seize nonthreatening contraband detected during a protective patdown search of the sort permitted by *Terry*. We think the answer is clearly that they may, so long as the officer's search stays within the bounds marked by *Terry*.

B

We have already held that police officers, at least under certain circumstances, may seize contraband detected during the lawful execution of a *Terry* search. * * *

The Court in [Michigan v. Long, 463 U.S. 1032, 103 S.Ct. 3469, 77 L.Ed.2d 1201 (1983)] justified this * * * holding by reference to our cases under the "plain-view" doctrine. Under that doctrine, if police are lawfully in a position from which they view an object, if its incriminating character is immediately apparent, and if the officers have a lawful right of access to the object, they may seize it without a warrant. If, however, the police lack probable cause to believe that an object in plain view is contraband without conducting some further search of the object—i.e., if "its incriminating character [is not] 'immediately apparent,' "—the plain-view doctrine cannot justify its seizure.

We think that this doctrine has an obvious application by analogy to cases in which an officer discovers contraband through the sense of touch during an otherwise lawful search. The rationale of the plain view doctrine is that if contraband is left in open view and is observed by a police officer from a lawful vantage point, there has been no invasion of a legitimate expectation of privacy and thus no "search" within the meaning of the Fourth Amendment—or at least no search independent of the initial intrusion that gave the officers their vantage point. The warrantless seizure of contraband that presents itself in this manner is deemed justified by the realization that resort to a neutral magistrate under such circumstances would often be impracticable and would do little to promote the objectives of the Fourth Amendment. The same can be said of tactile discoveries of contraband. If a police officer lawfully pats down a suspect's outer clothing and feels an object whose contour or mass makes its identity immediately apparent, there has been no invasion of the suspect's privacy beyond that already authorized by the officer's search for weapons; if the object is contraband, its warrantless seizure would be justified by the same practical considerations that inhere in the plain view context.

The Minnesota Supreme Court rejected an analogy to the plain-view doctrine on two grounds: first, its belief that "the sense of touch is inherently less immediate and less reliable than the sense of sight," and second, that "the sense of touch is far more intrusive into the personal privacy that is at the core of the [F]ourth [A]mendment." We have a somewhat different view. First, *Terry* itself demonstrates that the sense of touch is capable of revealing the nature of an object with sufficient reliability to support a seizure. The very premise of *Terry*, after all, is that officers will be able to detect the presence of weapons through the sense of touch and *Terry* upheld precisely such a seizure. Even if it were true that the sense of touch is generally less reliable than the sense of sight, that only suggests that officers will less often be able to justify seizures of unseen contraband. Regardless of whether the officer detects the contraband by sight or by touch, however, the Fourth Amendment's requirement that the officer have probable cause to believe that the item is contraband before seizing it ensures against excessively speculative seizures. The court's second concern—that touch is more intrusive into privacy than is sight—is inapposite in light of the fact that the intrusion the court fears has already been authorized by the lawful search for weapons. The seizure of an item whose identity is already known occasions no further invasion of privacy. Accordingly, the suspect's privacy interests are not advanced by a categorical rule barring the seizure of contraband plainly detected through the sense of touch.

III

It remains to apply these principles to the facts of this case. Respondent has not challenged the finding made by the trial court and affirmed by both the Court of Appeals and the State Supreme Court that the police were justified under *Terry* in stopping him and frisking him for weapons. Thus, the dispositive question before this Court is whether the officer who conducted the search was acting within the lawful bounds marked by *Terry* at the time he gained probable cause to believe that the lump in respondent's jacket was contraband. The State District Court did not make precise findings on this point, instead finding simply that the officer, after feeling "a small, hard object wrapped in plastic" in respondent's pocket, "formed the opinion that the object . . . was crack . . . cocaine." The District Court also noted that the officer made "no claim that he suspected this object to be a weapon," a finding affirmed on appeal. The Minnesota Supreme Court, after "a close examination of the record," held that the officer's own testimony "belies any notion that he 'immediately' "recognized the lump as crack cocaine. Rather, the court concluded, the officer determined that the lump was contraband only after "squeezing, sliding and otherwise manipulating the contents of the defendant's pocket"—a pocket which the officer already knew contained no weapon.

Under the State Supreme Court's interpretation of the record before it, it is clear that the court was correct in holding that the police officer in this case overstepped the bounds of the "strictly circumscribed" search for weapons allowed under *Terry*. Where, as here, "an officer who is executing a valid search for one item seizes a different item," this Court rightly "has been sensitive to the danger * * * that officers will enlarge a specific authorization, furnished by a warrant or an exigency, into the equivalent of a general warrant to rummage and seize at will." Texas v. Brown, 460 U.S. [730,] 748, 103 S.Ct. [1535,] 1546–47[, 75 L.Ed.2d 502 (1983)] (Stevens, J., concurring in judgment). Here, the officer's continued exploration of respondent's pocket after having concluded that it contained no weapon was unrelated to "[t]he sole justification of the search [under *Terry:*] . . . the protection of the police officer and others nearby." It therefore amounted to the sort of evidentiary search that *Terry* expressly refused to authorize, and that we have condemned in subsequent cases.

* * * Although the officer was lawfully in a position to feel the lump in respondent's pocket, because *Terry* entitled him to place his hands upon respondent's jacket, the court below determined that the incriminating character of the object was not immediately apparent to him. Rather, the officer determined that the item was contraband only after conducting a further search, one not authorized by *Terry* or by any other exception to the warrant requirement. Because this further search of respondent's pocket was constitutionally invalid, the seizure of the cocaine that followed is likewise unconstitutional.

IV

For these reasons, the judgment of the Minnesota Supreme Court is

Affirmed.

■ CHIEF JUSTICE REHNQUIST, with whom JUSTICE BLACKMUN and JUSTICE THOMAS join, concurring in part and dissenting in part.

I join Parts I and II of the Court's opinion. Unlike the Court, however, I would vacate the judgment of the Supreme Court of Minnesota and remand the case to that court for further proceedings.

The Court, correctly in my view, states that "the dispositive question before this Court is whether the officer who conducted the search was acting within the lawful bounds marked by Terry [v. Ohio, 392 U.S. 1, 88 S.Ct. 1868, 20 L.Ed.2d 889 (1968),] at the time he gained probable cause to believe that the lump in respondent's jacket was contraband." The Court then goes on to point out that the state trial court did not make precise findings on this point, but accepts the appellate findings made by the Supreme Court of Minnesota. I believe that these findings, like those of the trial court, are imprecise and not directed expressly to the question of the officer's probable cause to believe that the lump was contraband. Because the Supreme Court of Minnesota employed a Fourth Amendment analysis which differs significantly from that now adopted by this Court, I would vacate its judgment and remand the case for further proceedings there in the light of this Court's opinion.

NOTES

1. **Grounds for Weapons Search.** What constitutes grounds for a *Terry* weapons search is addressed by the Supreme Court in several additional cases. In Adams v. Williams, 407 U.S. 143, 92 S.Ct. 1921, 32 L.Ed.2d 612 (1972), the officer— Sgt. Connolly—was told the suspect was carrying drugs and had a gun at his waist. It was 2:15 a.m. when the officer approached the suspect seated in a car; the area was known to the officer as a high crime rate area. He tapped on the car window and asked the suspect to open the door. The suspect instead rolled down the window. At that point, the officer reached into the car and "removed" a loaded revolver from the suspect's waistband. The Court upheld the action, explaining:

> Sgt. Connolly had ample reason to fear for his safety. When Williams rolled down his window, rather than complying with the policeman's request to step out of the car so that his movements could more easily be seen, the revolver

allegedly at Williams' waist became an even greater threat. Under these circumstances the policeman's action in reaching to the spot where the gun was thought to be hidden constituted a limited intrusion designed to insure his safety, and we conclude that it was reasonable.

407 U.S. at 147–48, 92 S.Ct. at 1924, 32 L.Ed.2d at 618.

In Pennsylvania v. Mimms, 434 U.S. 106, 98 S.Ct. 330, 54 L.Ed.2d 331 (1977) (per curiam), an officer stopped a car driven by Mimms to issue him a traffic citation for having an expired license plate. When Mimms stepped out of the car, the officer observed a large bulge under Mimms' sports jacket. Under *Terry*, the Court held, the bulge permitted the officer to conclude Mimms posed a serious and present danger to the officer's safety. Thus, the officer properly conducted a pat down of Mimms. The pat down revealed Mimms was in fact armed.

The matter was again considered in Ybarra v. Illinois, 444 U.S. 85, 100 S.Ct. 338, 62 L.Ed.2d 238 (1979). Officers obtained a valid search warrant authorizing the search of the Aurora Tap Tavern and Greg, the bartender. When the officers entered the tavern in late afternoon, between 9 and 13 customers—including Ybarra—were present. All were "frisked" and the officer felt "a cigarette pack with objects in it" in Ybarra's pocket; he did not at that time remove it. Several minutes later, Ybarra was searched again, this time more thoroughly. Drugs were found in the cigarette package. The State argued the first patdown frisk was permissible under *Terry* and since this revealed probable cause to believe Ybarra was in possession of drugs, the second and thorough search was permissible as an exigent circumstances search made on probable cause. Without addressing whether the frisk gave rise to probable cause, a majority of the Court held the frisk invalid:

> The initial frisk of Ybarra was simply not supported by a reasonable belief that he was armed and presently dangerous, a belief which this Court has invariably held must form the predicate to a patdown of a person for weapons. When the police entered the Aurora Tap Tavern * * *, the lighting was sufficient for them to observe the customers. Upon seeing Ybarra, they neither recognized him as a person with a criminal history nor had any particular reason to believe that he might be inclined to assault them. Moreover, as Police Agent Johnson later testified, Ybarra, whose hands were empty, gave no indication of possessing a weapon, made no gestures or other actions indicative of an intent to commit an assault, and acted generally in a manner that was not threatening. At the suppression hearing, the most Agent Johnson could point to was that Ybarra was wearing a 3/4–length lumber jacket, clothing which the State admits could be expected on almost any tavern patron in Illinois in early March. In short, the State is unable to articulate any specific fact that would have justified a police officer at the scene in even suspecting that Ybarra was armed and dangerous.

> * * * The "narrow scope" of the *Terry* exception does not permit a frisk for weapons on less than reasonable belief or suspicion directed at the person to be frisked, even though that person happens to be on premises where an authorized narcotics search is taking place.

444 U.S. at 92–94, 100 S.Ct. at 343, 62 L.Ed.2d at 246–47.

2.   **Need to Begin With Patdown.** Is a weapons search under *Terry* always required to begin with a patdown? In Adams v. Williams, discussed in note 2 above, the officer apparently conducted no patdown but rather reached into the automobile and "removed" a gun from the suspect's waistband. The Court upheld the constitutionality of this action but did not discuss the officer's failure to conduct a preliminary patdown. How might this be justified?

D. TRAFFIC STOPS

EDITORS' INTRODUCTION: TRAFFIC STOPS AS A
DISTINGUISHABLE TYPE OF DETENTION

The Supreme Court and lower tribunals have long assumed that traffic stops are a type of detention different from arrests or investigatory field stops. Nevertheless, the case law arguably fails to make clear how, in at least some situations, a traffic stop should be distinguished from an arrest.

The Supreme Court first referred to traffic stops in United States v. Robinson, 414 U.S. 218, 94 S.Ct. 467, 38 L.Ed.2d 427 (1973). In a discussion of search incident to custodial arrest, it noted the court below "discussed its understanding of the law where the police officer makes what the court characterized as 'a routine traffic stop,' i.e., where the officer would simply issue a notice of violation and allow the offender to proceed." Since *Robinson* involved "a full-custody arrest of the violator," the Court did not reach the question discussed by the lower tribunal.

Citations as Alternatives to Custodial Arrest

The major alternative to "a full-custody arrest" as a law enforcement officer's response to observing a traffic offense, of course, is the issuance of what is varyingly called a citation, a "ticket," or in the language of the lower court in *Robinson*, a "notice of violation." A citation directs the cited person to appear, generally in a specified court, at some future time to respond to the official contention that he has committed an offense or violation. Failure to appear is generally a criminal offense. In many jurisdictions—including, as the principal case in this part indicates, Iowa— local nonconstitutional law gives officers considerable discretion whether, in the case of a traffic offense, to issue a citation or rather make a full custody arrest.

Some jurisdictions, however, limit officers' authority to make a full custody arrest for some minor offenses. A Minnesota rule, for example, provides:

> Law enforcement officers acting without a warrant, who have decided to proceed with prosecution, shall issue citations to persons subject to lawful arrest for misdemeanors, unless it reasonably appears to the officer that arrest or detention is necessary to prevent bodily harm to the accused or another or further criminal conduct, or that there is a substantial likelihood that the accused will fail to respond to a citation. The citation may be issued in lieu of an arrest, or if an arrest has been made, in lieu of continued detention.

Minn.R.Crim.Pro. 6.01, subd.1(1)(a).

A full custody arrest for some minor offenses or violations may violate the Fourth Amendment requirement that such seizures be reasonable. The Supreme Court has not addressed the matter, but one member of the tribunal has noted the issue. In Gustafson v. Florida, 414 U.S. 260, 94 S.Ct. 488, 38 L.Ed.2d 456 (1973), a companion case to *Robinson*, the Court upheld a search incident to a custodial arrest for driving without a license. Justice Stewart wrote separately, noting Gustafson had not contested the constitutional validity of his custodial arrest. "[A] persuasive claim might have been made in this case," Justice Stewart commented, "that the custodial arrest * * * for a minor traffic offense violated [Gustafson's] rights under the Fourth and Fourteenth Amendments."

The validity of full custody arrests for minor offenses was explored in State v. Jones, 1999 WL 76817 (Ohio App.) (unpublished), discretionary appeals allowed, 86 Ohio St.3d 1406, 711 N.E.2d 233 (1999), involving an arrest for jaywalking as prohibited by a city ordinance. The offense is a "minor misdemeanor," punishable by only a fine. Under an Ohio statute, an officer is barred from making an arrest for a minor misdemeanor and must issue a citation, unless one of four special circumstances exist. None existed in *Jones*, so the arrest violated Ohio law. The prosecution, however, argued the arrest did not violate the Fourth Amendment and thus evidence obtained by it was not inadmissible. Holding that the arrest did violate the Fourth Amendment, the court noted under Supreme Court case law common law informs the understanding as to what is unreasonable under the Fourth Amendment. At common law a warrantless arrest for a misdemeanor was permissible only if the offense took place in the presence of the officer and was a breach of the peace; this of course suggests warrantless arrests for misdemeanors are unreasonable in other situations.

More functionally, *Jones* reasoned, the Fourth Amendment requires an arrest be justified by some adequate state interest and this requirement is embodied in the constitutional requirement of probable cause. The weight of the underlying state interest is determined, at least in part, by state law. Where a state determines its interest reflected in a crime does not justify custodial arrests for that crime, the state interest is not sufficient to render a custodial arrest for that crime reasonable in Fourth Amendment terms. Probable cause, as required by Fourth Amendment law, means probable cause to believe the suspect has committed an offense for which state law authorizes a custodial arrest. *Jones* noted further:

> For a minor-misdemeanor offender, * * * the power of the police officer to arrest him creates a form of potential punishment that exceeds anything that could be meted out by a judge after a finding of guilt

Multiple Functions of Traffic Law Enforcement

The complexity of the law in this area is undoubtedly affected by the nature of traffic law's role in policing. Certainly, to some extent, law enforcement agencies properly regard traffic laws themselves as deserving of enforcement:

> [T]raffic problems are a quality-of-life issue nearly everywhere. If the essence of community policing is to be sensitive to citizen concerns, we cannot afford to ignore traffic enforcement. Citizens need to feel safe on the streets and highways—not only from careless and drunk drivers, but also from the violent quarrels that sometimes occur when hot-tempered, aggressive individuals act out because another driver "cut them off."

Earl M. Sweeney, Traffic Enforcement: New Uses for an Old Tool, 68 Police Chief 45 (1996). Aggressive traffic law enforcement may—perhaps because of the increase in resulting visibility of police officers—further other law enforcement objectives. Sweeney, for example, added:

> Many cities that are plagued by gang activities, illegal guns, open-air drug markets and drive-by shootings have discovered that saturating an area with traffic patrol shuts down these illegal operations.

In addition, traffic enforcement may be used as a means of investigating suspicions that particular persons are involved in more serious criminal behavior. Sweeney continued:

> [A]n alert police officer who "looks beyond the traffic ticket" and uses the motor vehicle stop to "sniff out" possible criminal behavior may be our most effective tool for interdicting criminals. Serious lawbreakers almost always have aggressive personalities that also show up in their driving behavior. They drive after drinking, speed, cross over solid center lines, run red lights and stop signs, and neglect to register their vehicles or renew their driver's licenses. And they pass through our communities every day on their way to or from holdups and burglaries, or en route in the transport of drugs or illegal loads of hazardous wastes. Many of them are apprehended in routine traffic stops—and still more could be—if we re-emphasized traffic patrol.

If traffic enforcement is a valuable tool for use against serious crime, how is it best used? In 1997, Indianapolis police implemented "directed patrol" programs in two high crime areas. In the first ("east"), officers tended to stop vehicles for any observed violation in order to create a sense of significantly increased police presence. In the second ("north") area, officers again used traffic stops but focused upon those motorists specifically suspected of involvement in nontraffic criminal activity. Officers made more stops in the first area, and every 100 stops resulted in 24.5 citations, 14.5 arrests, 1.1 felony arrests, and 0.34 seizures of illegal guns. In the second area, every 100 stops resulted in 49.2 citations, 30.6 arrests, 2.9 felony arrests and 0.085 seizures of illegal guns. Total gun crimes actually increased somewhat in the first area but dropped 29 percent in the second. Office of Justice Program, U.S. Department of Justice, Promising Strategies to Reduce Gun Violence 53–54, 95–96 (1999). This, of course, suggests that simply vigorous traffic enforcement is less effective than using stops to follow through on suspicions developed by other methods. But the more extensive use of warnings rather than citations in the first area may have muted the "zero tolerance" message the police sought to convey by the increased police presence.

A major issue, of course, is whether the legal rules relating to traffic stops should be affected by the likelihood that traffic stops are sometimes used for purposes other than simply enforcing traffic laws themselves.

Definition and Requirements of Traffic Stops

Judicial discussions—including those in the Supreme Court's case law—often assume traffic stops are self-defining. This, however, is not necessarily the case. Moreover, there is some question as to the basis required for a traffic stop. Further—as the first principal case reprinted here makes clear—there remains considerable question as to what officers may do during a traffic stop.

Implicit in a traffic stop is some particularized information suggesting the driver has committed a violation of a traffic law. As is discussed in the Editors' Introduction to the next part of this chapter, the Supreme Court has held the Fourth Amendment prohibits random or "suspicionless" stops of motorists to determine whether they lack valid driver's licenses or registration documents for the vehicles. Delaware v. Prouse, 440 U.S. 648, 99 S.Ct. 1391, 59 L.Ed.2d 660 (1979), so holding, made clear some focused showing of at least a basis for suspecting a driver of committing an offense is necessary for a traffic stop.

In Whren v. United States, 517 U.S. 806, 116 S.Ct. 1769, 135 L.Ed.2d 89 (1996), reprinted later in this chapter, the Supreme Court observed that an "[a]utomobile stop"—by which the Court apparently meant a routine traffic stop—"is reasonable where the police have probable cause to believe that a traffic violation has occurred." But is a traffic stop reasonable *only* if such probable cause exists? Or would a traffic stop to issue a citation be constitutionally permissible on reasonable suspicion the driver has committed a traffic violation? The issue seldom arises, of course, because traffic stops are nearly always supported by officers' testimony that they observed the drivers commit acts constituting violations of the traffic laws. Since such testimony constitutes probable cause, the cases present no occasion to consider whether less than probable cause might support a traffic stop. In *Whren,* for example, the parties apparently agreed that the officers had probable cause to believe the suspects committed multiple traffic violations.

The principal case reprinted next involved what all members of the Supreme Court apparently agreed was a nonarrest traffic stop. This agreement enabled the Court to address what the Fourth Amendment permits as incident to such a seizure.

Knowles v. Iowa

Supreme Court of the United States, 1998.
525 U.S. 113, 119 S.Ct. 484, 142 L.Ed.2d 492.

■ CHIEF JUSTICE REHNQUIST delivered the opinion of the Court.

An Iowa police officer stopped petitioner Knowles for speeding, but issued him a citation rather than arresting him. The question presented is whether such a procedure authorizes the officer, consistently with the Fourth Amendment, to conduct a full search of the car. We answer this question "no."

Knowles was stopped in Newton, Iowa, after having been clocked driving 43 miles per hour on a road where the speed limit was 25 miles per hour. The police officer issued a citation to Knowles, although under Iowa law he might have arrested him. The officer then conducted a full search of the car, and under the driver's seat he found a bag of marijuana and a "pot pipe." Knowles was then arrested and charged with violation of state laws dealing with controlled substances.

Before trial, Knowles moved to suppress the evidence so obtained. He argued that the search could not be sustained under the "search incident to arrest" exception recognized in United States v. Robinson, 414 U.S. 218, 94 S.Ct. 467, 38 L.Ed.2d 427 (1973), because he had not been placed under arrest. At the hearing on the motion to suppress, the police officer conceded that he had neither Knowles' consent nor probable cause to conduct the search. He relied on Iowa law dealing with such searches.

Iowa Code Ann. § 321.485(1)(a) (West 1997) provides that Iowa peace officers having cause to believe that a person has violated any traffic or motor vehicle equipment law may arrest the person and immediately take the person before a magistrate. Iowa law also authorizes the far more usual practice of issuing a citation in lieu of arrest or in lieu of continued custody after an initial arrest.[4] See Iowa Code Ann. § 805.1(1) (West Supp.1997). Section 805.1(4) provides that the issuance of a citation in lieu of an arrest "does not affect the officer's authority to conduct an otherwise lawful search." The Iowa Supreme Court has interpreted this provision as providing authority to officers to conduct a full-blown search of an automobile and driver in those cases where police elect not to make a custodial arrest and instead issue a citation—that is, a search incident to citation.

Based on this authority, the trial court denied the motion to suppress and found Knowles guilty. The Supreme Court of Iowa, sitting en banc, affirmed by a divided vote. * * * [T]he Iowa Supreme Court upheld the constitutionality of the search under a bright-line "search incident to citation" exception to the Fourth Amendment's warrant requirement, reasoning that so long as the arresting officer had probable cause to make a custodial arrest, there need not in fact have been a custodial arrest. We granted certiorari * * *. * * * Knowles did not argue below, and does not argue here, that the statute could never be lawfully applied. The question we therefore address is whether the search at issue, authorized as it was by state law, nonetheless violates the Fourth Amendment.

In *Robinson*, supra, we noted the two historical rationales for the "search incident to arrest" exception: (1) the need to disarm the suspect in order to take him into custody, and (2) the need to preserve evidence for later use at trial. But neither of these underlying rationales for the search incident to arrest exception is sufficient to justify the search in the present case.

We have recognized that the first rationale—officer safety—is " 'both legitimate and weighty.' "The threat to officer safety from issuing a traffic citation, however, is a good deal less than in the case of a custodial arrest. In *Robinson*, we stated that a custodial arrest involves "danger to an officer" because of "the extended exposure which follows the taking of a suspect into custody and transporting him to the police station." We recognized that "[t]he danger to the police officer flows from the fact of the

---

4. Iowa law permits the issuance of a citation in lieu of arrest for most offenses for which an accused person would be "eligible for bail." See Iowa Code Ann. § 805.1(1) (West Supp.1997). In addition to traffic and motor vehicle equipment violations, this would permit the issuance of a citation in lieu of arrest for such serious felonies as second-degree burglary, and first-degree theft, both bailable offenses under Iowa law. The practice in Iowa of permitting citation in lieu of arrest is consistent with law reform efforts.

arrest, and its attendant proximity, stress, and uncertainty, and not from the grounds for arrest." A routine traffic stop, on the other hand, is a relatively brief encounter and "is more analogous to a so-called '*Terry* stop' . . .than to a formal arrest." Berkemer v. McCarty, 468 U.S. 420, 437, 104 S.Ct. 3138, 82 L.Ed.2d 317 (1984). See also Cupp v. Murphy, 412 U.S. 291, 296, 93 S.Ct. 2000, 36 L.Ed.2d 900 (1973) ("Where there is no formal arrest . . .a person might well be less hostile to the police and less likely to take conspicuous, immediate steps to destroy incriminating evidence").

This is not to say that the concern for officer safety is absent in the case of a routine traffic stop. It plainly is not. But while the concern for officer safety in this context may justify the "minimal" additional intrusion of ordering a driver and passengers out of the car, it does not by itself justify the often considerably greater intrusion attending a full field-type search. Even without the search authority Iowa urges, officers have other, independent bases to search for weapons and protect themselves from danger. For example, they may order out of a vehicle both the driver, and any passengers; perform a "patdown" of a driver and any passengers upon reasonable suspicion that they may be armed and dangerous; conduct a "*Terry* patdown" of the passenger compartment of a vehicle upon reasonable suspicion that an occupant is dangerous and may gain immediate control of a weapon; and even conduct a full search of the passenger compartment, including any containers therein, pursuant to a custodial arrest.

Nor has Iowa shown the second justification for the authority to search incident to arrest—the need to discover and preserve evidence. Once Knowles was stopped for speeding and issued a citation, all the evidence necessary to prosecute that offense had been obtained. No further evidence of excessive speed was going to be found either on the person of the offender or in the passenger compartment of the car.

Iowa nevertheless argues that a "search incident to citation" is justified because a suspect who is subject to a routine traffic stop may attempt to hide or destroy evidence related to his identity (e. g., a driver's license or vehicle registration), or destroy evidence of another, as yet undetected crime. As for the destruction of evidence relating to identity, if a police officer is not satisfied with the identification furnished by the driver, this may be a basis for arresting him rather than merely issuing a citation. As for destroying evidence of other crimes, the possibility that an officer would stumble onto evidence wholly unrelated to the speeding offense seems remote.

In *Robinson*, we held that the authority to conduct a full field search as incident to an arrest was a "bright-line rule," which was based on the concern for officer safety and destruction or loss of evidence, but which did not depend in every case upon the existence of either concern. Here we are asked to extend that "bright-line rule" to a situation where the concern for officer safety is not present to the same extent and the concern for destruction or loss of evidence is not present at all. We decline to do so. The judgment of the Supreme Court of Iowa is reversed, and the cause remanded for further proceedings not inconsistent with this opinion.

It is so ordered.

NOTES

1. **Distinguishing Traffic Stops From Arrests.** Often, as in Iowa, an officer has authority to either issue a motor a citation for a traffic offense or make a full custody arrest. If in such situations the officer searches before actually issuing a citation, how should the courts determine whether the situation is an arrest permitting an incidental search or rather a nonarrest traffic stop that under *Knowles* does not permit such a search? The issue was raised during oral argument in *Knowles*. One member of the Court inquired of counsel for Knowles, Paul Rosenberg:

> QUESTION: * * * Suppose the officer had just said, I'm placing you under arrest, and he said those words before he searched the driver and the passenger and the inside of the car. * * *
>
> MR. ROSENBERG: If he had done that, then it would have been a valid search incident to a lawful arrest.
>
> QUESTION: So, the whole thing turns on whether the officer says you're under * * * arrest or here's a ticket.
>
> MR. ROSENBERG: Yes * * *.

During the argument by counsel for Iowa, Bridget A. Chambers, the following exchange took place:

> MS. CHAMBERS: * * * [U]nder Iowa law officers can arrest, search, and then subsequently release on citation. * * *
>
> QUESTION: Excuse me. They can arrest, search, and then say never mind the arrest?
>
> MS. CHAMBERS: Yes.
>
> QUESTION: Wow.

(Laughter.)

The questioning of Ms. Chambers continued:

> QUESTION: [T]he usual rule is there can be a search incident to an arrest. You want to turn it around and have an arrest incident to a search. And it seems to me that that's an abuse of authority. * * * If the officer arrests not intending really to arrest, that's an abuse of authority. You're not really proposing that this could happen, are you?
>
> MS. CHAMBERS: We're certainly not advocating that that should happen, and we're certainly not * * * not encouraging that. * * * [W]e think it could conceivably happen, and * * * [it is likely that this] wouldn't violate the Fourth Amendment * * *.

2. **Duration of Traffic Stops.** Are there Fourth Amendment limits on the duration of a traffic stop? In Ohio v. Robinette, 519 U.S. 33, 117 S.Ct. 417, 136 L.Ed.2d 347 (1996), Deputy Newsome stopped Robinette for speeding, asked for and received his driver's license, and ran a computer check which indicated that Robinette had no prior violations.

Newsome then asked Robinette to step out of his car, turned on his mounted video camera, issued a verbal warning to Robinette, and returned his license.

At this point, Newsome asked, "One question before you get gone: [A]re you carrying any illegal contraband in your car? Any weapons of any kind, drugs, anything like that?" Robinette answered "no" to these questions, after which Deputy Newsome asked if he could search the car. Robinette consented. In the car, Deputy Newsome discovered a small amount of marijuana and, in a film container, a pill which was later determined to be methylenedioxymeth-amphetamine (MDMA).

The Supreme Court granted review primarily to address the state court's holding that Robinette's consent was ineffective; this aspect of the case is discussed in Chapter 5. Robinette contended, however, the Court should not reach the consent issue because the state court had held the evidence inadmissible on an alternative basis. Before Newsome returned to Robinette's vehicle, he had determined not to give Robinette a ticket but rather to pursue his suspicion that Robinette might be in possession of drugs. "When the motivation behind a police officer's continued detention of a person stopped for a traffic violation is not related to the purpose of the original, constitutional stop, and when that continued detention is not based on articulable facts giving rise to a suspicion of some separate illegal activity justifying an extension of the detention," the state court explained, "the continued detention constitutes an illegal seizure." Thus the consent and search were all the tainted "fruit" of a detention that had become unreasonable. The Supreme Court, however, disagreed:

We think that under our recent decision in Whren v. United States, 517 U.S. 806, 116 S.Ct. 1769, 135 L.Ed.2d 89 (1996) [reprinted later in this chapter] * * *, the subjective intentions of the officer did not make the continued detention of respondent illegal under the Fourth Amendment. As we made clear in *Whren*, " 'the fact that [an] officer does not have the state of mind which is hypothecated by the reasons which provide the legal justification for the officer's action does not invalidate the action taken as long as the circum-stances, viewed objectively, justify that action.' * * * Subjective intentions play no role in ordinary, probable-cause Fourth Amendment analysis." * * *

519 U.S. at 38, 117 S.Ct. at 420–21, 136 L.Ed.2d at 354. It is not clear the Supreme Court intended by this discussion to reject the possibility that Deputy Newsome may have impermissibly extended the traffic stop. *Robinette* appears to reject only the state court's holding that the stop became unreasonable because the officer's subjective motivation had shifted from traffic matters to drug concerns.

On remand in *Robinette*, the Ohio Supreme Court reanalyzed the situation. In recognition of *Whren*, it first held that a continued detention resulting from a traffic stop becomes unreasonable "[w]hen [the] police officer's objective justification to continue detention * * * is not related to the purpose of the original stop," unless it is justified on some other ground. The Fourth Amendment permissibility of brief stops at sobriety checkpoints, the court continued, establishes the weight properly given to the strong policy in favor of quelling the drug trade. This policy also permits an officer who has made a proper traffic stop, pursuant to a drug interdiction policy, to briefly detain the motorist in order to ask him whether he is carrying any illegal drugs or weapons.

If during that continued detention reasonable suspicion develops, the Ohio court added, the officer may detain the motorist for a more in-depth investigation that may include soliciting consent to search. But where, as in *Robinette*, the questioning does not give rise to reasonable suspicion, the officer cannot reasonably continue to detain the motorist "to ask for and execute an intrusive search." State v. Robinette, 80 Ohio St.3d 234, 241, 685 N.E.2d 762, 768 (1997). Thus Robinette's detention became unreasonable, apparently after he responded negatively to New-some's inquiries about drugs and weapons.

3. **"Frisks" of Automobiles.** Under certain circumstances officers' right to conduct a protective weapons search extends beyond the person of a motorist and includes some parts of the automobile. Such searches are sometimes permissible during traffic stops.

In Michigan v. Long, 463 U.S. 1032, 103 S.Ct. 3469, 77 L.Ed.2d 1201 (1983), two Michigan sheriff's deputies, Howell and Lewis, were on routine patrol in a rural area. Shortly after midnight, they observed a car driven erratically and at excessive speed. When it swerved into a ditch, they stopped to investigate. Long, the only occupant of the vehicle, met the officers at the rear of the car which protruded from the ditch onto the road. Howell asked Long to produce his operator's license; Long did not respond until the request was repeated. When asked to produce the registration for the vehicle, Long again failed to respond. When this request was repeated, Long turned and walked towards the front open door on the driver's side of the vehicle. The officers followed Long and observed a large hunting knife on the floorboard of the vehicle. They then stopped Long and conducted a patdown; they found no weapons. Shining a flashlight into the car, one deputy noticed "something" protruding from under the armrest on the front seat. He entered the car, knelt, and lifted the armrest, revealing an open leather pouch on the seat. The officer then "determined" that the pouch contained marihuana. At issue before the Supreme Court was the propriety of the officers' action leading to the discovery of the marihuana as a *Terry*-type weapons search conducted on less than probable cause.

Neither *Terry's* language nor its rationale, Justice O'Connor concluded for the Court, required the right to search for weapons during a nonarrest detention be restricted to the person of the detained suspect. To the contrary, suspects confronted while in automobiles present special dangers to officers' safety because of their access to weapons that might be in the vehicles. Consequently, during a nonarrest detention of a suspect:

> the search of the passenger compartment of an automobile, limited to those areas in which a weapon might be placed or hidden, is permissible if the police officer possessed a reasonable belief based on "specific and articulable facts which, taken together with the rational inferences from those facts, reasonably warrant" the officers in believing that the suspect is dangerous and the suspect may gain immediate control of weapons. * * * If, while conducting a legitimate *Terry* search of the interior of the automobile, the officer should * * * discover contraband other than weapons, he clearly cannot be required to ignore the contraband, and the Fourth Amendment does not require its suppression in such circumstances.

463 U.S. at 1049–50, 103 S.Ct. at 3480–81, 77 L.Ed.2d at 1220. Turning to the facts before it, the Court held the deputies entertained the requisite reasonable fear for their safety. The rural nature of the area and late time of the stop were relevant. Further, the officers had reason to believe Long intoxicated and their pre-search observations disclosed a knife in the car. Although Long was, in some sense, under the "control" of the officers, he might still have been able to obtain and use weapons in the car. If released after the detention, he would in any event have had access to any such weapons. Even if methods other than the search were available to the officers to assure their safety, in contexts such as this in which quick decisions are crucial, the Court has "not required that officers adopt alternative means to ensure their safety in order to avoid the intrusion involved in a *Terry* encounter." Once begun, the search was properly limited. It was restricted to "those areas to which Long would generally have immediate control, and that could

contain a weapon." Examining the contents of the pouch was permissible, since the trial court determined the pouch "could have contained a weapon."

4. **Removal of Driver and Passengers from Stopped Vehicle.** Some protective action by officers during a traffic stop does not require even the justification demanded by the Court for the search in *Long*. This is the case, for example, with removal of persons from a stopped vehicle.

In Pennsylvania v. Mimms, 434 U.S. 106, 98 S.Ct. 330, 54 L.Ed.2d 331 (1977) (per curiam), an officer stopped Mimms for driving an automobile with an expired license plate, intending to issue a traffic citation. The officer asked Mimms to step out of the car and produce his owner's card and operator's license. When Mimms complied, the officer noticed a large bulge under Mimms' sports jacket. A frisk resulted in discovery of a revolver. The state court held ordering Mimms out of his car was unreasonable because the officer lacked any reason to believe criminal activity was afoot or Mimms posed a danger; the State conceded the officer had no reason to fear Mimms particularly. Reversing, the Supreme Court held the officers' action permissible. Conversing with a driver while standing exposed to traffic, it emphasized, creates a risk of injury to the officer. On the other hand, given the fact that the motorist had already been stopped, the additional intrusion involved in requiring the motorist to get out of the car "can only be described as *de minimis*." Once the officer observed the bulge in Mimms' jacket, the Court continued, *Terry* justified the officer's further action:

> The bulge in the jacket permitted the officer to conclude that Mimms was armed and thus posed a serious and present danger to the safety of the officer. In these circumstances, any man of "reasonable caution" would likely have conducted the "pat-down."

434 U.S. at 112, 98 S.Ct. at 334, 54 L.Ed.2d at 338.

In Maryland v. Wilson, 519 U.S. 408, 117 S.Ct. 882, 137 L.Ed.2d 41 (1997), *Mimms* was extended and the Court held that an officer making a traffic stop may order passengers to get out of a vehicle during the stop. Under *Mimms*, the Court reasoned, the reasonableness of such action depends on a balance between the public interests implicated and individuals' interest in personal security free of arbitrary interference by officers. Passenger removal furthers the same "legitimate and weighty" need for officer safety as was involved in *Mimms*. In fact, the Court added, "the fact that there is more than one occupant of the vehicle increases the possible sources of harm to the officer." That the persons involved are passengers rather than drivers does not significantly reduce the risk:

> It would seem that the possibility of a violent encounter stems not from the ordinary reaction of a motorist stopped for a speeding violation, but from the fact that evidence of a more serious crime might be encountered during the stop. And the motivation of a passenger to employ violence to prevent appre- hension of such a crime is every bit as great as that of the driver.

519 U.S. at 413, 117 S.Ct. at 886, 137 L.Ed.2d at 47–48.

Considering the public interest side of the balance, the Court acknowledged the case for suspicionless removal of passengers is "in one sense" weaker than that for removal of drivers. Although there is probable cause to believe the driver has committed an offense, there is no similar basis for stopping or detaining the passengers. Therefore, the passengers' personal liberty interests weigh more heavily against removal than did those of drivers. Nevertheless, the Court found this weightier liberty interest of minimal significance:

> [A]s a practical matter, the passengers are already stopped by virtue of the stop of the vehicle. The only change in their circumstances which will result from

ordering them out of the car is that they will be outside of, rather than inside of, the stopped car.

519 U.S. at 413–14, 117 S.Ct. at 886, 137 L.Ed.2d at 47. Consequently, "the additional intrusion on the passenger is minimal." The risk of harm to those involved "is minimized if the officers routinely exercise unquestioned command of the situation." The Fourth Amendment therefore permits officers making traffic stops to order passengers to get out of the cars pending completion of the stops.

Maryland urged the Court to hold an officer may forcibly detain a passenger for the duration of a stop. Wilson had not been detained after he was directed to get out of the car, the Court responded, and therefore the Court did not reach, and expressly reserved comment on, officers' power to detain passengers.

State v. Soto

Superior Court of New Jersey, 1996.[c]
324 N.J.Super. 66, 734 A.2d 350.

■ FRANCIS, J.S.C.

These are consolidated motions to suppress under the equal protection and due process clauses of the Fourteenth Amendment.[5] Seventeen defendants of African ancestry claim that their arrests on the New Jersey Turnpike south of exit 3 between 1988 and 1991 result from discriminatory enforcement of the traffic laws by the New Jersey State Police. After a lengthy hearing, I find defendants have established a *prima facie* case of selective enforcement which the State has failed to rebut requiring suppression of all contraband and evidence seized.

Defendants base their claim of institutional racism primarily on statistics. During discovery, each side created a database of all stops and arrests by State Police members patrolling the Turnpike between exits 1 and 7A out of the Moorestown Station for thirty-five randomly selected days between April 1988 and May 1991 from arrest reports, patrol charts, radio logs and traffic tickets. The databases are essentially the same. Both sides counted 3060 stops which the State found to include 1212 race identified stops (39.6%), the defense 1146 (37.4%).

To establish a standard against which to compare the stop data, the defense conducted a traffic survey and a violator survey. Dr. John Lamberth, Chairman of the Psychology Department at Temple University * * * designed both surveys.

The traffic survey was conducted over twenty-one randomly selected two and one-half hour sessions between June 11 and June 24, 1993 and between 8:00 a.m. and 8:00 p.m. at four sites, two northbound and two southbound, between exits 1 and 3 of the Turnpike. Teams supervised by Fred Last, Esq., of the Office of the Public Defender observed and recorded

---

c. The trial court granted the motion to suppress in 1996, and the State appealed. In 1999, the State dropped the appeal. At the request of the New Jersey Supreme Court's Committee on Opinions, the trial judge then submitted this opinion, written three years earlier, for publication.

5. The motions also include claims under the Fourth Amendment, but they were severed before the hearing to await future proceedings if not rendered moot by this decision.

the number of vehicles that passed them except for large trucks, tractor-trailers, buses and government vehicles, how many contained a "black" occupant and the state of origin of each vehicle. Of the 42,706 vehicles counted, 13.5% had a black occupant. * * *

The violator survey was conducted over ten sessions in four days in July 1993 by Mr. Last traveling between exits 1 and 3 in his vehicle at sixty miles per hour on cruise control after the speedometer had been calibrated and observing and recording the number of vehicles that passed him, the number of vehicles he passed and how many had a black occupant. Mr. Last counted a total of 2096 vehicles other than large trucks, tractortrailers, buses and government vehicles of which 2062 or 98.1% passed him going in excess of sixty miles per hour including 306 with a black occupant equaling about 15% of those vehicles clearly speeding. Multiple violators, that is those violating the speed limit and committing some other moving violation like tailgating, also equaled about 15% black. * * *

Using 13.5% as the standard or benchmark against which to compare the stop data, Dr. Lamberth found that 127 or 46.2% of the race identified stops between exits 1 and 3 were of blacks constituting an absolute disparity of 32.7%, a comparative disparity of 242% (32.7% divided by 13.5%) and 16.35 standard deviations. By convention, something is considered statistically significant if it would occur by chance fewer than five times in a hundred (over two standard deviations). * * *

Supposing that the disproportionate stopping of blacks was related to police discretion, the defense studied the traffic tickets issued by State Police members between exits 1 and 7A on the thirty-five randomly selected days broken down by State Police unit.[6] There are 533 racially identified tickets in the databases issued by either the now disbanded Radar Unit, the Tactical Patrol Unit or general road troopers ("Patrol Unit"). The testimony indicates that the Radar Unit focused mainly on speeders using a radar van and chase cars and exercised limited discretion regarding which vehicles to stop. The Tac–Pac concentrates on traffic problems at specific locations and exercises somewhat more discretion as regards which vehicles to stop. Responsible to provide general law enforcement, the Patrol Unit exercises by far the most discretion among the three units. From Mr. Last's count, Dr. Lamberth computed that 18% of the tickets issued by the Radar Unit were to blacks, 23.8% of the tickets issued by the Tac–Pac were to blacks while 34.2% of the tickets issued by the Patrol Unit were to blacks. South of exit 3, Dr. Lamberth computed that 19.4% of the tickets issued by the Radar Unit were to blacks, 0.0% of the tickets issued by the Tac–Pac were to blacks while 43.8% of the tickets issued by the Patrol Unit were to blacks. In his opinion, the Radar Unit percentages are statistically consistent with the standard established by the violator survey, but the differences between the Radar Unit and the Patrol Unit between both exits 1 and 3 and 1 and 7A are statistically significant or well in excess of two standard deviations.

6. Of the 3060 stops in the databases, 1292 are ticketed stops. Hence, no tickets were issued for nearly 60% of the stops.

The State presented the testimony of Dr. Leonard Cupingood to challenge or refute the statistical evidence offered by the defense. I found Dr. Cupingood is qualified to give expert testimony in the field of statistics * * *.

Dr. Cupingood had no genuine criticism of the defense traffic survey. Rather, he centered his criticism of the defense statistical evidence on the violator survey. Throughout his testimony he maintained that the violator survey failed to capture the relevant data which he opined was the racial mix of those speeders most likely to be stopped or the "tail of the distribution." * * * He was unclear, though, how he would design a study to ascertain in a safe way the vehicle going the fastest above the speed limit at a given time at a given location and the race of its occupants without involving the credibility of State Police members. In any event, his supposition that maybe blacks drive faster than whites above the speed limit was repudiated by all State Police members called by the State who were questioned about it. * * *

The defense [also] conducted a profile study * * *. It concentrated on the race identified stops of just blacks issued tickets and found that an adult black male was present in 88% of the cases where the gender of all occupants could be determined and that where gender and age could be determined, a black male 30 or younger was present in 63% of the cases. * * *

The defense did not rest on its statistical evidence alone. Along with the testimony of former troopers Kenneth Ruff and Kenneth Wilson about having been trained and coached to make race based profile stops but whose testimony is weakened by bias related to their not having been reappointed at the end of their terms, the defense elicited evidence through cross-examination of State witnesses and a rebuttal witness, Dr. James Fyfe, that the State Police hierarchy allowed, condoned, cultivated and tolerated discrimination between 1988 and 1991 in its crusade to rid New Jersey of the scourge of drugs.

Conjointly with the passage of the Comprehensive Drug Reform Act of 1987 and to advance the Attorney General's Statewide Action Plan for Narcotics Enforcement issued in January 1988 which "directed that the enforcement of our criminal drug laws shall be the highest priority law enforcement activity", Colonel Pagano formed the Drug Interdiction Training Unit (DITU) in late 1987 consisting of two supervisors and ten other members, two from each Troop selected for their successful seizure statistics, " . . . to actually patrol with junior road personnel and provide critical on-the-job training in recognizing potential violators." According to Colonel Pagano, the DITU program was intended to be one step beyond the existing coach program to impart to newer troopers insight into drug enforcement and the "criminal program" (patrol related arrests) in general. DITU was disbanded in or around July 1992.

[A]   glimpse of the work of DITU emerges from * * * the testimony of Sergeants Brian Caffrey and David Cobb. Sergeant Caffrey was the original assistant supervisor of DITU and became the supervisor in 1989. Sergeant Cobb was an original member of DITU and became the assistant supervisor in 1989. Sergeant Caffrey left DITU sometime in 1992, Sergeant Cobb sometime in 1991. Both testified that a major purpose of DITU was to teach trainees tip-offs and techniques about what to look for and do to talk or "dig" their way into a vehicle after, not before, a motor vehicle stop to effectuate patrol related arrests. Both denied teaching or using race as a tip-off either before or after a stop. Nevertheless, Sergeant Caffrey condoned a comment by a DITU trainer during the time he was the supervisor of DITU stating:

> "Trooper Fash previously had DITU training, and it showed in the way he worked. He has become a little reluctant to stop cars in lieu [sic] of the Channel 9 News Report. He was told as long as he uses Title 39 he can stop any car he wants. He enjoys DITU and would like to ride again."

As the defense observes in its closing brief, "Why would a trooper who is acting in a racially neutral fashion become reluctant to stop cars as a result of a news story charging that racial minorities were being targeted [by the New Jersey State Police]?" Even A.A.G. Ronald Susswein, Deputy Director of the Division of Criminal Justice, acknowledged that this comment is incomplete because it fails to add the caveat, "as long as he doesn't also use race or ethnicity." Further, Sergeant Caffrey testified that "ethnicity is something to keep in mind" albeit not a tip-off and that he taught attendees at both the annual State Police in-service training session in March 1987 and the special State Police in-service training sessions in July and August 1987 that Hispanics are mainly involved in drug trafficking and showed them the film Operation Pipeline wherein the ethnicity of those arrested, mostly Hispanics, is prominently depicted. Dr. Fyfe criticized Sergeant Caffrey's teaching Hispanics are mainly involved and his showing Operation Pipeline as well as the showing of the Jamaican Posse film wherein only blacks are depicted as drug traffickers at the 1989 annual State Police in-service training session saying trainers should not teach what they do not intend their trainees to act upon. At a minimum, teaching Hispanics are mainly involved in drug trafficking and showing films depicting mostly Hispanics and blacks trafficking in drugs at training sessions worked at cross-purposes with concomitant instruction pointing out that neither race nor ethnicity may be considered in making traffic stops.

Key corroboration for finding the State Police hierarchy allowed and tolerated discrimination came from Colonel Pagano. Colonel Pagano was Superintendent of the State Police from 1975 to February 1990. He testified there was a noisy demand in the 1980s to get drugs off the streets. In accord, Attorney General Cary Edwards and he made drug interdiction the number one priority of law enforcement. He helped formulate the Attorney General's Statewide Action Plan for Narcotics Enforcement and established DITU within the State Police. He kept an eye on DITU through conversations with staff officers and Sergeants Mastella and Caffrey and review of reports generated under the traditional reporting system * * *. He had no thought DITU would engage in constitutional violations. * * *

More telling, however, is what Colonel Pagano said and did, or did not do, in response to the Channel 9 expose entitled "Without Just Cause" which aired in 1989 and which troubled Trooper Fash and what he did not do in response to complaints of profiling from the NAACP and ACLU and these consolidated motions to suppress and similar motions in Warren and

Middlesex Counties. He said to Joe Collum of Channel 9 that "[violating rights of motorists was] of serious concern [to him], *but no where near* the concern that I think we have got to look to in trying to correct some of the problems we find with the criminal element in this State" and "the bottom line is that those stops were not made on the basis of race *alone.*" (emphasis added) Since perhaps these isolated comments were said inadvertently or edited out of context, a truer reflection of his attitude about claims of racism would appear to be his videotaped remarks shown all members of the State Police at roll call in conjunction with the WOR series. Thereon he clearly said that he did not want targeting or discriminatory enforcement and that "[w]hen you put on this uniform, you leave your biases and your prejudices behind." But he also said as regarded the charge of a Trenton school principal named Jones that he had been stopped on the Turnpike and threatened, intimidated and assaulted by a trooper, "We know that the teacher assaulted the trooper. He didn't have a driver's license or a registration *for his fancy new Mercedes.*" (emphasis added) And he called Paul McLemore, the first African–American trooper in New Jersey and now a practicing attorney and who spoke of discrimination within the ranks of the State Police, "an ingrate." And he told the members to "keep the heat on" and then assured them: " …[H]ere at Division Headquarters we'll make sure that when the wheels start to squeak, we'll do whatever we can to make sure that you're supported out in the field….Anything that goes toward implementing the Drug Reform Act is important. And, we'll handle the squeaky wheels here."

He admitted the Internal Affairs Bureau was not designed to investigate general complaints, so he could not refer the general complaints of discrimination to it for scrutiny. Yet he never requested the Analytical Unit to investigate stop data from radio logs, patrol charts and tickets or search and seizure data from arrest reports, operations reports, investigation reports and consent to search forms, not even after the Analytical Unit informed him in a report on arrests by region, race and crime that he had requested from it for his use in the WOR series that " …arrests are not a valid reflection of stops (data relative to stops with respect to race is not compiled)." The databases compiled for these motions attest, of course, to the fact that race identified stop data could have been compiled. He testified he could not launch an investigation into every general complaint because of limited resources and that there was insufficient evidence of discrimination in the Channel 9 series, the NAACP and ACLU complaints and the various motions to suppress for him to spend his "precious" resources. In short, he left the issue of discrimination up to the courts and months of testimony in this and other counties at State expense.

The right to be free from discrimination is firmly supported by the Fourteenth Amendment to the United States Constitution and the protections of Article I, paragraphs 1 and 5 of the New Jersey Constitution of 1947. * * * It is indisputable * * * that the police may not stop a motorist based on race or any other invidious classification.

Generally, however, the inquiry for determining the constitutionality of a stop or a search and seizure is limited to "whether the conduct of the law enforcement officer who undertook the [stop or] search was objectively reasonable, without regard to his or her underlying motives or intent." Thus, it has been said that the courts will not inquire into the motivation of a police officer whose stop of a vehicle was based upon a traffic violation committed in his presence. But where objective evidence establishes "that a police agency has embarked upon an officially sanctioned or *de facto* policy of targeting minorities for investigation and arrest," any evidence seized will be suppressed to deter future insolence in office by those charged with enforcement of the law and to maintain judicial integrity. State v. Kennedy, 247 N.J.Super. 21, 588 A.2d 834 (App.Div.1991).

Statistics may be used to make out a case of targeting minorities for prosecution of traffic offenses provided the comparison is between the racial composition of the motorist population violating the traffic laws and the racial composition of those arrested for traffic infractions on the relevant roadway patrolled by the police agency. While defendants have the burden of proving "the existence of purposeful discrimination," discriminatory intent may be inferred from statistical proof presenting a stark pattern or an even less extreme pattern in certain limited contexts. * * * [D]iscriminatory intent may be inferred from statistical proof in a traffic stop context probably because only uniform variables (Title 39 violations) are relevant to the challenged stops and the State has an opportunity to explain the statistical disparity. "[A] selection procedure that is susceptible of abuse ...supports the presumption of discrimination raised by the statistical showing." Castaneda v. Partida, 430 U.S. 482, 494, 97 S.Ct. 1272, 51 L.Ed.2d 498 (1977).

Once defendants expose a *prima facie* case of selective enforcement, the State generally cannot rebut it by merely calling attention to possible flaws or unmeasured variables in defendants' statistics. Rather, the State must introduce specific evidence showing that either there actually are defects which bias the results or the missing factors, when properly organized and accounted for, eliminate or explain the disparity. Nor will mere denials or reliance on the good faith of the officers suffice. Here, defendants have proven at least a *de facto* policy on the part of the State Police out of the Moorestown Station of targeting blacks for investigation and arrest between April 1988 and May 1991 both south of exit 3 and between exits 1 and 7A of the Turnpike. * * * The statistical disparities and standard deviations revealed are indeed stark. The discretion devolved upon general road troopers to stop any car they want as long as Title 39 is used evinces a selection process that is susceptible of abuse. The utter failure of the State Police hierarchy to monitor and control a crackdown program like DITU or investigate the many claims of institutional discrimination manifests its indifference if not acceptance. Against all this, the State submits only denials and * * * conjecture and flawed studies * * *.

The eradication of illegal drugs from our State is an obviously worthy goal, but not at the expense of individual rights. * * *

Motions granted.

E.   SOBRIETY CHECKPOINTS AND RELATED DETENTIONS

EDITORS' INTRODUCTION: SUSPICIONLESS STOPS

Arrests, *Terry* stops for investigation, and traffic stops all involve action based on suspicion focused upon the suspects. The criteria for determining the reasonableness of these seizures impose different standards for judging the adequacy of suspicion, or at least the basis for such suspicion. Those criteria all, however, address the adequacy of the facts to support a belief that the suspect is involved in criminal activity.

Some law enforcement action, in contrast, is permissible without regard to officers' suspicion the suspect is involved in criminal activity or any basis for such suspicion. This action may usefully be regarded as "suspicionless" law enforcement action.

Suspicionless action by officers is considered earlier in these materials. Thus searches incident to custodial arrests, addressed in subsection B(1) of this chapter, are suspicionless in the sense they are permissible regardless of whether the officers have any subjective concern that the suspects have evidence or weapons or whether the officers have any objective information supporting such concern.

This part considers the constitutionality of suspicionless stops of persons in certain situations. Eleven years before the principal case, the Supreme Court had refused to permit suspicionless stops of motorists in a different context. In Delaware v. Prouse, 440 U.S. 648, 99 S.Ct. 1391, 59 L.Ed.2d 660 (1979), the Court considered Delaware's contention that its police officers were permitted by the Fourth Amendment to stop any motorist to determine whether the driver was in possession of a valid driver's license and registration for the vehicle being driven. No suspicion that the driver lacked either was required, the state argued, nor did an officer need facts that would support any such suspicion. Holding that these suspicionless stops were unreasonable, the Court explained:

> We agree that the States have a vital interest in ensuring that only those qualified to do so are permitted to operate motor vehicles, that these vehicles are fit for safe operation, and hence that licensing, registration, and vehicle inspection requirements are being observed. * * *
>
> The question remains, however, whether in the service of these important ends the discretionary spot check is a sufficiently productive mechanism to justify the intrusion upon Fourth Amendment interests which such stops entail. On the record before us, that question must be answered in the negative. Given the alternative mechanisms available, both those in use and those that might be adopted, we are unconvinced that the incremental contribution to highway safety of the random spot check justifies the practice under the Fourth Amendment.
>
> The foremost method of enforcing traffic and vehicle safety regulations * * * is acting upon observed violations. Vehicle stops for traffic violations occur countless times each day; and on these occasions, licenses and registration papers are subject to inspection and drivers without them will be ascertained. Furthermore, drivers without licenses are presumably the less safe drivers whose propensities may well exhibit themselves. * * * The contribution to highway safety made by discretionary stops selected from among drivers generally will therefore be marginal at best. Furthermore, and again absent something more than mere assertion to the contrary, we find it difficult to believe

that the unlicensed driver would not be deterred by the possibility of being involved in a traffic violation or having some other experience calling for proof of his entitlement to drive but that he would be deterred by the possibility that he would be one of those chosen for a spot check. In terms of actually discovering unlicensed drivers or deterring them from driving, the spot check does not appear sufficiently productive to qualify as a reasonable law-enforcement practice under the Fourth Amendment.

Much the same can be said about the safety aspects of automobiles as distinguished from drivers. * * *

The marginal contribution to roadway safety possibly resulting from a system of spot checks cannot justify subjecting every occupant of every vehicle on the roads to a seizure—limited in magnitude compared to other intrusions but nonetheless constitutionally cognizable—at the unbridled discretion of law-enforcement officials. * * * This kind of standardless and unconstrained discretion is the evil the Court has discerned when in previous cases it has insisted that the discretion of the official in the field be circumscribed, at least to some extent. * * *

Accordingly, we hold that except in those situations in which there is at least articulable and reasonable suspicion that a motorist is unlicensed or that an automobile is not registered, or that either the vehicle or an occupant is otherwise subject to seizure for violation of law, stopping an automobile and detaining the driver in order to check his driver's license and the registration of the automobile are unreasonable under the Fourth Amendment. This holding does not preclude the State of Delaware or other States from developing methods for spot checks that involve less intrusion or that do not involve the unconstrained exercise of discretion. Questioning of all oncoming traffic at roadblock-type stops is one possible alternative. We hold only that persons in automobiles on public roadways may not for that reason alone have their travel and privacy interfered with at the unbridled discretion of police officers.

440 U.S. at 658–63, 99 S.Ct. at 1398–1401, 59 L.Ed.2d at 670–74. Justice Rehnquist dissented, noting the majority's statement concerning roadblocks "elevates the adage 'misery loves company' to a novel role in Fourth Amendment jurisprudence."

Prouse obviously invited the litigation of stops at "roadblock-type stops," and the issue was presented to the Court in the principal case that follows.

Michigan v. Sitz

Supreme Court of the United States, 1990.
496 U.S. 444, 110 S.Ct. 2481, 110 L.Ed.2d 412.

■ CHIEF JUSTICE REHNQUIST delivered the opinion of the Court.

This case poses the question whether a State's use of highway sobriety checkpoints violates the Fourth and Fourteenth Amendments to the United

States Constitution. We hold that it does not and therefore reverse the contrary holding of the Court of Appeals of Michigan.

Petitioners, the Michigan Department of State Police and its Director, established a sobriety checkpoint pilot program in early 1986. The Director appointed a Sobriety Checkpoint Advisory Committee comprising representatives of the State Police force, local police forces, state prosecutors, and the University of Michigan Transportation Research Institute. Pursuant to its charge, the Advisory Committee created guidelines setting forth procedures governing checkpoint operations, site selection, and publicity.

Under the guidelines, checkpoints would be set up at selected sites along state roads. All vehicles passing through a checkpoint would be stopped and their drivers briefly examined for signs of intoxication. In cases where a checkpoint officer detected signs of intoxication, the motorist would be directed to a location out of the traffic flow where an officer would check the motorist's driver's license and car registration and, if warranted, conduct further sobriety tests. Should the field tests and the officer's observations suggest that the driver was intoxicated, an arrest would be made. All other drivers would be permitted to resume their journey immediately.

The first—and to date the only—sobriety checkpoint operated under the program was conducted in Saginaw County with the assistance of the Saginaw County Sheriff's Department. During the hour-and-fifteen-minute duration of the checkpoint's operation, 126 vehicles passed through the checkpoint. The average delay for each vehicle was approximately 25 seconds. Two drivers were detained for field sobriety testing, and one of the two was arrested for driving under the influence of alcohol. A third driver who drove through without stopping was pulled over by an officer in an observation vehicle and arrested for driving under the influence.

On the day before the operation of the Saginaw County checkpoint, respondents filed a complaint in the Circuit Court of Wayne County seeking declaratory and injunctive relief from potential subjection to the checkpoints. * * * During pretrial proceedings, petitioners agreed to delay further implementation of the checkpoint program pending the outcome of this litigation.

After the trial, at which the court heard extensive testimony concerning, inter alia, the "effectiveness" of highway sobriety checkpoint programs, the court ruled that the Michigan program violated the Fourth Amendment and Art. 1, § 11, of the Michigan Constitution. On appeal, the Michigan Court of Appeals affirmed the holding that the program violated the Fourth Amendment and, for that reason, did not consider whether the program violated the Michigan Constitution. After the Michigan Supreme Court denied petitioners' application for leave to appeal, we granted certiorari.

To decide this case the [lower courts] performed a balancing test derived from our opinion in Brown v. Texas, 443 U.S. 47, 99 S.Ct. 2637, 61 L.Ed.2d 357 (1979) [which involved] "balancing the state's interest in preventing accidents caused by drunk drivers, the effectiveness of sobriety checkpoints in achieving that goal, and the level of intrusion on an individual's privacy caused by the checkpoints." * * *

As characterized by the Court of Appeals, the trial court's findings with respect to the balancing factors were that the State has "a grave and legitimate" interest in curbing drunken driving; that sobriety checkpoint programs are generally "ineffective" and, therefore, do not significantly further that interest; and that the checkpoints' "subjective intrusion" on individual liberties is substantial. According to the court, the record disclosed no basis for disturbing the trial court's findings, which were made within the context of an analytical framework prescribed by this Court for determining the constitutionality of seizures less intrusive than traditional arrests. * * *

[United States v.] Martinez–Fuerte, [428 U.S. 543, 96 S.Ct. 3074, 49 L.Ed.2d 1116 (1976) (reprinted in Chapter 5)], which utilized a balancing analysis in approving highway checkpoints for detecting illegal aliens, and Brown v. Texas, supra, are the relevant authorities here.

Petitioners concede, correctly in our view, that a Fourth Amendment "seizure" occurs when a vehicle is stopped at a checkpoint. The question thus becomes whether such seizures are "reasonable" under the Fourth Amendment.

It is important to recognize what our inquiry is NOT about. No allegations are before us of unreasonable treatment of any person after an actual detention at a particular checkpoint. As pursued in the lower courts, the instant action challenges only the use of sobriety checkpoints generally. We address only the initial stop of each motorist passing through a checkpoint and the associated preliminary questioning and observation by checkpoint officers. Detention of particular motorists for more extensive field sobriety testing may require satisfaction of an individualized suspicion standard.

No one can seriously dispute the magnitude of the drunken driving problem or the States' interest in eradicating it. * * *

Conversely, the weight bearing on the other scale—the measure of the intrusion on motorists stopped briefly at sobriety checkpoints—is slight. We reached a similar conclusion as to the intrusion on motorists subjected to a brief stop at a highway checkpoint for detecting illegal aliens. See *Martinez–Fuerte,* supra, at 558, 96 S.Ct. at 3083. We see virtually no difference between the levels of intrusion on law-abiding motorists from the brief stops necessary to the effectuation of these two types of checkpoints, which to the average motorist would seem identical save for the nature of the questions the checkpoint officers might ask. The trial court and the Court of Appeals[] thus[] accurately gauged the "objective" intrusion, measured by the duration of the seizure and the intensity of the investigation, as minimal.

With respect to what it perceived to be the "subjective" intrusion on motorists, however, the Court of Appeals found such intrusion substantial. The court first affirmed the trial court's finding that the guidelines governing checkpoint operation minimize the discretion of the officers on the scene. But the court also agreed with the trial court's conclusion that the checkpoints have the potential to generate fear and surprise in motorists. This was so because the record failed to demonstrate that approaching motorists would be aware of their option to make U-turns or turnoffs to avoid the checkpoints. On that basis, the court deemed the subjective intrusion from the checkpoints unreasonable.

We believe the Michigan courts misread our cases concerning the degree of "subjective intrusion" and the potential for generating fear and surprise. The "fear and surprise" to be considered are not the natural fear of one who has been drinking over the prospect of being stopped at a sobriety checkpoint but, rather, the fear and surprise engendered in law abiding motorists by the nature of the stop. * * * Here, checkpoints are selected pursuant to the guidelines, and uniformed police officers stop every approaching vehicle. The intrusion resulting from the brief stop at the sobriety checkpoint is for constitutional purposes indistinguishable from the checkpoint stops we upheld in *Martinez–Fuerte*.

The Court of Appeals went on to consider as part of the balancing analysis the "effectiveness" of the proposed checkpoint program. Based on extensive testimony in the trial record, the court concluded that the checkpoint program failed the "effectiveness" part of the test, and that this failure materially discounted petitioners' strong interest in implementing the program. We think the Court of Appeals was wrong on this point as well.

The actual language from Brown v. Texas, upon which the Michigan courts based their evaluation of "effectiveness," describes the balancing factor as "the degree to which the seizure advances the public interest." This passage from *Brown* was not meant to transfer from politically accountable officials to the courts the decision as to which among reasonable alternative law enforcement techniques should be employed to deal with a serious public danger. Experts in police science might disagree over which of several methods of apprehending drunken drivers is preferable as an ideal. But for purposes of Fourth Amendment analysis, the choice among such reasonable alternatives remains with the governmental officials who have a unique understanding of, and a responsibility for, limited public resources, including a finite number of police officers. * * *

Unlike [Delaware v. Prouse, 440 U.S. 648, 99 S.Ct. 1391, 59 L.Ed.2d 660 (1979)], this case involves neither a complete absence of empirical data nor a challenge to random highway stops. During the operation of the Saginaw County checkpoint, the detention of each of the 126 vehicles that entered the checkpoint resulted in the arrest of two drunken drivers. Stated as a percentage, approximately 1.5 percent of the drivers passing through the checkpoint were arrested for alcohol impairment. In addition, an expert witness testified at the trial that experience in other States demonstrated that, on the whole, sobriety checkpoints resulted in drunken driving arrests of around 1 percent of all motorists stopped. By way of comparison, the record from one of the consolidated cases in *Martinez–Fuerte,* showed that in the associated checkpoint, illegal aliens were found in only 0.12 percent of the vehicles passing through the checkpoint. The ratio of illegal aliens detected to vehicles stopped (considering that on occasion two or more illegal aliens were found in a single vehicle) was approximately 0.5 percent. We concluded that this "record ... provides a rather complete picture of the effectiveness of the San Clemente checkpoint", and we sustained its constitutionality. We see no justification for a different conclusion here.

In sum, the balance of the State's interest in preventing drunken driving, the extent to which this system can reasonably be said to advance that interest, and the degree of intrusion upon individual motorists who are briefly stopped, weighs in favor of the state program. We therefore hold that it is consistent with the Fourth Amendment. The judgment of the Michigan Court of Appeals is accordingly reversed, and the cause is remanded for further proceedings not inconsistent with this opinion.

Reversed.

■ JUSTICE STEVENS, with whom JUSTICE BRENNAN and JUSTICE MARSHALL join * * *, dissenting.

[T]he record in this case makes clear that a decision holding these suspicionless seizures unconstitutional would not impede the law enforcement community's remarkable progress in reducing the death toll on our highways. * * * [I]t seems inconceivable that a higher arrest rate could not have been achieved by more conventional means. * * *

[T]he Court today * * * overvalues the law enforcement interest in using sobriety checkpoints, undervalues the citizen's interest in freedom from random, unannounced investigatory seizures, and mistakenly assumes that there is "virtually no difference" between a routine stop at a permanent, fixed checkpoint and a surprise stop at a sobriety checkpoint. I believe this case is controlled by our * * * precedent[] condemning suspicionless random stops of motorists for investigatory purposes. Delaware v. Prouse, 440 U.S. 648, 99 S.Ct. 1391, 59 L.Ed.2d 660 (1979).

* * *

There is a critical difference between a seizure that is preceded by fair notice and one that is effected by surprise. That is one reason why a border search, or indeed any search at a permanent and fixed checkpoint, is much less intrusive than a random stop. A motorist with advance notice of the location of a permanent checkpoint has an opportunity to avoid the search entirely, or at least to prepare for, and limit, the intrusion on her privacy.

No such opportunity is available in the case of a random stop or a temporary checkpoint, which both depend for their effectiveness on the element of surprise. A driver who discovers an unexpected checkpoint on a familiar local road will be startled and distressed. She may infer, correctly, that the checkpoint is not simply "business as usual," and may likewise infer, again correctly, that the police have made a discretionary decision to focus their law enforcement efforts upon her and others who pass the chosen point.

This element of surprise is the most obvious distinction between the sobriety checkpoints permitted by today's majority and the interior border checkpoints approved by this Court in *Martinez–Fuerte*. The distinction casts immediate doubt upon the majority's argument, for *Martinez–Fuerte* is the only case in which we have upheld suspicionless seizures of motorists. But the difference between notice and surprise is only one of the important reasons for distinguishing between permanent and mobile checkpoints. With respect to the former, there is no room for discretion in either the timing or the location of the stop—it is a permanent part of the landscape. In the latter case, however, although the checkpoint is most frequently employed during the hours of darkness on weekends (because that is when drivers with alcohol in their blood are most apt to be found on the road), the police have extremely broad discretion in determining the exact timing and placement of the roadblock.

There is also a significant difference between the kind of discretion that the officer exercises after the stop is made. A check for a driver's license, or for identification papers at an immigration checkpoint, is far more easily standardized than is a search for evidence of intoxication. * * *

For all these reasons, I do not believe that this case is analogous to *Martinez–Fuerte*. In my opinion, the sobriety checkpoints are instead similar to—and in some respects more intrusive than—the random investigative stops that the Court held unconstitutional in * * * *Prouse*. * * *

I respectfully dissent.

NOTE

On remand, the Michigan courts held the roadblock at issue violated the Michigan Constitution's prohibition against unreasonable searches and seizures. Sitz v. Department of State Police, 443 Mich. 744, 506 N.W.2d 209 (1993), affirming 193 Mich.App. 690, 485 N.W.2d 135 (1992).

F. PRETEXT MOTIVATION

American courts have long disagreed on whether law enforcement activity objectively within legal limits can be successfully challenged on the basis that the officer's motive rendered it a "pretext" and, hence, invalid. Arrests and other detentions are probably attacked on this basis more frequently than other types of law enforcement activity. In the principal case that follows, the Supreme Court addressed the extent to which the Fourth Amendment provides a basis for this sort of attack.

There is considerable inconsistency in the terminology used in judicial discussions, but this inconsistency may reflect underlying conceptual confusion. Lower courts differ on precisely what constitutes a "pretext arrest." Moreover, there is confusion regarding the need to, or wisdom of, inquiring whether an arrest was made "on" various possible grounds and—to the extent such inquiries are undertaken—how to determine whether a particular arrest was made "on" a particular ground.

In connection with the pretext issue, consider the Supreme Court's willingness in other contexts to tie the validity of law enforcement action to officers' subjective state of mind. Reconsider, for example, the argument that an investigatory stop is invalid if the officer intended to detain the suspect longer than Fourth Amendment law permits; see the discussion in part C(1) of this chapter.

Whren v. United States

Supreme Court of the United States, 1996.
517 U.S. 806, 116 S.Ct. 1769, 135 L.Ed.2d 89.

■ JUSTICE SCALIA delivered the opinion of the Court.

In this case we decide whether the temporary detention of a motorist who the police have probable cause to believe has committed a civil traffic violation is inconsistent with the Fourth Amendment's prohibition against unreasonable seizures unless a reasonable officer would have been motivated to stop the car by a desire to enforce the traffic laws.

I

On the evening of June 10, 1993, plainclothes vice-squad officers of the District of Columbia Metropolitan Police Department were patrolling a "high drug area" of the city in an unmarked car. Their suspicions were aroused when they passed a dark Pathfinder truck with temporary license plates and youthful occupants waiting at a stop sign, the driver looking down into the lap of the passenger at his right. The truck remained stopped at the intersection for what seemed an unusually long time—more than 20 seconds. When the police car executed a U-turn in order to head back toward the truck, the Pathfinder turned suddenly to its right, without signaling, and sped off at an "unreasonable" speed. The policemen followed, and in a short while overtook the Pathfinder when it stopped behind other traffic at a red light. They pulled up alongside, and Officer Ephraim Soto stepped out and approached the driver's door, identifying himself as a police officer and directing the driver, petitioner Brown, to put the vehicle in park. When Soto drew up to the driver's window, he immediately observed two large plastic bags of what appeared to be crack cocaine in petitioner Whren's hands. Petitioners were arrested, and quantities of several types of illegal drugs were retrieved from the vehicle.

Petitioners were charged in a four-count indictment with violating various federal drug laws * * *. At a pretrial suppression hearing, they challenged the legality of the stop and the resulting seizure of the drugs. * * * The District Court denied the suppression motion * * *.

Petitioners were convicted of the counts at issue here. The Court of Appeals affirmed the convictions. * * * We granted certiorari.

II

The Fourth Amendment guarantees "[t]he right of the people to be secure in their persons, houses, papers, and effects, against unreasonable searches and seizures." Temporary detention of individuals during the stop of an automobile by the police, even if only for a brief period and for a limited purpose, constitutes a "seizure" of "persons" within the meaning of this provision. An automobile stop is thus subject to the constitutional imperative that it not be "unreasonable" under the circumstances. As a general matter, the decision to stop an automobile is reasonable where the police have probable cause to believe that a traffic violation has occurred.

Petitioners accept that Officer Soto had probable cause to believe that various provisions of the District of Columbia traffic code had been violated. See 18 D.C. Mun. Regs. §§ 2213.4 (1995) ("An operator shall . . . give full time and attention to the operation of the vehicle"); 2204.3 ("No person shall turn any vehicle . . . without giving an appropriate signal"); 2200.3 ("No person shall drive a vehicle . . . at a speed greater than is reasonable and prudent under the conditions"). They argue, however, that "in the unique context of civil traffic regulations" probable cause is not enough. Since, they contend, the use of automobiles is so heavily and minutely regulated that total compliance with traffic and safety rules is nearly impossible, a police officer will almost invariably be able to catch any given motorist in a technical violation. This creates the temptation to use traffic stops as a means of investigating other law violations, as to which no probable cause or even articulable suspicion exists. Petitioners, who are both black, further contend that police officers might decide which motorists to stop based on decidedly impermissible factors, such as the race of the car's occupants. To avoid this danger, they say, the Fourth Amendment test for traffic stops should be, not the normal one (applied by the Court of Appeals) of whether probable cause existed to justify the stop; but rather, whether a police officer, acting reasonably, would have made the stop for the reason given.

A

Petitioners contend that the standard they propose is consistent with our past cases' disapproval of police attempts to use valid bases of action against citizens as pretexts for pursuing other investigatory agendas. We are reminded that in Florida v. Wells, 495 U.S. 1, 4, 110 S.Ct. 1632, 1635, 109 L.Ed.2d 1 (1990), we stated that "an inventory search must not be used as a ruse for a general rummaging in order to discover incriminating evidence"; that in Colorado v. Bertine, 479 U.S. 367, 372, 107 S.Ct. 738, 741, 93 L.Ed.2d 739 (1987), in approving an inventory search, we apparently thought it significant that there had been "no showing that the police, who were following standard procedures, acted in bad faith or for the sole purpose of investigation"; and that in New York v. Burger, 482 U.S. 691, 716–717, n. 27, 107 S.Ct. 2636, 2651, n. 27, 96 L.Ed.2d 601 (1987), we observed, in upholding the constitutionality of a warrantless administrative inspection, that the search did not appear to be "a 'pretext' for obtaining evidence of . . . violation of . . . penal laws." But only an undiscerning reader would regard these cases as endorsing the principle that ulterior motives can invalidate police conduct that is justifiable on the basis of probable cause to believe that a violation of law has occurred. In each case we were addressing the validity of a search conducted in the absence of probable cause. Our quoted statements simply explain that the exemption from the need for probable cause (and warrant), which is accorded to searches made for the purpose of inventory or administrative regulation, is not accorded to searches that are not made for those purposes.

* * *

* * * Petitioners' difficulty is not simply a lack of affirmative support for their position. Not only have we never held, outside the context of inventory search or administrative inspection (discussed above), that an officer's motive invalidates objectively justifiable behavior under the Fourth

Amendment; but we have repeatedly held and asserted the contrary. In United States v. Villamonte–Marquez, 462 U.S. 579, 584, n. 3, 103 S.Ct. 2573, 2577, n. 3, 77 L.Ed.2d 22 (1983), we held that an otherwise valid warrantless boarding of a vessel by customs officials was not rendered invalid "because the customs officers were accompanied by a Louisiana state policeman, and were following an informant's tip that a vessel in the ship channel was thought to be carrying marihuana." We flatly dismissed the idea that an ulterior motive might serve to strip the agents of their legal justification. In United States v. Robinson, 414 U.S. 218, 94 S.Ct. 467, 38 L.Ed.2d 427 (1973), we held that a traffic-violation arrest (of the sort here) would not be rendered invalid by the fact that it was "a mere pretext for a narcotics search;" and that a lawful postarrest search of the person would not be rendered invalid by the fact that it was not motivated by the officer-safety concern that justifies such searches. And in Scott v. United States, 436 U.S. 128, 138, 98 S.Ct. 1717, 1723, 56 L.Ed.2d 168 (1978), in rejecting the contention that wiretap evidence was subject to exclusion because the agents conducting the tap had failed to make any effort to comply with the statutory requirement that unauthorized acquisitions be minimized, we said that "[s]ubjective intent alone ... does not make otherwise lawful conduct illegal or unconstitutional." We described *Robinson* as having established that "the fact that the officer does not have the state of mind which is hypothecated by the reasons which provide the legal justification for the officer's action does not invalidate the action taken as long as the circumstances, viewed objectively, justify that action."

We think these cases foreclose any argument that the constitutional reasonableness of traffic stops depends on the actual motivations of the individual officers involved. We of course agree with petitioners that the Constitution prohibits selective enforcement of the law based on considerations such as race. But the constitutional basis for objecting to intentionally discriminatory application of laws is the Equal Protection Clause, not the Fourth Amendment. Subjective intentions play no role in ordinary, probable-cause Fourth Amendment analysis.

B

Recognizing that we have been unwilling to entertain Fourth Amendment challenges based on the actual motivations of individual officers, petitioners disavow any intention to make the individual officer's subjective good faith the touchstone of "reasonableness." They insist that the standard they have put forward—whether the officer's conduct deviated materially from usual police practices, so that a reasonable officer in the same circumstances would not have made the stop for the reasons given—is an "objective" one.

But although framed in empirical terms, this approach is plainly and indisputably driven by subjective considerations. Its whole purpose is to prevent the police from doing under the guise of enforcing the traffic code what they would like to do for different reasons. Petitioners' proposed standard may not use the word "pretext," but it is designed to combat nothing other than the perceived "danger" of the pretextual stop, albeit only indirectly and over the run of cases. Instead of asking whether the individual officer had the proper state of mind, the petitioners would have us ask, in effect, whether (based on general police practices) it is plausible to believe that the officer had the proper state of mind.

Why one would frame a test designed to combat pretext in such fashion that the court cannot take into account actual and admitted pretext is a curiosity that can only be explained by the fact that our cases have foreclosed the more sensible option. If those cases were based only upon the evidentiary difficulty of establishing subjective intent, petitioners' attempt to root out subjective vices through objective means might make sense. But they were not based only upon that, or indeed even principally upon that. Their principal basis—which applies equally to attempts to reach subjective intent through ostensibly objective means—is simply that the Fourth Amendment's concern with "reasonableness" allows certain actions to be taken in certain circumstances, whatever the subjective intent. But even if our concern had been only an evidentiary one, petitioners' proposal would by no means assuage it. Indeed, it seems to us somewhat easier to figure out the intent of an individual officer than to plumb the collective consciousness of law enforcement in order to determine whether a "reasonable officer" would have been moved to act upon the traffic violation. While police manuals and standard procedures may sometimes provide objective assistance, ordinarily one would be reduced to speculating about the hypothetical reaction of a hypothetical constable—an exercise that might be called virtual subjectivity.

Moreover, police enforcement practices, even if they could be practicably assessed by a judge, vary from place to place and from time to time. We cannot accept that the search and seizure protections of the Fourth Amendment are so variable, and can be made to turn upon such trivialities.
* * *

III

In what would appear to be an elaboration on the "reasonable officer" test, petitioners argue that the balancing inherent in any Fourth Amendment inquiry requires us to weigh the governmental and individual interests implicated in a traffic stop such as we have here. That balancing, petitioners claim, does not support investigation of minor traffic infractions by plainclothes police in unmarked vehicles; such investigation only minimally advances the government's interest in traffic safety, and may indeed retard it by producing motorist confusion and alarm—a view said to be supported by the Metropolitan Police Department's own regulations generally prohibiting this practice. And as for the Fourth Amendment interests of the individuals concerned, petitioners point out that our cases acknowledge that even ordinary traffic stops entail "a possibly unsettling show of authority"; that they at best "interfere with freedom of movement, are inconvenient, and consume time" and at worst "may create substantial anxiety." That anxiety is likely to be even more pronounced when the stop is conducted by plainclothes officers in unmarked cars.

It is of course true that in principle every Fourth Amendment case, since it turns upon a "reasonableness" determination, involves a balancing of all relevant factors. With rare exceptions not applicable here, however, the result of that balancing is not in doubt where the search or seizure is based upon probable cause. * * *

Where probable cause has existed, the only cases in which we have found it necessary actually to perform the "balancing" analysis involved searches or seizures conducted in an extraordinary manner, unusually harmful to an individual's privacy or even physical interests—such as, for example, seizure by means of deadly force, see Tennessee v. Garner, 471 U.S. 1, 105 S.Ct. 1694, 85 L.Ed.2d 1 (1985), unannounced entry into a home, see Wilson v. Arkansas, 514 U.S. 927, 115 S.Ct. 1914, 131 L.Ed.2d 976 (1995), entry into a home without a warrant, see Welsh v. Wisconsin, 466 U.S. 740, 104 S.Ct. 2091, 80 L.Ed.2d 732 (1984), or physical penetration of the body, see Winston v. Lee, 470 U.S. 753, 105 S.Ct. 1611, 84 L.Ed.2d 662 (1985). The making of a traffic stop out-of-uniform does not remotely qualify as such an extreme practice, and so is governed by the usual rule that probable cause to believe the law has been broken "outbalances" private interest in avoiding police contact.

Petitioners urge as an extraordinary factor in this case that the "multitude of applicable traffic and equipment regulations" is so large and so difficult to obey perfectly that virtually everyone is guilty of violation, permitting the police to single out almost whomever they wish for a stop. But we are aware of no principle that would allow us to decide at what point a code of law becomes so expansive and so commonly violated that infraction itself can no longer be the ordinary measure of the lawfulness of enforcement. And even if we could identify such exorbitant codes, we do not know by what standard (or what right) we would decide, as petitioners would have us do, which particular provisions are sufficiently important to merit enforcement.

For the run-of-the-mine case, which this surely is, we think there is no realistic alternative to the traditional common-law rule that probable cause justifies a search and seizure.

* * *

Here the District Court found that the officers had probable cause to believe that petitioners had violated the traffic code. That rendered the stop reasonable under the Fourth Amendment, the evidence thereby discovered admissible, and the upholding of the convictions by the Court of Appeals for the District of Columbia Circuit correct.

Judgment affirmed.

NOTE: PRETEXT MOTIVATION UNDER STATE LAW

Despite *Whren*, state constitutional provisions may provide a basis for challenging law enforcement conduct as a pretext.

The Washington Supreme Court reaffirmed in State v. Ladson, 138 Wash.2d 343, 979 P.2d 833, 842 n. 10 (1999), that pretextual stops are unreasonable under the Washington constitution. Rejecting the Supreme Court's reasoning in *Whren*, the state tribunal explained the state constitution "requires we look beyond the formal justification for the stop to the actual one." It continued:

We note if we were to depart from our holdings and allow pretextual traffic stops, Washington citizens would lose their privacy every time they enter their automobiles. The traffic code is sufficiently extensive in its regulation that "[w]hether it be for failing to signal while changing lanes, driving with a headlight out, or not giving 'full time and attention' to the operation of the vehicle, virtually the entire driving population is in violation of some regulation as soon as they get in their cars, or shortly thereafter." Peter Shakow, Let He Who Never Has Turned Without Signaling Cast the First Stone: An Analysis of Whren v. United States, 24 Am. J.Crim. L. 627, 633 (1997) (footnote omitted). Thus, nearly every citizen would be subject to a *Terry* stop simply because he or she is in his or her car. But we have repeatedly affirmed that Washingtonians retain their privacy while in the automobile and we will do so today.

138 Wash.2d at 358 n. 10, 979 P.2d at 842 n. 10. In determining whether a particular stop is pretextual, the *Ladson* court added, a court "should consider the totality of the circumstances, including both the subjective intent of the officer as well as the objective reasonableness of the officer's behavior." Courts applying the *Ladson* analysis are likely to often give controlling significance to an officer's subjective motive. Thus in State v. DeSantiago, 983 P.2d 1173 (Wash.App.1999), the stop at issue was for a left turn made improperly because DeSantiago did not turn into the left hand lane of the street into which the turn was made. The trial court found the officer followed DeSantiago because he had observed DeSantiago leave a "narcotics hot spot" and "was looking for a basis to stop the vehicle." This established subjective pretext motivation, and for this reason the stop was unreasonable.

CHAPTER 5

"WARRANTLESS" SEARCHES

Analysis

EDITORS' INTRODUCTION: EXCEPTIONS TO BENCHMARK FOURTH AMENDMENT REQUIREMENTS

If law enforcement conduct constitutes a "search," the material in Chapters 2 and 3 made clear—as a general rule—certain benchmark Fourth Amendment requirements apply. Information amounting to "probable cause" to believe that the intrusion is justified must be present. In addition, officers must use the search warrant process and obtained a judicial determination that probable cause exists before the intrusion.

But the Fourth Amendment's reasonableness requirement has significant flexibility. In some situations, either or both of the benchmark demands may be modified or abandoned. Relaxation of these requirements was explored to some extent in Chapter 4, which considered officers' right to conduct certain searches as incidents to arrests or because of nonarrest police-citizen contacts. Other situations in which the Fourth Amendment's demands may deviate from the benchmark requirements are the subject of the present chapter.

Most of these situations involve law enforcement activity investigating whether a criminal offense has been committed and, if so, the offender's identity. But this is not always the case. Part B of this chapter considers the so-called "administrative" searches. These may be conducted by inspectors not law enforcement officers. Inspectors' primary objective may be to end violation of legal but noncriminal requirements by means other than criminal prosecution of those found in noncompliance with the law's demands. Whether a noncriminal objective justifies relaxation of Fourth Amendment requirements, of course, is among the issues raised by such inspections.

Each situation discussed in this chapter presents two categories of issues. The first concerns the requirement of a search warrant. In many situations, the issue is whether this requirement should be abandoned entirely and so-called "warrantless" searches regarded as reasonable. In other situations, however, the question is whether the warrant requirement should be retained but relaxed to accommodate special needs presented by the situation. In still others, the issue is whether Fourth Amendment reasonableness should be retained and modified so as to impose *more* stringent requirements than involved in the traditional warrant process considered in Chapter 3.

These situations are often discussed as if the only question is whether—and when—warrantless searches are reasonable. Many, however, also present issues in a second category, concerning possible changes in the traditional requirement of probable cause. If a decision is made to dispense with the warrant requirement, of course, Fourth Amendment reasonableness might still require that an officer have information amounting to probable cause before beginning the search. But in some situations persuasive arguments can be made for demanding only information meeting a less stringent standard or for dispensing entirely with any requirement that the officer have information indicating that a search is justified. Even if a warrant or court order is necessary, the standard for deciding whether that order or warrant can issue might demand less than traditional probable cause. In some situations involving unusually intrusive law enforcement conduct, the Fourth Amendment might permit a warrant to issue or a warrantless search conducted only under a *more* stringent standard than the traditional probable cause requirement.

The significance of these issues often results from the application of the plain view seizure rule, considered in part B(2) of Chapter 2. If law enforcement officers or other public officials are engaged in a proper, i.e., "reasonable," search and in the course of that search come upon items in plain view, they may often seize those items. Whether the search placing the items in the officers' plain view was proper will, in many cases, determine whether the seizure was permissible. If the officers came upon the items in the course of an unreasonable search, the discovery and seizure of the items is likely to be tainted "fruit" of the improper search.

The case law presented in this chapter consists entirely of United States Supreme Court decisions construing the Fourth Amendment requirement of reasonableness. State constitutional, statutory or case law may here as well as elsewhere impose more stringent requirements upon official activity than is mandated by the federal constitutional provision.

Several subsequent chapters address other areas of official conduct raising issues similar to those considered in this chapter. Electronic surveillance, for example, is considered in Chapter 6 and use of grand jury subpoenas is discussed in Chapter 9. Among the issues raised in Chapter 8 is the extent to which undercover law enforcement activity so intrudes upon privacy as to justify subjecting such activity to Fourth Amendment reasonableness requirements. If the Fourth Amendment were applied to this activity, the courts would have to address the extent and nature of the regulation which Fourth Amendment reasonableness imposes.

A. THE EMERGENCY DOCTRINE

The Supreme Court has upheld certain searches without warrants upon demonstrations that the officers reasonably believed delays necessary to apply for search warrants would result in destruction of the evidence or contraband sought. See Schmerber v. California, 384 U.S. 757, 86 S.Ct. 1826, 16 L.Ed.2d 908 (1966) (reprinted in Chapter 2), upholding a warrantless taking of a blood sample because delaying the process might result in the suspect's body eliminating alcohol from his system. But it remains unclear how great a risk the officer must perceive before a warrantless search becomes permissible.

Exigent circumstances—or "emergencies"—are generally treated by courts as dispensing only with the need for a warrant. The officer must still have probable cause to believe evidence or contraband will be found by the search. Perhaps, however, standards for determining when probable cause exists are relaxed when the officer was required to evaluate facts under the pressure of an emergency situation.

In a sense, the emergency exception is a benchmark for analysis of other situations that may dispense with the need for a warrant and perhaps probable cause. In regard to the warrant requirement, many other exceptions—such as that for certain vehicles—involve situations in which a claim might be made that an emergency exists. Fitting a case within one of the other exceptions, however, dispenses with the need for the prosecution to show that *on the facts of the particular case* delay to apply for a warrant would create sufficient risk of loss of the evidence or contraband. In considering the wisdom of various other more specific exceptions and their scope, the availability of the general emergency exception might usefully be kept in mind. If a case falls without any other exception, the prosecution always has the opportunity to demonstrate that, on the facts of the particular situation, the emergency exception applies.

Vale v. Louisiana

Supreme Court of the United States, 1970.
399 U.S. 30, 90 S.Ct. 1969, 26 L.Ed.2d 409.

■ MR. JUSTICE STEWART delivered the opinion of the Court.

The appellant, Donald Vale, was convicted in a Louisiana court on a charge of possessing heroin and was sentenced as a multiple offender to 15 years' imprisonment at hard labor. The Louisiana Supreme Court affirmed the conviction, rejecting the claim that evidence introduced at the trial was the product of an unlawful search and seizure. * * *

The evidence adduced at the pretrial hearing on a motion to suppress showed that on April 24, 1967, officers possessing two warrants for Vale's arrest and having information that he was residing at a specified address proceeded there in an unmarked car and set up a surveillance of the house. The evidence of what then took place was summarized by the Louisiana Supreme Court as follows:

"After approximately 15 minutes the officers observed a green 1958 Chevrolet drive up and sound the horn and after backing into a parking place, again blew the horn. At this juncture Donald Vale, who was well known to Officer Brady having arrested him twice in the previous month, was seen coming out of the house and walk up to the passenger side of the Chevrolet where he had a close brief conversation with the driver; and after looking up and down the street returned inside of the house. Within a few minutes he reappeared on the porch, and again cautiously looked up and down the street before proceeding to the passenger side of the Chevrolet, leaning through the window. From this the officers were convinced a narcotics sale had taken place. They returned to their car and immediately drove toward Donald Vale, and as they reached within approximately three car lengths from the accused, (Donald Vale) he looked up and, obviously recognizing the officers, turned around, walking quickly toward the house. At the same time the driver of the Chevrolet started to make his get away when the car was blocked by the police vehicle. The three officers promptly alighted from the car, whereupon Officers Soule and Laumann called to Donald Vale to stop as he reached the front steps of the house, telling him he was under arrest. Officer Brady at the same time, seeing the driver of the Chevrolet, Arizzio Saucier, whom the officers knew to be a narcotic addict, place something hurriedly in his mouth, immediately placed him under arrest and joined his co-officers. Because of the transaction they had just observed they, informed Donald Vale they were going to search the house, and thereupon advised him of his constitutional rights. After they all entered the front room, Officer Laumann made a cursory inspection of the house to ascertain if anyone else was present and within about three minutes Mrs. Vale and James Vale, mother and brother of Donald Vale, returned home carrying groceries and were informed of the arrest and impending search."

The search of a rear bedroom revealed a quantity of narcotics.

* * *

The Louisiana Supreme Court thought the search * * * supportable because it involved narcotics, which are easily removed, hidden, or destroyed. It would be unreasonable, the Louisiana court concluded, "to require the officers under the facts of the case to first secure a search warrant before searching the premises, as time is of the essence inasmuch as the officers never know whether there is anyone on the premises to be searched who could very easily destroy the evidence." Such a rationale could not apply to the present case, since by their own account the arresting officers satisfied themselves that no one else was in the house when they first entered the premises. But entirely apart from that point, our past decisions make clear that only in "a few specifically established and well-delineated" situations, may a warrantless search of a dwelling withstand constitutional scrutiny, even though the authorities have probable cause to conduct it. The burden rests on the State to show the existence of such an exceptional situation. And the record before us discloses none.

There is no suggestion that anyone consented to the search. The officers were not responding to an emergency. They were not in hot pursuit of a fleeing felon. Warden v. Hayden, 387 U.S. 294, 298–299, 87 S.Ct. 1642, 1645–1646, 18 L.Ed.2d 782. The goods ultimately seized were not in the process of destruction. Schmerber v. California, 384 U.S. 757, 770–771, 86 S.Ct. 1826, 1835–1836, 16 L.Ed.2d 908. Nor were they about to be removed from the jurisdiction.

The officers were able to procure two warrants for Vale's arrest. They also had information that he was residing at the address where they found him. There is thus no reason, so far as anything before us appears, to suppose that it was impracticable for them to obtain a search warrant as well. * * * We decline to hold that an arrest on the street can provide its own "exigent circumstance" so as to justify a warrantless search of the arrestee's house.

* * *

Reversed and remanded.

■ Mr. Justice Blackmun took no part in the consideration or decision of this case.

■ Mr. Justice Black, with whom The Chief Justice joins, dissenting.

* * *

[T]he police had probable cause to believe that Vale was engaged in a narcotics transfer, and that a supply of narcotics would be found in the house, to which Vale had returned after his first conversation, from which he had emerged furtively bearing what the police could readily deduce was a supply of narcotics, and toward which he hurried after seeing the police. But the police did not know then who else might be in the house. Vale's arrest took place near the house, and anyone observing from inside would surely have been alerted to destroy the stocks of contraband which the police believed Vale had left there. The police had already seen Saucier, the narcotics addict, apparently swallow what Vale had given him. Believing that some evidence had already been destroyed and that other evidence might well be, the police were faced with the choice of risking the immediate destruction of evidence or entering the house and conducting a search. I cannot say that their decision to search was unreasonable. Delay in order to obtain a warrant would have given an accomplice just the time he needed.

* * *

[T]he circumstances here were sufficiently exceptional to justify a search * * *. The Court recognizes that searches to prevent the destruction or removal of evidence have long been held reasonable by the Court. * * * It is only necessary to find that, given Vale's arrest in a spot readily visible to anyone in the house and the probable existence of narcotics inside, it was reasonable for the police to conduct an immediate search of the premises.

The Court, however, finds the search here unreasonable. First, the Court suggests that the contraband was not "in the process of destruction." None of the cases cited by the Court supports the proposition that "exceptional circumstances" exist only when the process of destruction has already begun. On the contrary we implied that those circumstances did exist when "evidence or contraband was *threatened* with removal or destruction." Johnson v. United States, [333 U.S. 10, 15, 68 S.Ct. 367, 369, 92 L.Ed. 436 (1948)] (emphasis added).

Second, the Court seems to argue that the search was unreasonable because the police officers had time to obtain a warrant. I agree that the opportunity to obtain a warrant is one of the factors to be weighed in determining reasonableness. But the record conclusively shows that there was no such opportunity here. As I noted above, once the officers had observed Vale's conduct in front of the house they had probable cause to believe that a felony had been committed and that immediate action was necessary. At no time after the events in front of Mrs. Vale's house would it have been prudent for the officers to leave the house in order to secure a warrant.

The Court asserts, however, that because the police obtained two warrants for Vale's arrest there is "no reason * * * to suppose that it was impracticable for them to obtain a search warrant as well." The difficulty is that the two arrest warrants on which the Court seems to rely so heavily were not issued because of any present misconduct of Vale's; they were issued because the bond had been increased for an earlier narcotics charge then pending against Vale. When the police came to arrest Vale, they knew only that his bond had been increased. There is nothing in the record to indicate that, absent the increased bond, there would have been probable cause for an arrest, much less a search. Probable cause for the search arose for the first time when the police observed the activity of Vale and Saucier in and around the house.

* * *

NOTES

1. In Minnesota v. Olson, 495 U.S. 91, 110 S.Ct. 1684, 109 L.Ed.2d 85 (1990), officers investigating a robbery-murder occurring about 6 a.m. on July 18, 1987 developed probable cause to believe Olson the driver of the getaway car. On July 19, they determined Olson was staying in a duplex unit occupied by Louanne and Julie Bergstrom. The occupant of the other duplex unit promised to call when Olson returned; officers were directed to stay away from the duplex in the interim. At 2:45 p.m., the neighbor called and told police Olson had returned. Officers surrounded the unit and telephoned Julie Bergstrom to tell her Olson should come out. The telephoning detective heard a male voice say, "[T]ell them I left." Julie said "Rob" had left. At 3 p.m., police entered and found Olson hiding in a closet. The Minnesota Supreme Court found this warrantless entry of the duplex was not justified by exigent circumstances. In the absence of hot pursuit, it reasoned, officers must have probable cause to believe the situation involved a risk of imminent destruction of evidence, the suspect's escape, or danger to police or persons inside or outside the dwelling. In assessing these risks, it also concluded, the crime's gravity and the likelihood the suspect is armed could be considered. Applying this standard, the state court held that the entry was unjustified. A majority of the Supreme Court held the state tribunal "applied essentially the correct standard in determining whether exigent circumstances existed." Moreover, it declined to disagree with the state court's "fact-specific application" of the standard:

> The [state] court pointed out that although a grave crime was involved, [Olson] "was known not to be the murderer but thought to be the driver of the getaway car," and that the police had already recovered the murder weapon. "The police knew that Louanne and Julie were with the suspect in the upstairs duplex with no suggestion of danger to them. Three or four Minneapolis police squads surrounded the house. The time was 3 p.m., Sunday.... It was evident the suspect was going nowhere. If he came out of the house he would have been promptly apprehended." We do not disturb the state court's judgment that these facts do not add up to exigent circumstances.

495 U.S. at 100–01, 110 S.Ct. at 1690, 109 L.Ed.2d at 96. Justice Kennedy joined with the "understanding" that the Court's discussion was not an endorsement of the state court's application of the standard. Chief Justice Rehnquist and Justice Blackmun dissented without opinion.

2. **"Hot Pursuit" Situations.** In Warden v. Hayden, 387 U.S. 294, 87 S.Ct. 1642, 18 L.Ed.2d 782 (1967), two cab drivers followed the armed robber of the cab company to a residence. A description of the robber and the drivers' information was relayed to police, who arrived at the residence within minutes. They knocked on the door and told the woman who answered they had reason to believe a robber had entered the house. The officers asked to search and the woman did not object. Hayden was found in an upstairs bedroom feigning sleep, and was arrested when no other male was found in the house. One officer was attracted to a bathroom adjoining that in which Hayden was found; in the flush tank of a toilet he found a shotgun and pistol. Another officer searching the cellar for the gun or money looked in a washing machine and found a jacket and trousers resembling what the fleeing robber wore. Under the mattress of Hayden's bed the officers found ammunition for the pistol and a cap. Additional ammunition was found in the drawer of the bedroom dresser. Upholding the admission of these items into evidence, the Su-

preme Court held that the entry of the premises and the search for the robber and his weapons without a warrant was reasonable, because delay might have endangered the officers or others. "[O]nly a thorough search of the house for persons or weapons could have insured that Hayden was the only man present and that the police had control of all weapons which could be used against them or to effect an escape."

Hayden is sometimes—as in the principal case—cited as a "hot pursuit" case. Was it? And how does hot pursuit expand officers' power to search?

3. **"Securing" Premises as Alternative to Searching.** If the officers in *Vale* could not conduct a warrantless search of the premises, could they have prevented Vale's mother and brother from entering the premises until the officers had time to apply for a search warrant? When—and even whether—officers may "secure" a residence pending application for and arrival of a search warrant remains uncertain. See Rawlings v. Kentucky, 448 U.S. 98, 106, 100 S.Ct. 2556, 2562, 65 L.Ed.2d 633, 643 (1980), assuming officers detaining occupants of a house for about an hour pending application for a warrant did so improperly. See also, Segura v. United States, 468 U.S. 796, 104 S.Ct. 3380, 82 L.Ed.2d 599 (1984).

If officers may secure premises pending application for a warrant, does this mean there are two levels of emergency? Perhaps one authorizes a warrantless search while the other permits only the securing of the premises pending application for a warrant.

4. **Crime Scenes.** In Mincey v. Arizona, 437 U.S. 385, 98 S.Ct. 2408, 57 L.Ed.2d 290 (1978), the Supreme Court rejected the proposition that emergency considerations justify a broad exception to the warrant requirement for scenes of even serious offenses such as homicides. Police officers entered Mincey's apartment to arrest him for possession of drugs. A police officer was shot and killed and Mincey was wounded. Officers secured the apartment and arrested Mincey and the other occupants. There then ensued four days of searching the apartment for evidence related to the homicide; two or three hundred items were seized and inventoried. No warrant was obtained. Mincey was convicted of murder and other offenses after a trial in which some of the seized items were introduced. The Arizona Supreme Court affirmed in part, holding the search permissible without a warrant because the place searched was a "murder scene." The Supreme Court reversed. That the premises were a crime scene did not itself dispense with the warrant requirement. Considered under the emergency doctrine, the search exceeded what emergency justification the case presented:

> All the persons in Mincey's apartment had been located before the investigating homicide officers arrived there and began their search. And a fourday search that included opening dresser drawers and ripping up carpets can hardly be rationalized in terms of the legitimate concerns that justify an emergency search.

437 U.S. at 393, 98 S.Ct. at 2414, 57 L.Ed.2d at 300. See also, Flippo v. West Virginia, ___ U.S. ___, 120 S.Ct. 7, 145 L.Ed.2d 16 (1999) (per curiam); Thompson v. Louisiana, 469 U.S. 17, 105 S.Ct. 409, 83 L.Ed.2d 246 (1984) (per curiam).

B. ADMINISTRATIVE INSPECTIONS AND SEARCHES OF LICENSED PREMISES

EDITOR'S' INTRODUCTION: "ADMINISTRATIVE" HOUSING CODE INSPECTIONS

The Fourth Amendment by its terms is not limited to traditional criminal investigation but is potentially applicable to any governmental activity meeting the threshold requirements of a "search" or a "seizure." Supreme Court case law, however, has tended to dilute the requirements of the Amendment when governmental activity has a purpose other than the location of evidence to use in a criminal prosecution.

Such dilution was clearly evidenced in Frank v. Maryland, 359 U.S. 360, 79 S.Ct. 804, 3 L.Ed.2d 877 (1959). The Health Code of the City of Baltimore required all dwellings be kept clean and free from rodent infestation. Health inspectors having "cause to suspect" a violation were authorized to demand entry to premises for purposes of inspection. Frank was convicted and fined $20 for refusing to permit an inspector to enter his premises to look for rats. Finding no federal constitutional defect in this conviction, a majority of the Supreme Court explained:

> The attempted inspection of appellant's home is merely to determine whether conditions exist which the Baltimore Health Code proscribes. If they do appellant is notified to remedy the infringing condition. No evidence for criminal prosecution is sought to be seized. * * * The power of inspection granted by the Baltimore City Code is strictly limited * * *. Valid grounds for suspicion of the existence of a nuisance must exist. * * * The inspection must be made in the day time. * * * Moreover, the inspector has no power to force entry * * *. A fine is imposed for resistance, but officials are not authorized to break past the unwilling occupant.
>
> Thus, not only does the inspection touch at most upon the periphery of the important interests safeguarded by the Fourteenth Amendment's protection against official intrusion, but it is hedged about with safeguards designed to make the least possible demand on the individual occupant, and to cause only the slightest restriction on his claims of privacy.

359 U.S. at 366–67, 79 S.Ct. at 808–09, 3 L.Ed. at 882. Against this, the Court continued, must be weighed the interests served by inspections:

> Time and experience have forcefully taught that the power to inspect dwelling places, either as a matter of systematic area-by-area search or * * * to treat a specific problem, is of indispensable importance to the maintenance of community health; a power that would be greatly hobbled by the blanket requirement of the safeguards necessary for a search of evidence for criminal acts.

359 U.S. at 372, 79 S.Ct. at 811, 3 L.Ed.2d at 885. In light of this, a five justice majority of the Court held the inspector's entry would not have been an unreasonable search and thus Frank was properly convicted of refusing to permit it.

Franks suggested warrants are unnecessary for administrative inspections. In 1967, however, the Court held that despite *Franks* the Fourth Amendment requires warrants for nonemergency Housing Code inspections of residences. Camara v. Municipal Court, 387 U.S. 523, 87 S.Ct. 1727, 18 L.Ed.2d 930 (1967). But it also held warrants authorizing such inspections need not be based upon probable cause to believe that each building to be inspected contains Code violations. Several considerations justified modification of the probable cause standard for this context. Code violations are a serious problem and so limiting inspectors would render effective enforcement impossible. Moreover, since "the inspections are neither personal in nature nor aimed at the discovery of evidence of crime, they involve a relatively limited invasion of the urban citizen's privacy." Consequently, the warrant process is appropriately modified in this context so as to permit warrants to issue for "area inspections"—inspections of all premises in a particular area based on conditions in the area as a whole rather than on knowledge of conditions in particular buildings. Thus:

> "probable cause" to issue a warrant to inspect must exist if reasonable legislative or administrative standards for conducting an area inspection are satisfied with respect to a particular dwelling. Such standards, which will vary with the municipal program being enforced, may be based upon the passage of time, the nature of the building (e.g., a multifamily apartment house), or the condition of the entire area, but they will not necessarily depend upon specific knowledge of the condition of the particular dwelling.

387 U.S. at 538, 87 S.Ct. at 1736, 18 L.Ed.2d at 941. In a companion case, the Court held the same general Fourth Amendment rules apply to administrative inspections of commercial premises and added that the nature of such premises might make them subject to inspection in more situations than permit inspections of private residence. See v. City of Seattle, 387 U.S. 541, 87 S.Ct. 1737, 18 L.Ed.2d 943 (1967).

The principal case in this section deals with inspections of heavily regulated businesses, which are permitted under even more relaxed Fourth Amendment standards than were applied in *Camara* and *See*.

New York v. Burger

Supreme Court of the United States, 1987.
482 U.S. 691, 107 S.Ct. 2636, 96 L.Ed.2d 601.

■ JUSTICE BLACKMUN delivered the opinion of the Court.

This case presents the question whether the warrantless search of an automobile junkyard, conducted pursuant to a statute authorizing such a search, falls within the exception to the warrant requirement for administrative inspections of pervasively regulated industries. The case also presents the question whether an otherwise proper administrative inspection is unconstitutional because the ultimate purpose of the regulatory statute pursuant to which the search is done—the deterrence of criminal behavior—is the same as that of penal laws, with the result that the inspection may disclose violations not only of the regulatory statute but also of the penal statutes.

I

Respondent Joseph Burger is the owner of a junkyard in Brooklyn, N.Y. His business consists, in part, of the dismantling of automobiles and the selling of their parts. His junkyard is an open lot with no buildings. A high metal fence surrounds it, wherein are located, among other things, vehicles and parts of vehicles. At approximately noon on November 17,

1982, Officer Joseph Vega and four other plainclothes officers, all members of the Auto Crimes Division of the New York City Police Department, entered respondent's junkyard to conduct an inspection pursuant to N.Y.Veh. & Traf.Law § 415–a5 (McKinney 1986). On any given day, the Division conducts from 5 to 10 inspections of vehicle dismantlers, automobile junkyards, and related businesses.

Upon entering the junkyard, the officers asked to see Burger's license[1] and his "police book"—the record of the automobiles and vehicle parts in his possession. Burger replied that he had neither a license nor a police book. The officers then announced their intention to conduct a § 415–a inspection. Burger did not object. In accordance with their practice, the officers copied down the Vehicle Inspection Numbers (VINs) of several vehicles and parts of vehicles that were in the junkyard. After checking these numbers against a police computer, the officers determined that respondent was in possession of stolen vehicles and parts. Accordingly, Burger was arrested and charged with five counts of possession of stolen property and one count of unregistered operation as a vehicle dismantler * * *.

In the Kings County Supreme Court, Burger moved to suppress the evidence obtained as a result of the inspection, primarily on the ground that § 415–a5 was unconstitutional. After a hearing, the court denied the motion. * * *

The New York Court of Appeals, however, reversed. In its view, § 415–a5 violated the Fourth Amendment's prohibition of unreasonable searches and seizures. According to the Court of Appeals, "[t]he fundamental defect [of § 415–a5] * * * is that [it] authorize[s] searches undertaken solely to uncover evidence of criminality and not to enforce a comprehensive regulatory scheme. The asserted 'administrative schem[e]' here [is], in reality, designed simply to give the police an expedient means of enforcing penal sanctions for possession of stolen property." * * * [W]e granted certiorari.

II

A

The Court long has recognized that the Fourth Amendment's prohibition on unreasonable searches and seizures is applicable to commercial premises, as well as to private homes. An owner or operator of a business thus has an expectation of privacy in commercial property, which society is prepared to consider to be reasonable. This expectation exists not only with respect to traditional police searches conducted for the gathering of criminal evidence but also with respect to administrative inspections designed to enforce regulatory statutes. See Marshall v. Barlow's, Inc., 436 U.S. 307,

---

1. An individual operating a vehicle-dismantling business in New York is required to have a license:

"Definition and registration of vehicle dismantlers. A vehicle dismantler is any person who is engaged in the business of acquiring motor vehicles or trailers for the purpose of dismantling the same for parts or reselling such vehicles as scrap. No person shall engage in the business of or operate as a vehicle dismantler unless there shall have been issued to him a registration in accordance with the provisions of this section. A violation of this subdivision shall be a class E felony." N.Y.Veh. & Traf.Laws 415–a1 (McKinney 1986).

312–313, 98 S.Ct. 1816, 1820–1821, 56 L.Ed.2d 305 (1978). An expectation of privacy in commercial premises, however, is different from, and indeed less than, a similar expectation in an individual's home. See Donovan v. Dewey, 452 U.S. 594, 598–599, 101 S.Ct. 2534, 2537–2538, 69 L.Ed.2d 262 (1981). This expectation is particularly attenuated in commercial property employed in "closely regulated" industries. The Court observed in *Marshall v. Barlow's, Inc.*: "Certain industries have such a history of government oversight that no reasonable expectation of privacy could exist for a proprietor over the stock of such an enterprise."

The Court first examined the "unique" problem of inspections of "closely regulated" businesses in two enterprises that had "a long tradition of close government supervision." In Colonnade Corp. v. United States, 397 U.S. 72, 90 S.Ct. 774, 25 L.Ed.2d 60 (1970), it considered a warrantless search of a catering business pursuant to several federal revenue statutes authorizing the inspection of the premises of liquor dealers. Although the Court disapproved the search because the statute provided that a sanction be imposed when entry was refused, and because it did not authorize entry without a warrant as an alternative in this situation, it recognized that "the liquor industry [was] long subject to close supervision and inspection."

We returned to this issue in United States v. Biswell, 406 U.S. 311, 92 S.Ct. 1593, 32 L.Ed.2d 87 (1972), which involved a warrantless inspection of the premises of a pawn shop operator, who was federally licensed to sell sporting weapons pursuant to the Gun Control Act of 1968, 82 Stat. 1213, 18 U.S.C. § 921 et seq. While noting that "[f]ederal regulation of the interstate traffic in firearms is not as deeply rooted in history as is governmental control of the liquor industry," we nonetheless concluded that the warrantless inspections authorized by the Gun Control Act would "pose only limited threats to the dealer's justifiable expectations of privacy." We observed: "When a dealer chooses to engage in this pervasively regulated business and to accept a federal license, he does so with the knowledge that his business records, firearms, and ammunition will be subject to effective inspection."

The "*Colonnade–Biswell*" doctrine, stating the reduced expectation of privacy by an owner of commercial premises in a "closely regulated" industry, has received renewed emphasis in more recent decisions. In *Marshall v. Barlow's, Inc.*, we noted its continued vitality but declined to find that warrantless inspections, made pursuant to the Occupational Safety and Health Act of 1970, 84 Stat. 1598, 29 U.S.C. §§ 657(a), of all businesses engaged in interstate commerce fell within the narrow focus of this doctrine. However, we found warrantless inspections made pursuant to the Federal Mine Safety and Health Act of 1977, 91 Stat. 1290, 30 U.S.C. § 801 et seq., proper because they were of a "closely regulated" industry. *Donovan v. Dewey*, supra.

Indeed, in Donovan v. Dewey, we declined to limit our consideration to the length of time during which the business in question—stone quarries— had been subject to federal regulation. We pointed out that the doctrine is essentially defined by "the pervasiveness and regularity of the federal regulation" and the effect of such regulation upon an owner's expectation of privacy. We observed, however, that "the duration of a particular regulatory scheme" would remain an "important factor" in deciding whether a warrantless inspection pursuant to the scheme is permissible.

B

Because the owner or operator of commercial premises in a "closely regulated" industry has a reduced expectation of privacy, the warrant and probable cause requirements, which fulfill the traditional Fourth Amendment standard of reasonableness for a government search, have lessened application in this context. Rather, we conclude that, as in other situations of "special need," where the privacy interests of the owner are weakened and the government interests in regulating particular businesses are concomitantly heightened, a warrantless inspection of commercial premises may well be reasonable within the meaning of the Fourth Amendment.

This warrantless inspection, however, even in the context of a pervasively regulated business, will be deemed to be reasonable only so long as three criteria are met. First, there must be a "substantial" government interest that informs the regulatory scheme pursuant to which the inspection is made. See Donovan v. Dewey, 452 U.S., at 602, 101 S.Ct., at 2540 ("substantial federal interest in improving the health and safety conditions in the Nation's underground and surface mines"); United States v. Biswell, 406 U.S., at 315, 92 S.Ct., at 1596 (regulation of firearms is "of central importance to federal efforts to prevent violent crime and to assist the States in regulating the firearms traffic within their borders"); Colonnade Corp. v. United States, 397 U.S., at 75, 90 S.Ct., at 776 (federal interest "in protecting the revenue against various types of fraud").

Second, the warrantless inspections must be "necessary to further [the] regulatory scheme." For example, in *Dewey* we recognized that forcing mine inspectors to obtain a warrant before every inspection might alert mine owners or operators to the impending inspection, thereby frustrating the purposes of the Mine Safety and Health Act—to detect and thus to deter safety and health violations.

Finally, "the statute's inspection program, in terms of the certainty and regularity of its application, [must] provid[e] a constitutionally adequate substitute for a warrant." In other words, the regulatory statute must perform the two basic functions of a warrant: it must advise the owner of the commercial premises that the search is being made pursuant to the law and has a properly defined scope, and it must limit the discretion of the inspecting officers. To perform this first function, the statute must be "sufficiently comprehensive and defined that the owner of commercial property cannot help but be aware that his property will be subject to periodic inspections undertaken for specific purposes." In addition, in defining how a statute limits the discretion of the inspectors, we have observed that it must be "carefully limited in time, place, and scope."

III

A

Searches made pursuant to § 415–a, in our view, clearly fall within this established exception to the warrant requirement for administrative inspections in "closely regulated" businesses. First, the nature of the regulatory statute reveals that the operation of a junkyard, part of which is devoted to vehicle dismantling, is a "closely regulated" business in the State of New York. The provisions regulating the activity of vehicle dismantling are extensive. An operator cannot engage in this industry without first obtaining a license, which means that he must meet the registration requirements and must pay a fee. Under § 415–a5(a), the operator must maintain a police book recording the acquisition and disposition of motor vehicles and vehicle parts, and make such records and inventory available for inspection by the police or any agent of the Department of Motor Vehicles. The operator also must display his registration number prominently at his place of business, on business documentation, and on vehicles and parts that pass through his business. Moreover, the person engaged in this activity is subject to criminal penalties, as well as to loss of license or civil fines, for failure to comply with these provisions. That other States besides New York have imposed similarly extensive regulations on automobile junkyards further supports the "closely regulated" status of this industry.

In determining whether vehicle dismantlers constitute a "closely regulated" industry, the "duration of [this] particular regulatory scheme," has some relevancy. Section 415–a could be said to be of fairly recent vintage, and the inspection provision of § 415–a5 was added only in 1979. But because the automobile is a relatively new phenomenon in our society and because its widespread use is even newer, automobile junkyards and vehicle dismantlers have not been in existence very long and thus do not have an ancient history of government oversight. * * *

The automobile junkyard business * * * is simply a new branch of an industry that has existed, and has been closely regulated, for many years. The automobile junkyard is closely akin to the secondhand shop or the general junkyard. Both share the purpose of recycling salvageable articles and components of items no longer usable in their original form. As such, vehicle dismantlers represent a modern, specialized version of a traditional activity.

In New York, general junkyards and secondhand shops long have been subject to regulation. * * * The history of government regulation of junk-related activities argues strongly in favor of the "closely regulated" status of the automobile junkyard.

Accordingly, in light of the regulatory framework governing his business and the history of regulation of related industries, an operator of a junkyard engaging in vehicle dismantling has a reduced expectation of privacy in this "closely regulated" business.

B

The New York regulatory scheme satisfies the three criteria necessary to make reasonable warrantless inspections pursuant to § 415–a5. First, the State has a substantial interest in regulating the vehicle-dismantling and automobile-junkyard industry because motor vehicle theft has increased in the State and because the problem of theft is associated with this industry. In this day, automobile theft has become a significant social problem, placing enormous economic and personal burdens upon the citizens of different States. * * * Because contemporary automobiles are made from standardized parts, the nationwide extent of vehicle theft and concern about it are understandable.

Second, regulation of the vehicle-dismantling industry reasonably serves the State's substantial interest in eradicating automobile theft. It is well established that the theft problem can be addressed effectively by controlling the receiver of, or market in, stolen property. Automobile junkyards and vehicle dismantlers provide the major market for stolen vehicles and vehicle parts. Thus, the State rationally may believe that it will reduce car theft by regulations that prevent automobile junkyards from becoming markets for stolen vehicles and that help trace the origin and destination of vehicle parts.

Moreover, the warrantless administrative inspections pursuant to § 415–a5 "are necessary to further [the] regulatory scheme." In this respect, we see no difference between these inspections and those approved by the Court in United States v. Biswell and Donovan v. Dewey. We explained in *Biswell:*

> "[I]f inspection is to be effective and serve as a credible deterrent, unannounced, even frequent, inspections are essential. In this context, the prerequisite of a warrant could easily frustrate inspection; and if the necessary flexibility as to time, scope, and frequency is to be preserved, the protections afforded by a warrant would be negligible."

Similarly, in the present case, a warrant requirement would interfere with the statute's purpose of deterring automobile theft accomplished by identifying vehicles and parts as stolen and shutting down the market in such items. Because stolen cars and parts often pass quickly through an automobile junkyard, "frequent" and "unannounced" inspections are necessary in order to detect them. In sum, surprise is crucial if the regulatory scheme aimed at remedying this major social problem is to function at all.

Third, § 415–a5 provides a "constitutionally adequate substitute for a warrant." The statute informs the operator of a vehicle dismantling business that inspections will be made on a regular basis. Thus, the vehicle dismantler knows that the inspections to which he is subject do not constitute discretionary acts by a government official but are conducted pursuant to statute. Section 415–a5 also sets forth the scope of the inspection and, accordingly, places the operator on notice as to how to comply with the statute. In addition, it notifies the operator as to who is authorized to conduct an inspection.

Finally, the "time, place, and scope" of the inspection is limited, to place appropriate restraints upon the discretion of the inspecting officers. The officers are allowed to conduct an inspection only "during [the] regular and usual business hours."[2] The inspections can be made only of vehicle-

---

2. Respondent contends that § 415–a5 is unconstitutional because it fails to limit the number of searches that may be conducted of a particular business during any given period. While such limitations, or the absence thereof, are a factor in an analysis of the adequacy of a particular statute, they are not determinative of the result so long as the statute, as a whole, places adequate limits upon the discretion of the inspecting officers. * * *

dismantling and related industries. And the permissible scope of these searches is narrowly defined: the inspectors may examine the records, as well as "any vehicles or parts of vehicles which are subject to the record keeping requirements of this section and which are on the premises."

IV

A search conducted pursuant to § 415–a5, therefore, clearly falls within the well-established exception to the warrant requirement for administrative inspections of "closely regulated" businesses. The Court of Appeals, nevertheless, struck down the statute as violative of the Fourth Amendment because, in its view, the statute had no truly administrative purpose but was "designed simply to give the police an expedient means of enforcing penal sanctions for possession of stolen property." The court rested its conclusion that the administrative goal of the statute was pretextual and that § 415–a5 really "authorize[d] searches undertaken solely to uncover evidence of criminality" particularly on the fact that, even if an operator failed to produce his police book, the inspecting officers could continue their inspection for stolen vehicles and parts. The court also suggested that the identity of the inspectors—police officers—was significant in revealing the true nature of the statutory scheme.

In arriving at this conclusion, the Court of Appeals failed to recognize that a State can address a major social problem both by way of an administrative scheme and through penal sanctions. Administrative statutes and penal laws may have the same ultimate purpose of remedying the social problem, but they have different subsidiary purposes and prescribe different methods of addressing the problem. An administrative statute establishes how a particular business in a "closely regulated" industry should be operated, setting forth rules to guide an operator's conduct of the business and allowing government officials to ensure that those rules are followed. Such a regulatory approach contrasts with that of the penal laws, a major emphasis of which is the punishment of individuals for specific acts of behavior.

* * *

Accordingly, to state that § 415–a5 is "really" designed to gather evidence to enable convictions under the penal laws is to ignore the plain administrative purposes of § 415–a, in general, and § 415–a5, in particular. If the administrative goals of § 415–a5 are recognized, the difficulty the Court of Appeals perceives in allowing inspecting officers to examine vehicles and vehicle parts even in the absence of records evaporates. The regulatory purposes of § 415–a5 certainly are served by having the inspecting officers compare the records of a particular vehicle dismantler with vehicles and vehicle parts in the junkyard. The purposes of maintaining junkyards in the hands of legitimate-business persons and of tracing vehicles that pass through these businesses, however, also are served by having the officers examine the operator's inventory even when the operator, for whatever reason, fails to produce the police book. Forbidding inspecting officers from examining the inventory in this situation would permit an illegitimate vehicle dismantler to thwart the purposes of the administrative scheme and would have the absurd result of subjecting his counterpart who maintained records to a more extensive search.

Nor do we think that this administrative scheme is unconstitutional simply because, in the course of enforcing it, an inspecting officer may discover evidence of crimes, besides violations of the scheme itself. The discovery of evidence of crimes in the course of an otherwise proper administrative inspection does not render that search illegal or the administrative scheme suspect.

Finally, we fail to see any constitutional significance in the fact that police officers, rather than "administrative" agents, are permitted to conduct the § 415–a5 inspection. The significance respondent alleges lies in the role of police officers as enforcers of the penal laws and in the officers' power to arrest for offenses other than violations of the administrative scheme. It is, however, important to note that state police officers, like those in New York, have numerous duties in addition to those associated with traditional police work. As a practical matter, many States do not have the resources to assign the enforcement of a particular administrative scheme to a specialized agency. So long as a regulatory scheme is properly administrative, it is not rendered illegal by the fact that the inspecting officer has the power to arrest individuals for violations other than those created by the scheme itself. In sum, we decline to impose upon the States the burden of requiring the enforcement of their regulatory statutes to be carried out by specialized agents.

V

Accordingly, the judgment of the New York Court of Appeals is reversed and the case is remanded to that court for further proceedings not inconsistent with this opinion.

It is so ordered.

■ JUSTICE BRENNAN, with whom JUSTICE MARSHALL joins, and with whom JUSTICE O'CONNOR joins as to all but Part III, dissenting.

Warrantless inspections of pervasively regulated businesses are valid if necessary to further an urgent state interest, and if authorized by a statute that carefully limits their time, place, and scope. I have no objection to this general rule. Today, however, * * * the Court renders virtually meaningless the general rule that a warrant is required for administrative searches of commercial property.

I

In See v. City of Seattle, 387 U.S. 541, 543, 87 S.Ct. 1737, 1739, 18 L.Ed.2d 943 (1967), we held that an administrative search of commercial property generally must be supported by a warrant. We make an exception to this rule, and dispense with the warrant requirement, in cases involving "closely regulated" industries, where we believe that the commercial operator's privacy interest is adequately protected by detailed regulatory schemes authorizing warrantless inspections. See Donovan v. Dewey, 452 U.S. 594, 599, 101 S.Ct. 2534, 2538, 69 L.Ed.2d 262 (1981). * * *

* * * In *Dewey* * * * we clarified that * * * it is "the pervasiveness and regularity of * * * regulation that ultimately determines whether a warrant is necessary to render an inspection program reasonable under the Fourth Amendment."

The provisions governing vehicle dismantling in New York simply are not extensive. A vehicle dismantler must register and pay a fee, display the registration in various circumstances, maintain a police book, and allow inspections. Of course, the inspections themselves cannot be cited as proof of pervasive regulation justifying elimination of the warrant requirement; that would be obvious bootstrapping. Nor can registration and recordkeeping requirements be characterized as close regulation. New York City, like many States and municipalities, imposes similar, and often more stringent, licensing, recordkeeping, and other regulatory requirements on a myriad of trades and businesses. Few substantive qualifications are required of an aspiring vehicle dismantler; no regulation governs the condition of the premises, the method of operation, the hours of operation, the equipment utilized, etc. * * *

In sum, if New York City's administrative scheme renders the vehicle-dismantling business closely regulated, few businesses will escape such a finding. Under these circumstances, the warrant requirement is the exception not the rule * * *.

II

Even if vehicle dismantling were a closely regulated industry, I would nonetheless conclude that this search violated the Fourth Amendment. The warrant requirement protects the owner of a business from the "unbridled discretion [of] executive and administrative officers," by ensuring that "reasonable legislative or administrative standards for conducting an . . . inspection are satisfied with respect to a particular [business]." In order to serve as the equivalent of a warrant, an administrative statute must create "a predictable and guided (governmental) presence," *Dewey*, 452 U.S., at 604, 101 S.Ct., at 2541. Section 415–a5 does not approach the level of "certainty and regularity of * * * application" necessary to provide "a constitutionally adequate substitute for a warrant."[3]

The statute does not inform the operator of a vehicle-dismantling business that inspections will be made on a regular basis; in fact, there is no assurance that any inspections at all will occur. There is neither an upper nor a lower limit on the number of searches that may be conducted at any given operator's establishment in any given time period. Neither the statute, nor any regulations, nor any regulatory body, provide limits or guidance on the selection of vehicle dismantlers for inspection. In fact, the State could not explain why Burger's operation was selected for inspection. * * *

---

3. I also dispute the contention that warrantless searches are necessary to further the regulatory scheme, because of the need for unexpected and/or frequent searches. If surprise is essential (as it usually is in a criminal case), a warrant may be obtained *ex parte*. If the State seeks to conduct frequent inspections, then the statute (or some regulatory authority) should somewhere inform the industry of that fact.

The Court also maintains that this statute effectively limits the scope of the search. We have previously found significant that "the standards with which a [business] operator is required to comply are all specifically set forth," reasoning that a clear and complete definition of potential administrative violations constitutes an implied limitation on the scope of any inspection. Plainly, a statute authorizing a search which can uncover no administrative violations is not sufficiently limited in scope to avoid the warrant requirement. This statute fails to tailor the scope of administrative inspection to the particular concerns posed by the regulated business. I conclude that "the frequency and purpose of the inspections [are left] to the unchecked discretion of Government officers." The conduct of the police in this case underscores this point. The police removed identification numbers from a walker and a wheelchair, neither of which fell within the statutory scope of a permissible administrative search.

The Court also finds significant that an operator is on notice as to who is authorized to search the premises; I do not find the statutory limitation—to "any police officer" or "agent of the commissioner"—significant. The sole limitation I see on a police search of the premises of a vehicle dismantler is that it must occur during business hours; otherwise it is open season. The unguided discretion afforded police in this scheme precludes its substitution for a warrant.

III

The fundamental defect in § 415–a5 is that it authorizes searches intended solely to uncover evidence of criminal acts. The New York Court of Appeals correctly found that § 415–a5 authorized a search of Burger's business "solely to discover whether defendant was storing stolen property on his premises." In the law of administrative searches, one principle emerges with unusual clarity and unanimous acceptance: the government may not use an administrative inspection scheme to search for criminal violations. * * *

Here the State has used an administrative scheme as a pretext to search without probable cause for evidence of criminal violations. It thus circumvented the requirements of the Fourth Amendment by altering the label placed on the search. * * *

Moreover, it is factually impossible that the search was intended to discover wrongdoing subject to administrative sanction. Burger stated that he was not registered to dismantle vehicles as required by § 415–a1, and that he did not have a police book, as required by § 415–a5(a). At that point he had violated every requirement of the administrative scheme. There is no administrative provision forbidding possession of stolen automobiles or automobile parts. The inspection became a search for evidence of criminal acts when all possible administrative violations had been uncovered.

The Court * * * implicitly holds that if an administrative scheme has certain goals and if the search serves those goals, it may be upheld even if no concrete administrative consequences could follow from a particular search. This is a dangerous suggestion, for the goals of administrative schemes often overlap with the goals of the criminal law. * * * If the

Fourth Amendment is to retain meaning in the commercial context, it must be applied to searches for evidence of criminal acts even if those searches would also serve an administrative purpose, unless that administrative purpose takes the concrete form of seeking an administrative violation.

IV

The implications of the Court's opinion, if realized, will virtually eliminate Fourth Amendment protection of commercial entities in the context of administrative searches. No State may require, as a condition of doing business, a blanket submission to warrantless searches for any purpose. I respectfully dissent.

NOTES

1. **Inspections and Searches Related to Arson Investigations.** The Supreme Court has explored the relationship among emergency, "administrative" warrant, and traditional searches for criminal evidence in the context of arson investigations. In Michigan v. Tyler, 436 U.S. 499, 98 S.Ct. 1942, 56 L.Ed.2d 486 (1978), firemen arrived at a furniture store ablaze at midnight and extinguished the fire by 4 a.m. Two plastic containers holding flammable liquid were discovered during the course of extinguishing the fire. Investigators were not able to conduct a thorough investigation of the scene when the fire was extinguished because of the darkness and the smoke. The fire chief returned at 9 a.m. the next morning and discovered some suspicious burn marks in the carpeting. Samples of the carpet were seized. Three weeks later a state fire inspector entered the premises several times and seized more items. No warrant was obtained. Tyler was subsequently tried for arson of the store. The items seized in both inspections and evidence derived from them was admitted over defense objection and Tyler was convicted.

The Supreme Court held this constitutional error. Firefighters do not need a warrant to enter a burning building and extinguish the fire, Justice Stewart's opinion for the Court explained. Moreover:

> Prompt determination of the fire's origin may be necessary to prevent its recurrence, as through the detection of continuing dangers such as faulty wiring or a defective furnace. Immediate investigation may also be necessary to preserve evidence from intentional or accidental destruction. * * * For these reasons, officials need no warrant to remain in a building for a reasonable time to investigate the cause of a blaze after it has been extinguished.

436 U.S. at 510, 98 S.Ct. at 1950, 56 L.Ed.2d at 498–99. But other entries require a warrant. Despite the fire, privacy interests may still be implicated. Burned premises are sometimes still used for living or business purposes after the fire. Private effects are often left at the scene of a fire. The court declined, however, to require a traditional search warrant for all post-fire entries. In some situations, an administrative warrant will suffice. Rejecting the argument administrative warrants serve no purpose, Justice Stewart explained for the Court:

> To secure a warrant to investigate the cause of a fire, an official must show more than the bare fact that a fire has occurred. The magistrate's duty is to assure that the proposed search will be reasonable, a determination that requires inquiry into the need for the intrusion on the one hand, and the threat of disruption of the occupant on the other. * * * Even though a fire victim's privacy must normally yield to the vital social objective of ascertaining the cause of the fire, the magistrate can perform the important function of preventing harassment by keeping that invasion to a minimum.

In addition, * * * [another] major function of the warrant is to provide the property owner with sufficient information to reassure him of the entry's legality.

436 U.S. at 507–08, 98 S.Ct. at 1949, 56 L.Ed.2d at 497. But, Justice Stewart continued:

[I]f the investigating officials find probable cause to believe that arson has occurred and require further access to gather evidence for a possible prosecution, they may obtain a warrant only upon a traditional showing of probable cause applicable to searches for evidence of crime.

436 U.S. at 512, 98 S.Ct. at 1951, 56 L.Ed.2d at 500. On the facts of the case, the Court concluded the entry on the morning after the fire was "no more than an actual continuation" of the firefighters' entry the previous night to extinguish the fire and to conduct an immediate investigation into its origin; therefore, no warrant was needed. But the later entries required a warrant. Since none had been secured, evidence obtained from those entries should not have been used against Tyler.

The Fourth Amendment need for a warrant to conduct post-fire inspections was before the Court again in Michigan v. Clifford, 464 U.S. 287, 104 S.Ct. 641, 78 L.Ed.2d 477 (1984). In *Clifford,* a majority of the Court's members appeared to reject *Tyler's* analysis. Justice Rehnquist, joined by the Chief Justice and Justices Blackmun and O'Connor, took the position that no warrant whatsoever is necessary for a post-fire investigation conducted within a reasonable time of a fire. Since the right to enter is contingent upon the happening of an event—a fire—over which authorities have no control, application of the warrant requirement is not necessary to regulate authorities' power to initiate searches. Property owners could be adequately assured of the legality of an inspection by providing inspectors with identification or by efforts to notify the owners before the inspection. 464 U.S. at 309, 104 S.Ct. at 655, 78 L.Ed.2d at 494–95 (Rehnquist, J., dissenting). Justice Stevens construed the Fourth Amendment as requiring a traditional search warrant for an unannounced entry. But an entry without any warrant would be reasonable, he concluded, if the inspector had either given the owner sufficient advance notice to enable him or an agent to be present at the inspection or had made a reasonable effort to provide such notice. 464 U.S. at 303, 104 S.Ct. at 652, 78 L.Ed.2d at 490 (Stevens, J., concurring in the judgment).

2.   Administrative-like considerations were held to justify considerable flexibility in the Fourth Amendment as it applies to searches of probationers in Griffin v. Wisconsin, 483 U.S. 868, 107 S.Ct. 3164, 97 L.Ed.2d 709 (1987). Application of Fourth Amendment standards to searches by a public employer of employee workplaces split the Court in O'Connor v. Ortega, 480 U.S. 709, 107 S.Ct. 1492, 94 L.Ed.2d 714 (1987).

C.   CONSENT SEARCHES

Evidence obtained by a search need not be excluded if the search was conducted pursuant to effective consent provided by a person with authority to give it. Effective consent means the absence of a warrant will not render evidence inadmissible, even if under general Fourth Amendment requirements a warrant is usually required for similar searches of the sort at issue. In addition, the officers need not have had information rising to the level of probable cause.

Consent searches present three major categories of issues. First are those related to the legal effectiveness of words appearing on their face to constitute consent to search; these are addressed in the first subsection that follows. Second are those related to the authority of the consenting person to consent to the search; these are addressed in the second subsection. Third are questions regarding the scope of authority resulting from particular consents; these are considered in the last subsection.

1.   THE EFFECTIVENESS OF CONSENT

The Supreme Court has long recognized that not all words or actions of consent are effective. In Amos v. United States, 255 U.S. 313, 41 S.Ct. 266, 65 L.Ed. 654 (1921), for example, officers testified that they went to Amos's residence and told the only person there, Amos' wife, they had come to search the premises. She opened the nearby store and the officers entered and searched. The Court held:

> The contention that the constitutional rights of defendant were waived when his wife admitted to his home the governmental officers * * * cannot be entertained. * * * [I]t is perfectly clear that, under the implied coercion here presented, no such waiver was intended or effected.

255 U.S. at 317, 41 S.Ct. at 268, 65 L.Ed. at 656. But under what circumstances will words of consent have full effect? In analyzing this problem, is it necessary or permissible to conceptualize consent as a "waiver" of the right to be free from searches in the absence of compliance with certain requirements, such as a search warrant based on probable cause? To the extent consent operates as a waiver, perhaps it must meet standards developed in other contexts for determining the effectiveness of a waiver of federal constitutional rights. These issues are addressed in the following case.

Schneckloth v. Bustamonte

Supreme Court of the United States, 1973.
412 U.S. 218, 93 S.Ct. 2041, 36 L.Ed.2d 854.

■ MR. JUSTICE STEWART delivered the opinion of the Court.

* * *

I.

The respondent was brought to trial in a California court upon a charge of possessing a check with intent to defraud. He moved to suppress the introduction of certain material as evidence against him on the ground that the material had been acquired through an unconstitutional search and seizure. In response to the motion, the trial judge conducted an evidentiary hearing where it was established that the material in question had been acquired by the State under the following circumstances:

While on routine patrol in Sunnyvale, California, at approximately 2:40 in the morning, Police Officer James Rand stopped an automobile when he observed that one headlight and its license plate light were burned out. Six men were in the vehicle. Joe Alcala and the respondent, Robert Busta-monte, were in the front seat with Joe Gonzales, the driver. Three older men were seated in the rear. When, in response to the policeman's question, Gonzales could not produce a driver's license, Officer Rand asked if any of the other five had any evidence of identification. Only Alcala produced a license, and he explained that the car was his brother's. After the six occupants had stepped out of the car at the officer's request and after two additional policemen had arrived, Officer Rand asked Alcala if he could search the car. Alcala replied, "Sure, go ahead." Prior to the search no one was threatened with arrest and, according to Officer Rand's uncon-tradicted testimony, it "was all very congenial at this time." Gonzales testified that Alcala actually helped in the search of the car, by opening the trunk and glove compartment. In Gonzales' words: " * * * the police officer asked Joe [Alcala], he goes, 'Does the trunk open?' And Joe said, 'Yes.' He went to the car and got the keys and opened up the trunk." Wadded up under the left rear seat, the police officers found three checks that had previously been stolen from a car wash.

[Bustamonte, by means never explained, had come into possession of a checkwriting machine previously stolen from a car wash. He, Alcala, and Gonzales had cashed at least one check from the machine. On the day prior to the stop in Sunnydale, the three had gone to San Jose to find other people willing to use false identification to cash checks written on the machine. The three passengers in the rear seat of the car at the time of the stop had joined the trio for this purpose. By the time Alcala gave his consent to the search, there were four police cars and an undetermined number of officers at the scene. The facts do not suggest that the officers connected the car and its occupants with the theft of the checkwriting machine or the passing of the checks before the search. Two of the older men seated in the rear seat had given inconsistent stories concerning the situation. One officer stated that permission to search the car was sought because things "just didn't fit in right." The search was quite intensive; the officers removed the rear seat from the car. After discovery of the checks, Gonzales "cooperated" with the officers and provided information that linked Bustamonte and the others to the checkwriting machine and the scheme to cash the forged checks. Editors.]

The trial judge denied the motion to suppress, and the checks in question were admitted in evidence at Bustamonte's trial. On the basis of this and other evidence he was convicted, and the California Court of Appeals for the First Appellate District affirmed the conviction. In agreeing that the search and seizure were constitutionally valid, the appellate court applied the standard earlier formulated by the Supreme Court of California in an opinion by then Justice Traynor: "Whether in a particular case an apparent consent was in fact voluntarily given or was in submission to an express or implied assertion of authority, is a question of fact to be determined in the light of all the circumstances." People v. Michael, 45 Cal.2d 751, 753, 290 P.2d 852, 854. The appellate court found that "[i]n the instant case the prosecution met the necessary burden of showing consent * * * since there were clearly circumstances from which the trial court could ascertain that consent had been freely given without coercion or submission to authority. Not only officer Rand, but Gonzales, the driver of the automobile, testified that Alcala's assent to the search of his brother's automobile was freely, even casually given. At the time of the request to search the automobile the atmosphere, according to Rand, was 'congenial' and there had been no discussion of any crime. As noted, Gonzales said Alcala even attempted to aid in the search." The California Supreme Court denied review.

Thereafter, the respondent sought a writ of habeas corpus in a federal district court. It was denied. On appeal, the Court of Appeals for the Ninth Circuit * * * set aside the District Court's order. The appellate court reasoned that a consent was a waiver of a person's Fourth and Fourteenth Amendment rights, and that the State was under an obligation to demonstrate not only that the consent had been uncoerced, but that it had been given with an understanding that it could be freely and effectively withheld. Consent could not be found, the court held, solely from the absence of coercion and a verbal expression of assent. Since the District Court had not determined that Alcala had *known* that his consent could be withheld and that he could have refused to have his vehicle searched, the Court of Appeals vacated the order denying the writ and remanded the case for further proceedings. We granted the State's petition for certiorari to determine whether the Fourth and Fourteenth Amendments require the showing thought necessary by the Court of Appeals.

II.

It is important to make it clear at the outset what is not involved in this case. The respondent concedes that a search conducted pursuant to a valid consent is constitutionally permissible. * * * And similarly the State concedes that "[w]hen a prosecutor seeks to rely upon consent to justify the lawfulness of a search he has the burden of proving that the consent was, in fact, freely and voluntarily given." Bumper v. North Carolina, 391 U.S. 543, 548, 88 S.Ct. 1788, 1792, 20 L.Ed.2d 797.

The precise question in this case, then, is what must the state prove to demonstrate that a consent was "voluntarily" given. * * *

A.

The most extensive judicial exposition of the meaning of "voluntariness" has been developed in those cases in which the Court has had to determine the "voluntariness" of a defendant's confession for purposes of the Fourteenth Amendment. * * * It is to that body of case law to which we turn for initial guidance on the meaning of "voluntariness" in the present context.

Those cases yield no talismanic definition of "voluntariness," mechanically applicable to the host of situations where the question has arisen. "The notion of 'voluntariness,'" Mr. Justice Frankfurter once wrote, "is itself an amphibian." Culombe v. Connecticut, 367 U.S. 568, 604–605, 81 S.Ct. 1860, 1880–1881, 6 L.Ed.2d 1037. It cannot be taken literally to mean a "knowing" choice. "Except where a person is unconscious or drugged or otherwise lacks capacity for conscious choice, all incriminating statements—even those made under brutal treatment—are 'voluntary' in the sense of representing a choice of alternatives. On the other hand, if 'voluntariness' incorporates notions of 'but-for' cause, the question should be whether the statement would have been made even absent inquiry or other official action. Under such a test, virtually no statement would be voluntary because very few people give incriminating statements in the absence of official action of some kind." It is thus evident that neither linguistics nor epistemology will provide a ready definition of the meaning of "voluntariness."

Rather, "voluntariness" has reflected an accommodation of the complex of values implicated in police questioning of a suspect. At one end of the spectrum is the acknowledged need for police questioning as a tool for the effective enforcement of criminal laws. Without such investigation, those who were innocent might be falsely accused, those who were guilty might wholly escape prosecution, and many crimes would go unsolved. In short, the security of all would be diminished. At the other end of the spectrum, is the set of values reflecting society's deeply felt belief that the criminal law cannot be used as an instrument of unfairness, and that the possibility of unfair and even brutal police tactics poses a real and serious threat to civilized notions of justice. "[I]n cases involving involuntary confessions, this Court enforces the strongly felt attitude of our society that important human values are sacrificed where an agency of the government, in the course of securing a conviction, wrings a confession out of an accused against his will."

This Court's decisions reflect a frank recognition that the Constitution requires the sacrifice of neither security nor liberty. The Due Process Clause does not mandate that the police forego all questioning, nor that they be given carte blanche to extract what they can from a suspect. "The ultimate test remains that which has been the only clearly established test in Anglo–American courts for two hundred years: the test of voluntariness. Is the confession the product of an essentially free and unconstrained choice by its maker? If it is, if he has willed to confess, it may be used against him. If it is not, if his will has been overborne and his capacity for self-determination critically impaired, the use of his confession offends due process." Culombe v. Connecticut, supra, 367 U.S., at 602, 81 S.Ct., at 1879.

In determining whether a defendant's will was overborne in a particular case, the Court has assessed the totality of all the surrounding circumstances—both the characteristics of the accused and the details of the interrogation. Some of the factors taken into account have included the youth of the accused, his lack of education, or his low intelligence, the lack of any advice to the accused of his constitutional rights, the length of detention, the repeated and prolonged nature of the questioning, and the use of physical punishment such as the deprivation of food or sleep. In all of these cases, the Court determined the factual circumstances surrounding the confession, assessed the psychological impact on the accused, and evaluated the legal significance of how the accused reacted.

The significant fact about all of these decisions is that none of them turned on the presence or absence of a single controlling criterion; each reflected a careful scrutiny of all the surrounding circumstances. In none of them did the Court rule that the Due Process Clause required the prosecution to prove as part of its initial burden that the defendant knew he had a right to refuse to answer the questions that were put. While the state of the accused's mind, and the failure of the police to advise the accused of his rights, were certainly factors to be evaluated in assessing the "voluntariness" of an accused's responses, they were not in and of themselves determinative.

B.

Similar considerations lead us to agree with the courts of California that the question whether a consent to a search was in fact "voluntary" or was the product of duress or coercion, express or implied, is a question of fact to be determined from the totality of all the circumstances. While knowledge of the right to refuse consent is one factor to be taken into account, the government need not establish such knowledge as the *sine qua non* of an effective consent. As with police questioning, two competing concerns must be accommodated in determining the meaning of a "voluntary" consent—the legitimate need for such searches and the equally important requirement of assuring the absence of coercion.

In situations where the police have some evidence of illicit activity, but lack probable cause to arrest or search, a search authorized by a valid consent may be the only means of obtaining important and reliable evidence. In the present case for example, while the police had reason to stop the car for traffic violations, the State does not contend that there was probable cause to search the vehicle or that the search was incident to a valid arrest of any of the occupants. Yet, the search yielded tangible evidence that served as a basis for a prosecution, and provided some assurance that others, wholly innocent of the crime, were not mistakenly brought to trial. And in those cases where there is probable cause to arrest or search, but where the police lack a warrant, a consent search may still be valuable. If the search is conducted and proves fruitless, that in itself may convince the police that an arrest with its possible stigma and embarrassment is unnecessary, or that a far more extensive search pursuant to a warrant is not justified. In short, a search pursuant to consent may result in considerably less inconvenience for the subject of the search, and, properly conducted, is a constitutionally permissible and wholly legitimate aspect of effective police activity.

But the Fourth and Fourteenth Amendments require that a consent not be coerced, by explicit or implicit means, by implied threat or covert force. For, no matter how subtly the coercion were applied, the resulting "consent" would be no more than a pretext for the unjustified police intrusion against which the Fourth Amendment is directed. * * *

The problem of reconciling the recognized legitimacy of consent searches with the requirement that they be free from any aspect of official coercion cannot be resolved by any infallible touchstone. To approve such searches without the most careful scrutiny would sanction the possibility of official coercion; to place artificial restrictions upon such searches would jeopardize their basic validity. Just as was true with confessions, the requirement of a "voluntary" consent reflects a fair accommodation of the constitutional requirements involved. In examining all the surrounding circumstances to determine if in fact the consent to search was coerced, account must be taken of subtly coercive police questions, as well as the possibly vulnerable subjective state of the person who consents. Those searches that are the product of police coercion can thus be filtered out without undermining the continuing validity of consent searches. In sum, there is no reason for us to depart in the area of consent searches, from the traditional definition of "voluntariness."

The approach of the Court of Appeals for the Ninth Circuit * * *, that the State must affirmatively prove that the subject of the search knew that he had a right to refuse consent, would, in practice, create serious doubt whether consent searches could continue to be conducted. There might be rare cases where it could be proved from the record that a person in fact affirmatively knew of his right to refuse—such as a case where he announced to the police that if he didn't sign the consent form, "you [police] are going to get a search warrant;" or a case where by prior experience and training a person had clearly and convincingly demonstrated such knowledge. But more commonly where there was no evidence of any coercion, explicit or implicit, the prosecution would nevertheless be unable to demonstrate that the subject of the search in fact had known of his right to refuse consent.

The very object of the inquiry—the nature of a person's subjective understanding—underlines the difficulty of the prosecution's burden under the rule applied by the Court of Appeals in this case. Any defendant who was the subject of a search authorized solely by his consent could effectively frustrate the introduction into evidence of the fruits of that search by simply failing to testify that he in fact knew he could refuse to consent. And the near impossibility of meeting this prosecutorial burden suggests why this Court has never accepted any such litmus-paper test of voluntariness. * * *

One alternative that would go far towards proving that the subject of a search did know he had a right to refuse consent would be to advise him of that right before eliciting his consent. That, however, is a suggestion that has been almost universally repudiated by both federal and state courts, and, we think, rightly so. For it would be thoroughly impractical to impose on the normal consent search the detailed requirements of an effective warning. Consent searches are part of the standard investigatory techniques of law enforcement agencies. They normally occur on the highway, or in a person's home or office, and under informal and unstructured conditions. The circumstances that prompt the initial request to search may develop quickly or be a logical extension of investigative police questioning. The police may seek to investigate further suspicious circumstances or to follow up leads developed in questioning persons at the scene of a crime. These situations are a far cry from the structured atmosphere of a trial where, assisted by counsel if he chooses, a defendant is informed of his trial rights. And, while surely a closer question, these situations are still immeasurably, far removed from "custodial interrogation" where * * * we found that the Constitution required certain now familiar warnings as a prerequisite to police interrogation. * * *

Consequently, we cannot accept the position of the Court of Appeals in this case that proof of knowledge of the right to refuse consent is a necessary prerequisite to demonstrating a "voluntary" consent. Rather it is only by analyzing all the circumstances of an individual consent that it can be ascertained whether in fact it was voluntary or coerced. It is this careful sifting of the unique facts and circumstances of each case that is evidenced in our prior decisions involving consent searches.

* * *

[I]f under all the circumstances it has appeared that the consent was not given voluntarily—that it was coerced by threats or force, or granted only in submission to a claim of lawful authority—then we have found the consent invalid and the search unreasonable. In *Bumper*, a 66-year-old Negro widow, who lived in a house located in a rural area at the end of an isolated mile-long dirt road, allowed four white law enforcement officials to search her home after they asserted they had a warrant to search the house. We held the alleged consent to be invalid, noting that "[w]hen a law enforcement officer claims authority to search a home under a warrant, he announces in effect that the occupant has no right to resist the search. The situation is instinct with coercion—albeit colorably lawful coercion. Where there is coercion there cannot be consent."

Implicit in all of these cases is the recognition that knowledge of a right to refuse is not a prerequisite of a voluntary consent. If the prosecution were required to demonstrate such knowledge, * * * [the] opinions would surely have focused upon the subjective mental state of the person who consented. Yet they did not.

In short, neither this Court's prior cases, nor the traditional definition of "voluntariness" requires proof of knowledge of a right to refuse as the *sine qua non* of an effective consent to a search.

C.

It is said, however, that a "consent" is a "waiver" of a person's rights under the Fourth and Fourteenth Amendments. The argument is that by allowing the police to conduct a search, a person "waives" whatever right he had to prevent the police from searching. It is argued that under the doctrine of Johnson v. Zerbst, 304 U.S. 458, 464, 58 S.Ct. 1019, 1023, 82 L.Ed. 1461, to establish such a "waiver" the state must demonstrate "an intentional relinquishment or abandonment of a known right or privilege."

But these standards were enunciated in *Johnson* in the context of the safeguards of a fair criminal trial. Our cases do not reflect an uncritical demand for a knowing and intelligent waiver in every situation where a person has failed to invoke a constitutional protection. As Mr. Justice Black once observed for the Court: " 'Waiver' is a vague term used for a great variety of purposes, good and bad, in the law." Green v. United States, 355 U.S. 184, 191, 78 S.Ct. 221, 226, 2 L.Ed.2d 199. * * *

The requirement of a "knowing" and "intelligent" waiver was articulated in a case involving the validity of a defendant's decision to forego a right constitutionally guaranteed to protect a fair trial and the reliability of the truth-determining process. Johnson v. Zerbst, supra, dealt with the denial of counsel in a federal criminal trial. There the Court held that under the Sixth Amendment a criminal defendant is entitled to the assistance of counsel, and that if he lacks sufficient funds to retain counsel, it is the Government's obligation to furnish him with a lawyer. * * * To preserve the fairness of the trial process the Court established an appropriately heavy burden on the government before waiver could be found—"an intentional relinquishment or abandonment of a known right or privilege."

Almost without exception the requirement of a knowing and intelligent waiver has been applied only to those rights which the Constitution guarantees to a criminal defendant in order to preserve a fair trial. Hence, and hardly surprisingly in view of the facts of *Johnson* itself, the standard of a knowing and intelligent waiver has most often been applied to test the validity of a waiver of counsel, either at trial, or upon a guilty plea. And the Court has also applied the *Johnson* criteria to assess the effectiveness of a waiver of other trial rights such as the right to confrontation, to a jury trial and to a speedy trial, and the right to be free from twice being placed in jeopardy. Guilty pleas have been carefully scrutinized to determine whether the accused knew and understood all the rights to which he would be entitled at trial, and that he had intentionally chosen to forego them. And the Court has evaluated the knowing and intelligent nature of the waiver of trial rights in trial-type situations, such as the waiver of the privilege against compulsory self-incrimination before an administrative agency or a congressional committee or the waiver of counsel in a juvenile proceeding.

The guarantees afforded a criminal defendant at trial also protect him at certain stages before the actual trial, and any alleged waiver must meet the strict standard of an intentional relinquishment of a "known" right. But the "trial" guarantees that have been applied to the "pretrial" stage of the criminal process are similarly designed to protect the fairness of the trial itself.

* * *

There is a vast difference between those rights that protect a fair criminal trial and the rights guaranteed under the Fourth Amendment. Nothing, either in the purposes behind requiring a "knowing" and "intelligent" waiver of trial rights, or in the practical application of such a requirement suggests that it ought to be extended to the constitutional guarantee against unreasonable searches and seizures.

A strict standard of waiver has been applied to those rights guaranteed to a criminal defendant to insure that he will be accorded the greatest possible opportunity to utilize every facet of the constitutional model of a fair criminal trial. Any trial conducted in derogation of that model leaves open the possibility that the trial reached an unfair result precisely because all the protections specified in the Constitution were not provided. A prime example is the right to counsel. For without that right, a wholly innocent accused faces the real and substantial danger that simply because of his lack of legal expertise he may be convicted. * * * The Constitution requires that every effort be made to see to it that a defendant in a criminal case has not unknowingly relinquished the basic protections that the Framers thought indispensable to a fair trial.

The protections of the Fourth Amendment are of a wholly different order, and have nothing whatever to do with promoting the fair ascertainment of truth at a criminal trial. Rather, * * * the Fourth Amendment protects the "security of one's privacy against arbitrary intrusion by the police. * * * " * * * The Fourth Amendment "is not an adjunct to the ascertainment of truth." The guarantees of the Fourth Amendment stand "as a protection of quite different constitutional values—values reflecting the concern of our society for the right of each individual to be let alone. To recognize this is no more than to accord those values undiluted respect."

Nor can it even be said that a search, as opposed to an eventual trial, is somehow "unfair" if a person consents to a search. While the Fourth and Fourteenth Amendments limit the circumstances under which the police can conduct a search, there is nothing constitutionally suspect in a person voluntarily allowing a search. The actual conduct of the search may be precisely the same as if the police had obtained a warrant. And, unlike those constitutional guarantees that protect a defendant at trial, it cannot be said every reasonable presumption ought to be indulged against voluntary relinquishment. We have only recently stated: "[I]t is no part of the policy underlying the Fourth and Fourteenth Amendments to discourage citizens from aiding to the utmost of their ability in the apprehension of criminals." Coolidge v. New Hampshire, 403 U.S. 443, 448, 91 S.Ct. 2022, 2049, 29 L.Ed.2d 564. Rather the community has a real interest in encouraging consent, for the resulting search may yield necessary evidence for the solution and prosecution of crime, evidence that may insure that a wholly innocent person is not wrongly charged with a criminal offense.

Those cases that have dealt with the application of the Johnson v. Zerbst rule make clear that it would be next to impossible to apply to a consent search the standard of "an intentional relinquishment or abandonment of a known right or privilege." To be true to *Johnson* and its progeny, there must be examination into the knowing and understanding nature of the waiver, an examination that was designed for a trial judge in the structured atmosphere of a courtroom. * * * It would be unrealistic to expect that in the informal, unstructured context of a consent search a policeman, upon pain of tainting the evidence obtained, could make the detailed type of examination demanded by *Johnson*. And, if for this reason a diluted form of "waiver" were found acceptable, that would itself be ample recognition of the fact that there is no universal standard that must be applied in every situation where a person forgoes a constitutional right.

Similarly, a "waiver" approach to consent searches would be thoroughly inconsistent with our decisions that have approved "third party consents." * * * [I]t is inconceivable that the Constitution could countenance the waiver of a defendant's right to counsel by a third party, or that a waiver could be found because a trial judge reasonably though mistakenly believed a defendant had waived his right to plead not guilty.

In short, there is nothing in the purposes or application of the waiver requirements of Johnson v. Zerbst that justifies, much less compels, the easy equation of a knowing waiver with a consent search. * * *

* * *

E.

Our decision today is a narrow one. We hold only that when the subject of a search is not in custody and the State attempts to justify a search on the basis of his consent, the Fourth and Fourteenth Amendments require that it demonstrate that the consent was in fact voluntarily given, and not the result of duress or coercion, express or implied. Voluntariness is a question of fact to be determined from all the circumstances, and while the subject's knowledge of a right to refuse is a factor to be taken into account, the prosecution is not required to demonstrate such knowledge as a prerequisite to establishing a voluntary consent. Because the California courts followed these principles in affirming the respondent's conviction, and because the Court of Appeals for the Ninth Circuit in remanding for an evidentiary hearing required more, its judgment must be reversed.

It is so ordered.

■ MR. JUSTICE MARSHALL, dissenting.

Several years ago, Mr. Justice Stewart reminded us that "[t]he Constitution guarantees * * * a society of free choice. Such a society presupposes the capacity of its members to choose." Ginsberg v. New York, 390 U.S. 629, 649, 88 S.Ct. 1274, 1285, 20 L.Ed.2d 195 (1968) (concurring opinion). I would have thought that the capacity to choose necessarily depends upon knowledge that there is a choice to be made. But today the Court reaches the curious result that one can choose to relinquish a constitutional right— the right to be free of unreasonable searches—without knowing that he has the alternative of refusing to accede to a police request to search. I cannot agree, and therefore dissent.

NOTES

1. **Consent From Person in Custody.** Despite the limitations the Court placed upon its holding in the principal case, the same analysis was soon applied to consent given by an arrested person. United States v. Watson, 423 U.S. 411, 96 S.Ct. 820, 46 L.Ed.2d 598 (1976).

2. **Suspect's Knowledge Search Would be Incriminating.** Does the fact the suspect was likely aware that a search would be fruitful suggest that the suspect's consent to the search was not voluntary? In United States v. Mendenhall, 446 U.S. 544, 100 S.Ct. 1870, 64 L.Ed.2d 497 (1980), Mendenhall was approached by two Drug Enforcement Administration agents at the Detroit Metropolitan Airport and agreed to accompany them to a nearby office. She consented to being searched. When told that the search would require her to remove her clothing, Mendenhall stated she had a plane to catch. The officer, however, assured her that if she were carrying no drugs "there would be no problem." After beginning to disrobe, Mendenhall took two small packages from her undergarments and handed them to the officer. One contained heroin. Upholding a lower court finding that Mendenhall's consent was voluntary, Justice Stewart's plurality opinion rejected the assertion that Mendenhall's consent was involuntary because she would not have voluntarily consented to a search she knew was likely to disclose incriminating narcotics. "[T]he question," he responded, "is not whether [she] acted in her ultimate self-interest, but whether she acted voluntarily." Nevertheless, he also noted the possibility that Mendenhall may have thought she was acting in self-

interest by voluntarily cooperating with the officers in a manner she perceived would result in later more lenient treatment.

3. **Consents During or After Traffic Stops.** Do consents solicited during traffic stops pose special risks justifying special Fourth Amendment requirements? In Ohio v. Robinette, 519 U.S. 33, 117 S.Ct. 417, 136 L.Ed.2d 347 (1996), Deputy Newsome stopped Robinette for speeding, asked for and received his driver's license, and ran a computer check which indicated Robinette had no prior violations.

> Newsome then asked Robinette to step out of his car, turned on his mounted video camera, issued a verbal warning to Robinette, and returned his license.
>
> At this point, Newsome asked, "One question before you get gone: [A]re you carrying any illegal contraband in your car? Any weapons of any kind, drugs, anything like that?" Robinette answered "no" to these questions, after which Deputy Newsome asked if he could search the car. Robinette consented. In the car, Deputy Newsome discovered a small amount of marijuana and, in a film container, a pill which was later determined to be methylenedioxymethamphetamine (MDMA).

The Ohio Supreme Court held the prosecution barred from establishing the consent was "an independent act of free will" by the officer's failure to follow what the court found to be the applicable Fourth Amendment law:

> This case demonstrates the need for this court to draw a bright line between the conclusion of a valid seizure and the beginning of a consensual exchange. * * *
>
> The transition between detention and a consensual exchange can be so seamless that the untrained eye may not notice that it has occurred. The undetectability of that transition may be used by police officers to coerce citizens into answering questions that they need not answer, or to allow a search of a vehicle that they are not legally obligated to allow.
>
> The present case offers an example of the blurring between a legal detention and an attempt at consensual interaction. Even assuming that Newsome's detention of Robinette was legal through the time when Newsome handed back Robinette's driver's license, Newsome then said, "One question *before you get gone*: are you carrying any illegal contraband in your car?" (Emphasis added.) Newsome tells Robinette that before he leaves Newsome wants to know whether Robinette is carrying any contraband. Newsome does not ask if he may ask a question, he simply asks it, implying that Robinette must respond before he may leave. The interrogation then continues. Robinette is never told that he is free to go or that he may answer the question at his option.
>
> Most people believe that they are validly in a police officer's custody as long as the officer continues to interrogate them. The police officer retains the upper hand and the accouterments of authority. That the officer lacks legal license to continue to detain them is unknown to most citizens, and a reasonable person would not feel free to walk away as the officer continues to address him.
>
> We are aware that consensual encounters between police and citizens are an important, and constitutional, investigative tool. However, citizens who have not been detained immediately prior to being encountered and questioned by police are more apt to realize that they need not respond to a police officer's questions. A "consensual encounter" immediately following a detention is likely to be imbued with the authoritative aura of the detention. Without a clear break from the detention, the succeeding encounter is not consensual at all.

Therefore, we are convinced that the right, guaranteed by the federal and Ohio Constitutions, to be secure in one's person and property requires that citizens stopped for traffic offenses be clearly informed by the detaining officer when they are free to go after a valid detention, before an officer attempts to engage in a consensual interrogation. Any attempt at consensual interrogation must be preceded by the phrase "At this time you legally are free to go" or by words of similar import.

73 Ohio St.3d at 654–55, 653 N.E.2d at 698–99.

The United States Supreme Court disagreed:

We have long held that the "touchstone of the Fourth Amendment is reasonableness." Reasonableness, in turn, is measured in objective terms by examining the totality of the circumstances.

In applying this test we have consistently eschewed bright-line rules, instead emphasizing the fact-specific nature of the reasonableness inquiry. * * *

The Fourth Amendment test for a valid consent to search is that the consent be voluntary, and "[v]oluntariness is a question of fact to be determined from all the circumstances." The Supreme Court of Ohio having held otherwise, its judgment is reversed, and the case is remanded for further proceedings not inconsistent with this opinion.

519 U.S. at 39–40, 117 S.Ct. at 421, 136 L.Ed.2d at 354–55.

On remand, the Ohio court assessed the voluntariness of Robinette's consent under *Bustamante* and Florida v. Royer (reprinted in Chapter 4) and concluded that the consent was not voluntary:

Newsome's words did not give Robinette any indication that he was free to go, but rather implied just the opposite—that Robinette was not free to go until he answered Newsome's additional questions. The timing of Newsome's immediate transition from giving Robinette the warning for speeding into questioning regarding contraband and the request to search is troubling. * * *

When these factors are combined with a police officer's superior position of authority, any reasonable person would have felt compelled to submit to the officer's questioning. While Newsome's questioning was not expressly coercive, the circumstances surrounding the request to search made the questioning impliedly coercive. * * * [A]n officer has discretion to issue a ticket rather than a warning to a motorist if the motorist becomes uncooperative. From the totality of the circumstances, it appears that Robinette merely submitted to "a claim of lawful authority" rather than consenting as a voluntary act of free will.

State v. Robinette, 80 Ohio St.3d 234, 244–45, 685 N.E.2d 762, 770–71 (1997).

2. AUTHORITY TO CONSENT: "THIRD PARTY" CONSENTS

EDITORS' INTRODUCTION: CONSENTS GIVEN BY THIRD PARTIES

In a substantial number of cases, law enforcement officers rely on consent provided by persons other than those against whom the discovered evidence is eventually offered at trial. The sufficiency of such consents was addressed in United States v. Matlock, 415 U.S. 164, 94 S.Ct. 988, 39 L.Ed.2d 242 (1974):

This Court left open in Amos v. United States, 255 U.S. 313, 317, 41 S.Ct. 266, 267, 65 L.Ed. 654 (1921), the question whether a wife's permission to search the residence in which she lived with her husband could "waive his constitutional rights," but more recent authority here clearly indicates that the consent of one who possesses common authority over premises or effects is valid as against the absent, nonconsenting person with whom that authority is shared. In Frazier v. Cupp, 394 U.S. 731, 740, 89 S.Ct. 1420, 1425, 22 L.Ed.2d 684 (1969), the Court "dismissed rather quickly" the contention that the consent of the petitioner's cousin to the search of a duffel bag, which was being used jointly by both men and had been left in the cousin's home, would not justify the seizure of petitioner's clothing found inside; joint use of the bag rendered the cousin's authority to consent to the search clear. Indeed, the Court was unwilling to engage in the "metaphysical subtleties" raised by Frazier's claim that his cousin only had permission to use one compartment within the bag. By allowing the cousin the use of the bag, and by leaving it in his house, Frazier was held to have assumed the risk that his cousin would allow someone else to look inside. * * * [W]hen the prosecution seeks to justify a warrantless search by proof of voluntary consent, it is not limited to proof that consent was given by the defendant, but may show that permission to search was obtained from a third party who possessed common authority over or other sufficient relationship to the premises or effect sought to be inspected.

415 U.S. at 170–71, 94 S.Ct. at 993, 39 L.Ed.2d at 249–50. The Court elaborated further:

Common authority is * * * not to be implied from the mere property interest a third party has in the premises. The authority which justifies the third-party consent does not rest upon the law of property, with its attendant historical and legal refinements, see Chapman v. United States, 365 U.S. 610, 81 S.Ct. 776, 5 L.Ed.2d 828 (1961) (landlord could not validly consent to the search of a house he had rented to another), Stoner v. California, 376 U.S. 483, 84 S.Ct. 889, 11 L.Ed.2d 856 (1964) (night hotel clerk could not validly consent to search of customer's room) but rests rather on mutual use of the property by persons generally having joint access or control for most purposes, so that it is reasonable to recognize that any of the cohabitants has the right to permit the inspection in his own right and that the others have assumed the risk that one of their number might permit the common area to be searched.

415 U.S. at 171 n. 7, 94 S.Ct. at 993 n. 7, 39 L.Ed.2d at 250 n. 7.

In *Matlock,* the officers searched a room in a house leased by Mr. and Mrs. Marshall and occupied by Mrs. Marshall, several of her children including Gayle Graff, Graff's three-year old son, and Matlock. Matlock was arrested in the yard. Several officers, without consulting Matlock, went to the door, met Mrs. Graff, and—after telling her they were looking for money and a gun—asked Graff if they could search the house. She consented. While going through an upstairs bedroom occupied by Matlock and Graff, officers found $4,995 in cash concealed in a diaper bag in the only closet in the room. At issue was the admissibility at the hearing on the motion to suppress of Graff's out-of-court statements concerning her joint occupancy of the bedroom and similar statements by both Graff and Matlock representing themselves as husband and wife. After finding the statements were admissible, the Court concluded the Government's evidence was sufficient to prove Graff's consent was "legally sufficient." But since the Court preferred that the trial court first pass on the sufficiency of the evidence in light of the *Matlock* opinion, it remanded the case for such reconsideration.

Suppose, however, the person giving consent lacks authority to give effective authorization for the search? This problem is considered in the following case.

Illinois v. Rodriguez

Supreme Court of the United States, 1990.
497 U.S. 177, 110 S.Ct. 2793, 111 L.Ed.2d 148.

■ JUSTICE SCALIA delivered the opinion of the Court.

In United States v. Matlock, 415 U.S. 164, 94 S.Ct. 988, 39 L.Ed.2d 242 (1974), this Court reaffirmed that a warrantless entry and search by law enforcement officers does not violate the Fourth Amendment's proscription of "unreasonable searches and seizures" if the officers have obtained the consent of a third party who possesses common authority over the premises. The present case presents an issue we expressly reserved in *Matlock*: whether a warrantless entry is valid when based upon the consent of a third party whom the police, at the time of the entry, reasonably believe to possess common authority over the premises, but who in fact does not do so.

I

Respondent Edward Rodriguez was arrested in his apartment by law enforcement officers and charged with possession of illegal drugs. The police gained entry to the apartment with the consent and assistance of Gail Fischer, who had lived there with respondent for several months. The relevant facts leading to the arrest are as follows.

On July 26, 1985, police were summoned to the residence of Dorothy Jackson on South Wolcott in Chicago. They were met by Ms. Jackson's daughter, Gail Fischer, who showed signs of a severe beating. She told the officers that she had been assaulted by respondent Edward Rodriguez earlier that day in an apartment on South California. Fischer stated that Rodriguez was then asleep in the apartment, and she consented to travel there with the police in order to unlock the door with her key so that the officers could enter and arrest him. During this conversation, Fischer several times referred to the apartment on South California as "our" apartment, and said that she had clothes and furniture there. It is unclear whether she indicated that she currently lived at the apartment, or only that she used to live there.

The police officers drove to the apartment on South California, accompanied by Fischer. They did not obtain an arrest warrant for Rodriguez, nor did they seek a search warrant for the apartment. At the apartment, Fischer unlocked the door with her key and gave the officers permission to enter. They moved through the door into the living room, where they observed in plain view drug paraphernalia and containers filled with white powder that they believed (correctly, as later analysis showed) to be cocaine. They proceeded to the bedroom, where they found Rodriguez asleep and discovered additional containers of white powder in two open attache cases. The officers arrested Rodriguez and seized the drugs and related paraphernalia.

Rodriguez was charged with possession of a controlled substance with intent to deliver. He moved to suppress all evidence seized at the time of his arrest, claiming that Fischer had vacated the apartment several weeks earlier and had no authority to consent to the entry. The Cook County Circuit Court granted the motion, holding that at the time she consented to the entry Fischer did not have common authority over the apartment. The Court concluded that Fischer was not a "usual resident" but rather an "infrequent visitor" at the apartment on South California, based upon its findings that Fischer's name was not on the lease, that she did not contribute to the rent, that she was not allowed to invite others to the apartment on her own, that she did not have access to the apartment when respondent was away, and that she had moved some of her possessions from the apartment. The Circuit Court also rejected the State's contention that, even if Fischer did not possess common authority over the premises, there was no Fourth Amendment violation if the police reasonably believed at the time of their entry that Fischer possessed the authority to consent.

The Appellate Court of Illinois affirmed the Circuit Court in all respects. The Illinois Supreme Court denied the State's Petition for Leave to Appeal, and we granted certiorari.

II

The Fourth Amendment generally prohibits the warrantless entry of a person's home, whether to make an arrest or to search for specific objects. The prohibition does not apply, however, to situations in which voluntary consent has been obtained, either from the individual whose property is searched, see Schneckloth v. Bustamonte, 412 U.S. 218, 93 S.Ct. 2041, 36 L.Ed.2d 854 (1973), or from a third party who possesses common authority over the premises. The State of Illinois contends that that exception applies in the present case.

As we stated in *Matlock,* "[c]ommon authority" rests "on mutual use of the property by persons generally having joint access or control for most purposes...." The burden of establishing that common authority rests upon the State. On the basis of this record, it is clear that burden was not sustained. The evidence showed that although Fischer, with her two small children, had lived with Rodriguez beginning in December 1984, she had moved out on July 1, 1985, almost a month before the search at issue here, and had gone to live with her mother. She took her and her children's clothing with her, though leaving behind some furniture and household effects. During the period after July 1 she sometimes spent the night at Rodriguez's apartment, but never invited her friends there, and never went there herself when he was not home. Her name was not on the lease nor did she contribute to the rent. She had a key to the apartment, which she said at trial she had taken without Rodriguez's knowledge (though she testified at the preliminary hearing that Rodriguez had given her the key). On these facts the State has not established that, with respect to the South California apartment, Fischer had "joint access or control for most purposes." To the contrary, the Appellate Court's determination of no common authority over the apartment was obviously correct.

III

A

The State contends that, even if Fischer did not in fact have authority to give consent, it suffices to validate the entry that the law enforcement officers reasonably believed she did. * * *

B

[R]espondent asserts that permitting a reasonable belief of common authority to validate an entry would cause a defendant's Fourth Amendment rights to be "vicariously waived." We disagree. We have been unyielding in our insistence that a defendant's waiver of his trial rights cannot be given effect unless it is "knowing" and "intelligent." We would assuredly not permit, therefore, evidence seized in violation of the Fourth Amendment to be introduced on the basis of a trial court's mere "reasonable belief"—derived from statements by unauthorized persons—that the defendant has waived his objection. But one must make a distinction between, on the one hand, trial rights that derive from the violation of constitutional guarantees and, on the other hand, the nature of those constitutional guarantees themselves. As we said in *Schneckloth*:

> "There is a vast difference between those rights that protect a fair criminal trial and the rights guaranteed under the Fourth Amendment. Nothing, either in the purposes behind requiring a 'knowing' and 'intelligent' waiver of trial rights, or in the practical application of such a requirement suggests that it ought to be extended to the constitutional guarantee against unreasonable searches and seizures."

What Rodriguez is assured by the trial right of the exclusionary rule, where it applies, is that no evidence seized in violation of the Fourth Amendment will be introduced at his trial unless he consents. What he is assured by the Fourth Amendment itself, however, is not that no government search of his house will occur unless he consents; but that no such search will occur that is "unreasonable." U.S. Const., Amdt. 4. There are various elements, of course, that can make a search of a person's house "reasonable"—one of which is the consent of the person or his cotenant. The essence of respondent's argument is that we should impose upon this element a requirement that we have not imposed upon other elements that regularly compel government officers to exercise judgment regarding the facts: namely, the requirement that their judgment be not only responsible but correct.

The fundamental objective that alone validates all unconsented government searches is, of course, the seizure of persons who have committed or are about to commit crimes, or of evidence related to crimes. But "reasonableness," with respect to this necessary element, does not demand that the government be factually correct in its assessment that that is what a search will produce. * * * If a magistrate, based upon seemingly reliable but factually inaccurate information, issues a warrant for the search of a house in which the sought-after felon is not present, has never been present, and was never likely to have been present, the owner of that house suffers one of the inconveniences we all expose ourselves to as the cost of living in a safe society; he does not suffer a violation of the Fourth Amendment.

* * *

It would be superfluous to multiply * * * examples. It is apparent that in order to satisfy the "reasonableness" requirement of the Fourth Amendment, what is generally demanded of the many factual determinations that must regularly be made by agents of the government—whether the magistrate issuing a warrant, the police officer executing a warrant, or the police officer conducting a search or seizure under one of the exceptions to the warrant requirement—is not that they always be correct, but that they always be reasonable. * * *

We see no reason to depart from this general rule with respect to facts bearing upon the authority to consent to a search. Whether the basis for such authority exists is the sort of recurring factual question to which law enforcement officials must be expected to apply their judgment; and all the Fourth Amendment requires is that they answer it reasonably. The Constitution is no more violated when officers enter without a warrant because they reasonably (though erroneously) believe that the person who has consented to their entry is a resident of the premises, than it is violated when they enter without a warrant because they reasonably (though erroneously) believe they are in pursuit of a violent felon who is about to escape.

* * *

[W]hat we hold today does not suggest that law enforcement officers may always accept a person's invitation to enter premises. Even when the invitation is accompanied by an explicit assertion that the person lives there, the surrounding circumstances could conceivably be such that a reasonable person would doubt its truth and not act upon it without further inquiry. As with other factual determinations bearing upon search and seizure, determination of consent to enter must "be judged against an objective standard: would the facts available to the officer at the moment * * * 'warrant a man of reasonable caution in the belief' "that the consenting party had authority over the premises? If not, then warrantless entry without further inquiry is unlawful unless authority actually exists. But if so, the search is valid.

* * *

In the present case, the Appellate Court found it unnecessary to determine whether the officers reasonably believed that Fischer had the authority to consent, because it ruled as a matter of law that a reasonable belief could not validate the entry. Since we find that ruling to be in error, we remand for consideration of that question. The judgment of the Illinois Appellate Court is reversed and remanded for further proceedings not inconsistent with this opinion.

So ordered.

■ Justice Marshall, with whom Justice Brennan and Justice Stevens join, dissenting.

* * *

The majority [concludes] that Fischer did not have authority to consent to the officers' entry of Rodriguez's apartment. The Court holds that the warrantless entry into Rodriguez's home was nonetheless valid if the officers reasonably believed that Fischer had authority to consent. The majority's defense of this position rests on a misconception of the basis for third-party consent searches. That such searches do not give rise to claims of constitutional violations rests not on the premise that they are "reasonable" under the Fourth Amendment, but on the premise that a person may voluntarily limit his expectation of privacy by allowing others to exercise authority over his possessions. Thus, an individual's decision to permit another "joint access [to] or control [over the property] for most purposes," United States v. Matlock, 415 U.S. 164, 171, n. 7, 94 S.Ct. 988, 993, n. 7, 39 L.Ed.2d 242 (1974), limits that individual's reasonable expectation of privacy and to that extent limits his Fourth Amendment protections. If an individual has not so limited his expectation of privacy, the police may not dispense with the safeguards established by the Fourth Amendment.

* * *

I

* * * We have * * * held that "a search or seizure carried out on a suspect's premises without a warrant is per se unreasonable, unless the police can show that it falls within one of a carefully defined set of exceptions." Coolidge v. New Hampshire, 403 U.S. 443, 474, 91 S.Ct. 2022, 2042, 29 L.Ed.2d 564 (1971). * * *

The Court has tolerated departures from the warrant requirement only when an exigency makes a warrantless search imperative to the safety of the police and of the community. The Court has often heard, and steadfastly rejected, the invitation to carve out further exceptions to the warrant requirement for searches of the home because of the burdens on police investigation and prosecution of crime. * * *

In the absence of an exigency, then, warrantless home searches and seizures are unreasonable under the Fourth Amendment. The weighty constitutional interest in preventing unauthorized intrusions into the home overrides any law enforcement interest in relying on the reasonable but potentially mistaken belief that a third party has authority to consent to such a search or seizure. Indeed, as the present case illustrates, only the minimal interest in avoiding the inconvenience of obtaining a warrant weighs in on the law enforcement side.

* * *

Unlike searches conducted pursuant to the recognized exceptions to the warrant requirement, third-party consent searches are not based on an exigency and therefore serve no compelling social goal. Police officers, when faced with the choice of relying on consent by a third party or securing a warrant, should secure a warrant, and must therefore accept the risk of error should they instead choose to rely on consent.

II

Our prior cases discussing searches based on third-party consent have never suggested that such searches are "reasonable." * * * As the Court's assumption-of-risk analysis makes clear, third-party consent limits a person's ability to challenge the reasonableness of the search only because that person voluntarily has relinquished some of his expectation of privacy by sharing access or control over his property with another person.

A search conducted pursuant to an officer's reasonable but mistaken belief that a third party had authority to consent is thus on an entirely different constitutional footing from one based on the consent of a third party who in fact has such authority. Even if the officers reasonably believed that Fischer had authority to consent, she did not, and Rodriguez's expectation of privacy was therefore undiminished. Rodriguez accordingly can challenge the warrantless intrusion into his home as a violation of the Fourth Amendment.

* * *

III

Acknowledging that the third party in this case lacked authority to consent, the majority seeks to rely on cases suggesting that reasonable but mistaken factual judgments by police will not invalidate otherwise reasonable searches. The majority reads these cases as establishing a "general rule" that "what is generally demanded of the many factual determinations that must regularly be made by agents of the government—whether the magistrate issuing a warrant, the police officer executing a warrant, or the police officer conducting a search or seizure under one of the exceptions to the warrant requirement—is not that they always be correct, but that they always be reasonable."

The majority's assertion, however, is premised on the erroneous assumption that third-party consent searches are generally reasonable. The cases the majority cites thus provide no support for its holding. * * * Because reasonable factual errors by law enforcement officers will not validate unreasonable searches, the reasonableness of the officer's mistaken belief that the third party had authority to consent is irrelevant.

* * *

IV

* * *

Instead of judging the validity of consent searches, as we have in the past, based on whether a defendant has in fact limited his expectation of privacy, the Court today carves out an additional exception to the warrant requirement for third-party consent searches without pausing to consider whether " 'the exigencies of the situation' make the needs of law enforcement so compelling that the warrantless search is objectively reasonable under the Fourth Amendment." Where this freefloating creation of "reasonable" exceptions to the warrant requirement will end, now that the Court has departed from the balancing approach that has long been part of our Fourth Amendment jurisprudence, is unclear. But by allowing a person to be subjected to a warrantless search in his home without his consent and without exigency, the majority has taken away some of the liberty that the Fourth Amendment was designed to protect.

NOTE

On remand, the Illinois Appellate Court remanded the case to the trial court for a factual hearing. The trial judge noted that Rodriguez had not been in further "trouble," and suggested the State reduce the charge. The State did so and Rodriguez pled guilty. Therefore, the Illinois courts did not further consider admissibility of the evidence seized during the search of the apartment. Interview with James W. Reilly, counsel for Edward Rodriguez.

3.   SCOPE OF CONSENT

If effective consent was given by a person with authority to provide it, defining the scope of that consent may present further problems. How extensive and intrusive a search is supported by particular words of consent? How should a court approach the task of construing words constituting consent to a search of some sort? The Supreme Court addressed these issues in the following case.

Florida v. Jimeno

Supreme Court of the United States, 1991.
500 U.S. 248, 111 S.Ct. 1801, 114 L.Ed.2d 297.

■ CHIEF JUSTICE REHNQUIST delivered the opinion of the Court.

* * *

This case began when a Dade County police officer, Frank Trujillo, overheard respondent, Enio Jimeno, arranging what appeared to be a drug transaction over a public telephone. Believing that respondent might be involved in illegal drug trafficking, Officer Trujillo followed his car. The officer observed respondent make a right turn at a red light without stopping. He then pulled respondent over to the side of the road in order to issue him a traffic citation. Officer Trujillo told respondent that he had been stopped for committing a traffic infraction. The officer went on to say that he had reason to believe that respondent was carrying narcotics in his car, and asked permission to search the car. He explained that respondent did not have to consent to a search of the car. Respondent stated that he had nothing to hide, and gave Trujillo permission to search the automobile. After two passengers stepped out of respondent's car, Officer Trujillo went to the passenger side, opened the door, and saw a folded, brown paper bag on the floorboard. The officer picked up the bag, opened it, and found a kilogram of cocaine inside.

Respondent was charged with possession with intent to distribute cocaine in violation of Florida law. Before trial, he moved to suppress the cocaine found in the bag on the ground that his consent to search the car did not extend to the closed paper bag inside of the car. The trial court granted the motion. It found that although respondent "could have assumed that the officer would have searched the bag" at the time he gave his consent, his mere consent to search the car did not carry with it specific consent to open the bag and examine its contents.

The Florida District Court of Appeal affirmed the trial court's decision to suppress the evidence of the cocaine. In doing so, the court established a *per se* rule that "consent to a general search for narcotics does not extend to 'sealed containers within the general area agreed to by the defendant.' " The Florida Supreme Court affirmed, relying upon its decision in State v. Wells, 539 So.2d 464 (1989) aff'd on other grounds, 495 U.S. 1, 110 S.Ct. 1632, 109 L.Ed.2d 1 (1990). We granted certiorari to determine whether consent to search a vehicle may extend to closed containers found inside the vehicle * * * and we now reverse the judgment of the Supreme Court of Florida.

The touchstone of the Fourth Amendment is reasonableness. The Fourth Amendment does not proscribe all state-initiated searches and seizures; it merely proscribes those which are unreasonable. Thus, we have long approved consensual searches because it is no doubt reasonable for the police to conduct a search once they have been permitted to do so. The standard for measuring the scope of a suspect's consent under the Fourth Amendment is that of "objective" reasonableness—what would the typical reasonable person have understood by the exchange between the officer and the suspect? The question before us, then, is whether it is reasonable for an officer to consider a suspect's general consent to a search of his car to include consent to examine a paper bag lying on the floor of the car. We think that it is.

The scope of a search is generally defined by its expressed object. In this case, the terms of the search's authorization were simple. Respondent granted Officer Trujillo permission to search his car, and did not place any explicit limitation on the scope of the search. Trujillo had informed respondent that he believed respondent was carrying narcotics, and that he would be looking for narcotics in the car. We think that it was objectively reasonable for the police to conclude that the general consent to search respondent's car included consent to search containers within that car which might bear drugs. A reasonable person may be expected to know that narcotics are generally carried in some form of a container. "Contraband goods rarely are strewn across the trunk or floor of a car." The authorization to search in this case, therefore, extended beyond the surfaces of the car's interior to the paper bag lying on the car's floor.

The facts of this case are therefore different from those in State v. Wells, supra, on which the Supreme Court of Florida relied in affirming the suppression order in this case. There the Supreme Court of Florida held that consent to search the trunk of a car did not include authorization to pry open a locked briefcase found inside the trunk. It is very likely unreasonable to think that a suspect, by consenting to the search of his trunk, has agreed to the breaking open of a locked briefcase within the trunk, but it is otherwise with respect to a closed paper bag.

Respondent argues, and the Florida trial court agreed with him, that if the police wish to search closed containers within a car they must separately request permission to search each container. But we see no basis for adding this sort of superstructure to the Fourth Amendment's basic test of objective reasonableness. A suspect may of course delimit as he chooses the scope of the search to which he consents. But if his consent would reasonably be understood to extend to a particular container, the Fourth Amendment provides no grounds for requiring a more explicit authorization. * * *

The judgment of the Supreme Court of Florida is accordingly reversed, and the case remanded for further proceedings not inconsistent with this opinion.

It is so ordered.

■ JUSTICE MARSHALL, with whom JUSTICE STEVENS joins, dissenting.

[A]nalysis of this question must start by identifying the differing expectations of privacy that attach to cars and closed containers. It is well established that an individual has but a limited expectation of privacy in the interior of his car. * * * In contrast, it is equally well established that an individual has a heightened expectation of privacy in the contents of a closed container. Luggage, handbags, paper bags, and other containers are common repositories for one's papers and effects, and the protection of these items from state intrusion lies at the heart of the Fourth Amendment. * * *

The distinct privacy expectations that a person has in a car as opposed to a closed container do not merge when the individual uses his car to transport the container. * * *

Because an individual's expectation of privacy in a container is distinct from, and far greater than, his expectation of privacy in the interior of his car, it follows that an individual's consent to a search of the interior of his car cannot necessarily be understood as extending to containers in the car. At the very least, general consent to search the car is ambiguous with respect to containers found inside the car. In my view, the independent and divisible nature of the privacy interests in cars and containers mandates that a police officer who wishes to search a suspicious container found during a consensual automobile search obtain additional consent to search the container. If the driver intended to authorize search of the container, he will say so; if not, then he will say no.[4] The only objection that the police could have to such a rule is that it would prevent them from exploiting the ignorance of a citizen who simply did not anticipate that his consent to search the car would be understood to authorize the police to rummage through his packages.

* * *

I dissent.

D. SEARCHES AND SEIZURES OF VEHICLES

Searches and seizures of vehicles have probably given rise to more difficulties than any other category of searches. In all of its vehicle search or seizure case law, the Supreme court has assumed citizens' privacy interest in vehicles and their contents is less than their privacy in homes and some other places:

> One has a lesser expectation of privacy in a motor vehicle because its function is transportation and it seldom serves as one's residence or as the repository of personal effects. A car has little capacity for escaping public scrutiny. It travels public thoroughfares where both its occupants and its contents are in plain view.

Cardwell v. Lewis, 417 U.S. 583, 590, 94 S.Ct. 2464, 2469, 41 L.Ed.2d 325, 335 (1974) (opinion of Blackmun, J., announcing the judgment of the Court).

Searches of vehicles may be permissible under several doctrines. The right to search a car "incident to" the arrest of a person in the car was considered in Chapter 4, as was the right to make a weapons search of some cars during nonarrest confrontations between officers and citizens. This chapter addresses two additional aspects of vehicle searches. The first subsection that follows presents the traditional "vehicle exception" to the requirement of a search warrant; the second subsection considers officers' ability to search containers found in vehicles searched under this doctrine.

1. THE "VEHICLE" EXCEPTION TO THE SEARCH WARRANT REQUIREMENTS

EDITORS' INTRODUCTION: "AUTOMOBILE" OR "VEHICLE" EXCEPTION

In two early cases, the Supreme Court recognized a right on the part of law enforcement officers to conduct warrantless searches of automobiles independent of any right the officers may have to arrest occupants. In Carroll v. United States, 267 U.S. 132, 45 S.Ct. 280, 69 L.Ed. 543 (1925), officers observed a car coming from the direction of Detroit, which they knew to be a location where much illicit liquor entered the United States. Several months earlier the officers, acting undercover, met with two men

---

4. Alternatively, the police could obtain such consent in advance by asking the indi-vidual for permission to search both the car and any closed containers found inside.

who agreed to sell them illicit liquor; the men came to the meeting in the same automobile. The officers stopped the car and searched it; they found 68 bottles of illicit liquor concealed under the seat upholstery. Finding the search reasonable, the Supreme Court noted there is

> a necessary difference between a search of a store, dwelling house or other structure in respect of which a proper official warrant readily may be obtained, and a search of a ship, motor boat, wagon or automobile for contraband goods, where it is not practicable to secure a warrant because the vehicle can be quickly moved out of the locality or jurisdiction in which the warrant must be sought.

267 U.S. at 153, 45 S.Ct. at 285, 69 L.Ed. at 551. The right of those using public highways to free passage without interruption or search, it continued, is adequately protected by the prohibition against search of vehicles "unless there is known to a competent official authorized to search, probable cause for believing that their vehicles are carrying contraband or illegal merchandise." Transporting the liquor was in violation of the National Prohibition Act. Those transporting it were guilty of a criminal offense; the first two offenses were misdemeanors but a third conviction constituted a felony. Carroll urged that federal law permitted a warrantless arrest for a misdemeanor only if the offense was committed in the officers' presence and consequently that the officers lacked authority to arrest him without a warrant. It followed, he argued, the officers should not be permitted to make a warrantless search related to a crime for which no warrantless arrest was permissible. The Court responded:

> The argument of defendants is based on the theory that the seizure in this case can only be * * * justified [on the ground that it was incident to a lawful arrest]. If their theory were sound, their conclusion would be. The validity of the seizure would turn wholly on the validity of the arrest without a seizure. But the theory is unsound. The right to search and the validity of the seizure are not dependent on the right to arrest. They are dependent on the reasonable cause the seizing officers has for belief that the contents of the automobile offend against the law. The seizure in such a proceeding comes before the arrest * * *. The character of the offense for which, after the contraband liquor is found and seized, the driver can be prosecuted does not affect the validity of the seizure.

267 U.S. at 158–59, 45 S.Ct. at 287, 69 L.Ed. at 553–54. The *Carroll* approach was reaffirmed in the second leading case, Brinegar v. United States, 338 U.S. 160, 69 S.Ct. 1302, 93 L.Ed. 1879 (1949), involving similar facts.

Chief Justice Burger's opinion for the Court in California v. Carney, 471 U.S. 386, 105 S.Ct. 2066, 85 L.Ed.2d 406 (1985), traced the evolution of the rationale for the vehicle exception as follows:

> [A]lthough ready mobility alone was perhaps the original justification for the vehicle exception, our later cases have made clear that ready mobility is not the only basis for the exception. The reasons for the vehicle exception, we have said, are twofold. "Besides the element of mobility, less rigorous warrant requirements govern because the expec-

tation of privacy with respect to one's automobile is significantly less than that relating to one's home or office." [South Dakota v. Opperman, 428 U.S. 364, 367, 96 S.Ct. 3092, 49 L.Ed.2d 1000 (1976)].

* * *

These reduced expectations of privacy derive not from the fact that the area to be searched is in plain view, but from the pervasive regulation of vehicles capable of traveling on the public roadway. As we explained in South Dakota v. Opperman * * * :

> "Automobiles, unlike homes, are subjected to pervasive and continuing governmental regulations and controls, including periodic inspection and licensing requirements. As an everyday occurrence, police stop and examine vehicles when license plates or inspection stickers have expired, or if other violations, such as exhaust fumes or excessive noise, are noted, or if headlights or other safety equipment are not in proper working order."

The public is fully aware that it is accorded less privacy in its automobiles because of this compelling governmental need for regulation. Historically, "individuals always [have] been on notice that movable vessels may be stopped and searched on facts giving rise to probable cause that the vehicle contains contraband, without the protection afforded by a magistrate's prior evaluation of those facts." [United States v.] Ross, [456 U.S. 798, 806 n. 8, 102 S.Ct. 2157, 2163 n. 8, 72 L.Ed.2d 572, 582 n. 8 (1982)].

471 U.S. at 391–92, 105 S.Ct. at 2069–70, 85 L.Ed.2d at 413–14.

Chambers v. Maroney

Supreme Court of the United States, 1970.
399 U.S. 42, 90 S.Ct. 1975, 26 L.Ed.2d 419.

■ MR. JUSTICE WHITE delivered the opinion of the Court.

The principal question in this case concerns the admissibility of evidence seized from an automobile, in which petitioner was riding at the time of his arrest, after the automobile was taken to a police station and was there thoroughly searched without a warrant.

* * *

I

During the night of May 20, 1963, a Gulf service station in North Braddock, Pennsylvania, was robbed by two men, each of whom carried and displayed a gun. The robbers took the currency from the cash register; the service station attendant, one Stephen Kovacich, was directed to place the coins in his righthand glove, which was then taken by the robbers. Two teenagers, who had earlier noticed a blue compact station wagon circling the block in the vicinity of the Gulf station, then saw the station wagon speed away from a parking lot close to the Gulf station. About the same time, they learned that the Gulf station had been robbed. They reported to police, who arrived immediately, that four men were in the station wagon and one was wearing a green sweater. Kovacich told the police that one of the men who robbed him was wearing a green sweater and the other was wearing a trench coat. A description of the car and the two robbers was broadcast over the police radio. Within an hour, a light blue compact station wagon answering the description and carrying four men was stopped by the police about two miles from the Gulf station. Petitioner was one of the men in the station wagon. He was wearing a green sweater and there was a trench coat in the car. The occupants were arrested and the car was driven to the police station. In the course of a thorough search of the car at the station, the police found concealed in a compartment under the dashboard two .38 caliber revolvers (one loaded with dumdum bullets), a righthand glove containing small change, and certain cards bearing the name of Raymond Havicon, the attendant at a Boron service station in McKeesport, Pennsylvania, who had been robbed at gunpoint on May 13, 1963. * * *

Petitioner was indicted for both robberies. * * * The materials taken from the station wagon were introduced into evidence, Kovacich identifying his glove and Havicon the cards taken in the May 13 robbery. Petitioner was sentenced to a term of four to eight years' imprisonment for the May 13 robbery and to a term of two to seven years' imprisonment for the May 20 robbery, the sentences to run consecutively. Petitioner did not take a direct appeal from these convictions. In 1965, petitioner sought a writ of habeas corpus in the state court, which denied the writ after a brief evidentiary hearing; the denial of the writ was affirmed on appeal in the Pennsylvania appellate courts. Habeas corpus proceedings were then commenced in the United States District Court for the Western District of Pennsylvania. An order to show cause was issued. Based on the State's response and the state court record, the petition for habeas corpus was denied without a hearing. The Court of Appeals for the Third Circuit affirmed and we granted certiorari.

II

We pass quickly the claim that the search of the automobile was the fruit of an unlawful arrest. Both the courts below thought the arresting officers had probable cause to make the arrest. We agree. Having talked to the teenage observers and to the victim Kovacich, the police had ample cause to stop a light blue compact station wagon carrying four men and to arrest the occupants, one of whom was wearing a green sweater and one of whom had a trench coat with him in the car.

Even so, the search that produced the incriminating evidence was made at the police station some time after the arrest and cannot be justified as a search incident to an arrest: "Once an accused is under arrest and in custody, then a search made at another place, without a warrant, is simply not incident to the arrest." Preston v. United States, 376 U.S. 364, 367, 84 S.Ct. 881, 883, 11 L.Ed.2d 777 (1964).

There are, however alternative grounds arguably justifying the search of the car in this case. * * * Here * * * the police had probable cause to believe that the robbers, carrying guns and the fruits of the crime, had fled the scene in a light blue compact station wagon which would be carrying four men, one wearing a green sweater and another wearing a trench coat. As the state courts correctly held, there was probable cause to arrest the occupants of the station wagon that the officers stopped; just as obviously was there probable cause to search the car for guns and stolen money.

In terms of the circumstances justifying a warrantless search, the Court has long distinguished between an automobile and a home or office. In Carroll v. United States, 267 U.S. 132, 45 S.Ct. 280, 69 L.Ed. 543 (1925), the issue was the admissibility in evidence of contraband liquor seized in a warrantless search of a car on the highway. After surveying the law from the time of the adoption of the Fourth Amendment onward, the Court held that automobiles and other conveyances may be searched without a warrant in circumstances that would not justify the search without a warrant of a house or an office, provided that there is probable cause to believe that the car contains articles that the officers are entitled to seize. * * * Finding that there was probable cause for the search and seizure at issue before it, the Court affirmed the convictions.

* * *

Neither *Carroll,* supra, nor other cases in this Court require or suggest that in every conceivable circumstance the search of an auto even with probable cause may be made without the extra protection for privacy that a warrant affords. But the circumstances that furnish probable cause to search a particular auto for particular articles are most often unforeseeable; moreover, the opportunity to search is fleeting since a car is readily movable. Where this is true, as in *Carroll* and the case before us now, if an effective search is to be made at any time, either the search must be made immediately without a warrant or the car itself must be seized and held without a warrant for whatever period is necessary to obtain a warrant for the search.

In enforcing the Fourth Amendment's prohibition against unreasonable searches and seizures, the Court has insisted upon probable cause as a minimum requirement for a reasonable search permitted by the Constitution. As a general rule, it has also required the judgment of a magistrate on the probable-cause issue and the issuance of a warrant before a search is made. Only in exigent circumstances will the judgment of the police as to probable cause serve as a sufficient authorization for a search. *Carroll,* supra, holds a search warrant unnecessary where there is probable cause to search an automobile stopped on the highway; the car is movable, the occupants are alerted, and the car's contents may never be found again if a warrant must be obtained. Hence an immediate search is constitutionally permissible. * * *[5]

* * *

Arguably, because of the preference for a magistrate's judgment, only the immobilization of the car should be permitted until a search warrant is

---

5. Following the car until a warrant can be obtained seems an impractical alternative since, among other things, the car may be taken out of the jurisdiction. Tracing the car and searching it hours or days later would of course permit instruments or fruits of crime to be removed from the car before the search.

obtained; arguably, only the "lesser" intrusion is permissible until the magistrate authorizes the "greater." But which is the "greater" and which the "lesser" intrusion is itself a debatable question and the answer may depend on a variety of circumstances. For constitutional purposes, we see no difference between on the one hand seizing and holding a car before presenting the probable cause issue to a magistrate and on the other hand carrying out an immediate search without a warrant. Given probable cause to search, either course is reasonable under the Fourth Amendment.

On the facts before us, the blue station wagon could have been searched on the spot when it was stopped since there was probable cause to search and it was a fleeting target for a search. The probable cause factor still obtained at the station house and so did the mobility of the car unless the Fourth Amendment permits a warrantless seizure of the car and the denial of its use to anyone until a warrant is secured. In that event there is little to choose in terms of practical consequences between an immediate search without a warrant and the car's immobilization until a warrant is obtained.[6] The same consequences may not follow where there is unforeseeable cause to search a house. But as *Carroll*, supra, held, for the purposes of the Fourth Amendment there is a constitutional difference between houses and cars.

* * *

Affirmed.

■ MR. JUSTICE HARLAN, concurring in part and dissenting in part.

* * *

Where officers have probable cause to search a vehicle on a public way, a * * * limited exception to the warrant requirement is reasonable * * * . I agree with the Court that they should be permitted to take the steps necessary to preserve evidence and to make a search possible. The Court holds that those steps include making a warrantless search of the entire vehicle on the highway * * * and indeed appears to go further and to condone the removal of the car to the police station for a warrantless search there at the convenience of the police. I cannot agree that this result is consistent with our insistence in other areas that departures from the warrant requirement strictly conform to the exigency presented.

[I]n the circumstances in which this problem is likely to occur the lesser intrusion will almost always be the simple seizure of the car for the period—perhaps a day—necessary to enable the officers to obtain a search warrant. * * * To be sure, one can conceive of instances in which the occupant, having nothing to hide and lacking concern for the privacy of the automobile, would be more deeply offended by a temporary immobilization of his vehicle than by a prompt search of it. However, such a person always remains free to consent to an immediate search, thus avoiding any delay.

---

6. It was not unreasonable in this case to take the car to the station house. All occupants in the car were arrested in a dark parking lot in the middle of the night. A careful search at that point was impractical and perhaps not safe for the officers, and it would serve the owner's convenience and the safety of his car to have the vehicle and the keys together at the station house.

Where consent is not forthcoming, the occupants of the car have an interest in privacy that is protected by the Fourth Amendment even where the circumstances justify a temporary seizure. * * * The Court's endorsement of a warrantless invasion of that privacy where another course would suffice is simply inconsistent with our repeated stress on the Fourth Amendment's mandate of "adherence to judicial processes."[7]

* * *

NOTES

1. The lower courts' occasional failures to fully grasp the scope of the vehicle exception was made clear in Pennsylvania v. Labron, 518 U.S. 938, 116 S.Ct. 2485, 135 L.Ed.2d 1031 (1996)(per curiam), involving two cases in which the Pennsylvania Supreme Court construed the United States Supreme Court's case law as requiring for the search of an automobile both probable cause and the presence of exigent circumstances. Summarily reversing, the United States Supreme Court majority explained:

> The Supreme Court of Pennsylvania held the rule permitting warrantless searches of automobiles is limited to cases where " 'unforeseen circumstances involving the search of an automobile [are] coupled with the presence of probable cause.' " (emphasis deleted). This was incorrect. * * * If a car is readily mobile and probable cause exists to believe it contains contraband, the Fourth Amendment * * * permits the police to search the vehicle without more.

518 U.S. at 940, 116 S.Ct. at 2487, 135 L.Ed.2d at 1035–36.

On remand, the Pennsylvania Supreme Court reinstated its original order in *Labron*, explaining that this order had in fact been based on article I, section 8 of the Pennsylvania Constitution: "The people shall be secure in their persons, houses, papers and possessions from unreasonable searches and seizures * * *." Case law applying the state provision, the court stressed, has long required both the existence of probable cause and the presence of exigent circumstances to justify a warrantless search of an automobile. Commonwealth v. Labron, 547 Pa. 344, 690 A.2d 228 (1997).

2. **Vehicles Subject to Search.** What vehicles are within the exception? In California v. Carney, 471 U.S. 386, 105 S.Ct. 2066, 85 L.Ed.2d 406 (1985), DEA agents received uncorroborated information that Carney's Dodge Mini Motor Home was being used by someone else for purposes of exchanging marihuana for sex. An agent observed Carney approach a youth in downtown San Diego; the two went to Carney's motor home, parked in a nearby lot. The shades of the motor home were drawn and the youth remained in it for about one and one-quarter hours. After the youth left, the agents stopped him and elicited from him that he had received marihuana in return for allowing Carney sexual contacts. At the agent's request, the youth knocked on the motor home door. Carney came out. An agent immediately entered and observed marihuana and related items. The Supreme Court, in an

---

7. Circumstances might arise in which it would be impracticable to immobilize the car for the time required to obtain a warrant—for example, where a single police officer must take arrested suspects to the station, and has no way of protecting the suspects' car during his absence. In such situations it might be wholly reasonable to perform an on-the-spot search based on probable cause. However, where nothing in the situation makes impracticable the obtaining of a warrant, I cannot join the Court in shunting aside that vital Fourth Amendment safeguard.

opinion by Chief Justice Burger, held the motor home was within the vehicle exception:

> While it is true that [Carney's] vehicle possessed some, if not many of the attributes of a home, it is equally clear that the vehicle falls clearly within the scope of the exception * * *. Like the automobile in *Carroll,* [Carney's] motor home was readily mobile. Absent the prompt search and seizure, it could readily have been moved beyond the reach of the police. Furthermore, the vehicle was licensed to "operate on public streets; [was] serviced in public places; ...and [was] subject to extensive regulation and inspection." Rakas v. Illinois, 439 U.S. 128, 154, n. 2, 99 S.Ct. 421, 436, n. 2, 58 L.Ed.2d 387 (1978) (Powell, J., concurring). And the vehicle was so situated that an objective observer would conclude that it was being used not as a residence, but as a vehicle. * * *
>
> Our application of the vehicle exception has never turned on the other uses to which a vehicle might be put. * * *

471 U.S. at 393–94, 105 S.Ct. at 2070, 85 L.Ed.2d at 414–15. The Court added:

> We need not pass on the application of the vehicle exception to a motor home that is situated in a way or place that objectively indicates that it is being used as a residence. Among the factors that might be relevant in determining whether a warrant would be required in such a circumstance is its location, whether the vehicle is readily mobile or instead, for instance, elevated on blocks, whether the vehicle is licensed, whether it is connected to utilities, and whether it has convenient access to a public road.

471 U.S. at 394 n. 3, 105 S.Ct. at 2071 n. 3, 85 L.Ed.2d at 415 n. 3. The information available to the agents, the Court also concluded, gave them "abundant probable cause" to enter and search the vehicle for evidence of a crime. As a result, the search was "reasonable" for Fourth Amendment purposes.

3. **Vehicles Parked in Public Places.** Does *Carney* also signal another expansion of the exception? Officers did not stop Carney's motor home but instead came upon it parked in an off-the-street lot. The Court's opinion equated "a vehicle * * * being used on the highways"—like those in *Carroll* and *Chambers*—with one—like Carney's motor home—"readily capable of such use and * * * found stationary in a place not regularly used for residential purposes." Justice Stevens commented:

> Until today, * * * the Court has never decided whether the practical justifications that apply to a vehicle stopped in transit on a public way apply with the same force to a vehicle parked in a lot near a court house where it could easily be detained while a warrant is issued.

471 U.S. at 403, 105 S.Ct. at 2075, 85 L.Ed.2d at 421 (Stevens, J., dissenting).

2.   SEARCHES OF CONTAINERS FOUND IN VEHICLES

In United States v. Chadwick, 433 U.S. 1, 97 S.Ct. 2476, 53 L.Ed.2d 538 (1977), discussed in subsection B(2) of Chapter 2, the Supreme Court held that in some circumstances officers may seize a "container" but not search it until they obtain a search warrant. Court have had particular difficulty applying *Chadwick* to containers found in vehicles. Issues of this sort have been considered already. New York v. Belton, reprinted in subsection B(2) of Chapter 4 considered an officer's right to search a container found in a vehicle that is being searched incident to a valid custodial arrest. This subsection focuses on containers in vehicles searched pursuant to the doctrine developed in Chambers v. Maroney.

The Supreme Court's struggle to properly develop *Chadwick* in this context, culminating in the principal case in this subsection, was reflected in several major cases decided between *Chadwick* and the principal case. Arkansas v. Sanders, 442 U.S. 753, 99 S.Ct. 2586, 61 L.Ed.2d 235 (1979), illustrates the Court's initial approach.

In *Sanders*, an informant of demonstrated reliability told a Little Rock officer that Sanders—who was known to both the informant and the officer—would arrive at a specific gate at the Municipal Airport that afternoon and would be carrying a green suitcase containing marihuana. During surveillance, the officers observed Sanders's arrival at the designated gate and followed him while he met another man and obtained a green suitcase from the airline baggage. Sanders and the other man hailed a taxi, placed the green suitcase in the trunk, and entered the taxi. Several blocks from the airport, the officers stopped the taxi, retrieved the green suitcase from the trunk, and searched it. They found marihuana. The Supreme Court concluded the officers had probable cause to believe the suitcase contained marihuana and that they acted properly in seizing the suitcase. But, it continued, search of the suitcase without a warrant offended the Fourth Amendment:

> A closed suitcase in the trunk of an automobile may be as mobile as the automobile in which it rides. But * * * the exigencies of mobility must be assessed at the point immediately before the search—after the police have seized the object to be searched and have it securely within their control. Once police have seized a suitcase, as they did here, the extent of its mobility is in no way affected by the place from which it was taken. Accordingly as a general rule there is no greater need for warrantless searches of luggage taken from automobiles than of luggage taken from other places.

442 U.S. at 763–64, 99 S.Ct. at 2593, 61 L.Ed.2d at 244–45. This approach was reconsidered in the principal case that follows.

California v. Acevedo

Supreme Court of the United States, 1991.
500 U.S. 565, 111 S.Ct. 1982, 114 L.Ed.2d 619.

■ JUSTICE BLACKMUN delivered the opinion of the Court.

This case requires us once again to consider the so-called "automobile exception" to the warrant requirement of the Fourth Amendment and its application to the search of a closed container in the trunk of a car.

I

On October 28, 1987, Officer Coleman of the Santa Ana, Cal., Police Department received a telephone call from a federal drug enforcement agent in Hawaii. The agent informed Coleman that he had seized a package containing marijuana which was to have been delivered to the Federal Express Office in Santa Ana and which was addressed to J.R. Daza at 805

West Stevens Avenue in that city. The agent arranged to send the package to Coleman instead. Coleman then was to take the package to the Federal Express office and arrest the person who arrived to claim it.

Coleman received the package on October 29, verified its contents, and took it to the Senior Operations Manager at the Federal Express office. At about 10:30 a.m. on October 30, a man, who identified himself as Jamie Daza, arrived to claim the package. He accepted it and drove to his apartment on West Stevens. He carried the package into the apartment.

At 11:45 a.m., officers observed Daza leave the apartment and drop the box and paper that had contained the marijuana into a trash bin. Coleman at that point left the scene to get a search warrant. About 12:05 p.m., the officers saw Richard St. George leave the apartment carrying a blue knapsack which appeared to be half full. The officers stopped him as he was driving off, searched the knapsack, and found 1½ pounds of marijuana.

At 12:30 p.m., respondent Charles Steven Acevedo arrived. He entered Daza's apartment, stayed for about 10 minutes, and reappeared carrying a brown paper bag that looked full. The officers noticed that the bag was the size of one of the wrapped marijuana packages sent from Hawaii. Acevedo walked to a silver Honda in the parking lot. He placed the bag in the trunk of the car and started to drive away. Fearing the loss of evidence, officers in a marked police car stopped him. They opened the trunk and the bag, and found marijuana.

Respondent was charged in state court with possession of marijuana for sale * * *. He moved to suppress the marijuana found in the car. The motion was denied. He then pleaded guilty but appealed the denial of the suppression motion.

The California Court of Appeal, Fourth District, concluded that the marijuana found in the paper bag in the car's trunk should have been suppressed. * * *

The Supreme Court of California denied the State's petition for review. * * *

We granted certiorari to reexamine the law applicable to a closed container in an automobile, a subject that has troubled courts and law enforcement officers since it was first considered in [United States v. Chadwick, 433 U.S. 1, 97 S.Ct. 2476, 53 L.Ed.2d 538 (1977)].

II

* * *

In United States v. Ross, 456 U.S. 798, 102 S.Ct. 2157, 72 L.Ed.2d 572, decided in 1982, we held that a warrantless search of an automobile under the *Carroll* doctrine could include a search of a container or package found inside the car when such a search was supported by probable cause. The warrantless search of Ross' car occurred after an informant told the police that he had seen Ross complete a drug transaction using drugs stored in the trunk of his car. The police stopped the car, searched it, and discovered in the trunk a brown paper bag containing drugs. We decided that the search of Ross' car was not unreasonable under the Fourth Amendment:

"The scope of a warrantless search based on probable cause is no narrower—and no broader—than the scope of a search authorized by a warrant supported by probable cause." Thus, "[i]f probable cause justifies the search of a lawfully stopped vehicle, it justifies the search of every part of the vehicle and its contents that may conceal the object of the search." In *Ross*, therefore, we clarified the scope of the *Carroll* doctrine as properly including a "probing search" of compartments and containers within the automobile so long as the search is supported by probable cause.

In addition to this clarification, *Ross* distinguished the *Carroll* doctrine from the separate rule that governed the search of closed containers. The Court had announced this separate rule, unique to luggage and other closed packages, bags, and containers, in United States v. Chadwick. In *Chadwick*, federal narcotics agents had probable cause to believe that a 200–pound double-locked footlocker contained marijuana. The agents tracked the locker as the defendants removed it from a train and carried it through the station to a waiting car. As soon as the defendants lifted the locker into the trunk of the car, the agents arrested them, seized the locker, and searched it. In this Court, the United States did not contend that the locker's brief contact with the automobile's trunk sufficed to make the *Carroll* doctrine applicable. Rather, the United States urged that the search of movable luggage could be considered analogous to the search of an automobile.

The Court rejected this argument because, it reasoned, a person expects more privacy in his luggage and personal effects than he does in his automobile. Moreover, it concluded that as "may often not be the case when automobiles are seized," secure storage facilities are usually available when the police seize luggage.

In Arkansas v. Sanders, 442 U.S. 753, 99 S.Ct. 2586, 61 L.Ed.2d 235 (1979), the Court extended *Chadwick's* rule to apply to a suitcase actually being transported in the trunk of a car. In *Sanders*, the police had probable cause to believe a suitcase contained marijuana. They watched as the defendant placed the suitcase in the trunk of a taxi and was driven away. The police pursued the taxi for several blocks, stopped it, found the suitcase in the trunk, and searched it. Although the Court had applied the *Carroll* doctrine to searches of integral parts of the automobile itself, (indeed, in *Carroll*, contraband whiskey was in the upholstery of the seats), it did not extend the doctrine to the warrantless search of personal luggage "merely because it was located in an automobile lawfully stopped by the police." Again, the *Sanders* majority stressed the heightened privacy expectation in personal luggage and concluded that the presence of luggage in an automobile did not diminish the owner's expectation of privacy in his personal items.

In *Ross*, the Court endeavored to distinguish between *Carroll*, which governed the *Ross* automobile search, and *Chadwick*, which governed the *Sanders* automobile search. It held that the *Carroll* doctrine covered searches of automobiles when the police had probable cause to search an entire vehicle, but that the *Chadwick* doctrine governed searches of luggage when the officers had probable cause to search only a container within the vehicle. Thus, in a *Ross* situation, the police could conduct a reasonable search under the Fourth Amendment without obtaining a warrant, whereas in a *Sanders* situation, the police had to obtain a warrant before they searched.

* * * *Ross* involved the scope of an automobile search [and] held that closed containers encountered by the police during a warrantless search of a car pursuant to the automobile exception could also be searched. Thus, this Court in *Ross* took the critical step of saying that closed containers in cars could be searched without a warrant because of their presence within the automobile. Despite the protection that *Sanders* purported to extend to closed containers, the privacy interest in those closed containers yielded to the broad scope of an automobile search.

III

* * *

* * * We now must decide the question deferred in *Ross*: whether the Fourth Amendment requires the police to obtain a warrant to open the sack in a movable vehicle simply because they lack probable cause to search the entire car. We conclude that it does not.

IV

Dissenters in *Ross* asked why the suitcase in *Sanders* was "more private, less difficult for police to seize and store, or in any other relevant respect more properly subject to the warrant requirement, than a container that police discover in a probable-cause search of an entire automobile?" We now agree that a container found after a general search of the automobile and a container found in a car after a limited search for the container are equally easy for the police to store and for the suspect to hide or destroy. In fact, we see no principled distinction in terms of either the privacy expectation or the exigent circumstances between the paper bag found by the police in *Ross* and the paper bag found by the police here. Furthermore, by attempting to distinguish between a container for which the police are specifically searching and a container which they come across in a car, we have provided only minimal protection for privacy and have impeded effective law enforcement.

The line between probable cause to search a vehicle and probable cause to search a package in that vehicle is not always clear, and separate rules that govern the two objects to be searched may enable the police to broaden their power to make warrantless searches and disserve privacy interests. We noted this in *Ross* in the context of a search of an entire vehicle. Recognizing that under Carroll [v. United States, 267 U.S. 132, 45 S.Ct. 280, 69 L.Ed. 543 (1925)], the "entire vehicle itself ... could be searched without a warrant," we concluded that "prohibiting police from opening immediately a container in which the object of the search is most likely to be found and instead forcing them first to comb the entire vehicle would actually exacerbate the intrusion on privacy interests." At the moment when officers stop an automobile, it may be less than clear whether they suspect with a high degree of certainty that the vehicle contains drugs in a bag or simply contains drugs. If the police know that they may open a bag only if they are actually searching the entire car, they may search more extensively than they otherwise would in order to establish the general probable cause required by *Ross*.

To the extent that the *Chadwick–Sanders* rule protects privacy, its protection is minimal. Law enforcement officers may seize a container and hold it until they obtain a search warrant. "Since the police, by hypothesis, have probable cause to seize the property, we can assume that a warrant will be routinely forthcoming in the overwhelming majority of cases." *Sanders,* 442 U.S., at 770, 99 S.Ct. at 2596 (dissenting opinion). And the police often will be able to search containers without a warrant, despite the *Chadwick–Sanders* rule, as a search incident to a lawful arrest. * * *

Finally, the search of a paper bag intrudes far less on individual privacy than does the incursion sanctioned long ago in *Carroll*. In that case, prohibition agents slashed the upholstery of the automobile. This Court nonetheless found their search to be reasonable under the Fourth Amendment. If destroying the interior of an automobile is not unreasonable, we cannot conclude that looking inside a closed container is. In light of the minimal protection to privacy afforded by the *Chadwick–Sanders* rule, and our serious doubt whether that rule substantially serves privacy interests, we now hold that the Fourth Amendment does not compel separate treatment for an automobile search that extends only to a container within the vehicle.

V

The *Chadwick–Sanders* rule not only has failed to protect privacy but it has also confused courts and police officers and impeded effective law enforcement. The conflict between the *Carroll* doctrine cases and the *Chadwick–Sanders* line has been criticized in academic commentary. * * *

The discrepancy between the two rules has led to confusion for law enforcement officers. For example, when an officer, who has developed probable cause to believe that a vehicle contains drugs, begins to search the vehicle and immediately discovers a closed container, which rule applies? The defendant will argue that the fact that the officer first chose to search the container indicates that his probable cause extended only to the container and that *Chadwick* and *Sanders* therefore require a warrant. On the other hand, the fact that the officer first chose to search in the most obvious location should not restrict the propriety of the search. The *Chadwick* rule, as applied in *Sanders,* has devolved into an anomaly such that the more likely the police are to discover drugs in a container, the less authority they have to search it. We have noted the virtue of providing " 'clear and unequivocal' guidelines to the law enforcement profession." The *Chadwick–Sanders* rule is the antithesis of a " 'clear and unequivocal' guideline."

* * *

VI

The interpretation of the *Carroll* doctrine set forth in *Ross* now applies to all searches of containers found in an automobile. In other words, the police may search without a warrant if their search is supported by probable cause. The Court in *Ross* put it this way:

> "The scope of a warrantless search of an automobile ... is not defined by the nature of the container in which the contraband is secreted. Rather, it is defined by the object of the search and the places in which there is probable cause to believe that it may be found."

It went on to note: "Probable cause to believe that a container placed in the trunk of a taxi contains contraband or evidence does not justify a search of the entire cab." We reaffirm that principle. In the case before us, the police had probable cause to believe that the paper bag in the automobile's trunk contained marijuana. That probable cause now allows a warrantless search of the paper bag. The facts in the record reveal that the police did not have probable cause to believe that contraband was hidden in any other part of the automobile and a search of the entire vehicle would have been without probable cause and unreasonable under the Fourth Amendment.

* * *

Until today, this Court has drawn a curious line between the search of an automobile that coincidentally turns up a container and the search of a container that coincidentally turns up in an automobile. The protections of the Fourth Amendment must not turn on such coincidences. We therefore interpret *Carroll* as providing one rule to govern all automobile searches. The police may search an automobile and the containers within it where they have probable cause to believe contraband or evidence is contained.

The judgment of the California Court of Appeal is reversed and the case is remanded to that court for further proceedings not inconsistent with this opinion.

It is so ordered.

■ JUSTICE SCALIA, concurring in the judgment.

* * *

I would reverse the judgment in the present case, not because a closed container carried inside a car becomes subject to the "automobile" exception to the general warrant requirement, but because the search of a closed container, outside a privately owned building, with probable cause to believe that the container contains contraband, and when it in fact does contain contraband, is not one of those searches whose Fourth Amendment reasonableness depends upon a warrant. For that reason I concur in the judgment of the Court.

■ JUSTICE WHITE, dissenting.

Agreeing as I do with most of JUSTICE STEVENS' opinion and with the result he reaches, I dissent and would affirm the judgment below.

■ JUSTICE STEVENS, with whom JUSTICE MARSHALL joins, dissenting.

* * *

The Court's statement that *Chadwick* and *Sanders* provide only "minimal protection to privacy," is * * * unpersuasive. Every citizen clearly has an interest in the privacy of the contents of his or her luggage, briefcase, handbag or any other container that conceals private papers and effects from public scrutiny. That privacy interest has been recognized repeatedly in cases spanning more than a century.

Under the Court's holding today, the privacy interest that protects the contents of a suitcase or a briefcase from a warrantless search when it is in public view simply vanishes when its owner climbs into a taxicab. Unquestionably * * * today's decision will result in a significant loss of individual privacy.

* * *

Even if the warrant requirement does inconvenience the police to some extent, that fact does not distinguish this constitutional requirement from any other procedural protection secured by the Bill of Rights. It is merely a part of the price that our society must pay in order to preserve its freedom. * * *

I respectfully dissent.

NOTE: CONTAINERS BELONGING TO PASSENGERS

Is ownership of a container relevant to whether it may be searched during a vehicle search? In Wyoming v. Houghton, 526 U.S. 295, 119 S.Ct. 1297, 143 L.Ed.2d 408 (1999), a Wyoming police officer made a traffic stop of an automobile driven by David Young. Houghton and another woman were passengers; both were sitting in the front seat. During the stop, the officer observed a hypodermic syringe in Young's pocket. When asked, Young reported he used the syringe to take drugs. The officer then, after removing the three occupants, began to search the car. He came upon a purse in the rear seat and, as he began to search it, Houghton claimed it as hers. Nevertheless, the officer continued to search the purse and discovered methamphetamine and drug paraphernalia. The Wyoming court held the drugs and paraphernalia could not be used in Houghton's prosecution. An officer's right to search a vehicle on probable cause to believe it contains contraband, the court reasoned, does not extent to a container the officer knows or should know belongs to a passenger not suspected of criminal activity—unless there was an opportunity for someone to conceal the contraband sought in that container.

The Supreme Court reversed. Justice Scalia's opinion for the Court reasoned the Court's automobile cases, and United States v. Ross, 456 U.S. 798, 806, 102 S.Ct. 2157, 72 L.Ed.2d 572 (1982), in particular, reflect a conclusion that the Framers would have regarded as reasonable a warrantless search of all containers in a vehicle regardless of ownership if those containers might conceal contraband the officer has probable cause to believe is in the vehicle. Reasonableness of a search, it continued, historically does not depend upon whether the owner of property is suspected of a crime but rather whether there is probable cause to believe seizable items are in or on the property. Further:

> Even if the historical evidence * * * were thought to be equivocal, we would find that the balancing of the relative interests weighs decidedly in favor of allowing searches of a passenger's belongings. Passengers, no less than drivers, possess a reduced expectation of privacy with regard to the property that they transport in cars * * *.

Whereas the passenger's privacy expectations are * * * considerably diminished, the governmental interests at stake are substantial. Effective law enforcement would be appreciably impaired without the ability to search a passenger's personal belongings when there is reason to believe contraband or evidence of criminal wrongdoing is hidden in the car. As in all car-search cases, the "ready mobility" of an automobile creates a risk that the evidence or contraband will be permanently lost while a warrant is obtained. In addition, a car passenger * * * will often be engaged in a common enterprise with the driver, and have the same interest in concealing the fruits or the evidence of their wrongdoing. A criminal might be able to hide contraband in a passenger's belongings as readily as in other containers in the car perhaps even surreptitiously, without the passenger's knowledge or permission. * * *

To be sure, these factors favoring a search will not always be present, but the balancing of interests must be conducted with an eye to the generality of cases. To require that the investigating officer have positive reason to believe that the passenger and driver were engaged in a common enterprise, or positive reason to believe that the driver had time and occasion to conceal the item in the passenger's belongings, surreptitiously or with friendly permission, is to impose requirements so seldom met that a "passenger's property" rule would dramatically reduce the ability to find and seize contraband and evidence of crime. Of course these requirements would not attach (under the Wyoming Supreme Court's rule) until the police officer knows or has reason to know that the container belongs to a passenger. But once a "passenger's property" exception to car searches became widely known, one would expect passenger-confederates to claim everything as their own. And one would anticipate a bog of litigation in the form of both civil lawsuits and motions to suppress in criminal trials involving such questions as whether the officer should have believed a passenger's claim of ownership, whether he should have inferred ownership from various objective factors, whether he had probable cause to believe that the passenger was a confederate, or to believe that the driver might have introduced the contraband into the package with or without the passenger's knowledge. When balancing the competing interests, our determinations of "reasonableness" under the Fourth Amendment must take account of these practical realities. We think they militate in favor of the needs of law enforcement, and against a personal-privacy interest that is ordinarily weak.

Finally, if we were to invent an exception from the historical practice * * *, it is perplexing why that exception should protect only property belonging to a passenger, rather than (what seems much more logical) property belonging to anyone other than the driver. * * *

526 U.S. at ___, 119 S.Ct. at 1302–03, 143 L.Ed.2d at 416–19. United States v. Di Re, 332 U.S. 581, 68 S.Ct. 222, 92 L.Ed. 210 (1948), the Court added, "held that probable cause to search a car did not justify a body search of a passenger." *Houghton* apparently did not disturb this holding.

Justice Breyer joined the *Houghton* majority opinion but wrote separately to comment on one aspect of the facts:

[It is important, in my view,] that the container here at issue, a woman's purse, was found at a considerable distance from its owner, who did not claim ownership until the officer discovered her identification while looking through it. Purses are special containers. They are repositories of especially personal items that people generally like to keep with them at all times. So I am tempted to say that a search of a purse involves an intrusion so similar to a search of one's person that the same rule should govern both. However, given this Court's prior cases, I cannot argue that the fact that the container was a purse automatically makes a legal difference, for the Court has warned against trying to make that kind of distinction. But I can say that it would matter if a woman's purse, like a man's billfold, were attached to her person. It might then amount to a kind of "outer clothing," which under the Court's cases would properly receive increased protection. In this case, the purse was separate from the person, and no one has claimed that, under those circumstances, the type of container makes a difference. For that reason, I join the Court's opinion.

526 U.S. at ___, 119 S.Ct. at 1304, 143 L.Ed.2d at 420 (Breyer, J., concurring).

Justice Stevens, joined by Justices Souter and Ginsburg, dissented:

In all of our prior cases applying the automobile exception to the Fourth Amendment's warrant requirement, either the defendant was the operator of the vehicle and in custody of the object of the search, or no question was raised as to the defendant's ownership or custody. In the only automobile case confronting the search of a passenger defendant—United States v. Di Re, 332 U.S. 581, 68 S.Ct. 222, 92 L.Ed. 210 (1948)—the Court held that the exception to the warrant requirement did not apply. In *Di Re*, as here, the information prompting the search directly implicated the driver, not the passenger. Today, instead of adhering to the settled distinction between drivers and passengers, the Court fashions a new rule that is based on a distinction between property contained in clothing worn by a passenger and property contained in a passenger's briefcase or purse. In cases on both sides of the Court's newly minted test, the property is in a "container" (whether a pocket or a pouch) located in the vehicle. Moreover, unlike the Court, I think it quite plain that the search of a passenger's purse or briefcase involves an intrusion on privacy that may be just as serious as was the intrusion in *Di Re*.

* * *

[I]n my view, the State's legitimate interest in effective law enforcement does not outweigh the privacy concerns at issue. I am as confident in a police officer's ability to apply a rule requiring a warrant or individualized probable cause to search belongings that areas in this case obviously owned by and in the custody of a passenger as is the Court in a "passenger-confederate[']s" ability to circumvent the rule. Certainly the ostensible clarity of the Court's rule is attractive. But that virtue is insufficient justification for its adoption. Moreover, a rule requiring a warrant or individualized probable cause to search passenger belongings is every bit as simple as the Court's rule; it simply protects more privacy.

* * *

Instead of applying ordinary Fourth Amendment principles to this case, the majority extends the automobile warrant exception to allow searches of passenger belongings based on the driver's misconduct. Thankfully, the Court's automobile-centered analysis limits the scope of its holding. But it does not justify the outcome in this case.

526 U.S. at ___, 119 S.Ct. at 1305–06, 143 L.Ed.2d at 420–23 (Stevens, J., dissenting).

3.   SEIZURE AND INVENTORY OF VEHICLES

EDITORS' INTRODUCTION: IMPOUNDMENT OF VEHICLES AND INVENTORYING OF IMPOUNDED VEHICLES

Two often-related issues frequently arise regarding official exercises of control over vehicles. One is officials' authority to seize or "impound" vehicles. The other is officers' authority to examine the contents of a properly seized vehicle, most often as part of "inventorying" those contents. Unfortunately, the Supreme Court's case law has focused more upon the power to inventory than on the power to seize.

Inventory Inspections of Seized Automobiles. Just as officers may inventory personal possessions of a person to be incarcerated after arrest (see subsection B(1) of Chapter 4), the Supreme Court held that the Fourth Amendment permits some inventory inspections of seized automobiles. The leading case is South Dakota v. Opperman, 428 U.S. 364, 96 S.Ct. 3092, 49 L.Ed.2d 1000 (1976). At 3 A.M., a Vermillion, South Dakota police officer noted Opperman's car parked in a downtown area in violation of an ordinance prohibiting parking in such areas between 2 a.m. and 6 a.m. He issued a citation and placed it on the windshield. After another officer issued a second citation at 10 a.m., the vehicle was "inspected" and towed to the city impound lot. At the lot, an officer noted a watch on the dashboard and other items of personal property on the back seat and floorboard. The locked car doors were opened and "using a standard inventory form, pursuant to police procedures, the officer inventoried the contents of the car * * *." The glove compartment was not locked; upon opening it, the officer discovered marihuana in a plastic bag. All items found in the car were removed to the police department for safekeeping. Opperman was prosecuted for possession of marihuana. His objection to the admissibility of the marihuana was overruled and he was convicted. Finding the police activity reasonable, a majority of the Supreme Court explained:

> When vehicles are impounded, local police departments generally follow a routine practice of securing and inventorying the automobiles' contents. These procedures developed in response to three distinct needs: the protection of the owner's property while it remains in police custody; the protection of the police against claims or disputes over lost or stolen property; and the protection of the police from potential danger. The practice has been viewed as essential to respond to incidents of theft or vandalism. In addition, police frequently attempt to determine whether a vehicle has been stolen and thereafter abandoned. * * *

> The decisions of this Court point unmistakably to the conclusion * * * that inventories pursuant to standard police procedures are reasonable.

> The Vermillion police were indisputably engaged in a caretaking search of a lawfully impounded automobile. The inventory was conducted only after the car had been impounded for multiple parking violations. The owner, having left his car illegally parked for an extended period, and thus subject to impoundment, was not present to make other arrangements for the safekeeping of his belongings. The inventory itself was prompted by the presence in plain view of a number of valuables inside the car. * * * [T]here is no suggestion whatever that this standard procedure * * * was a pretext concealing an investigatory motive.

428 U.S. at 369, 372, 375–76, 96 S.Ct. at 3097–99, 3100, 49 L.Ed.2d at 1005, 1007, 1009. Nor, the majority continued, was the inventory unlawful in scope because it extended to items not in plain view from outside the car:

> [O]nce the policeman was lawfully inside the car to secure the personal property in plain view, it was not unreasonable to open the unlocked glove compartment, to which vandals would have had ready and unobstructed access once inside the car.

428 U.S. at 376 n. 10, 96 S.Ct. at 3100 n. 10, 49 L.Ed.2d at 1009 n. 10.

Opperman's holding that certain vehicular inventory examinations are permissible was developed in the principal case in this subsection. An otherwise proper inventory examination is fatally tainted, however, if the vehicle's impoundment was an unreasonable seizure of it. Courts have considerable difficulty determining when impoundments of vehicles are reasonable.

Seizures or Impoundments of Automobiles. Despite the frequency with which police assume control over automobiles, the extent of officers' authority to impound vehicles is not well developed in case law. Police authority to impound in several situations is, however, quite settled. In *Opperman* itself, the Court commented, "The authority of police to seize and remove from the streets vehicles impeding traffic or threatening public safety and convenience is beyond challenge." Statutes in many jurisdictions authorize judicial proceedings for the forfeiture of some vehicles used illegally, such as in the commission of particular criminal offenses. When officers have probable cause to believe a vehicle subject to forfeiture under such provisions, they may seize the vehicle and hold it pending the completion of judicial forfeiture proceedings. Cf. Cooper v. California, 386 U.S. 58, 87 S.Ct. 788, 17 L.Ed.2d 730 (1967).

It has also been suggested that grounds for impoundment exist when— or at least when officers have reason to believe—the automobile has been abandoned or stolen, the automobile constitutes evidence of the commission of a crime or of someone's guilt of a crime, or the driver (as by reason of injury, intoxication or mental incapacitation) is unable to attend to the car. See State v. Singleton, 9 Wn.App. 327, 332–33, 511 P.2d 1396, 1399–1400 (1973).

Courts disagree regarding the propriety of vehicle impoundments made because the driver was arrested. Unfortunately, judicial discussions often do not clearly distinguish between validity of the initial impoundment and inventory inspection of a vehicle properly in official custody. In State v. Duncan, 77 Ohio Misc.2d 7, 665 N.E.2d 767 (Ohio Ct.Common Pleas 1996), however, the distinction was carefully made. Officers arrested Duncan at a hospital where he sought treatment for injuries sustained in an attempted robbery. They learned he had driven to the hospital alone in his mother's automobile which he was parked on the street near the hospital. Without seeking a warrant they searched the automobile and found drugs. When the admissibility of the drugs was challenged, the prosecution defended the search as an inventory inspection of a seized vehicle. The trial court ruled the prosecution had failed to establish the vehicle's seizure was reasonable:

No evidence was offered that the car was illegally parked or that its prolonged presence on the street would violate any parking laws. The police attempted to justify the impoundment on the ground that such action was necessary to protect the car from vandalism or theft.

Merely because the driver of a vehicle is taken into custody does not justify impoundment. The state must show that a law would be violated, that a danger would be posed to others if impoundment did not occur, that no reasonable alternative existed for safeguarding the vehicle, or that the impoundment was made pursuant to a reasonable police regulation. No evidence was presented that the vehicle was illegally parked or obstructed traffic. No evidence was presented that the defendant desired it to be towed for safekeeping or could not have called his mother (the owner of the car) or a friend to move the vehicle. The state has, thus, not sustained its burden of showing the reasonableness of towing this vehicle.

77 Ohio Misc.2d at 9, 665 N.E.2d at 769.

Colorado v. Bertine

Supreme Court of the United States, 1987.
479 U.S. 367, 107 S.Ct. 738, 93 L.Ed.2d 739.

■ CHIEF JUSTICE REHNQUIST delivered the opinion of the Court.

On February 10, 1984, a police officer in Boulder, Colorado, arrested respondent Steven Lee Bertine for driving while under the influence of alcohol. After Bertine was taken into custody and before the arrival of a tow truck to take Bertine's van to an impoundment lot,[8] a backup officer inventoried the contents of the van. The officer opened a closed backpack in which he found controlled substances, cocaine paraphernalia, and a large amount of cash. Bertine was subsequently charged with driving while under the influence of alcohol, unlawful possession of cocaine with intent to dispense, sell, and distribute, and unlawful possession of methaqualone. We are asked to decide whether the Fourth Amendment prohibits the State from proving these charges with the evidence discovered during the inventory of Bertine's van. We hold that it does not.

The backup officer inventoried the van in accordance with local police procedures, which require a detailed inspection and inventory of impounded vehicles. He found the backpack directly behind the frontseat of the van. Inside the pack, the officer observed a nylon bag containing metal canisters. Opening the canisters, the officer discovered that they contained cocaine, methaqualone tablets, cocaine paraphernalia, and $700 in cash. In an outside zippered pouch of the backpack, he also found $210 in cash in a

---

8. Section 772(a)(4) of the Boulder Revised Code authorizes police officers to impound vehicles when drivers are taken into custody. Section 772(a)(4) provides:

"A peace officer is authorized to remove or cause to be removed a vehicle from any street, parking lot, or driveway when:

(4) The driver of a vehicle is taken into custody by the police department." Boulder Rev.Code § 772(a)(4) (1981).

sealed envelope. After completing the inventory of the van, the officer had the van towed to an impound lot and brought the backpack, money, and contraband to the police station.

After Bertine was charged with the offenses described above, he moved to suppress the evidence found during the inventory search on the ground, inter alia, that the search of the closed backpack and containers exceeded the permissible scope of such a search under the Fourth Amendment. The Colorado trial court ruled that probable cause supported Bertine's arrest and that the police officers had made the decisions to impound the vehicle and to conduct a thorough inventory search in good faith. Although noting that the inventory of the vehicle was performed in a "somewhat slipshod" manner, the District Court concluded that "the search of the backpack was done for the purpose of protecting the owner's property, protection of the police from subsequent claims of loss or stolen property, and the protection of the police from dangerous instrumentalities." The court observed that the standard procedures for impounding vehicles mandated a "detailed inventory involving the opening of containers and the listing of [their] contents." Based on these findings, the court determined that the inventory search did not violate Bertine's rights under the Fourth Amendment of the United States Constitution. * * *

On the State's interlocutory appeal, the Supreme Court of Colorado [disagreed]. * * * The court recognized that in South Dakota v. Opperman, 428 U.S. 364, 96 S.Ct. 3092, 49 L.Ed.2d 1000 (1976), we had held inventory searches of automobiles to be consistent with the Fourth Amendment, and that in Illinois v. Lafayette, 462 U.S. 640, 103 S.Ct. 2605, 77 L.Ed.2d 65 (1983), we had held that the inventory search of personal effects of an arrestee at a police station was also permissible under that Amendment. The Supreme Court of Colorado felt, however, that our decisions in Arkansas v. Sanders, 442 U.S. 753, 99 S.Ct. 2586, 61 L.Ed.2d 235 (1979), and United States v. Chadwick, 433 U.S. 1, 97 S.Ct. 2476, 53 L.Ed.2d 538 (1977), holding searches of closed trunks and suitcases to violate the Fourth Amendment, meant that *Opperman* and *Lafayette* did not govern this case.

We granted certiorari to consider the important and recurring question of federal law decided by the Colorado Supreme Court. As that court recognized, inventory searches are now a well-defined exception to the warrant requirement of the Fourth Amendment. The policies behind the warrant requirement are not implicated in an inventory search, nor is the related concept of probable cause:

> "The standard of probable cause is peculiarly related to criminal investigations, not routine, noncriminal procedures.... The probable-cause approach is unhelpful when analysis centers upon the reasonableness of routine administrative caretaking functions, particularly when no claim is made that the protective procedures are a subterfuge for criminal investigations."

For these reasons, the Colorado Supreme Court's reliance on Arkansas v. Sanders, supra, and United States v. Chadwick, supra, was incorrect. Both of these cases concerned searches solely for the purpose of investigating criminal conduct, with the validity of the searches therefore dependent on the application of the probable-cause and warrant requirements of the Fourth Amendment.

By contrast, an inventory search may be "reasonable" under the Fourth Amendment even though it is not conducted pursuant to a warrant based upon probable cause. In *Opperman*, this Court assessed the reasonableness of an inventory search of the glove compartment in an abandoned automobile impounded by the police. We found that inventory procedures serve to protect an owner's property while it is in the custody of the police, to insure against claims of lost, stolen, or vandalized property, and to guard the police from danger. In light of these strong governmental interests and the diminished expectation of privacy in an automobile, we upheld the search. In reaching this decision, we observed that our cases accorded deference to police caretaking procedures designed to secure and protect vehicles and their contents within police custody.

In our more recent decision, *Lafayette*, a police officer conducted an inventory search of the contents of a shoulder bag in the possession of an individual being taken into custody. In deciding whether this search was reasonable, we recognized that the search served legitimate governmental interests similar to those identified in *Opperman*. We determined that those interests outweighed the individual's Fourth Amendment interests and upheld the search.

In the present case, as in *Opperman* and *Lafayette*, there was no showing that the police, who were following standardized procedures, acted in bad faith or for the sole purpose of investigation. In addition, the governmental interests justifying the inventory searches in *Opperman* and *Lafayette* are nearly the same as those which obtain here. In each case, the police were potentially responsible for the property taken into their custody. By securing the property, the police protected the property from unauthorized interference. Knowledge of the precise nature of the property helped guard against claims of theft, vandalism, or negligence. Such knowledge also helped to avert any danger to police or others that may have been posed by the property.

* * *

The Supreme Court of Colorado * * * expressed the view that the search in this case was unreasonable because Bertine's van was towed to a secure, lighted facility and because Bertine himself could have been offered the opportunity to make other arrangements for the safekeeping of his property. But the security of the storage facility does not completely eliminate the need for inventorying; the police may still wish to protect themselves or the owners of the lot against false claims of theft or dangerous instrumentalities. And while giving Bertine an opportunity to make alternative arrangements would undoubtedly have been possible, we said in *Lafayette*:

> "[T]he real question is not what 'could have been achieved,' but whether the Fourth Amendment requires such steps . . .
>
> "The reasonableness of any particular governmental activity does not necessarily or invariably turn on the existence of alternative 'less intrusive' means."

We conclude that here, as in *Lafayette*, reasonable police regulations relating to inventory procedures administered in good faith satisfy the Fourth Amendment, even though courts might as a matter of hindsight be able to devise equally reasonable rules requiring a different procedure.[9]

The Supreme Court of Colorado also thought it necessary to require that police, before inventorying a container, weigh the strength of the individual's privacy interest in the container against the possibility that the container might serve as a repository for dangerous or valuable items. We think that such a requirement is contrary to our decisions in *Opperman* and *Lafayette* * * *:

> "Even if less intrusive means existed of protecting some particular types of property, it would be unreasonable to expect police officers in the everyday course of business to make fine and subtle distinctions in deciding which containers or items may be searched and which must be sealed as a unit." *Lafayette*, supra, 462 U.S., at 648, 103 S.Ct., at 2610.

* * *

We reaffirm these principles here: " '[a] single familiar standard is essential to guide police officers, who have only limited time and expertise to reflect on and balance the social and individual interests involved in the specific circumstances they confront.' " *Lafayette*, supra, 462 U.S., at 648, 103 S.Ct., at 2610.

Bertine finally argues that the inventory search of his van was unconstitutional because departmental regulations gave the police officers discretion to choose between impounding his van and parking and locking it in a public parking place. The Supreme Court of Colorado did not rely on this argument in reaching its conclusion, and we reject it. Nothing in *Opperman* or *Lafayette* prohibits the exercise of police discretion so long as that discretion is exercised according to standard criteria and on the basis of something other than suspicion of evidence of criminal activity. Here, the discretion afforded the Boulder police was exercised in light of standardized criteria, related to the feasibility and appropriateness of parking and locking a vehicle rather than impounding it.[10] There was no showing that

---

9. We emphasize that, in this case, the trial court found that the Police Department's procedures mandated the opening of closed containers and the listing of their contents. Our decisions have always adhered to the requirement that inventories be conducted according to standardized criteria.

[T]he dissent suggests that the inventory here was not authorized by the standard procedures of the Boulder Police Department. Yet that court specifically stated that the procedure followed here was "officially authorized." In addition, the court did not disturb the trial court's finding that the police procedures for impounding vehicles required a detailed inventory of Bertine's van.

10. In arguing that the Boulder Police Department procedures set forth no stan-

dardized criteria guiding an officer's decision to impound a vehicle, the dissent selectively quotes from the police directive concerning the care and security of vehicles taken into police custody. The dissent fails to mention that the directive establishes several conditions that must be met before an officer may pursue the park-and-lock alternative. For example, police may not park and lock the vehicle where there is reasonable risk of damage or vandalism to the vehicle or where the approval of the arrestee cannot be obtained. Not only do such conditions circumscribe the discretion of individual officers, but they also protect the vehicle and its contents and minimize claims of property loss.

the police chose to impound Bertine's van in order to investigate suspected criminal activity.

While both *Opperman* and *Lafayette* are distinguishable from the present case on their facts, we think that the principles enunciated in those cases govern the present one. The judgment of the Supreme Court of Colorado is therefore

Reversed.

■ JUSTICE MARSHALL, with whom JUSTICE BRENNAN joins, dissenting.

[The] search [in this case]—it cannot legitimately be labeled an inventory—was unreasonable and violated the Fourth Amendment. * * * [I]t was not conducted according to standardized procedures. * * *

As the Court acknowledges, inventory searches are reasonable only if conducted according to standardized procedures. * * *

The Court today attempts to evade these clear prohibitions on unfettered police discretion by declaring that "the discretion afforded the Boulder police was exercised in light of standardized criteria, related to the feasibility and appropriateness of parking and locking a vehicle rather than impounding it." This vital assertion is flatly contradicted by the record in this case. The officer who conducted the inventory, Officer Reichenbach, testified at the suppression hearing that the decision not to "park and lock" respondent's vehicle was his "own individual discretionary decision." Indeed, application of these supposedly standardized "criteria" upon which the Court so heavily relies would have yielded a different result in this case. Since there was ample public parking adjacent to the intersection where respondent was stopped, consideration of "feasibility" would certainly have militated in favor of the "park and lock" option, not against it. I do not comprehend how consideration of "appropriateness" serves to channel a field officer's discretion; nonetheless, the "park and lock" option would seem particularly appropriate in this case, where respondent was stopped for a traffic offense and was not likely to be in custody for a significant length of time.

Indeed, the record indicates that *no* standardized criteria limit a Boulder police officer's discretion. According to a departmental directive, after placing a driver under arrest, an officer has three options for disposing of the vehicle. First, he can allow a third party to take custody. Second, the officer or the driver (depending on the nature of the arrest) may take the car to the nearest public parking facility, lock it, and take the keys. Finally, the officer can do what was done in this case: impound the vehicle, and search and inventory its contents, including closed containers.

Under the first option, the police have no occasion to search the automobile. Under the "park and lock" option, "[c]losed containers that give no indication of containing either valuables or a weapon *may not be opened and the contents searched* (i.e., inventoried)." Only if the police choose the third option are they entitled to search closed containers in the vehicle. Where the vehicle is not itself evidence of a crime,[11] as in this case,

---

11. Respondent's van was not evidence of a crime within the meaning of the departmental directive; Officer Reichenbach testified that it was not his practice to impound

the police apparently have totally unbridled discretion as to which proce-dure to use. Consistent with this conclusion, Officer Reichenbach testified that such decisions were left to the discretion of the officer on the scene.

Once a Boulder police officer has made this initial completely discre-tionary decision to impound a vehicle, he is given little guidance as to which areas to search and what sort of items to inventory. The arresting officer, Officer Toporek, testified at the suppression hearing as to what items would be inventoried: "That would I think be very individualistic as far as what an officer may or may not go into. I think whatever arouses his suspicious [sic] as far as what may be contained in any type of article in the car." In application, these so-called procedures left the breadth of the "inventory" to the whim of the individual officer. Clearly, "[t]he practical effect of this system is to leave the [owner] subject to the discretion of the official in the field."

Inventory searches are not subject to the warrant requirement because they are conducted by the government as part of a "community caretak-ing" function, "totally divorced from the detection, investigation, or acqui-sition of evidence relating to the violation of a criminal statute." Standard-ized procedures are necessary to ensure that this narrow exception is not improperly used to justify, after the fact, a warrantless investigative foray. Accordingly, to invalidate a search that is conducted without established procedures, it is not necessary to establish that the police actually acted in bad faith, or that the inventory was in fact a "pretext." By allowing the police unfettered discretion, Boulder's discretionary scheme * * * is unrea-sonable because of the " 'grave danger' of abuse of discretion."

* * *

NOTE: REQUIRED STANDARDIZED PROCEDURES

Bertine's emphasis upon the need for "standardized procedures" was developed in Florida v. Wells, 495 U.S. 1, 110 S.Ct. 1632, 109 L.Ed.2d 1 (1990). Officers examined the contents of a suitcase found in an impounded car. The state court held the search improper because no evidence was produced that the police agency had any policy concerning opening of closed containers found during inventory searches. The Supreme Court affirmed, reasoning that "absent [a policy with respect to the opening of closed containers encountered during an inventory search], the instant search was not sufficiently regulated to satisfy the Fourth Amendment * * *." Chief Justice Rehnquist, writing for the majority, explained:

> Our view that standardized criteria or established routine must regulate the opening of containers found during inventory searches is based on the principle that an inventory search must not be a ruse for a general rummaging in order to discover incriminating evidence. The policy or practice governing inventory searches should be designed to produce an inventory. The individual police officer must not be allowed so much latitude that inventory inspections are

all cars following an arrest for driving while under the influence of alcohol. The Memo-randum also requires the "approval of the arrestee" before the police can "park and lock" his car. In this case, however, respon-dent was never advised of this option and had no opportunity to consent. At the suppression hearing, he indicated that he would have consented to such a procedure.

turned into "a purposeful and general means of discovering evidence of crime," *Bertine,* supra, 479 U.S., at 376, 107 S.Ct., at 744 (Blackmun, J., concurring).

495 U.S. at 4, 110 S.Ct. at 1635, 109 L.Ed.2d at 6. He expressed disagreement, however, with the state court's comment that under *Bertine* the policy must mandate that either all or no containers be opened:

> A police officer may be allowed sufficient latitude whether a particular container should or should not be opened in light of the nature of the search and characteristics of the container itself. Thus, while policies of opening all containers or of opening no containers are unquestionably permissible, it would be equally permissible, for example, to allow the opening of closed containers whose contents officers determine they are unable to ascertain from examining the containers' exteriors. The allowance of the exercise of judgment based on concerns relevant to the purposes of an inventory search does not violate the Fourth Amendment.

495 U.S. at 4, 110 S.Ct. at 1635, 109 L.Ed.2d at 6–7.

Justice Brennan, joined by Justice Marshall, disagreed that the majority's dicta was consistent with *Bertine,* which he read as the Florida court had. Justice Blackmun agreed the Florida court was wrong in reading *Bertine* as requiring all or no containers be opened but complained the majority's dicta permitted too much flexibility:

> A State * * * probably could adopt a policy which requires the opening of all containers that are not locked, or a policy which requires the opening of all containers over or under a certain size, even though these policies do not call for the opening of all or no containers. In other words, a State has the discretion to choose a scheme that lies somewhere between the extremes identified by the Florida Supreme Court.

> It is an entirely different matter, however, to say, as this majority does, that an individual policeman may be afforded discretion in conducting an inventory search. The exercise of discretion by an individual officer, especially when it cannot be measured against objective, standard criteria, creates the potential for abuse of Fourth Amendment rights our earlier inventory search cases were designed to guard against.

495 U.S. at 11, 110 S.Ct. at 1639, 109 L.Ed.2d at 11 (Blackmun, J., concurring in the judgment). Justice Stevens agreed. 495 U.S. at 12, 110 S.Ct. at 1639, 109 L.Ed.2d at 11 (Stevens, J., concurring in the judgment).

E. SEARCHES AND SEIZURES AT OR NEAR INTERNATIONAL BORDERS

Searches and other law enforcement activity related to the international border have traditionally given rise to substantial concern. Statutory authority to conduct border-related activity consists of grants of authority to both the Bureau of Customs and the Department of Immigration. Customs officers are authorized in 19 U.S.C.A. § 482 to "stop, search, and examine * * * any vehicle, beast, or person, on which or whom he or they shall suspect there is merchandise which is subject to duty, or shall have been introduced into the United States in any manner contrary to law * * *" Under 19 U.S.C.A. § 1581(a), customs officers are authorized to board any vessel or vehicle and "search the vessel or vehicle and every part thereof and any person, trunk, package or cargo on board * * *." Immigration officers, on the other hand, are authorized by 8 U.S.C.A. § 1357(a)(1) to interrogate any person "believed to be an alien as to his right to be or remain in the United States * * *". They are also authorized to board any vessel, railway car or conveyance "within a reasonable distance" of any external border to search for persons who have illegally entered the country. 8 U.S.C.A. § 1357(a)(3). "Reasonable distance" is defined by regulation. Border patrol officers, as agents of the Department of Immigration, might be thought by the nature of their duties to have a more limited right to search than customs officials. But the Bureau of Customs has designates border patrol officers as customs agents and, in this latter capacity, they may search for things improperly brought over the border. See United States v. Thompson, 475 F.2d 1359 (5th Cir.1973).

Federal law enforcement activity conducted pursuant to this authority consists of several legally significant types. One, of course, is the process at the international border itself (and at the "functional equivalents" of the border) of searching and questioning persons and things actually then crossing the border. In addition, the Immigration and Naturalization Service conducts "area control" operations in the country's interior. These consist of traffic control operations and factory surveys to identify illegally entered aliens working at those places. See Immigration and Naturalization Service v. Delgado, 466 U.S. 210, 225 n. 1, 104 S.Ct. 1758, 1767 n. 1, 80 L.Ed.2d 247, 261 n. 1 (1984) (Brennan, J., concurring in part and dissenting in part). In regard to the traffic control operations, the Court has noted:

> The Border Patrol conducts three types of surveillance along inland roadways, all in the asserted interest of detecting the illegal importation of aliens. Permanent checkpoints are maintained at certain nodal intersections; temporary checkpoints are established from time to time at various places; and finally, there are roving patrols * * *.

Almeida-Sanchez v. United States, 413 U.S. 266, 268, 93 S.Ct. 2535, 2537, 37 L.Ed.2d 596, 600 (1973). The first subsection of this section deals with law enforcement activity at the border or its functional equivalents. In the second, "area control" operations are considered.

1. Enforcement Activity at the International Border

The Supreme Court did not have occasion, until the following principal case, to definitively address the limits that the federal constitution places upon law enforcement activity at the international border itself. But its basic position was clear in dictum:

> That searches made at the border, pursuant to the longstanding right of the sovereign to protect itself by stopping and examining persons and property crossing into this country, are reasonable simply by virtue of the fact that they occur at the border, should, by now, require no extended demonstration.

United States v. Ramsey, 431 U.S. 606, 616, 97 S.Ct. 1972, 1978, 52 L.Ed.2d 617, 626 (1977). These discussions left significant question as to the additional requirements applicable when the search is nonroutine or extraordinarily intrusive.

The Court has made clear at least some activity permissible at the border may also take place at other locations within the country's borders:

> [R]outine border search[s] * * * may in certain circumstances take place not only at the border itself, but at its functional equivalents as well. For example, searches at an established station near the border, at a point marking the confluence of two or more roads that extend from the border, might be functional equivalents of border searches. For another example, a search of the passengers and cargo of an airplane arriving at a St. Louis airport after a nonstop flight from Mexico City would clearly be the functional equivalent of a border search.

Almeida-Sanchez v. United States, 413 U.S. 266, 272–73, 93 S.Ct. 2535, 2539, 37 L.Ed.2d 596, 602–03 (1973).

United States v. Montoya de Hernandez

Supreme Court of the United States, 1985.
473 U.S. 531, 105 S.Ct. 3304, 87 L.Ed.2d 381.

■ JUSTICE REHNQUIST delivered the opinion of the Court.

Respondent Rosa Elvira Montoya de Hernandez * * * arrived at Los Angeles International Airport shortly after midnight, March 5, 1983, on Avianca Flight 080, a direct 10 hour flight from Bogota, Colombia. Her visa was in order so she was passed through Immigration and proceeded to the customs desk. At the customs desk she encountered Customs Inspector Talamantes, who reviewed her documents and noticed from her passport that she had made at least eight recent trips to either Miami or Los Angeles. Talamantes referred respondent to a secondary customs' desk for further questioning. At this desk Talamantes and another inspector asked respondent general questions concerning herself and the purpose of her trip. Respondent revealed that she spoke no English and had no family or friends in the United States. She explained in Spanish that she had come to the United States to purchase goods for her husband's store in Bogota. The customs inspectors recognized Bogota as a "source city" for narcotics. Respondent possessed $5,000 in cash, mostly $50 bills, but had no billfold. She indicated to the inspectors that she had no appointments with merchandise vendors, but planned to ride around Los Angeles in taxicabs visiting retail stores such as J.C. Penney and K–Mart in order to buy goods for her husband's store with the $5,000.

Respondent admitted that she had no hotel reservations, but stated that she planned to stay at a Holiday Inn. Respondent could not recall how her airline ticket was purchased. When the inspectors opened respondent's one small valise they found about four changes of "cold weather" clothing. Respondent had no shoes other than the highheeled pair she was wearing. Although respondent possessed no checks, waybills, credit cards, or letters of credit, she did produce a Colombian business card and a number of old receipts, waybills, and fabric swatches displayed in a photo album.

At this point Talamantes and the other inspector suspected that respondent was a "balloon swallower," one who attempts to smuggle narcotics into this country hidden in her alimentary canal. Over the years Inspector Talamantes had apprehended dozens of alimentary canal smugglers arriving on Avianca Flight 080.

The inspectors requested a female customs inspector to take respondent to a private area and conduct a patdown and strip search. During the search the female inspector felt respondent's abdomen area and noticed a firm fullness, as if respondent were wearing a girdle. The search revealed no contraband but the inspector noticed that respondent was wearing two pair of elastic underpants with a paper towel lining the crotch area.

When respondent returned to the customs area and the female inspector reported her discoveries, the inspector in charge told respondent that he suspected she was smuggling drugs in her alimentary canal. Respondent agreed to the inspector's request that she be x rayed at a hospital but in answer to the inspector's query stated that she was pregnant. She agreed to a pregnancy test before the x ray. Respondent withdrew the consent for an x ray when she learned that she would have to be handcuffed en route to the hospital. The inspector then gave respondent the option of returning to Colombia on the next available flight, agreeing to an x ray, or remaining in detention until she produced a monitored bowel movement that would confirm or rebut the inspectors' suspicions. Respondent chose the first option and was placed in a customs' office under observation. She was told that if she went to the toilet she would have to use a wastebasket in the women's restroom, in order that female customs inspectors could inspect her stool for balloons or capsules carrying narcotics. The inspectors refused respondent's request to place a telephone call.

Respondent sat in the customs office, under observation, for the remainder of the night. During the night customs officials attempted to place respondent on a Mexican airline that was flying to Bogota via Mexico City in the morning. The airline refused to transport respondent because she lacked a Mexican visa necessary to land in Mexico City. Respondent was not permitted to leave, and was informed that she would be detained until she agreed to an x ray or her bowels moved. She remained detained in the customs office under observation, for most of the time curled up in a chair leaning to one side. She refused all offers of food and drink, and refused to use the toilet facilities. The Court of Appeals noted that she exhibited symptoms of discomfort consistent with "heroic efforts to resist the usual calls of nature."

At the shift change at 4:00 p.m. the next afternoon, almost 16 hours after her flight had landed, respondent still had not defecated or urinated or partaken of food or drink. At that time customs officials sought a court order authorizing a pregnancy test, an x ray, and a rectal examination. The Federal Magistrate issued an order just before midnight that evening, which authorized a rectal examination and involuntary x ray, provided that the physician in charge considered respondent's claim of pregnancy. Respondent was taken to a hospital and given a pregnancy test, which later turned out to be negative. Before the results of the pregnancy test were known, a physician conducted a rectal examination and removed from respondent's rectum a balloon containing a foreign substance. Respondent was then placed formally under arrest. By 4:10 a.m. respondent had passed

6 similar balloons; over the next 4 days she passed 88 balloons containing a total of 528 grams of 80% pure cocaine hydrochloride.

After a suppression hearing the District Court admitted the cocaine in evidence against respondent. She was convicted of possession of cocaine with intent to distribute and unlawful importation of cocaine.

A divided panel of the United States Court of Appeals for the Ninth Circuit reversed respondent's convictions. The court noted that customs inspectors had a "justifiably high level of official skepticism" about respondent's good motives, but the inspectors decided to let nature take its course rather than seek an immediate magistrate's warrant for an x ray. Such a magistrate's warrant required a "clear indication" or "plain suggestion" that the traveler was an alimentary canal smuggler under previous decisions of the Court of Appeals. The court applied this required level of suspicion to respondent's case. The court questioned the "humanity" of the inspectors' decision to hold respondent until her bowels moved, knowing that she would suffer "many hours of humiliating discomfort" if she chose not to submit to the x-ray examination. The court concluded that under a "clear indication" standard "the evidence available to the customs officers when they decided to hold [respondent] for continued observation was insufficient to support the 16-hour detention."

The government contends that the customs inspectors reasonably suspected that respondent was an alimentary canal smuggler, and this suspicion was sufficient to justify the detention. In support of the judgment below respondent argues, *inter alia*, that reasonable suspicion would not support respondent's detention, and in any event the inspectors did not reasonably suspect that respondent was carrying narcotics internally.

The Fourth Amendment commands that searches and seizures be reasonable. What is reasonable depends upon all of the circumstances surrounding the search or seizure and the nature of the search or seizure itself. The permissibility of a particular law enforcement practice is judged by "balancing its intrusion on the individual's Fourth Amendment interests against its promotion of legitimate governmental interests."

Here the seizure of respondent took place at the international border. Since the founding of our Republic, Congress has granted the Executive plenary authority to conduct routine searches and seizures at the border, without probable cause or a warrant, in order to regulate the collection of duties and to prevent the introduction of contraband into this country. This Court has long recognized Congress' power to police entrants at the border. * * * Consistently, therefore, with Congress' power to protect the Nation by stopping and examining persons entering this country, the Fourth Amendment's balance of reasonableness is qualitatively different at the international border than in the interior. Routine searches of the persons and effects of entrants are not subject to any requirement of reasonable suspicion, probable cause, or warrant, and first-class mail may be opened without a warrant on less than probable cause. Automotive travelers may be stopped at fixed check points near the border without individualized suspicion even if the stop is based largely on ethnicity, and boats on inland waters with ready access to the sea may be hailed and boarded with no suspicion whatever.

These cases reflect longstanding concern for the protection of the integrity of the border. This concern is, if anything, heightened by the veritable national crisis in law enforcement caused by smuggling of illicit narcotics, and in particular by the increasing utilization of alimentary canal smuggling. This desperate practice appears to be a relatively recent addition to the smugglers' repertoire of deceptive practices, and it also appears to be exceedingly difficult to detect. * * *

Balanced against the sovereign's interests at the border are the Fourth Amendment rights of respondent. Having presented herself at the border for admission, and having subjected herself to the criminal enforcement powers of the Federal Government, respondent was entitled to be free from unreasonable search and seizure. But not only is the expectation of privacy less at the border than in the interior, but the Fourth Amendment balance between the interests of the Government and the privacy right of the individual is struck much more favorably to the Government at the border.

We have not previously decided what level of suspicion would justify a seizure of an incoming traveler for purposes other than a routine border search. The Court of Appeals held that the initial detention of respondent was permissible only if the inspectors possessed a "clear indication" of alimentary canal smuggling. This "clear indication" language comes from our opinion in Schmerber v. California, 384 U.S. 757, 86 S.Ct. 1826, 16 L.Ed.2d 908 (1966), but we think that the Court of Appeals misapprehended the significance of that phrase in the context in which it was used in *Schmerber*. The Court of Appeals for the Ninth Circuit viewed "clear indication" as an intermediate standard between "reasonable suspicion" and "probable cause." But we think that the words in *Schmerber* were used to indicate the necessity for particularized suspicion that the evidence sought might be found within the body of the individual, rather than as enunciating still a third Fourth Amendment threshold between "reasonable suspicion" and "probable cause."

No other court, including this one, has ever adopted *Schmerber's* "clear indication" language as a Fourth Amendment standard. * * * We do not think that the Fourth Amendment's emphasis upon reasonableness is consistent with the creation of a third verbal standard in addition to "reasonable suspicion" and "probable cause"; we are dealing with a constitutional requirement of reasonableness, * * * and subtle verbal gradations may obscure rather than elucidate the meaning of the provision in question.

We hold that the detention of a traveler at the border, beyond the scope of a routine customs search and inspection, is justified at its inception if customs agents, considering all the facts surrounding the traveler and her trip, reasonably suspect that the traveler is smuggling contraband in her alimentary canal.[12]

---

12. It is also important to note what we do *not* hold. Because the issues are not presented today we suggest no view on what level of suspicion, if any, is required for non-routine border searches such as strip, body cavity, or involuntary x-ray searches. Both parties would have us decide the issue of whether aliens possess lesser Fourth Amendment rights at the border; that question was

The "reasonable suspicion" standard has been applied in a number of contexts and effects a needed balance between private and public interests when law enforcement officials must make a limited intrusion on less than probable cause. It thus fits well into the situations involving alimentary canal smuggling at the border: this type of smuggling gives no external signs and inspectors will rarely possess probable cause to arrest or search, yet governmental interests in stopping smuggling at the border are high indeed. Under this standard officials at the border must have a "particularized and objective basis for suspecting the particular person" of alimentary canal smuggling.

The facts, and their rational inferences, known to customs inspectors in this case clearly supported a reasonable suspicion that respondent was an alimentary canal smuggler. We need not belabor the facts, including respondent's implausible story, that supported this suspicion. The trained customs inspectors had encountered many alimentary canal smugglers and certainly had more than an "inchoate and unparticularized suspicion or 'hunch,'" that respondent was smuggling narcotics in her alimentary canal. The inspectors' suspicion was a "'commonsense conclusio[n] about human behavior' upon which 'practical people,'—including government officials, are entitled to rely."

The final issue in this case is whether the detention of respondent was reasonably related in scope to the circumstances which justified it initially. In this regard we have cautioned that courts should not indulge in "unrealistic second-guessing," and we have noted that "creative judge[s], engaged in *post hoc* evaluations of police conduct can almost always imagine some alternative means by which the objectives of the police might have been accomplished." But "[t]he fact that the protection of the public might, in the abstract, have been accomplished by 'less intrusive' means does not, in itself, render the search unreasonable." Authorities must be allowed "to graduate their response to the demands of any particular situation." Here, respondent was detained *incommunicado* for almost 16 hours before inspectors sought a warrant; the warrant then took a number of hours to procure, through no apparent fault of the inspectors. This length of time undoubtedly exceeds any other detention we have approved under reasonable suspicion. But we have also consistently rejected hard-and-fast time limits. Instead, "common sense and ordinary human experience must govern over rigid criteria."

The rudimentary knowledge of the human body which judges possess in common with the rest of humankind tells us that alimentary canal smuggling cannot be detected in the amount of time in which other illegal activity may be investigated through brief *Terry*-type stops. It presents few, if any external signs; a quick frisk will not do, nor will even a strip search. In the case of respondent the inspectors had available, as an alternative to simply awaiting her bowel movement, an x ray. They offered her the alternative of submitting herself to that procedure. But when she refused that alternative, the customs inspectors were left with only two practical alternatives: detain her for such time as necessary to confirm their suspi-

not raised in either court below and we do
not consider it today.

cions, a detention which would last much longer than the typical *"Terry"* stop, or turn her loose into the interior carrying the reasonably suspected contraband drugs.

The inspectors in this case followed this former procedure. They no doubt expected that respondent, having recently disembarked from a 10hour direct flight with a full and stiff abdomen, would produce a bowel movement without extended delay. But her visible efforts to resist the call of nature, which the court below labeled "heroic," disappointed this expectation and in turn caused her humiliation and discomfort. Our prior cases have refused to charge police with delays in investigatory detention attributable to the suspect's evasive actions, and that principle applies here as well. Respondent alone was responsible for much of the duration and discomfort of the seizure.

Under these circumstances, we conclude that the detention in this case was not unreasonably long. It occurred at the international border, where the Fourth Amendment balance of interests leans heavily to the Government. At the border, customs officials have more than merely an investigative law enforcement role. They are also charged, along with immigration officials, with protecting this Nation from entrants who may bring anything harmful into this country, whether that be communicable diseases, narcotics, or explosives. In this regard the detention of a suspected alimentary canal smuggler at the border is analogous to the detention of a suspected tuberculosis carrier at the border: both are detained until their bodily processes dispel the suspicion that they will introduce a harmful agent into this country.

Respondent's detention was long, uncomfortable, indeed, humiliating; but both its length and its discomfort resulted solely from the method by which she chose to smuggle illicit drugs into this country. * * * [I]n the presence of articulable suspicion of smuggling in her alimentary canal, the customs officers were not required by the Fourth Amendment to pass respondent and her 88 cocaine-filled balloons into the interior. Her detention for the period of time necessary to either verify or dispel the suspicion was not unreasonable. The judgment of the Court of Appeals is therefore

Reversed.

■ JUSTICE STEVENS, concurring in the judgment.

If a seizure and a search of the person of the kind disclosed by this record may be made on the basis of reasonable suspicion, we must assume that a significant number of innocent persons will be required to undergo similar procedures. The rule announced in this case cannot, therefore, be supported on the ground that respondent's prolonged and humiliating detention "resulted solely from the method by which she chose to smuggle illicit drugs into this country."

The prolonged detention of respondent was, however, justified by a different choice that respondent made; she withdrew her consent to an x-ray examination that would have easily determined whether the reasonable suspicion that she was concealing contraband was justified. I believe that Customs agents may require that a nonpregnant person reasonably suspected of this kind of smuggling submit to an x-ray examination as an incident to a border search. I therefore concur in the judgment.

■ JUSTICE BRENNAN, with whom JUSTICE MARSHALL joins, dissenting.

* * *

I

Travelers at the national border are routinely subjected to questioning, pat-downs, and thorough searches of their belongings. These measures, which involve relatively limited invasions of privacy and which typically are conducted on all incoming travelers, do not violate the Fourth Amendment given the interests of "national self-protection reasonably requiring one entering the country to identify himself as entitled to come in, and his belongings as effects which may lawfully be brought in." Carroll v. United States, 267 U.S. 132, 154, 45 S.Ct. 280, 285, 69 L.Ed. 543 (1925). Individual travelers also may be singled out on "reasonable suspicion" and briefly held for further investigation. Cf. Terry v. Ohio, 392 U.S. 1, 88 S.Ct. 1868, 20 L.Ed.2d 889 (1968). At some point, however, further investigation involves such severe intrusions on the values the Fourth Amendment protects that more stringent safeguards are required. For example, the length and nature of a detention may, at least when conducted for criminal-investigative purposes, ripen into something approximating a full-scale custodial arrest—indeed, the arrestee, unlike the detainee in cases such as this, is at least given such basic rights as a telephone call, *Miranda* warnings, a bed, a prompt hearing before the nearest federal magistrate, an appointed attorney, and consideration of bail. In addition, border detentions may involve the use of such highly intrusive investigative techniques as body-cavity searches, x-ray searches, and stomach-pumping.

I believe that detentions and searches falling into these more intrusive categories are presumptively "reasonable" within the meaning of the Fourth Amendment only if authorized by a judicial officer. * * *

We have, to be sure, held that executive officials need not obtain prior judicial authorization where exigent circumstances would make such authorization impractical and counterproductive. In so holding, however, we have reaffirmed the general rule that "the police must, whenever practicable, obtain advance judicial approval of searches and seizures through the warrant procedure." * * *

The Government contends, however, that because investigative detentions of the sort that occurred in this case need not be supported by probable cause, no warrant is required given the phraseology of the Fourth Amendment's Warrant Clause. * * * Even assuming that border detentions and searches that become lengthy and highly intrusive need not be supported by probable cause, * * * this reasoning runs squarely contrary to the Court's administrative-warrant cases. * * *

Something has gone fundamentally awry in our constitutional jurisprudence when a neutral and detached magistrate's authorization is required before the authorities may inspect "the plumbing, heating, ventilation, gas, and electrical systems" in a person's home, investigate the back rooms of his workplace, or poke through the charred remains of his gutted garage, but *not* before they may hold him in indefinite involuntary isolation at the nation's border to investigate whether he might be engaged in criminal wrongdoing. * * *

The Court argues, however, that the length and "discomfort" of de Hernandez' detention "resulted *solely* from the method by which she chose to smuggle illicit drugs into this country," and it speculates that only her " 'heroic' "efforts prevented the detention from being brief and to the point. Although we now know that de Hernandez was indeed guilty of smuggling drugs internally, such *post hoc* rationalizations have no place in our Fourth Amendment jurisprudence, which demands that we "prevent hindsight from coloring the evaluation of the reasonableness of a search or seizure." At the time the authorities simply had, at most, a reasonable suspicion that de Hernandez might be engaged in such smuggling. * * * [W]ith all respect to the Court, it is not " 'unrealistic second-guessing' " to predict that an innocent traveler, locked away in *incommunicado* detention in unfamiliar surroundings in a foreign land, might well be so frightened and exhausted as to be unable so to "cooperate" with the authorities.

* * *

Finally, I disagree with JUSTICE STEVENS that de Hernandez' alternative "choice" of submitting to abdominal x-irradiation at the discretion of customs officials made this detention "justified." * * * [T]he crux of my disagreement is this: We have learned in our lifetimes, time and again, the inherent dangers that result from coupling unchecked "law enforcement" discretion with the tools of medical technology. * * * This should be so whether the intrusion is by incision, by stomach-pumping, or by exposure to x-irradiation. Because no exigent circumstances prevented the authorities from seeking a magistrate's authorization so to probe de Hernandez' abdominal cavity, the proffered alternative "choice" of a warrantless x-ray was just as impermissible as the 27-hour detention that actually occurred.

II

I believe that de Hernandez' detention violated the Fourth Amendment for an additional reason: it was not supported by probable cause. In the domestic context, a detention of the sort that occurred here would be permissible only if there were probable cause at the outset.

To be sure, it is commonly asserted that as a result of the Fourth Amendment's "border exception" there is no requirement of probable cause for such investigations. But the justifications for the border exception necessarily limit its breadth. The exception derives from the unquestioned and paramount interest in "national self-protection reasonably requiring one entering the country to identify himself as entitled to come in, and his belongings as effects which may be lawfully brought in." * * * Subject only to the other applicable guarantees of the Bill of Rights, this interest in "national self-protection" is plenary. Thus, as the Court notes, a suspected tuberculosis carrier may be detained at the border for medical testing and treatment as a condition of entry. As a condition of entry, the traveler may be subjected to exhaustive processing and examinations, and his belongings may be scrutinized with exacting care. I have no doubt as well that, *as a* *condition of entry,* travelers in appropriate circumstances may be required to excrete their bodily wastes for further scrutiny and to submit to diagnostic x-rays.

Contrary to the Court's reasoning, however, the Government in carrying out such immigration and customs functions does not simply have the two stark alternatives of either forcing a traveler to submit to such procedures or allowing him to "pass . . . into the interior." There is a third alternative: to instruct the traveler who refuses to submit to burdensome but reasonable conditions of entry that he is free to turn around and leave the country. In fact, I believe that the "reasonableness" of any burdensome requirement for entry is necessarily conditioned on the potential entrant's freedom to leave the country if he objects to that requirement. Surely the Government's manifest interest in preventing potentially excludable individuals carrying potential contraband from crossing our borders is fully vindicated if those individuals voluntarily decided not to cross the borders.

* * * If the traveler does not wish to consent to prolonged detentions or intrusive examinations, the nation's customs and immigration interests are fully served by sending the traveler on his way elsewhere. If the authorities nevertheless propose to detain the traveler for purposes of subjecting him to criminal investigation and possible arrest and punishment, they may do so only pursuant to constitutional safeguards applicable to everyone else in the country. Chief among those safeguards is the requirement that, except in limited circumstances not present here, custodial detentions occur only on probable cause. * * * That standard obviously is not met, and was not met here, simply by courier profiles, "common rumor or report, suspicion, or even 'strong reason to suspect.'" Because the contraband in this case was the fruit of the authorities' indefinite detention of Rosa de Hernandez without probable cause or a warrant, I would affirm the judgment of the Court of Appeals for the Ninth Circuit reversing her conviction.

2. BORDER-RELATED ENFORCEMENT ACTIVITY

Law enforcement activity conducted in the interior of the country is arguably less directly related to the federal government's interest in protecting the security of its borders. It also may intrude upon privacy and other concerns more significantly than activity occurring at the border. For these and other reasons, the Supreme Court has treated such law enforcement activity differently than law enforcement activity at the border or its functional equivalent. Most of the Court's case law, including the principal case in this subsection, deals with traffic control operations.

In United States v. Ortiz, 422 U.S. 891, 95 S.Ct. 2585, 45 L.Ed.2d 623 (1975), Border Patrol officers stopped Ortiz' automobile at a fixed checkpoint at San Clemente, California; the checkpoint is described and discussed in the principal case in this subsection. A search of the vehicle's trunk revealed three aliens and Ortiz was convicted of knowingly transporting illegal aliens. A unanimous Supreme Court invalidated the search of the automobile because it was conducted without probable cause to believe illegal aliens would be found. The government urged the probable cause requirement be found inapplicable for two reasons. First, careful selection of locations for checkpoints by high-level Border Patrol officials limited officers' discretion in stopping and searching cars. Second, checkpoints provided visible signs of officers' authority and demonstrated to stopped motorists that others were being stopped and searched as well; motorists were, as a result, less likely to be frightened or annoyed by the search and consequently the search was less intrusive upon privacy than other law enforcement activities. Rejecting the government's argument, the Court stressed that a search of a car, even under the conditions at issue, remains a substantial invasion of privacy. Moreover, only a small portion of cars passing through checkpoints were searched; throughout the system, less than 3% were examined. Officers manning the checkpoints exercised a degree of discretion in deciding which cars to search. "This degree of discretion," the Court observed, "is not consistent with the Fourth Amendment."

Evidence showed inspections of cars for illegal aliens typically included examinations of the trunk, under the hood, and beneath the chassis. Enclosed portions of trucks, campers and similar vehicles were also examined. But inspections sometimes became more rigorous. The Court noted in one case previously before it officers removed a back seat cushion because of reports aliens were found seated upright behind seats from which the springs had been removed. Not every aspect of the routine "inspections" necessarily constitutes a "search" for which probable cause is required, the Court commented. It found no occasion in the case "to define the exact limits of an automobile 'search.' "

United States v. Martinez–Fuerte

Supreme Court of the United States, 1976.
428 U.S. 543, 96 S.Ct. 3074, 49 L.Ed.2d 1116.

■ MR. JUSTICE POWELL delivered the opinion of the Court.

These cases involve criminal prosecutions for offenses relating to the transportation of illegal Mexican aliens. Each defendant was arrested at a permanent checkpoint operated by the Border Patrol away from the international border with Mexico, and each sought the exclusion of certain evidence on the ground that the operation of the checkpoint was incompatible with the Fourth Amendment. In each instance whether the Fourth Amendment was violated turns primarily on whether a vehicle may be stopped at a fixed checkpoint for brief questioning of its occupants even though there is no reason to believe the particular vehicle contains illegal aliens. We reserved this question last Term in United States v. Ortiz, 422 U.S. 891, 897 n. 3, 95 S.Ct. 2585, 2589, 45 L.Ed.2d 623 (1975). We hold today that such stops are consistent with the Fourth Amendment. We also hold that the operation of a fixed checkpoint need not be authorized in advance by a judicial warrant.

I

A

The respondents in No. 74–1560 are defendants in three separate prosecutions resulting from arrests made on three different occasions at the permanent immigration checkpoint on Interstate 5 near San Clemente, Cal. Interstate 5 is the principal highway between San Diego and Los Angeles, and the San Clemente checkpoint is 66 road miles north of the Mexican border. We previously have described the checkpoint as follows:

" 'Approximately one mile south of the checkpoint is a large black on yellow sign with flashing yellow lights over the highway stating "ALL VEHICLES, STOP AHEAD, 1 MILE." Three quarters of a mile further north are two black on yellow signs suspended over the highway with flashing lights stating "WATCH FOR BRAKE LIGHTS." At the checkpoint, which is also the location of a State of California weighing station, are two large signs with flashing red lights suspended over the highway. These signs each state "STOP HERE—U.S. OFFI-CERS." Placed on the highway are a number of orange traffic cones funneling traffic into two lanes where a Border Patrol agent in full dress uniform, standing behind a white on red "STOP" sign checks traffic. Blocking traffic in the unused lanes are official U.S. Border Patrol vehicles with flashing red lights. In addition, there is a permanent building which houses the Border Patrol office and temporary detention facilities. There are also floodlights for nighttime operation.' "

The "point" agent standing between the two lanes of traffic visually screens all northbound vehicles, which the checkpoint brings to a virtual, if not a complete, halt. Most motorists are allowed to resume their progress without any oral inquiry or close visual examination. In a relatively small number of cases the "point" agent will conclude that further inquiry is in order. He directs these cars to a secondary inspection area, where their occupants are asked about their citizenship and immigration status. The Government informs us that at San Clemente the average length of an investigation in the secondary inspection area is three to five minutes. A direction to stop in the secondary inspection area could be based on something suspicious about a particular car passing through the checkpoint, but the Government concedes that [the stop] at issue in No. 74–1560 was [not] based on any articulable suspicion. During the period when these stops were made, the checkpoint was operating under a magistrate's "warrant of inspection," which authorized the Border Patrol to conduct a routine-stop operation at the San Clemente location.

We turn now to the particulars of the stops involved in No. 74–1560, and the procedural history of the case. Respondent Amado Martinez-Fuerte approached the checkpoint driving a vehicle containing two female passengers. The women were illegal Mexican aliens who had entered the United States at the San Ysidro port of entry by using false papers and rendezvoused with Martinez-Fuerte in San Diego to be transported northward. At the checkpoint their car was directed to the secondary inspection area. Martinez-Fuerte produced documents showing him to be a lawful resident alien, but his passengers admitted being present in the country unlawfully. He was charged, *inter alia*, with two counts of illegally transporting aliens in violation of 8 U.S.C. § 1324(a)(2). He moved before trial to suppress all evidence stemming from the stop on the ground that the operation of the checkpoint was in violation of the Fourth Amendment. The motion to suppress was denied, and he was convicted on both counts after a jury trial.

* * *

Martinez-Fuerte appealed his conviction * * *. The Court of Appeals held, with one judge dissenting, that [the stop] violated the Fourth Amendment, concluding that a stop for inquiry is constitutional only if the Border Patrol reasonably suspects the presence of illegal aliens on the basis of articulable facts. It reversed Martinez-Fuerte's conviction * * *. We reverse and remand.

B

Petitioner in No. 75–5387, Rodolfo Sifuentes, was arrested at the permanent immigration checkpoint on U.S. Highway 77 near Sarita, Tex. Highway 77 originates in Brownsville, and it is one of the two major highways running north from the lower Rio Grande valley. The Sarita checkpoint is about 90 miles north of Brownsville, and 65–90 miles from the nearest points of the Mexican border. The physical arrangement of the checkpoint resembles generally that at San Clemente, but the checkpoint is operated differently in that the officers customarily stop all northbound motorists for a brief inquiry. Motorists whom the officers recognize as local inhabitants, however, are waved through the checkpoint without inquiry. Unlike the San Clemente checkpoint the Sarita operation was conducted without a judicial warrant.

Sifuentes drove up to the checkpoint without any visible passengers. When an agent approached the vehicle, however, he observed four passengers, one in the front seat and the other three in the rear, slumped down in the seats. Questioning revealed that each passenger was an illegal alien, although Sifuentes was a United States citizen. The aliens had met Sifuentes in the United States, by prearrangement, after swimming across the Rio Grande.

Sifuentes was indicted on four counts of illegally transporting aliens. He moved on Fourth Amendment grounds to suppress the evidence derived from the stop. The motion was denied and he was convicted after a jury trial. Sifuentes renewed his Fourth Amendment argument on appeal, contending primarily that stops made without reason to believe a car is transporting aliens illegally are unconstitutional. The United States Court of Appeals for the Fifth Circuit affirmed the conviction, * * * rul[ing] that routine checkpoint stops are consistent with the Fourth Amendment. We affirm.

II

The Courts of Appeals for the Ninth and the Fifth Circuits are in conflict on the constitutionality of a law enforcement technique considered important by those charged with policing the Nation's borders. Before turning to the constitutional question, we examine the context in which it arises.

A

It has been national policy for many years to limit immigration into the United States. Since July 1, 1968, the annual quota for immigrants from all independent countries of the Western Hemisphere, including Mexico, has been 120,000 persons. Many more aliens than can be accommodated under the quota want to live and work in the United States. Consequently, large numbers of aliens seek illegally to enter or to remain in the United States. We noted last Term that "[e]stimates of the number of illegal immigrants [already] in the United States vary widely. A conservative estimate in 1972 produced a figure of about one million, but the Immigration and Naturalization Service now suggests there may be as many as 10 or 12 million aliens illegally in the country." United States v. Brignoni-Ponce, 422 U.S. 873, 878, 95 S.Ct. 2574, 2578, 45 L.Ed.2d 607 (1975) (footnote omitted). It is estimated that 85% of the illegal immigrants are from Mexico, drawn by the fact that economic opportunities are significantly greater in the United States than they are in Mexico.

Interdicting the flow of illegal entrants from Mexico poses formidable law enforcement problems. The principal problem arises from surreptitious entries. The United States shares a border with Mexico that is almost 2,000 miles long, and much of the border area is uninhabited desert or thinly populated arid land. Although the Border Patrol maintains personnel, electronic equipment, and fences along portions of the border, it remains relatively easy for individuals to enter the United States without detection. It also is possible for an alien to enter unlawfully at a port of entry by the use of falsified papers or to enter lawfully but violate restrictions of entry in an effort to remain in the country unlawfully. Once within the country, the aliens seek to travel inland to areas where employment is believed to be available, frequently meeting by prearrangement with friends or professional smugglers who transport them in private vehicles.

The Border Patrol conducts three kinds of inland traffic-checking operations in an effort to minimize illegal immigration. Permanent checkpoints, such as those at San Clemente and Sarita, are maintained at or near intersections of important roads leading away from the border. They operate on a coordinated basis designed to avoid circumvention by smugglers and others who transport the illegal aliens. Temporary checkpoints, which operate like permanent ones, occasionally are established in other strategic locations. Finally, roving patrols are maintained to supplement the checkpoint system. See Almeida-Sanchez v. United States, 413 U.S. 266, 268, 93 S.Ct. 2535, 2537, 37 L.Ed.2d 596 (1973). In fiscal 1973, 175,511 deportable aliens were apprehended throughout the Nation by "line watch" agents stationed at the border itself. Traffic-checking operations in the interior apprehended approximately 55,300 more deportable aliens. Most of the traffic-checking apprehensions were at checkpoints, though precise figures are not available.

B

We are concerned here with permanent checkpoints, the locations of which are chosen on the basis of a number of factors. The Border Patrol believes that to assure effectiveness, a checkpoint must be (i) distant enough from the border to avoid interference with traffic in populated areas near the border, (ii) close to the confluence of two or more significant roads leading away from the border, (iii) situated in terrain that restricts vehicle passage around the checkpoint, (iv) on a stretch of highway compatible with safe operation, and (v) beyond the 25 mile zone in which "border passes" are valid.

The record in No. 74–1560 provides a rather complete picture of the effectiveness of the San Clemente checkpoint. Approximately 10 million cars pass the checkpoint location each year, although the checkpoint actually is in operation only about 70% of the time. In calendar year 1973, approximately 17,000 illegal aliens were apprehended there. During an eight-day period in 1974 that included the arrests involved in No. 74–1560, roughly 146,000 vehicles passed through the checkpoint during 124⅙ hours of operation. Of these, 820 vehicles were referred to the secondary inspection area, where Border Patrol agents found 725 deportable aliens in 171 vehicles. In all but two cases, the aliens were discovered without a conventional search of the vehicle. A similar rate of apprehensions throughout the year would have resulted in an annual total of over 33,000, although the Government contends that many illegal aliens pass through the checkpoint undetected. * * *

IV

It is agreed that checkpoint stops are "seizures" within the meaning of the Fourth Amendment. The defendants contend primarily that the routine stopping of vehicles at a checkpoint is invalid because *Brignoni–Ponce* must be read as proscribing any stops in the absence of reasonable suspicion. Sifuentes alternatively contends in No. 75–5387 that routine checkpoint stops are permissible only when the practice has the advance judicial authorization of a warrant. There was a warrant authorizing the stops at San Clemente but none at Sarita. As we reach the issue of a warrant requirement only if reasonable suspicion is not required, we turn first to whether reasonable suspicion is a prerequisite to a valid stop, a question to be resolved by balancing the interests at stake.

A

Our previous cases have recognized that maintenance of a traffic-checking program in the interior is necessary because the flow of illegal aliens cannot be controlled effectively at the border. We note here only the substantiality of the public interest in the practice of routine stops for inquiry at permanent checkpoints, a practice which the Government identifies as the most important of the traffic-checking operations. These checkpoints are located on important highways; in their absence such highways would offer illegal aliens a quick and safe route into the interior. Routine checkpoint inquiries apprehend many smugglers and illegal aliens who succumb to the lure of such highways. And the prospect of such inquiries forces others onto less efficient roads that are less heavily traveled, slowing their movement and making them more vulnerable to detection by roving patrols.

A requirement that stops on major routes inland always be based on reasonable suspicion would be impractical because the flow of traffic tends to be too heavy to allow the particularized study of a given car that would enable it to be identified as a possible carrier of illegal aliens. In particular, such a requirement would largely eliminate any deterrent to the conduct of well-disguised smuggling operations, even though smugglers are known to use these highways regularly.

B

While the need to make routine checkpoint stops is great, the consequent intrusion on Fourth Amendment interests is quite limited. The stop does intrude to a limited extent on motorists' right to "free passage without interruption," and arguably on their right to personal security. But it involves only a brief detention of travelers during which

> " '[a]ll that is required of the vehicle's occupants is a response to a brief question or two and possibly the production of a document evidencing a right to be in the United States.' "

Neither the vehicle nor its occupants are searched, and visual inspection of the vehicle is limited to what can be seen without a search. This objective intrusion—the stop itself, the questioning, and the visual inspection—also existed in roving-patrol stops. But we view checkpoint stops in a different light because the subjective intrusion—the generating of concern or even fright on the part of lawful travelers—is appreciably less in the case of a checkpoint stop. * * *

In *Brignoni–Ponce,* we recognized that Fourth Amendment analysis in this context also must take into account the overall degree of interference with legitimate traffic. We concluded there that random roving-patrol stops could not be tolerated because they "would subject the residents of * * * [border] areas to potentially unlimited interference with their use of the highways, solely at the discretion of Border Patrol officers. * * * [They] could stop motorists at random for questioning, day or night, anywhere within 100 air miles of the 2,000 mile border, on a city street, a busy highway, or a desert road * * *." There also was a grave danger that such unreviewable discretion would be abused by some officers in the field.

Routine checkpoint stops do not intrude similarly on the motoring public. First, the potential interference with legitimate traffic is minimal. Motorists using these highways are not taken by surprise as they know, or may obtain knowledge of, the location of the checkpoints and will not be stopped elsewhere. Second, checkpoint operations both appear to and actually involve less discretionary enforcement activity. The regularized manner in which established checkpoints are operated is visible evidence, reassuring to lawabiding motorists, that the stops are duly authorized and believed to serve the public interest. The location of a fixed checkpoint is not chosen by officers in the field, but by officials responsible for making overall decisions as to the most effective allocation of limited enforcement resources. We may assume that such officials will be unlikely to locate a checkpoint where it bears arbitrarily or oppressively on motorists as a class. And since field officers may stop only those cars passing the checkpoint, there is less room for abusive or harassing stops of individuals than there was in the case of roving-patrol stops. Moreover, a claim that a particular exercise of discretion in locating or operating a checkpoint is unreasonable is subject to post-stop judicial review.

The defendants arrested at the San Clemente checkpoint suggest that its operation involves a significant extra element of intrusiveness in that only a small percentage of cars are referred to the secondary inspection area, thereby "stigmatizing" those diverted and reducing the assurances provided by equal treatment of all motorists. We think defendants overstate the consequences. Referrals are made for the sole purpose of conducting a routine and limited inquiry into residence status that cannot feasibly be made of every motorist where the traffic is heavy. The objective intrusion of the stop and inquiry thus remains minimal. Selective referral may involve some annoyance, but it remains true that the stops should not be frightening or offensive because of their public and relatively routine nature. Moreover, selective referrals—rather than questioning the occupants of every car—tend to advance some Fourth Amendment interests by minimizing the intrusion on the general motoring public.

C

The defendants note correctly that to accommodate public and private interests some quantum of individualized suspicion is usually a prerequisite to a constitutional search or seizure. But the Fourth Amendment imposes no irreducible requirement of such suspicion. * * *

[H]ere * * * we deal neither with searches nor with the sanctity of private dwellings, ordinarily afforded the most stringent Fourth Amendment protection. * * * [O]ne's expectation of privacy in an automobile and of freedom in its operation are significantly different from the traditional expectation of privacy and freedom in one's residence. And the reasonableness of the procedures followed in making these checkpoint stops makes the resulting intrusion on the interests of motorists minimal. On the other hand, the purpose of the stops is legitimate and in the public interest, and the need for this enforcement technique is demonstrated by the records in the cases before us. Accordingly, we hold that the stops and questioning at issue may be made in the absence of any individualized suspicion at reasonably located checkpoints.[13]

---

13. [W]e deem the argument by the defendants in No. 74–1560 * * * to raise the question whether, even though a warrant is not required, it is unreasonable to locate a checkpoint at San Clemente.

We answer this question in the negative. As indicated above, the choice of checkpoint locations is an administrative decision that must be left largely within the discretion of the Border Patrol. We think the decision to locate a checkpoint at San Clemente was reasonable. The location meets the criteria prescribed by the Border Patrol to assure effectiveness and the evidence supports the view that the needs of law enforcement are furthered by this location. The absolute number of apprehensions at the checkpoint is high confirming Border Patrol judgment that significant numbers of illegal aliens regularly use Interstate 5 at this point. Also, San Clemente was selected as the location where traffic is lightest between San Diego and Los Angeles, thereby minimizing interference with legitimate traffic.

No question has been raised about the reasonableness of the location of the Sarita checkpoint.

We further believe that it is constitutional to refer motorists selectively to the secondary inspection area at the San Clemente checkpoint on the basis of criteria that would not sustain a roving-patrol stop. Thus, even if it be assumed that such referrals are made largely on the basis of apparent Mexican ancestry, we perceive no constitutional violation. As the intrusion here is sufficiently minimal that no particularized reason need exist to justify it, we think it follows that the Border Patrol officers must have wide discretion in selecting the motorists to be diverted for the brief questioning involved.

V

Sifuentes' alternative argument is that routine stops at a checkpoint are permissible only if a warrant has given judicial authorization to the particular checkpoint location and the practice of routine stops. A warrant requirement in these circumstances draws some support from [Camara v. Municipal Court, 387 U.S. 523, 87 S.Ct. 1727, 18 L.Ed.2d 930 (1967) (discussed in part B of this chapter)], where the Court held that, absent consent, an "area" warrant was required to make a building code inspection, even though the search could be conducted absent cause to believe that there were violations in the building searched.

We do not think, however, that *Camara* is an apt model. It involved the search of private residences, for which a warrant traditionally has been required. * * * [T]he strong Fourth Amendment interests that justify the warrant requirement in that context are absent here. The degree of intrusion upon privacy that may be occasioned by a search of a house hardly can be compared with the minor interference with privacy resulting from the mere stop for questioning as to residence. Moreover, the warrant requirement in *Camara* served specific Fourth Amendment interests to which a warrant requirement here would make little contribution. The Court there said:

> "[W]hen [an] inspector [without a warrant] demands entry, the occupant has no way of knowing whether enforcement of the municipal code involved requires inspection of his premises, no way of knowing the lawful limits of the inspector's power to search, and no way of knowing whether the inspector himself is acting under proper authorization."

A warrant provided assurance to the occupant on these scores. We believe that the visible manifestations of the field officers' authority at a checkpoint provide substantially the same assurances in this case.

Other purposes served by the requirement of a warrant also are inapplicable here. One such purpose is to prevent hindsight from coloring the evaluation of the reasonableness of a search or seizure. The reasonableness of checkpoint stops, however, turns on factors such as the location and method of operation of the checkpoint, factors that are not susceptible to the distortion of hindsight, and therefore will be open to post-stop review notwithstanding the absence of a warrant. Another purpose for a warrant requirement is to substitute the judgment of the magistrate for that of the searching or seizing officer. But the need for this is reduced when the decision to "seize" is not entirely in the hands of the officer in the field, and deference is to be given to the administrative decisions of higher ranking officials.

VI

In summary, we hold that stops for brief questioning routinely conducted at permanent checkpoints are consistent with the Fourth Amendment and need not be authorized by warrant. The principal protection of Fourth Amendment rights at checkpoints lies in appropriate limitations on the scope of the stop. We have held that checkpoint searches are constitutional only if justified by consent or probable cause to search. United States v. Ortiz, 422 U.S. 891, 95 S.Ct. 2585, 45 L.Ed.2d 623 (1975). And our holding today is limited to the type of stops described in this opinion. "[A]ny further detention must be based on consent or probable cause." United States v. Brignoni–Ponce, supra, at 882, 95 S.Ct., at 2580. None of the defendants in these cases argues that the stopping officers exceeded these limitations. Consequently, we affirm the judgment of the Court of Appeals for the Fifth Circuit, which had affirmed the conviction of Sifuentes. We reverse the judgment of the Court of Appeals for the Ninth Circuit and remand the case with directions to affirm the conviction of Martinez-Fuerte * * *.

It is so ordered.

■ MR. JUSTICE BRENNAN, with whom MR. JUSTICE MARSHALL joins, dissenting.

* * *

The Court assumes, and I certainly agree, that persons stopped at fixed checkpoints, whether or not referred to a secondary detention area, are "seized" within the meaning of the Fourth Amendment. Moreover, since the vehicle and its occupants are subjected to a "visual inspection," the intrusion clearly exceeds mere physical restraint, for officers are able to see more in a stopped vehicle than in vehicles traveling at normal speeds down the highway. As the Court concedes, the checkpoint stop involves essentially the same intrusions as a roving-patrol stop, yet the Court provides no principled basis for distinguishing checkpoint stops.

Certainly that basis is not provided in the Court's reasoning that the subjective intrusion here is appreciably less than in the case of a stop by a roving patrol. *Brignoni–Ponce* nowhere bases the requirement of reasonable suspicion upon the subjective nature of the intrusion. In any event, the subjective aspects of checkpoint stops, even if different from the subjective aspects of roving-patrol stops, just as much require some principled restraint on law enforcement conduct. The motorist whose conduct has been nothing but innocent—and this is overwhelmingly the case—surely resents his own detention and inspection. And checkpoints, unlike roving stops, detain thousands of motorists, a dragnet-like procedure offensive to the sensibilities of free citizens. Also, the delay occasioned by stopping hundreds of vehicles on a busy highway is particularly irritating.

In addition to overlooking these dimensions of subjective intrusion, the Court, without explanation, also ignores one major source of vexation. In abandoning any requirement of a minimum of reasonable suspicion, or even articulable suspicion, the Court in every practical sense renders meaningless, as applied to checkpoint stops, the *Brignoni–Ponce* holding that "standing alone [Mexican appearance] does not justify stopping all Mexican-Americans to ask if they are aliens." Since the objective is almost entirely the Mexican illegally in the country, checkpoint officials, uninhibited by any objective standards and therefore free to stop any or all motorists without explanation or excuse, wholly on whim, will perforce target motorists of Mexican appearance. The process will then inescapably discriminate against citizens of Mexican ancestry and Mexican aliens lawfully in this country for no other reason than that they unavoidably possess the same "suspicious" physical and grooming characteristics of illegal Mexican aliens.

* * *

The Court argues * * * that practicalities necessitate [upholding the stops]. * * *

As an initial matter, whatever force this argument may have, it cannot apply to the secondary detentions that occurred in No. 74–1560. Once a vehicle has been slowed and observed at a checkpoint, ample opportunity exists to formulate the reasonable suspicion which, if it actually exists, would justify further detention. * * *

The Court's rationale is also not persuasive because several of the factors upon which officers may rely in establishing reasonable suspicion are readily ascertainable, regardless of the flow of traffic. * * *

Finally, the Court's argument fails for more basic reasons. There is no principle in the jurisprudence of fundamental rights which permits constitutional limitations to be dispensed with merely because they cannot be conveniently satisfied. * * *

NOTES: "ROVING" PATROLS

1. The Supreme Court first addressed the effect of Fourth Amendment considerations upon the technique often described as conducting "roving" border patrols in Almeida–Sanchez v. United States, 413 U.S. 266, 93 S.Ct. 2535, 37 L.Ed.2d 596 (1973). Almeida–Sanchez's car was stopped and searched while traveling on highway 78 in California. Highway 78 runs east-west and although it meanders it does not touch the border; the point of the stop was 25 air miles north of the border. The Immigration and Nationality Act purports to authorize warrantless searches of automobiles or other conveyances for illegally entered aliens "within a reasonable distance from any external boundary of the United States," as authorized by regulations promulgated by the Attorney General. "Reasonable distance" was defined in such regulations as within 100 air miles from any external boundary. 8 C.F.R. § 287.1. Rejecting the argument that extraordinary needs of border enforcement justify searches such as that in the case, the Court held that the absence of probable cause or consent rendered the search unreasonable.

2. In United States v. Brignoni–Ponce, 422 U.S. 873, 95 S.Ct. 2574, 45 L.Ed.2d 607 (1975), the Court returned to roving patrol stops. Border Patrol officers stopped Brignoni–Ponce's car on Interstate Highway 5 in California south of San Clemente. The Government defended the stop on the ground the officers believed the three occupants of the vehicle to be of Mexican decent. When questioned, the occupants acknowledged the two passengers were aliens who had entered the country illegally.

At Brignoni–Ponce's trial for transportation of illegally entered aliens, evidence from the stop and questioning of the occupants was admitted over defense objection. The Supreme Court reversed the resulting conviction. It acknowledged the important need to enforce border security created special problems, but it rejected the argument that this need permitted law enforcement officers to stop motorists at random within 100 air miles of the border. Law enforcement needs are sufficiently met, the Court concluded, by officers' right to conduct brief field stops on reasonable suspicion. On the facts before it, however, the Government failed to show the officers harbored reasonable suspicion that Brignoni–Ponce's vehicle contained illegally entered aliens. In response to the Government's contention that the occupants' apparent Mexican ancestry supported the stop, the Court explained:

> [T]his factor alone would justify neither a reasonable belief that they were aliens, nor a reasonable belief that the car concealed other aliens who were illegally in the country. Large numbers of native-born and naturalized citizens have the physical characteristics identified with Mexican ancestry, and even in the border area a relatively small proportion of them are aliens. The likelihood that any given person of Mexican ancestry is an alien is high enough to make Mexican appearance a relevant factor, but standing alone it does not justify stopping all Mexican-Americans to ask if they are aliens.

422 U.S. at 886–87, 95 S.Ct. at 2583, 45 L.Ed.2d at 619–20. As to what other factors might contribute to the development of reasonable suspicion, the Court offered:

> Officers may consider the characteristics of the area in which they encounter a vehicle. Its proximity to the border, the usual patterns of traffic on the particular road, and previous experience with alien traffic are all relevant. They may also consider information about recent illegal border crossings in the area. The driver's behavior may be relevant, as erratic driving or obvious attempts to evade officers can support a reasonable suspicion. Aspects of the vehicle itself may justify suspicion. For instance, officers say that certain station wagons, with large compartments for fold-down seats or spare tires, are frequently used for transporting concealed aliens. The vehicle may appear to be heavily loaded, it may have an extraordinary number of passengers, or the officers may observe persons trying to hide. The Government also points out that trained officers can recognize the characteristic appearance of persons who live in Mexico, relying on such factors as the mode of dress and haircut. In all situations the officer is entitled to assess the facts in light of his experience in detecting illegal entry and smuggling.

422 U.S. at 884–85, 95 S.Ct. at 2582, 45 L.Ed.2d at 618–19. Where the factors amount to reasonable suspicion, the Court has held that a stop of a vehicle and questioning of the driver is permissible. United States v. Cortez, 449 U.S. 411, 101 S.Ct. 690, 66 L.Ed.2d 621 (1981).

F.   Extraordinarily Intrusive Searches

In all of the situations covered in the preceding parts of this chapter, attention has focused on whether or to what extent the benchmark requirements of probable cause and a traditional search warrant should be abandoned or diluted. But in other situations, it is at least arguable that those requirements should not only be retained but also tightened so as to impose greater limitations on police ability to search than are imposed in standard situations. One of those situations—surgical removal of evidence from the suspect's body—is covered in this section.

Winston v. Lee

Supreme Court of the United States, 1985.
470 U.S. 753, 105 S.Ct. 1611, 84 L.Ed.2d 662.

■ JUSTICE BRENNAN delivered the opinion of the Court.

* * *

I

A

At approximately 1 a.m. on July 18, 1982, Ralph E. Watkinson was closing his shop for the night. As he was locking the door, he observed someone armed with a gun coming toward him from across the street. Watkinson was also armed and when he drew his gun, the other person told him to freeze. Watkinson then fired at the other person, who returned his fire. Watkinson was hit in the legs, while the other individual, who appeared to be wounded in his left side, ran from the scene. The police arrived on the scene shortly thereafter, and Watkinson was taken by ambulance to the emergency room of the Medical College of Virginia (MCV) Hospital.

Approximately 20 minutes later, police officers responding to another call found respondent eight blocks from where the earlier shooting occurred. Respondent was suffering from a gunshot wound to his left chest area and told the police that he had been shot when two individuals attempted to rob him. An ambulance took respondent to the MCV Hospital. Watkinson was still in the MCV emergency room and, when respondent entered that room, said "[t]hat's the man that shot me." After an investigation, the police decided that respondent's story of having been himself the victim of a robbery was untrue and charged respondent with attempted robbery, malicious wounding, and two counts of using a firearm in the commission of a felony.

B

The Commonwealth shortly thereafter moved in state court for an order directing respondent to undergo surgery to remove an object thought to be a bullet lodged under his left collarbone. The court conducted several evidentiary hearings on the motion. At the first hearing, the Commonwealth's expert testified that the surgical procedure would take 45 minutes and would involve a three to four percent chance of temporary nerve damage, a one percent chance of permanent nerve damage, and a one-tenth of one percent chance of death. At the second hearing, the expert testified that on reexamination of respondent, he discovered that the bullet was not "back inside close to the nerves and arteries," as he originally had thought. Instead, he now believed the bullet to be located "just beneath the skin." He testified that the surgery would require an incision of only one and one-half centimeters (slightly more than one-half inch), could be performed under local anesthesia, and would result in "no danger on the basis that there's no general anesthesia employed."

The state trial judge granted the motion to compel surgery. Respondent petitioned the Virginia Supreme Court for a writ of prohibition and/or a writ of habeas corpus, both of which were denied. Respondent then brought an action in the United States District Court for the Eastern District of Virginia to enjoin the pending operation on Fourth Amendment grounds. The court refused to issue a preliminary injunction, holding that respondent's cause had little likelihood of success on the merits.

On October 18, 1982, just before the surgery was scheduled, the surgeon ordered that X rays be taken of respondent's chest. The X rays revealed that the bullet was in fact lodged two and one-half to three centimeters (approximately one inch) deep in muscular tissue in respondent's chest, substantially deeper than had been thought when the state court granted the motion to compel surgery. The surgeon now believed that a general anesthetic would be desirable for medical reasons.

Respondent moved the state trial court for a rehearing based on the new evidence. After holding an evidentiary hearing, the state trial court denied the rehearing and the Virginia Supreme Court affirmed. Respondent then returned to federal court, where he moved to alter or amend the judgment previously entered against him. After an evidentiary hearing, the District Court enjoined the threatened surgery. A divided panel of the Court of Appeals for the Fourth Circuit affirmed. We granted certiorari to consider whether a State may consistently with the Fourth Amendment compel a suspect to undergo surgery of this kind in a search for evidence of a crime.

II

The Fourth Amendment protects "expectations of privacy," see Katz v. United States, 389 U.S. 347, 88 S.Ct. 507, 19 L.Ed.2d 576 (1967)—the individual's legitimate expectations that in certain places and at certain times he has "the right to be let alone—the most comprehensive of rights and the right most valued by civilized men." Olmstead v. United States, 277 U.S. 438, 478, 48 S.Ct. 564, 572, 72 L.Ed. 944 (1928) (Brandeis, J., dissenting). Putting to one side the procedural protections of the warrant requirement, the Fourth Amendment generally protects the "security" of "persons, houses, papers, and effects" against official intrusions up to the point where the community's need for evidence surmounts a specified standard, ordinarily "probable cause." Beyond this point, it is ordinarily justifiable for the community to demand that the individual give up some part of his interest in privacy and security to advance the community's vital interests in law enforcement; such a search is generally "reasonable" in the Amendment's terms.

A compelled surgical intrusion into an individual's body for evidence, however, implicates expectations of privacy and security of such magnitude that the intrusion may be "unreasonable" even if likely to produce evidence of a crime. In Schmerber v. California, 384 U.S. 757, 86 S.Ct. 1826, 16 L.Ed.2d 908 (1966), we addressed a claim that the State had breached the Fourth Amendment's protection of the "right of the people to be secure in their *persons* . . . against unreasonable searches and seizures" (emphasis added) when it compelled an individual suspected of drunken driving to undergo a blood test. Schmerber had been arrested at a hospital while receiving treatment for injuries suffered when the automobile he was driving struck a tree. Despite Schmerber's objection, a police officer at the hospital had directed a physician to take a blood sample from him. Schmerber subsequently objected to the introduction at trial of evidence obtained as a result of the blood test.

The authorities in *Schmerber* clearly had probable cause to believe that he had been driving while intoxicated, and to believe that a blood test would provide evidence that was exceptionally probative in confirming this belief. Because the case fell within the exigent circumstances exception to the warrant requirement, no warrant was necessary. The search was not more intrusive than reasonably necessary to accomplish its goals. Nonetheless, Schmerber argued that the Fourth Amendment prohibited the authorities from intruding into his body to extract the blood that was needed as evidence.

Schmerber noted that "[t]he overriding function of the Fourth Amendment is to protect personal privacy and dignity against unwarranted intrusion by the State." * * * [W]e observed that these values were "basic to a free society." We also noted that "[b]ecause we are dealing with intrusions into the human body rather than with state interferences with property relationships or private papers—'houses, papers, and effects'—we write on a clean slate." The intrusion perhaps implicated Schmerber's most personal and deep-rooted expectations of privacy, and the Court recognized that Fourth Amendment analysis thus required a discerning inquiry into the facts and circumstances to determine whether the intrusion was justifiable. The Fourth Amendment neither forbids nor permits all such intrusions; rather, the Amendment's "proper function is to constrain, not against all intrusions as such, but against intrusions which are not justified in the circumstances, or which are made in an improper manner."

The reasonableness of surgical intrusions beneath the skin depends on a case-by-case approach, in which the individual's interests in privacy and security are weighed against society's interests in conducting the procedure. In a given case, the question whether the community's need for evidence outweighs the substantial privacy interests at stake is a delicate one admitting of few categorical answers. We believe that *Schmerber,* however, provides the appropriate framework of analysis for such cases.

Schmerber recognized that the ordinary requirements of the Fourth Amendment would be the threshold requirements for conducting this kind of surgical search and seizure. We noted the importance of probable cause. And we pointed out: "Search warrants are ordinarily required for searches of dwellings, and, absent an emergency, no less could be required where intrusions into the human body are concerned. . . . The importance of informed, detached and deliberate determinations of the issue whether or not to invade another's body in search of evidence of guilt is indisputable and great."

Beyond these standards, *Schmerber* 's inquiry considered a number of other factors in determining the "reasonableness" of the blood test. A crucial factor in analyzing the magnitude of the intrusion in *Schmerber* is the extent to which the procedure may threaten the safety or health of the individual. "[F]or most people [a blood test] involves virtually no risk, trauma, or pain." Moreover, all reasonable medical precautions were taken and no unusual or untested procedures were employed in *Schmerber,* the procedure was performed "by a physician in a hospital environment according to accepted medical practices." Notwithstanding the existence of probable cause, a search for evidence of a crime may be unjustifiable if it endangers the life or health of the suspect.

Another factor is the extent of intrusion upon the individual's dignitary interests in personal privacy and bodily integrity. Intruding into an individual's living room, eavesdropping upon an individual's telephone conversations, or forcing an individual to accompany police officers to the police station typically do not injure the physical person of the individual. Such intrusions do, however, damage the individual's sense of personal privacy and security and are thus subject to the Fourth Amendment's dictates. In noting that a blood test was "a commonplace in these days of periodic physical examinations," *Schmerber* recognized society's judgment that blood tests do not constitute an unduly extensive imposition on an individual's personal privacy and bodily integrity.

Weighed against these individual interests is the community's interest in fairly and accurately determining guilt or innocence. This interest is of course of great importance. We noted in *Schmerber* that a blood test is "a highly effective means of determining the degree to which a person is under the influence of alcohol." Moreover, there was "a clear indication that in fact [desired] evidence [would] be found" if the blood test were undertaken. Especially given the difficulty of proving drunkenness by other means, these considerations showed that results of the blood test were of vital importance if the State were to enforce its drunken driving laws. In *Schmerber,* we concluded that this state interest was sufficient to justify the intrusion, and the compelled blood test was thus "reasonable" for Fourth Amendment purposes.

III

Applying the *Schmerber* balancing test in this case, we believe that the Court of Appeals reached the correct result. The Commonwealth plainly had probable cause to conduct the search. In addition, all parties apparently agree that respondent has had a full measure of procedural protections and has been able fully to litigate the difficult medical and legal questions necessarily involved in analyzing the reasonableness of a surgical incision of this magnitude.[14] Our inquiry therefore must focus on the extent of the intrusion on respondent's privacy interests and on the State's need for the evidence.

The threats to the health or safety of respondent posed by the surgery are the subject of sharp dispute between the parties. Before the new revelations of October 18, the District Court found that the procedure could be carried out "with virtually no risk to [respondent]." On rehearing, however, with new evidence before it, the District Court held that "the

14. Because the State has afforded respondent the benefit of a full adversary presentation and appellate review, we do not reach the question whether the State may compel a suspect to undergo a surgical search of this magnitude for evidence absent such special procedural protections.

risks previously involved have increased in magnitude even as new risks are being added."

The Court of Appeals examined the medical evidence in the record and found that respondent would suffer some risks associated with the surgical procedure. One surgeon had testified that the difficulty of discovering the exact location of the bullet "could require extensive probing and retracting of the muscle tissue," carrying with it "the concomitant risks of injury to the muscle as well as injury to the nerves, blood vessels and other tissue in the chest and pleural cavity." The court further noted that "the greater intrusion and the larger incisions increase the risks of infection." Moreover, there was conflict in the testimony concerning the nature and the scope of the operation. One surgeon stated that it would take 15–20 minutes, while another predicted the procedure could take up to two and one-half hours. The court properly took the resulting uncertainty about the medical risks into account.

Both lower courts in this case believed that the proposed surgery, which for purely medical reasons required the use of a general anesthetic, would be an "extensive" intrusion on respondent's personal privacy and bodily integrity. When conducted with the consent of the patient, surgery requiring general anesthesia is not necessarily demeaning or intrusive. In such a case, the surgeon is carrying out the patient's own will concerning the patient's body and the patient's right to privacy is therefore preserved. In this case, however, the Court of Appeals noted that the Commonwealth proposes to take control of respondent's body, to "drug this citizen—not yet convicted of a criminal offense—with narcotics and barbiturates into a state of unconsciousness," and then to search beneath his skin for evidence of a crime. This kind of surgery involves a virtually total divestment of respondent's ordinary control over surgical probing beneath his skin.

The other part of the balance concerns the Commonwealth's need to intrude into respondent's body to retrieve the bullet. The Commonwealth claims to need the bullet to demonstrate that it was fired from Watkinson's gun, which in turn would show that respondent was the robber who confronted Watkinson. However, although we recognize the difficulty of making determinations in advance as to the strength of the case against respondent, petitioners' assertions of a compelling need for the bullet are hardly persuasive. The very circumstances relied on in this case to demonstrate probable cause to believe that evidence will be found tend to vitiate the Commonwealth's need to compel respondent to undergo surgery. The Commonwealth has available substantial additional evidence that respondent was the individual who accosted Watkinson on the night of the robbery. No party in this case suggests that Watkinson's entirely spontaneous identification of respondent at the hospital would be inadmissible. In addition, petitioners can no doubt prove that [respondent] was found a few blocks from Watkinson's store shortly after the incident took place. And petitioners can certainly show that the location of the bullet (under respondent's left collarbone) seems to correlate with Watkinson's report that the robber "jerked" to the left. The fact that the Commonwealth has available such substantial evidence of the origin of the bullet restricts the need for the Commonwealth to compel respondent to undergo the contemplated surgery.[15]

In weighing the various factors in this case, we therefore reach the same conclusion as the courts below. The operation sought will intrude substantially on respondent's protected interests. The medical risks of the operation, although apparently not extremely severe, are a subject of considerable dispute: the very uncertainty militates against finding the operation to be "reasonable." In addition, the intrusion on respondent's privacy interests entailed by the operation can only be characterized as severe. On the other hand, although the bullet may turn out to be useful to the Commonwealth in prosecuting respondent, the Commonwealth has failed to demonstrate a compelling need for it. We believe that in these circumstances the Commonwealth has failed to demonstrate that it would be "reasonable" under the terms of the Fourth Amendment to search for evidence of this crime by means of the contemplated surgery.

IV

The Fourth Amendment is a vital safeguard of the right of the citizen to be free from unreasonable governmental intrusions into any area in which he has a reasonable expectation of privacy. Where the Court has found a lesser expectation of privacy, or where the search involves a minimal intrusion on privacy interests, the Court has held that the Fourth Amendment's protections are correspondingly less stringent. Conversely, however, the Fourth Amendment's command that searches be "reasonable" requires that when the State seeks to intrude upon an area in which our society recognizes a significantly heightened privacy interest, a more substantial justification is required to make the search "reasonable." Applying these principles, we hold that the proposed search in this case would be "unreasonable" under the Fourth Amendment.

Affirmed.

◼ JUSTICE BLACKMUN and JUSTICE REHNQUIST concur in the judgment.

◼ CHIEF JUSTICE BURGER, concurring.

I join because I read the Court's opinion as not preventing detention of an individual if there are reasonable grounds to believe that natural bodily functions will disclose the presence of contraband materials secreted internally.

---

15. There are also some questions concerning the probative value of the bullet, even if it could be retrieved. The evidentiary value of the bullet depends on a comparison between markings, if any, on the bullet in respondent's shoulder and markings, if any, found on a test bullet that the police could fire from Watkinson's gun. However, the record supports some doubt whether this kind of comparison is possible. This is because the bullet's markings may have been corroded in the time that the bullet has been in respondent's shoulder, thus making it useless for comparison purposes. In addition, respondent argues that any given gun may be incapable of firing bullets that have a consistent set of markings. The record is devoid of any evidence that the police have attempted to testfire Watkinson's gun, and there thus remains the additional possibility that a comparison of bullets is impossible because Watkinson's gun does not consistently fire bullets with the same markings. However, because the courts below made no findings on this point, we hesitate to give it significant weight in our analysis.

CHAPTER 6

ELECTRONIC SURVEILLANCE

Analysis

Modern technology has resulted in the development of very sophisticated devices that can enhance the effectiveness of the human senses, especially sight and hearing. The use of these devices—often referred to as "electronic surveillance"—in criminal investigations is the subject of this chapter. Most attention is devoted to surveillance of the spoken word and this is the focus of the federal statute emphasized in this discussion. But other law enforcement techniques raise similar issues. Norwood, "Available Dark" Photography, Industrial Photography, Nov. 1971, at 24, for example, describes the electronic intensifier, which permits taking of photographs in very low light. This, he claims, permits law enforcement surveillance work to take place in "almost complete darkness." Excellent photographs of narcotics transactions have been taken, he continues, apparently in circumstances in which most persons would believe their actions not subject to "capture" on film or even—given the darkness—to visual observation by others.[1]

---

1. A number of courts have held that use of a light enhancing device to conduct nighttime surveillance does not involve a search under federal or state constitutions. Eg., United States v. Ward, 703 F.2d 1058, 1061 (8th Cir.1983); State v. Wacker, 317 Or. 419, 856 P.2d 1029, 1036 (Or.1993). But the Pennsylvania Supreme Court has commented:

> It is not necessary at this time and in this case to hold that every time a * * * device that "sees" through darkness is used by authorities to obtain evidence without a search warrant the evidence must be suppressed. However, when such a device is used for nine days to observe a private apartment frequented by other than those sought by the police, including two acts of sexual intercourse not involving the person, the subject for detection, for whom the surveillance was established, then the warrantless observation of a third floor apartment in darkness has truly impermissibly invaded privacy to which all citizens * * * are guaranteed by the Fourth Amendment.

Commonwealth v. Williams, 494 Pa. 496, 500, 431 A.2d 964, 966 (1981).

A. THE CONSTITUTIONAL BACKGROUND

EDITORS' NOTE: BACKGROUND OF FEDERAL AND STATE
ELECTRONIC SURVEILLANCE LAW

Electronic surveillance of communication is pervasively regulated by a number of federal statutes, most significantly legislation originally enacted as Title III of the Omnibus Crime Control and Safe Streets Act of 1968. It was somewhat modified by subsequent congressional action, most importantly 1986 legislation, The Federal Electronic Communications Privacy Act, codified as 18 U.S.C.A. §§ 2510–2522. The basic statute is still widely known as "Title III," and will be so described in this discussion. This statute is the subject of the second portion of this chapter.

Although Title III was based in part on legislation enacted earlier, it clearly reflected a new approach to the matter. This approach was molded by two important Supreme Court cases decided shortly before Congress's 1968 action.

In Berger v. New York, 388 U.S. 41, 87 S.Ct. 1873, 18 L.Ed.2d 1040 (1967), the Court considered the validity of New York's eavesdrop statute, which permitted eavesdropping pursuant to a court order issued under the statute. Assuming the conduct which the statute authorized constituted a search under the Fourth Amendment, the Court found several defects in the New York statute. First, the statute did not require the court order specify with particularity the crime under investigation, the "place" to be "searched," or the conversations to be "seized." Although the statute demanded identification of the persons whose conversations were to be overheard, this requirement was not sufficient to meet Fourth Amendment specificity needs. Second, the statute permitted officers serving the court order to seize all conversations of all persons coming into the area during a two-month period without regard to their connection to the crime under investigation. Therefore, the order authorized a series of intrusions pursuant to a single showing of probable cause, which might not constitute an adequate basis for each of the numerous intrusions authorized by the court order. Third, the two-month period of eavesdropping which the statute authorized permitted avoidance of the requirement of prompt execution of the order. Fourth, two-month extensions of the eavesdropping order could be obtained upon a showing continued eavesdropping would be "in the public interest." Such extensions violated the requirement of probable cause, which demands a showing of present probable cause for the authorized activity. Fifth, there was no provision for termination of the seizure once the conversation sought was overheard. Sixth, the statute had neither a requirement of notice to persons whose conversations were seized nor any reasonable substitute. Finally, the statute provided for no return on the court order and consequently left the use of conversations overheard and information obtained completely within the discretion of the officer.

The New York statute permitted the issuance of an eavesdrop order upon the "oath" of a prosecutor or high police official that "there is probable cause to believe that evidence of a crime may thus be obtained."

Whether orders issued on this basis complied with the Fourth Amendment's requirement that search warrants be issued only upon an adequate showing of probable cause was described by the Court as a serious question that did not have to be resolved in the case.

The Fourth Amendment requirements which *Berger* applied to the New York statute are significantly more stringent than those which the Court has applied to regular search warrants. Cady v. Dombrowski, 413 U.S. 433, 93 S.Ct. 2523, 37 L.Ed.2d 706 (1973), for example, strongly suggested there is no Fourth Amendment requirement of a return of a standard search warrant. Yet *Berger* indicated that a return may be constitutionally required for electronic surveillance. Of course, *Berger* did not make clear whether each of the defects identified by the Court in the New York statute constituted an application of a separate and independent constitutional requirement or, rather, whether the statute fell because of the totality of the deficiencies.

The second case, Katz v. United States, 389 U.S. 347, 88 S.Ct. 507, 19 L.Ed.2d 576 (1967), resolved the issue left unaddressed in *Berger*—whether electronic interception of the spoken word is a search under the Fourth Amendment.

In Olmstead v. United States, 277 U.S. 438, 48 S.Ct. 564, 72 L.Ed. 944 (1928), the Court found no infringement upon interests protected by the Fourth Amendment in the "tapping" of the defendant's telephone line accomplished without unlawful entry into (or onto) his premises. Section 605 of the Communications Act of 1934, however, barred "interception" of any interstate communication by wire. In Nardone v. United States, 302 U.S. 379, 58 S.Ct. 275, 82 L.Ed. 314 (1937), the Court held that Section 605 required the exclusion in federal criminal trials of the products of wiretaps that, under *Olmstead*, would not have involved searches under the Fourth Amendment. In Goldman v. United States, 316 U.S. 129, 62 S.Ct. 993, 86 L.Ed. 1322 (1942), the Court found no violation of the Fourth Amendment in the use of a "detectaphone" placed against an office wall to hear private conversations in the office next door because there was no "trespass" on the premises under surveillance. *Olmstead* and *Goldman* were generally regarded as establishing that surveillance did not amount to a search and therefore did not have to be reasonable in Fourth Amendment terms unless it involved some physical trespass on or into premises in which the subject had a privacy interest.

Katz, however, held that this trespass requirement was no longer controlling. In *Katz*, FBI agents attached an electronic listening and recording device to the outside of a public telephone booth. This device enabled them to overhear Katz's end of a telephone conversation he carried on in the booth, but involved no physical penetration of, or trespass into, the booth. Nevertheless, the Court held this a search. The Fourth Amendment protects people—and not merely areas—against unreasonable searches and seizures, Justice Stewart explained for the majority, and consequently "the reach of that Amendment cannot turn upon the presence or absence of a physical intrusion into any given enclosure." Since Katz reasonably expected, when he used the booth, that his words would "not be broadcast to the world," he had a privacy interest in the content of those words that was infringed by the agents' use of the recording and listening device. The result of *Katz*, Justice Harlan noted in his concurrence, is that any surveillance resulting in obtaining information the subjects actually and reasonably believed was relatively private constitutes a search and must be scrutinized under Fourth Amendment reasonableness standards. 389 U.S. at 361, 88 S.Ct. at 516–17, 19 L.Ed.2d at 587–88 (Harlan, J., concurring).

The Senate Judiciary Report on Title III noted both *Berger* and *Katz*. It further commented that Title III was drafted to meet the constitutional criteria for electronic surveillance delineated in *Berger* and to "conform with" *Katz*. Senate Report No. 1097, 90th Congress, 2nd Session, 1968, U.S. Code Congressional and Administrative News, 1968, Vol. 2, 2112, at 2153.

The Supreme Court has not addressed the facial validity of the electronic surveillance statute. It has given no indication in its numerous decisions dealing with the statute that the statute suffers from the fatal defects *Berger* found in the New York provision. Lower courts have upheld Title III against constitutional attacks. E.g., United States v. Sklaroff, 506 F.2d 837 (5th Cir.1975), cert. denied 423 U.S. 874, 96 S.Ct. 142, 46 L.Ed.2d 105; United States v. Tortorello, 480 F.2d 764 (2d Cir.1973), cert. denied 414 U.S. 866, 94 S.Ct. 63, 38 L.Ed.2d 86; United States v. Cox, 449 F.2d 679 (8th Cir. 1971), cert. denied 406 U.S. 934, 92 S.Ct. 1783, 32 L.Ed.2d 136 (1972).

B.   The Federal Statute and Its Application

EDITORS' INTRODUCTION: A SUMMARY OF THE FEDERAL ELECTRONIC COMMUNICATIONS PRIVACY ACT ("TITLE III")

Title III was originally enacted in 1968. It has been amended several times. One federal court commented that another tribunal "might have put the matter too mildly" when that second tribunal noted that the statute "is famous (if not infamous) for its lack of clarity." United States v. Smith, 155 F.3d 1051, 1055 (9th Cir.1998). The following is a summary of the current provisions.

Coverage and Prohibitions

The essence of Title III is its prohibition against the interception of any wire, oral or electronic communication. 18 U.S.C.A. § 2511(1)(a).

Title III distinguishes among "wire communications," "oral communications," and "electronic communications." All three are covered, but in somewhat different ways.

A "wire communication" is defined as an aural transfer that in whole or part uses wire, cable or other "like connection." It must at some point involve the human voice. An "oral communication" is defined as "any oral communication uttered by a person exhibiting an expectation that such communication is not subject to interception under circumstances justifying such expectation."

In 1986, Title III was expanded to protect electronic communications. An "electronic communication" is defined as a transfer of signs, signals, images, data or intelligence by means of wire, radio, or similar means. Thus it includes such innovations as electronic mail, facsimile transmissions, and video teleconferences. 18 U.S.C.A. § 2510.

"Intercept" is defined as "the aural or other acquisition of the contents of any wire, electronic, or oral communication through the use of any electronic, mechanical, or other device." 18 U.S.C.A. § 2510(4). "Electronic, mechanical, or other device" is defined as "any device or apparatus which can be used to intercept a wire or oral communication." Specifically designated as not such devices are telephone or telegraph equipment furnished to a user and used in the ordinary course of business (i.e., an extension phone) and a hearing aid or similar device used to correct subnormal hearing to not better than normal. 18 U.S.C.A. § 2510(5).

Exceptions Permitting Interception

Several exceptions to the statute's general prohibition permit interception of communications covered by Title III. First, a party to the conversation or a person authorized by one of the parties to the communication may intercept the communication. 18 U.S.C.A. § 2511(2)(c), (d).

Second, federal law enforcement officers may intercept communications in certain emergency situations. The situations must be believed to involve "immediate danger of death or serious physical injury" or "conspiratorial activities threatening the national security interest or * * * characteristic of organized crime." Application for a court order approving the interception must be made within 48 hours. 18 U.S.C.A. § 2518(7).

Third—and most important—the statute provides for federal law enforcement agencies to obtain court orders from federal judges authorizing certain interceptions. 18 U.S.C.A. § 2516. Further, the statute authorizes states to enact statutes permitting state law enforcement officers to obtain similar court orders from state judges "in conformity with" the provisions of Title III. 18 U.S.C.A. § 2516(2). In the absence of an order obtained pursuant to a state "enabling" statute, the federal statute bars state law enforcement officers from engaging in the conduct prohibited by the statute.

Interceptions Under Court Order

The process of applying for, obtaining, and serving a court order permitting otherwise prohibited interceptions under the statute is complex and best considered in several steps.

(1) Offenses Involved

An application may be made to a federal court for interception of wire or oral communications only if the surveillance is sought to obtain evidence of certain enumerated offenses. State statutes may authorize court orders only to obtain evidence regarding "murder, kidnapping, gambling, robbery, bribery, extortion, or dealing in narcotic drugs, marihuana or other dangerous drugs, or other crime dangerous to life, limb, or property, and punishable by imprisonment for more than one year * * * or any conspiracy to commit any of the foregoing offenses." 18 U.S.C.A. § 2516(2). An application for authorization to intercept electronic communications may be made for any federal felony.

(2) Authorization

An application for interception of wire or oral communications may be made to a federal court for a surveillance order only if application is authorized by certain high level members of the Attorney General's staff. 18 U.S.C.A. § 2516(1). Any assistant United States Attorney may authorize application for an electronic communications intercept. A state procedure must require authorization by the principal prosecuting attorney of the state or of a political subdivision of the state. 18 U.S.C.A. § 2516(2).

(3) Application Contents

The contents of the application are governed by 18 U.S.C.A. § 2518(1):

Each application for an order authorizing or approving the interception of a wire, oral, or electronic communication * * * shall be made in writing upon oath or affirmation to a judge of competent jurisdiction and shall state the applicant's authority to make such application. Each application shall include the following information:

(a) the identity of the investigative or law enforcement officer making the application, and the officer authorizing the application;

(b) a full and complete statement of the facts and circumstances relied upon by the applicant, to justify his belief that an order should be issued, including (i) details as to the particular offense that has been, is being, or is about to be committed, (ii) * * * a particular description of the nature and location of the facilities from which or the place where the communication is to be intercepted, (iii) a particular description of the type of communications sought to be intercepted, (iv) the identity of the person, if known, committing the offense and whose communications are to be intercepted;

(c) a full and complete statement as to whether or not other investigative procedures have been tried and failed or why they reasonably appear to be unlikely to succeed if tried or to be too dangerous;

(d) a statement of the period of time for which the interception is required to be maintained. If the nature of the investigation is such that the authorization for interception should not automatically terminate when the described type of communication has been first obtained, a particular description of facts establishing probable cause to believe that additional communications of the same type will occur thereafter;

(e) a full and complete statement of the facts concerning all previous applications known to the individual authorizing and making the application, made to any judge for authorization to intercept, or for approval of interceptions of, wire, oral, or electronic communications involving any of the same persons, facilities or places specified in the application, and the action taken by the judge on each such application; and

(f) where the application is for the extension of an order, a statement setting forth the results thus far obtained from the interception, or a reasonable explanation of the failure to obtain such results.

(4) Judicial Function and Issuance of Order

The judge to whom the application is made may require the applicant to furnish additional testimony or evidence in support of the application. 18 U.S.C.A. § 2518(2). An *ex parte* order authorizing interception may be issued:

if the judge determines on the basis of the facts submitted by the applicant that—

(a) there is probable cause for belief that an individual is committing, has committed, or is about to commit [an offense for which an order may be issued];

(b) there is probable cause for belief that particular communications concerning that offense will be obtained through such interception;

(c) normal investigative procedures have been tried and have failed or reasonably appear to be unlikely to succeed if tried or to be too dangerous; [and]

(d) * * * there is probable cause for belief that the facilities from which, or the place where, the wire or oral communications are to be intercepted are being used, or are about to be used, in connection with the commission of such offense, or are leased to, listed in the name of, or commonly used by such person.

18 U.S.C.A. § 2518(3).

(5) Contents of Order

Under 18 U.S.C.A. § 2518(4), each order shall specify:

(a) the identity of the person, if known, whose communications are to be intercepted;

(b) the nature and location of the communications facilities as to which, or the place where, authority to intercept is granted;

(c) a particular description of the type of communication sought to be intercepted, and a statement of the particular offense to which it relates;

(d) the identity of the agency authorized to intercept the communications, and of the person authorizing the application; and

(e) the period of time during which such interception is authorized, including a statement as to whether or not the interception shall automatically terminate when the described communication has been first obtained.

Further, every order must contain a provision "that the authorization to intercept shall be executed as soon as practicable, [and] shall be conducted in such a way as to minimize the interception of communications not otherwise subject to interception under this chapter * * *." 18 U.S.C.A. § 2518(5).

The period of time during which interception may be authorized is only as long as is necessary to achieve the objective of the order, but never longer than thirty days. Each order must contain a directive that the interception "must terminate upon attainment of the authorized objective." 18 U.S.C.A. § 2518(5).

Upon request of the applicant, the judge "shall" include in the order a directive that a communication common carrier, landlord, custodian "or other person" shall furnish the officers with "all information, facilities, and technical assistance necessary to accomplish the interception unobtrusively." Such persons are compensated at prevailing rates. 18 U.S.C.A. § 2518(4).

The judge may also include a requirement the officers submit progress reports at designated intervals. These reports may require a showing as to what progress has been made toward achievement of the authorized objective and the need for continued interception. 18 U.S.C.A. § 2518(6).

(6) Service of the Intercept Order

The statute contains very few provisions relating directly to the manner in which the court order is to be served. Some limits on execution of orders, however, can be read into the provisions discussed above. It is clear, for example, the statute contemplates compliance with the order's provisions that the interception occur as soon as practicable and that it be conducted in such a manner as to minimize the interception of communications not subject to interception. Further, assistance from landlords and other persons may be obtained.

The statute does explicitly direct that the contents of any intercepted communications "shall, if possible, be recorded on tape or wire or other comparable device" and that this be done "in such way as will protect the recording from editing or other alteration." 18 U.S.C.A. § 2518(8)(a).

In Dalia v. United States, 441 U.S. 238, 99 S.Ct. 1682, 60 L.Ed.2d 177 (1979), the Supreme Court upheld covert entry of private premises by agents to install a listening device whose use was authorized by a court order. Such entries are not inherently unreasonable under the Fourth Amendment, it reasoned, and the statute does not prohibit them. Nor is it necessary the court order specifically authorize such covert entry. The precise manner in which search warrants are to be served, Justice Powell noted for the majority, has always been left to the discretion of the officers executing the order, subject to later judicial review for "reasonableness." There is no need, the Court concluded, to depart from this approach in the electronic surveillance area.

(7) Extensions

Extensions of an intercept order may be granted. But an application for such an extension must comply with the requirements for applications for an initial order and an extension may be granted only if the judge makes the determinations required for an initial order. Extensions may be for no longer than is necessary to achieve the purposes for which they are granted and may never exceed thirty days. 18 U.S.C.A. § 2518(5).

(8) Return to Court

The statute does not specifically impose a requirement of a return of the order to the issuing court. But immediately upon the expiration of the order, any recordings made of intercepted communications are to "be made available" to the judge, sealed, and shall be retained in custody as ordered by the court. 18 U.S.C.A. § 2518(8)(a). The provisions for notice (discussed below) assume some communication to the court from the serving agency or officers, if not a formal return.

(9) Notice

The statute contains two provisions for notice to persons whose communications may have been intercepted. Within a reasonable time, but not more than ninety days after denial of an application or the termination of an interception authorized by an order, an inventory is to be served on certain persons. This inventory is to include notice of (a) the fact of the entry of the order or the application; (b) the date of the entry and the period of authorized, approved or disapproved interception, or the denial of the application; and (c) the fact that, during the period, communications were or were not intercepted. An inventory is to be served on persons named in the application or order and "such other parties to the intercepted communications as the judge may determine in his discretion that is in the interest of justice." On an *ex parte* showing of good cause, the service of the inventory may be postponed. 18 U.S.C.A. § 2518(8)(d).

The second provision focuses upon use of results of surveillance. If the contents of an intercepted communication or evidence derived from such communications are to be used or disclosed in any trial, hearing or "other proceeding," each party must be given, no less than ten days before the proceedings, a copy of the court order and the application. 18 U.S.C.A. § 2518(9).

"Roving" Interception Orders

As a result of 1986 legislation, interception orders sometimes need not specify the specific location of the facilities where or from which the communications are to be intercepted. These orders are often called "roving" orders, since they give law enforcement officers considerable flexibility regarding where to intercept the targeted communications.

If the order permits interception of oral communications, the judge must find—on the basis of facts contained in the application—specifying the facilities is not "practical."

If the order is to permit interception of wire or electronic communications, the judge must find—again on the basis of the facts in the application—there is probable cause to believe the actions of the person whose communications are sought "could have the effect of thwarting interception from a specified facility." 18 U.S.C.A. § 2518(11).

An earlier version of these provisions was found constitutional over arguments they violate the Fourth Amendment requirements established in Berger v. New York, 388 U.S. 41, 87 S.Ct. 1873, 18 L.Ed.2d 1040 (1967). See United States v. Gaytan, 74 F.3d 545, 553 (5th Cir.1996).

Intercepted Communications Concerning Nontarget Offenses

Officers serving a court order authorizing the interception of communications related to a specified offense may overhear communications concerning other offenses. What is required to enable law enforcement officers to use the information obtained by intercepting such nontarget communications depends upon the use the officers seek to make of them.

The statute provides officers may disclose the contents of these communications to other law enforcement officers to the extent that such action is appropriate to the proper performance of the intercepting officer's official duties. Further, the officer may use the contents of these communications in the proper performance of his duties.

An officer may, however, disclose the contents of such communications in testimony given in an official proceeding only:

> when authorized or approved by a judge of competent jurisdiction where such judge finds on subsequent application that the contents were otherwise intercepted in accordance with the provisions of this chapter. Such application shall be made as soon as practicable.

18 U.S.C.A. § 2517(5). One court has explained:

> The danger inherent in disclosure without judicial approval is that the original application may have been a subterfuge, that is, the government, not having probable cause to obtain a wiretap for some crime, might obtain it by purporting to investigate a different crime. We have acknowledged the potential for this kind of abuse. We have therefore held that a court, when faced with evidence of other crimes obtained in the course of a wiretap, may allow its disclosure only if it determines that:
>
> > the original order was lawfully obtained, that it was sought in good faith and not as a subterfuge search, and that the communication was, in fact, incidentally intercepted during the course of a lawfully executed order.

United States v. Barnes, 47 F.3d 963, 964–65 (8th Cir.1995).

But the necessary judicial authorization can be easily obtained. Courts have held, for example, that if, in applying for an extension of the original interception order, the Government discloses it has intercepted communications regarding other offenses, the court's action in granting the extension is authorization to use those communications. United States v. London, 66 F.3d 1227, 1235 (1st Cir.1995). In *Barnes*, the court held that if the Government uses such nontarget communications to obtain an indictment, it may obtain the necessary judicial approval after-the-fact, that is, after it uses the communications in testimony before the grand jury.

Remedies for Violation of the Statute

The statute provides several remedies for a violation of its provisions. "Intentional" violations are punishable as criminal offenses and carry penalties of a fine or imprisonment for not more than five years, or both. 18 U.S.C.A. § 2511. A civil cause of action is also created and provisions are made for recovery of attorney's fees, punitive damages, and actual damages not less than liquidated damages computed at the rate of $100 a day for each day of violation or $10,000, whichever is higher. 18 U.S.C.A. § 2520.

Title III has its own exclusionary sanction in 18 U.S.C.A. § 2515:

Whenever any wire or oral communication has been intercepted, no part of the contents of such communication and no evidence derived therefrom may be received in evidence in any trial, hearing, or other proceeding in or before any court, grand jury, department, officer, agency, regulatory body, legislative committee, or other authority of the United States, a State, or a political subdivision thereof if the disclosure of that information would be in violation of this chapter.

"Any aggrieved person" may move to suppress the contents of an intercepted communication or evidence derived from it on the following grounds:

(i) the communication was unlawfully intercepted;

(ii) the order of authorization or approval under which it was intercepted is insufficient on its face; or

(iii) the interception was not made in conformity with the order of authorization or approval.

18 U.S.C.A. § 2518(10)(a). "Aggrieved person" is defined as "a person who was a party to any intercepted wire, oral, or electronic communication or a person against whom the interception was directed." 18 U.S.C.A. § 2510(11).

To some extent, this statutory exclusionary remedy is broader than that of the Fourth Amendment. In Gelbard v. United States, 408 U.S. 41, 92 S.Ct. 2357, 33 L.Ed.2d 179 (1972), for example, the Court held that witnesses who had been subpoenaed before a grand jury could invoke 18 U.S.C.A. § 2515. Thus, they could not be cited for contempt for refusal to answer questions based upon information obtained in violation of the statute. It may not follow, however, that an indictment is subject to attack by a defendant on the basis that the grand jury considered or relied upon evidence obtained in violation of the statute.

Perhaps the most perplexing problem is the determination of what noncompliance with the statutory procedures requires suppression of the results of an interception. In United States v. Giordano, 416 U.S. 505, 94 S.Ct. 1820, 40 L.Ed.2d 341 (1974), the Supreme Court held the Congressional intention was to provide for suppression where "there is failure to satisfy any of those statutory requirements that directly and substantially implement the congressional intent to limit the use of intercept procedures to those situations clearly calling for the employment of this extraordinary investigative device." In *Giordano*, the application for the court order recited that it had been approved by a designated Assistant Attorney

General; evidence showed, however, that the Executive Assistant to the Attorney General approved it. Finding the requirement of approval by the Attorney General or a designated Assistant Attorney General was one that directly and substantially implemented the congressional purpose, the Court held the products of the order must be suppressed under 18 U.S.C.A. § 2515. In United States v. Chavez, 416 U.S. 562, 94 S.Ct. 1849, 40 L.Ed.2d 380 (1974), however, the application recited that it had been approved by the Assistant Attorney General although the facts showed the Attorney General himself had approved it. The statute's requirement that the application accurately state which of the several authorized persons approved it, held the Court, was not so directly and substantially related to the Congressional purpose as to require suppression of the products of the surveillance.

If there is a violation of a statutory requirement that brings 18 U.S.C.A. § 2515 into play, does it require suppression of evidence or information obtained *before* that violation took place? In United States v. Donovan, 429 U.S. 413, 97 S.Ct. 658, 50 L.Ed.2d 652 (1977), the defendant did not receive post-interception notice because the government left the defendant's name off the list of persons whose conversations were intercepted. This omission, the Supreme Court held, violated the statute, since the government had exclusive access to this information and thus was obligated to provide a full list. But, it continued, this violation of the notice provision of the statute was not "retroactive" in the sense that it would render the earlier interceptions unlawful and therefore subject to suppression.

Section 2518(8)(a), requiring officers record intercepted conversations and make the recording available to the judge, also directs the recording sealed under the judge's direction. This is to occur "[i]mmediately upon the expiration" of the order or any extensions that are authorized. In United States v. Ojeda Rios, 495 U.S. 257, 110 S.Ct. 1845, 109 L.Ed.2d 224 (1990), no seal was immediately obtained as the statute directs. Section 2518(8)(a) provides the seal "or a satisfactory explanation for the absence thereof, shall be a prerequisite for the use or disclosure" of a communication intercepted under the statute or evidence derived from such a communication. Thus, the Court observed, the statute contains its own "explicit exclusionary remedy." It continued:

> The presence or absence of a seal does not in itself establish the integrity of electronic surveillance tapes [but] is a means of ensuring that subsequent to its placement on a tape, the Government has no opportunity to tamper with, alter, or edit the conversations that have been recorded.

495 U.S. at 263, 110 S.Ct. at 1849, 109 L.Ed.2d at 234. Next, it rejected the Government's argument that evidence was admissible if the Government provided an explanation that was not "satisfactory" but showed the offered recording authentic. Under the language of the statute, proof that no tampering with the recording occurred in the particular case is not an adequate substitute for a "satisfactory explanation" for the failure to have the recording sealed. There was also evidence that the attorney supervising the investigation misconstrued the statute as requiring no effort on the

Government's part to have the recording sealed until there was a "meaningful hiatus" in the investigation as a whole. This interpretation, the Court held, was an objectively reasonable—although ultimately incorrect—reading of the law. If offered to the trial court, it would constitute a "satisfactory explanation" for the absence of a seal timely secured. The case was remanded for a determination as to whether the Government had presented this explanation to the trial court at the suppression hearing.

Determining Whether Surveillance Occurred

Defendants may experience difficulty in determining whether law enforcement investigations leading to their prosecutions involved activity actually or potentially subject to the statutory provisions. Unless defendants can establish that activity of this sort occurred, they are in no position to claim government evidence the "fruit" of impermissible surveillance.

Such defendants can sometimes invoke a federal statute that provides:

upon a claim by a party aggrieved that evidence is admissible because it is the * * * product of an unlawful act * * * the opponent of the claim shall affirm or deny the occurrence of the alleged unlawful act.

18 U.S.C.A. § 3504(a)(1). Thus a defendant can claim illegal surveillance and the government must affirm or deny it.

The specificity which lower courts have required of governmental claims that no such surveillance took place depends upon the specificity of and support for the defendant's assertion it did. Where only a general unsupported claim is made by the defendant, a general denial by the government has been held to suffice. A more specific claim supported by facts indicating surveillance was conducted may require the government to conduct a more comprehensive inquiry of agencies with surveillance capabilities before its denial will be accepted. See Matter of Grand Jury, 529 F.2d 543 (3d Cir.1976).

If it is established illegal surveillance took place and the defendant has "standing" to raise the matter, the defense is entitled to access to records of that surveillance. It is not sufficient for the trial judge to examine the records *in camera* and turn over to the defense those records the judge determines "arguably relevant" to the proceedings. Alderman v. United States, 394 U.S. 165, 89 S.Ct. 961, 22 L.Ed.2d 176 (1969). The Court reached a different result where the defendant did not establish which intercepted conversations he participated in and therefore had standing to challenge. In this situation, the trial judge acted properly in examining the recordings of the intercepted conversations *in camera* and disclosing to the defense only those to which the defendant was a party. Taglianetti v. United States, 394 U.S. 316, 89 S.Ct. 1099, 22 L.Ed.2d 302 (1969).

State Statutes

Section 2516(2) authorizes states to enact legislation permitting state court judges to issue to state law enforcement officers—"in conformity with section 2518 of [the federal statute]"—a court order authorizing interceptions otherwise barred by the federal statute. As of December 31, 1998, forty two states (as well as the District of Columbia and the Virgin Islands) had such legislation. Administrative Office of the United States Courts, Report on Applications for Orders Authorizing or Approving the Interception of Wire or Oral Communications for the Period January 1 Through December 31, 1998. These statutes raise a number of issues, including the extent to which state legislation must embody provisions identical or similar to the federal statute.

States are free to enact legislation providing those subject to investigations with more protection than the federal statute extends. Some states, for example, prohibit the interception of communications even by a party to the conversation if the other party does not consent. The Pennsylvania statute was held to cover the action of a police officer in secretly recording conversations with persons the officer stopped for traffic violations. Commonwealth v. McIvor, 448 Pa.Super. 98, 670 A.2d 697 (1996), appeal denied, 547 Pa. 753, 692 A.2d 564 (1997).

NOTES

1. **Pen Registers and "Trap and Trace" Devices.** In 1986 Congress passed legislation covering devices enabling law enforcement officers to ascertain numbers dialed *from* particular telephones (pen registers) or the numbers from which calls are placed *to* particular telephones ("trap and trace" devices). These devices do not intercept the contents of calls.

Use of these devices would otherwise be free of statutory or constitutional limitation. In United States v. New York Telephone Co., 434 U.S. 159, 98 S.Ct. 364, 54 L.Ed.2d 376 (1977), the Court held that pen registers are not covered by Title III because they do not intercept communications. Two years later, in Smith v. Maryland, 442 U.S. 735, 99 S.Ct. 2577, 61 L.Ed.2d 220 (1979), discussed in Chapter 2, the Court held that use of a pen register does not constitute a search.

As a general rule under the 1986 legislation, use of these devices by law enforcement authorities or private persons is prohibited without a court order. 18 U.S.C.A. § 3121(a). Authorization to use them without an order is provided for certain emergency situations. 18 U.S.C.A. § 3125.

An application for an order authorizing use of one of these devices is required to include "a certification by the applicant that the information likely to be obtained is relevant to an ongoing criminal investigation being conducted by [a law enforcement agency]." 18 U.S.C.A. § 3122(b). States may provide for state officers to obtain similar orders.

The role of the court to which application must be made is minimal. The statute provides that upon finding the applicant has made the required certification, "the court shall issue an ex parte order authorizing [use of the devices]." 18 U.S.C.A. § 3123(a). The order is to state the offense to which the information likely to be obtained relates, the identity of the person who is the subject of the investigation, and the number and location of the telephone line to which the device is to be attached. 18 U.S.C.A. § 3123(b). An agency using an authorized device is to employ "technology reasonably available" that "restricts the recording or decoding of electronic or other impulses to the dialing and signaling information utilized in call processing." 18 U.S.C.A. § 3121(c).

The statute provides that a person who knowingly violates the general prohibition against use of these devices is subject to criminal conviction. 18 U.S.C.A. § 3121(d). It contains no provision for exclusion of evidence resulting from law enforcement activity conducted in violation of its provisions. There is authority for the proposition that such evidence may be used. See United States v. Thompson, 936 F.2d 1249, 1249–50 (11th Cir.1991). State statutes have been similarly construed. Thus in State v. Cain, 670 So.2d 515 (La.App.1996), the court explained:

> We find * * * that there is no statutory or constitutional basis to require exclusion of evidence gathered from a pen register that was authorized without compliance with [the state statute authorizing court orders]. We recognize that there is little incentive for law enforcement officials to comply with the procedural requirements for obtaining authorization for a pen register when there is no sanction for the failure to comply. However, absent a constitutionally protected privacy interest with regard to the numbers dialed from one's home, it is for the legislature to determine what, if any, consequence will flow from the failure to comply with the procedures it has established for obtaining a pen register.

670 So.2d at 520.

2. **Accessing or Intercepting "Stored" Communications.** The Stored Communication Act, 18 U.S.C. §§ 2701–2710, covers wire or electronic communications while in electronic storage. It prohibits any person without authorization from accessing a facility through which an electronic communication service is provided and thereby obtaining access to a stored communication. 18 U.S.C.A. § 2701(a). A governmental agency may obtain a search warrant authorizing the provider of such services to disclose the content of a stored communication. 18 U.S.C.A. § 2703(a).

The statute provides a civil action for damages that may be invoked by any person aggrieved by a violation of the chapter. 18 U.S.C.A. § 2707(a). If a court finds a violation of the statute occurred and the circumstances raise a question as to whether governmental agency's employee willfully or intentionally committed the violation, the agency or department is to initiate a proceeding to determine whether disciplinary action is warranted against the employee. 18 U.S.C.A. § 2707(d). But the statute also provides, "The remedies and sanctions described in this chapter are the only judicial remedies and sanctions for nonconstitutional violations of this chapter." 18 U.S.C.A. § 2708. Thus the statute provides no basis for challenging the admissibility of evidence obtained as a result of violation of its requirements.

The relationship between this statute and Title III is uncertain. In United States v. Smith, 155 F.3d 1051 (9th Cir.1998), the court considered whether in a federal criminal trial the Government was barred from using evidence resulting from a private person's action in obtaining access to the defendant's voice mail system and retrieving a message stored in his "mailbox." If this action violated only The Stored Communication Act, the court held, exclusion would not be required because the Act's provisions bar an exclusionary remedy. But a person who not only accesses the voice mail system in violation of the Act but obtains the contents of a stored communication violates the federal wiretap statute. The private person in *Smith* obtained the contents of a stored communication in a manner violating the wiretap statute. Thus the exclusionary provision of the wiretap statute demanded exclusion of the resulting evidence.

3. **Silent Video Surveillance.** No federal statute covers video surveillance conducted for domestic law enforcement purposes where the device does not record voices. Such surveillance is regulated when conducted for purposes of gathering information for foreign intelligence by the Foreign Intelligence Surveillance Act, 50 U.S.C. §§ 1801–1811. See generally, United States v. Koyomejian, 970 F.2d 536 (9th Cir.1992) (en banc).

United States v. Kahn

Supreme Court of the United States, 1974.
415 U.S. 143, 94 S.Ct. 977, 39 L.Ed.2d 225.

■ MR. JUSTICE STEWART delivered the opinion of the Court.

On March 20, 1970, an attorney from the United States Department of Justice submitted an application for an order authorizing a wiretap interception pursuant to Title III of the Omnibus Crime Control and Safe Streets Act of 1970, 18 U.S.C.A. §§ 2510–2520, to Judge William J. Campbell of the United States District Court for the Northern District of Illinois. The affidavit accompanying the application contained information indicating that the respondent, Irving Kahn, was a bookmaker who operated from his residence and used two home telephones to conduct his business. The affidavit also noted that the Government's informants had stated that they would refuse to testify against Kahn, that telephone company records alone would be insufficient to support a bookmaking conviction, and that physical surveillance or normal search-and-seizure techniques would be unlikely to produce useful evidence. The application therefore concluded that "normal investigative procedures reasonably appear to be unlikely to succeed," and asked for authorization to intercept wire communications of Irving Kahn and "others as yet unknown" over two named telephone lines, in order that information concerning the gambling offenses might be obtained.

Judge Campbell entered an order, pursuant to 18 U.S.C.A. § 2518, approving the application. He specifically found that there was probable cause to believe that Irving Kahn and "others as yet unknown" were using the two telephones to conduct an illegal gambling business, and that normal investigative techniques were unlikely to succeed in providing federal officials with sufficient evidence to successfully prosecute such crimes. The order authorized special agents of the F.B.I. to "intercept wire communications of Irving Kahn and others as yet unknown" to and from the two named telephones concerning gambling activities.

The authorization order further provided that status reports were to be filed with Judge Campbell on the fifth and 10th days following the date of the order, showing what progress had been made towards achievement of the order's objective, and describing any need for further interceptions. The first such report, filed with Judge Campbell on March 25, 1970, indicated that the wiretap had been terminated because its objectives had been attained. The status report gave a summary of the information garnered by the interceptions, stating in part that on March 21, Irving Kahn made two telephone calls from Arizona to his wife at their home in Chicago and discussed gambling wins and losses, and that on the same date Minnie Kahn, Irving's wife, made two telephone calls from the intercepted telephones to a person described in the status report as "a known gambling figure," with whom she discussed various kinds of betting information.

Both Irving and Minnie Kahn were subsequently indicted for using a facility in interstate commerce to promote, manage, and facilitate an illegal gambling business, in violation of 19 U.S.C.A. § 1952. The Government prosecutor notified the Kahns that he intended to introduce into evidence at trial the conversations intercepted under the court order. The Kahns in turn filed motions to suppress the conversations. These motions were heard by Judge Thomas R. McMillen in the Northern District of Illinois, who, in an unreported opinion, granted the motion to suppress. * * * [A]ll * * * conversations in which Minnie Kahn was a participant were suppressed as being outside the scope of Judge Campbell's order, on the ground that Minnie Kahn was not a person "as yet unknown" to the federal authorities at the time of the original application.

The Government filed an interlocutory appeal from the suppression order. A divided panel of the United States Court of Appeals for the Seventh Circuit affirmed that part of the District Court's order suppressing all conversations of Minnie Kahn, * * *. The court held that under the wiretap order all intercepted conversations had to meet two requirements before they could be admitted into evidence:

> "(1) that Irving Kahn be a party to the conversations, and (2) that his conversations intercepted be with 'others as yet unknown.' "

The court then construed the statutory requirements of 18 U.S.C.A. §§ 2518(1)(b)(iv) and 2518(4)(a) that the person whose communications are to be intercepted is to be identified if known, as excluding from the term "others as yet unknown" any "persons whom careful investigation by the government would disclose were probably using the Kahn telephones in conversations for illegal activities." Since the Government in this case had not shown that further investigation of Irving Kahn's activities would not have implicated Minnie in the gambling business, the Court of Appeals felt that Mrs. Kahn was not a "person as yet unknown" within the purview of Judge Campbell's order.

We granted the Government's petition for certiorari, in order to resolve a seemingly important issue involving the construction of this relatively new federal statute.

At the outset, it is worth noting what issues are not involved in this case. First, we are not presented with an attack upon the constitutionality of any part of Title III of the Omnibus Crime Control and Safe Streets Act of 1970. Secondly, review of this interlocutory order does not involve any questions as to the propriety of the Justice Department's internal procedures in authorizing the application for the wiretap. Finally, no argument is presented that the federal agents failed to conduct the wiretap here in such a manner as to minimize the interception of innocent conversations. The question presented is simply whether the conversations that the Government wishes to introduce into evidence at the respondents' trial are made inadmissible by the "others as yet unknown" language of Judge Campbell's order or by the corresponding statutory requirements of Title III.

In deciding that Minnie Kahn was not a person "as yet unknown" within the meaning of the wiretap order, the Court of Appeals relied heavily on an expressed objective of Congress in the enactment of Title III: the protection of the personal privacy of those engaging in wire communications. In light of this clear congressional concern, the Court of Appeals reasoned, the Government could not lightly claim that a person whose conversations were intercepted was "unknown" within the meaning of

Title III. Thus, it was not enough that Mrs. Kahn was not known to be taking part in any illegal gambling business at the time that the Government applied for the wiretap order; in addition, the court held that the Government was required to show that such complicity would not have been discovered had a thorough investigation of Mrs. Kahn been conducted before the wiretap application.

In our view, neither the legislative history nor the specific language of Title III compels this conclusion. To be sure, Congress was concerned with protecting individual privacy when it enacted this statute. But it is also clear that Congress intended to authorize electronic surveillance as a weapon against the operations of organized crime. There is, of course, some tension between these two stated congressional objectives, and the question of how Congress struck the balance in any particular instance cannot be resolved simply through general reference to the statute's expressed concern for the protection of individual privacy. Rather, the starting point, as in all statutory construction, is the precise wording chosen by Congress in enacting Title III.

Section 2518(1) of Title 18, United States Code Annotated, sets out in detail the requirements for the information to be included in an application for an order authorizing the interception of wire communications. The sole provision pertaining to the identification of persons whose communications are to be intercepted is contained in § 2518(1)(b)(iv), which requires that the application state "the identity of the person, if known, *committing the offense* and whose communications are to be intercepted." (Emphasis supplied.) This statutory language would plainly seem to require the naming of a specific person in the wiretap application only when law enforcement officials believe that such an individual is actually committing one of the offenses specified in 18 U.S.C.A. § 2516. Since it is undisputed here that Minnie Kahn was not known to the Government to be engaging in gambling activities at the time the interception order was sought, the failure to include her name in the application would thus seem to comport with the literal language of § 2518(1)(b)(v).

Moreover, there is no reason to conclude that the omission of Minnie Kahn's name from the actual wiretap order was in conflict with any of the provisions of Title III. Section 2518(4)(a) requires that the order specify "the identity of the person, if known, whose communications are to be intercepted." Since the judge who prepares the order can only be expected to learn of the target individual's identity through reference to the original application, it can hardly be inferred that this statutory language imposes any broader requirement than the identification provisions of § 2518(1)(b)(iv).

In effect, the Court of Appeals read these provisions of § 2518 as if they required that the application and order identify "all persons, known or discoverable, who are committing the offense and whose communications are to be intercepted." But that is simply not what the statute says: identification is required only of those "known" to be "committing the offense." Had Congress wished to engraft a separate requirement of "discoverability" onto the provisions of Title III, it surely would have done so in language plainer than that now embodied in § 2518.

Moreover, the Court of Appeals' interpretation of § 2518 would have a broad impact. A requirement that the Government fully investigate the possibility that any likely user of a telephone was engaging in criminal activities before applying for an interception order would greatly subvert the effectiveness of the law enforcement mechanism that Congress constructed. In the case at hand, the Court of Appeals' holding would require the complete investigation not only of Minnie Kahn, but also of the two teenaged Kahn children and other frequenters of the Kahn residence before a wiretap order could be applied for. If the telephone were in a store or an office, the Government might well be required to investigate everyone who had access to it—in some cases, literally hundreds of people—even though there was no reason to suspect that any of them were violating any criminal law. It is thus open to considerable doubt that such a requirement would ultimately serve the interests of individual privacy. In any event, the statute as actually drafted contains no intimation of such total investigative demands.

In arriving at its reading of § 2518, the Court of Appeals seemed to believe that taking the statute at face value would result in a wiretap order amounting to a "virtual general warrant," since the law enforcement authorities would be authorized to intercept communications of anyone who talked on the named telephone line. But neither the statute nor the wiretap order in this case would allow the federal agents such total unfettered discretion. By its own terms, the wiretap order in this case conferred authority to intercept only communications "concerning the above-described [gambling] offenses." Moreover, in accord with the statute the order required the agents to execute the warrant in such a manner as to minimize the interception of any innocent conversations. And the order limited the length of any possible interception to 15 days, while requiring status reports as to the progress of the wiretap to be submitted to the District Judge every five days, so that any possible abuses might be quickly discovered and halted. Thus, the failure of the order to specify that Mrs. Kahn's conversations might be the subject of interception hardly left the executing agents free to seize at will every communication that came over the wire—and there is no indication that such abuses took place in this case.[2]

We conclude, therefore, that Title III requires the naming of a person in the application or interception order only when the law enforcement authorities have probable cause to believe that that individual is "committing the offense" for which the wiretap is sought. Since it is undisputed that the Government had no reason to suspect Minnie Kahn of complicity in the gambling business before the wire interceptions here began, it

---

2. The fallacy in the Court of Appeals' "general warrant" approach may be illustrated by examination of an analogous conventional search and seizure. If a warrant had been issued, upon a showing of probable cause, to search the Kahn residence for physical records of gambling operations, there could be no question that a subsequent seizure of such records bearing Minnie Kahn's handwriting would be fully lawful, despite the fact that she had not been identified in the warrant nor independently investigated. In fact, as long as the property to be seized is described with sufficient specificity, even a warrant failing to name the owner of the premises at which a search is directed, while not the best practice, has been held to pass muster under the Fourth Amendment. * * *

follows that under the statute she was among the class of persons "as yet unknown" covered by Judge Campbell's order.

The remaining question is whether, under the actual language of Judge Campbell's order, only those intercepted conversations to which Irving Kahn himself was a party are admissible in evidence at the Kahn's trial, as the Court of Appeals concluded. The effect of such an interpretation of the wiretap order in this case would be to exclude from evidence the intercepted conversations between Minnie Kahn and the "known gambling figure" concerning betting information. Again, we are unable to read either the District Court order or the underlying provisions of Title III as requiring such a result.

The order signed by Judge Campbell in this case authorized the Government to "intercept wire communications of Irving Kahn and others as yet unknown to and from two telephones, subscribed to by Irving Kahn." The order does not refer to conversations *between* Irving Kahn and others; rather, it describes "communications *of* Irving Kahn and others as yet unknown" to and from the target telephones. To read this language as requiring that Irving Kahn be a party to every intercepted conversation would not only involve a substantial feat of verbal gymnastics, but would also render the phrase "and others as yet unknown" quite redundant, since Kahn perforce could not communicate except with others.

Moreover, the interpretation of the wiretap authorization adopted by the Court of Appeals is at odds with one of the stated purposes of Judge Campbell's order. The District Judge specifically found that the wiretap was needed to "reveal the identities of [Irving Kahn's] confederates, their places of operation, and the nature of the conspiracy involved." It is evident that such information might be revealed in conversations to which Irving Kahn was not a party. For example, a confederate might call in Kahn's absence, and leave either a name, a return telephone number, or an incriminating message. Or, one of Kahn's associates might himself come to the family home and employ the target telephones to conduct the gambling business. It would be difficult under any circumstances to believe that a District Judge meant such intercepted conversations to be inadmissible at any future trial; given the specific language employed by Judge Campbell in the wiretap order today before us, such a conclusion is simply untenable.

Nothing in Title III requires that, despite the order's language, it must be read to exclude Minnie Kahn's communications. As already noted, 18 U.S.C.A. §§ 2518(1)(b)(iv) and 2518(4)(a) require identification of the person committing the offense only "if known." The clear implication of this language is that when there is probable cause to believe that a particular telephone is being used to commit an offense but no particular person is identifiable, a wire interception order may, nevertheless, properly issue under the statute. It necessarily follows that Congress could not have intended that the authority to intercept must be limited to those conversations *between* a party named in the order and others, since at least in some cases, the order might not name any specific party at all.

For these reasons, we hold that the Court of Appeals was in error when it interpreted the phrase "others as yet unknown" so as to exclude conversations involving Minnie Kahn from the purview of the wiretap order. We further hold that neither the language of Judge Campbell's order nor that of Title III requires the suppression of legally intercepted conversations to which Irving Kahn was not himself a party.

Accordingly, the judgment of the Court of Appeals is reversed, and the case is remanded to that court for further proceedings consistent with this opinion.

It is so ordered.

NOTES

1. **Need To Name Persons Not Principal Target.** Suppose the investigating officers had information indicating Minnie Kahn was involved in the bookmaking operation. Would the failure to name her in the application have been improper? In United States v. Donovan, 429 U.S. 413, 97 S.Ct. 658, 50 L.Ed.2d 652 (1977), the Court rejected the argument that the statute required the applicant for a surveillance order to identify only the principal target of the surveillance. "[A] wiretap application," held the Court, "must name an individual if the Government has probable cause to believe that the individual is engaged in the criminal activity under investigation and expects to intercept the individual's conversations over the target telephone."

2. **Exclusionary Penalty for Failing to Name Persons.** Suppose the Government had information indicating Minnie Kahn was involved and nevertheless failed to identify her in the application. Would this omission require exclusion of the results of the surveillance? In *Donovan*, the Court held the failure to name such a person did not require exclusion of the results of the surveillance. The majority concluded that § 2518(1)(b)(iv) does not play a "substantive role" with respect to judicial authorization of intercept orders:

> [Despite noncompliance with § 2518(1)(b)(iv)] the statutorily imposed preconditions to judicial authorization were satisfied, and the issuing judge was simply unaware that additional persons might be overheard engaging in incriminating conversations. In no meaningful sense can it be said that the presence of that information as to additional targets would have precluded judicial authorization of the intercept. * * * [T]he instant intercept is lawful because the application provided sufficient information to enable the issuing judge to determine that the statutory preconditions were satisfied.

429 U.S. at 436, 97 S.Ct. at 672, 50 L.Ed.2d at 673. The Court noted, however, there was no suggestion the Government agents "intentionally" failed to identify the person or omitting this person's name resulted in the person's failure to receive the mandatory inventory notice required by § 2518(8)(d).

3. **Proof that Other Investigative Procedures Would Not Suffice.** Under section 2518(3)(c), the judge who issued the intercept order in *Kahn* determined, "on the basis of the facts submitted by the applicant," that "normal investigative procedures have been tried and have failed or reasonably appear to be unlikely to succeed if tried or to be too dangerous." If Kahn challenged the sufficiency of the evidence to support such a determination, should such a challenge have succeeded? The application apparently did not explain why the applicant believed physical surveillance or "normal search and seizure techniques" would not produce useful evidence. Could the issuing judge have made an "independent" determination of the matter required by section 2518(3)(c)? If this determination was not supported by adequate facts submitted by the applicant, would the absence of the supporting facts invalidate the order and require suppression of its "fruits"?

4. **Minimization of Interception of Innocent Communications.** In *Kahn*, the Court noted no argument had been made that the officers failed to conduct the wiretap in such a manner as to minimize the interception of innocent conversations. But suppose such an argument had been made? Were the officers justified in listening to the conversations between Irving and Minnie Kahn? Between Minnie and an unidentified person? Suppose the officers had listened to conversations between the two teenage Kahn children and their friends. Would it make any difference whether all of these conversations were listened to? Whether any effort was made to identify conversations that should not be listened to in the future, at least in their entirety? If the officers violated the "minimization" requirement, what impact would this violation have upon the admissibility of information obtained during interception of conversations clearly within the order's authorization?

The leading Supreme Court decision, Scott v. United States, 436 U.S. 128, 98 S.Ct. 1717, 56 L.Ed.2d 168 (1978), involved an investigation of a conspiracy to distribute heroin. An intercept order was issued and, for the month of the surveillance, the officers intercepted and recorded all conversations over the telephone described in the order. Forty percent of the calls were ultimately determined to relate to the conspiracy under investigation. The agent in charge of the investigation testified that, although he was aware of the minimization requirement, he made no effort to avoid the interception of innocent calls. The Court rejected the argument that this was bad faith which itself violated the statute. Objective circumstances, not the officers' subjective intent, determine the legality of the actions:

> [B]lind reliance on the percentage of nonpertinent calls intercepted is not a sure guide * * * . Such percentages may provide assistance, but there are surely cases * * * where the percentage of nonpertinent calls is relatively high and yet their interception was still reasonable. Many of the nonpertinent calls may have been very short. Others may have been one-time-only calls. Still other calls may have been ambiguous in nature or apparently involved guarded or coded language. In all these circumstances agents can hardly be expected to know that the calls are not pertinent prior to their termination.

> [I]t is also important to consider the circumstances of the wiretap. For example, when the investigation is focusing on what is thought to be a widespread conspiracy more extensive surveillance may be justified in an attempt to determine the precise scope of the enterprise. And it is possible that many more of the conversations will be permissibly interceptable because they will involve one or more of the co-conspirators. The type of use to which the telephone is normally put may also have some bearing on the extent of minimization required. For example, if the agents are permitted to tap a public telephone because one individual is thought to be placing bets over the phone, substantial doubts as to minimization may arise if the agents listen to every call which goes out over that phone regardless of who places the call. On the other hand, if the phone is located in the residence of a person thought to be the head of a major drug ring, a contrary conclusion may be indicated.

> [I]t may be important to determine at exactly what point during the authorized period the investigation was made. During the early stages of surveillance the agents may be forced to intercept all calls to establish categories of nonpertinent calls which will not be intercepted thereafter. Interception of these same types of calls might be unreasonable later on, however, once the nonpertinent categories have been established and it is clear that this particular conversation is of that type. Other situations may arise where patterns of nonpertinent calls do not appear. In these circumstances it may not be

unreasonable to intercept almost every short conversation because the determination of relevancy cannot be made before the call is completed.

436 U.S. at 140–41, 98 S.Ct. at 1724–25, 56 L.Ed.2d at 179–80.

On the facts of the case, the majority found no violation of the minimization requirement despite the high percentage of nonpertinent calls intercepted. Many of the nonpertinent calls were short and many were ambiguous in nature, making characterization impossible until the call was terminated. Further, the agents' conduct must be considered in light of the fact that the crime under investigation was a wide-ranging conspiracy with a large number of participants. The Court noted, but did not reach, the argument that, if the agents violated the minimization requirements, suppression is required only of those conversations improperly intercepted, not of all intercepted conversations.

Justice Brennan, joined by Justice Marshall, dissented. The majority, he suggested, undercut that portion of *Kahn's* reasoning which relied upon the minimization requirement to answer the contention that the holding in *Kahn* would authorize general search warrants.

5. **Actual Use and Effect of Electronic Surveillance Legislation.** The federal statute requires periodic reports by judges and prosecutors concerning applications, orders, and interceptions. These reports are apparently intended to develop and maintain a pool of information useful in evaluating the continued wisdom of making these law enforcement devices available under the limitations and restrictions imposed by present federal and state legislation. The reports are made to the Administrative Office of the United States Courts, which issues yearly reports summarizing information collected for the previous year. See, e.g., Administrative Office of the United States Courts, 1998 Wiretap Report, covering the period from January 1, 1998 through December 31, 1998. Several aspects of this information for recent years are especially useful.

Statutory authorization of electronic surveillance exists in 31 states, the District of Columbia and the federal system.

During 1998, 1,329 applications were granted for authorization of wire, oral, or electronic surveillance—566 were granted by federal judges and 763 by state judges. Only 2 applications were denied in 1998. During the 11 years from 1988 through 1988, a total of only 5 applications were denied by the judiciary; 11,000 applications were granted.

The number of orders issued has been increasing. In 1988, federal judges issued 293 orders and in 1993 they issued 450. In 1988, state judges issues 445 orders and in 1993 they issued 526.

The average number of interceptions per day ranged from zero to 427 for each device. The average number of persons whose conversations were intercepted was 129 per installed intercept and the average number of conversations intercepted was 1,251. About 25 percent of those conversations produced incriminating evidence.

The best measure of the effectiveness of electronic surveillance would be the number of persons arrested and convicted as a result of intercepts who would not otherwise have been arrested and convicted. That information, however, is not available. The Administrative Office does provide the numbers of arrests and convictions reported as resulting from intercept orders. There is often considerable lapse of time from the year in which an intercept occurs to when an arrest or a conviction is obtained. The Administrative Office's 1998 Report provides information on arrests and convictions reported as resulting from intercept orders installed in the years from 1987 through 1997. In 1993, 976 federal and statute intercept orders were issued and 938 resulted in actual installation of intercepts. The results of those 1993 intercepts were reported as follows:

	1993	1994	1995	1996	1997	Total
Arrests Made During Year	2,428	981	390	130	109	4,038
Convictions During Year	413	912	538	233	179	2,275

The 938 intercepts made in 1993, then, resulted in 2,275 convictions.

CHAPTER 7

INTERROGATION AND CONFESSIONS

Analysis

EDITORS' INTRODUCTION: CONFESSIONS AND CONFESSIONS LAW IN THE CONTEXT OF MODERN LAW ENFORCEMENT

Among traditional law enforcement techniques are the collection and preservation of suspects' out-of-court statements and, in some situations, active elicitation or encouragement of such statements. These techniques and the legal issues they raise are the subjects of this chapter.

Terminology: Confessions, Admissions, and Exculpatory Statements

When prosecutors offer defendants' out-of-court self-incriminating statements into evidence against them, courts sometimes distinguished between a "confession"—a statement admitting or acknowledging all facts necessary for conviction of the crime charged—and an "admission"—an acknowledgement of one or more facts that tend to establish guilt but not of all elements of the crime. Moreover, both are sometimes distinguished from an "exculpatory" statement, a statement which, at the time it was made, was intended to exculpate rather than incriminate the speaker, but which later is offered to prove the speaker's guilt. Prosecutors often use exculpatory statements by of proving that a suspect gave a false explanation of incriminating circumstances; this is offered to prove that the suspect was conscious of his or her guilt and, therefore, that the suspect is in fact guilty. It is doubtful that these distinctions have much significance today.

Basic Issues and Policy Considerations

The legal doctrines related to the admissibility of confessions raise two basic questions: First, when should a confession be excluded as a means of discouraging or punishing inappropriate law enforcement behavior? Second, when should a confession be excluded because—without regard to the existence or nonexistence of any "fault" on the part of law enforcement personnel—it was given in circumstances that make its use unacceptable? There is substantial overlap between these two matters, but it is also clear the admissibility of confessions is sometimes attacked on the basis of factors which cannot be the fault of law enforcement officers or other government agents.

In addressing these and other questions raised in this chapter—what rules should govern the admissibility of confessions and how should these rules be interpreted and applied—it is important to identify various and sometimes competing policy considerations involved. The government, of course, has an obvious interest in being able to use reliable evidence of defendants' guilt of crimes; confessions are traditionally regarded as exceptionally reliable evidence of guilt. In Hopt v. Utah, 110 U.S. 574, 584–85, 4 S.Ct. 202, 207, 28 L.Ed. 262, 267 (1884), the Court explained:

A confession, if freely and voluntarily made, is evidence of the most satisfactory character. Such a confession * * * "is deserving of the highest credit, because it is presumed to flow from the strongest sense of guilt, and, therefore, it is admitted as proof of the crime to which it refers." * * * [T]he presumption upon which weight is given to such evidence [is] * * * that one who is innocent will not imperil his safety or prejudice his interests by an untrue statement * * * .

How important confessions are to securing convictions is a matter of dispute. It is clear that in some cases, available evidence other than the confession would result in conviction. In others, it seems certain the confession is essential to proof of guilt. Project, Interrogations in New Haven: The Impact of Miranda, 76 Yale L.J. 1519 (1967), studied the investigation of 90 cases. In 49 questioning was successful, i.e., it resulted in a self-incriminating statement. But the researchers concluded that in only 4 cases (8%) was questioning "necessary," in the sense that other evidence available would not have been sufficient to prove guilt. But Seeburger and Wettick, Miranda in Pittsburgh—A Statistical Study, 29 U.Pitt.L.Rev. 1 (1967), studied two samples of cases and concluded that confessions were necessary to conviction in 24.7% and 32.8% of those cases.

Reliability of Confessions

To some extent, legal requirements relating to interrogation and the admissibility of confessions are concerned with confessions' reliability. In this regard, why is *exclusion* of confessions appropriate? Why not simply trust juries to consider the credibility of evidence that defendants confessed and give that evidence the weight it deserves?

Defendants are entitled—as a matter of federal constitutional law—to the opportunity to persuade judges and juries that confessions should not be believed because of the manner in which they were elicited. In Crane v. Kentucky, 476 U.S. 683, 106 S.Ct. 2142, 90 L.Ed.2d 636 (1986), the defense moved before trial to suppress Crane's confession to the murder for which he was to be tried. A pretrial hearing was held on the motion, at which Crane testified he had been detained for questioning in a windowless room for some time, as many as six officers had been present during the questioning, he had unsuccessfully made repeated requests to contact his family and he had been badgered into making a false confession. Several police officers' testimonies contradicted this version of the facts and the trial court held the confession admissible. At trial, the prosecution introduced the confession into evidence. The defense contended in response that contradictions in the confession and the circumstances under which it was given meant the jury should not believe it. In support of this, the defense unsuccessfully attempted to introduce before the jury evidence concerning the interrogation during which the defendant made the confession. The state supreme court affirmed the resulting conviction, reasoning that evidence relating only to the "voluntariness" of a confession is not admissible before the jury. While evidence relating to the "credibility" of the confession is admissible, the court reasoned, all of Crane's offered evidence went only to voluntariness. A unanimous Supreme Court, speaking through Justice O'Connor, reversed:

> Whether rooted directly in the due process clause of the Fourteenth Amendment or in the Compulsory Process or Confrontation clauses of the Sixth Amendment, the Constitution guarantees criminal defendants "a meaningful opportunity to present a complete defense." We break no new ground in observing that an essential component of procedural fairness is an opportunity to be heard. That opportunity would be an empty one if the State were permitted to exclude compe-

tent, reliable evidence bearing on the credibility of a confession when such evidence is central to the defendant's claim of innocence. * * *

Under these principles, the Kentucky courts erred in foreclosing [Crane's] efforts to introduce testimony about the environment in which the police secured his confession. * * * [E]vidence about the manner in which a confession was obtained is often highly relevant to its reliability and credibility.

476 U.S. at 690–91, 106 S.Ct. at 2146–47, 90 L.Ed.2d at 645.

In view of defendants' right to challenge confessions' voluntariness before trial juries, why is exclusion of confessions ever justified on reliability grounds? Are jurors likely to be insensitive to evidence that should cause them to disregard a confession as unreliable? Perhaps the need to discourage police actions that, in general, tend to result in inaccurate confessions requires that the law provide an especially strong disincentive for engaging in such action. Such a disincentive might best be provided by completely excluding confessions rather than giving the prosecution opportunities to convince juries that such confessions ought to be credited.

Should confession law encourage police to elicit self-incriminating admissions from suspects and prosecutors to use them in trying cases? Or, should it attempt to discourage either or both? Courts sometimes assume restrictions on the admissibility of confessions will encourage law enforcement officers to seek out more reliable evidence of accuseds' guilt. Whether such evidence is available and—if so—whether confession law can successfully encourage officers to obtain it is not clear.

The number and significance of inaccurate convictions is a matter of longstanding controversy. Richard A. Leo and Richard J. Ofshe, The Consequences of False Confessions: Deprivations of Liberty and Miscarriages of Justice in the Age of Psychological Interrogation, 88 J.Crim.L. & Crim. 429 (1998), presented 60 cases involving what they characterized as proven false confessions (34 cases), highly probable false confessions (18 cases) and probable false confessions (8 cases). In 29 of the 60 cases the confessing defendant was convicted. Currently used interrogation techniques, they maintained, encourage inaccurate confessions. Further, law enforcement officers are not trained to be sensitive to this risk. Law enforcement officers, prosecutors, and jurors, moreover, "treat confession evidence with such deference that it outweighs strong evidence of a defendant's innocence." Leo and Ofshe concluded that "the problems caused by police-induced false confessions are significant, recurrent, and deeply troubling."

As might be expected, the claims of Leo and Ofshe have not gone unchallenged. Paul G. Cassell, The Guilty and the "Innocent": An Examination of Alleged Cases of Wrongful Conviction From False Confessions, 22 Harv. J. L. & Pub.Policy 523 (1999), maintained that in nine of the cases in which Leo and Ofshe claimed false confessions led to convictions there was substantial evidence supporting the guilt of the accused and that these persons were most likely guilty. Cassell suggested current interrogation techniques pose a worrisome risk of inducing false confessions only if the suspects are mentally retarded.

Nonevidentiary Law Enforcement Objectives

The undeniable fact that interrogation and resulting statements may serve a number of law enforcement objectives other than securing admissible evidence of suspects' guilt of criminal offenses complicates confession law. See Project, Interrogation in New Haven: The Impact of Miranda, 76 Yale L.J. 1519, 1593–96 (1967). For example, confessions may be useful or necessary for identifying accomplices to an offense. While a confession may not be admissible against the accomplice, it may direct law enforcement officers to other information and admissible evidence of the accomplice's guilt. And statements may be used to "clear" crimes for purposes of internal police records. If a case is "cleared"—even if no prosecution results—the police books are closed and no further resources will be expended on it. Further, a law enforcement agency's effectiveness is often judged in part by its clearance rate, so such agencies have a strong incentive to seek information permitting them to close cases even if no criminal prosecutions are possible or likely. Statements elicited by interrogation may serve a variety of other functions. Statements may permit the recovery of stolen property or of weapons that might otherwise be available to persons for future crimes. Or the statements may be used for "intelligence" purposes, to allocate resources most effectively, and to make various decisions as to how to proceed with the "policing" job.

In considering matters raised in this chapter, consider whether the law should be concerned with police techniques serving these functions as well as those designed to secure admissible evidence for courtroom use. Is exclusion of statements offered in criminal trials sufficient response to such problems as exist? Or should the law seek to discourage techniques such as interrogation even when those techniques are not intended to and will not result in the use against the suspect of a self-incriminating statement? If so, how might this be done?

Concerns Unrelated to Reliability

There are almost certainly considerations other than accuracy that should be accommodated in confession law. Suspects may have legitimate interests in being free from use against them of some law enforcement techniques, even if those techniques pose no danger of eliciting inaccurate statements. Encouraging suspects to incriminate themselves in some circumstances and by use of some techniques may be inconsistent with the manner in which human beings—even those believed on adequate grounds to be guilty of crimes—should be treated. There has, of course, been little brief made for the position that suspects should never be permitted to incriminate themselves or that all self-incriminating admissions should be rejected at trial. As then-Justice Rehnquist commented, "[The Supreme Court] has never held that an accused is constitutionally protected from his inability to keep quiet * * * ." United States v. Henry, 447 U.S. 264, 297, 100 S.Ct. 2183, 2201, 65 L.Ed.2d 115, 140 (1980) (Rehnquist, J., dissenting).

But suspects may have a legitimate interest in being encouraged or permitted to incriminate themselves only when they have certain information concerning the consequences of doing so and the alternatives available to them. Dix, Mistake, Ignorance, Expectation of Benefit, and the Modern Law of Confessions, 1975 Wash.U.L.Q. 275, 330–31, argued:

> A major objective of the law of confessions * * * should be * * * assuring that a person who confesses does so with as complete an understanding of his tactical position as possible. This, of course, would require awareness not only of his abstract legal rights, but also of his practical ability to implement those rights in light of his factual situation and of the tactical wisdom of asserting them.

Should this be one of the law's objectives in this area? If the act of making a confession as a practical matter assures conviction, perhaps a confession should be regarded as a "waiver" of the right to trial and the right to have the state prove guilt beyond a reasonable doubt. Waivers of important trial rights must, under prevailing law, be "knowing" and "intelligent" as well as "voluntary." Johnson v. Zerbst, 304 U.S. 458, 58 S.Ct. 1019, 82 L.Ed. 1461 (1938). Arguably, decisions to confess, then, should be given legal effect only if they were "knowing" and "intelligent" in this sense. It may follow that legal rules should discourage interrogation in situations likely to result in confessions failing these requirements. Further, perhaps confessions should be regarded as admissible only if they meet these standards.

The material in this chapter reflects to some extent a progression of developments. The first part develops the requirement that a confession be "voluntary," the traditional doctrine governing admissibility of confessions. Consider the reasons why the Supreme Court may have been dissatisfied with this doctrine as a means for dealing with what the Court perceived to be the problems presented by confessions in general and custodial interrogation in particular. That such dissatisfaction existed is made clear by the Court's 1966 action in Miranda v. Arizona, the subject of Part B of this chapter. Given the nature of the *Miranda* rules and their subsequent development, have they lived up to the Court's 1966 expectations? Do they adequately deal with the problems presented by custodial interrogation? What alternatives should be considered? How should they be evaluated? The third part of this chapter deals with suspects' Sixth Amendment right to counsel. Consider how this meshes with the voluntariness rule and the *Miranda* requirements.

Requirement of Corroboration or "Independent" Proof of the Corpus Delicti.

The doctrines discussed in this chapter relating to the admissibility of confessions must be distinguished from the very different requirement of "corroboration." The requirement of corroboration is often put as a demand that the prosecution, in order to prove guilt beyond a reasonable doubt, produce evidence other than an out-of-court confession by the defendant. This other evidence is often required to show the *corpus delicti,* that is, that the crime charged was committed *by someone.* The evidence independent of the confession need not tend to show that the defendant committed the crime. Nor need it be sufficient in itself to prove commission of the crime beyond a reasonable doubt. The confession can be the only evidence tending to show that the defendant committed the offense; the corroborating evidence can be considered together with the confession in determining whether the prosecution has proven guilt beyond a reasonable doubt. In some states, the requirement has been incorporated into statute. Section 60.50 of New York's Criminal Procedure Law, for example, provides that a conviction is not permitted "solely upon evidence of a confession made by [the defendant] without additional proof that the offense charged has been committed."

The requirement is sometimes stated as one addressing the admissibility of a confession—a confession is not admissible unless the prosecution has first introduced other evidence showing that the charged offense was committed. But trial judges have great discretion over the order of proof. A trial judge is therefore unlikely to commit reversible error even under this formulation of the requirement by admitting a confession, if the prosecution later in the case produces other evidence showing the charged offense was committed. See generally, McCormick on Evidence § 145 (5th ed. 1999).

In some jurisdictions, the requirement is somewhat more flexible than one of independent proof of the *corpus delicti*. In federal litigation, for example, the Supreme Court has held that in order for a conviction to be upheld the Government must have introduced "substantial independent evidence which would tend to establish the trustworthiness of the [defendant's] statement." Opper v. United States, 348 U.S. 84, 93, 75 S.Ct. 158, 164, 99 L.Ed. 101, 109 (1954). This is the requirement applied by the Court in Wong Sun v. United States, 371 U.S. 471, 83 S.Ct. 407, 9 L.Ed.2d 441 (1963), reprinted in Chapter 1. However the requirement is formulated, it is in effect a requirement that a confession be corroborated by some other evidence at trial in order to justify the conviction of the defendant.

Like the voluntariness rule, the requirement of corroboration is based upon concern regarding the accuracy of out-of-court self-incriminating statements. In *Opper* the Court explained:

> [O]ur concept of justice that finds no man guilty until proven has led our state and federal courts generally to refuse conviction on testimony concerning confessions of the accused not made by him at the trial of his case. * * * [T]he doubt persists that the zeal of the agencies of prosecution to protect the peace, the self-interest of the accomplice, the maliciousness of an enemy or the aberration or weakness of the accused under the strain of suspicion may tinge or warp the facts of the confession. Admissions, retold at trial, are much like hearsay, that is, statements not made at the pending trial. They had neither the compulsion of the oath nor the test of cross-examination.

348 U.S. at 89–90, 75 S.Ct. at 162–63, 99 L.Ed. at 106–07. Despite its concern with the accuracy of confessions and trials, however, the requirement of corroboration has not been incorporated into any federal constitutional doctrine and remains exclusively a matter of state or local definition of evidence sufficiency.

Statutory Provisions Related to Confessions

There have been relatively few legislative efforts addressing confession issues. The federal statute set out in part B(6) of this chapter is one of the few such efforts. The American Law Institute's Model Code of Pre-Arraignment Procedure (Official Draft, 1975) offers a more comprehensive effort.

Article 150 deals with Exclusion of Statements and some portions of Article 140, Conditions of Investigation During Custody of an Arrested Person, are also relevant to confession issues.

A.   THE REQUIREMENT OF "VOLUNTARINESS"

EDITORS' INTRODUCTION: DEVELOPMENT, CONTENT, AND CURRENT SIGNATURE OF THE VOLUNTARINESS REQUIREMENT

Because of the widespread publicity given the *Miranda* decision, contemporary discussions of "confession law" tend to revolve around the *Miranda* requirements. An adequate understanding of the reasons for the "*Miranda* revolution," however, demands acquaintance with pre-*Miranda* voluntariness law. In addition, the voluntariness requirement is not without current significance. If *Miranda* does not apply to a given situation, the voluntariness requirement is likely to be the major consideration in determining whether a confession can be used in evidence. If a confession is inadmissible to prove a defendant's guilt because of the *Miranda* requirements, its availability to impeach the defendant's credibility—should the defendant testify at trial—apparently depends in part upon the voluntariness of the admission. Even if *Miranda* applies to a situation, there is a high likelihood that the effectiveness of the suspect's waiver of the rights to silence and to counsel will be at issue. Traditional voluntariness law undoubtedly bears upon the appropriate resolution of such matters. Further, if a suspect has given several confessions and *Miranda* was violated only during the elicitation of the first, the admissibility of the later confessions depends largely or entirely upon their voluntariness.

Development of the Federal Constitutional Requirement. In its first confession case, Hopt v. Utah, 110 U.S. 574, 4 S.Ct. 202, 28 L.Ed. 262 (1884), the United States Supreme Court treated the admissibility of an incriminating statement as a matter of federal evidence law. The admissibility of such statements, the Court noted, "so largely depends upon the special circumstances connected with the confession, that it is difficult, if not impossible, to formulate a rule that will comprehend all cases." But, it then held, the case could be resolved by "the weight of authority," which stated a confession is involuntary and inadmissible if

> the confession appears to have been made either in consequence of inducements of a temporal nature, held out by one in authority, touching the charge preferred, or because of a threat or promise by or in the presence of such person, which, operating upon the fears or hopes of the accused, in reference to the charge, deprive him of that freedom of will or self-control essential to make his confession voluntary within the meaning of the law.

110 U.S. at 585, 4 S.Ct. at 207–08, 28 L.Ed. at 266–67.

Thirteen years later, in Bram v. United States, 168 U.S. 532, 18 S.Ct. 183, 42 L.Ed. 568 (1897), the Court commented that "[i]n criminal trials, in the courts of the United States wherever a question arises whether a confession is incompetent because not voluntary, the issue is controlled by that portion of the fifth amendment to the constitution of the United States, commanding that no person 'shall be compelled in any criminal case, to be a witness against himself.' " The Fifth Amendment privilege, the Court continued, was a crystallization of the common law voluntariness rule existing at the time of the adoption of the Constitution. The "principle by which the admissibility of the confession of an accused person is to be determined is expressed in the textbooks," the high tribunal added, and it then cited with approval the following passage from 3 Russell on Crimes 478 (6th ed.):

> [A] confession, in order to be admissible, must be free and voluntary; that is, must not be extracted by any sort of threats or violence, nor obtained by any direct or implied promises, however slight, nor by the exertion of any improper influence.

The Fifth Amendment privilege against compelled self-incrimination was not held binding upon the states until Malloy v. Hogan, 378 U.S. 1, 84 S.Ct. 1489, 12 L.Ed.2d 653 (1964). But, beginning with Brown v. Mississippi, 297 U.S. 278, 56 S.Ct. 461, 80 L.Ed. 682 (1936), the Supreme Court imposed Constitutional limitations upon the use of confessions in state criminal trials through application of the Fourteenth Amendment's general requirement of due process. Although earlier cases suggested some difference between the due process requirement and the *Bram* Fifth Amendment rules, in 1966 the Court commented that "[t]he decisions of this Court have guaranteed the same procedural protection for the defendant whether his confession was used in a federal or state court." Miranda v. Arizona, 384 U.S. 436, 464 n. 33, 86 S.Ct. 1602, 1623 n. 33, 16 L.Ed.2d 694, 717–18 n. 33 (1966).

Not only has the "voluntariness" requirement been imposed as a matter of federal constitutional law, but state courts have universally accepted it as a matter of state constitutional doctrine. It is clear, then, that an appreciation of the need for and significance of subsequent developments in the legal standards governing the admissibility of confessions in American courts requires an understanding of this concept of voluntariness.

Content of the Voluntariness Requirement. In Blackburn v. Alabama, 361 U.S. 199, 80 S.Ct. 274, 4 L.Ed.2d 242 (1960), the Supreme Court observed that "a complex of values underlies the stricture against use by the state of confessions which, by way of convenient shorthand, this Court terms involuntary, and the role played by each in any situation varies according to the particular circumstances of the case." The Court commented further upon these values:

> The abhorrence of society to the use of involuntary confessions does not turn alone on their inherent untrustworthiness. It also turns on the deep-rooted feeling that the police must obey the law while enforcing the law; that in the end life and liberty can be as much endangered from illegal methods used to convict those thought to be criminals as from the actual criminals themselves. Accordingly, the actions of police in obtaining confessions * * * come under scrutiny * * *.

Spano v. New York, 360 U.S. 315, 320–21, 79 S.Ct. 1202, 1205–06, 3 L.Ed.2d 1265, 1270 (1959).

Brown and many early cases involved "coerced" confessions—that is, confessions stimulated by improper violence or the threat of such violence. In *Brown,* for example, police beat the suspects and told them such beatings would continue until the suspects provided confessions of the substance desired by the officers. But in subsequent cases the Court extended the prohibition against involuntary confessions far beyond such coerced statements.

Overbearing of the Will. In Blackburn v. Alabama, the Court noted that "coercion can be mental as well as physical and * * * the blood of the accused is not the only hallmark of an unconstitutional inquisition." In Spano v. New York, the Court observed:

> [A]s * * * the methods used to extract confessions [become] more sophisticated, our duty to enforce federal constitutional protections does not cease. It only becomes more difficult because of the more delicate judgments to be made.

360 U.S. at 321, 79 S.Ct. at 1206, 3 L.Ed.2d at 1271. In cases lacking overt brutality, the Court has applied a "totality of the circumstances" analysis. Justice Frankfurter authored the classic statement of this approach:

> No single litmus-paper test for constitutionally-impermissible interrogation has been evolved: neither extensive cross questioning * * *; nor undue delay in arraignment * * *; nor failure to caution a prisoner * * *; nor refusal to permit communication with friends and legal counsel at stages in the proceeding when the prisoner is still only a suspect * * *.
>
> Each of these factors, in company with all of the surrounding circumstances—the duration and conditions of detention (if the confessor has been detained), the manifest attitude of the police towards him, his physical and mental state, the diverse pressures which sap or sustain his powers of resistance and self-control—is relevant. The ultimate test remains * * *: * * * Is the confession the product of an essentially free and unconstrained choice by its maker? * * * [I]f his will has been overborne and his capacity for self-determination critically impaired, the use of his confession offends due process.

Culombe v. Connecticut, 367 U.S. 568, 601–02, 81 S.Ct. 1860, 1878–79, 6 L.Ed.2d 1037, 1057–58 (1961).

Greenwald v. Wisconsin, 390 U.S. 519, 88 S.Ct. 1152, 20 L.Ed.2d 77 (1968) (per curiam), illustrated application of the test. Although the case was decided by the Supreme Court after *Miranda, Miranda's* nonretroactivity meant that it did not govern the admissibility of the confession. The facts were as follows:

> [Greenwald], who has a ninth-grade education, was arrested on suspicion of burglary shortly before 10:45 on the evening of January 20, 1965. He was taken to a police station. He was suffering from high blood pressure, a condition for which he was taking medication twice a day. [He] had last taken food and medication, before his arrest, at 4

p.m. He did not have medication with him at the time of the arrest. At the police station [he] was interrogated from 10:45 until midnight. He was not advised of his constitutional rights. [He] repeatedly denied guilt. No incriminating statements were made at this time.

[He] was booked and fingerprinted and, sometime after 2 a.m., he was taken to a cell in the city jail. A plank fastened to the wall served as his bed. [He] claims he did not sleep. At 6 a.m., [he] was led from the cell to a "bullpen." At 8:30 he was placed in a lineup. At 8:45, his interrogation recommenced. It was conducted by several officers at a time, in a small room. [Greenwald] testified that in the course of the morning he was not offered food and that he continued to be without medication. For an hour or two he refused to answer any questions. When he did speak, it was to deny, once again, his guilt.

Sometime after 10 a.m., [Greenwald] was asked to write out a confession. He refused, stating that "it was against my constitutional rights" and that he was "entitled to have a lawyer." These statements were ignored. No further reference was made to an attorney, by [Greenwald] or by the police officers.

At about 11 a.m. [Greenwald] began a series of oral admissions culminating in a full oral confession at about 11:30. At noon he was offered food. The confession was reduced to writing about 1 p.m. Just before the confession was reduced to writing, [he] was advised of his constitutional rights. According to his testimony, he confessed because "I knew they weren't going to leave me alone until I did."

Considering the totality of these circumstances, a majority of the Court held the Wisconsin Supreme Court had erred in finding that Greenwald's statements "were the product of his free and rational choice." Justice Stewart, joined by two other members of the Court, read the circumstances as adequately supporting the state court's conclusion:

[Greenwald] was nearly 30 years old and was by no means a stranger to the criminal law. He was questioned for little more than an hour one evening and for less than four hours the next morning. He was neither abused nor threatened and was promised no benefit for confessing. * * * [H]e himself testified that, during his interrogation, "he knew he had a constitutional right to refuse to answer any questions, * * * he knew anything he said could be used against him, and * * * he knew he had a constitutional right to retain counsel." Moreover, * * * [he] himself testified that at no time between his arrest and his confession did he express to anyone a desire for food or for medication.

390 U.S. at 521–22, 88 S.Ct. at 1154, 20 L.Ed.2d at 80 (Stewart, J., dissenting).

As applied in cases such as *Greenwald*, does the voluntariness case law provide a meaningful standard for determining the admissibility of confessions? Judge Posner of the Seventh Circuit suggested not:

[W]hether a confession is voluntary is not really a fact, but a characterization. There is indeed no "faculty of will" inside our heads that has two states, on and off, such that through careful reconstruction of events the observer can determine whether the switch was on when the defendant was confessing. * * *

[C]ourts have not been successful in devising a standard that will determine in a consistent fashion when confessions should be excluded on grounds of involuntariness. Of course if the confession is unreliable, it should go out, along with other unreliable evidence. It is on this basis that confessions extracted by torture are excluded. But in most cases in which a confession is sought to be excluded because involuntary, there is little likelihood that the inducements placed before the defendant were so overpowering as to induce an untrue confession. The courts in such cases retreat to the proposition that a confession, to be admissible, must be the product of a free choice. [B]ut [this] is just the faculty of will approach, and, as the courts are beginning to suspect, it leads nowhere. Taken seriously it would require the exclusion of virtually all fruits of custodial interrogation, since few choices to confess can be thought truly "free" when made by a person who is incarcerated and is being questioned by armed officers without the presence of counsel or anyone else to give him moral support. The formula is not taken seriously. * * * [V]ery few incriminating statements, custodial or otherwise, are held to be involuntary, though few are the product of a choice that the interrogators left completely free.

United States v. Rutledge, 900 F.2d 1127, 1128–29 (7th Cir.1990) (Posner, J.).

Promises. The traditional requirement of voluntariness mandated exclusion of a confession obtained as a result of a promise or inducement, made by a person in a position of authority, concerning the criminal charges to which the defendant confessed. See generally, Dix, Mistake, Ignorance, Expectation of Benefit, and the Modern Law of Confessions, 1975 Wash.U.L.Q. 275 (1975). As the language from *Bram* set out above suggests, the Supreme Court appeared to incorporate this traditional requirement into the due process voluntariness standard.

The Supreme Court addressed the modern constitutional significance of promises in Arizona v. Fulminante, 499 U.S. 279, 111 S.Ct. 1246, 113 L.Ed.2d 302 (1991). Fulminante was a prisoner in a federal correctional facility and had begun to receive "rough treatment" from other inmates because of a rumor he had killed a child. Sarivola was a fellow inmate who was also an informant for the Federal Bureau of Investigation. Federal agents encouraged Sarivola to elicit information about the killing from Fulminante. Sarivola then offered to protect Fulminante from other inmates if Fulminante told him about the matter. Fulminante admitted the killing to Sarivola. At Fulminante's trial for the murder of the child, the prosecution successfully offered his confession. On appeal, the Arizona Supreme Court reversed, holding the confession inadmissible. The Supreme Court granted review to consider the State's contention that the Arizona Supreme Court had incorrectly applied a standard under which the confession was involuntary upon proof that "but for" the "promise" by Sarivola, Fulminante would not have made the confession. The Supreme Court noted the *Bram* language but made clear that this 1897 discussion's statement of voluntariness was no longer accurate federal constitutional law:

Although the Court noted in *Bram* that a confession cannot be obtained by " 'any direct or implied promises, however slight, nor by the exertion of any improper influence,' " it is clear this passage from *Bram* * * * does not state the standard for determining the voluntariness of a confession * * *.

499 U.S. at 285, 111 S.Ct. at 1251, 113 L.Ed.2d at 315. But it further found the Arizona court had properly applied a totality of the circumstances analysis. Although the question was a "close one," the majority concluded the Arizona court acceptably found the confession involuntary:

The Arizona Supreme Court found a credible threat of physical violence unless Fulminante confessed. Our cases have made clear that a finding of coercion need not depend upon actual violence by a government agent; a credible threat is sufficient. * * * [T]he Arizona Supreme Court found that it was fear of physical violence, absent protection from his friend (and Government agent) Sarivola, which motivated Fulminante to confess. Accepting the Arizona court's finding, permissible on this record, that there was a credible threat of physical violence, we agree with its conclusion that Fulminante's will was overborne in such a way as to render his confession the product of coercion.

499 U.S. at 287, 111 S.Ct. at 1252–53, 113 L.Ed.2d at 316–17.

Deception. Despite the case law's traditionally rigid prohibition against promises, American courts developed no similar voluntariness rule barring police officers from deceiving suspects during interrogation. Some courts have traditionally held that deception is simply not a basis for regarding a confession involuntary. In Commonwealth v. Graham, 408 Pa. 155, 182 A.2d 727 (1962), for example, a female police employee attended a lineup, pointed to the defendant, and said, "That's the man." The Pennsylvania Supreme Court expressed emphatic disapproval of the action, but held that the deception did not amount to legal duress or coercion rendering the confession inadmissible. Some courts have stated the voluntariness requirement so as to leave open the possibility that at least some deception affects admissibility. In People v. Everett, 10 N.Y.2d 500, 225 N.Y.S.2d 193, 180 N.E.2d 556 (1962), for example, an officer misrepresented to a murder suspect that the victim had only been injured and had identified the suspect as his assailant. "Deception alone will not render a confession invalid," the New York court held, "unless the deceiving acts amount to a deprivation of due process." On the facts before it, the court found no aggravation of the sort necessary to violate due process.

Others courts have indicated that deception would render a confession involuntary only if the deception was likely to induce a false confession. In applying this test, however, the courts have been reluctant to find that particular deception created the required risk of a false statement. E.g., People v. Castello, 194 Cal. 595, 229 P. 855 (1924) (inaccurate statement by officer that defendant had been seen stealing the property was not such as to produce an untrue confession and therefore did not render confession inadmissible).

The Supreme Court did not address the relationship between deception and the federal due process standard until Frazier v. Cupp, 394 U.S. 731,

89 S.Ct. 1420, 22 L.Ed.2d 684 (1969). (Although *Frazier* was decided after *Miranda, Miranda's* requirements did not apply to the confession there at issue and therefore its admissibility turned upon its voluntariness.) Police interrogated Frazier; he denied committing the offense and claimed to have been with his cousin, Rawls, on the night of the crime. The officer then falsely told Frazier that Rawls had confessed to the murder. Subsequently, Frazier decided to make a statement. The trial court, over defense objection, admitted the statement at Frazier's trial.

The Supreme Court found no violation of the due process standard. It noted that Frazier had received a "partial warning" of his constitutional rights, the questioning was of short duration, and Frazier was "a mature individual of normal intelligence." Without citation of authority or discussion of the relevant considerations, the Court then commented, "The fact that the police misrepresented the statement that Rawls made is, while relevant, insufficient in our view to make this otherwise voluntary confession inadmissible."

Burden of Proof. If the prosecution offers a confession against a defendant, the prosecution must prove the voluntariness of that confession. In Lego v. Twomey, 404 U.S. 477, 92 S.Ct. 619, 30 L.Ed.2d 618 (1972), however, the Court held that the federal Constitution required only that voluntariness be proved by a preponderance of the evidence. No basis existed, the majority reasoned, to believe that rulings made under the preponderance of the evidence standard have been unreliable or otherwise wanting in quality. Consequently, the prosecution's ability to put confessions before juries need not be further impeded by a need to prove voluntariness beyond a reasonable doubt. States, of course, remain free to impose such a higher standard as a matter of state law.

Harmless Error. Earlier Supreme Court discussions suggested that if on appeal an appellate court determined that the trial judge had erroneously admitted an involuntary confession, reversal of the conviction for a new trial was always necessary. Admission of such a confession, in other words, could not be "harmless error." In Arizona v. Fulminante, discussed earlier in this Introductory Note as addressing promises made to suspects, a bare majority of the Supreme Court held that even admission of an involuntary confession could be harmless error if the appellate court is convinced beyond a reasonable doubt that the confession did not contribute to the defendant's conviction. Trial errors generally are subject to the harmless error rule, the Court concluded, and insufficient reason exists to treat involuntary confessions any differently. Admission of such a confession is not a "structural defect[ ] in the constitution of the trial mechanism, which def[ies] analysis by 'harmless error' standards." Nor is the admission of such a confession a type of error that should always require reversal because it "transcends the criminal process." On the facts of *Fulminante,* however, the State failed to meet its burden of establishing beyond a reasonable doubt that the confession did not contribute to Fulminante's conviction. Therefore, his conviction was reversed.

* * *

The principal case in this section reflects a major conceptual development of the federal constitutional voluntariness doctrine. In addition to the statements raising the due process voluntariness concern discussed in those parts of the opinions reprinted here, the defendant made other statements to which *Miranda* applied. The Supreme Court's holdings on the *Miranda* issues are discussed in Part B of this chapter.

Colorado v. Connelly

Supreme Court of the United States, 1986.
479 U.S. 157, 107 S.Ct. 515, 93 L.Ed.2d 473.

■ CHIEF JUSTICE REHNQUIST delivered the opinion of the Court.

* * *

I

On August 18, 1983, Officer Patrick Anderson of the Denver Police Department was in uniform, working in an off-duty capacity in downtown Denver. Respondent Francis Connelly approached Officer Anderson and, without any prompting, stated that he had murdered someone and wanted to talk about it. Anderson immediately advised respondent that he had the right to remain silent, that anything he said could be used against him in court, and that he had the right to an attorney prior to any police questioning. See Miranda v. Arizona, 384 U.S. 436, 86 S.Ct. 1602, 16 L.Ed.2d 694 (1966). Respondent stated that he understood these rights but he still wanted to talk about the murder. Understandably bewildered by this confession, Officer Anderson asked respondent several questions. Connelly denied that he had been drinking, denied that he had been taking any drugs, and stated that, in the past, he had been a patient in several mental hospitals. Officer Anderson again told Connelly that he was under no obligation to say anything. Connelly replied that it was "all right," and that he would talk to Officer Anderson because his conscience had been bothering him. To Officer Anderson, respondent appeared to understand fully the nature of his acts.

Shortly thereafter, Homicide Detective Stephen Antuna arrived. Respondent was again advised of his rights, and Detective Antuna asked him "what he had on his mind." Respondent answered that he had come all the way from Boston to confess to the murder of Mary Ann Junta, a young girl whom he had killed in Denver sometime during November 1982. Respondent was taken to police headquarters, and a search of police records revealed that the body of an unidentified female had been found in April 1983. Respondent openly detailed his story to Detective Antuna and Sergeant Thomas Haney, and readily agreed to take the officers to the scene of the killing. Under Connelly's sole direction, the two officers and respondent proceeded in a police vehicle to the location of the crime. Respondent pointed out the exact location of the murder. Throughout this episode, Detective Antuna perceived no indication whatsoever that respondent was suffering from any kind of mental illness.

Respondent was held overnight. During an interview with the public defender's office the following morning, he became visibly disoriented. He began giving confused answers to questions, and for the first time, stated that "voices" had told him to come to Denver and that he had followed the directions of these voices in confessing. Respondent was sent to a state hospital for evaluation. He was initially found incompetent to assist in his own defense. By March 1984, however, the doctors evaluating respondent determined that he was competent to proceed to trial.

At a preliminary hearing, respondent moved to suppress all of his statements. Doctor Jeffrey Metzner, a psychiatrist employed by the state hospital, testified that respondent was suffering from chronic schizophrenia and was in a psychotic state at least as of August 17, 1983, the day before he confessed. Metzner's interviews with respondent revealed that respondent was following the "voice of God." This voice instructed respondent to withdraw money from the bank, to buy an airplane ticket, and to fly from Boston to Denver. When respondent arrived from Boston, God's voice became stronger and told respondent either to confess to the killing or to commit suicide. Reluctantly following the command of the voices, respondent approached Officer Anderson and confessed.

Dr. Metzner testified that, in his expert opinion, respondent was experiencing "command hallucinations." This condition interfered with respondent's "volitional abilities; that is, his ability to make free and rational choices." Dr. Metzner further testified that Connelly's illness did not significantly impair his cognitive abilities. Thus, respondent understood the rights he had when Officer Anderson and Detective Antuna advised him that he need not speak. Dr. Metzner admitted that the "voices" could in reality be Connelly's interpretation of his own guilt, but explained that in his opinion, Connelly's psychosis motivated his confession.

On the basis of this evidence the Colorado trial court decided that respondent's statements must be suppressed because they were "involuntary." * * *

The Colorado Supreme Court affirmed. * * *

II

The Due Process Clause of the Fourteenth Amendment provides that no State shall "deprive any person of life, liberty, or property, without due process of law." Just last Term, in Miller v. Fenton, 474 U.S. 104, 109, 106 S.Ct. 445, 449, 88 L.Ed.2d 405 (1985), we held that by virtue of the Due Process Clause "certain interrogation techniques, either in isolation or as applied to the unique characteristics of a particular suspect, are so offensive to a civilized system of justice that they must be condemned." * * * [T]he cases considered by this Court * * * have focused upon the crucial element of police overreaching. While each confession case has turned on its own set of factors justifying the conclusion that police conduct was oppressive, all have contained a substantial element of coercive police conduct. Absent police conduct causally related to the confession, there is simply no basis for concluding that any state actor has deprived a criminal defendant of due process of law. Respondent correctly notes that as interrogators have turned to more subtle forms of psychological persuasion, courts have found the mental condition of the defendant a more significant factor in the "voluntariness" calculus. But this fact does not justify a conclusion that a defendant's mental condition, by itself and apart from its relation to official coercion, should ever dispose of the inquiry into constitutional "voluntariness."

Respondent relies on Blackburn v. Alabama, 361 U.S. 199, 80 S.Ct. 274, 4 L.Ed.2d 242 (1960), and Townsend v. Sain, 372 U.S. 293, 83 S.Ct. 745, 9 L.Ed.2d 770 (1963), for the proposition that the "deficient mental condition of the defendants in those cases was sufficient to render their confessions involuntary." But respondent's reading of *Blackburn* and *Townsend* ignores the integral element of police overreaching present in both cases. In *Blackburn,* the Court found that the petitioner was probably insane at the time of his confession and the police learned during the interrogation that Blackburn had a history of mental problems. The police exploited this weakness with coercive tactics: "the eight- to nine-hour sustained interrogation in a tiny room which was upon occasion literally filled with police officers; the absence of Blackburn's friends, relatives, or legal counsel; [and] the composition of the confession by the Deputy Sheriff rather than by Blackburn." These tactics supported a finding that the confession was involuntary. Indeed, the Court specifically condemned police activity that "wrings a confession out of an accused against his will." *Townsend* presented a similar instance of police wrongdoing. In that case, a police physician had given Townsend a drug with truth-serum properties. The subsequent confession, obtained by officers who knew that Townsend had been given drugs, was held involuntary. These two cases demonstrate that while mental condition is surely relevant to an individual's susceptibility to police coercion, mere examination of the confessant's state of mind can never conclude the due process inquiry.

Our "involuntary confession" jurisprudence is entirely consistent with the settled law requiring some sort of "state action" to support a claim of violation of the Due Process Clause of the Fourteenth Amendment. The Colorado trial court, of course, found that the police committed no wrongful acts, and that finding has been neither challenged by the respondent nor disturbed by the Supreme Court of Colorado. The latter court, however, concluded that sufficient state action was present by virtue of the admission of the confession into evidence in a court of the State.

The difficulty with the approach of the Supreme Court of Colorado is that it fails to recognize the essential link between coercive activity of the State, on the one hand, and a resulting confession by a defendant, on the other. The flaw in respondent's constitutional argument is that it would expand our previous line of "voluntariness" cases into a far-ranging requirement that courts must divine a defendant's motivation for speaking or acting as he did even though there be no claim that governmental conduct coerced his decision.

The most outrageous behavior by a private party seeking to secure evidence against a defendant does not make that evidence inadmissible under the Due Process Clause. * * * Moreover, suppressing respondent's statements would serve absolutely no purpose in enforcing constitutional guarantees. The purpose of excluding evidence seized in violation of the

Constitution is to substantially deter future violations of the Constitution. Only if we were to establish a brand new constitutional right—the right of a criminal defendant to confess to his crime only when totally rational and properly motivated—could respondent's present claim be sustained.

We have previously cautioned against expanding "currently applicable exclusionary rules by erecting additional barriers to placing truthful and probative evidence before state juries." * * * We abide by that counsel now. "[T]he central purpose of a criminal trial is to decide the factual question of the defendant's guilt or innocence," and while we have previously held that exclusion of evidence may be necessary to protect constitutional guarantees, both the necessity for the collateral inquiry and the exclusion of evidence deflect a criminal trial from its basic purpose. Respondent would now have us require sweeping inquiries into the state of mind of a criminal defendant who has confessed, inquiries quite divorced from any coercion brought to bear on the defendant by the State. We think the Constitution rightly leaves this sort of inquiry to be resolved by state laws governing the admission of evidence and erects no standard of its own in this area. A statement rendered by one in the condition of respondent might be proved to be quite unreliable, but this is a matter to be governed by the evidentiary laws of the forum, see, e.g., Fed.Rule Evid. 601, and not by the Due Process Clause of the Fourteenth Amendment. "The aim of the requirement of due process is not to exclude presumptively false evidence, but to prevent fundamental unfairness in the use of evidence, whether true or false." Lisenba v. California, 314 U.S. 219, 236, 62 S.Ct. 280, 290, 86 L.Ed. 166 (1941).

We hold that coercive police activity is a necessary predicate to the finding that a confession is not "voluntary" within the meaning of the Due Process Clause of the Fourteenth Amendment. We also conclude that the taking of respondent's statements, and their admission into evidence, constitute no violation of that Clause.

* * *

IV

The judgment of the Supreme Court of Colorado is accordingly reversed, and the cause remanded for further proceedings not inconsistent with this opinion.

■ JUSTICE BRENNAN, with whom JUSTICE MARSHALL joins, dissenting.

* * * Because I believe that the use of a mentally ill person's involuntary confession is antithetical to the notion of fundamental fairness embodied in the Due Process Clause, I dissent.

* * *

The absence of police wrongdoing should not, by itself, determine the voluntariness of a confession by a mentally ill person. The requirement that a confession be voluntary reflects a recognition of the importance of free will and of reliability in determining the admissibility of a confession, and thus demands an inquiry into the totality of the circumstances surrounding the confession.

* * *

We have never confined our focus to police coercion, because the value of freedom of will has demanded a broader inquiry. The confession cases decided by this Court * * * have focused upon both police overreaching and free will. While it is true that police overreaching has been an element of every confession case to date, it is also true that in every case the Court has made clear that ensuring that a confession is a product of free will is an independent concern. The fact that involuntary confessions have always been excluded in part because of police overreaching signifies only that this is a case of first impression. Until today, we have never upheld the admission of a confession that does not reflect the exercise of free will.

[I]f state action is required, police overreaching is not its only relevant form. The Colorado Supreme Court held that the trial court's admission of the involuntary confession into evidence is also state action. * * *

The instant case starkly highlights the danger of admitting a confession by a person with a severe mental illness. The trial court made no findings concerning the reliability of Mr. Connelly's involuntary confession, since it believed that the confession was excludable on the basis of involuntariness. However, the overwhelming evidence in the record points to the unreliability of Mr. Connelly's delusional mind. * * *

Moreover, the record is barren of any corroboration of the mentally ill defendant's confession. No physical evidence links the defendant to the alleged crime. Police did not identify the alleged victim's body as the woman named by the defendant. Mr. Connelly identified the alleged scene of the crime, but it has not been verified that the unidentified body was found there or that a crime actually occurred there. There is not a shred of competent evidence in this record linking the defendant to the charged homicide. There is only Mr. Connelly's confession.

Minimum standards of due process should require that the trial court find substantial indicia of reliability, on the basis of evidence extrinsic to the confession itself, before admitting the confession of a mentally ill person into evidence. I would require the trial court to make such a finding on remand. To hold otherwise allows the State to imprison and possibly to execute a mentally ill defendant based solely upon an inherently unreliable confession.

* * *

NOTES

1. **Relevance of Accuracy.** While the unreliability of involuntary confessions may be among the rationales for excluding them, the accuracy of a particular confession is irrelevant to its due process voluntariness. In Rogers v. Richmond, 365 U.S. 534, 81 S.Ct. 735, 5 L.Ed.2d 760 (1961), the police misrepresented to defendant that they were about to bring his wife into the stationhouse for questioning. The trial judge held the resulting confession admissible because the police pretense "had

no tendency to produce a confession that was not in accord with the truth." The United States Supreme Court reversed the conviction:

> From a fair reading of * * * [the record] we cannot but conclude that the question whether Rogers' confessions were admissible was answered by reference to a legal standard which took into account the circumstance of probable truth or falsity. And this is not a permissible standard under the Due Process Clause of the Fourteenth Amendment. The attention of the trial court should have been focused * * * on the question whether the behavior of the State's law enforcement officials was such as to overbear petitioner's will to resist and to bring about confessions not freely self-determined—a question to be answered with complete disregard of whether or not petitioner in fact spoke the truth.

365 U.S. at 543–44, 81 S.Ct. at 741, 5 L.Ed.2d at 768.

2. **Violation of "Prompt Presentation" Requirements.** Rule 5(a) of the Federal Rules of Criminal Procedure demands presentation of an arrested person before a judicial officer without "unnecessary delay." Most if not all states have similar requirements of "prompt presentation" of arrested suspects. In part, prompt presentation minimizes the opportunity for coercive or otherwise improper interrogation techniques. At the arrestee's appearance before the magistrate, the arrestee may be given information concerning the charges pending and may be informed by the judge regarding legal rights. Moreover, provision may be made for pretrial release. What is the effect upon the admissibility of a confession of a delay in presenting the accused before a magistrate in accordance with these requirements?

In McNabb v. United States, 318 U.S. 332, 63 S.Ct. 608, 87 L.Ed. 819 (1943), the Supreme Court held that under its supervisory power it would require exclusion of a confession made by a defendant after federal officers who had the defendant in custody failed to comply with a statutory predecessor to Rule 5(a) demanding prompt presentation. The Court later applied the same exclusionary rule to Rule 5(a). Upshaw v. United States, 335 U.S. 410, 69 S.Ct. 170, 93 L.Ed. 100 (1948). In Mallory v. United States, 354 U.S. 449, 77 S.Ct. 1356, 1 L.Ed.2d 1479 (1957), the Court considered the meaning of "unnecessary delay" under Rule 5(a), and made clear this was to be defined so as to minimize the opportunity for custodial interrogation:

> Circumstances may justify a brief delay between arrest and arraignment, as for instance, where the story volunteered by the accused is susceptible of quick verification through third parties. But the delay must not be of a nature to give opportunity for the extraction of a confession.

354 U.S. at 455, 77 S.Ct. at 1360, 1 L.Ed.2d at 1483. The delay in the case before it, the Court held, was "unnecessary" because a magistrate was readily available and the defendant was not presented only because the officers desired the opportunity for interrogation.

The Supreme Court has never held the *McNabb-Mallory* rule in any way binding on the states. Instead, a showing that a confession was obtained during an improper delay in presenting the defendant before a magistrate has always been regarded as merely one factor to consider in determining the confession's due process voluntariness. Of course, this lack of any federal constitutional prompt presentation requirement is no bar to states adopting, as a matter of state law, an exclusionary rule requiring the suppression of confessions made during a period of delay violative of the state's prompt presentation requirement.

As a matter of federal law, Congress has modified the *McNabb-Mallory* rule. Under 18 U.S.C.A. § 3501(c), other portions of which are reprinted later in subsection B(6) of this chapter, a confession offered against a federal criminal defendant is not to be excluded solely because of delay in presenting a defendant before a magistrate if the confession is voluntary and made within six hours following the defendant's taking into custody. Further, a confession obtained after a six-hour period is not to be excluded on delay grounds alone if the delay is found reasonable, considering the distance traveled to a judicial officer and the means of transportation available to the officers.

Precisely what effect flows from the federal statute is unclear. The Supreme Court has, for example, noted but not passed on the contention that the statute mandates suppression of a confession made during improper delay in presenting a suspect before a magistrate if the confession is made after the six hour "safe harbor" period has expired. United States v. Alvarez–Sanchez, 511 U.S. 350, 355–56, 114 S.Ct. 1599, 1602–03, 114 L.Ed.2d 319, 326–27 (1994).

3. **Violation of Fourth Amendment Right to Probable Cause Determination.** Under Gerstein v. Pugh, 420 U.S. 103, 95 S.Ct. 854, 43 L.Ed.2d 54 (1975), an unindicted defendant arrested without a warrant has a Fourth Amendment right to a "prompt" judicial determination of probable cause. County of Riverside v. McLaughlin, 500 U.S. 44, 111 S.Ct. 1661, 114 L.Ed.2d 49 (1991), made clear that promptness generally requires such probable cause determinations be made within 48 hours of arrests. These determinations may—but need not—be made when the defendants go before magistrates pursuant to the statutory provisions discussed in note 2, above. If an arrested defendant is not provided with the probable cause determination required under *Gerstein* and *McLaughlin,* is a confession given during that detention—and after the defendant was entitled to a probable cause determination—inadmissible as the fruit of the Fourth Amendment violation?

The issue was noted but not addressed by the Supreme Court in Powell v. Nevada, 511 U.S. 79, 84–85, 114 S.Ct. 1280, 1283–84, 128 L.Ed.2d 1, 7–8 (1994). Justice Thomas, joined by the Chief Justice, argued in *Powell* that the Court should reach the issue. He further offered an analysis that would render suppression inappropriate in some and perhaps all such cases. Powell was arrested on November 3, 1989 after he brought a badly injured child to a hospital for treatment. On November 7, he made a statement admitting abusing the child. Later on the 7th, a magistrate determined the arrest was supported by probable cause; the magistrate relied upon facts recited in a "declaration of arrest" prepared by officers within an hour of Powell's arrest. On these facts, Justice Thomas reasoned, the November 7th statement need not be suppressed:

[S]uppression of petitioner's statement would not be appropriate because the statement was not a product of the *McLaughlin* violation.

Our decisions make clear "that evidence will not be excluded as 'fruit' [of an unlawful act] unless the illegality is at least the 'but for' cause of the discovery of the evidence." * * *

Contrary to petitioner's arguments, the violation of *McLaughlin* (as opposed to his arrest and custody) bore no causal relationship whatsoever to his November 7 statement. The timing of the probable cause determination would have affected petitioner's statement only if a proper hearing at or before the 48–hour mark would have resulted in a finding of no probable cause. Yet, as the Magistrate found, the police had probable cause to suspect petitioner of child abuse, and there is no suggestion that the delay in securing a determination of probable cause permitted the police to gather additional evidence to be presented to the Magistrate. On the contrary, the Magistrate based his determination on the facts included in the declaration of arrest that was completed within an hour of petitioner's arrest. Thus, if the probable cause determination had been made within 48 hours as required by *McLaughlin,* the same information would have been presented, the same result would have been obtained, and none of the circumstances of petitioner's custody would have been altered.

Moreover, it cannot be argued that the *McLaughlin* error somehow made petitioner's custody unlawful and thereby rendered the statement the product of unlawful custody. Because the arresting officers had probable cause to arrest petitioner, he was lawfully arrested at the hospital. The presumptively unconstitutional delay in securing a judicial determination of probable cause during a period of lawful custody did not render that custody illegal. We have never suggested that lawful custody becomes unlawful due to a failure to obtain a prompt judicial finding of probable cause—that is, probable cause does not disappear if not judicially determined within 48 hours.

511 U.S. at 89–91 114 S.Ct. at 1286–87, 128 L.Ed.2d at 10–12 (Thomas, J., dissenting). Since the confession was not the product of illegal governmental activity, he added, "conventional attenuation principles are inapplicable in this case * * *."

4. **Adequacy of Voluntariness Requirement.** Was the voluntariness requirement insufficient to protect suspects' interests during custodial interrogation? Schulhofer, Confessions and the Court, 79 Mich.L.Rev. 865, 869–72 (1981), summarized a number of defects which critics found in the due process voluntariness requirement. It failed to provide specific guidance to law enforcement on which questioning tactics were and were not permissible. The "elusive task of balancing" invited trial judges to give weight to their subjective preferences and discouraged appellate review; judicial review of police activity was therefore impaired. Often, the critical issue was one of fact—what happened in the interrogation room—resulting in "swearing matches" between officers and defendants; defendants generally lost. And despite the requirement, considerable pressure was placed on suspects to confess, those with special weaknesses were especially susceptible to such pressure, and even physical brutality was not effectively enough discouraged.

For a general discussion of the voluntariness requirement concluding it is the only constitutional restraint that can justifiably be imposed upon police interrogation, see Grano, Voluntariness, Free Will and the Law of Confessions, 65 Va.L.Rev. 859 (1979).

B. Self-Incrimination and *Miranda's* Right to Counsel

Beginning with Escobedo v. Illinois, 378 U.S. 478, 84 S.Ct. 1758, 12 L.Ed.2d 977 (1964), the Supreme Court began to shift away from the voluntariness requirement as the major federal constitutional means of addressing what it perceived to be the continuing problems posed by police questioning of suspects in custody. This shift was completed two years later in Miranda v. Arizona, 384 U.S. 436, 86 S.Ct. 1602, 16 L.Ed.2d 694 (1966).

The *Miranda* decision itself is presented in the first subsection of this section. The second subsection addresses the task of determining those situations to which *Miranda* applies. The next presents one aspect of *Miranda* that has undergone considerable evolution—the right to prevent questioning. Subsection four considers what has become a major problem area in *Miranda* law—the existence and validity of waivers of the *Miranda* rights. In the fifth subsection, attention is turned to a particularly troublesome problem concerning remedy—a defendant's potential right to exclusion of evidence obtained as a factual result of an inadmissible confession.

Finally, the last subsection considers the impact of the *Miranda* requirements and the Congressional effort to "overrule" the decision.

1.   THE *MIRANDA* DECISION

EDITORS' INTRODUCTION: THE *MIRANDA* RIGHTS

Miranda v. Arizona is, of course, one of the most widely-known and controversial decisions of the "Warren Court." To put the decision in doctrinal perspective, it is necessary to understand that before *Miranda* there was substantial support for the proposition that police interrogation did not—directly, at least—implicate the Fifth Amendment privilege against compelled self-incrimination. The privilege, it was widely considered, applied only where the suspect could be the subject of "legal compulsion," that is, compulsion authorized by law, to answer questions. In a courtroom or before a grand jury a witness can be penalized for contempt of court for refusing to respond to questions; thus the court applies "legal" compulsion to the witness and consequently the situation implicated the privilege. Police officers, on the other hand, have no legal right to impose penalties upon suspects who refuse to answer the officers' questions. Consequently, although police interrogation could give rise to an involuntary confession, it could not directly violate the Fifth Amendment privilege.

In addition, even where the privilege against compelled self-incrimination applies, it is, as a general rule, violated only if a person first specifically claims a right under the privilege to refuse to answer a question and then is nevertheless encouraged to answer. Unless the person first claims the privilege, he has not been "compelled" to incriminate himself within the meaning of the privilege. It follows from this, of course, that—again, as a general rule—the government has no obligation before or during questioning to inform the person of the privilege. The person has the obligation to assert the privilege. See Minnesota v. Murphy, 465 U.S. 420, 427, 104 S.Ct. 1136, 1142, 79 L.Ed.2d 409, 418–19 (1984).

Miranda first determined that police custodial interrogation of a person implicated interests of the person protected by the Fifth Amendment, and thus that provision. The Court then proceeded to define the requirements of the Fifth Amendment in this context.

Subsequent judicial discussion and development of *Miranda* sometimes emphasized the identification of so-called *"per se"* rules. The precise meaning of this characterization of some *Miranda* requirements is not always clear. Perhaps, however, it is best considered as describing the relationship between a legal requirement and the exclusionary remedy. A *per se* requirement, then, is one that, when violated, automatically demands the exclusion of resulting evidence. Police violation of other requirements, on the other hand, may not require exclusion of resulting evidence unless other considerations apply. In the *Miranda* context, for example, violation of some requirements announced in the decision or subsequent case law might require the exclusion of resulting evidence only if it rendered the suspect's waiver of the right to remain silent involuntary or otherwise ineffective.

Whatever the terminology used, it is important in identifying and understanding the *Miranda* rights to separate two matters. One, of course, is the contents of the requirements which case law places upon law enforcement officers. The other, however, is the relationship between violation of these requirements and the admissibility of suspects' self-incriminating statements and other evidence obtained as the result of such statements.

Miranda v. Arizona

Supreme Court of the United States, 1966.
384 U.S. 436, 86 S.Ct. 1602, 16 L.Ed.2d 694.

■ MR. CHIEF JUSTICE WARREN delivered the opinion of the Court.

The cases before us raise questions which go to the roots of our concepts of American criminal jurisprudence: the restraints society must observe consistent with the Federal Constitution in prosecuting individuals for crime. More specifically, we deal with the admissibility of statements obtained from an individual who is subjected to custodial police interrogation and the necessity for procedures which assure that the individual is accorded his privilege under the Fifth Amendment to the Constitution not to be compelled to incriminate himself.

* * *

Our holding will be spelled out with some specificity in the pages which follow but briefly stated it is this: the prosecution may not use statements, whether exculpatory or inculpatory, stemming from custodial interrogation of the defendant unless it demonstrates the use of procedural safeguards effective to secure the privilege against self-incrimination. By custodial interrogation, we mean questioning initiated by law enforcement officers after a person has been taken into custody or otherwise deprived of his freedom of action in any significant way. As for the procedural safeguards to be employed, unless other fully effective means are devised to inform accused persons of their right of silence and to assure a continuous opportunity to exercise it, the following measures are required. Prior to any questioning, the person must be warned that he has a right to remain silent, that any statement he does make may be used as evidence against him, and that he has a right to the presence of an attorney, either retained or appointed. The defendant may waive effectuation of these rights, provided the waiver is made voluntarily, knowingly and intelligently. If, however, he indicates in any manner and at any stage of the process that he wishes to consult with an attorney before speaking there can be no questioning. Likewise, if the individual is alone and indicates in any manner that he does not wish to be interrogated, the police may not question him. The mere fact that he may have answered some questions or volunteered some statements on his own does not deprive him of the right to refrain from answering any further inquiries until he has consulted with an attorney and thereafter consents to be questioned.

I.

* * *

An understanding of the nature and setting of * * * in-custody interrogation is essential to our decisions today. The difficulty in depicting what transpires at such interrogations stems from the fact that in this country they have largely taken place incommunicado. From extensive factual studies undertaken in the early 1930's, including the famous Wickersham Report to Congress by a Presidential Commission, it is clear that police violence and the "third degree" flourished at that time. In a series of cases decided by this Court long after these studies, the police resorted to physical brutality—beatings, hanging, whipping—and to sustained and protracted questioning incommunicado in order to extort confessions. * * *

[Situations involving brutality] are undoubtedly the exception now, but they are sufficiently widespread to be the object of concern. Unless a proper limitation upon custodial interrogation is achieved—such as these decisions will advance—there can be no assurance that practices of this nature will be eradicated in the foreseeable future.

* * * .

[T]he modern practice of in-custody interrogation is psychologically rather than physically oriented. * * * "[T]his Court has recognized that coercion can be mental as well as physical, and that the blood of the accused is not the only hallmark of an unconstitutional inquisition." Blackburn v. State of Alabama, 361 U.S. 199, 206, 80 S.Ct. 274, 279, 4 L.Ed.2d 242 (1960). Interrogation still takes place in privacy. Privacy results in secrecy and this in turn results in a gap in our knowledge as to what in fact goes on in the interrogation rooms. A valuable source of information about present police practices, however, may be found in various police manuals and texts which document procedures employed with success in the past, and which recommend various other effective tactics. These texts are used by law enforcement agencies themselves as guides. It should be noted that these texts professedly present the most enlightened and effective means presently used to obtain statements through custodial interrogation. By considering these texts and other data, it is possible to describe procedures observed and noted around the country.

The officers are told by the manuals that the "principal psychological factor contributing to a successful interrogation is privacy—being alone with the person under interrogation." The efficacy of this tactic has been explained as follows:

> "If at all practicable, the interrogation should take place in the investigator's office or at least in a room of his own choice. The subject should be deprived of every psychological advantage. In his own home he may be confident, indignant, or recalcitrant. He is more keenly aware of his rights and more reluctant to tell of his indiscretions or criminal behavior within the walls of his home. Moreover his family and other friends are nearby, their presence lending moral support. In his office, the investigator possesses all the advantages. The atmosphere suggests the invincibility of the forces of the law."

To highlight the isolation and unfamiliar surroundings, the manuals instruct the police to display an air of confidence in the suspect's guilt and from outward appearance to maintain only an interest in confirming certain details. The guilt of the subject is to be posited as a fact. The interrogator should direct his comments toward the reasons why the subject committed the act, rather than court failure by asking the subject whether he did it. Like other men, perhaps the subject has had a bad family life, had an unhappy childhood, had too much to drink, had an unrequited desire for women. The officers are instructed to minimize the moral seriousness of the offense, to cast blame on the victim or on society. These tactics are designed to put the subject in a psychological state where his story is but an elaboration of what the police purport to know already—that he is guilty. Explanations to the contrary are dismissed and discouraged.

The texts thus stress that the major qualities an interrogator should possess are patience and perseverance. One writer describes the efficacy of these characteristics in this manner:

"In the preceding paragraphs emphasis has been placed on kindness and stratagems. The investigator will, however, encounter many situations where the sheer weight of his personality will be the deciding factor. Where emotional appeals and tricks are employed to no avail, he must rely on an oppressive atmosphere of dogged persistence. He must interrogate steadily and without relent, leaving the subject no prospect of surcease. He must dominate his subject and overwhelm him with his inexorable will to obtain the truth. He should interrogate for a spell of several hours pausing only for the subject's necessities in acknowledgment of the need to avoid a charge of duress that can be technically substantiated. In a serious case, the interrogation may continue for days, with the required intervals for food and sleep, but with no respite from the atmosphere of domination. It is possible in this way to induce the subject to talk without resorting to duress or coercion. The method should be used only when the guilt of the subject appears highly probable."

The manuals suggest that the suspect be offered legal excuses for his actions in order to obtain an initial admission of guilt. Where there is a suspected revenge-killing, for example, the interrogator may say:

"Joe, you probably didn't go out looking for this fellow with the purpose of shooting him. My guess is, however, that you expected something from him and that's why you carried a gun—for your own protection. You knew him for what he was, no good. Then when you met him he probably started using foul, abusive language and he gave some indication that he was about to pull a gun on you, and that's when you had to act to save your own life. That's about it, isn't it, Joe?"

Having then obtained the admission of shooting, the interrogator is advised to refer to circumstantial evidence which negates the self-defense explanation. This should enable him to secure the entire story. One text notes that "Even if he fails to do so, the inconsistency between the subject's original denial of the shooting and his present admission of at least doing the shooting will serve to deprive him of a self-defense 'out' at the time of trial."

When the techniques described above prove unavailing, the texts recommend they be alternated with a show of some hostility. One ploy often used has been termed the "friendly-unfriendly" or the "Mutt and Jeff" act:

" * * * In this technique, two agents are employed. Mutt, the relentless investigator, who knows the subject is guilty and is not going to waste any time. He's sent a dozen men away for this crime and he's going to send the subject away for the full term. Jeff, on the other hand, is obviously a kindhearted man. He has a family himself. He has a brother who was involved in a little scrape like this. He disapproves of Mutt and his tactics and will arrange to get him off the case if the subject will cooperate. He can't hold Mutt off for very long. The subject would be wise to make a quick decision. The technique is applied by having both investigators present while Mutt acts out his role. Jeff may stand by quietly and demur at some of Mutt's tactics. When Jeff makes his plea for cooperation, Mutt is not present in the room."

The interrogators sometimes are instructed to induce a confession out of trickery. The technique here is quite effective in crimes which require identification or which run in series. In the identification situation, the interrogator may take a break in his questioning to place the subject among a group of men in a lineup. "The witness or complainant (previously coached, if necessary) studies the lineup and confidently points out the subject as the guilty party." Then the questioning resumes "as though there were now no doubt about the guilt of the subject." A variation on this technique is called the "reverse lineup":

"The accused is placed in a lineup, but this time he is identified by several fictitious witnesses or victims who associated him with different offenses. It is expected that the subject will become desperate and confess to the offense under investigation in order to escape from the false accusations."

The manuals also contain instructions for police on how to handle the individual who refuses to discuss the matter entirely or who asks for an attorney or relatives. The examiner is to concede him the right to remain silent. "This usually has a very undermining effect. First of all, he is disappointed in his expectation of an unfavorable reaction on the part of the interrogator. Secondly, a concession of this right to remain silent impresses the subject with the apparent fairness of his interrogator." After this psychological conditioning, however, the officer is told to point out the incriminating significance of the suspect's refusal to talk:

"Joe, you have a right to remain silent. That's your privilege and I'm the last person in the world who'll try to take it away from you. If that's the way you want to leave this, O. K. But let me ask you this. Suppose you were in my shoes and I were in yours and you called me in to ask me about this and I told you, 'I don't want to answer any of your questions.' You'd think I had something to hide, and you'd probably be right in thinking that. That's exactly what I'll have to think about you, and so will everybody else. So let's sit here and talk this whole thing over."

Few will persist in their initial refusal to talk, it is said, if this monologue is employed correctly.

In the event that the subject wishes to speak to a relative or an attorney, the following advice is tendered:

> "[T]he interrogator should respond by suggesting that the subject first tell the truth to the interrogator himself rather than get anyone else involved in the matter. If the request is for an attorney, the interrogator may suggest that the subject save himself or his family the expense of any such professional service, particularly if he is innocent of the offense under investigation. The interrogator may also add, 'Joe, I'm only looking for the truth, and if you're telling the truth, that's it. You can handle this by yourself.' "

From these representative samples of interrogation techniques, the setting prescribed by the manuals and observed in practice becomes clear. In essence, it is this: To be alone with the subject is essential to prevent distraction and to deprive him of any outside support. The aura of confidence in his guilt undermines his will to resist. He merely confirms the preconceived story the police seek to have him describe. Patience and persistence, at times relentless questioning, are employed. To obtain a confession, the interrogator must "patiently maneuver himself or his quarry into a position from which the desired objective may be attained." When normal procedures fail to produce the needed result, the police may resort to deceptive stratagems such as giving false legal advice. It is important to keep the subject off balance, for example, by trading on his insecurity about himself or his surroundings. The police then persuade, trick, or cajole him out of exercising his constitutional rights.

Even without employing brutality, the "third degree" or the specific stratagems described above, the very fact of custodial interrogation exacts a heavy toll on individual liberty and trades on the weakness of individuals.
* * *

In those cases before us today * * * we might not find the defendants' statements to have been involuntary in traditional terms. * * * The fact remains that in none of these cases did the officers undertake to afford appropriate safeguards at the outset of the interrogation to insure that the statements were truly the product of free choice.

It is obvious that such an interrogation environment is created for no purpose other than to subjugate the individual to the will of his examiner. This atmosphere carries its own badge of intimidation. To be sure, this is not physical intimidation, but it is equally destructive of human dignity. The current practice of incommunicado interrogation is at odds with one of our Nation's most cherished principles—that the individual may not be compelled to incriminate himself. Unless adequate protective devices are employed to dispel the compulsion inherent in custodial surroundings, no statement obtained from the defendant can truly be the product of his free choice.

From the foregoing, we can readily perceive an intimate connection between the privilege against self-incrimination and police custodial questioning. * * *

II.

* * *

The question in these cases is whether the [Fifth Amendment] privilege is fully applicable during a period of custodial interrogation. * * * We are satisfied that all the principles embodied in the privilege apply to informal compulsion exerted by law-enforcement officers during in-custody questioning. An individual swept from familiar surroundings into police custody, surrounded by antagonistic forces, and subjected to the techniques of persuasion described above cannot be otherwise than under compulsion to speak. As a practical matter, the compulsion to speak in the isolated setting of the police station may well be greater than in courts or other official investigations, where there are often impartial observers to guard against intimidation or trickery.

* * *

III.

* * * We have concluded that without proper safeguards the process of in-custody interrogation of persons suspected or accused of crime contains inherently compelling pressures which work to undermine the individual's will to resist and to compel him to speak where he would not otherwise do so freely. In order to combat these pressures and to permit a full opportunity to exercise the privilege against self-incrimination, the accused must be adequately and effectively apprised of his rights and the exercise of those rights must be fully honored.

It is impossible for us to foresee the potential alternatives for protecting the privilege which might be devised by Congress or the States in the exercise of their creative rulemaking capacities. Therefore we cannot say that the Constitution necessarily requires adherence to any particular solution for the inherent compulsions of the interrogation process as it is presently conducted. Our decision in no way creates a constitutional straitjacket which will handicap sound efforts at reform, nor is it intended to have this effect. We encourage Congress and the States to continue their laudable search for increasingly effective ways of protecting the rights of the individual while promoting efficient enforcement of our criminal laws. However, unless we are shown other procedures which are at least as effective in apprising accused persons of their right of silence and in assuring a continuous opportunity to exercise it, the following safeguards must be observed.

At the outset, if a person in custody is to be subjected to interrogation, he must first be informed in clear and unequivocal terms that he has the right to remain silent. For those unaware of the privilege, the warning is needed simply to make them aware of it—the threshold requirement for an intelligent decision as to its exercise. More important, such a warning is an absolute prerequisite in overcoming the inherent pressures of the interrogation atmosphere. It is not just the subnormal or woefully ignorant who succumb to an interrogator's imprecations, whether implied or expressly stated, that the interrogation will continue until a confession is obtained or that silence in the face of accusation is itself damning and will bode ill when presented to a jury. Further, the warning will show the individual that his interrogators are prepared to recognize his privilege should he choose to exercise it.

The Fifth Amendment privilege is so fundamental to our system of constitutional rule and the expedient of giving an adequate warning as to the availability of the privilege so simple, we will not pause to inquire in individual cases whether the defendant was aware of his rights without a warning being given. Assessments of the knowledge the defendant possessed, based on information as to his age, education, intelligence, or prior contact with authorities, can never be more than speculation; a warning is a clearcut fact. More important, whatever the background of the person interrogated, a warning at the time of the interrogation is indispensable to overcome its pressures and to insure that the individual knows he is free to exercise the privilege at that point in time.

The warning of the right to remain silent must be accompanied by the explanation that anything said can and will be used against the individual in court. This warning is needed in order to make him aware not only of the privilege, but also of the consequences of forgoing it. It is only through an awareness of these consequences that there can be any assurance of real understanding and intelligent exercise of the privilege. Moreover, this warning may serve to make the individual more acutely aware that he is faced with a phase of the adversary system—that he is not in the presence of persons acting solely in his interest.

The circumstances surrounding in-custody interrogation can operate very quickly to overbear the will of one merely made aware of his privilege by his interrogators. Therefore, the right to have counsel present at the interrogation is indispensable to the protection of the Fifth Amendment privilege under the system we delineate today. Our aim is to assure that the individual's right to choose between silence and speech remains unfettered throughout the interrogation process. A once-stated warning, delivered by those who will conduct the interrogation, cannot itself suffice to that end among those who most require knowledge of their rights. A mere warning given by the interrogators is not alone sufficient to accomplish that end. * * * Even preliminary advice given to the accused by his own attorney can be swiftly overcome by the secret interrogation process. * * * Thus, the need for counsel to protect the Fifth Amendment privilege comprehends not merely a right to consult with counsel prior to questioning, but also to have counsel present during any questioning if the defendant so desires.

The presence of counsel at the interrogation may serve several significant subsidiary functions as well. If the accused decides to talk to his interrogators, the assistance of counsel can mitigate the dangers of untrustworthiness. With a lawyer present the likelihood that the police will practice coercion is reduced, and if coercion is nevertheless exercised the lawyer can testify to it in court. The presence of a lawyer can also help to guarantee that the accused gives a fully accurate statement to the police and that the statement is rightly reported by the prosecution at trial.

An individual need not make a preinterrogation request for a lawyer. While such request affirmatively secures his right to have one, his failure to ask for a lawyer does not constitute a waiver. No effective waiver of the right to counsel during interrogation can be recognized unless specifically made after the warnings we here delineate have been given. The accused who does not know his rights and therefore does not make a request may be the person who most needs counsel. * * *

Accordingly we hold that an individual held for interrogation must be clearly informed that he has the right to consult with a lawyer and to have the lawyer with him during interrogation under the system for protecting the privilege we delineate today. As with the warnings of the right to remain silent and that anything stated can be used in evidence against him, this warning is an absolute prerequisite to interrogation. No amount of circumstantial evidence that the person may have been aware of this right will suffice to stand in its stead. Only through such a warning is there ascertainable assurance that the accused was aware of this right.

If an individual indicates that he wishes the assistance of counsel before any interrogation occurs, the authorities cannot rationally ignore or deny his request on the basis that the individual does not have or cannot afford a retained attorney. The financial ability of the individual has no relationship to the scope of the rights involved here. The privilege against self-incrimination secured by the Constitution applies to all individuals. The need for counsel in order to protect the privilege exists for the indigent as well as the affluent. In fact, were we to limit these constitutional rights to those who can retain an attorney, our decisions today would be of little significance. The cases before us as well as the vast majority of confession cases with which we have dealt in the past involve those unable to retain counsel. While authorities are not required to relieve the accused of his poverty, they have the obligation not to take advantage of indigence in the administration of justice. * * *

In order fully to apprise a person interrogated of the extent of his rights under this system then, it is necessary to warn him not only that he has the right to consult with an attorney, but also that if he is indigent a lawyer will be appointed to represent him. Without this additional warning, the admonition of the right to consult with counsel would often be understood as meaning only that he can consult with a lawyer if he has one or has the funds to obtain one. The warning of a right to counsel would be hollow if not couched in terms that would convey to the indigent—the person most often subjected to interrogation—the knowledge that he too has a right to have counsel present. As with the warnings of the right to remain silent and of the general right to counsel, only by effective and express explanation to the indigent of this right can there be assurance that he was truly in a position to exercise it.[1]

---

1. While a warning that the indigent may have counsel appointed need not be given to the person who is known to have an attorney or is known to have ample funds to secure one, the expedient of giving a warning is too simple and the rights involved too

Once warnings have been given, the subsequent procedure is clear. If the individual indicates in any manner, at any time prior to or during questioning, that he wishes to remain silent, the interrogation must cease.[2] At this point he has shown that he intends to exercise his Fifth Amendment privilege; any statement taken after the person invokes his privilege cannot be other than the product of compulsion, subtle or otherwise. Without the right to cut off questioning, the setting of in-custody interrogation operates on the individual to overcome free choice in producing a statement after the privilege has been once invoked. If the individual states that he wants an attorney, the interrogation must cease until an attorney is present. At that time, the individual must have an opportunity to confer with the attorney and to have him present during any subsequent questioning. If the individual cannot obtain an attorney and he indicates that he wants one before speaking to police, they must respect his decision to remain silent.

* * *

If the interrogation continues without the presence of an attorney and a statement is taken, a heavy burden rests on the government to demonstrate that the defendant knowingly and intelligently waived his privilege against self-incrimination and his right to retained or appointed counsel. * * * This Court has always set high standards of proof for the waiver of constitutional rights, Johnson v. Zerbst, 304 U.S. 458, 58 S.Ct. 1019, 82 L.Ed. 1461 (1938), and we reassert these standards as applied to in-custody interrogation. Since the State is responsible for establishing the isolated circumstances under which the interrogation takes place and has the only means of making available corroborated evidence of warnings given during incommunicado interrogation, the burden is rightly on its shoulders.

An express statement that the individual is willing to make a statement and does not want an attorney followed closely by a statement could constitute a waiver. But a valid waiver will not be presumed simply from the silence of the accused after warnings are given or simply from the fact that a confession was in fact eventually obtained. * * * Moreover, where in-custody interrogation is involved, there is no room for the contention that the privilege is waived if the individual answers some questions or gives some information on his own prior to invoking his right to remain silent when interrogated.

Whatever the testimony of the authorities as to waiver of rights by an accused, the fact of lengthy interrogation or incommunicado incarceration before a statement is made is strong evidence that the accused did not validly waive his rights. In these circumstances the fact that the individual eventually made a statement is consistent with the conclusion that the compelling influence of the interrogation finally forced him to do so. It is

important to engage in *ex post facto* inquiries into financial ability when there is any doubt at all on that score.

2. If an individual indicates his desire to remain silent, but has an attorney present, there may be some circumstances in which further questioning would be permissible. In the absence of evidence of overbearing, statements then made in the presence of counsel might be free of the compelling influence of the interrogation process and might fairly be construed as a waiver of the privilege for purposes of these statements.

inconsistent with any notion of a voluntary relinquishment of the privilege. Moreover, any evidence that the accused was threatened, tricked, or cajoled into a waiver will, of course, show that the defendant did not voluntarily waive his privilege. The requirement of warnings and waiver of rights is a fundamental with respect to the Fifth Amendment privilege and not simply a preliminary ritual to existing methods of interrogation.

The warnings required and the waiver necessary in accordance with our opinion today are, in the absence of a fully effective equivalent, prerequisites to the admissibility of any statement made by a defendant. * * *

Our decision is not intended to hamper the traditional function of police officers in investigating crime. When an individual is in custody on probable cause, the police may, of course, seek out evidence in the field to be used at trial against him. Such investigation may include inquiry of persons not under restraint. General on-the-scene questioning as to facts surrounding a crime or other general questioning of citizens in the factfinding process is not affected by our holding. It is an act of responsible citizenship for individuals to give whatever information they may have to aid in law enforcement. In such situations the compelling atmosphere inherent in the process of in-custody interrogation is not necessarily present.

In dealing with statements obtained through interrogation, we do not purport to find all confessions inadmissible. Confessions remain a proper element in law enforcement. Any statement given freely and voluntarily without any compelling influences is, of course, admissible in evidence. The fundamental import of the privilege while an individual is in custody is not whether he is allowed to talk to the police without the benefit of warnings and counsel, but whether he can be interrogated. There is no requirement that police stop a person who enters a police station and states that he wishes to confess to a crime, or a person who calls the police to offer a confession or any other statement he desires to make. Volunteered statements of any kind are not barred by the Fifth Amendment and their admissibility is not affected by our holding today.

* * *

V.

Because of the nature of the problem and because of its recurrent significance in numerous cases, we have to this point discussed the relationship of the Fifth Amendment privilege to police interrogation without specific concentration on the facts of the cases before us. We turn now to these facts to consider the application to these cases of the constitutional principles discussed above. In each instance, we have concluded that statements were obtained from the defendant under circumstances that did not meet constitutional standards for protection of the privilege.

No. 759. Miranda v. Arizona

On March 13, 1963, petitioner, Ernesto Miranda, was arrested at his home and taken in custody to a Phoenix police station. He was there identified by the complaining witness. The police then took him to "Interrogation Room No. 2" of the detective bureau. There he was questioned by two police officers. The officers admitted at trial that Miranda was not advised that he had a right to have an attorney present. Two hours later, the officers emerged from the interrogation room with a written confession signed by Miranda. At the top of the statement was a typed paragraph stating that the confession was made voluntarily, without threats or promises of immunity and "with full knowledge of my legal rights, understanding any statement I make may be used against me."

At his trial before a jury, the written confession was admitted into evidence over the objection of defense counsel, and the officers testified to the prior oral confession made by Miranda during the interrogation. Miranda was found guilty of kidnapping and rape. He was sentenced to 20 to 30 years' imprisonment on each count, the sentences to run concurrently. On appeal, the Supreme Court of Arizona held that Miranda's constitutional rights were not violated in obtaining the confession and affirmed the conviction. In reaching its decision, the court emphasized heavily the fact that Miranda did not specifically request counsel.

We reverse. From the testimony of the officers and by the admission of respondent, it is clear that Miranda was not in any way apprised of his right to consult with an attorney and to have one present during the interrogation, nor was his right not to be compelled to incriminate himself effectively protected in any other manner. Without these warnings the statements were inadmissible. The mere fact that he signed a statement which contained a typed-in clause stating that he had "full knowledge" of his "legal rights" does not approach the knowing and intelligent waiver required to relinquish constitutional rights.

* * *

[The Court's discussion of the facts of the other cases is omitted. Editors.]

Judgment of Supreme Court of California in No. 584 affirmed.

■ MR. JUSTICE CLARK, dissenting in Nos. 759, 760, and 761, and concurring in the result in No. 584.

* * * Since there is at this time a paucity of information and an almost total lack of empirical knowledge on the practical operation of requirements truly comparable to those announced by the majority, I would be more restrained lest we go too far too fast.

* * *

Custodial interrogation has long been recognized as "undoubtedly an essential tool in effective law enforcement." Haynes v. State of Washington, 373 U.S. 503, 515, 83 S.Ct. 1336, 1344, 10 L.Ed.2d 513 (1963). Recognition of this fact should put us on guard against the promulgation of doctrinaire rules. * * *

The rule prior to today * * * depended upon "a totality of circumstances evidencing an involuntary * * * admission of guilt." * * *

I would continue to follow that rule. Under the "totality of circumstances" rule * * *, I would consider in each case whether the police officer prior to custodial interrogation added the warning that the suspect might have counsel present at the interrogation, and further, that a court would appoint one at his request if he was too poor to employ counsel. In the absence of warnings, the burden would be on the State to prove that counsel was knowingly and intelligently waived or that in the totality of the circumstances, including the failure to give the necessary warnings, the confession was clearly voluntary.

* * *

[The dissenting opinions of Justice Harlan, with whom Justices Stewart and White joined, and of Justice White, with whom Justices Harlan and Stewart joined, are omitted.]

NOTES

1. **Terminology of the Warnings.** How much deviation from the language used by the majority in *Miranda* is permissible in giving suspects *Miranda* warnings? In California v. Prysock, 453 U.S. 355, 101 S.Ct. 2806, 69 L.Ed.2d 696 (1981) (per curiam), the sixteen year old suspect was warned and questioned in the presence of his mother. The officer first told Prysock "you have the right to remain silent," "if you give up your right to remain silent, anything you say can and will be used as evidence against you in a court of law," and "you have the right to talk to a lawyer before you are questioned, have him present with you while you are being questioned, and all during the questioning." He was also told, "you have the right to have a lawyer appointed to represent you at no cost to yourself." This was all tape recorded. There was then a brief off-the-record discussion between the suspect's mother and the officer. The officer later testified that in this discussion, the mother asked if a lawyer would be available later if the suspect did not request one at this time. According to the officer, he responded by saying:

> That he would have an attorney when he went to Court. And that he could have one at this time if he wished one. He could terminate the statement at any time he so desired.

Following the warnings, Prysock consented to questioning without an attorney and admitted the killing. This confession was later used against him in his murder trial, and he was convicted. On appeal, however, the intermediate California appellate court reversed. Emphasizing its view that the rigidity of the *Miranda* requirements affords police clear guidance, the court held Prysock had not been adequately informed that the services of a free attorney were available to him prior to the impending questioning. The Supreme Court reversed. It read the state court as establishing "a flat rule that the content of *Miranda* warnings be a virtual incantation of the precise language contained in the *Miranda* opinion" and holding the warnings here defective because of the order in which they were given. In fact, the Court stressed, "no talismanic incantation" is required to satisfy *Miranda*. The warnings given Prysock adequately conveyed to him that he had a right to an appointed attorney prior to and during questioning. The Court stressed, however, that warnings might be inadequate if the reference to the right to counsel was linked with some future point in time after the police interrogation. It cited with apparent approval United States v. Garcia, 431 F.2d 134 (9th Cir.1970), holding inadequate a statement to the defendant that she could "have an attorney appointed to represent you when you first appear before the U.S. Commissioner or the Court.''

In Duckworth v. Eagan, 492 U.S. 195, 109 S.Ct. 2875, 106 L.Ed.2d 166 (1989), Eagan was given warnings that, in regard to the right to counsel, included:

> You have a right to talk to a lawyer for advice before we ask you any questions, and to have him with you during questioning. You have this right to the advice and presence of a lawyer even if you cannot afford to hire one. We have no way of giving you a lawyer, but one will be appointed for you, if you wish, if and when you go to court. If you wish to answer questions now without a lawyer present, you have the right to stop answering questions at any time. You also have the right to stop answering at any time until you've talked to a lawyer.

By a 5–to–4 vote, the Supreme Court held this complied with *Miranda*. Chief Justice Rehnquist wrote for the Court rejecting Eagan's argument that the "if and when you go to court" phrase rendered the warning confusing and insufficient:

> First, this instruction accurately described the procedure for the appointment of counsel in Indiana. Under Indiana law, counsel is appointed at the defendant's initial appearance in court, and formal charges must be filed at or before that hearing. We think it must be relatively commonplace for a suspect, after receiving *Miranda* warnings, to ask when he will obtain counsel. The "if and and when you go to court" advice simply anticipates that question. Second, *Miranda* does not require that attorneys be producible on call, but only that the suspect be informed, as here, that he has the right to an attorney before and during questioning, and that an attorney would be appointed for him if he could not afford one. The Court in *Miranda* emphasized that it was not suggesting that "each police station must have a 'station house lawyer' present at all times to advise prisoners." If the police cannot provide appointed counsel, *Miranda* requires only that the police not question a suspect unless he waives his right to counsel. Here, [Eagan] did just that.

495 U.S. at 204, 109 S.Ct. at 2880–81, 106 L.Ed.2d at 177–78.

2. **Impeachment Use of Confessions Violating *Miranda*.** The "impeachment exception" to many exclusionary sanctions, discussed in Chapter 1, has been applied to confessions in a manner which distinguishes between the requirements of *Miranda* and voluntariness.

In Harris v. New York, 401 U.S. 222, 91 S.Ct. 643, 28 L.Ed.2d 1 (1971), the majority acknowledged language in *Miranda* could be read as barring the use of a confession obtained in violation of *Miranda* for any purpose. Nevertheless, the Court held a statement obtained after a warning failing to inform the defendant of his right to appointed counsel could be used to impeach the defendant when he took the stand at trial and testified in a manner inconsistent with the statement. "[T]he trustworthiness of the evidence satisfies legal standards," the majority commented, and the confession would undoubtedly aid the jury in evaluating the defendant's credibility as well as determining whether he perjured himself during testimony. Turning to the need to exclude such confessions as a means of deterring violation of the *Miranda* requirements, the majority concluded "sufficient deterrence flows when the evidence in question is made unavailable to the prosecution in its case in chief."

In Oregon v. Hass, 420 U.S. 714, 95 S.Ct. 1215, 43 L.Ed.2d 570 (1975), Hass was arrested and given complete *Miranda* warnings. Although Hass said he wanted to telephone a lawyer, an officer continued to interrogate him without the presence of counsel; he made an incriminating statement. This statement was used for impeachment at trial after Hass took the stand and testified to facts contrary to those in the confession. The Supreme Court found no impropriety in use of the statement at Hass' trial. The dissent contended the case was distinguishable from *Harris*:

> [A]fter *Harris*, police had some incentive for following *Miranda* by warning an accused of his right to remain silent and his right to counsel. If the warnings were given, the accused might still make a statement which could be used in the prosecution's case in chief. [But where the warnings are given and the suspect indicates a desire for counsel], police have almost no incentive for following *Miranda's* requirement that "[i]f the individual states that he wants an attorney, the interrogation must cease until an attorney is present." * * * If the requirement is followed there will almost surely be no statement since the attorney will advise the accused to remain silent. If, however, the requirement is disobeyed, the police may obtain a statement which can be used for impeachment if the accused has the temerity to testify in his own defense.

420 U.S. at 725, 95 S.Ct. at 1222, 43 L.Ed.2d at 579 (Brennan, J., dissenting). Thus the need to exclude the confession to encourage compliance with *Miranda* was greater in the case before the Court than in *Harris*. The majority, in contrast, characterized the possibility of an officer proceeding on the basis suggested by the dissent as "speculative." "If, in a given case," it concluded, "the officer's conduct amounts to an abuse, that case, like those involving coercion or duress, may be taken care of when it arises measured by the traditional standards for evaluating voluntariness and trustworthiness."

In Mincey v. Arizona, 437 U.S. 385, 98 S.Ct. 2408, 57 L.Ed.2d 290 (1978), however, the Court reaffirmed involuntary statements could not be used even for impeachment of a testifying defendant. This is apparently because such statements—unlike the statements in *Harris* and *Hass*—do not satisfy legal standards of trustworthiness.

3.   **Use of Suspects' Silence.** A defendant's silence under circumstances in which a reasonable, innocent person would have denied guilt is, generally speaking, admissible to prove the defendant's guilt as a "tacit" confession. See McCormick, Evidence § 161 (5th ed. 1999). *Miranda*, however, imposes some limitations on the admissibility of such silence. In Doyle v. Ohio, 426 U.S. 610, 96 S.Ct. 2240, 49 L.Ed.2d 91 (1976), Doyle was charged with sale of marijuana based on a transaction arranged by one Bonnell, a police informant. None of the narcotics agents who had the transaction under surveillance actually saw the alleged transfer of the marijuana from Doyle to Bonnell. At trial, Doyle took the stand and testified that the arrangement had actually been for Bonnell to sell marijuana to him. On cross examination, the prosecution elicited Doyle's admission that after being arrested and given the *Miranda* warnings he had not told this version of the incident to the arresting officers. Reversing Doyle's conviction, the Supreme Court held that silence after being given the *Miranda* warnings could not be used even for impeachment. Silence after *Miranda* warnings cannot, under *Doyle*, even be used to rebut a defendant's claim of insanity. Wainwright v. Greenfield, 474 U.S. 284, 106 S.Ct. 634, 88 L.Ed.2d 623 (1986).

In Fletcher v. Weir, 455 U.S. 603, 102 S.Ct. 1309, 71 L.Ed.2d 490 (1982) (per curiam), the Court characterized *Doyle* as resting not upon the ambiguity of suspects' silence but the fundamental unfairness of using silence against defendants after they have received governmental assurances that there is a right to remain silent. The Court found no federal constitutional barrier to the use of a defendant's silence after arrest but before *Miranda* warnings, at least where silence was used to impeach the defendant after he took the witness stand at trial and testified to an exculpatory version of the events. Where the *Miranda* warnings were not given, the Court reasoned, no assurances of a right to remain silent were provided and thus there is no unfairness in using the defendants' silence. Whether in such situations a defendant's silence is a sufficiently reliable indicator he lied during direct examination, the Court commented, is a decision each State is entitled to make as a matter of State evidence law policy.

Doyle imposes no federal constitutional bar to the use of *prearrest* silence to impeach a testifying defendant. Jenkins v. Anderson, 447 U.S. 231, 100 S.Ct. 2124, 65 L.Ed.2d 86 (1980). Nor does *Miranda* bar questioning of a testifying defendant concerning inconsistent statements made after arrest and receipt of *Miranda* warnings. Such a defendant has chosen to speak rather than remain silent so there is no impermissible use of silence as prohibited by *Doyle*. Anderson v. Charles, 447 U.S. 404, 100 S.Ct. 2180, 65 L.Ed.2d 222 (1980) (per curiam).

2.   APPLICABILITY OF *MIRANDA*

EDITORS' INTRODUCTION: "THRESHOLD" ISSUES AND EXCEPTIONS

Soon after the *Miranda* decision, the Court rejected arguments that its requirements be limited to stationhouse interrogation or at least not applied to custodial questioning conducted in surroundings familiar to the suspect. Orozco v. Texas, 394 U.S. 324, 89 S.Ct. 1095, 22 L.Ed.2d 311 (1969), held *Miranda* applicable to questioning of Orozco in his own bedroom by four officers who entered the bedroom and awoke, arrested, and questioned him.

The *Miranda* opinion itself made clear that the requirements established by the case did not apply to all out-of-court confessions or statements by defendants. Rather, those requirements must be respected only in situations involving both "custody" and "interrogation." When these threshold requirements for the application of *Miranda* are met is addressed in the two subsections that follow. The Court has also considered arguments for exceptions releasing officers from the *Miranda* requirements in situations involving what is at least "technically" custodial interrogation.

Public Safety Exception

A "public safety" exception to the *Miranda* requirements, applicable despite the existence of both custody and interrogation, was adopted and applied in New York v. Quarles, 467 U.S. 649, 104 S.Ct. 2626, 81 L.Ed.2d 550 (1984).

In *Quarles*, a woman approached two New York police officers and reported that she had just been raped by a man who entered a nearby supermarket carrying a gun. Upon arrival at the supermarket, one officer (Kraft) entered the store and the other radioed for assistance. Officer Kraft quickly observed Quarles, who met the woman's description. Apparently upon seeing Officer Kraft, Quarles ran towards the rear of the store. Kraft drew his weapon and pursued Quarles. Although he lost sight of Quarles for several seconds, Officer Kraft soon saw him again and ordered Quarles to stop and place his hands over his head. Several other officers had since arrived. Kraft approached Quarles and, upon frisking him, discovered he was wearing an empty shoulder holster. Quarles was handcuffed. Kraft then, without providing any *Miranda* warnings, asked Quarles where the gun was. Nodding in the direction of some empty cartons, Quarles responded by saying, "The gun is over there." Kraft searched the area and found a loaded .38 caliber revolver. Quarles was then warned under *Miranda* and agreed to answer questions without an attorney present. In response to questions by Kraft, Quarles admitted ownership of the gun and explained how he had acquired it. Before Quarles' trial for criminal possession of a weapon, the trial court considered the admissibility of the revolver, his pre-warning statement, "The gun is over there," and his post-warning admissions. Both the gun and the pre-warning statement were held inadmissible because of Officer Kraft's failure to comply with *Miranda* before asking about the gun's location; the post-warning admissions were excluded as tainted by the preceding *Miranda* violation.

By a five-to-four vote, the Supreme Court reversed. *Miranda* had not been violated, it held, because Officer Kraft's actions came within a "narrow exception" to *Miranda* for situations in which the officer's question is prompted by concern for the public safety. This exception, Justice Rehnquist explained for the Court, is consistent with *Miranda's* rationale. In most situations, the cost of respecting *Miranda's* requirements is the possibility of fewer convictions; this cost is acceptable given the value of the *Miranda* requirements in protecting the underlying right to freedom from compelled self-incrimination. But where in addition compliance with the *Miranda* requirement pose an immediate risk to public safety, the cost becomes unacceptably high:

> We decline to place officers such as Officer Kraft in the untenable position of having to consider, often in a matter of seconds, whether it best serves society for them to ask the necessary questions without the *Miranda* warnings and render whatever probative evidence they uncover inadmissible, or for them to give the warnings in order to preserve the admissibility of evidence they might uncover but possibly damage or destroy their ability to obtain that evidence and neutralize the volatile situation confronting them.

467 U.S. at 657–58, 104 S.Ct. at 2632, 81 L.Ed.2d at 558. On the facts before it, the Court found sufficient risk to public safety. Officer Kraft had reason to believe the gun was somewhere in the store where it might be retrieved by an accomplice of Quarles or discovered by a store employee or customer.

The state court had declined to apply a public safety exception because of its perception that there was no indication that Officer Kraft was actually motivated by a desire to protect himself or the public. This, the Court reasoned, was not controlling:

> [T]he availability of [the] exception does not depend upon the motivation of the individual officer involved. In a kaleidoscopic situation such as the one confronting these officers, where spontaneity rather than adherence to a police manual is necessarily the order of the day, the application of the exception * * * should not be made to depend on *post hoc* findings at a suppression hearing concerning the subjective motivation of the arresting officer.

467 U.S. at 656, 104 S.Ct. at 2631, 81 L.Ed.2d at 557.

The Supreme Court observed it was presented with no claim that Quarles's pre-warning statement was "actually compelled by police conduct which overcame his will to resist." Quarles was free to argue on remand that his statement was "coerced under traditional due process standards." The Court's holding, Justice Rehnquist emphasized, was not a rejection of this argument; he explained, "we merely reject the * * * argument * * * that the statement must be *presumed* compelled because of Officer Kraft's failure to read [Quarles] his *Miranda* warnings." 467 U.S. at 655 n. 5, 104 S.Ct. at 2631 n. 5, 81 L.Ed.2d at 556 n. 5 (emphasis in original).

Routine Booking Question Exception

A plurality of the Court recognized another exception in Pennsylvania v. Muniz, 496 U.S. 582, 110 S.Ct. 2638, 110 L.Ed.2d 528 (1990). After his arrest for drunk-driving, Muniz was taken to the stationhouse. During the ensuing procedure, and without complying with *Miranda*, an officer asked Muniz his name, address, height, weight, eye color, date of birth, and current age. This was videotaped. Justice Brennan, writing for a plurality of four justices, explained why the plurality regarded his answers admissible:

> We agree with amicus United States * * * that Muniz's answers to these * * * questions are * * * admissible because the questions fall within a "routine booking question" exception which exempts from *Miranda's* coverage questions to secure the "biographical data necessary to complete booking or pretrial services." Brief for the United States as Amicus Curiae 12 * * *. The state court found that the first seven questions were "requested for recordkeeping purposes only," and therefore the questions appear reasonably related to the police's administrative concerns. In this context, therefore, the * * * questions * * * fall outside the protections of *Miranda* and the answers thereto need not be suppressed.

495 U.S. at 601–02, 110 S.Ct. at 2650, 110 L.Ed.2d at 552. He added:

> As amicus United States explains, "[r]ecognizing a 'booking exception' to *Miranda* does not mean, of course, that any question asked during the booking process falls within that exception. Without obtaining a waiver of the suspect's *Miranda* rights, the police may not ask questions, even during booking, that are designed to elicit incriminatory admissions." Brief for United States as Amicus Curiae 13.

495 U.S. at 602 n. 14, 110 S.Ct. at 2650 n. 14, 110 L.Ed.2d at 552 n. 14.

Although these exceptions may render *Miranda* inapplicable to some situations, the major limitations on the scope of the decision arise from the requirements of, first, interrogation and, second, custody. The following two subsections address these prerequisites to the application of *Miranda*.

a. THE REQUIREMENT OF "INTERROGATION"

Unless a suspect in custody is subjected to "interrogation," *Miranda* has no applicability. Thus when a statement is "volunteered" by a suspect, it is admissible despite the failure to comply with *Miranda* requirements.

Rhode Island v. Innis

Supreme Court of the United States, 1980.
446 U.S. 291, 100 S.Ct. 1682, 64 L.Ed.2d 297.

■ MR. JUSTICE STEWART delivered the opinion of the Court.

* * * The issue in this case is whether the respondent was "interrogated" in violation of the standards promulgated in the *Miranda* opinion.

I.

On the night of January 12, 1975, John Mulvaney, a Providence, R. I., taxicab driver, disappeared after being dispatched to pick up a customer. His body was discovered four days later buried in a shallow grave in Coventry, R. I. He had died from a shotgun blast aimed at the back of his head.

On January 17, 1975, shortly after midnight, the Providence police received a telephone call from Gerald Aubin, also a taxicab driver, who reported that he had just been robbed by a man wielding a sawed-off shotgun. Aubin further reported that he had dropped off his assailant near Rhode Island College in a section of Providence known as Mount Pleasant. While at the Providence police station waiting to give a statement, Aubin noticed a picture of his assailant on a bulletin board. Aubin so informed one of the police officers present. The officer prepared a photo array, and again Aubin identified a picture of the same person. That person was the respondent. Shortly thereafter, the Providence police began a search of the Mount Pleasant area.

At approximately 4:30 a. m. on the same date, Patrolman Lovell, while cruising the streets of Mount Pleasant in a patrol car, spotted the respondent standing in the street facing him. When Patrolman Lovell stopped his car, the respondent walked towards it. Patrolman Lovell then arrested the respondent, who was unarmed, and advised him of his so-called *Miranda* rights. While the two men waited in the patrol car for other police officers to arrive, Patrolman Lovell did not converse with the respondent other than to respond to the latter's request for a cigarette.

Within minutes, Sergeant Sears arrived at the scene of the arrest, and he also gave the respondent the *Miranda* warnings. Immediately thereafter, Captain Leyden and other police officers arrived. Captain Leyden advised the respondent of his *Miranda* rights. The respondent stated that he understood those rights and wanted to speak with a lawyer. Captain Leyden then directed that the respondent be placed in a "caged wagon," a four-door police car with a wire screen mesh between the front and rear seats, and be driven to the central police station. Three officers, Patrolmen Gleckman, Williams, and McKenna, were assigned to accompany the respondent to the central station. They placed the respondent in the vehicle and shut the doors. Captain Leyden then instructed the officers not to question the respondent or intimidate or coerce him in any way. The three officers then entered the vehicle, and it departed.

While en route to the central station, Patrolman Gleckman initiated a conversation with Patrolman McKenna concerning the missing shotgun. As Patrolman Gleckman later testified:

"A. At this point, I was talking back and forth with Patrolman McKenna stating that I frequent this area while on patrol and [that because a school for handicapped children is located nearby,] there's a lot of handicapped children running around in this area, and God forbid one of them might find a weapon with shells and they might hurt themselves.''

Patrolman McKenna apparently shared his fellow officer's concern:

"A. I more or less concurred with him [Gleckman] that it was a safety factor and that we should, you know, continue to search for the weapon and try to find it.''

While Patrolman Williams said nothing, he overheard the conversation between the two officers:

"A. He [Gleckman] said it would be too bad if the little—I believe he said girl—would pick up the gun, maybe kill herself.''

The respondent then interrupted the conversation, stating that the officers should turn the car around so he could show them where the gun was located. At this point, Patrolman McKenna radioed back to Captain Leyden that they were returning to the scene of the arrest, and that the respondent would inform them of the location of the gun. At the time the respondent indicated that the officers should turn back, they had traveled no more than a mile, a trip encompassing only a few minutes.

The police vehicle then returned to the scene of the arrest where a search for the shotgun was in progress. There, Captain Leyden again advised the respondent of his *Miranda* rights. The respondent replied that he understood those rights but that he "wanted to get the gun out of the way because of the kids in the area in the school.'' The respondent then led the police to a nearby field, where he pointed out the shotgun under some rocks by the side of the road.

On March 20, 1975, a grand jury returned an indictment charging the respondent with the kidnapping, robbery, and murder of John Mulvaney. Before trial, the respondent moved to suppress the shotgun and the statements he had made to the police regarding it. After an evidentiary hearing at which the respondent elected not to testify, the trial judge found that the respondent had been "repeatedly and completely advised of his *Miranda* rights.'' He further found that it was "entirely understandable that [the officers in the police vehicle] would voice their concern [for the safety of the handicapped children] to each other.'' The judge then concluded that the respondent's decision to inform the police of the location of the shotgun was "a waiver, clearly, and on the basis of the evidence that I have heard, and [sic] intelligent waiver, of his [*Miranda*] right to remain silent.'' Thus, without passing on whether the police officers had in fact "interrogated'' the respondent, the trial court sustained the admissibility of the shotgun and testimony related to its discovery. That evidence was later introduced at the respondent's trial, and the jury returned a verdict of guilty on all counts.

* * *

II

* * *

In the present case, the parties are in agreement that the respondent was fully informed of his *Miranda* rights and that he invoked his *Miranda* right to counsel when he told Captain Leyden that he wished to consult with a lawyer. It is also uncontested that the respondent was "in custody" while being transported to the police station.

The issue, therefore, is whether the respondent was "interrogated" by the police officers in violation of the respondent's undisputed right under *Miranda* to remain silent until he had consulted with a lawyer. In resolving this issue, we first define the term "interrogation" under *Miranda* before turning to a consideration of the facts of this case.

A

The starting point for defining "interrogation" in this context is, of course, the Court's *Miranda* opinion. There the Court observed that "[b]y custodial interrogation, we mean *questioning* initiated by law enforcement officers after a person has been taken into custody or otherwise deprived of his freedom of action in any significant way." This passage and other references throughout the opinion to "questioning" might suggest that the *Miranda* rules were to apply only to those police interrogation practices that involve express questioning of a defendant while in custody.

We do not, however, construe the *Miranda* opinion so narrowly. The concern of the Court in *Miranda* was that the "interrogation environment" created by the interplay of interrogation and custody would "subjugate the individual to the will of his examiner" and thereby undermine the privilege against compulsory self-incrimination. The police practices that evoked this concern included several that did not involve express questioning. For example, one of the practices discussed in *Miranda* was the use of lineups in which a coached witness would pick the defendant as the perpetrator. This was designed to establish that the defendant was in fact guilty as a predicate for further interrogation. A variation on this theme discussed in *Miranda* was the so-called "reverse line-up" in which a defendant would be identified by coached witnesses as the perpetrator of a fictitious crime, with the object of inducing him to confess to the actual crime of which he was suspected in order to escape the false prosecution. The Court in *Miranda* also included in its survey of interrogation practices the use of psychological ploys, such as to "posi[t]" "the guilt of the subject," to "minimize the moral seriousness of the offense," and "to cast blame on the victim or on society." It is clear that these techniques of persuasion, no less than express questioning, were thought, in a custodial setting, to amount to interrogation.

This is not to say, however, that all statements obtained by the police after a person has been taken into custody are to be considered the product of interrogation. * * * It is clear * * * that the special procedural safeguards outlined in *Miranda* are required not where a suspect is simply taken into custody, but rather where a suspect in custody is subjected to interrogation. "Interrogation," as conceptualized in the *Miranda* opinion, must reflect a measure of compulsion above and beyond that inherent in custody itself.

We conclude that the *Miranda* safeguards come into play whenever a person in custody is subjected to either express questioning or its functional equivalent. That is to say, the term "interrogation" under *Miranda* refers not only to express questioning, but also to any words or actions on the part of the police (other than those normally attendant to arrest and custody) that the police should know are reasonably likely to elicit an incriminating response from the suspect. The latter portion of this definition focuses primarily upon the perceptions of the suspect, rather than the intent of the police. This focus reflects the fact that the *Miranda* safeguards were designed to vest a suspect in custody with an added measure of protection against coercive police practices, without regard to objective proof of the underlying intent of the police. A practice that the police should know is reasonably likely to evoke an incriminating response from a suspect thus amounts to interrogation.[3] But, since the police surely cannot be held accountable for the unforeseeable results of their words or actions, the definition of interrogation can extend only to words or actions on the part of police officers that they *should have known* were reasonably likely to elicit an incriminating response.[4]

B

Turning to the facts of the present case, we conclude that the respondent was not "interrogated" within the meaning of *Miranda*. It is undisputed that the first prong of the definition of "interrogation" was not satisfied, for the conversation between Patrolmen Gleckman and McKenna included no express questioning of the respondent. Rather, that conversation was, at least in form, nothing more than a dialogue between the two officers to which no response from the respondent was invited.

Moreover, it cannot be fairly concluded that the respondent was subjected to the "functional equivalent" of questioning. It cannot be said, in short, that Patrolmen Gleckman and McKenna should have known that their conversation was reasonably likely to elicit an incriminating response from the respondent. There is nothing in the record to suggest that the officers were aware that the respondent was peculiarly susceptible to an appeal to his conscience concerning the safety of handicapped children. Nor is there anything in the record to suggest that the police knew that the respondent was unusually disoriented or upset at the time of his arrest.[5]

---

3. This is not to say that the intent of the police is irrelevant, for it may well have a bearing on whether the police should have known that their words or actions were reasonably likely to evoke an incriminating response. In particular, where a police practice is designed to elicit an incriminating response from the accused, it is unlikely that the practice will not also be one which the police should have known was reasonably likely to have that effect.

4. Any knowledge the police may have had concerning the unusual susceptibility of a defendant to a particular form of persuasion might be an important factor in determining whether the police should have known that their words or actions were reasonably likely to elicit an incriminating response from the suspect.

5. The record in no way suggests that the officers' remarks were *designed* to elicit a response. It is significant that the trial judge, after hearing the officers' testimony, concluded that it was "entirely understandable that [the officers] would voice their concern [for the safety of the handicapped children] to each other."

The case thus boils down to whether, in the context of a brief conversation, the officers should have known that the respondent would suddenly be moved to make a self-incriminating response. Given the fact that the entire conversation appears to have consisted of no more than a few offhand remarks, we cannot say that the officers should have known that it was reasonably likely that Innis would so respond. This is not a case where the police carried on a lengthy harangue in the presence of the suspect. Nor does the record support the respondent's contention that, under the circumstances, the officers' comments were particularly "evocative." It is our view, therefore, that the respondent was not subjected by the police to words or actions that the police should have known were reasonably likely to elicit an incriminating response from him.

The Rhode Island Supreme Court erred * * * in equating "subtle compulsion" with interrogation. That the officers' comments struck a responsive cord is readily apparent. Thus, it may be said, as the Rhode Island Supreme Court did say, that the respondent was subjected to "subtle compulsion." But that is not the end of the inquiry. It must also be established that a suspect's incriminating response was the product of words or actions on the part of the police that they should have known were reasonably likely to elicit an incriminating response.[6] This was not established in the present case.

* * *

■ MR. JUSTICE STEVENS, dissenting.

* * *

[I]n order to give full protection to a suspect's right to be free from any interrogation at all [after he has invoked his right to cut off questioning], the definition of "interrogation" must include any police statement or conduct that has the same purpose or effect as a direct question. Statements that appear to call for a response from the suspect, as well as those that are designed to do so, should be considered interrogation. By prohibiting only those relatively few statements or actions that a police officer should know are likely to elicit an incriminating response, the Court today accords a suspect considerably less protection. Indeed, * * * this new definition will almost certainly exclude every statement that is not punctuated with a question mark from the concept of "interrogation."

* * *

In any event, I think the Court is clearly wrong in holding, as a matter of law, that Officer Gleckman should not have realized that his statement was likely to elicit an incriminating response. * * *

The Court's assumption that criminal suspects are not susceptible to appeals to conscience is directly contrary to the teachings of police interro-

---

6. By way of example, if the police had done no more than to drive past the site of the concealed weapon while taking the most direct route to the police station, and if the respondent, upon noticing for the first time the proximity of the school for handicapped children, had blurted out that he would show the officers where the gun was located, it could not seriously be argued that this "subtle compulsion" would have constituted "interrogation" within the meaning of the *Miranda* opinion.

gation manuals, which recommend appealing to a suspect's sense of morality as a standard and often successful interrogation technique. Surely the practical experience embodied in such manuals should not be ignored in a case such as this in which the record is devoid of any evidence—one way or the other—as to the susceptibility of suspects in general or of Innis in particular.

Moreover, there is evidence in the record to support the view that Officer Gleckman's statement was intended to elicit a response from Innis. Officer Gleckman, who was not regularly assigned to the caged wagon, was directed by a police captain to ride with respondent to the police station. Although there is a dispute in the testimony, it appears that Gleckman may well have been riding in the back seat with Innis. The record does not explain why, notwithstanding the fact that respondent was handcuffed, unarmed, and had offered no resistance when arrested by an officer acting alone, the captain ordered Officer Gleckman to ride with respondent. It is not inconceivable that two professionally trained police officers concluded that a few well-chosen remarks might induce respondent to disclose the whereabouts of the shotgun. This conclusion becomes even more plausible in light of the emotionally charged words chosen by Officer Gleckman ("God forbid" that a "little girl" should find the gun and hurt herself).

NOTES

1. *Innis* was applied in Arizona v. Mauro, 481 U.S. 520, 107 S.Ct. 1931, 95 L.Ed.2d 458 (1987). Mauro was arrested after he approached authorities, volunteered he had killed his young son, and led authorities to the victim's body. At the stationhouse, he was advised of his *Miranda* rights. He told officers he did not want to make any more statements until his lawyer was present. Questioning then ceased. Meanwhile, Mauro's wife, who had been questioned by other officers, asked to speak to him. After discussion, the officer in charge (Sergeant Allen) permitted this. Mrs. Mauro was taken to the office in which Mauro was held. The couple was told they could speak only if an officer remained present and the officer—Detective Manson—then placed a tape recorder in plain sight. A brief conversation ensued in which Mrs. Mauro expressed despair regarding the situation and Mauro urged his wife not to answer questions until a lawyer was present. At trial, Mauro presented a defense of insanity. The state then in rebuttal sought to prove the conversation between Mauro and his wife to show that Mauro was functioning in a sane fashion. The defense objected that the conversation was the result of "interrogation" conducted in violation of *Miranda* because Mauro had invoked his right to counsel which barred further "interrogation" until a lawyer was present. Nevertheless, the evidence was admitted. By a 5–4 vote, the Supreme Court found no *Miranda* defect. The majority noted some uncertainty in the record as to whether Mauro was given advance notice that his wife would be coming to speak with him. Assuming no notice was provided, however, the Court explained:

> The sole issue * * * is whether the officers' * * * actions rose to the level of interrogation—that is, in the language of *Innis,* whether they were the "functional equivalent" of police interrogation. We think it is clear under both *Miranda* and *Innis* that Mauro was not interrogated. * * * Detective Manson asked Mauro no questions about the crime or his conduct. Nor is it suggested— or supported by any evidence—that Sergeant Allen's decision to allow Mauro's wife to see him was the kind of psychological ploy that properly could be treated as the functional equivalent of interrogation.

There is no evidence that the officers sent Mrs. Mauro in to see her husband for the purpose of eliciting incriminating statements. * * * [T]he weakness of Mauro's claim that he was interrogated is underscored by examining the situation from his perspective. We doubt that a suspect, told by officers that his wife will be allowed to speak to him, would feel that he was being coerced to incriminate himself in any way. * * * Officers do not interrogate a suspect simply by hoping that he will incriminate himself. * * * Mauro was not subjected to compelling influences, psychological ploys, or direct questioning. Thus, his volunteered statements cannot properly be considered the result of police interrogation.

481 U.S. at 527–29, 107 S.Ct. at 1935–37, 95 L.Ed.2d at 467–68. Justice Stevens, joined by Justices Brennan, Marshall and Blackmun, dissented.

2. **Request for Submission to Blood Alcohol Test.** In *Innis,* the Court indicated "interrogation" did not include police words or activity "normally attendant to arrest and custody." In South Dakota v. Neville, 459 U.S. 553, 103 S.Ct. 916, 74 L.Ed.2d 748 (1983), relying on this *Innis* dictum, the Court held that a request a suspect submit to a blood alcohol test is not "interrogation." Justice O'Connor explained for the Court:

> The police inquiry * * * is highly regulated by state law, and is presented in virtually the same words to all suspects. It is similar to a police request to submit to fingerprinting or photography.

459 U.S. at 564 n. 15, 103 S.Ct. at 923 n. 15, 74 L.Ed.2d at 759 n. 15.

b. THE REQUIREMENT OF "CUSTODY"

EDITORS' INTRODUCTION: *MIRANDA'S* CUSTODY PREREQUISITE

The requirement of custody has given rise to more Supreme Court consideration than the requirement of interrogation. In Oregon v. Mathiason, 429 U.S. 492, 97 S.Ct. 711, 50 L.Ed.2d 714 (1977) (per curiam), the Court made clear that the need for custody was firm. *Miranda* would not be applied where custody was lacking, *Mathiason* held, even if the situation presented a "coercive environment" in some sense.

The custody need not be for the offense that is the subject of the questioning. In Mathis v. United States, 391 U.S. 1, 88 S.Ct. 1503, 20 L.Ed.2d 381 (1968), police questioned the suspect while the suspect was in prison serving a sentence for an offense unrelated to that under investigation. Rejecting the argument that *Miranda* applied only to suspects in custody for the offense that was the subject of the interrogation, the majority explained that such a limitation would "[go] against the whole purpose of the *Miranda* decision * * *."

When custody exists has presented a source of continuing controversy. In *Mathiason*, the Court concluded a parolee who appeared at a police station in response to an officer's request for a discussion was not in custody for purposes of *Miranda*. The majority explained, *"Miranda* warnings are required only where there has been such a restriction on a person's freedom as to render him 'in custody.' "

The Court developed and applied the *Mathiason* standard for custody in California v. Beheler, 463 U.S. 1121, 103 S.Ct. 3517, 77 L.Ed.2d 1275 (1983) (per curiam). Beheler himself called police after he and several others attempted to rob a drug dealer and one of the others killed the dealer. He admitted his participation and consented to a search of his backyard; the murder weapon was located there, as he said it would be. That evening, he agreed to accompany officers to the stationhouse. The officers told him he was not under arrest. During a thirty minute interview, he again acknowledged his participation. He was told his statement would be evaluated by the district attorney and he was then permitted to leave. The stationhouse statement was admitted over defense objection at Beheler's trial for aiding and abetting first degree murder. An intermediate California appellate court, however, held admission of the statement violated *Miranda,* reasoning that the prosecution had failed to meet its burden of establishing lack of custody. *Mathiason* was distinguished on several grounds: (a) the interview with Beheler took place soon after the offense, while that with Mathiason occurred 25 days after the crime under investigation; (b) the officers had more information implicating Beheler than had been available against Mathiason at the time of his interview; (c) Beheler had been drinking and was emotionally upset; and (d) Beheler was not a parolee and therefore lacked a parolee's incentive to cooperate with law enforcement officers by voluntarily consenting to an interview.

The Supreme Court reversed. Under *Mathiason,* it explained, "the ultimate inquiry is simply whether there is a 'formal arrest or restraint on freedom of movement' of the degree associated with a formal arrest." Considerations (a) and (b) summarized above, it continued, are irrelevant to this inquiry. Properly framed, the issue presented "is whether *Miranda* warnings are required if the suspect is not placed under arrest, voluntarily comes to the police station, and is allowed to leave unhindered by the police after a brief interview." Since its past decisions clearly directed a negative answer, the Court reversed the decision of the California appellate tribunal.

Similarly, a probationer who appeared at his probation officer's office in response to her request for a meeting with the officer was not in custody under *Mathiason* and *Beheler.* Minnesota v. Murphy, 465 U.S. 420, 104 S.Ct. 1136, 79 L.Ed.2d 409 (1984).

In 1994, the Court returned to the custody problem in Stansbury v. California, 511 U.S. 318, 114 S.Ct. 1526, 128 L.Ed.2d 293 (1994) (per curiam). Officers investigating the rape and murder of a ten year old girl learned that on the day of her death the victim had been seen talking to Stansbury, an ice cream truck driver. At 11:00 p.m., four officers went to Stansbury's trailer home and asked if he would accompany them to the police station to answer some questions. He agreed. During subsequent questioning conducted without *Miranda* warnings, Stansbury made incriminating admissions. The state court held the statement nevertheless admissible, stressing in part that suspicion had not focused on Stansbury until he made the statement. The Supreme Court responded:

> Our decisions make clear that the initial determination of custody depends on the objective circumstances of the interrogation, not on the subjective views harbored by either the interrogating officers or the person being questioned. * * *
>
> [A] police officer's subjective view that the individual under questioning is a suspect, if undisclosed, does not bear upon the question whether the individual is in custody for purposes of *Miranda.* The

same principle obtains if an officer's undisclosed assessment is that the person being questioned is not a suspect. In either instance, one cannot expect the person under interrogation to probe the officer's innermost thoughts. Save as they are communicated or otherwise manifested to the person being questioned, an officer's evolving but unarticulated suspicions do not affect the objective circumstances of an interrogation or interview, and thus cannot affect the *Miranda* custody inquiry. * * *

An officer's knowledge or beliefs may bear upon the custody issue if they are conveyed, by word or deed, to the individual being questioned. Those beliefs are relevant only to the extent they would affect how a reasonable person in the position of the individual being questioned would gauge the breadth of his or her " 'freedom of action.' " Even a clear statement from an officer that the person under interrogation is a prime suspect is not, in itself, dispositive of the custody issue, for some suspects are free to come and go until the police decide to make an arrest. The weight and pertinence of any communications regarding the officer's degree of suspicion will depend upon the facts and circumstances of the particular case. In sum, an officer's views concerning the nature of an interrogation, or beliefs concerning the potential culpability of the individual being questioned, may be one among many factors that bear upon the assessment whether that individual was in custody, but only if the officer's views or beliefs were somehow manifested to the individual under interrogation and would have affected how a reasonable person in that position would perceive his or her freedom to leave. (Of course, instances may arise in which the officer's undisclosed views are relevant in testing the credibility of his or her account of what happened during an interrogation; but it is the objective surroundings, and not any undisclosed views, that control the *Miranda* custody inquiry.)

511 U.S. at 523–25, 114 S.Ct. at 1529–30, 128 L.Ed.2d at 298–300. The state court's analysis suggested the court may have regarded the officers' subjective beliefs regarding Stansbury's status "as significant in and of themselves, rather than as relevant only to the extent they influenced the objective conditions surrounding his interrogation." Nevertheless, the parties disagreed on whether the objective facts in the record supported a finding that Stansbury was in custody. Concluding the state court should consider this question in the first instance, the Supreme Court reversed the judgment of the state tribunal and remanded the case "for further proceedings not inconsistent with this opinion."

On remand, the California Supreme Court held that under the analysis directed by the Supreme Court's opinion, the record supported the trial court's finding that Stansbury was not in custody. "[T]he record indicates," the state court concluded, "that a reasonable person in defendant's shoes would not consider that he or she was in custody." It stressed that the officers informed Stansbury he was a possible witness and asked him to come to the station. They invited him to sit in the front seat of their vehicle. Further:

the nature of the interview in this case, which was brief and not accusatory, would not convey to the reasonable person the impression that he or she was in custody, despite the fact that the interview took place in an interview room in the jail area of the police station.

People v. Stansbury, 9 Cal.4th 824, 832, 889 P.2d 588, 592, 38 Cal.Rptr.2d 394, 398 (1995).

Stansbury emphasized suspects' perceptions regarding their ability to break off interactions with police. Nevertheless, the following principal case makes clear that custody does not depend entirely upon whether such a perception exists.

Berkemer v. McCarty

Supreme Court of the United States, 1984.
468 U.S. 420, 104 S.Ct. 3138, 82 L.Ed.2d 317.

■ JUSTICE MARSHALL delivered the opinion of the Court.

This case presents two related questions: First, does our decision in Miranda v. Arizona, 384 U.S. 436, 86 S.Ct. 1602, 16 L.Ed.2d 694 (1966), govern the admissibility of statements made during custodial interrogation by a suspect accused of a misdemeanor traffic offense? Second, does the roadside questioning of a motorist detained pursuant to a traffic stop constitute custodial interrogation for the purposes of the doctrine enunciated in *Miranda?*

I

A

The parties have stipulated to the essential facts. On the evening of March 31, 1980, Trooper Williams of the Ohio State Highway Patrol observed respondent's car weaving in and out of a lane on Interstate Highway 270. After following the car for two miles, Williams forced respondent to stop and asked him to get out of the vehicle. When respondent complied, Williams noticed that he was having difficulty standing. At that point, "Williams concluded that [respondent] would be charged with a traffic offense and, therefore, his freedom to leave the scene was terminated." However, respondent was not told that he would be taken into custody. Williams then asked respondent to perform a field sobriety test, commonly known as a "balancing test." Respondent could not do so without falling.

While still at the scene of the traffic stop, Williams asked respondent whether he had been using intoxicants. Respondent replied that "he had consumed two beers and had smoked several joints of marijuana a short time before." Respondent's speech was slurred, and Williams had difficulty understanding him. Williams thereupon formally placed respondent under arrest and transported him in the patrol car to the Franklin County Jail.

At the jail, respondent was given an intoxilyzer test to determine the concentration of alcohol in his blood. The test did not detect any alcohol whatsoever in respondent's system. Williams then resumed questioning respondent in order to obtain information for inclusion in the State

Highway Patrol Alcohol Influence Report. Respondent answered affirmatively a question whether he had been drinking. When then asked if he was under the influence of alcohol, he said, "I guess, barely." Williams next asked respondent to indicate on the form whether the marihuana he had smoked had been treated with any chemicals. In the section of the report headed "Remarks," respondent wrote, "No ang[el] dust or PCP in the pot. Rick McCarty."

At no point in this sequence of events did Williams or anyone else tell respondent that he had a right to remain silent, to consult with an attorney, and to have an attorney appointed for him if he could not afford one.

B

Respondent was charged with operating a motor vehicle while under the influence of alcohol and/or drugs * * *. Under Ohio law, that offense is a first-degree misdemeanor and is punishable by fine or imprisonment for up to 6 months. Incarceration for a minimum of 3 days is mandatory.

Respondent moved to exclude the various incriminating statements he had made to Patrolman Williams on the ground that introduction into evidence of those statements would violate the Fifth Amendment insofar as he had not been informed of his constitutional rights prior to his interrogation. When the trial court denied the motion, respondent pleaded "no contest" and was found guilty. He was sentenced to 90 days in jail, 80 of which were suspended, and was fined $300, $100 of which were suspended.

On appeal [in the state courts, respondent's conviction was affirmed.]

Respondent then filed an action for a writ of habeas corpus in the District Court for the Southern District of Ohio. The District Court dismissed the petition * * *.

A divided panel of the Court of Appeals for the Sixth Circuit reversed, holding that "*Miranda* warnings must be given to *all* individuals prior to custodial interrogation, whether the offense investigated be a felony or a misdemeanor traffic offense." * * *

We granted certiorari * * *.

II

* * *

In the years since the decision in *Miranda,* we have frequently reaffirmed the central principle established by that case: if the police take a suspect into custody and then ask him questions without informing him of the rights enumerated above, his responses cannot be introduced into evidence to establish his guilt.

Petitioner asks us to carve an exception out of the foregoing principle. When the police arrest a person for allegedly committing a misdemeanor traffic offense and then ask him questions without telling him his constitutional rights, petitioner argues, his responses should be admissible against him. We cannot agree.

One of the principal advantages of the doctrine that suspects must be given warnings before being interrogated while in custody is the clarity of that rule. * * * The exception to *Miranda* proposed by petitioner would substantially undermine this crucial advantage of the doctrine. The police often are unaware when they arrest a person whether he may have committed a misdemeanor or a felony. * * * It would be unreasonable to expect the police to make guesses as to the nature of the criminal conduct at issue before deciding how they may interrogate the suspect.

* * *

We hold * * * that a person subjected to custodial interrogation is entitled to the benefit of the procedural safeguards enunciated in *Miranda,* regardless of the nature or severity of the offense of which he is suspected or for which he was arrested.

The * * * statements made by respondent at the County Jail were inadmissible. There can be no question that respondent was "in custody" at least as of the moment he was formally placed under arrest and instructed to get into the police car. Because he was not informed of his constitutional rights at that juncture, respondent's subsequent admissions should not have been used against him.

III

To assess the admissibility of the self-incriminating statements made by respondent prior to his formal arrest, we are obliged to address a second issue concerning the scope of our decision in *Miranda:* whether the road-side questioning of a motorist detained pursuant to a routine traffic stop should be considered "custodial interrogation." Respondent urges that it should, on the ground that *Miranda* by its terms applies whenever "a person has been taken into custody *or otherwise deprived of his freedom of action in any significant way.*" Petitioner contends that a holding that every detained motorist must be advised of his rights before being questioned would constitute an unwarranted extension of the *Miranda* doctrine.

It must be acknowledged at the outset that a traffic stop significantly curtails the "freedom of action" of the driver and the passengers, if any, of the detained vehicle. Under the law of most States, it is a crime either to ignore a policeman's signal to stop one's car or, once having stopped, to drive away without permission. Certainly few motorists would feel free either to disobey a directive to pull over or to leave the scene of a traffic stop without being told they might do so. * * *

However, we decline to accord talismanic power to the phrase in the *Miranda* opinion emphasized by respondent. Fidelity to the doctrine announced in *Miranda* requires that it be enforced strictly, but only in those types of situations in which the concerns that powered the decision are implicated. Thus, we must decide whether a traffic stop exerts upon a detained person pressures that sufficiently impair his free exercise of his privilege against self-incrimination to require that he be warned of his constitutional rights.

Two features of an ordinary traffic stop mitigate the danger that a person questioned will be induced "to speak where he would not otherwise do so freely." First, detention of a motorist pursuant to a traffic stop is presumptively temporary and brief. The vast majority of roadside detentions last only a few minutes. A motorist's expectations, when he sees a policeman's light flashing behind him, are that he will be obliged to spend a short period of time answering questions and waiting while the officer checks his license and registration, that he may then be given a citation, but that in the end he most likely will be allowed to continue on his way. In this respect, questioning incident to an ordinary traffic stop is quite different from stationhouse interrogation, which frequently is prolonged, and in which the detainee often is aware that questioning will continue until he provides his interrogators the answers they seek.[7]

Second, circumstances associated with the typical traffic stop are not such that the motorist feels completely at the mercy of the police. To be sure, the aura of authority surrounding an armed, uniformed officer and the knowledge that the officer has some discretion in deciding whether to issue a citation, in combination, exert some pressure on the detainee to respond to questions. But other aspects of the situation substantially offset these forces. Perhaps most importantly, the typical traffic stop is public, at least to some degree. Passersby, on foot or in other cars, witness the interaction of officer and motorist. This exposure to public view both reduces the ability of an unscrupulous policeman to use illegitimate means to elicit self-incriminating statements and diminishes the motorist's fear that, if he does not cooperate, he will be subjected to abuse. The fact that the detained motorist typically is confronted by only one or at most two policemen further mutes his sense of vulnerability. In short, the atmosphere surrounding an ordinary traffic stop is substantially less "police dominated" than that surrounding the kinds of interrogation at issue in *Miranda* itself, and in the subsequent cases in which we have applied *Miranda*.

In both of these respects, the usual traffic stop is more analogous to a so-called *"Terry* stop," see Terry v. Ohio, 392 U.S. 1, 88 S.Ct. 1868, 20 L.Ed.2d 889 (1968), than to a formal arrest. Under the Fourth Amendment, we have held, a policeman who lacks probable cause but whose "observations lead him reasonably to suspect" that a particular person has committed, is committing, or is about to commit a crime, may detain that person briefly in order to "investigate the circumstances that provoke suspicion." "[T]he stop and inquiry must be 'reasonably related in scope to the justification for their initiation.' " Typically, this means that the officer may ask the detainee a moderate number of questions to determine his identity and to try to obtain information confirming or dispelling the officer's suspicions. But the detainee is not obliged to respond. And, unless the detainee's answers provide the officer with probable cause to arrest him, he must then be released. The comparatively nonthreatening character of detentions of this sort explains the absence of any suggestion in our

---

7. The brevity and spontaneity of an ordinary traffic stop also reduces the danger that the driver through subterfuge will be made to incriminate himself. One of the investigative techniques that *Miranda* was designed to guard against was the use by police of various kinds of trickery—such as "Mutt and Jeff" routines—to elicit confessions from suspects. A police officer who stops a suspect on the highway has little chance to develop or implement a plan of this sort.

opinions that *Terry* stops are subject to the dictates of *Miranda*. The similarly noncoercive aspect of ordinary traffic stops prompts us to hold that persons temporarily detained pursuant to such stops are not "in custody" for the purposes of *Miranda*.

Respondent contends that to "exempt" traffic stops from the coverage of *Miranda* will open the way to widespread abuse. Policemen will simply delay formally arresting detained motorists, and will subject them to sustained and intimidating interrogation at the scene of their initial detention. * * * The net result, respondent contends, will be a serious threat to the rights that the *Miranda* doctrine is designed to protect.

We are confident that the state of affairs projected by respondent will not come to pass. It is settled that the safeguards prescribed by *Miranda* become applicable as soon as a suspect's freedom of action is curtailed to a "degree associated with formal arrest." If a motorist who has been detained pursuant to a traffic stop thereafter is subjected to treatment that renders him "in custody" for practical purposes, he will be entitled to the full panoply of protections prescribed by *Miranda*.

Admittedly, our adherence to the doctrine just recounted will mean that the police and lower courts will continue occasionally to have difficulty deciding exactly when a suspect has been taken into custody. Either a rule that *Miranda* applies to all traffic stops or a rule that a suspect need not be advised of his rights until he is formally placed under arrest would provide a clearer, more easily administered line. However, each of these two alternatives has drawbacks that make it unacceptable. The first would substantially impede the enforcement of the nation's traffic laws—by compelling the police either to take the time to warn all detained motorists of their constitutional rights or to forgo use of self-incriminating statements made by those motorists—while doing little to protect citizens' Fifth Amendment rights. The second would enable the police to circumvent the constraints on custodial interrogations established by *Miranda*.

Turning to the case before us, we find nothing in the record that indicates that respondent should have been given *Miranda* warnings at any point prior to the time Trooper Williams placed him under arrest. For the reasons indicated above, we reject the contention that the initial stop of respondent's car, by itself, rendered him "in custody." And respondent has failed to demonstrate that, at any time between the initial stop and the arrest, he was subjected to restraints comparable to those associated with a formal arrest. Only a short period of time elapsed between the stop and the arrest. At no point during that interval was respondent informed that his detention would not be temporary. Although Trooper Williams apparently decided as soon as respondent stepped out of his car that respondent would be taken into custody and charged with a traffic offense, Williams never communicated his intention to respondent. A policeman's unarticulated plan has no bearing on the question whether a suspect was "in custody" at a particular time; the only relevant inquiry is how a reasonable man in the suspect's position would have understood his situation. Nor do other aspects of the interaction of Williams and respondent support the contention that respondent was exposed to "custodial interrogation" at the scene of the stop. From aught that appears in the stipulation of facts, a single

police officer asked respondent a modest number of questions and requested him to perform a simple balancing test at a location visible to passing
motorists. Treatment of this sort cannot fairly be characterized as the
functional equivalent of formal arrest.

We conclude, in short, that respondent was not taken into custody for
the purposes of *Miranda* until Williams arrested him. Consequently, the
statements respondent made prior to that point were admissible against
him.

IV

[W]e agree with the Court of Appeals that respondent's postarrest
statements should have been suppressed but conclude that respondent's
prearrest statements were admissible * * *.

Accordingly, the judgment of the Court of Appeals is

Affirmed.

NOTES

1. **Modified Warnings for Field Stop Situations.** Insofar as a suspect
subjected to a nonarrest detention is not "in custody," *Miranda* is entirely inapplicable. But are there—or should there be—any requirements for interrogation in
such circumstances, other than the apparent demand that any resulting admissions
be voluntary? Should, for example, the Court have considered whether a modified
version of *Miranda* rights might be required by risks posed to suspects' Fifth
Amendment interests in traffic stop situations? Might this be required when
nonarrest detention is rather an investigatory field stop concerning a serious
offense?

The American Law Institute's Model Code of Pre-Arraignment Procedure
proposed the following alternatives to govern questioning during nonarrest stops for
investigation:

(5) *Questioning of Suspects.*

(a) *Warnings.* If a law enforcement officer stops any person who he
suspects or has reasonable cause to suspect may have committed a crime, the
officer shall warn such person as promptly as is reasonable under the circumstances, and in any case before engaging in any sustained questioning

(i) that such person is not obligated to say anything, and anything he says
may be used in evidence against him,

(ii) that within twenty minutes he will be released unless he is arrested.[,]

[(iii) that if he is arrested he will be taken to a police station where he may
promptly communicate by telephone with counsel, relatives or friends, and

(iv) that he will not be questioned unless he wishes, and that if he wishes
to consult a lawyer or have a lawyer present during questioning, he will not be
questioned at this time, and that after being taken to the stationhouse a lawyer
will be furnished him prior to questioning if he is unable to obtain one.]

(b) *Limitations on Questioning.* No law enforcement officer shall question
a person detained pursuant to the authority of this Section who he suspects or
has reasonable cause to suspect may have committed a crime, if such person
has indicated in any manner that he does not wish to be questioned, or that he
wishes to consult counsel before submitting to any questioning.

A Model Code of Pre-Arraignment Procedure § 110.2 (Official Draft 1975).

2. **Demand for Identifying Information.** In Brown v. Texas, 443 U.S. 47, 99 S.Ct. 2637, 61 L.Ed.2d 357 (1979), Brown was convicted under a Texas statute which made it a criminal offense for a person to refuse to give his name and address to an officer "who has lawfully stopped him and requested the information." The Supreme Court found the officers who stopped Brown had insufficient information to amount to reasonable suspicion Brown was engaged or had engaged in criminal conduct. Under these circumstances, it concluded, Brown could not be punished for refusing to identify himself. The Court specifically noted, however, it was not addressing whether a person could be punished for refusing to identify himself "in the context of a lawful investigatory stop which satisfies Fourth Amendment requirements."

3.   The Right to Prevent Questioning

EDITORS' INTRODUCTION: SUSPECTS' RIGHT UNDER *MIRANDA* TO AVOID INTERROGATION

Miranda itself suggested that among the rights of those covered by the opinion is the right to avoid questioning and, perhaps, other efforts by law enforcement officers to persuade suspects to cooperate. The Supreme Court's development of this aspect of *Miranda* is the major post-*Miranda* expansion of the Fifth Amendment law applicable to police interrogation.

The leading post-*Miranda* case is Edwards v. Arizona, 451 U.S. 477, 101 S.Ct. 1880, 68 L.Ed.2d 378 (1981). On January 19, Edwards was arrested on a complaint charging a variety of crimes. He was interrogated by several officers and discussed the possibility of "making a deal." Eventually he said to the interrogating officer, "I want an attorney before making a deal." Questioning ceased and he was taken to a jail cell. The Supreme Court explained what happened next:

> At 9:15 the next morning, two detectives, colleagues of the officer who had interrogated Edwards the previous night, came to the jail and asked to see Edwards. When the detention officer informed Edwards that the detectives wished to speak with him, he replied that he did not want to talk to anyone. The guard told him that "he had" to talk and then took him to meet with the detectives. The officers identified themselves, stated they wanted to talk to him, and informed him of his *Miranda* rights. Edwards was willing to talk, but he first wanted to hear the taped statement of the alleged accomplice who had implicated him. After listening to the tape for several minutes, * * * [h]e * * * implicated himself in the crime.

The Court held that his incriminating statement was inadmissible. It explained:

> *Miranda* itself indicated that the assertion of the right to counsel was a significant event and that once exercised by the accused, "the interrogation must cease until an attorney is present." * * * We reconfirm th[is] view[] and, to lend [it] substance, emphasize that it is inconsistent with *Miranda* and its progeny for the authorities, at their instance, to reinterrogate an accused in custody if he has clearly asserted his right to counsel.

[T]he officers conducting the interrogation on the evening of January 19 ceased interrogation when Edwards requested counsel as he had been advised he had the right to do. * * * [W]ithout making counsel available to Edwards, the police returned to him the next day. This was not at his suggestion or request. Indeed, Edwards informed the detention officer that he did not want to talk to anyone. At the meeting, the detectives told Edwards that they wanted to talk to him and again advised him of his *Miranda* rights. Edwards stated that he would talk, but what prompted this action does not appear. * * * We think it is clear that Edwards was subjected to custodial interrogation on January 20 * * *, and that this occurred at the instance of the authorities. His statement made without having had access to counsel, did not amount to a valid waiver and hence was inadmissible.

451 U.S. at 485–87, 101 S.Ct. at 1883–84, 68 L.Ed.2d at 386–88.

Edwards has been treated as recognizing and implementing a right on the part of those who have invoked their right to counsel not to be interrogated until and unless counsel is present. Neither *Edwards* nor the cases following it distinguished between interrogation in the common sense of that term—questioning aimed at eliciting a self-incriminating admission—and what might usefully be called a ''reapproach'' to a suspect—an approach to a suspect designed to persuade the suspect to submit to questioning without counsel's presence. Apparently *Edwards* regarded a reapproach in this sense as interrogation barred by the suspect's invocation of the right to counsel. Essentially, then, *Edwards* holds that if a suspect invokes the right to counsel, until the attorney is present the suspect cannot be subjected to either efforts to persuade him to admit guilt (literal interrogation) or attempts to persuade him to submit to such efforts to persuade him to admit guilt (a reapproach not involving literal interrogation).

Edwards Rule Not ''Offense Specific''

Edwards' prohibition against further interrogation applies even if officers reapproach the suspect concerning an offense unrelated to that under discussion when the suspect invoked his right to counsel. In this sense, the *Edwards* Fifth Amendment rule—unlike the Sixth Amendment *Edwards*-like rule discussed in part C of this chapter—is not ''offense specific.''

This was established in Arizona v. Roberson, 486 U.S. 675, 108 S.Ct. 2093, 100 L.Ed.2d 704 (1988). Officers called to the scene of a break-in arrested Roberson for the burglary. This took place on April 16, 1985. After the arresting officer gave him his *Miranda* warnings, Roberson responded that he ''wanted a lawyer before answering any questions.'' The officer noted this in his written report. Three days later, another officer approached Roberson, who was still in custody, regarding a burglary committed on April 15. This officer had not read the arresting officer's report and was unaware Roberson had invoked his right to counsel. After warning Roberson and questioning him, the second officer obtained from Roberson an admission to the April 15 offense. A majority of the Supreme Court held this was inadmissible under *Edwards*. Once a suspect invokes his right to counsel, Justice Stevens reasoned for the Court, *Edwards* bars further interrogation (until a lawyer is provided) even if that subsequent interrogation concerns an offense unrelated to the offense involved in the first interrogation session. Roberson's invocation of his right to counsel during questioning about the April 15 break-in, therefore, barred the second officer from reapproaching him even though that reapproach concerned the separate April 15 offense. The rationale for *Edwards*—that a suspect's invocation of the right to counsel raises a "presumption" that the suspect believes himself incapable of undergoing questioning without the help of an attorney—applies even if the further interrogation concerns a different offense. The rigid *Edwards* rule is justified in order to vigorously discourage police activity creating an especially high risk of an involuntary waiver; the Court found no basis for concluding "that police engaged in separate investigations will be any less eager than police involved in only one inquiry to question a suspect in custody." Suspects like Roberson might have good reason to speak with police about a different offense or at least to learn from police what the new investigation concerns so they can decide whether or not to make a statement, the Court acknowledged. But:

> the suspect, having requested counsel, can determine how to deal with the separate investigations with counsel's advice. Further, even if the police have decided temporarily not to provide counsel, they are free to inform the suspect of the facts of the second investigation as long as such communication does not constitute interrogation.

486 U.S. at 687, 108 S.Ct. at 2101, 100 L.Ed.2d at 717. The second officer's ignorance that Roberson had invoked his right to counsel was of no significance, the Court continued. *Edwards* focuses upon the suspect's state of mind rather than that of the officer. *Miranda* creates a "need to determine whether the suspect has requested counsel." This need exists whether further investigation concerns the same or a different offense or the same or a different interrogator. Failure to honor a request for counsel, the Court concluded, "cannot be justified by the lack of diligence of a particular officer."

Justice Kennedy, joined by the Chief Justice, dissented. When officers reapproach a suspect concerning a separate crime, he reasoned, "the danger of badgering is minimal and insufficient to justify a rigid *per se* rule." Suspects' interests, in this type of situation, are adequately protected by the officers' need to provide the "known and tested warnings" and the prosecution's obligation to prove any waivers were voluntary. When persons are arrested for one offense, it is frequently learned that they are "wanted for questioning" with regard to other offenses. The majority's approach, Justice Kennedy complained, will often bar officers, even those representing a jurisdiction other than the arresting one, from such questioning. "The majority's rule is not necessary to protect the rights of suspects, and it will in many instances deprive our nationwide law enforcement network of a legitimate investigative technique now routinely used to resolve major crimes." 486 U.S. at 688, 108 S.Ct. at 2102, 100 L.Ed.2d at 718 (Kennedy, J., dissenting).

Suspect Initiated Discussion

Edwards described its holding as inapplicable to situations in which "the accused himself initiates further communications, exchanges or conversations with the police." This qualification to the *Edwards* rule was developed in Oregon v. Bradshaw, 462 U.S. 1039, 103 S.Ct. 2830, 77 L.Ed.2d 405 (1983).

Bradshaw was asked to accompany a police officer to the station for further investigation of a traffic accident in which one Reynolds, a minor, had been killed. After being given full *Miranda* warnings, Bradshaw acknowledged furnishing Reynolds with liquor but denied other involvement. He was then placed under arrest for furnishing liquor to a minor and again advised of his *Miranda* rights. A police officer informed him that the officer believed Bradshaw was driving the vehicle in which Reynolds had been killed. After denying this, Bradshaw said, "I do want an attorney before it goes very much further." The officer immediately stopped the conversation.

"Sometime later" officers transported Bradshaw about ten or fifteen miles to a jail. Before or during this trip, Bradshaw asked one of the officers, "Well, what is going to happen to me?" The officer responded, "You do not have to talk to me. You have requested an attorney and I don't want you talking to me unless you so desire because anything you say— because—since you have requested an attorney, you know, it has to be at your own free will." Bradshaw stated he understood. A conversation then took place between Bradshaw and the officer concerning where Bradshaw would be taken and the offense with which he would be charged. The officer suggested Bradshaw take a lie detector test and Bradshaw agreed. The next day, after an officer again read him the *Miranda* rights, Bradshaw took the test. Afterwards, he admitted driving the vehicle and passing out because of intoxication. At his subsequent trial, his post-polygraph test statement was admitted into evidence. A state appellate tribunal, however, held admission of the confession violated *Edwards* and reversed.

Without an opinion of the Court, the Supreme Court found no violation of *Miranda* and *Edwards*. The Court's judgment was announced in an opinion authored by Justice Rehnquist and joined in by three other justices. In this opinion, Justice Rehnquist explained:

> [In *Edwards,*] we held that after the right to counsel had been asserted by an accused, further interrogation of the accused should not take place "unless the accused himself initiates further communication, exchanges, or conversations with the police." This was in effect a prophylactic rule, designed to protect an accused in police custody from being badgered by police officers * * *.

> But even if a conversation taking place after the accused had "expressed his desire to deal with the police only through counsel," is initiated by the accused, where reinterrogation follows, the burden remains upon the prosecution to show that subsequent events indicated a waiver of the Fifth Amendment right to have counsel present during the interrogation.

462 U.S. at 1044, 103 S.Ct. at 2834, 77 L.Ed.2d at 411–12. A suspect "initiates" a conversation under *Edwards* only by inquiries which can "be fairly said to represent a desire on the part of an accused to open up a more generalized discussion relating directly or indirectly to the investigation."

Other inquiries, such as requests for water to drink or access to a telephone, are "routine incidents of the custodial relationship" and generally do not amount to an initiation of a conversation within the meaning of *Edwards*.

No violation of the *Edwards* "rule" took place in *Bradshaw*, Justice Rehnquist then concluded:

> Although ambiguous, [Bradshaw's] question in this case as to what was going to happen to him evinced a willingness and a desire for a generalized discussion about the investigation; it was not merely a necessary inquiry arising out of the incidents of the custodial relationship. It could reasonably have been interpreted by the officer as relating generally to the investigation.

462 U.S. at 1045–46, 103 S.Ct. at 2835, 77 L.Ed.2d at 412–13. Progressing to whether the waiver was valid, Justice Rehnquist found no reason to dispute the conclusions of the lower courts that the waiver was voluntary and intelligent. Justice Powell provided the fifth vote to affirm. He did not join Justice Rehnquist's opinion but concurred on the ground the issue should be the voluntariness of Bradshaw's waiver and the record showed the waiver was voluntary.

Justice Marshall, joined by three other members of the Court, dissented. He agreed with Justice Rehnquist that under *Edwards* an accused "initiates" further communication with police only by conduct demonstrating a desire to discuss the subject matter of the investigation. But, he added, this "obviously" means "communication or dialogue *about the subject matter of the criminal investigation*." (emphasis in original). Turning to the facts before the Court, Justice Marshall construed Bradshaw's inquiry as expressing no more than a desire to find out where the officers were taking him. It did not concern the subject matter of the investigation and therefore did not express a desire to discuss that subject matter. As a result, the officer's actions violated *Edwards' per se* rule and the subsequent confession was inadmissible under *Miranda*.

Effect of Invoking Right to Silence

The *Edwards* rule is limited to situations in which the accused invokes the right to counsel. Six years before *Edwards*, in Michigan v. Mosley, 423 U.S. 96, 96 S.Ct. 321, 46 L.Ed.2d 313 (1975), the Court refused to completely bar officers from reapproaching a suspect who invoked his right to remain silent. *Mosley* explained:

> The issue in this case * * * is whether the conduct of the Detroit police that led to Mosley's incriminating statement did in fact violate the *Miranda* "guidelines," so as to render the statement inadmissible in evidence against Mosley at his trial. Resolution of the question turns almost entirely on the interpretation of a single passage in the *Miranda* opinion * * *:
>
> > Once warnings have been given, the subsequent procedure is clear. If the individual indicates in any manner, at any time prior to or during questioning, that he wishes to remain silent, the interrogation must cease. At this point he has shown that he intends to exercise his Fifth Amendment privilege; any statement

taken after the person invokes his privilege cannot be other than the product of compulsion, subtle or otherwise. Without the right to cut off questioning, the setting of in-custody interrogation operates on the individual to overcome free choice in producing a statement after the privilege has been once invoked.

This passage states that "the interrogation must cease" when the person in custody indicates that "he wishes to remain silent." It does not state under what circumstances, if any, a resumption of questioning is permissible. The passage could be literally read to mean that a person who has invoked his "right to silence" can never again be subjected to custodial interrogation by any police officer at any time or place on any subject. Another possible construction of the passage would characterize "any statement taken after the person invokes his privilege" as "the product of compulsion" and would therefore mandate its exclusion from evidence, even if it were volunteered by the person in custody without any further interrogation whatever. Or the passage could be interpreted to require only the immediate cessation of questioning, and to permit a resumption of interrogation after a momentary respite.

It is evident that any of these possible literal interpretations would lead to absurd and unintended results. To permit the continuation of custodial interrogation after a momentary cessation would clearly frustrate the purposes of *Miranda* by allowing repeated rounds of questioning to undermine the will of the person being questioned. At the other extreme, a blanket prohibition against the taking of voluntary statements or a permanent immunity from further interrogation, regardless of the circumstances, would transform the *Miranda* safeguards into wholly irrational obstacles to legitimate police investigative activity, and deprive suspects of an opportunity to make informed and intelligent assessments of their interests. Clearly, therefore, neither this passage nor any other passage in the *Miranda* opinion can sensibly be read to create a per se proscription of indefinite duration upon any further questioning by any police officer on any subject, once the person in custody has indicated a desire to remain silent.

423 U.S. at 100–03, 96 S.Ct. at 325–26, 46 L.Ed.2d at 316–21. *Edwards* distinguished *Mosley* on the basis that the request made in *Mosley*—"a request to remain silent"—was not the request for counsel that triggers the *Edwards* bar to all further interrogation.

The prosecution may have greater difficulty showing that a suspect effectively waived his rights if the facts show that the suspect was reapproached after invoking the right to silence; this is considered in subsection B(4) of this chapter. But under *Mosley*, a suspect who invokes only the right to silence is protected by no absolute prohibition against officers reapproaching him.

Davis v. United States

Supreme Court of the United States, 1994.
512 U.S. 452, 114 S.Ct. 2350, 129 L.Ed.2d 362.

■ JUSTICE O'CONNOR delivered the opinion of the Court.

In Edwards v. Arizona, 451 U.S. 477, 101 S.Ct. 1880, 68 L.Ed.2d 378 (1981), we held that law enforcement officers must immediately cease questioning a suspect who has clearly asserted his right to have counsel present during custodial interrogation. In this case we decide how law enforcement officers should respond when a suspect makes a reference to counsel that is insufficiently clear to invoke the *Edwards* prohibition on further questioning.

I

Pool brought trouble—not to River City, but to the Charleston Naval Base. Petitioner, a member of the United States Navy, spent the evening of October 2, 1988, shooting pool at a club on the base. Another sailor, Keith Shackleton, lost a game and a $30 wager to petitioner, but Shackleton refused to pay. After the club closed, Shackleton was beaten to death with a pool cue on a loading dock behind the commissary. The body was found early the next morning.

The investigation by the Naval Investigative Service (NIS) gradually focused on petitioner. Investigative agents determined that petitioner was at the club that evening, and that he was absent without authorization from his duty station the next morning. The agents also learned that only privately owned pool cues could be removed from the club premises, and that petitioner owned two cues—one of which had a bloodstain on it. The agents were told by various people that petitioner either had admitted committing the crime or had recounted details that clearly indicated his involvement in the killing.

On November 4, 1988, petitioner was interviewed at the NIS office. As required by military law, the agents advised petitioner that he was a suspect in the killing, that he was not required to make a statement, that any statement could be used against him at a trial by court-martial, and that he was entitled to speak with an attorney and have an attorney present during questioning. Petitioner waived his rights to remain silent and to counsel, both orally and in writing.

About an hour and a half into the interview, petitioner said, "Maybe I should talk to a lawyer." According to the uncontradicted testimony of one of the interviewing agents, the interview then proceeded as follows:

> "[We m]ade it very clear that we're not here to violate his rights, that if he wants a lawyer, then we will stop any kind of questioning with him, that we weren't going to pursue the matter unless we have it clarified is he asking for a lawyer or is he just making a comment about a lawyer, and he said, [']No, I'm not asking for a lawyer,' and then he continued on, and said, 'No, I don't want a lawyer.' "

After a short break, the agents reminded petitioner of his rights to remain silent and to counsel. The interview then continued for another hour, until petitioner said, "I think I want a lawyer before I say anything else." At that point, questioning ceased.

At his general court-martial, petitioner moved to suppress statements made during the November 4 interview. The Military Judge denied the motion * * *. Petitioner was convicted on one specification of unpremeditated murder * * *. The Navy–Marine Corps Court of Military Review affirmed.

The United States Court of Military Appeals granted discretionary review and affirmed. The court recognized that the state and federal courts have developed three different approaches to a suspect's ambiguous or equivocal request for counsel:

> "Some jurisdictions have held that any mention of counsel, however ambiguous, is sufficient to require that all questioning cease. Others have attempted to define a threshold standard of clarity for invoking the right to counsel and have held that comments falling short of the threshold do not invoke the right to counsel. Some jurisdictions ... have held that all interrogation about the offense must immediately cease whenever a suspect mentions counsel, but they allow interrogators to ask narrow questions designed to clarify the earlier statement and the [suspect's] desires respecting counsel."

Applying the third approach, the court held that petitioner's comment was ambiguous, and that the NIS agents properly clarified petitioner's wishes with respect to counsel before continuing questioning him about the offense.

* * *

II

[W]e held in Miranda v. Arizona, 384 U.S. 436, 469473, 86 S.Ct. 1602, 16251627, 16 L.Ed.2d 694 (1966), that a suspect subject to custodial interrogation has the right to consult with an attorney and to have counsel present during questioning, and that the police must explain this right to him before questioning begins. * * * If the suspect effectively waives his right to counsel after receiving the *Miranda* warnings, law enforcement officers are free to question him. But if a suspect requests counsel at any time during the interview, he is not subject to further questioning until a lawyer has been made available or the suspect himself reinitiates conversation. This "second layer of prophylaxis for the *Miranda* right to counsel," is "designed to prevent police from badgering a defendant into waiving his previously asserted *Miranda* rights." * * * "It remains clear, however, that this prohibition on further questioning—like other aspects of *Miranda* is not itself required by the Fifth Amendment's prohibition on coerced confessions, but is instead justified only by reference to its prophylactic purpose." Connecticut v. Barrett, [479 U.S. 523, 528, 107 S.Ct. 828, 832, 93 L.Ed.2d 920 (1987)].

The applicability of the " 'rigid' prophylactic rule" of *Edwards* requires courts to "determine whether the accused *actually invoked* his right to counsel." Smith v. Illinois, [469 U.S. 91, 95, 105 S.Ct. 490, 492 83 L.Ed.2d 488 (1984) (per curiam)] (emphasis added). To avoid difficulties of proof and to provide guidance to officers conducting interrogations, this is an objective inquiry. Invocation of the *Miranda* right to counsel "requires, at a minimum, some statement that can reasonably be construed to be an expression of a desire for the assistance of an attorney." McNeil v. Wisconsin, [501 U.S. 171, 178, 111 S.Ct. 2204, 2209, 115 L.Ed.2d 158

(1991)]. But if a suspect makes a reference to an attorney that is ambiguous or equivocal in that a reasonable officer in light of the circumstances would have understood only that the suspect might be invoking the right to counsel, our precedents do not require the cessation of questioning.

Rather, the suspect must unambiguously request counsel. * * * Although a suspect need not "speak with the discrimination of an Oxford don," he must articulate his desire to have counsel present sufficiently clearly that a reasonable police officer in the circumstances would understand the statement to be a request for an attorney. If the statement fails to meet the requisite level of clarity, *Edwards* does not require that the officers stop questioning the suspect.

We decline petitioner's invitation to extend *Edwards* and require law enforcement officers to cease questioning immediately upon the making of an ambiguous or equivocal reference to an attorney. The rationale underlying *Edwards* is that the police must respect a suspect's wishes regarding his right to have an attorney present during custodial interrogation. But when the officers conducting the questioning reasonably do not know whether or not the suspect wants a lawyer, a rule requiring the immediate cessation of questioning "would transform the *Miranda* safeguards into wholly irrational obstacles to legitimate police investigative activity," because it would needlessly prevent the police from questioning a suspect in the absence of counsel even if the suspect did not wish to have a lawyer present. Nothing in *Edwards* requires the provision of counsel to a suspect who consents to answer questions without the assistance of a lawyer. In *Miranda* itself, we expressly rejected the suggestion "that each police station must have a 'station house lawyer' present at all times to advise prisoners, and held instead that a suspect must be told of his right to have an attorney present and that he may not be questioned after invoking his right to counsel." We also noted that if a suspect is "indecisive in his request for counsel," the officers need not always cease questioning.

We recognize that requiring a clear assertion of the right to counsel might disadvantage some suspects who—because of fear, intimidation, lack of linguistic skills, or a variety of other reasons—will not clearly articulate their right to counsel although they actually want to have a lawyer present. But the primary protection afforded suspects subject to custodial interrogation is the *Miranda* warnings themselves. * * * A suspect who knowingly and voluntarily waives his right to counsel after having that right explained to him has indicated his willingness to deal with the police unassisted. Although *Edwards* provides an additional protection—if a suspect subsequently requests an attorney, questioning must cease—it is one that must be affirmatively invoked by the suspect.

In considering how a suspect must invoke the right to counsel, we must consider the other side of the *Miranda* equation: the need for effective law enforcement. Although the courts ensure compliance with the *Miranda* requirements through the exclusionary rule, it is police officers who must actually decide whether or not they can question a suspect. The *Edwards* rule—questioning must cease if the suspect asks for a lawyer—provides a bright line that can be applied by officers in the real world of investigation and interrogation without unduly hampering the gathering of information. But if we were to require questioning to cease if a suspect makes a statement that might be a request for an attorney, this clarity and ease of application would be lost. Police officers would be forced to make difficult judgment calls about whether the suspect in fact wants a lawyer even though he has not said so, with the threat of suppression if they guess wrong. We therefore hold that, after a knowing and voluntary waiver of the *Miranda* rights, law enforcement officers may continue questioning until and unless the suspect clearly requests an attorney.

Of course, when a suspect makes an ambiguous or equivocal statement it will often be good police practice for the interviewing officers to clarify whether or not he actually wants an attorney. That was the procedure followed by the NIS agents in this case. Clarifying questions help protect the rights of the suspect by ensuring that he gets an attorney if he wants one, and will minimize the chance of a confession being suppressed due to subsequent judicial second-guessing as to the meaning of the suspect's statement regarding counsel. But we decline to adopt a rule requiring officers to ask clarifying questions. If the suspect's statement is not an unambiguous or unequivocal request for counsel, the officers have no obligation to stop questioning him.

* * *

The courts below found that petitioner's remark to the NIS agents "Maybe I should talk to a lawyer" was not a request for counsel, and we see no reason to disturb that conclusion. The NIS agents therefore were not required to stop questioning petitioner, though it was entirely proper for them to clarify whether petitioner in fact wanted a lawyer. Because there is no ground for suppression of petitioner's statements, the judgment of the Court of Military Appeals is

Affirmed.

■ JUSTICE SOUTER, with whom JUSTICE BLACKMUN, JUSTICE STEVENS, and JUSTICE GINSBURG join, concurring in the judgment.

* * *

I agree with the majority that the Constitution does not forbid law enforcement officers to pose questions (like those directed at Davis) aimed solely at clarifying whether a suspect's ambiguous reference to counsel was meant to assert his Fifth Amendment right. Accordingly I concur in the judgment affirming Davis's conviction, resting partly on evidence of statements given after agents ascertained that he did not wish to deal with them through counsel. I cannot, however, join in my colleagues' further conclusion that if the investigators here had been so inclined, they were at liberty to disregard Davis's reference to a lawyer entirely, in accordance with a general rule that interrogators have no legal obligation to discover what a custodial subject meant by an ambiguous statement that could reasonably be understood to express a desire to consult a lawyer. * * * The concerns of fairness and practicality that have long anchored our *Miranda* case law point to a different response: when law enforcement officials "reasonably do not know whether or not the suspect wants a lawyer," they should stop their interrogation and ask him to make his choice clear.

I

A

While the question we address today is an open one, its answer requires coherence with nearly three decades of case law addressing the relationship between police and criminal suspects in custodial interrogation. Throughout that period, two precepts have commanded broad assent: that the *Miranda* safeguards exist " 'to assure that *the individual's right to choose* between speech and silence remains unfettered throughout the interrogation process,' " and that the justification for *Miranda* rules, intended to operate in the real world, "must be consistent with ... practical realities." A rule barring government agents from further interrogation until they determine whether a suspect's ambiguous statement was meant as a request for counsel fulfills both ambitions. It assures that a suspect's choice whether or not to deal with police through counsel will be "scrupulously honored," and it faces both the real-world reasons why misunderstandings arise between suspect and interrogator and the real-world limitations on the capacity of police and trial courts to apply fine distinctions and intricate rules.

B

Tested against the same two principles, the approach the Court adopts does not fare so well. First, as the majority expressly acknowledges, criminal suspects who may (in *Miranda*'s words) be "thrust into an unfamiliar atmosphere and run through menacing police interrogation procedures, would seem an odd group to single out for the Court's demand of heightened linguistic care." A substantial percentage of them lack anything like a confident command of the English language; many are "woefully ignorant;" and many more will be sufficiently intimidated by the interrogation process or overwhelmed by the uncertainty of their predicament that the ability to speak assertively will abandon them.[8] * * *

Nor may the standard governing waivers as expressed in these statements be deflected away by drawing a distinction between initial waivers of *Miranda* rights and subsequent decisions to reinvoke them, on the theory that so long as the burden to demonstrate waiver rests on the government, it is only fair to make the suspect shoulder a burden of showing a clear subsequent assertion. *Miranda* itself discredited the legitimacy of any such distinction. The opinion described the object of the warning as being to assure "a continuous opportunity to exercise [the right of silence]." "[C]on-

---

8. Social science confirms what common sense would suggest, that individuals who feel intimidated or powerless are more likely to speak in equivocal or nonstandard terms when no ambiguity or equivocation is meant. See W. O'Barr, Linguistic Evidence: Language, Power, and Strategy in the Courtroom 61–71 (1982). Suspects in police interrogation are strong candidates for these effects. Even while resort by the police to the "third degree" has abated since *Miranda*, the basic forms of psychological pressure applied by police appear to have changed less. Compare, e.g., *Miranda*, supra, 384 U.S., at 449, 86 S.Ct., at 1615 (" '[T]he principal psychological factor contributing to a successful interrogation is privacy' ") (quoting F. Inbau & J. Reid, Criminal Interrogations and Confessions 1 (1962)), with F. Inbau, J. Reid, & J. Buckley, Criminal Interrogation and Confessions 24 (3d ed. 1986) ("The principal psychological factor contributing to a successful interrogation is privacy").

tinuous opportunity" suggests an unvarying one, governed by a common standard of effectiveness. * * *

The Court defends as tolerable the certainty that some poorly expressed requests for counsel will be disregarded on the ground that *Miranda* warnings suffice to alleviate the inherent coercion of the custodial interrogation. But, "[a] once-stated warning, delivered by those who will conduct the interrogation, cannot itself suffice" to "assure that the . . . right to choose between silence and speech remains unfettered throughout the interrogation process." * * *

[I]t is easy, amidst the discussion of layers of protection, to lose sight of a real risk in the majority's approach, going close to the core of what the Court has held that the Fifth Amendment provides. The experience of the timid or verbally inept suspect (whose existence the Court acknowledges) may not always closely follow that of the defendant in Edwards v. Arizona (whose purported waiver of his right to counsel, made after having invoked the right, was held ineffective, lest police be tempted to "badge[r]" others like him). * * * When a suspect understands his (expressed) wishes to have been ignored (and by hypothesis, he has said something that an objective listener could "reasonably," although not necessarily, take to be a request), in contravention of the "rights" just read to him by his interrogator, he may well see further objection as futile and confession (true or not) as the only way to end his interrogation.

* * *

The other justifications offered for the "requisite level of clarity" rule are that, whatever its costs, it will further society's strong interest in "effective law enforcement," and maintain the "ease of application," that has long been a concern of our *Miranda* jurisprudence. With respect to the first point, the margin of difference between the clarification approach advocated here and the one the Court adopts is defined by the class of cases in which a suspect, if asked, would make it plain that he meant to request counsel (at which point questioning would cease). While these lost confessions do extract a real price from society, it is one that *Miranda* itself determined should be borne.

As for practical application, while every approach, including the majority's, will involve some "difficult judgment calls,"[9] the rule argued for here would relieve the officer of any responsibility for guessing "whether the suspect in fact wants a lawyer even though he hasn't said so." To the contrary, it would assure that the "judgment call" will be made by the party most competent to resolve the ambiguity, who our case law has always assumed should make it: the individual suspect.

9. In the abstract, nothing may seem more clear than a "clear statement" rule, but in police stations and trial courts the question, "how clear is clear?" is not so readily answered. When a suspect says, "uh, yeah, I'd like to do that" after being told he has a right to a lawyer, has he "clearly asserted" his right? Compare Smith v. Illinois, [469 U.S. 91, 97, 105 S.Ct. 490, 493, 83 L.Ed.2d 488 (1984) (per curiam)] (statement was " 'neither indecisive nor ambiguous' ") (citation omitted), with id., at 101, 105 S.Ct., at 495 496 (REHNQUIST, J., dissenting) (questioning clarity) * * *

As a practical matter, of course, the primary arbiters of "clarity" will be the interrogators themselves, who tend as well to be courts' preferred source in determining the precise words a suspect used. And when an inculpatory statement has been obtained as a result of an unrecorded, incommunicado interrogation, these officers rarely lose "swearing matches" against criminal defendants at suppression hearings.

II

Although I am convinced that the Court has taken the wrong path; I am not persuaded by petitioner's contention, that even ambiguous statements require an end to all police questioning. I recognize that the approach petitioner urges on us can claim some support from our case law, most notably in the "indicates in any manner" language of *Miranda*, and I do not deny that the rule I endorse could be abused by "clarifying" questions that shade subtly into illicitly badgering a suspect who wants counsel. But petitioner's proposal is not entirely in harmony with all the major themes of *Miranda* case law, its virtues and demerits being the reverse images of those that mark the Court's rule. While it is plainly wrong, for example, to continue interrogation when the suspect wants it to stop (and so indicates), the strong bias in favor of individual choice may also be disserved by stopping questioning when a suspect wants it to continue (but where his statement might be understood otherwise). The costs to society of losing confessions would, moreover, be especially hard to bear where the suspect, if asked for his choice, would have chosen to continue. One need not sign the majority's opinion here to agree that resort to the rule petitioner argues for should be had only if experience shows that less drastic means of safeguarding suspects' constitutional rights are not up to the job.

* * *

Our cases are best respected by a rule that when a suspect under custodial interrogation makes an ambiguous statement that might reasonably be understood as expressing a wish that a lawyer be summoned (and questioning cease), interrogators' questions should be confined to verifying whether the individual meant to ask for a lawyer. While there is reason to expect that trial courts will apply today's ruling sensibly (without requiring criminal suspects to speak with the discrimination of an Oxford don) and that interrogators will continue to follow what the Court rightly calls "good police practice" * * *, I believe that the case law under *Miranda* does not allow them to do otherwise.

NOTES

1. **Invoking the *Edwards* Bar to Questioning.** The Supreme Court has held a suspect has a Sixth Amendment right to counsel that applies—among other times—during police interrogation. This right is invoked, the Court has assumed, if a suspect appears in court with counsel representing him. The Sixth Amendment right, unlike the *Miranda–Edwards* right as construed in *Roberson,* is "offense-specific," meaning it only bars officers from approaching the suspect concerning the same offense. This chapter considers these holdings in part C. Action by a defendant

sufficient to invoke the Sixth Amendment right to counsel, however, does not necessarily invoke the *Edwards* rule under *Miranda* and the Fifth Amendment.

In McNeil v. Wisconsin, 501 U.S. 171, 111 S.Ct. 2204, 115 L.Ed.2d 158 (1991), the defendant was arrested for robbery and appeared before a court commissioner who set bail. A public defender represented him at that appearance. A detective later approached McNeil concerning an unrelated burglary and murder. McNeil was warned of his *Miranda* rights and waived them; he then gave a statement incriminating himself in those offenses. The Supreme Court "accepted" that McNeil's appearance before the commissioner with an attorney invoked his Sixth Amendment right to counsel with regard to the robbery. But it held that this action did not invoke McNeil's *Miranda* right to counsel so as to trigger the *Edwards* rule. Justice Scalia explained for the Court:

> [*Edwards*] requires, at a minimum, some statement that can reasonably be construed to be an expression of a desire for the assistance of an attorney *in dealing with custodial interrogation by the police.*

501 U.S. at 178, 111 S.Ct. at 2209, 115 L.Ed.2d at 169 (emphasis in original). Invoking the Sixth Amendment right to counsel concerning an offense for which one has been judicially charged does not suffice. Specifically, and with reference to the facts of *McNeil,* the Court explained, "[r]equesting the assistance of an attorney at a bail hearing does not bear that construction."

The *McNeil* Court also rejected a rule that invoking the Sixth Amendment right to counsel automatically gives the suspect the protection of *Edwards*. Such a rule would impede law enforcement objectives, it reasoned, since suspects are often given counsel in their first formal court appearance.

> Thus * * * most persons in pretrial custody for serious offenses would be *unapproachable* by police officers suspecting them of involvement in other crimes, *even though they have never expressed any unwillingness to be questioned.*

501 U.S. at 181, 111 S.Ct. at 2210, 115 L.Ed.2d at 170 (emphasis in original). The rule would provide only insignificant protection for suspects:

> If a suspect does not wish to communicate with the police except through an attorney, he can simply tell them that when they give him the *Miranda* warnings. There is not the remotest chance that he will feel "badgered" by their asking to talk to him without counsel present, since the subject will not be the charge on which he has already requested counsel's assistance * * * and he will not have rejected uncounseled interrogation on *any* subject before (for in that event *Edwards* would preclude initiation of the interview).

501 U.S. at 180, 111 S.Ct. at 2210, 115 L.Ed.2d at 170.

2. **"Anticipatory" Invocation of the Right to Counsel.** The *McNeil* dissenters suggested the majority's distinction will be nullified by lawyers who, on behalf of their clients, will routinely and at the first court appearance announce that their clients are invoking *Miranda* rights. Responding, Justice Scalia questioned whether these and other "anticipatory" invocations of *Miranda* rights would be effective:

> We have * * * never held that a person can invoke his *Miranda* rights anticipatorily, in a context other than "custodial interrogation"—which a preliminary hearing will not always, or even usually, involve. If the *Miranda* right to counsel can be invoked at a preliminary hearing, it could be argued, there is no logical reason why it could not be invoked by a letter prior to arrest, or indeed even prior to identification as a suspect. Most rights must be asserted when the government seeks to take the action they protect against. The fact

that we have allowed the *Miranda* right to counsel, once asserted, to be effective with respect to future custodial interrogation does not necessarily mean that we will allow it to be asserted initially outside the context of custodial interrogation, with similar future effect.

501 U.S. at 182 n. 3, 111 S.Ct. at 2211 n. 3, 115 L.Ed.2d at 171 n. 3.

3. **Presence of Attorney Required Under *Edwards*.** In Minnick v. Mississippi, 498 U.S. 146, 111 S.Ct. 486, 112 L.Ed.2d 489 (1990), Minnick was interviewed by FBI agents. He told them, "Come back Monday when I have a lawyer." The federal officers ended the interview. Minnick later met with a lawyer appointed to represent him and spoke with that attorney—perhaps by telephone—on several other occasions. A state officer then interviewed Minnick after warning him of his *Miranda* rights; Minnick refused to sign a waiver form but talked with the officer and made incriminating admissions. The state court declined to apply *Edwards,* reasoning that in *Edwards* the Supreme Court indicated that the bar to further interrogation applies only "until counsel has been made available to [the suspect];" the consultations between Minnick and his lawyer established counsel had been "made available." Justice Scalia, joined by the Chief Justice, agreed, arguing that *Edwards* should cease to apply after the initial consultation between the suspect and his attorney:

> The suspect then knows he had an advocate on his side, and that the police will permit him to consult that advocate. He almost certainly also has a heightened awareness (above what the *Miranda* warning itself will provide) of his right to remain silent * * *.

498 U.S. at 162, 111 S.Ct. at 496, 112 L.Ed.2d at 503 (Scalia, J., dissenting).

The *Minnick* majority, however, concluded otherwise. Justice Kennedy explained for the Court:

> [W]e * * * hold that when counsel is requested, interrogation must cease, and officials may not reinstate interrogation without counsel present, whether or not the accused has consulted with his attorney.
>
> We consider our ruling to be an appropriate and necessary application of the *Edwards* rule. A single consultation with an attorney does not remove the suspect from persistent attempts by officials to persuade him to waive his right, or from the coercive pressures that accompany custody and that may increase as custody is prolonged. * * *
>
> The exception proposed * * * would undermine the advantages flowing from *Edwards'* "clear and unequivocal" character. * * * [It] would leave far from certain the sort of consultation required to displace *Edwards. * * *
>
> [We are also concerned] that the suspect whose counsel is prompt would lose the protection of *Edwards,* while the one whose counsel is dilatory would not. There is more than irony in this rule. There is a strong possibility that it would distort the proper concept of the attorney's duty to the client and set us on a course at odds with what ought to be effective representation.

498 U.S. at 153–55, 111 S.Ct. at 491–92, 112 L.Ed.2d at 498–99.

4.   WAIVER OF THE *MIRANDA* RIGHTS

EDITORS' INTRODUCTION: WAIVER ISSUES

As *Miranda* makes clear, the constitutionally-required foundation for admissibility of a self-incriminating statement made during custodial interrogation is proof that the defendant "knowingly and intelligently waived his privilege against self-incrimination and [unless a lawyer was present during the interrogation] his right to retained or appointed counsel." The *Miranda* Court clearly believed that counsel's presence when a suspect decides to confess would reduce the difficulty of determining whether that waiver of the right to remain silent was effective. In most cases, however, counsel will not have been present during the interrogation. Consequently, waiver issues have become more prominent in *Miranda* law.

Analysis is helped by distinguishing between the need for the prosecution to prove two different matters. First is that the defendant made a choice that might constitute waiver. Second is that a choice made by the defendant was effective. The two inquiries raise different concerns. What is necessary to prove a choice, for example, is a much different question than what is necessary to prove that a choice was sufficiently voluntary and intelligent and therefore effective.

Burden of Proof. The burden of proof regarding *Miranda* waivers was addressed in Colorado v. Connelly, 479 U.S. 157, 107 S.Ct. 515, 93 L.Ed.2d 473 (1986). The state court had held that the prosecution must establish waivers of the rights to counsel and to remain silent by "clear and convincing evidence." Agreeing that the prosecution bears the burden of proof, the Supreme Court held this burden of proof is by only a preponderance of the evidence. Lego v. Twomey, 404 U.S. 477, 92 S.Ct. 619, 30 L.Ed.2d 618 (1972), the Court noted, established that the prosecution need prove the voluntariness of a confession only by a preponderance of the evidence. "[A] waiver of the auxiliary protections established in *Miranda*," *Connelly* reasoned "should require no higher a burden of proof."

Express Waivers Not Required. No "express" waiver of *Miranda* rights is required; an "implied waiver" is sufficient. The Supreme Court has left somewhat unclear precisely what is required for proof of an implied waiver.

In North Carolina v. Butler, 441 U.S. 369, 99 S.Ct. 1755, 60 L.Ed.2d 286 (1979), the North Carolina Supreme Court was held to have erred in applying a *per se* rule requiring an express waiver. "[A] court may find an intelligent and understanding rejection of counsel in situations where the defendant did not expressly state as much," Justice Stewart explained for the Court. He continued:

> The question is not one of form, but rather whether the defendant in fact knowingly and voluntarily waived the rights delineated in *Miranda*. * * * [M]ere silence is not enough. That does not mean that the defendant's silence, coupled with an understanding of his rights and a course of conduct indicating waiver, may never support a conclusion that a defendant has waived his rights. * * * [I]n at least some cases waiver can be clearly inferred from the actions and words of the person interrogated.

441 U.S. at 373, 99 S.Ct. at 1757, 60 L.Ed.2d at 292.

Distinguishing Different Waivers. Often discussions assume that one waiver or set of waivers is at issue. But often this is not the case. Suppose a suspect, after officers gave her the required warnings, agrees to talk with officers in the absence of an attorney. After two hours of discussion, the suspect makes a self-incriminating admission. Are the suspect's waivers of the right to counsel and the right to silence identical? Clearly not. Her waiver of the right to counsel occurred before interrogation began; her waiver of the right to remain silent occurred only when she made the admission.

This distinction is important because intervening events may bear upon the effectiveness of one waiver but not the other. Suppose, for example, that during a two hour discussion officers inform a suspect that she will not be presented before a judge until the officers have what they regard as a satisfactory statement from her. If the suspect had already waived her right to counsel during interrogation, this threat could not affect the effectiveness of this waiver. (Perhaps, however, her continued willingness to undergo questioning without a lawyer is a continuing waiver of the right to counsel rendered involuntary after the threat was made.) In any case, if, in response to this threat, the suspect decides to give an incriminating statement and thereby waive her right to silence, it is much clearer this waiver was fatally tainted by the threat.

Effectiveness of Waivers: In General. The criteria to be used in determining the effectiveness of *Miranda* waivers were distinguished and to some extent developed in Edwards v. Arizona, 451 U.S. 477, 101 S.Ct. 1880, 68 L.Ed.2d 378 (1981).

Before making his oral confession, given during a custodial interrogation, Edwards insisted he did not want his confession recorded because it could then be used against him in court. The interrogating detectives explained that an unrecorded oral confession could also be used against him. Edwards then made an incriminating statement. Prior to trial, defense counsel moved to suppress the confession on the ground that, despite the detectives' efforts, Edwards did not understand the admissibility of an oral confession and therefore the waiver of his rights was not knowingly made. The trial judge found the confession to have been "voluntary" and denied the motion to suppress. On appeal, the Arizona Supreme Court regarded the applicable standard as that discussed in Schneckloth v. Bustamonte, 412 U.S. 218, 93 S.Ct. 2041, 36 L.Ed.2d 854 (1973) (reprinted in Chapter 5), dealing with the voluntariness of a consent to search. It posed the question as whether, based on the totality of the circumstances, the trial court's conclusions that the defendant's action in confessing was knowing and intelligent and that his will had not been overborne were "clear and manifest error." It found no such error.

The Supreme Court held that the Arizona Supreme Court had not adequately considered whether Edwards had effectively relinquished his right to counsel. Under *Miranda,* it explained, the "voluntariness" of a consent or an admission, on the one hand, and the existence of a knowing and intelligent waiver, on the other, "are discrete inquiries." However sound the state court's conclusion regarding the "voluntariness" of Edwards' confession, the tribunal did not adequately address the *Miranda* waiver issue:

> [W]aivers of counsel must not only be voluntary, but must also constitute a knowing and intelligent relinquishment or abandonment of a known right or privilege * * *. [N]either the trial court nor the

Arizona Supreme Court undertook to focus on whether Edwards understood his right to counsel and intelligently and knowingly relinquished it. It is thus apparent that the decision below misunderstood the requirement for finding a valid waiver of the right to counsel * * *.

451 U.S. at 482–84, 101 S.Ct. at 1883–84, 68 L.Ed.2d at 385–86.

Under *Edwards*, the effectiveness of *Miranda* waivers clearly requires separate consideration of voluntariness and intelligence.

Effectiveness of Waivers: Voluntariness. The prosecution must prove a suspect's *Miranda* waivers were "voluntary." But what does this mean? How does the standard for determining voluntariness in this context compare with the criterion under the due process standard for determining the voluntariness of a confession?

Colorado v. Connelly, 479 U.S. 157, 107 S.Ct. 515, 93 L.Ed.2d 473 (1986), reprinted in part in section A of this chapter on general due process voluntariness, also addressed the voluntariness of *Miranda* waivers. After passing on the admissibility of the Connelly's confessions made before he was placed in custody, the Court assumed that once Officer Anderson handcuffed Connelly *Miranda* became applicable. It then turned to the state court's determination that Connelly had not effectively waived his *Miranda* rights regarding statements he made under custodial interrogation:

> The Supreme Court of Colorado in addressing this question relied on the testimony of the court-appointed psychiatrist to the effect that [Connelly] was not capable of making a "free decision with respect to his constitutional right of silence * * * and his constitutional right to confer with a lawyer before talking to the police."
>
> We think that the Supreme Court of Colorado erred in importing into this area of constitutional law notions of "free will" that have no place there. There is obviously no reason to require more in the way of a "voluntariness" inquiry in the *Miranda* waiver context than in the Fourteenth Amendment confession context. The sole concern of the Fifth Amendment, on which *Miranda* was based, is governmental coercion. * * * The voluntariness of a waiver of this privilege has always depended on the absence of police overreaching, not on "free choice" in any broader sense of the word. * * *
>
> [Connelly]   urges this Court to adopt his "free will" rationale, and to find an attempted waiver invalid whenever the defendant feels compelled to waive his rights by reason of any compulsion, even if the compulsion does not flow from the police. But such treatment of the waiver issue would "cut this Court's holding in [*Miranda*] completely loose from its own explicitly stated rationale." *Miranda* protects defendants against government coercion leading them to surrender rights protected by the Fifth Amendment; it goes no further than that. [Connelly's] perception of coercion flowing from the "voice of God," however important or significant such a perception might be in other disciplines, is a matter to which the United States Constitution does not speak.

479 U.S. at 169–71, 107 S.Ct. at 523–24, 93 L.Ed.2d at 486–87.

Effectiveness of Waivers: Intelligence. Edwards made clear that the requirement of an intelligent or knowing waiver is separate from, and requires different proof than, the need for voluntariness.

Perhaps this should have been clear from Tague v. Louisiana, 444 U.S. 469, 100 S.Ct. 652, 62 L.Ed.2d 622 (1980). Tague's confession given during custodial interrogation was offered at his trial for robbery. At a pretrial hearing on the admissibility of the statement, the officer who had taken the confession testified that he had read Tague the *Miranda* rights from a card, that he could not presently remember what those rights were, that he could not recall whether he had asked Tague whether he understood the rights, and that he "couldn't say yes or no" whether he rendered any tests to determine whether Tague was literate or otherwise capable of understanding the rights. The confession was admitted and Tague was convicted. On appeal, the Supreme Court of Louisiana affirmed, reasoning that "absent a clear and readily apparent lack thereof, it can be presumed that a person has capacity to understand [the *Miranda* rights], and the burden is on the one claiming a lack of capacity to show that lack." Without oral argument and in a *per curiam* opinion, the Supreme Court reversed. The Louisiana courts had impermissibly relied upon a presumption that one given the *Miranda* warnings understands the rights involved; such a presumption is inconsistent with the burden placed by *Miranda* on the state to show a knowing and intelligent waiver of the rights. Turning to the facts of the case, the Court continued:

> In this case no evidence at all was introduced to prove that [Tague] knowingly and intelligently waived his rights before making the inculpatory statement. The statement was therefore inadmissible.

441 U.S. at 471, 100 S.Ct. at 653, 62 L.Ed.2d at 625. As *Edwards* reaffirmed the next year, *Tague* held that the prosecution must address and prove that a *Miranda* waiver was intelligent.

But what precisely must a suspect know or understand in order to render intelligent his decisions to forego the assistance of counsel, his right to remain silent, or both? The principal case in this subsection addresses this question.

Suppose a defendant's waiver is "unintelligent," but for reasons not attributable to law enforcement officers' misconduct. *Connelly* made clear a *Miranda* waiver cannot be rendered *involuntary* by the defendant's mental impairment, where there is no law enforcement misconduct. Is it possible, however, that even in the absence of police misconduct, such mental impairment might nevertheless prevent a suspect from adequately understanding his right to counsel and therefore render his decision to relinquish it *unintelligent*?

In *Connelly,* the Supreme Court noted the Colorado Supreme Court's opinion could be read as finding Connelly's waiver invalid "on other grounds." This was apparently a reference to the state court's comment that Connelly's mental impairment had rendered him unable to make an "intelligent" decision. The Colorado court's analysis was influenced by "its mistaken view of 'voluntariness' in the constitutional sense," the *Connelly* majority stated. It thus reversed the state court's judgment "in its entirety," although it commented that on remand the state court was free to reconsider other issues in a manner not inconsistent with the opinion of the Court. Justice Brennan, dissenting, construed the majority's comment as permitting the state court to find that despite the absence of any official compulsion, Connelly's mental illness demonstrated that the prosecution had failed to meet *Miranda's* requirement of a knowing and intelligent waiver.

Scope of Waiver. The scope of effective waivers, especially those of the right to counsel, may raise difficult questions. One such problem was presented by Wyrick v. Fields, 459 U.S. 42, 103 S.Ct. 394, 74 L.Ed.2d 214 (1982). Fields had agreed to a polygraph test and had waived his right to counsel during that procedure. After the examination, the agent who administered the examination told Fields there had been some deceit and asked Fields if he could explain why his answers were bothering him. In the resulting discussion, Fields made incriminating admissions. He argued that neither he nor the lawyer who advised him prior to the waiver anticipated questioning after the examination and, therefore, his waiver of counsel had not extended to such post-examination questioning. Rejecting this contention, the Court explained:

> [I]t would have been unreasonable for Fields and his attorneys to assume that Fields would not be informed of the polygraph readings and asked to explain any unfavorable results. Moreover, Fields had been informed that he could stop the questioning at any time, and could request at any time that his lawyer join him. Merely disconnecting the polygraph equipment could not remove this knowledge from Fields' mind.

459 U.S. 47–48, 103 S.Ct. at 396, 74 L.Ed.2d at 214. Does this mean that the scope of a waiver is not defined by what the defendant actually understood it would cover but rather by what, in the exercise of reasonable care, he should have known it would be treated by police as covering?

Empirical Information on Suspects' Understanding of Miranda. Consideration of whether the Supreme Court has most appropriately formulated *Miranda* waiver law may be facilitated by information concerning what suspects might in actual fact understand as a result of *Miranda* warnings.

Grisso, Juveniles' Capacity to Waive Miranda Rights: An Empirical Analysis, 68 Cal.L.Rev. 1134 (1980), for purposes of comparison with juveniles, studied the results of giving *Miranda* warnings to 203 adult parolees and 57 adults employed in custodial services and university and hospital maintenance crews. He concluded a significant proportion of these adults did not learn the underlying rights from the *Miranda* warnings. 42.3% of the subjects were able accurately to paraphrase all four of the *Miranda* rights after the warning; 57.7% were not. The most commonly misunderstood part of the warning concerned the right to the presence of counsel; 14.6% of the subjects were unable to paraphrase this accurately. In an effort to avoid the effect of facility in verbal expression, Geiss administered a true-false test containing 12 questions to the subjects. 76.5% received a score of 10–12 correct responses; another 18.9% scored 7 to 9 correct answers. But 4.6% of the subjects scored only 5 or 6 correct answers. A further test consisted of questioning the subjects concerning a hypothetical interrogation situation. 89–95% of the subjects recognized the adversarial nature of the interrogation, the role of the subject's lawyer in it, and the lawyers' need for full information concerning the events. But many of the subjects failed to understand the effect which the privilege against self-incrimination would have later in the courtroom. 42.9% believed that they would have to later explain their criminal involvement in court if questioned by the judge. This suggests a significant proportion of *Miranda* waivers may be influenced by the suspects' perception that they will later be compelled to answer questions concerning the situation. Such suspects might reason that since they will have to explain the situation to authorities at some point, they might as well do it during police questioning.

Moran v. Burbine

Supreme Court of the United States, 1986.
475 U.S. 412, 106 S.Ct. 1135, 89 L.Ed.2d 410.

■ JUSTICE O'CONNOR delivered the opinion of the Court.

After being informed of his rights pursuant to Miranda v. Arizona, 384 U.S. 436, 86 S.Ct. 1602, 16 L.Ed.2d 694 (1966), and after executing a series of written waivers, respondent confessed to the murder of a young woman. * * * The question presented is whether either the conduct of the police or respondent's ignorance of the attorney's efforts to reach him taints the validity of the waivers and therefore requires exclusion of the confessions.

I

On the morning of March 3, 1977, Mary Jo Hickey was found unconscious in a factory parking lot in Providence, Rhode Island. Suffering from injuries to her skull apparently inflicted by a metal pipe found at the scene, she was rushed to a nearby hospital. Three weeks later she died from her wounds.

Several months after her death, the Cranston, Rhode Island police arrested respondent and two others in connection with a local burglary. Shortly before the arrest, Detective Ferranti of the Cranston police force had learned from a confidential informant that the man responsible for Ms. Hickey's death lived at a certain address and went by the name of "Butch." Upon discovering that respondent lived at that address and was known by that name, Detective Ferranti informed respondent of his *Miranda* rights. When respondent refused to execute a written waiver, Detective Ferranti spoke separately with the two other suspects arrested on the breaking and entering charge and obtained statements further implicating respondent in Ms. Hickey's murder. At approximately 6:00 p.m., Detective Ferranti telephoned the police in Providence to convey the information he had uncovered. An hour later, three officers from that department arrived at the Cranston headquarters for the purpose of questioning respondent about the murder.

That same evening, at about 7:45 p.m., respondent's sister telephoned the Public Defender's Office to obtain legal assistance for her brother. Her sole concern was the breaking and entering charge, as she was unaware that respondent was then under suspicion for murder. She asked for Richard Casparian who had been scheduled to meet with respondent earlier that afternoon to discuss another charge unrelated to either the break-in or the murder. As soon as the conversation ended, the attorney who took the call attempted to reach Mr. Casparian. When those efforts were unsuccessful, she telephoned Allegra Munson, another Assistant Public Defender, and told her about respondent's arrest and his sister's subsequent request that the office represent him.

At 8:15 p.m., Ms. Munson telephoned the Cranston police station and asked that her call be transferred to the detective division. In the words of the Supreme Court of Rhode Island * * * the conversation proceeded as follows:

"A male voice responded with the word 'Detectives.' Ms. Munson identified herself and asked if Brian Burbine was being held; the person responded affirmatively. Ms. Munson explained to the person that Burbine was represented by attorney Casparian who was not available; she further stated that she would act as Burbine's legal counsel in the event that the police intended to place him in a lineup or question him. The unidentified person told Ms. Munson that the police would not be questioning Burbine or putting him in a lineup and that they were through with him for the night. Ms. Munson was not informed that the Providence Police were at the Cranston police station or that Burbine was a suspect in Mary's murder."

At all relevant times, respondent was unaware of his sister's efforts to retain counsel and of the fact and contents of Ms. Munson's telephone conversation.

Less than an hour later, the police brought respondent to an interrogation room and conducted the first of a series of interviews concerning the murder. Prior to each session, respondent was informed of his *Miranda* rights, and on three separate occasions he signed a written form acknowledging that he understood his right to the presence of an attorney and explicitly indicating that he "[did] not want an attorney called or appointed for [him]" before he gave a statement. Uncontradicted evidence at the suppression hearing indicated that at least twice during the course of the evening, respondent was left in a room where he had access to a telephone, which he apparently declined to use. Eventually, respondent signed three written statements fully admitting to the murder.

Prior to trial, respondent moved to suppress the statements. The court denied the motion, finding that respondent had received the *Miranda* warnings and had "knowingly, intelligently, and voluntarily waived his privilege against self-incrimination [and] his right to counsel." Rejecting the contrary testimony of the police, the court found that Ms. Munson did telephone the detective bureau on the evening in question, but concluded that "there was no * * * conspiracy or collusion on the part of the Cranston Police Department to secrete this defendant from his attorney." In any event, the court held, the constitutional right to request the presence of an attorney belongs solely to the defendant and may not be asserted by his lawyer. Because the evidence was clear that respondent never asked for the services of an attorney, the telephone call had no relevance to the validity of the waiver or the admissibility of the statements.

The jury found respondent guilty of murder in the first degree, and he appealed to the Supreme Court of Rhode Island. A divided court rejected his contention that the Fifth and Fourteenth Amendments to the Constitution required the suppression of the inculpatory statements and affirmed the conviction. * * *

After unsuccessfully petitioning the United States District Court for the District of Rhode Island for a writ of habeas corpus, respondent appealed to the Court of Appeals for the First Circuit. That court reversed. * * *

We granted certiorari to decide whether a prearraignment confession preceded by an otherwise valid waiver must be suppressed either because the police misinformed an inquiring attorney about their plans concerning the suspect or because they failed to inform the suspect of the attorney's efforts to reach him. We now reverse.

* * *

II

* * *

Respondent * * * contends * * * that the confessions must be suppressed because the police's failure to inform him of the attorney's telephone call deprived him of information essential to his ability to knowingly waive his Fifth Amendment rights. In the alternative, he suggests that to fully protect the Fifth Amendment values served by *Miranda,* we should extend that decision to condemn the conduct of the Providence police. We address each contention in turn.

A

Echoing the standard first articulated in Johnson v. Zerbst, 304 U.S. 458, 464, 58 S.Ct. 1019, 1023, 82 L.Ed. 1461 (1938), *Miranda* holds that "[t]he defendant may waive effectuation" of the rights conveyed in the warnings "provided the waiver is made voluntarily, knowingly and intelligently." The inquiry has two distinct dimensions. First the relinquishment of the right must have been voluntary in the sense that it was the product of a free and deliberate choice rather than intimidation, coercion or deception. Second, the waiver must have been made with a full awareness both of the nature of the right being abandoned and the consequences of the decision to abandon it. Only if the "totality of the circumstances surrounding the interrogation" reveal both an uncoerced choice and the requisite level of comprehension may a court properly conclude that the *Miranda* rights have been waived.

Under this standard, we have no doubt that respondent validly waived his right to remain silent and to the presence of counsel. The voluntariness of the waiver is not at issue. As the Court of Appeals correctly acknowledged, the record is devoid of any suggestion that police resorted to physical or psychological pressure to elicit the statements. Indeed it appears that it was respondent, and not the police, who spontaneously initiated the conversation that led to the first and most damaging confession. Nor is there any question about respondent's comprehension of the full panoply of rights set out in the *Miranda* warnings and of the potential consequences of a decision to relinquish them. Nonetheless, the Court of Appeals believed that the "[d]eliberate or reckless" conduct of the police, in particular their failure to inform respondent of the telephone call, fatally undermined the validity of the otherwise proper waiver. We find this conclusion untenable as a matter of both logic and precedent.

Events occurring outside of the presence of the suspect and entirely unknown to him surely can have no bearing on the capacity to comprehend and knowingly relinquish a constitutional right. Under the analysis of the Court of Appeals, the same defendant, armed with the same information and confronted with precisely the same police conduct, would have knowingly waived his *Miranda* rights had a lawyer not telephoned the police station to inquire about his status. Nothing in any of our waiver decisions or in our understanding of the essential components of a valid waiver requires so incongruous a result. No doubt the additional information would have been useful to respondent; perhaps even it might have affected his decision to confess. But we have never read the Constitution to require that the police supply a suspect with a flow of information to help him calibrate his self interest in deciding whether to speak or stand by his rights. Once it is determined that a suspect's decision not to rely on his rights was uncoerced, that he at all times knew he could stand mute and request a lawyer, and that he was aware of the state's intention to use his statements to secure a conviction, the analysis is complete and the waiver is valid as a matter of law. The Court of Appeals' conclusion to the contrary was in error.

Nor do we believe that the level of the police's culpability in failing to inform respondent of the telephone call has any bearing on the validity of the waiver. In light of the state-court findings that there was no "conspiracy or collusion" on the part of the police, we have serious doubts about whether the Court of Appeals was free to conclude that their conduct constituted "deliberate or reckless irresponsibility." But whether intentional or inadvertent, the state of mind of the police is irrelevant to the question of the intelligence and voluntariness of respondent's election to abandon his rights. Although highly inappropriate, even deliberate deception of an attorney could not possibly affect a suspect's decision to waive his *Miranda* rights unless he were at least aware of the incident. Nor was the failure to inform respondent of the telephone call the kind of "trick[ery]" that can vitiate the validity of a waiver. Granting that the "deliberate or reckless" withholding of information is objectionable as a matter of ethics, such conduct is only relevant to the constitutional validity of a waiver if it deprives a defendant of knowledge essential to his ability to understand the nature of his rights and the consequences of abandoning them. Because respondent's voluntary decision to speak was made with full awareness and comprehension of all the information *Miranda* requires the police to convey, the waivers were valid.

B

At oral argument respondent acknowledged that a constitutional rule requiring the police to inform a suspect of an attorney's efforts to reach him would represent a significant extension of our precedents. He contends, however, that the conduct of the Providence police was so inimical to the Fifth Amendment values *Miranda* seeks to protect that we should read that decision to condemn their behavior. Regardless of any issue of waiver, he urges, the Fifth Amendment requires the reversal of a conviction if the police are less than forthright in their dealings with an attorney or if they fail to tell a suspect of a lawyer's unilateral efforts to contact him. Because the proposed modification ignores the underlying purposes of the *Miranda* rules and because we think that the decision as written strikes the proper balance between society's legitimate law enforcement interests and the protection of the defendant's Fifth Amendment rights, we decline the invitation to further extend *Miranda's* reach.

At the outset, while we share respondent's distaste for the deliberate misleading of an officer of the court, reading *Miranda* to forbid police deception of an *attorney* "would cut [the decision] completely loose from its own explicitly stated rationale." As is now well established, "[t]he * * * *Miranda* warnings are 'not themselves rights protected by the Constitution but [are] instead measures to insure that the [suspect's] right against compulsory self-incrimination [is] protected.'" Their objective is not to mold police conduct for its own sake. Nothing in the Constitution vests in us the authority to mandate a code of behavior for state officials wholly unconnected to any federal right or privilege. The purpose of the *Miranda* warnings instead is to dissipate the compulsion inherent in custodial interrogation and, in so doing, guard against abridgement of the suspect's Fifth Amendment rights. Clearly, a rule that focuses on how the police treat an attorney—conduct that has no relevance at all to the degree of compulsion experienced by the defendant during interrogation—would ignore both *Miranda's* mission and its only source of legitimacy.

Nor are we prepared to adopt a rule requiring that the police inform a suspect of an attorney's efforts to reach him. While such a rule might add marginally to *Miranda's* goal of dispelling the compulsion inherent in custodial interrogation, overriding practical considerations counsel against its adoption. As we have stressed on numerous occasions, "[o]ne of the principal advantages" of *Miranda* is the ease and clarity of its application. We have little doubt that the approach urged by respondent and endorsed by the Court of Appeals would have the inevitable consequence of muddying *Miranda's* otherwise relatively clear waters. The legal questions it would spawn are legion: To what extent should the police be held accountable for knowing that the accused has counsel? Is it enough that someone in the station house knows, or must the interrogating officer himself know of counsel's efforts to contact the suspect? Do counsel's efforts to talk to the suspect concerning one criminal investigation trigger the obligation to inform the defendant before interrogation may proceed on a wholly separate matter? We are unwilling to modify *Miranda* in manner that would so clearly undermine the decision's central "virtue of informing police and prosecutors with specificity * * * what they may do in conducting [a] custodial interrogation, and of informing courts under what circumstances statements obtained during such interrogation are not admissible.''

Moreover, problems of clarity to one side, reading *Miranda* to require the police in each instance to inform a suspect of an attorney's efforts to reach him would work a substantial and, we think, inappropriate shift in the subtle balance struck in that decision. Custodial interrogations implicate two competing concerns. On the one hand, "the need for police questioning as a tool for effective enforcement of criminal laws" cannot be doubted. Admissions of guilt are more than merely "desirable"; they are essential to society's compelling interest in finding, convicting and punishing those who violate the law. On the other hand, the Court has recognized that the interrogation process is "inherently coercive" and that, as a consequence, there exists a substantial risk that the police will inadvertently traverse the fine line between legitimate efforts to elicit admissions and constitutionally impermissible compulsion. *Miranda* attempted to reconcile these opposing concerns by giving the *defendant* the power to exert some control over the course of the interrogation. Declining to adopt the more extreme position that the actual presence of a lawyer was necessary to dispel the coercion inherent in custodial interrogation, the Court found that the suspect's Fifth Amendment rights could be adequately protected by less intrusive means. Police questioning, often an essential part of the investigatory process, could continue in its traditional form, the Court held, but only if the suspect clearly understood that, at any time, he could bring the proceeding to a halt or, short of that, call in an attorney to give advice and monitor the conduct of his interrogators.

The position urged by respondent would upset this carefully drawn approach in a manner that is both unnecessary for the protection of the Fifth Amendment privilege and injurious to legitimate law enforcement. Because, as *Miranda* holds, full comprehension of the rights to remain silent and request an attorney are sufficient to dispel whatever coercion is inherent in the interrogation process, a rule requiring the police to inform the suspect of an attorney's efforts to contact him would contribute to the protection of the Fifth Amendment privilege only incidentally, if at all. This minimal benefit, however, would come at a substantial cost to society's legitimate and substantial interest in securing admissions of guilt. Indeed, the very premise of the Court of Appeals was not that awareness of Ms. Munson's phone call would have dissipated the coercion of the interrogation room, but that it might have convinced respondent not to speak at all. Because neither the letter nor purposes of *Miranda* require this additional handicap on otherwise permissible investigatory efforts, we are unwilling to expand the *Miranda* rules to require the police to keep the suspect abreast of the status of his legal representation.

We acknowledge that a number of state courts have reached a contrary conclusion. * * * Nothing we say today disables the States from adopting different requirements for the conduct of its employees and officials as a matter of state law. We hold only that the Court of Appeals erred in construing the Fifth Amendment to the Federal Constitution to require the exclusion of respondent's three confessions.

IV

Finally, respondent contends that the conduct of the police was so offensive as to deprive him of the fundamental fairness guaranteed by the Due Process Clause of the Fourteenth Amendment. Focusing primarily on the impropriety of conveying false information to an attorney, he invites us to declare that such behavior should be condemned as violative of canons fundamental to the " 'traditions and conscience of our people.' " Rochin v. California, 342 U.S. 165, 169, 72 S.Ct. 205, 208, 96 L.Ed. 183 (1952). We do not question that on facts more egregious than those presented here police deception might rise to a level of a due process violation. * * * We hold only that, on these facts, the challenged conduct falls short of the kind of misbehavior that so shocks the sensibilities of civilized society as to warrant a federal intrusion into the criminal processes of the States.

We hold therefore that the Court of Appeals erred in finding that the Federal Constitution required the exclusion of the three inculpatory statements. Accordingly, we reverse and remand for proceedings consistent with this opinion.

So ordered.

■ JUSTICE STEVENS, with whom JUSTICE BRENNAN and JUSTICE MARSHALL join, dissenting.

* * *

II

Well-settled principles of law lead inexorably to the conclusion that the failure to inform Burbine of the call from his attorney makes the subsequent waiver of his constitutional rights invalid. * * * [T]his Court has sometimes relied on a case-by-case totality of the circumstances analysis. We have found, however, that some custodial interrogation situations require strict presumptions against the validity of a waiver. *Miranda* established that a waiver is not valid in the absence of certain warnings. * * * In these circumstances, the waiver is invalid as a matter of law * * *. Like the failure to give warnings * * *, police deception of a suspect through omission of information regarding attorney communications greatly exacerbates the inherent problems of incommunicado interrogation and requires a clear principle to safeguard the presumption against the waiver of constitutional rights. As in those situations [involving a failure to warn], the police deception should render a subsequent waiver invalid.

* * *

III

The Court makes the * * * argument that requiring police to inform a suspect of his attorney's communications to and about him is not required because it would upset the careful "balance" of *Miranda*. Despite its earlier notion that the attorney's call is an "outside event" that has "no bearing" on a knowing and intelligent waiver, the majority does acknowledge that information of attorney Munson's call "would have been useful to respondent" and "might have affected his decision to confess." Thus, a rule requiring the police to inform a suspect of an attorney's call would have two predictable effects. It would serve *"Miranda's* goal of dispelling the compulsion inherent in custodial interrogation" and it would disserve the goal of custodial interrogation because it would result in fewer confessions. By a process of balancing these two concerns, the Court finds the benefit to the individual outweighed by the "substantial cost to society's legitimate and substantial interest in securing admissions of guilt."

The Court's balancing approach is profoundly misguided. The cost of suppressing evidence of guilt will always make the value of a procedural safeguard appear "minimal," "marginal," or "incremental." Indeed, the value of any trial at all seems like a "procedural technicality" when balanced against the interest in administering prompt justice to a murderer or a rapist caught redhanded. The individual interest in procedural safeguards that minimize the risk of error is easily discounted when the fact of guilt appears certain beyond doubt.

What is the cost of requiring the police to inform a suspect of his attorney's call? It would decrease the likelihood that custodial interrogation will enable the police to obtain a confession. This is certainly a real cost, but it is the same cost that this Court has repeatedly found necessary to preserve the character of our free society and our rejection of an inquisitorial system. * * *

If the Court's cost benefit analysis were sound, it would justify a repudiation of the right to a warning about counsel itself. There is only a difference in degree between a presumption that advice about the immediate availability of a lawyer would not affect the voluntariness of a decision to confess, and a presumption that every citizen knows that he has a right to remain silent and therefore no warnings of any kind are needed. In either case, the withholding of information serves precisely the same law enforcement interests. And in both cases, the cost can be described as nothing more than an incremental increase in the risk that an individual will make an unintelligent waiver of his rights.

* * *

IV

The Court also argues that a rule requiring the police to inform a suspect of an attorney's efforts to reach him would have an additional cost: it would undermine the "clarity" of the rule of the *Miranda* case. This argument is not supported by any reference to the experience in the States that have adopted such a rule. * * *

* * *

V

At the time attorney Munson made her call to the Cranston Police Station, she was acting as Burbine's attorney. Under ordinary principles of agency law the deliberate deception of Munson was tantamount to deliberate deception of her client. If an attorney makes a mistake in the course of her representation of her client, the client must accept the consequences of that mistake. It is equally clear that when an attorney makes an inquiry on behalf of her client, the client is entitled to a truthful answer. Surely the client must have the same remedy for a false representation to his lawyer that he would have if he were acting *pro se* and had propounded the question himself.

* * *

The possible reach of the Court's opinion is stunning. For the majority seems to suggest that police may deny counsel all access to a client who is being held. * * * [I]t has been widely accepted that police may not simply deny attorneys access to their clients who are in custody. * * * The Court today seems to assume that this view was error—that, from the federal constitutional perspective, the lawyer's access is, as a question from the Court put it in oral argument, merely "a matter of prosecutorial grace." * * *

VI

The Court devotes precisely five sentences to its conclusion that the police interference in the attorney's representation of Burbine did not violate the Due Process Clause. In the majority's view, the due process analysis is a simple "shock the conscience" test. Finding its conscience troubled, but not shocked, the majority rejects the due process challenge.

* * *

In my judgment, police interference in the attorney-client relationship is the type of governmental misconduct on a matter of central importance to the administration of justice that the Due Process Clause prohibits. Just as the police cannot impliedly promise a suspect that his silence will not be used against him and then proceed to break that promise, so too police cannot tell a suspect's attorney that they will not question the suspect and then proceed to question him. Just as the government cannot conceal from a suspect material and exculpatory evidence, so too the government cannot conceal from a suspect the material fact of his attorney's communication.

* * *

VII

This case turns on a proper appraisal of the role of the lawyer in our society. If a lawyer is seen as a nettlesome obstacle to the pursuit of wrongdoers—as in an inquisitorial society—then the Court's decision today makes a good deal of sense. If a lawyer is seen as an aid to the understanding and protection of constitutional rights—as in an accusatorial society—then today's decision makes no sense at all.

Like the conduct of the police in the Cranston station on the evening of June 29, 1977, the Court's opinion today serves the goal of insuring that the perpetrator of a vile crime is punished. Like the police on that June night as well, however, the Court has trampled on well-established legal principles and flouted the spirit of our accusatorial system of justice.

I respectfully dissent.

NOTES

1. **Knowledge of Subject Matter of Interrogation.** A suspect can apparently effectively waive the *Miranda* rights concerning an interrogation even if that suspect fails to understand the subjects the officers will purse by the interrogation.

In Colorado v. Spring, 479 U.S. 564, 107 S.Ct. 851, 93 L.Ed.2d 954 (1987), an informant told officers of the federal Bureau of Alcohol, Tobacco, and Firearms (ATF) that John Spring was engaged in the transportation of stolen firearms and admitted to the informant he had once shot a companion during a hunting trip in Colorado. The agents set up a "sting" operation in Kansas City, Missouri, and, during a purchase of firearms from Spring, the agents arrested him. Agents advised of his *Miranda* rights at the scene of the arrest. After being taken to the ATF office in Kansas City, he was again advised of his rights and signed a written form stating he understood and waived his rights and he was willing to answer questions and make a statement. After questioning him about the firearms transaction, the ATF agents asked Spring about homicides. He "ducked his head" and mumbled, "I shot another guy once." But when asked specifically about the Colorado killing, he "paused," "ducked his head again," and denied the shooting. The interview ended.

About two months later, Colorado law enforcement officials interviewed Spring while he remained in custody on the federal charges. He was given his *Miranda* warnings and signed another written form indicating he understood his rights and was willing to waive them. When the officers told him they wished to question him about the Colorado homicide, Spring responded that he wanted to "get it off his chest" and confessed to the murder. A written statement was prepared and Springs read, edited and signed it. The Colorado Supreme Court held that admission of Spring's written statement in his trial for the murder violated *Miranda*. His waiver of *Miranda* rights during the interview with ATF agents was not voluntary and intelligent, the state tribunal reasoned, because the agents failed to inform him that the questioning would involve the homicide and such a failure to inform the suspect of the offenses at issue is a factor in evaluating voluntariness and intelligence. His written statement during the later interview with state officers, in turn, was the "fruit" of his earlier and improper interrogation.

The Supreme Court reversed, reasoning in an opinion by Justice Powell that no violation of *Miranda* occurred during the interview of Spring by the ATF agents:

> [T]here is no allegation that Spring failed to understand the basic privilege guaranteed by the Fifth Amendment. Nor is there any allegation that he misunderstood the consequences of speaking freely to the law enforcement officials. * * * [T]he trial court was indisputably correct in finding that Spring's waiver was made knowingly and intelligently within the meaning of *Miranda*.

* * *

> * * * We have held that a valid waiver does not require that an individual be informed of all information "useful" in making his decision or all information that "might . . . affec[t] his decision to confess." Moran v. Burbine, 475 U.S. [412, 422, 106 S.Ct. 1135, 1142, 89 L.Ed.2d 410 (1986)]. * * * [This] additional information could affect only the wisdom of a *Miranda* waiver, not its essentially voluntary and knowing nature. Accordingly, the failure of law enforcement officials to inform Spring of the subject matter of the interrogation could not affect Spring's decision to waive his Fifth Amendment privilege in a constitutionally significant manner.

* * *

[W]e hold that a suspect's awareness of all the possible subjects of questioning in advance of interrogation is not relevant to determining whether the suspect voluntarily, knowingly, and intelligently waived his Fifth Amendment privilege.

479 U.S. at 575–77, 107 S.Ct. at 858–59, 93 L.Ed.2d at 966–68.

2. **Limited or Qualified Waiver.** Can a suspect limit what police officers can do during an interrogation session by qualifying or limiting the waiver? One Supreme Court decision suggests so.

In Connecticut v. Barrett, 479 U.S. 523, 107 S.Ct. 828, 93 L.Ed.2d 920 (1987), Barrett signed an acknowledgment that he had been given the *Miranda* warnings. He then stated to the officers several times that he would not give them any written statement, at least until his lawyer was present. He added, however, that he had "no problem" in talking with them about the incident for which he had been arrested. During the following interrogation sessions, he made oral admissions of involvement in a sexual assault. At trial, testimony concerning these admissions was permitted over defense objection. The state appellate court—emphasizing that requests for counsel are not to be narrowly construed—held that Barrett's response to his *Miranda* warnings invoked his right to counsel and the subsequent conversations resulting in his oral admissions constituted prohibited interrogation without the presence of an attorney. The Supreme Court reversed:

Barrett's limited requests for counsel * * * were accompanied by affirmative announcements of his willingness to speak with the authorities. The fact that officials took the opportunity provided by Barrett to obtain an oral confession is quite consistent with the Fifth Amendment. *Miranda* gives the defendant a right to choose between speech and silence, and Barrett chose to speak. * * * Here * * * Barrett made clear his intentions, and they were honored by police. To conclude that [Barrett] invoked his right to counsel for all purposes requires not a broad interpretation of an ambiguous statement, but a disregard of the ordinary meaning of [Barrett's] statement.

479 U.S. at 529–30, 107 S.Ct. at 832, 93 L.Ed.2d at 928. Justice Brennan concurred, explaining "a partial waiver of the right to counsel, without more, invariably will be ambiguous." But here, Barrett's partial waiver was accompanied by express waiver of his right to silence, which removed the ambiguity.

3. **Reapproach of Suspect Who Invoked Right to Silence.** A suspect who invokes the right to remain silent raises no bar to being reapproached by officers, as is discussed in subsection B(3) of this chapter. Under Michigan v. Mosley, 423 U.S. 96, 96 S.Ct. 321, 46 L.Ed.2d 313 (1975), however, the fact that the suspect was reapproached after so invoking that right may increase the prosecution's burden of proving that his waivers were effective.

After Mosley was arrested, a Detective Cowie sought to question him about a specific robbery of a White Tower Restaurant. When Mosley said he did not want to answer any questions about the robbery, Cowie ceased the questioning and had Mosley taken to a cell. Several hours later, another officer—Detective Hill—had Mosley brought to an interrogation room for questioning concerning the fatal shooting of one Leroy Williams during a robbery of the 101 Ranch Bar. Hill gave Mosley *Miranda* warnings and Mosley signed a notification form. During the following 15 minute interrogation, Mosley admitted being involved in the slaying. Addressing the prosecution's ability to use that admission in evidence, the Supreme Court first determined that a suspect's invocation of his right to remain silent "can[not] sensibly be read to create a *per se* proscription of indefinite duration upon any further questioning by any police officer on any subject, once the person in custody has indicated a desire to remain silent." It then continued:

We * * * conclude that the admissibility of statements obtained after the person in custody has decided to remain silent depends under *Miranda* on whether his "right to cut off questioning" was "scrupulously honored."

A review of the circumstances leading to Mosley's confession reveals that his "right to cut off questioning" was fully respected in this case. Before his initial interrogation, Mosley was carefully advised that he was under no obligation to answer any questions and could remain silent if he wished. He orally acknowledged that he understood the *Miranda* warnings and then signed a printed notification-of-rights form. When Mosley stated that he did not want to discuss the robberies, Detective Cowie immediately ceased the interrogation and did not try either to resume the questioning or in any way to persuade Mosley to reconsider his position. After an interval of more than two hours, Mosley was questioned by another police officer at another location about an unrelated holdup murder. He was given full and complete *Miranda* warnings at the outset of the second interrogation. He was thus reminded again that he could remain silent and could consult with a lawyer, and was carefully given a full and fair opportunity to exercise these options. The subsequent questioning did not undercut Mosley's previous decision not to answer Detective Cowie's inquiries. Detective Hill did not resume the interrogation about the White Tower Restaurant robbery * * *, but instead focused exclusively on the Leroy Williams homicide, a crime different in nature and in time and place of occurrence from the robberies for which Mosley had been arrested and interrogated by Detective Cowie. Although it is not clear from the record how much Detective Hill knew about the earlier interrogation, his questioning of Mosley about an unrelated homicide was quite consistent with a reasonable interpretation of Mosley's earlier refusal to answer any questions about the robberies.

This is not a case, therefore, where the police failed to honor a decision of a person in custody to cut off questioning, either by refusing to discontinue the interrogation upon request or by persisting in repeated efforts to wear down his resistance and make him change his mind. In contrast to such practices, the police here immediately ceased the interrogation, resumed questioning only after the passage of a significant period of time and the provision of a fresh set of warnings, and restricted the second interrogation to a crime that had not been a subject of the earlier interrogation.

423 U.S. at 104–06, 96 S.Ct. 326–27, 46 L.Ed.2d at 321–22.

4. **Effect of Deception on Effectiveness of Waivers.** What is the effect of police officers' deception before or during interrogation to which *Miranda* applies? The issue was urged in *Spring*, discussed in note 1 above, but the Court held that it was not raised. The ATF agents' failure to inform Spring that he would be questioned about the homicide did not constitute "trickery":

This Court has never held that mere silence by law enforcement officials as to the subject matter of an interrogation is "trickery" sufficient to invalidate a suspect's waiver of *Miranda* rights, and we expressly decline to so hold today.

479 U.S. at 576, 107 S.Ct. at 858, 93 L.Ed.2d at 967. Therefore it was not addressing, the Court noted, the validity of waivers when law enforcement officials made "an affirmative misrepresentation * * * as to the scope of the interrogation * * *."

Miranda itself contains language suggesting that waivers will be rendered ineffective by proof that the defendant "was * * * tricked * * * into [the] waiver." Frazier v. Cupp, discussed in the Editors' Introduction to part A of this chapter, addressed the effect of deception upon due process voluntariness. Although it was decided after *Miranda, Frazier* did not acknowledge potential tension between its holding and the discussion in *Miranda*. Perhaps, then, *Frazier's* approach is not necessarily applicable when the issue is the validity of a *Miranda* waiver.

5. **Intoxication.** What effect does a suspect's intoxication have upon the effectiveness of a waiver of the *Miranda* rights? In Berkemer v. McCarty, 468 U.S. 420, 104 S.Ct. 3138, 82 L.Ed.2d 317 (1984), reprinted in subsection B(2)(b) of this chapter, the Court noted:

> [W]e are asked to consider what a State must do in order to demonstrate that a suspect who might have been under the influence of drugs or alcohol when subjected to custodial interrogation nevertheless understood and freely waived his constitutional rights. * * * We prefer to defer resolution of [this matter] to a case in which law enforcement authorities have at least attempted to inform the suspect of rights to which he is indisputably entitled.

468 U.S. at 434 n. 21, 104 S.Ct. at 3147 n. 21, 82 L.Ed.2d at 331 n. 21. In light of *Connelly,* discussed in the Editors' Introduction to this subsection, is intoxication relevant at all in the absence of law enforcement overreaching of some sort?

6. The requirements of an intelligent *Miranda* waiver are also addressed in Oregon v. Elstad, reprinted in the next subsection. Reevaluate what is necessary for a waiver to be effective after considering *Elstad*.

5. "FRUITS" OF AN INADMISSIBLE CONFESSION

Fourth Amendment case law has firmly established that when a defendant shows a violation of his Fourth Amendment rights, Mapp v. Ohio and its progeny require exclusion of what is often called all "fruit of the poisonous tree." This requirement, and various limitations and exceptions that might affect it, were developed in Part B of Chapter 1. The principal case in this subsection, however, establishes that the "fruit of the poisonous tree" rule is not necessarily applicable in some situations in which the poisonous tree is a violation of the Supreme Court's case law dealing with interrogation limitations.

Oregon v. Elstad

Supreme Court of the United States, 1985.
470 U.S. 298, 105 S.Ct. 1285, 84 L.Ed.2d 222.

■ JUSTICE O'CONNOR delivered the opinion of the Court.

This case requires us to decide whether an initial failure of law enforcement officers to administer the warnings required by Miranda v. Arizona, 384 U.S. 436, 86 S.Ct. 1602, 16 L.Ed.2d 694 (1966), without more, "taints" subsequent admissions made after a suspect has been fully advised of and has waived his *Miranda* rights. * * *

I

In December, 1981, the home of Mr. and Mrs. Gilbert Gross, in the town of Salem, Polk County, Ore., was burglarized. Missing were art objects and furnishings valued at $150,000. A witness to the burglary contacted the Polk County Sheriff's Office, implicating respondent Michael Elstad, an 18-year-old neighbor and friend of the Grosses' teenage son. Thereupon, Officers Burke and McAllister went to the home of respondent Elstad, with a warrant for his arrest. Elstad's mother answered the door.

She led the officers to her son's room where he lay on his bed, clad in shorts and listening to his stereo. The officers asked him to get dressed and to accompany them into the living room. Officer McAllister asked respondent's mother to step into the kitchen, where he explained that they had a warrant for her son's arrest for the burglary of a neighbor's residence. Officer Burke remained with Elstad in the living room. He later testified:

> "I sat down with Mr. Elstad and I asked him if he was aware of why Detective McAllister and myself were there to talk with him. He stated no, he had no idea why we were there. I then asked him if he knew a person by the name of Gross, and he said yes, he did, and also added that he heard that there was a robbery at the Gross house. And at that point I told Mr. Elstad that I felt he was involved in that, and he looked at me and stated, 'Yes, I was there.' "

The officers then escorted Elstad to the back of the patrol car. As they were about to leave for the Polk County Sheriff's office, Elstad's father arrived home and came to the rear of the patrol car. The officers advised him that his son was a suspect in the burglary. Officer Burke testified that Mr. Elstad became quite agitated, opened the rear door of the car and admonished his son: "I told you that you were going to get into trouble. You wouldn't listen to me. You never learn."

Elstad was transported to the Sheriff's headquarters and approximately one hour later, Officers Burke and McAllister joined him in McAllister's office. McAllister then advised respondent for the first time of his *Miranda* rights, reading from a standard card. Respondent indicated he understood his rights, and, having these rights in mind, wished to speak with the officers. Elstad gave a full statement, explaining that he had known that the Gross family was out of town and had been paid to lead several acquaintances to the Gross residence and show them how to gain entry through a defective sliding glass door. The statement was typed, reviewed by respondent, read back to him for correction, initialed and signed by Elstad and both officers. As an afterthought, Elstad added and initialed the sentence, "After leaving the house Robby & I went back to [the] van & Robby handed me a small bag of grass." Respondent concedes that the officers made no threats or promises either at his residence or at the Sheriff's office.

Respondent was charged with first-degree burglary. He was represented at trial by retained counsel. Elstad waived his right to a jury and his case was tried by a Circuit Court Judge. Respondent moved at once to suppress his oral statement and signed confession. He contended that the statement he made in response to questioning at his house "let the cat out of the bag," citing United States v. Bayer, 331 U.S. 532, 67 S.Ct. 1394, 91 L.Ed. 1654 (1947), and tainted the subsequent confession as "fruit of the poisonous tree," citing Wong Sun v. United States, 371 U.S. 471, 83 S.Ct. 407, 9 L.Ed.2d 441 (1963). The judge ruled that the statement, "I was there," had to be excluded because the defendant had not been advised of his *Miranda* rights. The written confession taken after Elstad's arrival at the Sheriff's office, however, was admitted in evidence. The court found:

> "[H]is written statement was given freely, voluntarily and knowingly by the defendant after he had waived his right to remain silent and

have counsel present which waiver was evidenced by the card which the defendant had signed. [It] was not tainted in any way by the previous brief statement between the defendant and the Sheriff's Deputies that had arrested him."

Elstad was found guilty of burglary in the first degree. He received a 5year sentence and was ordered to pay $18,000 in restitution.

Following his conviction, respondent appealed to the Oregon Court of Appeals * * *. The Court of Appeals reversed respondent's conviction, identifying the crucial constitutional inquiry as "whether there was a sufficient break in the stream of events between [the] inadmissible statement and the written confession to insulate the latter statement from the effect of what went before." The Oregon court concluded:

"Regardless of the absence of actual compulsion, the coercive impact of the unconstitutionally obtained statement remains, because in a defendant's mind it has sealed his fate. It is this impact that must be dissipated in order to make a subsequent confession admissible. In determining whether it has been dissipated, lapse of time, and change of place from the original surroundings are the most important considerations."

Because of the brief period separating the two incidents, the "cat was sufficiently out of the bag to exert a coercive impact on [respondent's] later admissions."

The State of Oregon petitioned the Oregon Supreme Court for review, and review was declined. This Court granted certiorari to consider the question whether the Self–Incrimination Clause of the Fifth Amendment requires the suppression of a confession, made after proper *Miranda* warnings and a valid waiver of rights, solely because the police had obtained an earlier voluntary but unwarned admission from the defendant.

II

The arguments advanced in favor of suppression of respondent's written confession rely heavily on metaphor. One metaphor, familiar from the Fourth Amendment context, would require that respondent's confession, regardless of its integrity, voluntariness, and probative value, be suppressed as the "tainted fruit of the poisonous tree" of the *Miranda* violation. A second metaphor questions whether a confession can be truly voluntary once the "cat is out of the bag." Taken out of context, each of these metaphors can be misleading. They should not be used to obscure fundamental differences between the role of the Fourth Amendment exclusionary rule and the function of *Miranda* in guarding against the prosecutorial use of compelled statements as prohibited by the Fifth Amendment. The Oregon court assumed and respondent here contends that a failure to administer *Miranda* warnings necessarily breeds the same consequences as police infringement of a constitutional right, so that evidence uncovered following an unwarned statement must be suppressed as "fruit of the poisonous tree." We believe this view misconstrues the nature of the protections afforded by *Miranda* warnings and therefore misreads the consequences of police failure to supply them.

A

* * *

Respondent's contention that his confession was tainted by the earlier failure of the police to provide *Miranda* warnings and must be excluded as "fruit of the poisonous tree" assumes the existence of a constitutional violation. This figure of speech is drawn from Wong Sun v. United States, in which the Court held that evidence and witnesses discovered as a result of a search in violation of the Fourth Amendment must be excluded from evidence. * * *

But * * * a procedural *Miranda* violation differs in significant respects from violations of the Fourth Amendment, which have traditionally mandated a broad application of the "fruits" doctrine. * * *

The *Miranda* exclusionary rule * * * serves the Fifth Amendment and sweeps more broadly than the Fifth Amendment itself. It may be triggered even in the absence of a Fifth Amendment violation. The Fifth Amendment prohibits use by the prosecution in its case in chief only of *compelled* testimony. Failure to administer *Miranda* warnings creates a presumption of compulsion. Consequently, unwarned statements that are otherwise voluntary within the meaning of the Fifth Amendment must nevertheless be excluded from evidence under *Miranda*. Thus, in the individual case, *Miranda's* preventive medicine provides a remedy even to the defendant who has suffered no identifiable constitutional harm.

But the *Miranda* presumption, though irrebutable for purposes of the prosecution's case in chief, does not require that the statements and their fruits be discarded as inherently tainted. Despite the fact that patently *voluntary* statements taken in violation of *Miranda* must be excluded from the prosecution's case, the presumption of coercion does not bar their use for impeachment purposes on cross-examination. Harris v. New York, 401 U.S. 222, 91 S.Ct. 643, 28 L.Ed.2d 1 (1971). * * *

In Michigan v. Tucker, [417 U.S. 433, 94 S.Ct. 2357, 41 L.Ed.2d 182 (1974)], the Court was asked to extend the *Wong Sun* fruits doctrine to suppress the testimony of a witness for the prosecution whose identity was discovered as the result of a statement taken from the accused without benefit of full *Miranda* warnings. * * * [T]he *Tucker* Court noted that neither the general goal of deterring improper police practices nor the Fifth Amendment goal of assuring trustworthy evidence would be served by suppression of the witness' testimony. The unwarned confession must, of course, be suppressed, but the Court ruled that introduction of the third-party witness' testimony did not violate Tucker's Fifth Amendment rights.

We believe that this reasoning applies with equal force when the alleged "fruit" of a noncoercive *Miranda* violation is neither a witness nor an article of evidence but the accused's own voluntary testimony. As in *Tucker,* the absence of any coercion or improper tactics undercuts the twin rationales—trustworthiness and deterrence—for a broader rule. * * * If errors are made by law enforcement officers in administering the prophylactic *Miranda* procedures, they should not breed the same irremediable consequences as police infringement of the Fifth Amendment itself. It is an unwarranted extension of *Miranda* to hold that a simple failure to administer the warnings, unaccompanied by any actual coercion or other circumstances calculated to undermine the suspect's ability to exercise his free will so taints the investigatory process that a subsequent voluntary and informed waiver is ineffective for some indeterminate period. Though *Miranda* requires that the unwarned admission must be suppressed, the admissibility of any subsequent statement should turn in these circumstances solely on whether it is knowingly and voluntarily made.

B

The Oregon court, however, believed that the unwarned remark compromised the voluntariness of respondent's later confession. It was the court's view that the prior *answer* and not the unwarned questioning impaired respondent's ability to give a valid waiver and that only lapse of time and change of place could dissipate what it termed the "coercive impact" of the inadmissible statement. When a prior statement is actually coerced, the time that passes between confessions, the change in place of interrogations, and the change in identity of the interrogators all bear on whether that coercion has carried over into the second confession. The failure of police to administer *Miranda* warnings does not mean that the statements received have actually been coerced, but only that courts will presume the privilege against compulsory self-incrimination has not been intelligently exercised. Of the courts that have considered whether a properly warned confession must be suppressed because it was preceded by an unwarned but clearly voluntary admission, the majority have explicitly or implicitly recognized that [the] requirement of a break in the stream of events is inapposite. In these circumstances, a careful and thorough administration of *Miranda* warnings serves to cure the condition that rendered the unwarned statement inadmissible. The warning conveys the relevant information and thereafter the suspect's choice whether to exercise his privilege to remain silent should ordinarily be viewed as an "act of free will." Wong Sun v. United States, 371 U.S., at 486, 83 S.Ct., at 416.

The Oregon court nevertheless identified a subtle form of lingering compulsion, the psychological impact of the suspect's conviction that he has let the cat out of the bag and, in so doing, has sealed his own fate. But endowing the psychological effects of *voluntary* unwarned admissions with constitutional implications would, practically speaking, disable the police from obtaining the suspect's informed cooperation even when the official coercion proscribed by the Fifth Amendment played no part in either his warned or unwarned confessions. * * *

This Court has never held that the psychological impact of voluntary disclosure of a guilty secret qualifies as state compulsion or compromises the voluntariness of a subsequent informed waiver. The Oregon court, by adopting this expansive view of Fifth Amendment compulsion, effectively immunizes a suspect who responds to pre-*Miranda* warning questions from the consequences of his subsequent informed waiver of the privilege of remaining silent. This immunity comes at a high cost to legitimate law enforcement activity, while adding little desirable protection to the individual's interest in not being *compelled* to testify against himself. When neither the initial nor the subsequent admission is coerced, little justification exists for permitting the highly probative evidence of a voluntary confession to be irretrievably lost to the factfinder.

There is a vast difference between the direct consequences flowing from coercion of a confession by physical violence or other deliberate means calculated to break the suspect's will and the uncertain consequences of disclosure of a "guilty secret" freely given in response to an unwarned but noncoercive question, as in this case. * * * Certainly, in respondent's case, the causal connection between any psychological disadvantage created by his admission and his ultimate decision to cooperate is speculative and attenuated at best. It is difficult to tell with certainty what motivates a suspect to speak. A suspect's confession may be traced to factors as disparate as "a prearrest event such as a visit with a minister," Dunaway v. New York, [442 U.S. 200, 220, 99 S.Ct. 2248, 2261, 60 L.Ed.2d 824, 841 (1979)] (STEVENS, J., concurring), or an intervening event such as the exchange of words respondent had with his father. We must conclude that, absent deliberately coercive or improper tactics in obtaining the initial statement, the mere fact that a suspect has made an unwarned admission does not warrant a presumption of compulsion. A subsequent administration of *Miranda* warnings to a suspect who has given a voluntary but unwarned statement ordinarily should suffice to remove the conditions that precluded admission of the earlier statement. In such circumstances, the finder of fact may reasonably conclude that the suspect made a rational and intelligent choice whether to waive or invoke his rights.

III

Though belated, the reading of respondent's rights was undeniably complete. McAllister testified that he read the *Miranda* warnings aloud from a printed card and recorded Elstad's responses. There is no question that respondent knowingly and voluntarily waived his right to remain silent before he described his participation in the burglary. It is also beyond dispute that respondent's earlier remark was voluntary, within the meaning of the Fifth Amendment. Neither the environment nor the manner of either "interrogation" was coercive. The initial conversation took place at midday, in the living room area of respondent's own home, with his mother in the kitchen area, a few steps away. Although in retrospect the officers testified that respondent was then in custody, at the time he made his statement he had not been informed that he was under arrest. The arresting officers' testimony indicates that the brief stop in the living room before proceeding to the station house was not to interrogate the suspect but to notify his mother of the reason for his arrest.

The state has conceded the issue of custody and thus we must assume that Burke breached *Miranda* procedures in failing to administer *Miranda* warnings before initiating the discussion in the living room. This breach may have been the result of confusion as to whether the brief exchange qualified as "custodial interrogation" or it may simply have reflected Burke's reluctance to initiate an alarming police procedure before McAllister had spoken with respondent's mother. Whatever the reason for Burke's oversight, the incident had none of the earmarks of coercion. Nor did the officers exploit the unwarned admission to pressure respondent into waiving his right to remain silent.

Respondent, however, has argued that he was unable to give a fully *informed* waiver of his rights because he was unaware that his prior statement could not be used against him. Respondent suggests that Deputy McAllister, to cure this deficiency, should have added an additional warning to those given him at the Sheriff's office. Such a requirement is neither practicable nor constitutionally necessary. In many cases, a breach of *Miranda* procedures may not be identified as such until long after full *Miranda* warnings are administered and a valid confession obtained. The standard *Miranda* warnings explicitly inform the suspect of his right to consult a lawyer before speaking. Police officers are ill equipped to pinch-hit for counsel, construing the murky and difficult questions of when "custody" begins or whether a given unwarned statement will ultimately be held admissible.

This Court has never embraced the theory that a defendant's ignorance of the full consequences of his decisions vitiates their voluntariness. * * * [T]he Court has refused to find that a defendant who confesses, after being falsely told that his codefendant has turned state's evidence, does so involuntarily. Frazier v. Cupp, 394 U.S. 731, 739, 89 S.Ct. 1420, 1424, 22 L.Ed.2d 684 (1969). The Court has also rejected the argument that a defendant's ignorance that a prior coerced confession could not be admitted in evidence compromised the voluntariness of his guilty plea. McMann v. Richardson, [397 U.S. 759, 769, 90 S.Ct. 1441, 1448, 25 L.Ed.2d 763, 772 (1970)]. Likewise, in California v. Beheler, [463 U.S. 1121, 103 S.Ct. 3517, 77 L.Ed.2d 1275 (1983)], the Court declined to accept defendant's contention that, because he was unaware of the potential adverse consequences of statements he made to the police, his participation in the interview was involuntary. Thus we have not held that the *sine qua non* for a knowing and voluntary waiver of the right to remain silent is a full and complete appreciation of all of the consequences flowing from the nature and the quality of the evidence in the case.

IV

When police ask questions of a suspect in custody without administering the required warnings, *Miranda* dictates that the answers received be presumed compelled and that they be excluded from evidence at trial in the State's case in chief. The Court has carefully adhered to this principle, permitting a narrow exception only where pressing public safety concerns demanded. The Court today in no way retreats from the bright line rule of *Miranda*. We do not imply that good faith excuses a failure to administer *Miranda* warnings; nor do we condone inherently coercive police tactics or methods offensive to due process that render the initial admission involuntary and undermine the suspect's will to invoke his rights once they are read to him. A handful of courts has, however, applied our precedents relating to confessions obtained under coercive circumstances to situations involving wholly voluntary admissions, requiring a passage of time or break in events before a second, fully warned statement can be deemed voluntary. Far from establishing a rigid rule, we direct courts to avoid one; there is no warrant for presuming coercive effect where the suspect's initial inculpatory statement, though technically in violation of *Miranda*, was voluntary. The relevant inquiry is whether, in fact, the second statement was also voluntarily made. As in any such inquiry, the finder of fact must examine the surrounding circumstances and the entire course of police conduct with respect to the suspect in evaluating the voluntariness of his statements. The fact that a suspect chooses to speak after being informed of his rights is, of course, highly probative. We find that the dictates of *Miranda* and the goals of the Fifth Amendment proscription against use of compelled testimony are fully satisfied in the circumstances of this case by barring use of the unwarned statement in the case in chief. No further purpose is served by imputing "taint" to subsequent statements obtained pursuant to a voluntary and knowing waiver. We hold today that a suspect who has once responded to unwarned yet uncoercive questioning is not thereby disabled from waiving his rights and confessing after he has been given the requisite *Miranda* warnings.

The judgment of the Court of Appeals of Oregon is reversed, and the case is remanded for further proceedings not inconsistent with this opinion.

It is so ordered.

■ JUSTICE BRENNAN, with whom JUSTICE MARSHALL joins, dissenting.

* * *

This Court has had long experience with the problem of confessions obtained after an earlier confession has been illegally secured. Subsequent confessions in these circumstances are not *per se* inadmissible, but the prosecution must demonstrate facts "sufficient to insulate the [subsequent] statement from the effect of all that went before." Clewis v. Texas, 386 U.S. 707, 710, 87 S.Ct. 1338, 1340, 18 L.Ed.2d 423 (1967). * * *

One of the factors that can vitiate the voluntariness of a subsequent confession is the hopeless feeling of an accused that he has nothing to lose by repeating his confession, even where the circumstances that rendered his first confession illegal have been removed. As the Court observed in United States v. Bayer, 331 U.S., at 540, 67 S.Ct., at 1398:

> "[A]fter an accused has once let the cat out of the bag by confessing, no matter what the inducement, he is never thereafter free of the psychological and practical disadvantages of having confessed. He can never get the cat back in the bag. The secret is out for good. In such a sense, a later confession always may be looked upon as a fruit of the first."

* * *

Our precedents did not develop in a vacuum. They reflect an understanding of the realities of police interrogation and the everyday experience of lower courts. Expert interrogators, far from dismissing a first admission or confession as creating merely a "speculative and attenuated" disadvantage for a suspect, understand that such revelations frequently lead directly to a full confession. Standard interrogation manuals advise that "[t]he securing of the first admission is the biggest stumbling block. * * * *" A. Aubry & R. Caputo, Criminal Interrogation 290 (3d ed. 1980). If this first admission can be obtained, "there is every reason to expect that the first admission will lead to others, and eventually to the full confession."

> "For some psychological reason which does not have to concern us at this point 'the dam finally breaks as a result of the first leak' with regards to the tough subject. * * * Any structure is only as strong as its weakest component, and total collapse can be anticipated when the weakest part first begins to sag."

* * *

One police practice that courts have frequently encountered involves the withholding of *Miranda* warnings until the end of an interrogation session. Specifically, the police escort a suspect into a room, sit him down and, without explaining his Fifth Amendment rights or obtaining a knowing and voluntary waiver of those rights, interrogate him about his suspected criminal activity. If the police obtain a confession, it is then typed up, the police hand the suspect a pen for his signature, and—just before he signs—the police advise him of his *Miranda* rights and ask him to proceed. Alternatively, the police may call a stenographer in after they have obtained the confession, advise the suspect for the first time of his *Miranda* rights, and ask him to repeat what he has just told them. In such circumstances, the process of giving *Miranda* warnings and obtaining the final confession is " 'merely a formalizing, a setting down almost as a scrivener does, [of] what ha[s] already taken [place].' " People v. Raddatz, 91 Ill.App.2d 425, 430, 235 N.E.2d 353, 356 (1968) (quoting trial court). In such situations, where "it was all over except for reading aloud and explaining the written waiver of the *Miranda* safeguards," courts have time and again concluded that "[t]he giving of the *Miranda* warnings before reducing the product of the day's work to written form could not undo what had been done or make legal what was illegal." People v. Bodner, 75 App.Div.2d 440, 448, 430 N.Y.S.2d 433, 438 (1980).

There are numerous variations on this theme. Police may obtain a confession in violation of *Miranda* and then take a break for lunch or go home for the evening. When questioning is resumed, this time preceded by *Miranda* warnings, the suspect is asked to "clarify" the earlier illegal confession and to provide additional information. Or he is led by one of the interrogators into another room, introduced to another official, and asked to repeat his story. The new officer then gives the *Miranda* warnings and asks the suspect to proceed. Alternatively, the suspect might be questioned by arresting officers "in the field" and without *Miranda* warnings, as was young Elstad in the instant case. After making incriminating admissions or a confession, the suspect is then brought into the stationhouse and either questioned by the same officers again or asked to repeat his earlier statements to another officer.

* * *

I would have thought that the Court, instead of dismissing the "cat out of the bag" presumption out of hand, would have accounted for these practical realities. * * * Expert interrogators and experienced lower-court judges will be startled, to say the least, to learn that the connection between multiple confessions is "speculative" and that a subsequent rendition of *Miranda* warnings "ordinarily" enables the accused in these circumstances to exercise his "free will" and to make "a rational and intelligent choice whether to waive or invoke his rights." * * *

The correct approach, administered for almost 20 years by most courts with no untoward results, is to presume that an admission or confession obtained in violation of *Miranda* taints a subsequent confession unless the prosecution can show that the taint is so attenuated as to justify admission of the subsequent confession. * * *

The Court today refuses to apply the derivative-evidence rule even to the extent necessary to deter objectively unreasonable failures by the authorities to honor a suspect's *Miranda* rights. Incredibly, faced with an obvious violation of *Miranda*, the Court asserts that it will not countenance suppression of a subsequent confession in such circumstances where the authorities have acted "legitimate[ly]" and have not used "improper tactics." One can only respond: whither went *Miranda*?

* * *

I dissent.

■ JUSTICE STEVENS, dissenting.

The Court concludes its opinion with a carefully phrased statement of its holding:

> "We hold today that a suspect who has once responded to unwarned yet uncoercive questioning is not thereby disabled from waiving his rights and confessing after he has been given the requisite *Miranda* warnings."

I find nothing objectionable in such a holding. Moreover, because the Court expressly endorses the "bright line rule of *Miranda*," which conclusively presumes that incriminating statements obtained from a suspect in custody without administering the required warnings are the product of compulsion, and because the Court places so much emphasis on the special facts of this case, I am persuaded that the Court intends its holding to apply only to a narrow category of cases in which the initial questioning of the suspect was made in a totally uncoercive setting and in which the first confession obviously had no influence on the second. I nevertheless dissent because even such a narrowly confined exception is inconsistent with the Court's prior cases, because the attempt to identify its boundaries in future cases will breed confusion and uncertainty in the administration of criminal justice, and because it denigrates the importance of one of the core constitutional rights that protects every American citizen from the kind of tyranny that has flourished in other societies.

* * *

For me, the most disturbing aspect of the Court's opinion is its somewhat opaque characterization of the police misconduct in this case. The Court appears ambivalent on the question whether there was any constitutional violation. This ambivalence is either disingenuous or completely lawless. This Court's power to require state courts to exclude probative self-incriminatory statements rests entirely on the premise that the use of such evidence violates the Federal Constitution. The same constitutional analysis applies whether the custodial interrogation is actually coercive or irrebuttably presumed to be coercive. If the Court does not accept that premise, it must regard the holding in the *Miranda* case itself, as well as all of the Federal jurisprudence that has evolved from that decision, as nothing more than an illegitimate exercise of raw judicial power. If the Court accepts the proposition that respondent's self-incriminatory statement was inadmissible, it must also acknowledge that the Federal Constitution protected him from custodial police interrogation without first being advised of his right to remain silent.

The source of respondent's constitutional protection is the Fifth Amendment's privilege against compelled self-incrimination that is secured against state invasion by the Due Process Clause of the Fourteenth Amendment. Like many other provisions of the Bill of Rights, that provision is merely a procedural safeguard. It is, however, the specific provision that protects all citizens from the kind of custodial interrogation that was once employed by the Star Chamber, by "the Germans of the 1930's and early 1940's," and by some of our own police departments only a few decades ago. Custodial interrogation that violates that provision of the Bill of Rights is a classic example of a violation of a constitutional right.

I respectfully dissent.

6.   Legislative "Modification" of *Miranda*

EDITORS' INTRODUCTION: THE EFFECT OF *MIRANDA*

Despite the outcry following the *Miranda* decision, some evidence suggests its impact was relatively slight. Early research efforts and the problems of such studies are summarized and discussed in The American Law Institute's, A Model Code of Pre-Arraignment Procedure Part II (Study Draft No. 1, 1968). See also Medalie, Zeitz and Alexander, Custodial Police Interrogation in our Nation's Capitol: The Attempt to Implement Miranda, 66 Mich.L.Rev. 1347 (1968).

Project, Interrogations in New Haven: The Impact of Miranda, 76 Yale L.J. 1519 (1965), compared the success of interrogations involving warnings and others in which the suspects received no warnings. Paradoxically, the questioning was *more* successful in those cases in which the subject was warned. The researchers' analysis of the conduct of 81 warned suspects suggested the warning affected the interrogation result for only eight. Three refused to talk; two of these had received advice of counsel. Three others made oral incriminating statements but refused to sign written statements. One admitted his guilt but refused to sign a statement implicating others, and another confessed after consulting an attorney and being advised to do so. The minor impact of the warnings, the study concluded, was not surprising in light of the process observed:

> In the first place, although most interrogations were not intimidating, they were designed to discourage any initiative on the part of the suspect. * * * [T]he warnings * * * were often intoned in a manner designed to minimize or negate their importance and effectiveness. * * * [U]nless the detectives made it absolutely clear what the warn-

ing meant—which they rarely did—most suspects appeared unable to grasp their significance.

Perhaps equally important, almost every person arrested * * * had committed the crime for which he was arrested and knew that the police had evidence of this. When he remained silent, the police would confront him with the evidence. Most suspects apparently felt compelled to give some alibi. Usually they lied and in doing so were caught in their lie. From then on the process was all downhill—from the suspect's point of view. Once a suspect said anything he usually had taken the first step towards incriminating himself.

In addition * * *, the warnings did not have an impact on a number of suspects who, knowing they were guilty, apparently saw no point in denying their guilt. Perhaps previous exposure to the process made them believe silence was futile—several of the defendants we interviewed expressed this belief.

Finally, the warnings had no apparent impact on the behavior of the suspects who seemingly believed they were giving exculpatory statements. * * * Most of those who began by attempting to justify their actions ended by incriminating themselves to some degree.

Id. at 1571–72.

Seeburger and Wettick, *Miranda* in Pittsburgh—A Statistical Study, 29 U.Pitt.L.Rev. 1 (1967), compared cases before and after *Miranda* and produced somewhat different results. The percentage of cases in which suspects made confessions dropped from 54.4% to 37.5% after *Miranda*; in robbery cases, the drop was from 62.4% to 36.7%. The percentage of cases in which confessions were necessary for conviction did not decrease after *Miranda*. Nevertheless, the conviction rate did not drop significantly after *Miranda*. This, the authors suggested, might be explained by grand juries' refusals to indict in the post-*Miranda* cases in which the defendants gave no confessions and in which a confession was essential to conviction, or by the dismissal of these cases at arraignment. Turning to the clearance rate for the crimes studied, the authors concluded the post-*Miranda* clearance rate actually exceeded the pre-*Miranda* rate by a small percentage.

The Seeburger and Wettick study was conducted soon after the *Miranda* decision. It may, then, reflect in part problems of transition as law enforcement adjusted to the new requirements. Certainly the study does not reflect any effects of post-*Miranda* decisions reducing the effect of the seminal case. Nevertheless, some changes seem certain to have occurred after—and perhaps—because of *Miranda*. Gerald Caplan has noted widespread agreement (although no firm evidence) on some matters:

Before *Miranda*, charges of physical force, questioning in relays, and sustained incommunicado detention were common; after *Miranda*, they became far less frequent.

Caplan, Book Review, 93 Yale L.J. 1375, 1382–83 (1984).

A recent reexamination of the empirical studies conducted on *Miranda* challenged the widespread perception that these studies indicated only minimal results. Cassell, *Miranda's* Social Costs: An Empirical Reassessment, 90 Nw.U.L.Rev. 387 (1966). Professor Cassell contended that "the existing empirical data supports the tentative estimate that *Miranda* has led to lost cases against almost four percent of all criminal suspects in this country who are questioned." A "lost case," he explained, is one in which a confession is needed to convict and, because of *Miranda*, the suspect did not confess. While a lost case is not necessarily one that would have resulted in a conviction, Professor Cassell added, most of the lost cases are probably ones that would have resulted in convictions. Finding that the data permits a "very rough" quantitative estimate of the effect of *Miranda* on plea bargaining, he concluded the decision resulted in more favorable plea bargains in about the same percent of cases. Id. At 445–46.

Turning to the significance of the various *Miranda* requirements, he concluded that advising suspects of their right to remain silent does not appear the critical factor. Instead, he argued, the rules barring questioning explain the results, given that about 20% of suspects invoke their rights and thus cannot be questioned. In the absence of the *Miranda* "cutoff" rules, he indicated, officers could be expected to successfully persuade some of these suspects to make incriminating statements. He also suggested "*Miranda's* greatest cost" is its blocking of searches for new approaches to custodial interrogation that might better reconcile society's need to apprehend offenders and suspects' interest in avoiding coercive questioning. Although *Miranda* purported to invite exploration of alternatives, he argued, the Court's failure to indicate the acceptability of specific alternatives rendered the invitation an empty one.

Professor Cassell acknowledged the drop in the confession rate might be a benefit rather than a cost of *Miranda* if it reflected the results of police inability to use coercive techniques. He concluded, however, that although direct evidence is lacking the indirect indications suggest it is "quite unlikely" that a reduction in police coercion explains the confession rate drop he attributed to *Miranda*. Id., at 478.

Professor Cassell and a colleague themselves conducted a study of the effect of *Miranda* in Salt Lake City, Utah by examining a sample of felony cases presented to the District Attorney for screening and possible prosecution and comparing the results with what they concluded were general pre-*Miranda* facts. Cassell and Hayman, Police Interrogation in the 1990s: An Empirical Study of the Effects of *Miranda*, 43 U.C.L.A.L.Rev. 839 (1966). 21% of the Salt Lake City suspects were not questioned, leading the authors to conclude that questioning rates have declined since *Miranda*. Of those questioned, 83.7% waived their *Miranda* rights, 7.0% requested an attorney, 4.7% invoked their right to silence, and another 4.7% refused to execute a waiver or otherwise invoked their rights. Turning to the productivity of questioning, the study concluded that successful questioning—questioning producing a statement useful to the prosecution—occurred in 33.3% of all the cases and in 42.2% of the cases in which the suspects were questioned. After determining that the available evidence indicated a 55% to 60% success rate in interrogations before *Miranda*, the authors concluded that their data suggested "*Miranda* has hampered law enforcement efforts to obtain incriminating statements." The strength of the evidence police had at the time of the questioning was strongly correlated with the productivity of questioning; questioning was productive in 55.6% of cases in which the available evidence was overwhelming and in only 26.3% of the cases in which it was weak.

Cassell would respond to what he believes to be the current state of affairs by eliminating the right of suspects to counsel during prearraignment interrogation, imposing no requirement of a waiver of rights before interrogation, and eliminating the requirement that interrogation halt upon the suspect's request for counsel or assertion of the right to remain silent. He would require a modified warning telling a suspect he has a right to silence and anything he says can be used as evidence. The suspect would also be told he has a right to be represented when brought before a judge and that the judge will appoint an attorney if necessary. He would add the admonition that the officers are required to bring the suspect before the judge without necessary delay. Balancing this retreat from *Miranda*, he would require the videotaping of all stationhouse interrogations and audiotaping of field custodial interrogations.

Professor Schulhofer responded at length to Professor Cassell in Schulhofer, *Miranda's* Practical Effect: Substantial Benefits and Vanishingly Small Social Costs, 90 Nw.U.L.Rev. 500 (1996). He reevaluated the empirical studies and concluded that *Miranda* has been shown to have resulted in lost convictions "in at most 0.78% of serious criminal cases." Does this suggest *Miranda* has so little impact it is not worth defending? Schulhofer claimed not, reasoning that *Miranda* has changed the nature of interrogation and the basis for suspects' confessing. Modern police questioning, he argued, has become "an elaborate 'confidence game,' "in which the officer dupes the suspect into believing he can help himself by revealing information. As a result:

> [T]oday's suspects typically confess not because of fear of mistreatment but primarily because of misplaced confidence in their own ability to talk their way out of trouble. * * * [C]onfessions are now most the result of persuasion and the suspect's overconfidence, not of pressure and fear.

90 Nw.U.L.Rev. at 561–62. Cassell replied in Cassell, All Benefits, No Costs: The Grand Illusion of Miranda's Defenders, 90 Nw.U.L.Rev. 1084 (1996). See also, Thomas, Plain Talk About the *Miranda* Empirical Debate: A "Steady–State" Theory of Confessions, 43 U.C.L.A. L. Rev. 933 (1996).

Professor Cassell and a colleague have also challenged the conventional wisdom that *Miranda* neither caused nor was followed by a sustained fall in the clearance rate for major offenses. Paul G. Cassell and Richard Fowles, Handcuffing the Cops? A Thirty-year Perspective on *Miranda's* Harmful Effect on law Enforcement, 50 Stan.L.Rev. 1055 (1998). They subjected clearance rate data to regression analysis, and concluded *Miranda* affected clearance rates for robbery, larceny, vehicle theft, and burglary, but not for homicide, rape or assault. Specifically:

> [W]ithout *Miranda*, the number of crimes cleared would have been substantially higher—by as much as 6.6–29.7% for robbery, 6.2–28.9% for burglary, 0.4–11.9% for larceny, and 12.8–45.4% for vehicle theft. * * * As many as 36,000 robberies, 82,000 burglaries, 163,000 larce-

nies, and 78,000 vehicle thefts remain uncleared each year as a result of *Miranda*.

50 Stan.L.Rev. at 1126.

Lawyer-sociologist Richard Leo conducted research of a quite different kind. His results were reported in Leo, Inside the Interrogation Room, 86 J.Crim. & Crim. 266 (1996). Leo observed 122 interrogations of felony suspects in an unidentified city and reviewed sixty videotaped interrogations from two other localities. Of the 175 suspects to whose interrogations *Miranda* applied, 38 (22%) invoked their rights. Leo noted that this is a higher percentage than is assumed by "conventional wisdom." Of the suspects who waived their rights (and who were therefore interrogated), more than three-fourths (76%) made some sort of incriminating statement and about one-third made full confessions. In only four cases, he concluded, did police tactics constitute coercion, and even in these the coercion was psychological rather than physical.

Suspects with felony criminal records, Leo reported, were four times as likely as those with no record to invoke *Miranda* rights. He found no relationship between success of the interrogation and the class, race, or gender of the suspects, victims, or officers, the age of the suspects, the strength of the evidence against the suspects, or the suspect's criminal record. Success of the interrogation was related to the number of tactics officers used and the length of the interrogation—the longer the interrogation and the more tactics used, the more fruitful the interrogation.

Distinguishing among techniques, Leo noted that in almost all cases officers confronted the suspect with existing evidence of his guilt and appealed to his self-interest. In 30% of the cases, officers confronted the suspect with *false* evidence of guilt. Leo found that success tended to be achieved by (1) identifying contradictions in the suspect's denial of involvement; (2) offering a moral justification or psychological excuse for the criminal behavior; (3) praise or flattery; (4) appealing to the suspect's conscience; and (5) appealing to the importance of cooperating with authorities.

Whether a suspect made an incriminating statement or not had a significant effect on the processing of the case. Suspects who made such statements were 20% more likely to be charged, 24% less likely to have charges dismissed, 25% more likely to have their cases resolved by plea bargaining (which meant a conviction in 98% of the cases), and 26% more likely to be convicted.

Leo commented further on the implications of his research in Leo, The Impact of *Miranda* Revisited, 86 J.Crim.L. & Crim. 621 (1996). He suggested compliance with *Miranda* is often a social process orchestrated to predispose suspects towards voluntarily waiving their rights. Leo described the detectives he observed employing three kinds of "subtle psychological strategies." The first was "conditioning," a process in which the officer makes pleasant small talk with the suspect or strikes up a conversation about some point of common interest (such as sports), sometimes while going through the routine booking questions. These practices, Leo concluded, were "intended to disarm the suspect, to lower his anxiety levels, to improve his opinion of the detective, and to create a social psychological setting conducive to both a *Miranda* waiver as well as to subsequent admissions."

A second strategy—which Leo called "de-emphasizing"—consisted of downplaying the potential importance of the *Miranda* rights. This was accomplished in either or both of two ways. One consisted of "blending the *Miranda* warning into the ebb and flow of pre-interrogation conversation by not doing or saying anything unusual when reading the warnings so that the suspect paid no special attention to the admonition." The other method of de-emphasizing was to call the suspect's attention to the "anomalous status" of the warnings, as by characterizing them as a mere formality required prior to questioning or by suggesting the suspect himself can probably recite them as a result of television viewing.

The third strategy—persuasion—consisted of explicit although often subtle attempts to persuade the suspect to waive the rights. For example, officers sometimes emphasized that the police already had the victim's side of the story and thus suggested that this would become in some sense an "official" version unless the suspect talked to the officers. Alternatively, officers sometimes indicated the purpose of the session was to inform the suspect of the evidence against him and what was likely to happen. They would then add that this could be done only if the suspect waived the rights.

Leo suggested the effectiveness of these techniques is more important in explaining why so many suspects waive their *Miranda* rights than other possibilities sometimes offered, such as suggestions that suspects do not actually understand the rights or are impermissibly induced to waive them. These negotiating strategies developed by police to minimize *Miranda's* potential obstacle, he concluded, "usually remain within the letter of *Miranda*, but frequently they straddle the ambiguous margins of legality."

Whatever the "real" facts, *Miranda* was followed by widespread pressure for some countermeasures to the decision. In 1968, Congress passed legislation—codified as 18 U.S.C.A. § 3501 and reprinted following this Introductory Note—designed "to offset the harmful effects of the [Supreme] Court decisions" dealing with the admissibility of confessions, primarily *Miranda*. S.Rep. No. 1097, 90th Cong., 2nd S. (1968), U.S.Code Cong. & Adm.News. Vol. 2, p. 2112, at 2127. Explaining the need for the legislation, the Senate Judiciary Committee stated:

> The committee is convinced * * * that the rigid and inflexible requirements of the majority opinion in the *Miranda* case are unreasonable, unrealistic, and extremely harmful to law enforcement. Instance after instance are documented in the transcript [of the subcommittee hearings] where the most vicious criminals have gone unpunished, even though they had voluntarily confessed their guilt.

Id. at 2132.

Despite the apparent significance of the statute, issues concerning it almost never came before the federal courts until the principal case reprinted in this subsection following the statute. The reason for this drew the ire of one member of the Supreme Court in Davis v. United States, 512

U.S. 452, 457 n. *, 512 U.S. 452, 114 S.Ct. 2350, 2354 n. *, 129 L.Ed.2d 362, 370 note * (1994), reprinted in part in subsection B(3) of this chapter.

In *Davis*, the Court declined the invitation of some amici to consider 18 U.S.C.A. § 3501, explaining that the Government had not relied upon the statute. Justice Scalia concurred in an opinion expressing frustration with the Government's continuing failure to rely on section 3501. "[W]ith limited exceptions," he noted, "the provision has been studiously avoided by every Administration, not only in this court but in the lower courts, since its enactment more than 25 years ago." He then added:

> [T]he refusal to consider arguments not raised is a sound prudential practice, rather than a statutory or constitutional mandate, and there are times when prudence dictates the contrary. As far as I am concerned, such a time will have arrived when a case that comes within the terms of this statute is next presented to us.

* * *

* * * Section 3501 of Title 18 is a provision of law directed to the courts, reflecting the people's assessment of the proper balance to be struck between concern for persons interrogated in custody and the needs of effective law enforcement. We shirk our duty if we systematically disregard that statutory command simply because the Justice Department systematically declines to remind us of it.

* * * The point is whether our continuing refusal to consider § 3501 is consistent with the Third Branch's obligation to decide according to the law. I think it is not.

512 U.S. at 464–65, 114 S.Ct. at 2358, 129 L.Ed.2d at 374–5 (Scalia, J., concurring).

OMNIBUS CRIME CONTROL AND SAFE STREETS ACT OF 1968

18 U.S.C.A.

§ 3501.   Admissibility of Confessions

(a) In any criminal prosecution brought by the United States or by the District of Columbia, a confession * * * shall be admissible in evidence if it is voluntarily given. Before such confession is received in evidence, the trial judge shall, out of the presence of the jury, determine any issue as to voluntariness. If the trial judge determines that the confession was voluntarily made it shall be admitted in evidence and the trial judge shall permit the jury to hear relevant evidence on the issue of voluntariness and shall instruct the jury to give such weight to the confession as the jury feels it deserves under all the circumstances.

(b) The trial judge in determining the issue of voluntariness shall take into consideration all the circumstances surrounding the giving of the confession, including (1) the time elapsing between arrest and arraignment of the defendant making the confession, if it was made after arrest and before arraignment, (2) whether such defendant knew the nature of the offense with which he was charged or of which he was suspected at the time of making the confession, (3) whether or not such defendant was advised or knew that he was not required to make any statement and that any such statement could be used against him, (4) whether or not such defendant had been advised prior to questioning of his right to the assistance of counsel; and (5) whether or not such defendant was without the assistance of counsel when questioned and when giving such confession.

The presence or absence of any of the abovementioned factors to be taken into consideration by the judge need not be conclusive on the issue of voluntariness of the confession.

* * *

United States v. Dickerson

United States Court of Appeals, Fourth Circuit, 1999.
166 F.3d 667.

■ Before WILLIAMS and MICHAEL, CIRCUIT JUDGES, and KISER, SENIOR UNITED STATES DISTRICT JUDGE FOR THE WESTERN DISTRICT OF VIRGINIA, sitting by designation.

■ WILLIAMS, CIRCUIT JUDGE:[a]

[Defendant Charles T. Dickerson was taken into custody after a witness to a bank robbery reported the license number of the getaway car and that vehicle was traced to him. Without giving Dickerson *Miranda* warnings, federal officers questioned him at length. He gave several statements admitting being the driver but he named Jimmy Rochester as the actual robber. When Rochester was apprehended, he gave a statement naming Dickerson as the driver in a series of eleven bank robberies.

Dickerson moved to suppress both his statement and that of Rochester, arguing that his statement was involuntary and obtained in violation of *Miranda* and that Rochester's statement was the tainted fruit of his statement. The district court held that Dickerson's confession was obtained in violation of *Miranda* and suppressed it. It refused, however, to suppress Rochester's statement, reasoning that fruits of a *Miranda* violation need not be excluded. Although fruits of an involuntary confession must be suppressed, it added, Dickerson's confession was voluntary and hence did not taint Rochester's statement.

The Government exercised its right to take an interlocutory appeal from the order suppressing Dickerson's confession. It did not, however, rely on 18 U.S.C.A. § 3501. In a 1997 unreported case, the Court of Appeals had ordered the Department of Justice to address the effect of the statute on a confession. In response, Attorney General Reno notified Congress that the Department would not defend the constitutionality of § 3501 in the lower federal courts. She acted pursuant to 2 U.S.C.A. § 288k(b), which requires the Department to notify Congress whenever the Department will not defend the constitutionality of a federal statute. The Department also filed a brief in the Court of Appeals taking the same position. It has not,

a. Some material from footnotes to the original opinion has been incorporated into the text.

however, decided whether in an appropriate case it would ask the United States Supreme Court to overrule or modify *Miranda.*

On the merits of the Government's appeal, the Court of Appeals reasoned that in light of the district court's finding that the confession was voluntary, the court erred in suppressing the confession simply because of a *Miranda* violation if 18 U.S.C.A. § 3501 is constitutionally valid. Thus it turned to that question. Editors.]

* * * Does Congress possess the authority to supersede the irrebuttable presumption created in *Miranda* that any unwarned statement to the police is involuntary, and therefore inadmissible?

* * *

In City of Boerne v. Flores, 521 U.S. 507, 117 S.Ct. 2157, 138 L.Ed.2d 624 (1997), the Court recently held that Congress does not possess the legislative authority to supersede a Supreme Court decision construing the Constitution. See id. 177 S.Ct. at 2172 (refusing to enforce federal statute establishing more narrow test for violation of the Free Exercise Clause than prior test established by Supreme Court). On the other hand, Congress possesses the legislative authority to overrule judicially created rules of evidence and procedure that are not required by the Constitution. See Palermo v. United States, 360 U.S. 343, 345, 348, 79 S.Ct. 1217, 3 L.Ed.2d 1287 (1959) (upholding federal statute establishing more narrow disclosure of *Jenks* material than prior rule established by Supreme Court); see also Carlisle v. United States, 517 U.S. 416, 426, 116 S.Ct. 1460, 134 L.Ed.2d 613 (1996) (noting that the federal courts may formulate rules of evidence and procedure so long as they do not conflict with an Act of Congress); Vance v. Terrazas, 444 U.S. 252, 265, 100 S.Ct. 540, 62 L.Ed.2d 461 (1980) (upholding statute altering the evidentiary standard for expatriation proceedings established by the Supreme Court because prior standard created by the Court was not required by "the Constitution"). In fact, the power of the Supreme Court to prescribe nonconstitutional "rules of procedure and evidence for the federal courts exists only in the absence of a relevant Act of Congress." *Palermo*, 360 U.S. at 353 n. 11, 79 S.Ct. 1217.

Whether Congress has the authority to enact § 3501, therefore, turns on whether the rule set forth by the Supreme Court in *Miranda* is required by the Constitution. If it is, Congress lacked the authority to enact § 3501, and *Miranda* continues to control the admissibility of confessions in federal court. If it is not required by the Constitution, then Congress possesses the authority to supersede *Miranda* legislatively, and § 3501 controls the admissibility of confessions in federal court.

* * *

We begin our analysis * * * with the Supreme Court's decision in *Miranda*. Several passages in Chief Justice Warren's opinion for the Court suggest that the warnings safeguard rights guaranteed by the Constitution. See, e.g., *Miranda*, 384 U.S. at 490 (noting that the privilege against self-incrimination is guaranteed by the Constitution). Surprisingly, the sixty-page opinion does not specifically state the basis for its holding that a statement obtained from a suspect without the warnings would be presumed involuntary. The Court strongly suggested, however, that the basis for the rule was identical to that set forth in [McNabb v. United States, 318 U.S. 332, 63 S.Ct. 608, 87 L.Ed. 819 (1943) (exercising its supervisory power over the federal courts, Supreme Court held that federal courts must exclude all incriminating statements, including voluntary confessions, obtained during an unreasonable delay between a defendant's arrest and initial appearance) and Mallory v. United States, 354 U.S. 449, 77 S.Ct. 1356, 1 L.Ed.2d 1479 (1957) (affirming the holding of *McNabb* under Rule 5(a) of the Federal Rules of Criminal Procedure)]. In particular, just as the "supervisory" rule set forth in *McNabb* and *Mallory* permitted the Court to avoid the constitutional issues associated with federal interrogations, the rule set forth in *Miranda* would allow the Court to avoid the constitutional issues associated with state interrogations.

Although the Court failed to specifically state the basis for its holding in *Miranda*, it did specifically state what the basis was not. At no point does the Court refer to the warnings as constitutional rights. Indeed, the Court acknowledged that the Constitution did not require the warnings, disclaimed any intent to create a "constitutional straightjacket," repeatedly referred to the warnings as "procedural safeguards," and invited Congress and the States "to develop their own safeguards for [protecting] the privilege."

Since deciding *Miranda*, the Supreme Court consistently (and repeatedly) has referred to the warnings as "prophylactic," New York v. Quarles, 467 U.S. 649, 654, 104 S.Ct. 2626, 81 L.Ed.2d 550 (1984), and "not themselves rights protected by the Constitution," Michigan v. Tucker, 417 U.S. 433, 444, 94 S.Ct. 2357, 41 L.Ed.2d 182 (1974); see also Davis v. United States, 512 U.S. 452, 457, 458, 114 S.Ct. 2350, 129 L.Ed.2d 362 (1994) (referring to *Miranda* warnings as "a series of recommended procedural safeguards"); Withrow v. Williams, 507 U.S. 680, 690, 691, 113 S.Ct. 1745, 123 L.Ed.2d 407 (1993) (acknowledging that *"Miranda's* safeguards are not constitutional in character"); Duckworth v. Eagan, 492 U.S. 195, 203, 109 S.Ct. 2875, 106 L.Ed.2d 166 (1989) (noting that the *Miranda* warnings are not required by the Constitution); Connecticut v. Barrett, 479 U.S. 523, 528, 107 S.Ct. 828, 93 L.Ed.2d 920 (1987) (noting that "the *Miranda* Court adopted prophylactic rules designed to insulate the exercise of Fifth Amendment rights"); Oregon v. Elstad, 470 U.S. 298, 306, 105 S.Ct. 1285, 84 L.Ed.2d 222 (1985) (noting that the *Miranda* exclusionary rule "may be triggered even in the absence of a Fifth Amendment violation").

* * *

Of particular importance here, the Court in *Elstad* made the following observation about *Miranda*:

> The *Miranda* exclusionary rule, however, serves the Fifth Amendment and sweeps more broadly than the Fifth Amendment itself. It may be triggered even in the absence of a Fifth Amendment violation. The Fifth Amendment prohibits use by the prosecution in its case in chief only of compelled testimony. Failure to administer *Miranda* warnings creates a presumption of compulsion. Consequently, un-

warned statements that are otherwise voluntary within the meaning of the Fifth Amendment must nevertheless be excluded from evidence under *Miranda*. Thus, in the individual case, *Miranda's* preventive medicine provides a remedy even to the defendant who has suffered no identifiable constitutional harm.

But the *Miranda* presumption, though irrebuttable for purposes of the prosecution's case in chief, does not require that the statements and their fruits be discarded as inherently tainted. Despite the fact that patently voluntary statements taken in violation of *Miranda* must be excluded from the prosecution's case, the presumption of coercion does not bar their use for impeachment purposes on cross-examination.

Id. at 306–07, 105 S.Ct. 1285 (internal footnotes and citations omitted).

In light of the foregoing cases, it is certainly "well established that the failure to deliver *Miranda* warnings is not itself a constitutional violation." United States v. Elie, 111 F.3d 1135, 1142 (4th Cir.1997) (citing Supreme Court cases). As a consequence, the irrebuttable presumption created by the Court in *Miranda* that a confession obtained without the warnings is presumed involuntary is *a fortiori* not required by the Constitution. Accordingly, Congress necessarily possesses the legislative authority to supersede the conclusive presumption created by *Miranda* pursuant to its authority to prescribe the rules of procedure and evidence in the federal courts.

The dissent does not dispute that the applicability of § 3501 turns on whether *Miranda* is a constitutional rule. Even more telling, after considering the merits, the dissent is unable to conclude that *Miranda's* conclusive presumption is, in fact, required by the Constitution. In the end, the dissent poses only the following rhetorical question: "If *Miranda* is not a constitutional rule, why does the Supreme Court continue to apply it in prosecutions arising in state courts." * * * [A]lthough the dissent raises an interesting academic question, the answer to why the Supreme Court applies *Miranda* in prosecutions arising in state courts has no bearing on our conclusion that *Miranda's* conclusive presumption is not required by the Constitution.

It is worth recalling that Congress not only acted in response to the Court's invitation, see *Miranda*, 384 U.S. at 490, 86 S.Ct. 1602 (inviting Congress and the States "to develop their own safeguards for [protecting] the privilege"), but that the Court in *Miranda* had acted in the absence of a relevant Act of Congress. It is well established that the Court's power to prescribe nonconstitutional "rules of procedure and evidence for the federal courts exists only in the absence of a relevant Act of Congress." *Palermo*, 360 U.S. at 353 n. 11, 79 S.Ct. 1217. Thus, just as the Court was free to create an irrebuttable presumption that statements obtained without certain procedural safeguards are involuntary, Congress was free to overrule that judicially created rule.

To be sure, the *Miranda* warnings were meant to safeguard the Fifth Amendment privilege against self-incrimination. Indeed, under § 3501 any statement obtained in violation of the privilege must be suppressed. Thus, we cannot say that Congress's decision to eliminate the irrebuttable presumption created by *Miranda* lessens the protections afforded by the privilege. Indeed, the Court has recognized that *Miranda's* irrebuttable presumption goes beyond what is required to protect the privilege. As a result, even "patently voluntary statements . . . must be excluded." *Elstad*, 470 U.S. at 307, 105 S.Ct. 1285. In enacting § 3501, Congress simply recognized the need to offset the harmful effects created by *Miranda's* irrebuttable presumption. No longer will criminals who have voluntarily confessed their crimes be released on mere technicalities.

In addition to recognizing the harmful effects created by *Miranda's* irrebuttable presumption, Congress concluded that the Court's justification for the conclusive presumption that custodial interrogations were inherently coercive and intimidating was simply incorrect as an empirical matter. See S.Rep. No. 901097 (1968), reprinted in 1968 U.S.C.C.A.N. 2112. During the subcommittee hearings, Senator Arlen Specter, then the district attorney of the City of Philadelphia, pointed out

> that the so-called third degree methods deplored by the Supreme Court and cited as a basis for their opinion in *Miranda* is not a correct portrayal of what actually goes on in police stations across the country. While there are isolated cases of police using coercive tactics, this is the exception rather than the rule.

Id. at 2134. Similarly, the final committee report concluded that the basis for the conclusive presumption in *Miranda* was faulty. Id. at 2142 (noting that the "data supporting the [Court's] conclusion of inherent coercion in custodial interrogation were drawn solely from police manuals and texts which may or may not have been followed"); id. at 2134 (noting that "while coercive practices might have been approved 30 years ago, they have no place in modern police techniques"); id. (finding that "the Court overreacted to defense claims that police brutality is widespread").

In sum, Congress, utilizing its superior factfinding ability, concluded that custodial interrogations were not inherently coercive. As Senator Sam Ervin noted at the time § 3501 was enacted:

> A decision of the Supreme Court, if it is based on a factual assumption which is incorrect, may be subject to Congress' power to legislate. The Supreme Court has no right to make . . . determinations based on unsound factual assumptions. I don't believe the great majority of law enforcement officers in the United States are such disreputable people that they have to have the criminals protected against them.

Hearings on the Supreme Court Before the Subcomm. on Separation of Powers of the Senate Comm. on the Judiciary, 90th Cong. 25 (1968). Senator Ervin's observation concerning Congress's authority to overrule Supreme Court decisions, whether or not correct as a general matter, is certainly correct when applied to judicially created presumptions. It is well established that a conclusive presumption "should not be applied . . . in situations where the generalization is incorrect as an empirical matter." Coleman v. Thompson, 501 U.S. 722, 737, 111 S.Ct. 2546, 115 L.Ed.2d 640 (1991). In fact, "the justification for a conclusive presumption disappears when application of the presumption will not reach the correct result most of the time." According to congressional findings, the basis for *Miranda's* conclusive presumption is incorrect as an empirical matter, and the presumption does not reach the correct result, i.e., suppressing only coerced confessions, most of the time that it is applied. As a result, Congress, pursuant to its authority to prescribe the rules of procedure and evidence in the federal courts, was justified in abandoning the conclusive presumption when it enacted § 3501.

Finally, lest there be any confusion on the matter, nothing in today's opinion provides those in law enforcement with an incentive to stop giving the now familiar *Miranda* warnings. As noted above, those warnings are among the factors a district court should consider when determining whether a confession was voluntarily given. See 18 U.S.C.A. § 3501(b). Indeed, federal courts rarely find confessions obtained in technical compliance with *Miranda* to be involuntary under the Fifth Amendment. Thus, providing the four *Miranda* warnings is still the best way to guarantee a finding of voluntariness.

In the end, and after an exhaustive review of the relevant authority, we are convinced that § 3501 enacted at the invitation of the Supreme Court and pursuant to Congress's unquestioned power to establish the rules of procedure and evidence in the federal courts is constitutional. * * * [W]e find that the admissibility of confessions in federal court is governed by 18 U.S.C.A. § 3501 (West 1985), rather than *Miranda* * * *. Accordingly, the district court's order suppressing the statements Dickerson made * * * is reversed, and the case is remanded for further proceedings.

REVERSED AND REMANDED

■ MICHAEL, CIRCUIT JUDGE, dissenting * * *:

* * * In pressing § 3501 into the prosecution of a case against the express wishes of the Department of Justice, the majority takes on more than any court should. I therefore respectfully dissent. * * *

* * * The majority holds that § 3501 governs the admissibility of confessions in federal court because *Miranda* is not a constitutional rule. I don't know whether it is or not, but before I had to decide, I would want thoughtful lawyers on both sides to answer one question for me. If *Miranda* is not a constitutional rule, why does the Supreme Court continue to apply it in prosecutions arising in state courts? This question illustrates that the § 3501 issue is so sweeping that we should not be delving into it on our own. In this case, we should follow our usual practice of deciding only the issues raised by the parties.

* * *

NOTES

1. The Senate Judiciary Committee's report on the bill enacting section 3501 defended the proposal by citing the passage in the *Miranda* majority opinion which encouraged legislative searches "for increasingly effective ways of protecting the rights of the individual while promoting efficient enforcement of our criminal laws." It then concluded:

> The committee feels that it is obvious * * * that the overwhelming weight of judicial opinion in this country is that the voluntariness test does not offend

the Constitution or deprive a defendant of any Constitutional right. No one can predict with any assurance what the Supreme Court might at some future date decide if these provisions are enacted. The committee has concluded that this approach to the balancing of the rights of society and the rights of the individual served us well over the years, that it is constitutional and that Congress should adopt it. After all, the *Miranda* decision itself was by a bare majority of one, and with increasing frequency the Supreme Court has reversed itself. The committee feels that by the time the issue of constitutionality would reach the Supreme Court, the probability rather is that this legislation would be upheld.

S.Rep. No. 1097, supra, at 2138.

2. **Judicially-Supervised Interrogation.** An alternative approach would be to authorize interrogation by or under the supervision of a judicial officer. An early brief for such a procedure was Kauper, Judicial Examination of the Accused—A Remedy for the Third Degree, 30 Mich.L.Rev. 1224 (1932). A "modernized" version of Kauper's proposal was presented in Kamisar, Kauper's "Judicial Examination of the Accused" Forty Years Later—Some Comments on a Remarkable Article, 73 Mich.L.Rev. 15, 23–24, 27, 32 (1974):

> 1. A person taken into custody because of, or charged with, a crime to which an interrogation relates, may be questioned only in the presence of and under the supervision of a judicial officer.

> 2. The person shall immediately (that is, as soon as humanly possible) be brought before a judicial officer who shall, before questioning begins, determine the existence of the grounds for detention or arrest.

> 3. The judicial officer shall give the person the familiar *Miranda* warnings and, in addition, inform him that if he is subsequently prosecuted his refusal to answer any questions will be disclosed at trial.

> 4. A complete written record shall be kept of the judicial examinations; the information of rights, any waiver thereof, and any questioning shall be recorded upon a sound recording device; and the suspect shall be so informed.

> 5. The questions shall be asked by police officers or prosecuting attorneys rather than the judicial officer, but only in the presence of the judicial officer, who may intervene to prevent abuse.

Would such a procedure be desirable? Would it be constitutional?

3. **Recording Requirements.** Another reform urged by many is the recording of custodial interrogation and suspects' resulting statements. The Model Code of Pre–Arraignment Procedure, for example, proposed a requirement that sound recordings be made of warnings, waivers, questioning, and statements made in response to questioning. Model Code of Pre–Arraignment Procedure § 130.4(3) (Official Draft 1975). The Alaska Supreme Court has read the state's constitutional due process demand as requiring electronic recording of custodial interrogations. Stephan v. State, 711 P.2d 1156, 1162 (Alaska 1985).

The Minnesota Supreme Court has adopted a recording requirement, but stopped short of mandating suppression of all self-incriminating statements related to noncompliance with this requirement:

> [I]n the exercise of our supervisory power to insure the fair administration of justice, we hold that all custodial interrogation including any information about rights, any waiver of those rights, and all questioning shall be electronically recorded where feasible and must be recorded when questioning occurs at a place of detention. If law enforcement officers fail to comply with this recording requirement, any statements the suspect makes in response to the interroga-

tion may be suppressed at trial. The parameters of the exclusionary rule applied to evidence of statements obtained in violation of these requirements must be decided on a case-by-case basis. Following the approach recommended by the drafters of the Model Code of Pre–Arraignment Procedure, suppression will be required of any statements obtained in violation of the recording requirement if the violation is deemed "substantial." This determination is to be made by the trial court after considering all relevant circumstances bearing on substantiality * * *.

State v. Scales, 518 N.W.2d 587, 592 (Minn.1994). Although a recording requirement is often urged on other courts, they have generally refused to impose such a demand. See State v. James, 237 Conn. 390, 431–34, 678 A.2d 1338, 1359–60 (1996). An extensive argument for videotaping is made in Leo, The Impact of *Miranda* Revisited, 86 J.Crim.L. & Crim. 621, 681–92 (1996).

An intermediate Indiana court concluded the Indiana Constitution imposed no duty on law enforcement officers to record custodial interrogations in places of detention. It added, however:

[A]lthough we impose no legal obligation, we discern few instances in which law enforcement officers would be justified in failing to record custodial interrogations in places of detention. Disputes regarding the circumstances of an interrogation would be minimized, in that a tape recording preserves undisturbed that which the mind may forget. In turn, the judiciary would be relieved of much of the burden of resolving disputes involving differing recollections of events which occurred. Moreover, the recording would serve to protect police officers against false allegations that a confession was not obtained voluntarily. Therefore, in light of the slight inconvenience and expense associated with the recording of custodial interrogations in their entirety, it is strongly recommended, as a matter of sound policy, that law enforcement officers adopt this procedure.

In the absence of an electronic recording of a custodial interrogation in a place of detention, we also note that the following consequences may ensue:

"[D]efense counsel is entitled to pursue the failure of the police to record a defendant's statements. Counsel may, for example, inquire of a testifying police officer ... whether he or she was aware of the availability of recorders to use during the questioning of suspects. Counsel may argue to a jury and to a judge as factfinder that the failure of the police to record electronically statements made in a place of custody should be considered in deciding the voluntariness of any statement, whether the defendant was properly advised of his rights, and whether any statement attributed to the defendant was made." Commonwealth v. Diaz (1996), 422 Mass. 269, 661 N.E.2d 1326, 1329.

Stoker v. State, 692 N.E.2d 1386, 1390, 1390 n. 11 (Ind.App.1998) (footnote incorporated into text).

C.   Sixth Amendment Right to Counsel

EDITORS' INTRODUCTION: SIXTH AMENDMENT RIGHT TO COUNSEL DURING POLICE QUESTIONING

In a series of cases beginning with Massiah v. United States, 377 U.S. 201, 84 S.Ct. 1199, 12 L.Ed.2d 246 (1964), the Supreme Court held the Sixth Amendment right to counsel applied to law enforcement undercover efforts to elicit self-incriminating statements occurring after the investigation had progressed to a certain point. This is considered further in Chapter 8. In Brewer v. Williams, 430 U.S. 387, 97 S.Ct. 1232, 51 L.Ed.2d 424 (1977), however, the Court held that the Sixth Amendment also applied to overt police interrogations occurring after the case had progressed far enough to trigger the Sixth Amendment. As the principal case in this section makes clear, this holding presented the Court with the difficult task of determining how suspects' rights are affected when their *Miranda* rights are supplemented (or perhaps preempted) by the Sixth Amendment right to counsel.

The Court's application of the Sixth Amendment to overt interrogation raises several other issues. One, of course, is when in this context the Sixth Amendment attaches. Another is the extent to which the Sixth Amendment embodies a prohibition against reapproaching a suspect as is imposed by the Fifth Amendment right to counsel under Edwards v. Arizona, 451 U.S. 477, 101 S.Ct. 1880, 68 L.Ed.2d 378 (1981).

Attachment of the Sixth Amendment. In *Williams,* the Court noted some uncertainty as to when the progress of an investigation triggered the Sixth Amendment but stated it certainly provides its protection "at or after the time that judicial proceedings have been initiated against [a suspect]— 'whether by way of formal charge, preliminary hearing, information or arraignment.' Kirby v. Illinois, [406 U.S. 682, 689, 92 S.Ct. 1877, 1882, 32 L.Ed.2d 411 (1972)]." The Court's citation to *Kirby,* an eyewitness identification decision, indicated attachment of the Sixth Amendment to interrogations poses the same problem raised by application of the provision to lineups and similar law enforcement techniques; this is considered in Chapter 10.

In *Williams,* a magistrate had issued an arrest warrant for Williams. Police took him into custody on that warrant and presented before a judge. Williams was then "committed" to confinement in jail. Thus, the Court held, judicial proceedings had been initiated. In Edwards v. Arizona, 451 U.S. 477, 480 n. 7, 101 S.Ct. 1880, 1882–83 n. 7, 68 L.Ed.2d 378, 383 n. 7 (1981), however, the Court noted but did not reach the prosecution's contention that under Arizona state law adversary judicial proceedings did not begin until the filing of an indictment or information or perhaps at a preliminary hearing if one was held.

Michigan v. Jackson, 475 U.S. 625, 106 S.Ct. 1404, 89 L.Ed.2d 631 (1986), made clear that "arraignment" triggers the Sixth Amendment right. Police questioned Jackson after he was arrested and "arraigned." The State argued that judicial proceedings had not been initiated, but the Court responded, "In view of the clear language in our decisions about the significance of arraignment, the State's argument is untenable."

Unfortunately, *Jackson* did not make clear what the Court meant by the term "arraignment." Apparently, at least in the *Jackson* context, the term refers to the defendant's appearance required by Mich.Comp.Laws Anno. § 764.13:

> A peace officer who has arrested a person for an offense without a
> warrant shall without unnecessary delay take the person arrested

before a magistrate of the judicial district in which the offense is charged to have been committed, and shall present to the magistrate a complaint stating the charge against the person arrested.

The Michigan courts have referred to this appearance as an "arraignment." E.g., People v. White, 392 Mich. 404, 424, 221 N.W.2d 357, 366 (1974). In *Williams*, however, the Court quoted language from Powell v. Alabama, 287 U.S. 45, 47, 53 L.Ed. 55, 59, 77 L.Ed. 158 (1932), that used the word "arraignment" in a different sense. Under the Alabama procedure discussed in *Powell*, the arraignment was a postindictment appearance before the trial court at which a defendant entered a plea. This appearance or its equivalent continues to be formally designated the "arraignment" under the procedural law of many jurisdictions. E.g., Fed.R.Crim.P. 10 (arraignment "shall consist of reading the indictment or information to the defendant * * * and calling on him to plead thereto").

Nevertheless, *Jackson* appeared to indicate unequivocally that if police after arrest present a suspect before a magistrate for purposes of a judicial warning and perhaps the setting of bail, judicial proceedings are initiated and the Sixth Amendment attaches.

The Court has refused to move application of the provision to an earlier point. In Moran v. Burbine, 475 U.S. 412, 106 S.Ct. 1135, 89 L.Ed.2d 410 (1986) (reprinted in part in subsection B(4) of this chapter), the defendant argued that Sixth Amendment applied to his interrogation. He acknowledged that "adversary judicial proceedings" had not yet begun, but urged that in some situations at least the Sixth Amendment is triggered before that point. Specifically, he argued the importance of custodial interrogation is such that the Sixth Amendment creates a right to noninterference with an attorney's dealings with a client-suspect if the attorney-client relationship has been formed and custodial interrogation begins. The Supreme Court, however, rejected the proposition that an attorney-client relationship independently triggers the Sixth Amendment right to counsel:

> As a practical matter, it makes little sense to say that the Sixth Amendment right to counsel attaches at different times depending on the fortuity of whether the suspect or his family happened to have retained counsel prior to interrogation. More importantly, the suggestion that the existence of an attorney-client relationship itself triggers the protections of the Sixth Amendment misconceives the underlying purpose of the right to counsel. The Sixth Amendment's intended function is not to wrap a protective cloak around the attorney-client relationship for its own sake any more than it is to protect a suspect from the consequences of his own candor. Its purpose, rather, is to assure than in any "criminal prosecutio[n]," U.S. Const., Amdt. 6, the accused shall not be left to his own devices in facing the " 'prosecutorial forces of organized society.' " Maine v. Moulton, [474 U.S. 159, 169, 106 S.Ct. 477, 484, 88 L.Ed.2d 481 (1985)]. By its very terms, it becomes applicable only when the government's role shifts from investigation to accusation. * * * [L]ooking to the initiation of adversary judicial proceedings, far from being mere formalism, is fundamental to the proper application of the Sixth Amendment right to counsel. * * *

[U]ntil such time as the " 'government has committed itself to prosecute, and ... the adverse positions of the government and defendant have solidified' " the Sixth amendment right to counsel does not attach. [United States v. Gouveia, 467 U.S. 180, 189, 104 S.Ct. 2292, 2298, 81 L.Ed.2d 146 (1984)].

475 U.S. at 430–32, 106 S.Ct. at 1145–46, 89 L.Ed.2d at 427–28.

Application of Edwards *Rule.* In *Jackson,* the Court held the *Edwards* rule as developed in the *Miranda* context, see subsection B(3) of this chapter, also applied in Sixth Amendment situations. This prohibition against reapproach of a suspect who invokes the right to counsel applies somewhat differently where it arises because the suspect has invoked the Sixth Amendment right to counsel.

Police arrested the two defendants in *Jackson* and presented them before a magistrate for "arraignment." At this arraignment they requested that counsel be appointed for them. The records left unclear whether the magistrate first offered to appoint counsel and, if so, in what terms; those records also left uncertain the terms of the defendants' requests for counsel. Later, while the defendants were still in custody, they were approached by police officers, given *Miranda* warnings, and—apparently after agreeing to submit to questioning without counsels' presence—made incriminating statements. A majority of the Supreme Court agreed with the Michigan Supreme Court that the Sixth Amendment required the suppression of these statements. The arraignment caused the defendants' Sixth Amendment right to counsel to attach, so the issue was whether the officers reapproach violated a Sixth Amendment version of the *Edwards* rule. The Sixth Amendment right to counsel includes an *Edwards*-like prohibition against reapproach, because "the Sixth Amendment right to counsel at a postarraignment interrogation requires at least as much protection as does the Fifth Amendment right to counsel at any custodial interrogation." The State argued that the defendants did not trigger this bar to any approach by officers seeking to interrogate the defendants; the defendants could have intended their request for counsel to refer only to counsel for trial and other formal legal purposes and not for purposes of representation during further questioning. But the Court responded:

> [I]t is the State that has the burden of establishing a valid waiver. Doubts must be resolved in favor of protecting the constitutional claim. This settled approach to questions of waiver requires us to give a broad, rather than a narrow, interpretation to a defendant's request for counsel—we presume that the defendant requests the lawyer's services at every critical stage of the prosecution. We thus reject the State's suggestion * * *.

475 U.S. at 633, 106 S.Ct. at 1409, 89 L.Ed.2d at 640. In a footnote, the Court commented further:

> In construing respondents' request for counsel, we do not, of course, suggest that the right to counsel turns on such a request. Rather, we construe the defendant's request for counsel as an extremely important fact in considering the validity of a subsequent waiver in response to police-initiated interrogation.

475 U.S. at 633 n. 6, 106 S.Ct. at 1409 n. 6, 89 L.Ed.2d at 640 n. 6. The Court summarized its holding:

> We * * * hold that, if police initiate interrogation after a defendant's assertion, at an arraignment or similar proceeding, of his right to counsel, any waiver of the defendant's right to counsel for that police-initiated interrogation is invalid.

475 U.S. at 636, 106 S.Ct. at 1411, 89 L.Ed.2d at 642.

But the *Edwards* rule as applied in some Sixth Amendment situations has less impact than it has when applied in *Miranda* contexts. If a suspect invokes the right to counsel during police questioning to which *Miranda* applies, *Edwards* as construed in *Roberson* (discussed in subsection B(3) of this chapter) means that officers cannot reapproach the suspect until a lawyer is present even if the subject of their inquiries is a different offense. In McNeil v. Wisconsin, 501 U.S. 171, 111 S.Ct. 2204, 115 L.Ed.2d 158 (1991), the Supreme Court held that in the Sixth Amendment context *Edwards* was not so broad.

Police arrested McNeil for a West Allis, Wisconsin armed robbery and brought him before a court commissioner on that charge. McNeil was represented by a public defender at this appearance. The commissioner set bail and scheduled a preliminary examination. Subsequently, officers approached McNeil seeking to question him about a robbery-murder committed in Caledonia, Wisconsin. After the officers warned McNeil under *Miranda,* he waived his rights and made several statements admitting participation in the Caledonia crimes. The Supreme Court assumed the Sixth Amendment right to counsel attached by virtue of McNeil's court appearance. It also assumed by appearing with counsel McNeil invoked his Sixth Amendment right with regard to the West Allis robbery. But it rejected McNeil's claim that under *Edwards* and *Roberson* this meant that the officers were barred from reapproaching him concerning the Caledonia crimes.

The Sixth Amendment right to counsel, the *McNeil* majority explained, "is offense-specific." It does not attach until prosecution commences, and its *Edwards* effect is similarly "offense-specific." Thus a suspect's invocation of the Sixth Amendment right to counsel does not bar officers from reapproaching the suspect regarding offenses as to which he does not yet have a Sixth Amendment right to counsel. McNeil "provided the statements at issue here before his Sixth Amendment right to counsel with respect to the Caledonia offenses had been (or could have been) invoked." Therefore, the Sixth Amendment did not bar the use of those statements against him.

* * *

When the Sixth Amendment is triggered, what effect does it have upon the legal status of a suspect undergoing custodial interrogation, above and beyond what is dictated by *Miranda* and the Fifth Amendment? Justice Marshall has suggested waivers of the Sixth Amendment right to counsel should be subjected to greater scrutiny than waivers of *Miranda* rights. A waiver of the former, he urged, should require a greater comprehension of the consequences than a waiver of the latter. See Fields v. Wyrick, 464 U.S.

1020, 1022–23, 104 S.Ct. 556, 557, 78 L.Ed.2d 728, 729 (1983) (Marshall, J., dissenting from denial of certiorari). The following case, to some extent, confronts this general question.

Patterson v. Illinois

Supreme Court of the United States, 1988.
487 U.S. 285, 108 S.Ct. 2389, 101 L.Ed.2d 261.

■ JUSTICE WHITE delivered the opinion of the Court.

In this case, we are called on to determine whether the interrogation of petitioner after his indictment violated his Sixth Amendment right to counsel.

I

Before dawn on August 21, 1983, petitioner and other members of the "Vice Lords" street gang became involved in a fight with members of a rival gang, the "Black Mobsters." Some time after the fight, a former member of the Black Mobsters, James Jackson, went to the home where the Vice Lords had fled. A second fight broke out there, with petitioner and three other Vice Lords beating Jackson severely. The Vice Lords then put Jackson into a car, drove to the end of a nearby street, and left him face down in a puddle of water. Later that morning, police discovered Jackson, dead, where he had been left.

That afternoon, local police officers obtained warrants for the arrest of the Vice Lords, on charges of battery and mob action, in connection with the first fight. One of the gang members who was arrested gave the police a statement concerning the first fight; the statement also implicated several of the Vice Lords (including petitioner) in Jackson's murder. A few hours later, petitioner was apprehended. Petitioner was informed of his rights under Miranda v. Arizona, 384 U.S. 436, 86 S.Ct. 1602, 16 L.Ed.2d 694 (1966), and volunteered to answer questions put to him by the police. Petitioner gave a statement concerning the initial fight between the rival gangs, but denied knowing anything about Jackson's death. Petitioner was held in custody the following day, August 22, as law enforcement authorities completed their investigation of the Jackson murder.

On August 23, a Cook County grand jury indicted petitioner and two other gang members for the murder of James Jackson. Police officer Michael Gresham, who had questioned petitioner earlier, removed him from the lockup where he was being held, and told petitioner that because he had been indicted he was being transferred to the Cook County jail. Petitioner asked Gresham which of the gang members had been charged with Jackson's murder, and upon learning that one particular Vice Lord had been omitted from the indictments, asked: "[W]hy wasn't he indicted, he did everything." Petitioner also began to explain that there was a witness who would support his account of the crime.

At this point, Gresham interrupted petitioner, and handed him a *Miranda* waiver form. The form contained five specific warnings, as suggested by this Court's *Miranda* decision, to make petitioner aware of his right to counsel and of the consequences of any statement he might make to police. Gresham read the warnings aloud, as petitioner read along with him. Petitioner initialed each of the five warnings, and signed the waiver form. Petitioner then gave a lengthy statement to police officers concerning the Jackson murder; petitioner's statement described in detail the role of each of the Vice Lords—including himself—in the murder of James Jackson.

Later that day, petitioner confessed involvement in the murder for a second time. This confession came in an interview with Assistant State's Attorney (ASA) George Smith. At the outset of the interview, Smith reviewed with petitioner the *Miranda* waiver he had previously signed, and petitioner confirmed that he had signed the waiver and understood his rights. Smith went through the waiver procedure once again: reading petitioner his rights, having petitioner initial each one, and sign a waiver form. In addition, Smith informed petitioner that he was a lawyer working with the police investigating the Jackson case. Petitioner then gave another inculpatory statement concerning the crime.

Before trial, petitioner moved to suppress his statements, arguing that they were obtained in a manner at odds with various constitutional guarantees. The trial court denied these motions, and the statements were used against petitioner at his trial. The jury found petitioner guilty of murder, and petitioner was sentenced to a 24–year prison term.

On appeal, petitioner argued that he had not "knowingly and intelligently" waived his Sixth Amendment right to counsel before he gave his uncounseled postindictment confessions. Petitioner contended that the warnings he received, while adequate for the purposes of protecting his *Fifth* Amendment rights as guaranteed by *Miranda,* did not adequately inform him of his *Sixth* Amendment right to counsel. The Illinois Supreme Court, however, rejected, this theory * * *.

II

There can be no doubt that petitioner had the right to have the assistance of counsel at his postindictment interviews with law enforcement authorities. Our cases make it plain that the Sixth Amendment guarantees this right to criminal defendants. Michigan v. Jackson, 475 U.S. 625, 629–630, 106 S.Ct. 1404, 1407–1408, 89 L.Ed.2d 631 (1986); Brewer v. Williams, 430 U.S. 387, 398–401, 97 S.Ct. 1232, 1239–1241, 51 L.Ed.2d 424 (1977); Massiah v. United States, 377 U.S. 201, 205–207, 84 S.Ct. 1199, 1202–1204, 12 L.Ed.2d 246 (1964).[10] Petitioner asserts that the questioning that produced his incriminating statements violated his Sixth Amendment right to counsel in two ways.

---

10. We note as a matter of some significance that petitioner had not retained, or accepted by appointment, a lawyer to represent him at the time he was questioned by authorities. Once an accused has a lawyer, a distinct set of constitutional safeguards aimed at preserving the sanctity of the attorney-client relationship takes effect. See Maine v. Moulton, 474 U.S. 159, 176, 106 S.Ct. 477, 487–88, 88 L.Ed.2d 481 (1985). The State conceded as much at argument.

A

Petitioner's first claim is that because his Sixth Amendment right to counsel arose with his indictment, the police were thereafter barred from initiating a meeting with him. He equates himself with a preindictment suspect who, while being interrogated, asserts his Fifth Amendment right to counsel; under Edwards v. Arizona, 451 U.S. 477, 101 S.Ct. 1880, 68 L.Ed.2d 378 (1981), such a suspect may not be questioned again unless he initiates the meeting.

* * *

At bottom, petitioner's theory cannot be squared with our rationale in *Edwards,* the case he relies on for support. * * * Preserving the integrity of an accused's choice to communicate with police only through counsel is the essence of *Edwards* and its progeny—not barring an accused from making an *initial* election as to whether he will face the State's officers during questioning with the aid of counsel, or go it alone. If an accused "knowingly and intelligently" pursues the latter course, we see no reason why the uncounseled statements he then makes must be excluded at his trial.

B

Petitioner's principal and more substantial claim is that questioning him without counsel present violated the Sixth Amendment because he did not validly waive his right to have counsel present during the interviews. Since it is clear that after the *Miranda* warnings were given to petitioner, he not only voluntarily answered questions without claiming his right to silence or his right to have a lawyer present to advise him but also executed a written waiver of his right to counsel during questioning, the specific issue posed here is whether this waiver was a "knowing and intelligent" waiver of his Sixth Amendment right.[11] See *Brewer v. Williams,* S.Ct. at 1240–41, 1242; Johnson v. Zerbst, 304 U.S. 458, 464–465, 58 S.Ct. 1019, 1023, 82 L.Ed.2d 1461 (1938).

In the past, this Court has held that a waiver of the Sixth Amendment right to counsel is valid only when it reflects "an intentional relinquishment or abandonment of a known right or privilege." *Johnson v. Zerbst,* supra, at 464, 58 S.Ct. at 1023. In other words, the accused must "kno[w] what he is doing" so that "his choice is made with eyes open." Adams v. United States ex rel. McCann, 317 U.S. 269, 279, 63 S.Ct. 236, 242, 87 L.Ed.2d 268 (1942). In a case arising under the Fifth Amendment, we described this requirement as "a full awareness [of] both the nature of the right being abandoned and the consequences of the decision to abandon it." Moran v. Burbine, 475 U.S. 412, 421, 106 S.Ct. 1135, 1141, 89 L.Ed.2d 410 (1986). Whichever of these formulations is used, the key inquiry in a case such as this one must be: Was the accused, who waived his Sixth Amendment rights during postindictment questioning, made sufficiently aware of his right to have counsel present during the questioning, and of the possible consequences of a decision to forgo the aid of counsel? In this case, we are convinced that by admonishing petitioner with the *Miranda* warn-

---

11. * * * [T]he voluntariness of petitioner's confession is not before us.

ings, respondent has met this burden and that petitioner's waiver of his right to counsel at the questioning was valid.

First, the *Miranda* warnings given petitioner made him aware of his right to have counsel present during the questioning. By telling petitioner that he had a right to consult with an attorney, to have a lawyer present while he was questioned, and even to have a lawyer appointed for him if he could not afford to retain one on his own, Officer Gresham and ASA Smith conveyed to petitioner the sum and substance of the rights that the Sixth Amendment provided him. * * * There is little more petitioner could have possibly been told in an effort to satisfy this portion of the waiver inquiry.

Second, the *Miranda* warnings also served to make petitioner aware of the consequences of a decision by him to waive his Sixth Amendment rights during postindictment questioning. Petitioner knew that any statement that he made could be used against him in subsequent criminal proceedings. This is the ultimate adverse consequence petitioner could have suffered by virtue of his choice to make uncounseled admissions to the authorities. This warning also sufficed—contrary to petitioner's claim here—to let him know what a lawyer could "do for him" during the postindictment questioning: namely, advise petitioner to refrain from making any such statements. By knowing what could be done with any statements he might make, and therefore, what benefit could be obtained by having the aid of counsel while making such statements, petitioner was essentially informed of the possible consequences of going without counsel during questioning. If petitioner nonetheless lacked "a full and complete appreciation of all of the consequences flowing" from his waiver, it does not defeat the State's showing that the information it provided to him satisfied the constitutional minimum.

Our conclusion is supported by petitioner's inability, in the proceedings before this Court, to articulate with precision what additional information should have been provided to him before he would have been competent to waive his right to counsel. All that petitioner's brief and reply brief suggest is petitioner should have been made aware of his "right under the Sixth Amendment to the broad protection of counsel"—a rather nebulous suggestion—and the "gravity of [his] situation." But surely this latter "requirement" (if it is one) was met when Officer Gresham informed petitioner that he had been formally charged with the murder of James Jackson. Under close questioning on this same point at argument, petitioner likewise failed to suggest any meaningful additional information that he should have been, but was not, provided in advance of his decision to waive his right to counsel. * * *

As a general matter, then, an accused who is admonished with the warnings prescribed by this Court in *Miranda,* has been sufficiently apprised of the nature of his Sixth Amendment rights, and of the consequences of abandoning those rights, so that his waiver on this basis will be considered a knowing and intelligent one.[12]

---

12. This does not mean, of course, that all Sixth Amendment challenges to the conduct of postindictment questioning will fail whenever the challenged practice would pass constitutional muster under *Miranda.* For example, we have permitted a *Miranda* waiv-

C

We consequently reject petitioner's argument, which has some acceptance from courts and commentators, that since "the sixth amendment right [to counsel] is far superior to that of the fifth amendment right" and since "[t]he greater the right the greater the loss from a waiver of that right," waiver of an accused's Sixth Amendment right to counsel should be "more difficult" to effectuate than waiver of a suspect's Fifth Amendment rights. While our cases have recognized a "difference" between the Fifth Amendment and Sixth Amendment rights to counsel, and the "policies" behind these Constitutional guarantees, we have never suggested that one right is "superior" or "greater" than the other, nor is there any support in our cases for the notion that because a Sixth Amendment right may be involved, it is more difficult to waive than the Fifth Amendment counterpart.

Instead, we have taken a more pragmatic approach to the waiver question—asking what purposes a lawyer can serve at the particular stage of the proceedings in question, and what assistance he could provide to an accused at that stage—to determine the scope of the Sixth Amendment right to counsel, and the type of warnings and procedures that should be required before a waiver of that right will be recognized.

At one end of the spectrum, we have concluded there is no Sixth Amendment right to counsel whatsoever at a postindictment photographic display identification, because this procedure is not one at which the accused "require[s] aid in coping with legal problems or assistance in meeting his adversary." At the other extreme, recognizing the enormous importance and role that an attorney plays at a criminal trial, we have imposed the most rigorous restrictions on the information that must be conveyed to a defendant, and the procedures that must be observed, before permitting him to waive his right to counsel at trial. In these extreme cases, and in others that fall between these two poles, we have defined the scope of the right to counsel by a pragmatic assessment of the usefulness of counsel to the accused at the particular proceeding, and the dangers to the accused of proceeding without counsel. An accused's waiver of his right to counsel is "knowing" when he is made aware of these basic facts.

Applying this approach, it is our view that whatever warnings suffice for *Miranda's* purposes will also be sufficient in the context of postindictment questioning. The State's decision to take an additional step and commence formal adversarial proceedings against the accused does not

---

er to stand where a suspect was not told that his lawyer was trying to reach him during questioning; in the Sixth Amendment context, this waiver would not be valid. See Moran v. Burbine, 475 U.S., at 424, 428, 106 S.Ct. at 1142–43, 1145. Likewise a surreptitious conversion between an undercover police officer and an indicted suspect would not give rise to any *Miranda* violation as long as the "interrogation" was not in a custodial setting; however, once the accused is indicted, such questioning would be prohibited.

Thus, because the Sixth Amendment's protection of the attorney-client relationship—"the right to rely on counsel as a 'medium' between [the accused] and the State"—extends beyond *Miranda's* protection of the Fifth Amendment right to counsel, there will be cases where a waiver which would be valid under *Miranda* will not suffice for Sixth Amendment purposes.

substantially increase the value of counsel to the accused at questioning, or expand the limited purpose that an attorney serves when the accused is questioned by authorities. With respect to this inquiry, we do not discern a substantial difference between the usefulness of a lawyer to a suspect during custodial interrogation, and his value to an accused at postindictment questioning.

Thus, we require a more searching or formal inquiry before permitting an accused to waive his right to counsel at trial than we require for a Sixth Amendment waiver during postindictment questioning—*not* because postindictment questioning is "less important" than a trial (the analysis that petitioner's "hierarchical" approach would suggest)—but because the full "dangers and disadvantages of self-representation," during questioning are less substantial and more obvious to an accused than they are at trial. Because the role of counsel at questioning is relatively simple and limited, we see no problem in having a waiver procedure at that stage which is likewise simple and limited. So long as the accused is made aware of the "dangers and disadvantages of self-representation" during postindictment questioning, by use of the *Miranda* warnings, his waiver of his Sixth Amendment right to counsel at such questioning is "knowing and intelligent."

III

Before confessing to the murder of James Jackson, petitioner was meticulously informed by authorities of his right to counsel, and of the consequences of any choice not to exercise that right. On two separate occasions, petitioner elected to forgo the assistance of counsel, and speak directly to officials concerning his role in the murder. Because we believe that petitioner's waiver of his Sixth Amendment rights was "knowing and intelligent," we find no error in the decision of the trial court to permit petitioner's confessions to be used against him. Consequently, the judgment of the Illinois Supreme Court is

Affirmed.

■ JUSTICE BLACKMUN, dissenting.

I agree with most of what Justice Stevens says in his dissenting opinion. I, however, merely would hold that after formal adversary proceedings against a defendant have been commenced, the Sixth Amendment mandates that the defendant not be " 'subject to further interrogation by the authorities until counsel has been made available to him, unless the accused himself initiates further communication, exchanges, or conversations with the police.' " Michigan v. Jackson, 475 U.S. 625, 626, 106 S.Ct. 1404, 1406, 89 L.Ed.2d 631 (1986), quoting Edwards v. Arizona, 451 U.S. 477, 484–485, 101 S.Ct. 1880, 1884–1885, 68 L.Ed.2d 378 (1981).

* * *

■ JUSTICE STEVENS, with whom JUSTICE BRENNAN and JUSTICE MARSHALL join, dissenting.

The Court should not condone unethical forms of trial preparation by prosecutors or their investigators. In civil litigation it is improper for a lawyer to communicate with his or her adversary's client without either notice to opposing counsel or the permission of the court. An attempt to obtain evidence for use at trial by going behind the back of one's adversary would be not only a serious breach of professional ethics but also a manifestly unfair form of trial practice. In the criminal context, the same ethical rules apply and, in my opinion, notions of fairness that are at least as demanding should also be enforced.

* * *

The question that this case raises * * * is at what point in the adversary process does it become impermissible for the prosecutor, or his or her agents, to conduct such private interviews with the opposing party? Several alternatives are conceivable: when the trial commences, when the defendant has actually met and accepted representation by his or her appointed counsel, when counsel is appointed, or when the adversary process commences. In my opinion, the Sixth Amendment right to counsel demands that a firm and unequivocal line be drawn at the point at which adversary proceedings commence.

* * *

Today, however * * * the Court backs away from the significance previously attributed to the initiation of formal proceedings. In the majority's view, the purported waiver of counsel in this case is properly equated with that of an unindicted suspect. Yet, * * * important differences separate the two. The return of an indictment, or like instrument, substantially alters the relationship between the state and the accused. Only after a formal accusation has "the government * * * committed itself to prosecute, and only then [have] the adverse positions of government and defendant * * * solidified." Moreover, the return of an indictment also presumably signals the government's conclusion that it has sufficient evidence to establish a prima facie case. As a result, any further interrogation can only be designed to buttress the government's case; authorities are no longer simply attempting " 'to solve a crime.' " Given the significance of the initiation of formal proceedings and the concomitant shift in the relationship between the state and the accused, I think it quite wrong to suggest that *Miranda* warnings—or for that matter, any warnings offered by an adverse party—provide a sufficient basis for permitting the undoubtedly prejudicial—and, in my view, unfair—practice of permitting trained law enforcement personnel and prosecuting attorneys to communicate with as-of-yet unrepresented criminal defendants.

It is well settled that there is a strong presumption against waiver of Sixth Amendment protections. Warnings offered by an opposing party, whether detailed or cursory, simply cannot satisfy this high standard.

The majority premises its conclusion that *Miranda* warnings lay a sufficient basis for accepting a waiver of the right to counsel on the assumption that those warnings make clear to an accused "what a lawyer could 'do for him' during the postindictment questioning: namely, advise [him] to refrain from making any [incriminating] statements." Yet, this is surely a gross understatement of the disadvantage of proceeding without a lawyer and an understatement of what a defendant must understand to make a knowing waiver. The *Miranda* warnings do not, for example, inform the accused that a lawyer might examine the indictment for legal sufficiency before submitting his or her client to interrogation or that a lawyer is likely to be considerably more skillful at negotiating a plea bargain and that such negotiations may be most fruitful if initiated prior to any interrogation. Rather, the warnings do not even go so far as to explain to the accused the nature of the charges pending against him—advice that a court would insist upon before allowing a defendant to enter a guilty plea with or without the presence of an attorney. Without defining precisely the nature of the inquiry required to establish a valid waiver of the Sixth Amendment right to counsel, it must be conceded that at least minimal advice is necessary—the accused must be told of the "dangers and disadvantages of self-representation."

Yet, once it is conceded that certain advice is required and that after indictment the adversary relationship between the state and the accused has solidified, it inescapably follows that a prosecutor may not conduct private interviews with a charged defendant. * * * [T]here are ethical constraints that prevent a prosecutor from giving legal advice to an uncounseled adversary. Thus, neither the prosecutor nor his or her agents can ethically provide the unrepresented defendant with the kind of advice that should precede an evidence-gathering interview after formal proceedings have been commenced. Indeed, in my opinion even the *Miranda* warnings themselves are a species of legal advice that is improper when given by the prosecutor after indictment.

Moreover, there are good reasons why such advice is deemed unethical, reasons that extend to the custodial, postindictment setting with unequaled strength. First, the offering of legal advice may lead an accused to underestimate the prosecuting authorities' true adversary posture. For an incarcerated defendant—in this case, a 17–year–old who had been in custody for 44 hours at the time he was told of the indictment—the assistance of someone to explain why he is being held, the nature of the charges against him, and the extent of his legal rights, may be of such importance as to overcome what is perhaps obvious to most, that the prosecutor is a foe and not a friend. Second, the adversary posture of the parties, which is not fully solidified until formal charges are brought, will inevitably tend to color the advice offered. As hard as a prosecutor might try, I doubt that it is possible for one to wear the hat of an effective advisor to a criminal defendant while at the same time wearing the hat of a law enforcement authority. Finally, regardless of whether or not the accused actually understands the legal and factual issues involved and the state's role as an adversary party, advice offered by a lawyer (or his or her agents) with such an evident conflict of interest cannot help but create a public perception of unfairness and unethical conduct. And as we held earlier this Term, "courts have an independent interest in ensuring that criminal trials are conducted within the ethical standards of the profession and that legal proceedings appear fair to all who observe them." Wheat v. United States, 486 U.S. 153, 160, 108 S.Ct. 1692, 1697, 100 L.Ed.2d 140 (1988). This interest is a factor that may be considered in deciding whether to override a defendant's waiver of his or her Sixth Amendment right to conflict free representation, and likewise, should be considered in determining whether a waiver based on advice offered by the criminal defendant's adversary is ever appropriate.

In sum, without a careful discussion of the pitfalls of proceeding without counsel, the Sixth Amendment right cannot properly be waived. An adversary party, moreover, cannot adequately provide such advice. As a result, once the right to counsel attaches and the adversary relationship between the state and the accused solidifies, a prosecutor cannot conduct a private interview with an accused party without "dilut[ing] the protection afforded by the right to counsel." Although this ground alone is reason enough to never permit such private interviews, the rule also presents the added virtue of drawing a clear and easily identifiable line at the point between the investigatory and adversary stages of a criminal proceeding. Such clarity in definition of constitutional rules that govern criminal proceedings is important to the law enforcement profession as well as to the private citizen. It is true, of course, that the interest in effective law enforcement would benefit from an opportunity to engage in incommunicado questioning of defendants who, for reasons beyond their control, have not been able to receive the legal advice from counsel to which they are constitutionally entitled. But the Court's singleminded concentration on that interest might also lead to the toleration of similar practices at any stage of the trial. I think it clear that such private communications are intolerable not simply during trial, but at any point after adversary proceedings have commenced.

I therefore respectfully dissent.

NOTE

In a footnote, *Patterson* cited Moran v. Burbine, 475 U.S. 412, 428, 106 S.Ct. 1135, 1144, 89 L.Ed.2d 410, 425 (1986) (reprinted in subsection B(4) of this chapter), in which the Court "readily agreed" that once the Sixth Amendment right to counsel attached, "it follows that the police may not interfere with the efforts of a defendant's attorney to act as a 'medium' between [the suspect] and the State' during the interrogation." Burbine's waiver, apparently, would not have been effective if the events had occurred after his Sixth Amendment right to counsel had attached. Why?

CHAPTER 8

UNDERCOVER INVESTIGATIONS

Analysis

EDITORS' INTRODUCTION: UNDERCOVER LAW ENFORCEMENT ACTIVITIES AND SPECIAL CONCERN

Police undercover investigations present a sufficiently unique situation to deserve separate consideration. Such investigations pose unusually difficult problems for legal control of law enforcement conduct. Since undercover activities inherently involve deception, officers' actions may infringe upon subjects' interest in privacy more than do other types of law enforcement investigatory conduct. In addition, however, undercover investigations necessarily involve low visibility decisionmaking. Consequently, decisions whether to conduct such investigations or to use particular investigatory techniques in particular investigations are comparatively less open to scrutiny, evaluation, and control.

Many analyses of undercover investigations—both legal discussions and others—fail to carefully identify the underlying concerns. The risk that undercover investigations will stimulate criminal acts which would not otherwise be committed is, of course, among the considerations. In addition, such investigations may unjustifiably infringe upon subjects' interest in privacy. Deception—or other activities always or sometimes involved in undercover work—may bring a law enforcement agency into public disrepute because some regard these tactics as inherently "wrong" when employed by government agencies. These concerns might be further refined— what the subjects' interest in "privacy" is, for example, obviously could be more carefully developed. Too often, however, discussions fail to make any effort whatsoever to define and evaluate the real underlying concerns.

Perhaps because of this failure to identify and discuss the underlying considerations, the legal situation of undercover investigations and specific techniques used in such investigations is confused. Many doctrines relate to undercover police work but judicial opinions and other discussions often suggest available legal tools are inadequate to deal with problems presented by some undercover police activity. This chapter is divided into sections each focusing upon a doctrine affecting undercover investigations. First, the traditional law of entrapment is presented. Next explored is the Sixth Amendment right to counsel and its effect upon the elicitation and overhearing by undercover personnel of self-incriminating admissions made by defendants. Finally, the third section addresses the application of the Fourth Amendment's right to be free from unreasonable searches and seizures in this context.

Two categories of undercover law enforcement activities are usefully distinguished. The first involves surveillance by an undercover investigator. Surveillance may be visual observation or involve overhearing communications. It may lead to the officer gaining possession of physical evidence, as where the subject of the surveillance, unaware of the agent's official status, entrusts items to the agent.

Surveillance must be contrasted with the other category of investigation, consisting of the undercover investigator actively stimulating the subject of the investigation to commit an offense at a time and place which make it feasible or easier for law enforcement officers to obtain proof of commission of the offense. L. Tiffany, D. McIntyre and D. Rotenberg, Detection of Crime 273 (1967) and Rotenberg, The Police Detection Practice of Encouragement: Lewis v. United States and Beyond, 4 Hous.L.Rev. 609 (1967), used the phrase "encouragement" to describe this tactic. Dix, Undercover Investigations and Police Rulemaking, 53 Texas L.Rev. 203, 215 (1975), preferred the phrase, "an offer * * * of the opportunity to commit an offense under controlled conditions." Whatever the practice is called, however, it raises considerations different than—or perhaps additional to—those triggered by surveillance. Tactics within both categories involve deception and therefore some possible invasion of the subject's expectation of privacy. The manipulation of the subject involved in encouragement, however, arguably constitutes a significantly greater invasion of that interest. In addition, encouragement creates a greater danger of stimulating the commission of offenses that would not otherwise be committed and of involving police agents in the commission of criminal acts.

A.   ENTRAPMENT

Traditional law has responded to concerns regarding undercover investigations with the doctrine of entrapment. There is, however, some reason to doubt whether entrapment provides an effective incentive for law enforcement to avoid misuse of undercover investigations.

Much dispute regarding entrapment law revolves around whether the controlling standard should be the "subjective" or the "objective" one. The Supreme Court's case law defining the entrapment defense under federal criminal law is a leading model supporting the subjective approach, and in the principal case following the Court adheres to its traditional subjective approach.

United States v. Russell

Supreme Court of the United States, 1973.
411 U.S. 423, 93 S.Ct. 1637, 36 L.Ed.2d 366.

■ MR. JUSTICE REHNQUIST delivered the opinion of the Court.

Respondent Richard Russell was charged in three counts of a five count indictment returned against him and codefendants John and Patrick Connolly. After a jury trial in the District Court, in which his sole defense was entrapment, respondent was convicted on all three counts of having unlawfully manufactured and processed methamphetamine ("speed") and of having unlawfully sold and delivered that drug * * *. He was sentenced to concurrent terms of two years in prison for each offense, the terms to be suspended on the condition that he spend six months in prison and be placed on probation for the following three years. On appeal the United States Court of Appeals for the Ninth Circuit, one judge dissenting, reversed the conviction solely for the reason that an undercover agent supplied an essential chemical for manufacturing the methamphetamine which formed the basis of respondent's conviction. The court concluded that as a matter of law "a defense to a criminal charge may be founded upon an intolerable degree of governmental participation in the criminal enterprise." We granted certiorari, and now reverse that judgment.

There is little dispute concerning the essential facts in this case. On December 7, 1969, Joe Shapiro, an undercover agent for the Federal Bureau of Narcotics and Dangerous Drugs, went to respondent's home on Whidbey Island in the State of Washington where he met with respondent and his two codefendants, John and Patrick Connolly. Shapiro's assignment was to locate a laboratory where it was believed that methamphetamine was being manufactured illicitly. He told the respondent and the Connollys that he represented an organization in the Pacific Northwest that was interested in controlling the manufacture and distribution of methamphetamine. He then made an offer to supply the defendants with the chemical phenyl–2–propanone, an essential ingredient in the manufacture of methamphetamine, in return for one-half of the drug produced. This offer was made on the condition that Agent Shapiro be shown a sample of the drug which they were making and the laboratory where it was being produced.

During the conversation Patrick Connolly revealed that he had been making the drug since May 1969 and since then had produced three pounds of it. John Connolly gave the agent a bag containing a quantity of methamphetamine that he represented as being from "the last batch that we made." Shortly thereafter, Shapiro and Patrick Connolly left respondent's house to view the laboratory which was located in the Connolly house on Whidbey Island. At the house Shapiro observed an empty bottle bearing the chemical label phenyl-2-propanone.

By prearrangement Shapiro returned to the Connolly house on December 9, 1969, to supply 100 grams of propanone and observe the chemical reaction. When he arrived he observed Patrick Connolly and the respondent cutting up pieces of aluminum foil and placing them in a large flask. There was testimony that some of the foil pieces accidentally fell on the floor and were picked up by the respondent and Shapiro and put into the flask.[1] Thereafter Patrick Connolly added all of the necessary chemicals, including the propanone brought by Shapiro, to make two batches of methamphetamine. The manufacturing process having been completed the following morning, Shapiro was given one-half of the drug and respondent kept the remainder. Shapiro offered to buy, and the respondent agreed to sell, part of the remainder for $60.

About a month later Shapiro returned to the Connolly house and met with Patrick Connolly to ask if he was still interested in their "business arrangement." Connolly replied that he was interested but that he had recently obtained two additional bottles of phenyl-2-propanone and would not be finished with them for a couple of days. He provided some additional methamphetamine to Shapiro at that time. Three days later Shapiro returned to the Connolly house with a search warrant and, among other items, seized an empty 500-gram bottle of propanone and a 100-gram bottle, not the one he had provided, that was partially filled with the chemical.

There was testimony at the trial of respondent and Patrick Connolly that phenyl-2-propanone was generally difficult to obtain. At the request of the Bureau of Narcotics and Dangerous Drugs, some chemical supply firms had voluntarily ceased selling the chemical.

At the close of the evidence, and after receiving the District Judge's standard entrapment instruction,[2] the jury found the respondent guilty on all counts charged. On appeal the respondent conceded that the jury could have found him predisposed to commit the offenses, but argued that on the facts presented there was entrapment as a matter of law. The Court of Appeals agreed, although it did not find the District Court had misconstrued or misapplied the traditional standards governing the entrapment defense. Rather, the court in effect expanded the traditional notion of entrapment, which focuses on the predisposition of the defendant, to mandate dismissal of a criminal prosecution whenever the court determines that there has been "an intolerable degree of governmental participation in the criminal enterprise." In this case the court decided that the conduct of the agent in supplying a scarce ingredient essential for the manufacture of a controlled substance established that defense.

---

1. Agent Shapiro did not otherwise participate in the manufacture of the drug or direct any of the work.

2. The District Judge stated the governing law on entrapment as follows: "Where a person has the willingness and the readiness to break the law, the mere fact that the government agent provides what appears to be a favorable opportunity is not entrapment." He then instructed the jury to acquit respondent if it had a "reasonable doubt whether the defendant had the previous intent or purpose to commit the offense * * * and did so only because he was induced or persuaded by some officer or agent of the government." No exception was taken by respondent to this instruction.

This new defense was held to rest on either of two alternative theories. One theory is based on * * * lower court decisions which have found entrapment, regardless of predisposition, whenever the government supplies contraband to the defendants. The second theory, a nonentrapment rationale, is based on a recent Ninth Circuit decision that reversed a conviction because a government investigator was so enmeshed in the criminal activity that the prosecution of the defendants was held to be repugnant to the American criminal justice system. Greene v. United States, 454 F.2d 783 (C.A.9 1971). The court below held that these two rationales constitute the same defense and that only the label distinguishes them. In any event, it held that "[b]oth theories are premised on fundamental concepts of due process and evince the reluctance of the judiciary to countenance 'overzealous law enforcement.' "

This Court first recognized and applied the entrapment defense in Sorrells v. United States, 287 U.S. 435, 53 S.Ct. 210, 77 L.Ed. 413 (1932). In *Sorrells*, a federal prohibition agent visited the defendant while posing as a tourist and engaged him in conversation about their common war experiences. After gaining the defendant's confidence the agent asked for some liquor, was twice refused, but upon asking a third time the defendant finally capitulated, and was subsequently prosecuted for violating the National Prohibition Act.

Chief Justice Hughes, speaking for the Court, held that as a matter of statutory construction the defense of entrapment should have been available to the defendant. Under the theory propounded by the Chief Justice, the entrapment defense prohibits law enforcement officers from instigating criminal acts by persons "otherwise innocent in order to lure them to its commission and to punish them." Thus, the thrust of the entrapment defense was held to focus on the intent or predisposition of the defendant to commit the crime. "[I]f the defendant seeks acquittal by reason of entrapment he cannot complain of an appropriate and searching inquiry into his own conduct and predisposition as bearing upon that issue."

Justice Roberts concurred in the result but was of the view "that courts must be closed to the trial of a crime instigated by the government's own agents." The difference in the view of the majority and the concurring opinions is that in the former the inquiry focuses on the predisposition of the defendant, whereas in the latter the inquiry focuses on whether the government "instigated the crime."

In 1958 the Court again considered the theory underlying the entrapment defense and expressly reaffirmed the view expressed by the *Sorrells* majority. Sherman v. United States, 356 U.S. 369, 78 S.Ct. 819, 2 L.Ed.2d 848 (1958). In *Sherman* the defendant was convicted of selling narcotics to a government informer. As in *Sorrells* it appears that the government agent gained the confidence of the defendant and, despite initial reluctance, the defendant finally acceded to the repeated importunings of the agent to commit the criminal act. On the basis of *Sorrells*, this Court reversed the affirmance of the defendant's conviction.

In affirming the theory underlying *Sorrells*, Chief Justice Warren for the Court, held that "[t]o determine whether entrapment has been established, a line must be drawn between the trap for the unwary innocent and the trap for the unwary criminal." Justice Frankfurter stated in a concurring opinion that he believed Justice Roberts had the better view in *Sorrells* and would have framed the question to be asked in an entrapment defense in terms of "whether the police conduct revealed in the particular case falls below standards * * * for the proper use of governmental power."

In the instant case respondent asks us to reconsider the theory of the entrapment defense as it is set forth in the majority opinions in *Sorrells* and *Sherman*. His principal contention is that the defense should rest on constitutional grounds. He argues that the level of Shapiro's involvement in the manufacture of the methamphetamine was so high that a criminal prosecution for the drug's manufacture violates the fundamental principles of due process. The respondent contends that the same factors that led this Court to apply the exclusionary rule to illegal searches and seizures, and confessions should be considered here. But he would have the Court go further in deterring undesirable official conduct by requiring that any prosecution be barred absolutely because of the police involvement in criminal activity. The analogy is imperfect in any event, for the principal reason behind the adoption of the exclusionary rule was the government's "failure to observe its own laws." * * * [T]he government's conduct here violated no independent constitutional right of the respondent. Nor did Shapiro violate any federal statute or rule or commit any crime in infiltrating the respondent's drug enterprise.

Respondent would overcome this basic weakness in his analogy to the exclusionary rule cases by having the Court adopt a rigid constitutional rule that would preclude any prosecution when it is shown that the criminal conduct would not have been possible had not an undercover agent "supplied an indispensable means to the commission of the crime that could not have been obtained otherwise, through legal or illegal channels." Even if we were to surmount the difficulties attending the notion that due process of law can be embodied in fixed rules, and those attending respondent's particular formulation, the rule he proposes would not appear to be of significant benefit to him. For on the record presented it appears that he cannot fit within the terms of the very rule he proposes.

The record discloses that although the propanone was difficult to obtain it was by no means impossible. The defendants admitted making the drug both before and after those batches made with the propanone supplied by Shapiro. Shapiro testified that he saw an empty bottle labeled phenyl-2-propanone on his first visit to the laboratory on December 7, 1969. And when the laboratory was searched pursuant to a search warrant on January 10, 1970, two additional bottles labeled phenyl-2-propanone were seized. Thus, the facts in the record amply demonstrate that the propanone used in the illicit manufacture of methamphetamine not only *could* have been obtained without the intervention of Shapiro but was in fact obtained by these defendants.

While we may some day be presented with a situation in which the conduct of law enforcement agents is so outrageous that due process principles would absolutely bar the government from invoking judicial processes to obtain a conviction, cf. Rochin v. California, 342 U.S. 165, 72

S.Ct. 205, 96 L.Ed. 183 (1952), the instant case is distinctly not of that breed. Shapiro's contribution of propanone to the criminal enterprise already in process was scarcely objectionable. The chemical is by itself a harmless substance and its possession is legal. While the government may have been seeking to make it more difficult for drug rings, such as that of which respondent was a member, to obtain the chemical, the evidence described above shows that it nonetheless was obtainable. The law enforcement conduct here stops far short of violating that "fundamental fairness, shocking to the universal sense of justice," mandated by the Due Process Clause of the Fifth Amendment.

The illicit manufacture of drugs is not a sporadic, isolated criminal incident, but a continuing, though illegal, business enterprise. In order to obtain convictions for illegally manufacturing drugs, the gathering of evidence of past unlawful conduct frequently proves to be an all but impossible task. Thus in drug-related offenses law enforcement personnel have turned to one of the only practicable means of detection: the infiltration of drug rings and a limited participation in their unlawful present practices. Such infiltration is a recognized and permissible means of apprehension; if that be so, then the supply of some item of value that the drug ring requires must, as a general rule, also be permissible. For an agent will not be taken into the confidence of the illegal entrepreneurs unless he has something of value to offer them. Law enforcement tactics such as this can hardly be said to violate "fundamental fairness" or "shocking to the universal sense of justice."

Respondent also urges, as an alternative to his constitutional argument, that we broaden the nonconstitutional defense of entrapment in order to sustain the judgment of the Court of Appeals. This Court's opinions in Sorrells v. United States, supra, and Sherman v. United States, supra, held that the principal element in the defense of entrapment was the defendant's predisposition to commit the crime. Respondent conceded in the Court of Appeals, as well he might, "that he may have harbored a predisposition to commit the charged offenses." Yet he argues that the jury's refusal to find entrapment under the charge submitted to it by the trial court should be overturned and the views of Justices Roberts and Frankfurter, concurring in *Sorrells* and *Sherman,* respectively, which make the essential element of the defense turn on the type and degree of governmental conduct, be adopted as the law.

We decline to overrule these cases. *Sorrells* is a precedent of long standing that has already been once reexamined in *Sherman* and implicitly there reaffirmed. Since the defense is not of a constitutional dimension, Congress may address itself to the question and adopt any substantive definition of the defense that it may find desirable.

Critics of the rule laid down in *Sorrells* and *Sherman* have suggested that its basis in the implied intent of Congress is largely fictitious, and have pointed to what they conceive to be the anomalous difference between the treatment of a defendant who is solicited by a private individual and one who is entrapped by a government agent. Questions have been likewise raised as to whether "predisposition" can be factually established with the requisite degree of certainty. Arguments such as these, while not devoid of appeal, have been twice previously made to this Court, and twice rejected by it, first in *Sorrells* and then in *Sherman*.

We believe that at least equally cogent criticism has been made of the concurring views in these cases. Commenting in *Sherman* on Justice Roberts' position in *Sorrells* that "although the defendant could claim that the Government had induced him to commit the crime, the Government could not reply by showing that the defendant's criminal conduct was due to his own readiness and not to the persuasion of government agents," Chief Justice Warren quoted the observation of Judge Learned Hand in an earlier stage of that proceeding:

> " 'Indeed, it would seem probable that, if there were no reply [to the claim of inducement], it would be impossible ever to secure convictions of any offences which consist of transactions that are carried on in secret.' "

Nor does it seem particularly desirable for the law to grant complete immunity from prosecution to one who himself planned to commit a crime, and then committed it, simply because government undercover agents subjected him to inducements which might have seduced a hypothetical individual who was not so predisposed. * * *

Several decisions of the United States district courts and courts of appeals have undoubtedly gone beyond this Court's opinions in *Sorrells* and *Sherman* in order to bar prosecutions because of what they thought to be for want of a better term "overzealous law enforcement." But the defense of entrapment enunciated in those opinions was not intended to give the federal judiciary a "chancellor's foot" veto over law enforcement practices of which it did not approve. The execution of the federal laws under our Constitution is confined primarily to the Executive Branch of the Government, subject to applicable constitutional and statutory limitations and to judicially fashioned rules to enforce those limitations. We think that the decision of the Court of Appeals in this case quite unnecessarily introduces an unmanageably subjective standard which is contrary to the holdings of this Court in *Sorrells* and *Sherman*.

Those cases establish that entrapment is a relatively limited defense. It is rooted not in any authority of the Judicial Branch to dismiss prosecutions for what it feels to have been "overzealous law enforcement," but instead in the notion that Congress could not have intended criminal punishment for a defendant who has committed all the elements of a prescribed offense, but who was induced to commit them by the government.

* * *

Respondent's concession in the Court of Appeals that the jury finding as to predisposition was supported by the evidence is, therefore, fatal to his claim of entrapment. He was an active participant in an illegal drug manufacturing enterprise which began before the government agent appeared on the scene, and continued after the government agent had left the scene. He was, in the words of *Sherman,* supra, not an "unwary innocent" but an "unwary criminal." The Court of Appeals was wrong, we believe, when it sought to broaden the principle laid down in *Sorrells* and *Sherman*. Its judgment is therefore reversed.

Reversed.

■ MR. JUSTICE STEWART, with whom MR. JUSTICE BRENNAN and MR. JUSTICE MARSHALL join, dissenting.

It is common ground that "[t]he conduct with which the defense of entrapment is concerned is the *manufacturing* of crime by law enforcement officials and their agents." Lopez v. United States, 373 U.S. 427, 434, 83 S.Ct. 1381, 1385, 10 L.Ed.2d 462 (1963). For the Government cannot be permitted to instigate the commission of a criminal offense in order to prosecute someone for committing it. * * * It is to prevent this situation from occurring in the administration of federal criminal justice that the defense of entrapment exists. But the Court has been sharply divided as to the proper basis, scope, and focus of the entrapment defense, and as to whether, in the absence of a conclusive showing, the issue of entrapment is for the judge or the jury to determine.

I.

In Sorrells v. United States, supra, and Sherman v. United States, supra, the Court took what might be called a "subjective" approach to the defense of entrapment. In that view, the defense is predicated on an unexpressed intent of Congress to exclude from its criminal statutes the prosecution and conviction of persons, "otherwise innocent," who have been lured to the commission of the prohibited act through the Government's instigation. * * * The Court today adheres to this approach.

The concurring opinion of Mr. Justice Roberts, joined by Justices Brandeis and Stone, in the *Sorrells* case, and that of Mr. Justice Frankfurter, joined by Justices Douglas, Harlan, and Brennan, in the *Sherman* case, took a different view of the entrapment defense. In their concept, the defense is not grounded on some unexpressed intent of Congress to exclude from punishment under its statutes those otherwise innocent persons tempted into crime by the Government, but rather on the belief that "the methods employed on behalf of the Government to bring about conviction cannot be countenanced." Thus, the focus of this approach is not on the propensities and predisposition of a specific defendant, but on "whether the police conduct revealed in the particular case falls below [the] standards, to which common feelings respond, for the proper use of governmental power." Phrased another way, the question is whether—regardless of the predisposition to crime of the particular defendant involved—the governmental agents have acted in such a way as is likely to instigate or create a criminal offense. Under this approach, the determination of the lawfulness of the Government's conduct must be made—as it is on all questions involving the legality of law enforcement methods—by the trial judge, not the jury.

In my view, this objective approach to entrapment advanced by the concurring opinions in *Sorrells* and *Sherman* is the only one truly consistent with the underlying rationale of the defense. Indeed, the very basis of the entrapment defense itself demands adherence to an approach that focuses on the conduct of the governmental agents, rather than on whether the defendant was "predisposed" or "otherwise innocent." I find it impossible to believe that the purpose of the defense is to effectuate some unexpressed congressional intent to exclude from its criminal statutes persons who committed a prohibited act, but would not have done so except for the Government's inducements. * * *

The purpose of the entrapment defense, then, cannot be to protect persons who are "otherwise innocent." Rather, it must be to prohibit unlawful governmental activity in instigating crime. * * * If that is so, then whether the particular defendant was "predisposed" or "otherwise innocent" is irrelevant; and the important question becomes whether the Government's conduct in inducing the crime was beyond judicial toleration.

Moreover, a test that makes the entrapment defense depend on whether the defendant had the requisite predisposition permits the introduction into evidence of all kinds of hearsay, suspicion, and rumor—all of which would be inadmissible in any other context—in order to prove the defendant's predisposition. It allows the prosecution, in offering such proof, to rely on the defendant's bad reputation or past criminal activities, including even rumored activities of which the prosecution may have insufficient evidence to obtain an indictment, and to present the agent's suspicions as to why they chose to tempt this defendant. This sort of evidence is not only unreliable, as the hearsay rule recognizes; but it is also highly prejudicial, especially if the matter is submitted to the jury, for, despite instructions to the contrary, the jury may well consider such evidence as probative not simply of the defendant's predisposition, but of his guilt of the offense with which he stands charged.

More fundamentally, focusing on the defendant's innocence or predisposition has the direct effect of making what is permissible or impermissible police conduct depend upon the past record and propensities of the particular defendant involved. Stated another way, this subjective test means that the Government is permitted to entrap a person with a criminal record or bad reputation, and then to prosecute him for the manufactured crime, confident that his record or reputation itself will be enough to show that he was predisposed to commit the offense anyway.

* * *

[W]hen the agents' involvement in criminal activities goes beyond the mere offering of such an opportunity and when their conduct is of a kind that could induce or instigate the commission of a crime by one not ready and willing to commit it, then—regardless of the character or propensities of the particular person induced—I think entrapment has occurred. For in that situation, the Government has engaged in the impermissible manufacturing of crime, and the federal courts should bar the prosecution in order to preserve the institutional integrity of the system of federal criminal justice.

II.

In the case before us, I think that the District Court erred in submitting the issue of entrapment to the jury, with instructions to acquit only if it had a reasonable doubt as to the respondent's predisposition to committing the crime. Since, under the objective test of entrapment, predisposition is irrelevant and the issue is to be decided by the trial judge, the Court of Appeals, I believe, would have been justified in reversing the conviction on this basis alone. But since the appellate court did not remand for consideration of the issue by the District Judge under an objective standard, but rather found entrapment as a matter of law and directed that the indictment be dismissed, we must reach the merits of the respondent's entrapment defense.

Since, in my view, it does not matter whether the respondent was predisposed to commit the offense of which he was convicted, the focus must be, rather, on the conduct of the undercover government agent. What the agent did here was to meet with a group of suspected producers of methamphetamine, including the respondent; to request the drug; to offer to supply the chemical phenyl-2-propanone in exchange for one-half of the methamphetamine to be manufactured therewith; and, when that offer was accepted, to provide the needed chemical ingredient, and to purchase some of the drug from the respondent.

It is undisputed that phenyl-2-propanone is an essential ingredient in the manufacture of methamphetamine; that it is not used for any other purpose; and that, while its sale is not illegal, it is difficult to obtain, because a manufacturer's license is needed to purchase it, and because many suppliers, at the request of the Federal Bureau of Narcotics and Dangerous Drugs, do not sell it at all. It is also undisputed that the methamphetamine which the respondent was prosecuted for manufacturing and selling was all produced on December 10, 1969, and that all the phenyl-2-propanone used in the manufacture of that batch of the drug was provided by the government agent. In these circumstances, the agent's undertaking to supply this ingredient to the respondent, thus making it possible for the Government to prosecute him for manufacturing an illicit drug with it, was, I think, precisely the type of governmental conduct that the entrapment defense is meant to prevent.

* * *

I would affirm the judgment of the Court of Appeals.

NOTES

1. **Predisposition Independent of the Undercover Investigation.** The Supreme Court's application of federal entrapment law in Jacobson v. United States, 503 U.S. 540, 112 S.Ct. 1535, 118 L.Ed.2d 174 (1992), may have imposed new demands on undercover activity. Specifically, federal entrapment law may now require the Government to respond to a claim of entrapment by showing the defendant's predisposition was independent of—and perhaps existed before—the undercover investigation.

In 1984, federal postal inspectors examining the records of a California book store found the name of a customer, Keith Jacobson. Jacobson, a Nebraska farmer, had purchased by mail two magazines Bare Boys I and Bare Boys II before federal legislation made criminal receipt through the mail of sexually explicit depictions of children. In January 1985 a postal inspector sent Jacobson a letter purporting to come from the fictitious American Hedonist Society. The letter included a membership application and represented that the Society believed that its members had the "right to read what we desire, the right to discuss similar interests with those who share our philosophy, and finally that we have the right to seek pleasure without restrictions being placed on us by outdated puritan morality." Jacobson joined the organization and returned a sexual attitude questionnaire asking him to rank on a scale of one to four his enjoyment of various sexual materials, one being "really enjoy," two being "enjoy," three being "somewhat enjoy," and four being "do not enjoy." He ranked the entry "[p]re-teen sex" as a two, but indicated he was opposed to pedophilia.

In May 1986, Jacobson was sent a solicitation from a second fictitious consumer research company, "Midlands Data Research," seeking a response from those who "believe in the joys of sex and the complete awareness of those lusty and youthful lads and lasses of the neophite [sic] age." He responded: "Please feel free to send me more information, I am interested in teenage sexuality. Please keep my name confidential." Postal authorities then sent him material purporting to come from another fictitious unit, "Heartland Institute for a New Tomorrow" or HINT. The material explained HINT was "an organization founded to protect and promote sexual freedom and freedom of choice. We believe that arbitrarily imposed legislative sanctions restricting your sexual freedom should be rescinded through the legislative process." A survey was enclosed and in response Jacobson indicated his interest in "[p]reteen sex-homosexual" material was above average, but not high.

A Government "prohibited mail specialist" began writing to Jacobson, using the pseudonym "Carl Long." The letters employed a tactic known as "mirroring," in which the investigator reflects interests expressed by the person under investigation. Jacobson indicated his primary interest was in "male-male items," and elaborated

> "As far as my likes are concerned, I like good looking young guys (in their late teens and early 20's) doing their thing together."

After writing two letters, Jacobson discontinued the correspondence.

In March 1987, a second Government agency, the Customs Service, using the fictitious name "Produit Outaouais," mailed Jacobson a brochure advertising photographs of young boys engaging in sex. Petitioner placed an order that was never filled.

The Postal Service then wrote to Jacobson as the "Far Eastern Trading Company Ltd." Its letter began:

> "As many of you know, much hysterical nonsense has appeared in the American media concerning 'pornography' and what must be done to stop it from coming across your borders. This brief letter does not allow us to give much comments; however, why is your government spending millions of dollars to exercise international censorship while tons of drugs, which makes yours the world's most crime ridden country are passed through easily."

It continued:

> "[W]e have devised a method of getting these to you without prying eyes of U.S. Customs seizing your mail * * *. After consultations with American solicitors, we have been advised that once we have posted our material through your system, it cannot be opened for any inspection without authorization of a judge."

Jacobson responded with a request for more information, and was sent a catalogue. He ordered Boys Who Love Boys, a pornographic magazine depicting young boys engaged in various sexual activities. Postal authorities arranged a controlled delivery of a photocopy of the magazine, and Jacobson was arrested.

Jacobson was prosecuted for violating the Child Protection Act of 1984 by receiving through the mails a visual depiction involving a minor engaged in sexually explicit conduct. At trial, he asserted a defense of entrapment. He testified that, when he received the initial Bare Boys magazines, he was shocked because he expected to receive photographs of young men 18 years or older. A search of Jacobson's home revealed no evidence that Jacobson collected or was actively interested in child pornography. When asked why he placed the order for Boys Who Love Boys, he responded:

> "Well, the statement was made of all the trouble and the hysteria over pornography and I wanted to see what the material was. It didn't describe the—I didn't know for sure what kind of sexual action they were referring to in the Canadian letter * * *."

The jury rejected his defense and convicted him.

The Supreme Court, by a 5 to 4 vote, reversed. Since the Government did not dispute its inducing Jacobson's commission of the offense, the majority explained, it had the burden of proving him predisposed to violate the law before the Government directed its attention to him. It failed to do so:

> [A]lthough he had become predisposed to break the law by May 1987, it is our view that the Government did not prove that this predisposition was independent and not the product of the attention that the Government had directed at [Jacobson] since January 1985.

The prosecution's evidence of predisposition falls into two categories: evidence developed prior to the Postal Service's mail campaign, and that developed during the course of the investigation. The sole piece of preinvestigation evidence is petitioner's 1984 order and receipt of the Bare Boys magazines. But this is scant if any proof of petitioner's predisposition to commit an illegal act, the criminal character of which a defendant is presumed to know. * * *

Furthermore, petitioner was acting within the law at the time he received these magazines. * * * Evidence of predisposition to do what once was lawful is not, by itself, sufficient to show predisposition to do what is not illegal, for there is a common understanding that most people obey the law even when they disapprove of it. * * *

The prosecution's evidence gathered during the investigation also fails to carry the Government's burden. [Jacobson's] responses to the many communications prior to the ultimate criminal act were at most indicative of certain personal inclinations, including a predisposition to view photographs of preteen sex and a willingness to promote a given agenda by supporting lobbying organizations. Even so, [his] responses hardly support an inference that he would commit the crime of receiving child pornography through the mails. * * *

On the other hand, the strong arguable inference is that, by waving the banner of individual rights and disparaging the legitimacy and constitutionality of efforts to restrict the availability of sexually explicit materials, the Government not only excited petitioner's interest in sexually explicit materials banned by law but also exerted substantial pressure on petitioner to obtain and read such material as part of a fight against censorship and the infringement of individual rights. * * *

Because * * * the prosecution failed, as a matter of law, to adduce evidence to support the jury verdict that petitioner was predisposed, independent of the

Government's acts and beyond a reasonable doubt, to violate the law by receiving child pornography through the mails, we reverse the Court of Appeals' judgment affirming the conviction of Keith Jacobson.

503 U.S. at 550–54, 112 S.Ct. at 1541–43, 118 L.Ed.2d at 185–86.

The dissenters indicated the majority held "Government conduct may be considered to create a predisposition to commit a crime, even before any Governmental action to induce the commission of the crime." This, they maintained, changed federal entrapment doctrine which has traditionally asked whether the defendant was predisposed before the Government induced the commission of the crime. They predicted the majority's approach would be often relied upon by defendants:

> [A]fter this case, every defendant will claim that something the Government agent did before soliciting the crime "created" a predisposition that was not there before. For example, a bribe taker will claim that the description of the amount of money available was so enticing that it implanted a disposition to accept the bribe later offered. A drug buyer will claim that the description of the drug's purity and effects was so tempting that it created the urge to try it for the first time. In short, the Court's opinion could be read to prohibit the Government from advertising the seductions of criminal activity as part of its sting operation, for fear of creating a predisposition in its suspects. * * *

503 U.S. at 557, 112 S.Ct. at 1545, 118 L.Ed.2d at 190 (O'Connor, J., dissenting).

2. **Requirement of Reasonable Suspicion to Target Suspect for Investigation.** Does *Jacobson*, perhaps in combination with Fourth Amendment law, impose a requirement that officers have reasonable suspicion a person is predisposed to commit an offense before targeting him, perhaps with a view towards offering him an opportunity to commit the offense? The courts have concluded no such requirement exists. United States v. Aibejeris, 28 F.3d 97, 99 (11th Cir.1994); United States v. Harvey, 991 F.2d 981, 989–93 (2d Cir.1993); Commonwealth v. Mance, 539 Pa. 282, 286–89, 652 A.2d 299, 301–02 (1995).

3. **Provision of Contraband for Offense.** The phenyl-2-propanone provided to the defendants by the officer in *Russell* was not contraband, i.e., its possession by persons like the defendants was not itself criminal. Suppose officers provide contraband for use in the commission of an offense?

In Hampton v. United States, 425 U.S. 484, 96 S.Ct. 1646, 48 L.Ed.2d 113 (1976), Hampton and Hutton, a Drug Enforcement Administration informant, sold heroin to federal undercover officers. At his trial for distribution of heroin, Hampton testified Hutton provided the heroin and suggested selling it; other testimony suggested Hampton provided the drug. The defense requested an instruction that Hampton was entitled to acquittal if the jury found the heroin sold supplied to Hampton by a government informer. The instruction was denied, Hampton was convicted, and appeal followed. The Supreme Court, with Justice Stevens not participating, affirmed but without an opinion of the Court. Justice Rehnquist, joined by the Chief Justice and Justice White, concluded *Russell* "ruled out the possibility that the defense of entrapment could ever be based upon governmental misconduct in a case, such as this one, where the predisposition of the defendant to commit the crime was established." He continued:

> The limitations of the Due Process Clause of the Fifth Amendment come into play only when the Government activity in question violates some protected right of the *defendant*. Here, * * * the police, the Government informant, and the defendant acted in concert with one another. * * * If the police engage in illegal activity in concert with a defendant beyond the scope of their duties the remedy lies, not in freeing the equally culpable defendant, but in prosecut-

ing the police under the applicable provisions of state or federal law. But the police conduct here no more deprived defendant of any right secured to him by the United States Constitution than did the police conduct in *Russell* deprive Russell of any rights.

425 U.S. at 490–91, 96 S.Ct. at 1650, 48 L.Ed.2d at 119. Justice Powell, joined by Justice Blackmun, concurred in the judgment. Given that the phenyl-2-propanone in *Russell* was difficult to obtain and useful only in the manufacture of methamphetamine, he found no difference between providing it and providing heroin. *Russell*, he concluded, controlled. Turning to the Due Process argument, he acknowledged "the doctrinal and practical difficulties of delineating limits to police involvement in crimes that do not focus upon predisposition, as Government participation ordinarily will be fully justified in society's 'war with the criminal classes.' " But given that Hampton's Due Process claim could be rejected as controlled by *Russell*, he was unwilling to join the plurality's broad language rejecting such claims in all cases of government involvement in crime.

4. **Expansive Objective "Due Process" Formulations of Entrapment.** The objective approach to entrapment as generally construed provides for the defense only if the officers' conduct violates objective limits designed to discourage law enforcement conduct tending to generate the commission of crime. The Supreme Court of Alaska, for example, defined entrapment under its objective standard as follows:

> [U]nlawful entrapment occurs when a public law enforcement official * * * induces another person to commit * * * an offense by persuasion which would be effective to persuade an average person, other than one who is ready and willing, to commit such an offense.

Grossman v. State, 457 P.2d 226, 229 (Alaska 1969).

Some courts, however, impose more rigorous limits on undercover investigations, often on due process related grounds. The New Mexico Supreme Court, for example, held that defendants are entitled to argue to juries that their situations present entrapment under either a subjective or objective approach. It also recognized a second type of "objective entrapment," based on due process of law as guaranteed by the State Constitution. Under this doctrine, a defendant is entitled to dismissal of the prosecution if the judge determines the law enforcement conduct employed in the investigation so exceeded the standards of proper investigation that the public's confidence in the fair and honorable administration of justice would be shaken by such conduct. State v. Vallejos, 123 N.M. 739, 945 P.2d 957 (1997). It continued:

> In order to provide some benchmarks, we have surveyed the factors and criteria other jurisdictions use when a defendant raises the objective entrapment defense, the outrageous government conduct defense, or the due process defense. We recognize two broad categories of impropriety: unconscionable methods and illegitimate purposes.

> * * *

> While police may engage in some degree of deception in their efforts to detect certain sorts of crime that are difficult to detect otherwise, police may not employ unconscionable methods in their attempts to ferret out crime. We find the following examples to be helpful as indicia of unconscionability: "coaxing a defendant into a circular transaction;" "[giving defendant] free heroin until he [is] addicted and then play[ing] on [his] addiction to persuade [him] to purchase heroin and cocaine for an undercover police agent;" an extreme plea of desperate illness; an appeal based primarily on sympathy or friendship; an offer of inordinate gain or a promise of excessive profit; persis-

tent solicitation to overcome a defendant's demonstrated hesitancy; the use of brutality or physical or psychological coercion to induce the commission of a crime; an offer to sell drugs to one in a drug rehabilitation program; employment of contingent fee agreements with informants, by which a key witness has "what amounts to a financial stake in criminal convictions;" "unjustified intrusion into citizens' privacy and autonomy;" the inducement of others to engage in violence or the threat of violence against innocent parties; the use of provocateurs sent into political organizations to suggest the commission of crimes; excessive involvement by the police in creating the crime; the "manufacture [of] a crime from whole cloth;" and the " 'engineer[ing] and direct[ion of] the criminal enterprise from start to finish.' "

Police also violate due process when they ensnare a defendant in an operation guided by an illegitimate purpose. "Illegitimate purpose" is not capable of being defined with great precision. However, other courts have described improper purposes in a number of ways. In West Virginia, a court considers whether police have ensnared a defendant "solely for the purpose of generating criminal charges and without any motive to prevent further crime or protect the public at large." The New York Court of Appeals has suggested that due process is violated when "the record reveals simply a desire to obtain a conviction . . . [rather than] to prevent further crime or protect the populace."

123 N.M. at 744–45, 945 P.2d at 962–63.

In *Vallejos*, the court found no objective entrapment. Other courts applying similar approaches, however, have found law enforcement conduct impermissible. In Soohoo v. State, 737 So.2d 1108 (Fla.App.1999), for example, the court held the due process prohibition against egregious governmental conduct required dismissal of the charges. Soohoo was charged with purchasing two kilos of cocaine from a confidential informant. The informant, seeking to reduce his sentence for drug offenses, was operating under the loose supervision of an officer. Explaining its conclusion, the court stressed, first, the informant offered to help the defendant sell the cocaine if the defendant would purchase five kilos. Second, the informant responded to the defendant's interest in one kilo by offering a second kilo on credit. In addition, the court emphasized the officer supervising the informant gave him what the court considered too much leeway in structuring the transaction.

Similarly, in State v. Grubb, 319 N.J.Super. 407, 725 A.2d 707 (1999), the appellate court, finding the drug defendant entitled to acquittal under "common law objective entrapment," emphasized the investigating officers had insufficient justification for targeting and investigating the defendant as a criminal suspect. The investigation was triggered when another suspect, who became an informant, reported that he had a deal pending to purchase Clenbuterol from Grubb, but the officers failed to conduct sufficient inquiry to determine that Clenbuterol was not a steroid as the officers suspected. The *Grubb* court also stressed the officers exercised insufficient supervision over the informant.

B.   ELICITATION OF SELF-INCRIMINATING STATEMENTS

EDITORS' INTRODUCTION: APPLICATION OF THE FIFTH AND SIXTH AMENDMENTS TO UNDERCOVER INVESTIGATIONS

The two major federal constitutional limits on law enforcement officers' ability to elicit self-incriminating admissions from suspects are the Fifth Amendment prohibition against compelled self-incrimination, as developed in Miranda v. Arizona, 384 U.S. 436, 86 S.Ct. 1602, 16 L.Ed.2d 694

(1966), and the Sixth Amendment right to counsel. Both doctrines, as they apply to general law enforcement questioning of suspects, are developed in Chapter 7. When self-incriminating admissions are obtained or overheard by undercover officers or informants working as agents of officers, the situation—and the law—is considerably different.

Does an undercover officer passively overhearing self-incriminating admissions made by a suspect engage in action that triggers self-incrimination protection? This was addressed in Hoffa v. United States, 385 U.S. 293, 87 S.Ct. 408, 17 L.Ed.2d 374 (1966), reprinted in part later in this chapter. *Hoffa* considered the argument that testimony by a government informer concerning incriminating admissions made by the defendant in the former's presence violated the defendant's Fifth Amendment privilege against compelled self-incrimination. It was clear that if the informer had disclosed his status he would not have been permitted by the defendant to overhear the conversations. The Court held:

> [A]   necessary element of compulsory self-incrimination is some kind of compulsion. * * * [No] claim has been or could be made that [Hoffa's] incriminating statements were the product of any sort of coercion, legal or factual. The * * * conversations * * * were wholly voluntary. For that reason, if for no other, it is clear that no right protected by the Fifth Amendment privilege against compulsory self-incrimination was violated in this case.

384 U.S. at 304, 87 S.Ct. at 414–15, 17 L.Ed.2d at 383.

Does *Miranda* apply when an undercover officer or informant actively persuades a suspect to make incriminating admissions? This was addressed in Illinois v. Perkins, 496 U.S. 292, 110 S.Ct. 2394, 110 L.Ed.2d 243 (1990). Police learned from a former prison acquaintance of Perkins that Perkins had admitted a homicide. Upon locating Perkins in a local jail, police placed the former acquaintance and an undercover officer in the same cellblock. After the former acquaintance introduced them, the officer engaged Perkins in conversations and encouraged Perkins to admit the offense and relate details of its commission. Failure to comply with *Miranda* in this process, the Court held, did not render Perkins's admissions subject to suppression.

> Conversations between suspects and undercover agents do not implicate the concerns underlying *Miranda*. The essential ingredients of a "police-dominated atmosphere" and compulsion are not present when an incarcerated person speaks freely to someone he believes to be a fellow inmate. Coercion is determined from the perspective of the suspect. * * * When a suspect considers himself in the company of cellmates and not officers, the coercive atmosphere is lacking. * * * When the suspect has no reason to think that the listeners have official power over him, it should not be assumed that his words are motivated by the reaction he expects from his listeners. * * *
>
> *Miranda* forbids coercion, not mere strategic deception by taking advantage of a suspect's misplaced trust in one he supposes to be a fellow prisoner. * * *

496 U.S. at 296–97, 110 S.Ct. at 2397, 110 L.Ed.2d at 251.

As a result of these decisions, federal constitutional regulation of law enforcement conduct in this area is achieved through the Sixth and Fourteenth Amendments right to counsel. The seminal case is Massiah v. United States, 377 U.S. 201, 84 S.Ct. 1199, 12 L.Ed.2d 246 (1964). Massiah, Colson, and others were arrested and indicted for drug offenses; Massiah and Colson were released on bail. Massiah retained a lawyer. Unknown to Massiah, Colson decided to cooperate with the government agents in their continuing investigation, and permitted the installation of a radio transmitter in his car. One evening, Colson and Massiah had a lengthy conversation while sitting in Colson's parked automobile. A federal agent listened over his radio to the conversation, which included several incriminating admissions by Massiah. At Massiah's trial, the agent was permitted to testify as to these admissions. The Supreme Court held this constitutional error:

> We hold that [Massiah] was denied the basic protection of [the Sixth Amendment right to counsel] when there was used against him at his trial evidence of his own incriminating words, which federal agents had deliberately elicited from him after he had been indicted and in the absence of his counsel.

377 U.S. at 206, 84 S.Ct. at 1203, 12 L.Ed.2d at 250. The principal case in this section explores the ramifications of *Massiah*.

United States v. Henry

Supreme Court of the United States, 1980.
447 U.S. 264, 100 S.Ct. 2183, 65 L.Ed.2d 115.

■ MR. CHIEF JUSTICE BURGER delivered the opinion of the Court.

We granted certiorari to consider whether respondent's Sixth Amendment right to the assistance of counsel was violated by the admission at trial of incriminating statements made by respondent to his cellmate, an undisclosed government informant, after indictment and while in custody.

I.

The Janaf Branch of the United Virginia Bank/Seaboard National in Norfolk, Va., was robbed in August 1972. Witnesses saw two men wearing masks and carrying guns enter the bank while a third man waited in the car. No witnesses were able to identify respondent Henry as one of the participants. About an hour after the robbery, the getaway car was discovered. Inside was found a rent receipt signed by one "Allen R. Norris" and a lease, also signed by Norris, for a house in Norfolk. Two men, who were subsequently convicted of participating in the robbery, were arrested at the rented house. Discovered with them were the proceeds of the robbery and the guns and masks used by the gunman.

Government agents traced the rent receipt to Henry; on the basis of this information, Henry was arrested in Atlanta, Ga., in November 1972. Two weeks later he was indicted for armed robbery under 18 U.S.C.A. § 2113(a) and (d). He was held pending trial in the Norfolk City Jail. Counsel was appointed on November 27.

On November 21, 1972, shortly after Henry was incarcerated, government agents working on the Janaf robbery contacted one Nichols, an inmate at the Norfolk City Jail, who for some time prior to this meeting had been engaged to provide confidential information to the Federal Bureau of Investigation as a paid informant. Nichols was then serving a sentence on local forgery charges. The record does not disclose whether the agent contacted Nichols specifically to acquire information about Henry or the Janaf robbery.

Nichols informed the agent that he was housed in the same cellblock with several federal prisoners awaiting trial, including Henry. The agent told him to be alert to any statements made by the federal prisoners, but not to initiate any conversation with or question Henry regarding the bank robbery. In early December, after Nichols had been released from jail, the agent again contacted Nichols, who reported that he and Henry had engaged in conversation and that Henry had told him about the robbery of the Janaf bank. Nichols was paid for furnishing the information.

When Henry was tried in March 1973, an agent of the Federal Bureau of Investigation testified concerning the events surrounding the discovery of the rental slip and the evidence uncovered at the rented house. Other witnesses also connected Henry to the rented house, including the rental agent who positively identified Henry as the "Allen R. Norris" who had rented the house and had taken the rental receipt described earlier. A neighbor testified that prior to the robbery she saw Henry at the rented house with John Luck, one of the two men who had by the time of Henry's trial been convicted for the robbery. In addition, palm prints found on the lease agreement matched those of Henry.

Nichols testified at trial that he had "an opportunity to have some conversations with Mr. Henry while he was in the jail," and that Henry told him that on several occasions he had gone to the Janaf Branch to see which employees opened the vault. Nichols also testified that Henry described to him the details of the robbery and stated that the only evidence connecting him to the robbery was the rental receipt. The jury was not informed that Nichols was a paid government informant.

On the basis of this testimony, Henry was convicted of bank robbery and sentenced to a term of imprisonment of 25 years. On appeal he raised no Sixth Amendment claims. His conviction was affirmed, and his petition to this Court for a writ of certiorari was denied.

On August 28, 1975, Henry moved to vacate his sentence * * *. At this stage, he stated that he had just learned that Nichols was a paid government informant and alleged that he had been intentionally placed in the same cell with Nichols so that Nichols could secure information about the robbery. Thus, Henry contended that the introduction of Nichols' testimony violated his Sixth Amendment right to the assistance of counsel. The District Court denied the motion without a hearing. The Court of Appeals, however, reversed and remanded for an evidentiary inquiry into "whether the witness [Nichols] was acting as a government agent during his interviews with Henry."

On remand, the District Court requested affidavits from the government agents. An affidavit was submitted describing the agent's relationship with Nichols and relating the following conversation:

> "I recall telling Nichols at this time to be alert to any statements made by these individuals [the federal prisoners] regarding the charges against them. I specifically recall telling Nichols that he was not to question Henry or these individuals about the charges against them, however, if they engaged him in conversation or talked in front of him, he was requested to pay attention to their statements. I recall telling Nichols not to initiate any conversations with Henry regarding the bank robbery charges against Henry, but that if Henry initiated the conversations with Nichols, I requested Nichols to pay attention to the information furnished by Henry."

The agent's affidavit also stated that he never requested anyone affiliated with the Norfolk City Jail to place Nichols in the same cell with Henry.

The District Court again denied Henry's § 2255 motion, concluding that Nichols' testimony at trial did not violate Henry's Sixth Amendment right to counsel. The Court of Appeals reversed and remanded, holding that the actions of the government impaired the Sixth Amendment rights of the defendant under Massiah v. United States, 377 U.S. 201, 84 S.Ct. 1199, 12 L.Ed.2d 246 (1964). The court noted that Nichols had engaged in conversation with Henry and concluded that if by association, by general conversation, or both, Nichols had developed a relationship of trust and confidence with Henry such that Henry revealed incriminating information, this constituted interference with the right to the assistance of counsel under the Sixth Amendment.

II.

* * *

The question here is whether under the facts of this case, a government agent "deliberately elicited" incriminating statements from Henry within the meaning of *Massiah*. Three factors are important. First, Nichols was acting under instructions as a paid informant for the government; second, Nichols was ostensibly no more than a fellow inmate of Henry; and third, Henry was in custody and under indictment at the time he was engaged in conversation by Nichols.

The Court of Appeals viewed the record as showing that Nichols deliberately used his position to secure incriminating information from Henry when counsel was not present and held that conduct attributable to the government. Nichols had been a paid government informant for more than a year; moreover, the FBI agent was aware that Nichols had access to Henry and would be able to engage him in conversations without arousing Henry's suspicion. The arrangement between Nichols and the agent was on a contingent fee basis; Nichols was to be paid only if he produced useful information. This combination of circumstances is sufficient to support the Court of Appeals' determination. Even if the agent's statement is accepted that he did not intend that Nichols would take affirmative steps to secure incriminating information, he must have known that such propinquity likely would lead to that result.

The Government argues that the federal agents instructed Nichols not to question Henry about the robbery. Yet according to his own testimony, Nichols was not a passive listener; rather, he had "some conversations with Mr. Henry" while he was in jail and Henry's incriminatory statements were "the product of this conversation." * * *

* * *

It is undisputed that Henry was unaware of Nichols' role as a government informant. The Government argues that this Court should apply a less rigorous standard under the Sixth Amendment where the accused is prompted by an undisclosed undercover informant than where the accused is speaking in the hearing of persons he knows to be government officers. That line of argument, however, seeks to infuse Fifth Amendment concerns against compelled self-incrimination into the Sixth Amendment protection of the right to the assistance of counsel. An accused speaking to a known government agent is typically aware that his statements may be used against him. The adversary positions at that stage are well established; the parties are then "arms length" adversaries.

When the accused is in the company of a fellow inmate who is acting by prearrangement as a government agent, the same cannot here be said. Conversation stimulated in such circumstances may elicit information that an accused would not intentionally reveal to persons known to be government agents. Indeed, the *Massiah* Court noted that if the Sixth Amendment "is to have any efficacy it must apply to indirect and surreptitious interrogations as well as those conducted in the jailhouse." The Court pointedly observed that Massiah was more seriously imposed upon because he did not know that his codefendant was a government agent.

Moreover, the concept of a knowing and voluntary waiver of Sixth Amendment rights does not apply in the context of communications with an undisclosed undercover informant acting for the government. In that setting Henry, being unaware that Nichols was a government agent expressly commissioned to secure evidence, cannot be held to have waived his right to the assistance of counsel.

Finally Henry's incarceration at the time he was engaged in conversation by Nichols is also a relevant factor. As a ground for imposing the prophylactic requirements in Miranda v. Arizona, 384 U.S. 436, 467, 86 S.Ct. 1602, 1624, 16 L.Ed.2d 694 (1966), this Court noted the powerful psychological inducements to reach for aid when a person is in confinement. While the concern in *Miranda* was limited to custodial police interrogation, the mere fact of custody imposes pressures on the accused; confinement may bring into play subtle influences that will make him particularly susceptible to the ploys of undercover government agents. The Court of Appeals determined that on this record the incriminating conversations between Henry and Nichols were facilitated by Nichols' conduct and apparent status as a person sharing a common plight. That Nichols had managed to gain the confidence of Henry, as the Court of Appeals determined, is confirmed by Henry's request that Nichols assist him in his escape plans when Nichols was released from confinement.

Under the strictures of the Court's holdings on the exclusion of evidence, we conclude that the Court of Appeals did not err in holding that Henry's statements to Nichols should not have been admitted at trial. By intentionally creating a situation likely to induce Henry to make incriminating statements without the assistance of counsel, the government violated Henry's Sixth Amendment right to counsel. This is not a case where, in Justice Cardozo's words, "the constable blundered," People v. Defore, 242 N.Y. 13, 21, 150 N.E. 585, 587 (1926); rather, it is one where the "constable" planned an impermissible interference with the right to the assistance of counsel.

The judgment of the Court of Appeals for the Fourth Circuit is affirmed.

■ MR. JUSTICE BLACKMUN, with whom MR. JUSTICE WHITE joins, dissenting.

* * *

I.

Massiah mandates exclusion only if a federal agent "deliberately elicited" statements from the accused in the absence of counsel. The word "deliberately" denotes intent. *Massiah* ties this intent to the act of elicitation, that is, to conduct that draws forth a response. Thus *Massiah*, by its own terms, covers only action undertaken with the specific intent to evoke an inculpatory disclosure.

* * *

[W]hile claiming to retain the "deliberately elicited" test, the Court really forges a new test that saps the word "deliberately" of all significance. The Court's extension of *Massiah* would cover even a "negligent" triggering of events resulting in reception of disclosures. This approach, in my view, is unsupported and unwise.

* * *

II.

In my view, the Court not only missteps in forging a new *Massiah* test; it proceeds to misapply the very test it has created. The new test requires a showing that the agent created a situation "likely to induce" the production of incriminatory remarks, and that the informant in fact "prompted" the defendant. Even accepting the most capacious reading of both this language and the facts, I believe that neither prong of the Court's test is satisfied.

A.   *"Likely to Induce."* In holding that Coughlin's actions were likely to induce Henry's statements, the Court relies on three facts: a contingent fee arrangement; Henry's assumption that Nichols was just a cellmate; and Henry's incarceration.

* * *

* * * I question whether the existence of a contingent fee arrangement is at all significant. The reasonable conclusion of an informant like Nichols would be that, whatever the arrangement, he would *not* be remunerated if he breached his promise; yet the Court asks us to infer that Coughlin's conversation with Nichols "likely would lead" Nichols to engage in the very conduct which Coughlin told him to avoid.

The Court also emphasizes that Henry was "unaware that Nichols was a government agent." One might properly assign this factor some importance, were it not for Brewer v. Williams, 430 U.S. 387, 97 S.Ct. 1232, 51 L.Ed.2d 424 (1977). In that case, the Court explicitly held that the fact "[t]hat the incriminating statements were elicited surreptitiously in the *Massiah* case, and otherwise here, is *constitutionally irrelevant*." (Emphasis added.) The Court's teeter-tottering with this factor in *Massiah* analysis can only induce confusion.

Finally, the Court notes that Henry was incarcerated when he made his statements to Nichols. The Court's emphasis of the "subtle influences" exerted by custody, however, is itself too subtle for me. This is not a case of a custodial encounter with police, in which the Government's display of power might overcome the free will of the accused. The relationship here was "social" and relaxed. Henry did not suspect that Nichols was connected with the FBI. Moreover, even assuming that "subtle influences" might encourage a detainee to talk about his crime, there are certainly counterbalances of at least equal weight. Since, in jail, "official surveillance has traditionally been the order of the day," and a jailmate has obvious incentives to assist authorities, one may expect a detainee to act with corresponding circumspection. * * *

* * * .

B.   *"Prompting."* All Members of the Court agree that Henry's statements were properly admitted if Nichols did not "prompt" him. The record, however, gives no indication that Nichols "stimulated" Henry's remarks with "affirmative steps to secure incriminating information." Certainly the known facts reveal nothing more than "a jailhouse informant who had been instructed to overhear conversations and to engage a criminal defendant in some conversations." The scant record demonstrates only that Nichols "had 'an opportunity to have some conversations with Mr. Henry while he was in the jail.'" "Henry had engaged [Nichols] in conversation," "had requested Nichols' assistance," and "had talked to Nichols about the bank robbery charges against him." Thus, we know only that Nichols and Henry had conversations, hardly a startling development, given their location in the same cellblock in a city jail. We know nothing about the nature of these conversations, particularly whether Nichols subtly or otherwise focused attention on the bank robberies. Indeed, to the extent the record says anything at all, it supports the inference that it was Henry, not Nichols, who "engaged" the other "in some conversations," and who was the moving force behind any mention of the crime. I cannot believe that *Massiah* requires exclusion when a cellmate previously unknown to the defendant and asked only to keep his ears open says: "It's a nice day," and the defendant responds: "It would be nicer if I hadn't robbed that bank." * * *

■ MR. JUSTICE REHNQUIST, dissenting.

* * *

The doctrinal underpinnings of *Massiah* have been largely left unexplained, and the result in this case, as in *Massiah*, is difficult to reconcile with the traditional notions of the role of an attorney. Here, as in *Massiah*, the accused was not prevented from consulting with his counsel as often as he wished. No meetings between the accused and his counsel were disturbed or spied upon. And preparation for trial was not obstructed. * * *

Once the accused has been made aware of his rights, it is his responsibility to decide whether or not to exercise them. If he voluntarily relinquishes his rights by talking to authorities, or if he decides to disclose incriminating information to someone whom he mistakenly believes will not report it to the authorities, he is normally accountable for his actions and must bear any adverse consequences that result. Such information has not in any sense been obtained because the accused's will has been overborne, nor does it result from any "unfair advantage" that the State has over the accused: the accused is free to keep quiet and to consult with his attorney if he so chooses. In this sense, the decision today and the result in *Massiah* are fundamentally inconsistent with traditional notions of the role of the attorney that underlie the Sixth Amendment right to counsel.

* * *

* * * This Court has never held that an accused is constitutionally protected from his inability to keep quiet, whether or not he has been encouraged by third party citizens to voluntarily make incriminating remarks. I do not think the result should be different merely because the government has encouraged a third party informant to report remarks obtained in this fashion. When an accused voluntarily chooses to make an incriminatory remark in these circumstances, he knowingly assumes the risk that his confidant may be untrustworthy.

* * *

The fact that police carry on undercover activities should not automatically be transmuted because formal criminal proceedings have begun. * * * [T]he mere bringing of formal proceedings does not necessarily mean that an undercover investigation or the need for it has terminated. A person may be arrested on the basis of probable cause arising in the immediate aftermath of an offense and during early stages of investigation, but before the authorities have had an opportunity to investigate fully his connection with the crime. And for the criminal, there is no rigid dichotomy between the time before commencement of former criminal proceedings and the time after such proceedings have begun. Once out on bail the accused remains free to continue his criminal activity, and very well may decide to do so. * * * I would hold that the Government's activity here is merely a continuation of their lawful authority to use covert operations in investigating a criminal case after formal proceedings have commenced.

NOTES

1. **Passive Informants.** If an informant overhears an incriminating admission by a defendant but did not elicit it, does the Sixth Amendment bar the use of this admission? The principal case suggests not, and this has been reaffirmed.

In Kuhlmann v. Wilson, 477 U.S. 436, 106 S.Ct. 2616, 91 L.Ed.2d 364 (1986), Wilson was arrested and arraigned on charges relating to a robbery-murder. He was placed in a cell with prisoner Benny Lee; the cell provided them with a view of the garage at which the crimes were committed. Unknown to Wilson, Lee had entered into an arrangement under which he agreed to listen to Wilson's conversations and report them to police. Lee was instructed not to ask Wilson any questions but to "keep his ears open." Wilson soon told Lee that, although he was present at the robbery and murder, he did not know the perpetrators and was not involved in the crime. According to his later testimony, Lee responded that the story "didn't sound too good" and "things didn't look too good for him." At another point, Lee testified he had told Wilson, "[Y]ou better come up with a better story because that one doesn't sound too cool to me * * *." Several days later, Wilson told Lee another version of the events, admitting guilty participation. At Wilson's state trial, the trial judge found Wilson's admissions to Lee "spontaneous" and "unsolicited" and admitted them. In subsequent federal habeas corpus litigation, the Supreme Court held Wilson entitled to no relief. Acknowledging that it had never expressly addressed whether the Sixth Amendment bars the admission of statements overheard yet not elicited by an informant, the majority resolved the issue:

> [T]he primary concern of the *Massiah* line of decisions is secret interrogation by investigatory techniques that are the equivalent of direct police interrogation. Since "the Sixth Amendment is not violated whenever—by luck or happenstance—the State obtains incriminating statements from the accused after the right to counsel has attached," a defendant does not make out a violation of that right simply by showing that an informant, either through prior arrangement or voluntarily, reported his incriminating statements to the police. Rather, the defendant must demonstrate that the police and their informant took some action, beyond merely listening, that was designed deliberately to elicit incriminating remarks.

477 U.S. at 459, 106 S.Ct. at 2630, 91 L.Ed.2d at 384–85. The record in the case, the majority concluded, did not permit a federal habeas corpus court to find, under this standard, Wilson's Sixth Amendment rights violated.

2. **Target Suspected of Several Crimes.** Special problems are presented when a suspect is believed involved in multiple crimes. If the suspect's Sixth Amendment right to counsel under *Massiah* and *Henry* attaches, may law enforcement officers nevertheless seek to elicit admissions to other offenses under investigation?

In Maine v. Moulton, 474 U.S. 159, 106 S.Ct. 477, 88 L.Ed.2d 481 (1985), both Moulton and one Colson were indicted for theft by receiving stolen property. Colson contacted police; he reported that he had received anonymous threatening telephone calls and that Moulton suggested the two kill Gary Elwell, a state witness. Other witnesses in the case reported to authorities that they had also received threats. The police made and Colson accepted a deal under which he would cooperate with authorities in return for no further charges being brought against him. During later telephone conversations with Colson, Moulton suggested the two meet to plan their defense to the charges. For purposes of this meeting, Colson was equipped with a body wire transmitter to record what was said; according to police testimony, the device was provided for Colson's safety in the event Moulton realized he was cooperating with authorities and to record any further threats to witnesses

Moulton might make. During the conversation, Moulton offered that the plan for killing Elwell would not work. There was extended discussion concerning the falsification of alibis and Colson encouraged Moulton to make a number of incriminating admissions concerning the crime for which he had been indicted. At Moulton's later theft trial, the state successfully offered into evidence those portions of the recorded conversations in which Moulton made admissions concerning the crime charged. One portion of the discussion concerning false alibis was admitted, but no part of the conversation concerning the killing of the witness was offered. Moulton was convicted.

The Supreme Court reversed, reasoning that admission of the conversations violated Moulton's Sixth Amendment rights as developed in *Massiah* and *Henry*. The majority rejected the prosecution's argument that the evidence was admissible because the police activity was legitimately intended to investigate matters other than the theft offense for which Moulton was indicted—the threats to Colson and Moulton's plan to kill Elwell:

> To allow the admission of evidence obtained from the accused in violation of his Sixth Amendment right whenever the police assert an alternative, legitimate reason for their surveillance invites abuse by law enforcement personnel in the form of fabricated investigations and risks the evisceration of the Sixth Amendment right recognized in *Massiah*. * * * Consequently, incriminating statements pertaining to pending charges are inadmissible at the trial of those charges, notwithstanding the fact that the police were also investigating other crimes, if, in obtaining this evidence, the State violated the Sixth Amendment by knowingly circumventing the accused's right to the assistance of counsel.

474 U.S. at 180, 106 S.Ct. at 489, 88 L.Ed.2d at 498–99. Because Moulton's *Massiah* right was violated, the use of the evidence in his theft trial was improper. The Court also offered:

> On the other hand, to exclude evidence pertaining to charges as to which the Sixth Amendment right to counsel had not attached at the time the evidence was obtained, simply because other charges were pending at that time, would unnecessarily frustrate the public's interest in the investigation of criminal activities.

474 U.S. at 180, 106 S.Ct. at 489, 88 L.Ed.2d at 498. It added:

> Incriminating statements pertaining to other crimes, as to which the Sixth Amendment right has not yet attached are, of course, admissible at the trial of those offenses.

474 U.S. at 180 n. 16, 106 S.Ct. at 489 n. 16, 88 L.Ed.2d at 499 n. 16.

C. UNDERCOVER SURVEILLANCE AS A "SEARCH" (AND RELATED MATTERS)

The Fourth Amendment's prominence in federal constitutional regulation of other aspects of law enforcement investigatory behavior suggests the provision would be appropriate as a means of limiting, but not prohibiting, certain aspects of undercover investigations. This, of course, would be possible only if some or all of the activities of undercover officers and agents constituted "searches" or "seizures" within the meaning of the Fourth Amendment. Whether this is the case is addressed in the principal case in this section.

Hoffa v. United States

Supreme Court of the United States, 1966.
385 U.S. 293, 87 S.Ct. 408, 17 L.Ed.2d 374.

■ MR. JUSTICE STEWART delivered the opinion of the Court.

Over a period of several weeks in the late autumn of 1962 there took place in a federal court in Nashville, Tennessee, a trial by jury in which James Hoffa was charged with violating a provision of the Taft-Hartley Act. That trial, known in the present record as the Test Fleet trial, ended with a hung jury. The petitioners now before us—James Hoffa, Thomas Parks, Larry Campbell, and Ewing King—were tried and convicted in 1964 for endeavoring to bribe members of that jury. The convictions were affirmed by the Court of Appeals. A substantial element in the Government's proof that led to the convictions of these four petitioners was contributed by a witness named Edward Partin, who testified to several incriminating statements which he said petitioners Hoffa and King had made in his presence during the course of the Test Fleet trial. Our grant of certiorari was limited to the single issue of whether the Government's use in this case of evidence supplied by Partin operated to invalidate these convictions.

* * *

The controlling facts can be briefly stated. The Test Fleet trial, in which James Hoffa was the sole individual defendant, was in progress between October 22 and December 23, 1962, in Nashville, Tennessee. James Hoffa was president of the International Brotherhood of Teamsters. During the course of the trial he occupied a three-room suite in the Andrew Jackson Hotel in Nashville. One of his constant companions throughout the trial was the petitioner King, president of the Nashville local of the Teamsters Union. Edward Partin, a resident of Baton Rouge, Louisiana, and a local Teamsters Union official there, made repeated visits to Nashville during the period of the trial. On these visits he frequented the Hoffa hotel suite, and was continually in the company of Hoffa and his associates, including King, in and around the hotel suite, the hotel lobby, the courthouse, and elsewhere in Nashville. During this period Partin made frequent reports to a federal agent named Sheridan concerning conversations he said Hoffa and King had had with him and with each other, disclosing endeavors to bribe members of the Test Fleet jury. Partin's reports and his subsequent testimony at the petitioners' trial unquestionably contributed, directly or indirectly, to the convictions of all four of the petitioners.

The chain of circumstances which led Partin to be in Nashville during the Test Fleet trial extended back at least to September of 1962. At that time Partin was in jail in Baton Rouge on a state criminal charge. He was also under a federal indictment for embezzling union funds, and other indictments for state offenses were pending against him. Between that time and Partin's initial visit to Nashville on October 22 he was released on bail on the state criminal charge, and proceedings under the federal indictment were postponed. On October 8, Partin telephoned Hoffa in Washington, D. C., to discuss local union matters and Partin's difficulties with the authorities. In the course of this conversation Partin asked if he could see Hoffa to confer about these problems, and Hoffa acquiesced. Partin again called

Hoffa on October 18 and arranged to meet him in Nashville. During this period Partin also consulted on several occasions with federal law enforcement agents, who told him that Hoffa might attempt to tamper with the Test Fleet jury, and asked him to be on the lookout in Nashville for such attempts and to report to the federal authorities any evidence of wrongdoing that he discovered. Partin agreed to do so.

After the Test Fleet trial was completed, Partin's wife received four monthly installment payments of $300 from government funds, and the state and federal charges against Partin were either dropped or not actively pursued.

[W]e proceed upon the premise that Partin was a government informer from the time he first arrived in Nashville on October 22, and that the Government compensated him for his services as such. It is upon that premise that we consider the constitutional issues presented.

* * *

I.

It is contended that only by violating the petitioner's rights under the Fourth Amendment was Partin able to hear the petitioner's incriminating statements in the hotel suite, and that Partin's testimony was therefore inadmissible * * *. The argument is that Partin's failure to disclose his role as a government informer vitiated the consent that the petitioner gave to Partin's repeated entries into the suite, and that by listening to the petitioner's statements Partin conducted an illegal "search" for verbal evidence.

The preliminary steps of this argument are on solid ground. A hotel room can clearly be the object of Fourth Amendment protection as much as a home or an office. The Fourth Amendment can certainly be violated by guileful as well as by forcible intrusions into a constitutionally protected area. And the protections of the Fourth Amendment are surely not limited to tangibles, but can extend as well to oral statements.

Where the argument falls is in its misapprehension of the fundamental nature and scope of Fourth Amendment protection. What the Fourth Amendment protects is the security a man relies upon when he places himself or his property within a constitutionally protected area, be it his home or his office, his hotel room or his automobile. There he is protected from unwarranted governmental intrusion. And when he puts something in his filing cabinet, in his desk drawer, or in his pocket, he has the right to know it will be secure from an unreasonable search or an unreasonable seizure. * * *

In the present case, however, it is evident that no interest legitimately protected by the Fourth Amendment is involved. It is obvious that the petitioner was not relying on the security of his hotel suite when he made the incriminating statements to Partin or in Partin's presence. Partin did not enter the suite by force or by stealth. He was not a surreptitious eavesdropper. Partin was in the suite by invitation, and every conversation which he heard was either directed to him or knowingly carried on in his presence. The petitioner, in a word, was not relying on the security of the hotel room; he was relying upon his misplaced confidence that Partin would not reveal his wrongdoing. As counsel for the petitioner himself points out, some of the communications with Partin did not take place in the suite at all, but in the "hall of the hotel," in the "Andrew Jackson Hotel lobby," and "at the courthouse."

Neither this Court nor any member of it has ever expressed the view that the Fourth Amendment protects a wrongdoer's misplaced belief that a person to whom he voluntarily confides his wrongdoing will not reveal it. Indeed, the Court unanimously rejected that very contention less than four years ago in Lopez v. United States, 373 U.S. 427, 83 S.Ct. 1381, 10 L.Ed.2d 462. * * * In the words of the dissenting opinion in *Lopez*, "The risk of being overheard by an eavesdropper or betrayed by an informer or deceived as to the identity of one with whom one deals is probably inherent in the conditions of human society. It is the kind of risk we necessarily assume whenever we speak."

Adhering to these views, we hold that no right protected by the Fourth Amendment was violated in the present case.

* * *

IV.

Finally, the petitioner claims that even if there was no violation [of any of his specific federal constitutional rights], the judgment of conviction must nonetheless be reversed. The argument is based upon the Due Process Clause of the Fifth Amendment. The "totality" of the Government's conduct during the Test Fleet trial operated, it is said, to " 'offend those canons of decency and fairness which express the notions of justice of English-speaking peoples even toward those charged with the most heinous offenses' (Rochin v. [People of] California, 342 U.S. 165, 169 [72 S.Ct. 205, 208, 96 L.Ed. 183])."

The argument boils down to a general attack upon the use of a government informer as "a shabby thing in any case," and to the claim that in the circumstances of this particular case the risk that Partin's testimony might be perjurious was very high. Insofar as the general attack upon the use of informers is based upon historic "notions" of "English-speaking peoples," it is without historical foundation. In the words of Judge Learned Hand, "Courts have countenanced the use of informers from time immemorial; in cases of conspiracy, or in other cases when the crime consists of preparing for another crime, it is usually necessary to rely upon them or upon accomplices because the criminals will almost certainly proceed covertly. * * * " United States v. Dennis, 2 Cir., 183 F.2d 201, at 224.

This is not to say that a secret government informer is to the slightest degree more free from all relevant constitutional restrictions than is any other government agent. It *is* to say that the use of secret informers is not *per se* unconstitutional.

The petitioner is quite correct in the contention that Partin, perhaps even more than most informers, may have had motives to lie. But it does not follow that his testimony was untrue, nor does it follow that his testimony was constitutionally inadmissible. The established safeguards of the Anglo-American legal system leave the veracity of a witness to be tested by cross-examination, and the credibility of his testimony to be determined by a properly instructed jury. At the trial of this case, Partin was subjected to rigorous cross-examination, and the extent and nature of his dealings with federal and state authorities were insistently explored. The trial judge instructed the jury, both specifically and generally, with regard to assessing Partin's credibility. The Constitution does not require us to upset the jury's verdict.

Affirmed.

NOTES

1. **Use of Transmitters or Recorders.** If an undercover agent uses electronic devices, does the investigation involve a search? Should it make any difference whether the undercover agent merely records a conversation with the suspect, or causes it to be transmitted for hearing (and perhaps recording) by others?

In United States v. White, 401 U.S. 745, 91 S.Ct. 1122, 28 L.Ed.2d 453 (1971), White was charged with drug transactions with a government informer, Harvey Jackson. Jackson had carried a radio transmitter concealed on his person and nearby government agents listened to the transaction by this means. At trial, Jackson was not available and, over objection, the trial judge permitted the government agents to testify to what they overheard; White was convicted. On appeal, the Court of Appeals read On Lee v. United States, 343 U.S. 747, 72 S.Ct. 967, 96 L.Ed. 1270 (1952), as holding that use of such a transmitting device did not make Jackson's conduct a search. But it further read Katz v. United States, 389 U.S. 347, 88 S.Ct. 507, 19 L.Ed.2d 576 (1967), as overruling On Lee. Under Katz, it continued, Jackson's activity was a search conducted without a warrant. Therefore the agents' testimony was inadmissible. The Supreme Court reversed. In an opinion announcing the judgment of the Court and joined by three other members of the Court, Justice White relied upon two grounds. First, the Court of Appeals erred in reading Katz as overruling On Lee:

> If the conduct and revelations of an agent operating without electronic equipment do not invade the defendant's constitutionally justifiable expectations of privacy, neither does a simultaneous recording of the same conversation made by the agent or by others from transmissions received from the agent to whom the defendant is talking and whose trustworthiness the defendant necessarily risks.

401 U.S. at 751, 91 S.Ct. at 1126, 28 L.Ed.2d at 458. Second, under Desist v. United States, 394 U.S. 244, 89 S.Ct. 1030, 22 L.Ed.2d 248 (1969), Katz was not to be applied to surveillance which—like that in On Lee—took place before the decision in Katz. Judged by pre-Katz law, i.e., On Lee, the facts presented no search.

Justices Harlan, Marshall, and Douglas dissented separately; each expressed the view that Desist was wrongly decided and should not be followed. All also took the position that On Lee should no longer be regarded as controlling, and that Jackson's activity implicated the Fourth Amendment. Justice Harlan explained:

> The critical question * * * is whether under our system of government, as reflected in the Constitution, we should impose on our citizens the risk of the electronic listener or observer without at least the protection of a warrant requirement.

This question must, in my view, be answered by assessing the nature of a particular practice and the likely extent of its impact on the individual's sense of security balanced against the utility of the conduct as a technique of law enforcement. * * *

The impact of the practice of third-party bugging must, I think, be considered such as to undermine that confidence and sense of security in dealing with one another that is characteristic of individual relationships between citizens in a free society. It goes beyond the impact on privacy occasioned by the ordinary type of "informer" investigation * * *. The argument of the plurality opinion, to the effect that it is irrelevant whether secrets are revealed by the mere tattletale or the transistor, ignores the differences occasioned by third-party monitoring and recording which insures full and accurate disclosure of all that is said, free of the possibility of error and oversight that inheres in human reporting.

401 U.S. at 786–87, 91 S.Ct. at 1143, 28 L.Ed.2d at 478–79. Overruling *On Lee*, he stressed, would not end third-party monitoring of informants but rather prevent law enforcement officers from engaging in the practice "unless they first had probable cause to suspect an individual of involvement in illegal activities and had tested their version of the facts before a detached judicial officer." Justice Harlan noted that recording of a transaction by an informer-participant (without transmission of it to others) was not at issue. He observed, however, that such a situation might be distinguished on the ground the informer may renege and not provide the recording to the Government; where transmission of the conversation is involved, however, the intrusion involved in providing the government with a documented record of the conversation "is instantaneous."

Justice Marshall expressed the view that in light of *Katz*, *On Lee* "cannot be considered viable." Justice Douglas' general discussion strongly suggested he would regard either participant recording or transmission as a search.

Justice Brennan concurred in the result on the ground that, under *Desist*, the case was controlled by *On Lee*. But he further offered that in his view "current Fourth Amendment jurisprudence interposes a warrant requirement not only in cases of third-party electronic monitoring * * * but also in cases of electronic recording by a government agent of a face-to-face conversation with a criminal suspect." Justice Black also concurred in the result only. He expressed disagreement with the plurality's reliance upon *Desist* because, in his view, exclusionary rule cases should be applied retroactively. But relying upon his dissent in *Katz*, he took the position that eavesdropping by electronic means cannot constitute a search (i.e., *Katz* was wrongly decided) and therefore Jackson's activities did not constitute a search for Fourth Amendment purposes.

Does *White* settle the issue of transmission of a conversation by an undercover agent? Justices Brennan, Douglas, Marshall and Harlan expressed the view that Jackson's conduct constituted a search under the Fourth Amendment; the four Justices in the plurality were obviously committed to the opposite position. Justice Black's action can be characterized as a refusal to address the effect of *Katz* upon this situation because he regarded *Katz* as wrongly decided.

Despite the Government's apparent victory in *White*, on October 16, 1972, the United States Attorney General issued a memorandum requiring Department of Justice approval for all consensual monitoring of nontelephone conversations by federal departments or agencies. If fewer than 48 hours are available to obtain such approval or if exigent circumstances preclude an effort to secure Department of Justice approval, the head of the department or agency (or someone designated by the head) may authorize the action. In United States v. Caceres, 440 U.S. 741, 99 S.Ct. 1465, 59 L.Ed.2d 733 (1979), the Supreme Court refused to require the exclusion in a federal criminal trial of evidence obtained in violation of Internal Revenue Service regulations adopted pursuant to the Attorney General's memorandum.

2. **Literal "Searches" Conducted by Undercover Officers.** Is the Fourth Amendment applicable if an undercover officer engages in a more traditional "search," as contrasted with the efforts to overhear conversations involved in *Hoffa*? The leading case is Gouled v. United States, 255 U.S. 298, 41 S.Ct. 261, 65 L.Ed. 647 (1921). Army intelligence personnel suspected Gouled of involvement in a scheme to defraud the Government. They discovered an enlisted man assigned to intelligence, Cohen, was a business associate of Gouled and directed him to visit Gouled to see what he could learn. The formal certificate before the Supreme Court stated that Cohen came to Gouled's office during his absence on the pretense of making a friendly call, gained admission to the office, and—in a manner not detailed—found and seized a certain document later admitted at trial. The Solicitor General, however, urged this version of the facts was not supported by the only evidence directly bearing upon the matter, Cohen's own testimony. Cohen testified that Gouled was in his office when he arrived and the two chatted; when Gouled stepped out for a moment, Cohen took the document at issue from the top of Gouled's desk. The Court's opinion stated that Cohen "pretending to make a friendly call upon the defendant gained admission to his office and in his absence * * * seized and carried away" the document. It is not clear whether Gouled, if present at the time of Cohen's visit, was aware of Cohen's status as an army intelligence agent.

The Court held that the manner in which the document was obtained constituted an unreasonable search within the meaning of the Fourth Amendment.

> [W]hether entrance to the home or office of a person suspected of crime be obtained * * * by stealth, or through social acquaintance, or in the guise of a business call, and whether the owner be present or not when [the officer] enters, any search and seizure subsequently and secretly made in his absence falls within the scope of the prohibition of the Fourth Amendment * * *.

255 U.S. at 306, 41 S.Ct. at 264, 65 L.Ed. at 651.

Gouled can be read as holding only that if an undercover officer obtains consent to enter premises or to inspect items through deception, he cannot exceed the scope of that consent. Thus the decision may rest upon the proposition that Cohen's entry into the office, although pursuant to consent obtained by deception, was permissible. When he approached the desk, rummaged through the papers (if he did so), or seized the document, however, he exceeded the scope of that consent and his conduct was no longer supportable on the basis of the consent. It is also possible, however, to read *Gouled* more broadly as imposing or at least suggesting more stringent limitations upon some undercover activities.

CHAPTER 9

GRAND JURY INVESTIGATIVE FUNCTIONS

Analysis

EDITORS' INTRODUCTION: GRAND JURY INVESTIGATIVE POWERS

The grand jury serves two distinct functions. One is a screening function; the grand jury evaluates evidence supporting possible charges and returns an indictment only in those cases in which the evidence amounts to at least probable cause to believe the accused committed the offense. The other is an investigatorial function: the grand jury sometimes develops information that is of value in determining whether grounds for a charge exist and—perhaps incidentally—in proving that charge at the defendant's criminal trial. The second function is the subject of this chapter.

The unique advantage the grand jury has as an investigatorial agency is its subpoena power. Unlike police officers or prosecutors, the grand jury can compel persons, under threat of contempt, to appear, be sworn, and—in absence of a legal privilege—to accurately answer questions. Note, The Grand Jury—Its Investigatory Powers and Limitations, 37 Minn.L.Rev. 586, 606 (1953). See also, Note, The Grand Jury as an Investigatory Body, 74 Harv.L.Rev. 590 (1961). In addition, a grand jury subpoena can direct persons to bring with them papers, documents, or physical items for production to the grand jury. A subpoena directing appearance for oral testimony is often called a subpoena *ad testificandum*, while a subpoena directing the production of items is called a subpoena *duces tecum*. See State ex rel. Pollard v. Criminal Court, 263 Ind. 236, 329 N.E.2d 573 (1975).

Investigatory Role

The grand jury's investigatory role developed out of its function in screening charges. Although the government often presented a proposed criminal charge to the grand jury for consideration, grand juries were traditionally free to act on their own knowledge and return charges on this basis. Costello v. United States, 350 U.S. 359, 362, 76 S.Ct. 406, 408, 100 L.Ed. 397, 402 (1956). Moreover, the grand jury could develop its own information even in the absence of a proposed criminal charge submitted by the government. See Hale v. Henkel, 201 U.S. 43, 26 S.Ct. 370, 50 L.Ed. 652 (1906). The authority to subpoena witnesses and documents developed as an aid in performing the duty to develop information to use in deciding whether to return formal criminal charges. The Supreme Court has commented:

> [T]he grand jury * * * plays an important role in fair and effective law enforcement * * * . Because its task is to inquire into the existence of possible criminal conduct and to return only well-founded indictments, its investigative powers are necessarily broad. "It is a grand inquest, a body with powers of investigation and inquisition, the scope of whose inquiries is not to be limited narrowly by questions of propriety or forecasts of the probable results of the investigation, or by doubts whether any particular individual will be found properly subject to an accused action of crime." Blair v. United States, 250 U.S. 273, 282, 39 S.Ct. 468, 471, 63 L.Ed. 979 (1919). Hence, the grand jury's authority to subpoena witnesses is not only historic * * * but essential to its task.

Branzburg v. Hayes, 408 U.S. 665, 687–88, 92 S.Ct. 2646, 2660, 33 L.Ed.2d 626, 643–44 (1972).

The traditional absence of legal limitations upon the grand jury's inquiries—both their scope and method—is justified on the need for full information, the absence of danger of abuse of the power due in large part to the lay composition of the groups, and the difficulty of imposing such limitations without unduly impeding the work of the bodies. In Costello v. United States, for example, the Court described the grand jury as "a body of laymen, free from technical rules, acting in secret, pledged to indict no one because of prejudice and to free no one because of special favor." Clearly the Court regarded the solemn nature of grand jury service and the absence of a professional or occupational bias in favor of law enforcement as sufficient to prevent abuse of the grand jury's investigatorial powers—at least in light of the disruption and cost entailed in any efforts to regulate those powers by legal means.

Grand Jury Subpoena Power

The grand jury typically has the authority to invoke the subpoena power of the court which called the grand jury into existence. In theory, the grand jury decides whether to compel appearance of a witness and the court determines whether to issue the subpoena. But in practice the situation may be far different:

> [A]lthough like all federal court subpoenas grand jury subpoenas are issued in the name of the district court over the signature of the clerk, they are issued pro forma and in blank to anyone requesting them. The court exercises no prior control whatsoever over their use. * * * [A]lthough grand jury subpoenas are occasionally discussed as if they were instrumentalities of the grand jury, they are in fact almost universally instrumentalities of the United States Attorney's office or

of some other investigative or prosecutorial department of the executive branch.

In re Grand Jury Proceedings, 486 F.2d 85, 90 (3d Cir.1973).

A grand jury may not itself punish an actual or potential witness for failing to respond to the subpoena or for declining to answer questions. Only the court which called the grand jury into existence can exercise contempt power. See 28 U.S.C.A. § 1826. In the federal system, the scenario often develops as follows: A witness appears before the grand jury but refuses to answer questions put. The refusal is brought to the attention of the judge, who considers the witness's reasons, if any, for refusing to answer. The judge then orders the witness to testify. The witness is returned to the grand jury room. If the witness persists in refusing to respond, the matter goes back to the judge and contempt proceedings begin. See Note, Coercive Contempt and the Federal Grand Jury, 79 Colum.L.Rev. 735, 746 n. 83 (1979). In the contempt proceeding, the witness has an opportunity to assert defenses, i.e., any legal reason for declining to answer. 28 U.S.C.A. § 1826(a) provides for contempt sanctions if a witness has refused to comply with a court order "without just cause." If found in contempt, the witness may be confined until s/he is willing to comply. But such confinement cannot, generally, extend beyond the term of the grand jury. Shillitani v. United States, 384 U.S. 364, 86 S.Ct. 1531, 16 L.Ed.2d 622 (1966). A witness found in contempt can also be given a "criminal contempt" penalty, which generally provides no provision for escape from the penalty by complying with the initial order or directive. The Supreme Court indicated in *Shillitani*, however, that the lower federal courts should regard so-called "civil" contempt as the preferred response to an uncooperative witness.

Independence of Grand Jury

Perhaps the major issue in structuring grand jury investigation tools is the extent to which some characteristics of the body render it less susceptible to abuse than other investigatorial agencies. It is traditionally regarded as an independent body, in part because its screening and indictment functions assume such independence; this independence is assumed carry over into its use of the subpoena power for purposes of investigation.

Detractors of the grand jury argue that it is in fact not independent because prosecutors tend to dominate grand juries. Prosecutors are generally given the right to be present during the investigatory stages of the grand jury process, although they may not remain in the chamber for the jury's deliberation and vote on a proposed indictment. E.g., Fed.R.Crim. Pro. 6(d). Although prosecutors have no formal legal power to control the grand jury, they have immense practical authority. Prosecutors generally propose avenues of inquiry, subpoena witnesses, question witnesses when they appear, and advise the grand jurors concerning all matters. One commentator, after noting the "plain fact" of the prosecutor's dominance over the grand jury, concluded:

The real evil of the grand jury system—its viciousness, if you will—lies not so much in the fact that the grand jury is * * * the prosecutor's alter ego, as it does in our pretensions that it is actually an informed and independent quasi-judicial organ, a pretension which misrepresents the prosecutor's unilateral action as the product of stately proceedings conducted by judicial standards. Therefore, * * * the grand jury * * * ironically * * * encourages abuses by allowing the prosecuting authority to carry on its work with complete anonymity and with effects greatly magnified by the accompanying judicial rites.

Antell, The Modern Grand Jury: Benighted Supergovernment, 51 A.B.A.J. 153, 156 (1965).

"One Man" Grand Juries

A number of jurisdictions have curious procedures for judicial participation in the investigation of suspected criminal offenses that somewhat resembles the traditional grand jury. These procedures are more streamlined because they provide for inquiry by single judges. See Conn.Gen.Stat. §§ 54–47b–54–47(h) (providing for "investigatory grand jury" that may consist of a single judge); Mich.Con.Law § 767.3. In some jurisdictions, a judge functioning in this capacity is labeled a "special inquiry" judge. See Idaho Code §§ 19.1116–19.1123 (enacted in 1980); Wash.Rev.Code Ann. § 10.27.170; Okla.Stat.Ann. § 21–951 (limited to possible violation of gambling laws). More traditionally, judges operating under such a procedure are referred to as "one man" grand juries. See In re Slattery, 310 Mich. 458, 461, 17 N.W.2d 251, 252 (1945). The judge typically has the power to subpoena witnesses, compel testimony with the contempt power, and grant immunity to witnesses. At the conclusion of the inquiry, the judge may issue a report or direct the apprehension of the suspect (if probable cause is found), but does not appear to have authority to return formal charges. Authority to bring formal charges remains in the traditional grand jury, if the jurisdiction affords defendants the right to grand jury indictment, or in the prosecutor. See State v. Manning, 86 Wn.2d 272, 543 P.2d 632 (1975).

The rationale for this procedure was discussed by the Michigan Supreme Court in In re Colacasides, 379 Mich. 69, 150 N.W.2d 1 (1967):

Experience has demonstrated * * * that regularly constituted law enforcement agencies sometimes are unable effectively and lawfully to enforce the laws, particularly with respect to corrupt conduct by officers of government and conspiratorial criminal activity on an organized and continuing basis. Our experience has also demonstrated that the common-law 23-man grand jury is unwieldy and ineffective for the investigation of such crimes in a modern, industrialized, and mobile society. It has demonstrated also that corruption in government and organized crime are susceptible to discovery and prosecution if the investigative body has the power to compel some participants therein to testify by enforcing attendance of witness by subpoena and granting immunity from prosecution, but police agencies in this country do not possess such extraordinary power. * * * Traditionally in this country, such extraordinary power has been entrusted only to judicial officers. * * *

This dilemma has been resolved * * * by [the] unique one-man grand jury, comprised of a judicial officer who can properly exercise the

subpoena power and the power to grant immunity to compel testimony.
* * *

379 Mich. at 89–90, 150 N.W.2d at 11.

If procedural protections for suspects in police investigations are properly relaxed in traditional grand jury inquiries, is such relaxation also appropriate when the inquiry is conducted by such a one man grand jury or special inquiry judge? A Michigan court read that state's statutes as permitting a witness to have counsel present during questioning by a one man grand jury but not during an appearance before a traditional grand jury. Responding to the argument that this difference violated the equal protection rights of persons appearing before traditional grand juries, the court summarily concluded "the significant differences" between the two types of proceedings justified the different rights to counsel. People v. Blachura, 59 Mich.App. 664, 667, 229 N.W.2d 877, 879 (1975).

* * *

This chapter contains two sections addressing two aspects of the grand jury's investigatory function. The first addresses the subpoena power and the extent to which it is subject to Fourth Amendment requirements placed upon law enforcement investigation. The second considers the applicability of the Fifth Amendment privilege against compelled self-incrimination in this context and more specifically the need to afford grand jury witnesses the procedural incidents of that privilege applying in traditional law enforcement investigations.

In connection with these issues, consider the recommendation of the National Advisory Commission on Criminal Justice Standards and Goals that the subpoena power presently reposing in the grand jury be given to prosecutors. The Commission's proposal would require a prosecutor using the subpoena power to permit the subject's attorney to be present during the questioning, provide an attorney if the subject desires one but is unable to provide any, and warn the subject concerning his rights including the privilege against self-incrimination. This would formally give the subpoena power to those who, in the Commission's judgment, already exercise it as a practical matter. The result, according to the Commission, would be a "workable and efficient alternative to the grand jury in many criminal cases," which could be used "at even less danger to the interests of the subjects, who often are inadequately protected by existing grand jury procedures." National Advisory Commission on Criminal Justice Standards and Goals, Courts 244–45 (1973). In some jurisdictions, prosecutors already have subpoena power under certain circumstances. Del.Code Ann. tit. 29 § 2504(4); Kan.Stat.Ann. § 22–3101(2). Under the Comprehensive Drug Abuse Prevention and Control Act of 1970, the Attorney General has the power to subpoena witnesses, compel testimony, and require the production of records. 21 U.S.C.A. § 876. This authority has been delegated to special agents in charge of the Drug Enforcement Administration. Such agent's exercise of the subpoena power was upheld in United States v. Hossbach, 518 F.Supp. 759 (E.D.Pa.1980).

A. THE SUBPOENA POWER

A person required by subpoena to appear before a grand jury to testify or participate in the grand jury's investigation could reasonably be regarded as seized within the meaning of the Fourth Amendment. If this is the nature of compelled appearance and participation, the courts would have to consider the circumstances under which such seizures are "reasonable" for Fourth Amendment purposes. The Fourth Amendment significance of grand juries' exercise of the subpoena power is the major issue addressed by the cases in this section.

United States v. Dionisio

Supreme Court of the United States, 1973.
410 U.S. 1, 93 S.Ct. 764, 35 L.Ed.2d 67.

■ MR. JUSTICE STEWART delivered the opinion of the Court.

A special grand jury was convened in the Northern District of Illinois in February 1971, to investigate possible violations of federal criminal statutes relating to gambling. In the course of its investigation the grand jury received in evidence certain voice recordings that had been obtained pursuant to court orders.

The grand jury subpoenaed approximately 20 persons, including the respondent Dionisio, seeking to obtain from them voice exemplars for comparison with the recorded conversations that had been received in evidence. Each witness was advised that he was a potential defendant in a criminal prosecution. Each was asked to examine a transcript of an intercepted conversation, and to go to a nearby office of the United States Attorney to read the transcript into a recording device. The witnesses were advised that they would be allowed to have their attorneys present when they read the transcripts. Dionisio and other witnesses refused to furnish the voice exemplars, asserting that these disclosures would violate their rights under the Fourth and Fifth Amendments.

The Government then filed separate petitions in the United States District Court to compel Dionisio and the other witnesses to furnish the voice exemplars to the grand jury. The petitions stated that the examplars were "essential and necessary" to the grand jury investigation, and that they would "be used solely as a standard of comparison in order to determine whether or not the witness is the person whose voice was intercepted * * * ."

Following a hearing, the district judge rejected the witnesses' constitutional arguments and ordered them to comply with the grand jury's request. He reasoned * * * there would be no Fourth Amendment violation, because the grand jury subpoena did not itself violate the Fourth Amendment, and the order to produce the voice exemplars would involve no unreasonable search and seizure within the proscription of that Amendment * * * . When Dionisio persisted in his refusal to respond to the grand jury's directive, the District Court adjudged him in civil contempt and ordered him committed to custody until he obeyed the court order, or until the expiration of 18 months.

The Court of Appeals for the Seventh Circuit reversed. It * * * concluded that to compel the voice recordings would violate the Fourth Amendment. In the Court's view, the grand jury was "seeking to obtain the voice exemplars of the witnesses by the use of its subpoena powers because probable cause did not exist for their arrest or for some other, less unusual, method of compelling the production of the exemplars." The Court found that the Fourth Amendment applied to grand jury process, and that "under the fourth amendment law enforcement officials may not compel the production of physical evidence absent a showing of the reasonableness of the seizure. * * * "

* * *

The Court of Appeals held that the Fourth Amendment required a preliminary showing of reasonableness before a grand jury witness could be compelled to furnish a voice exemplar, and that in this case the proposed "seizures" of the voice exemplars would be unreasonable because of the large number of witnesses summoned by the grand jury and directed to produce such exemplars. We disagree.

The Fourth Amendment guarantees that all people shall be "secure in their persons, houses, papers, and effects, against unreasonable searches and seizures * * *." Any Fourth Amendment violation in the present setting must rest on a lawless governmental intrusion upon the privacy of "persons" rather than on interference with "property relationships or private papers." Schmerber v. California, 384 U.S. 757, 767, 86 S.Ct. 1826, 1833, 16 L.Ed.2d 908. In Terry v. Ohio, 392 U.S. 1, 88 S.Ct. 1868, 20 L.Ed.2d 889, the Court explained the protection afforded to "persons" in terms of the statement in Katz v. United States, 389 U.S. 347, 88 S.Ct. 507, 19 L.Ed.2d 576, that "the Fourth Amendment protects people, not places," and concluded that "wherever an individual may harbor a reasonable 'expectation of privacy,' * * * he is entitled to be free from unreasonable governmental intrusion."

[T]he obtaining of physical evidence from a person involves a potential Fourth Amendment violation at two different levels—the "seizure" of the "person" necessary to bring him into contact with government agents, and the subsequent search for and seizure of the evidence. * * * The constitutionality of the compulsory production of exemplars from a grand jury witness necessarily turns on the same dual inquiry—whether either the initial compulsion of the person to appear before the grand jury, or the subsequent directive to make a voice recording is an unreasonable "seizure" within the meaning of the Fourth Amendment.

It is clear that a subpoena to appear before a grand jury is not a "seizure" in the Fourth Amendment sense, even though that summons may be inconvenient or burdensome. Last Term we again acknowledged what has long been recognized, that "[c]itizens generally are not constitutionally immune from grand jury subpoenas * * *." Branzburg v. Hayes, 408 U.S. 665, 682, 92 S.Ct. 2646, 2656, 33 L.Ed.2d 626.

* * *

[This is] recent reaffirmation[] of the historically grounded obligation of every person to appear and give his evidence before the grand jury. "The personal sacrifice involved is a part of the necessary contribution of the individual to the welfare of the public." Blair v. United States, 250 U.S. 273, 281, 39 S.Ct. 468, 471, 63 L.Ed. 979. And while the duty may be "onerous" at times, it is "necessary to the administration of justice."

The compulsion exerted by a grand jury subpoena differs from the seizure effected by an arrest or even an investigative "stop" in more than civic obligation. For, as Judge Friendly wrote for the Court of Appeals for the Second Circuit:

"The latter is abrupt, is effected with force or the threat of it and often in demeaning circumstances, and, in the case of arrest, results in a record involving social stigma. A subpoena is served in the same manner as other legal process; it involves no stigma whatever; if the time for appearance is inconvenient, this can generally be altered; and it remains at all times under the control and supervision of a court." United States v. Doe (Schwartz) 457 F.2d 895, 898 (1972).

* * *

This is not to say that a grand jury subpoena is some talisman that dissolves all constitutional protections. The grand jury cannot require a witness to testify against himself. * * * The Fourth Amendment provides protection against a grand jury subpoena *duces tecum* too sweeping in its terms "to be regarded as reasonable." Hale v. Henkel, 201 U.S. 43, 76, 26 S.Ct. 370, 379, 50 L.Ed. 652. And last Term, in the context of a First Amendment claim, we indicated that the Constitution could not tolerate the transformation of the grand jury into an instrument of oppression: "Official harassment of the press undertaken not for purposes of law enforcement but to disrupt a reporter's relationship with his news sources would have no justification. Grand juries are subject to judicial control and subpoenas to motions to quash. We do not expect courts will forget that grand juries must operate within the limits of the First Amendment as well as the Fifth." Branzburg v. Hayes, 408 U.S. 665, 707–708, 92 S.Ct. 2646, 2669–2670, 33 L.Ed.2d 626.

But we are here faced with no such constitutional infirmities in the subpoena to appear before the grand jury or in the order to make the voice recordings. There is * * * no valid Fifth Amendment claim. There was no order to produce private books and papers, and no sweeping subpoena *duces tecum*. And even if *Branzburg* be extended beyond its First Amendment moorings and tied to a more generalized due process concept, there is still no indication in this case of the kind of harassment that was of concern there.

The Court of Appeals found critical significance in the fact that the grand jury had summoned approximately 20 witnesses to furnish voice exemplars. We think that fact is basically irrelevant to the constitutional issues here. The grand jury may have been attempting to identify a number of voices on the tapes in evidence, or it might have summoned the 20 witnesses in an effort to identify one voice. But whatever the case, "[a] grand jury's investigation is not fully carried out until every available clue has been run down and all witnesses examined in every proper way to find if a crime has been committed * * *." United States v. Stone, 2 Cir., 429 F.2d 138, 140. As the Court recalled last Term, "Because its task is to inquire into the existence of possible criminal conduct and to return only well-founded indictments, its investigative powers are necessarily broad." Branzburg v. Hayes, 408 U.S., at 688, 92 S.Ct., at 2659. The grand jury may well find it desirable to call numerous witnesses in the course of an investigation. It does not follow that each witness may resist a subpoena on the ground that too many witnesses have been called. Neither the order to Dionisio to appear, nor the order to make a voice recording was rendered unreasonable by the fact that many others were subjected to the same compulsion.

But the conclusion that Dionisio's compulsory appearance before the grand jury was not an unreasonable "seizure" is the answer to only the first part of the Fourth Amendment inquiry here. Dionisio argues that the grand jury's subsequent directive to make the voice recording was itself an infringement of his rights under the Fourth Amendment. We cannot accept that argument.

In Katz v. United States, supra, we said that the Fourth Amendment provides no protection for what "a person knowingly exposes to the public, even in his own home or office * * *." The physical characteristics of a person's voice, its tone and manner, as opposed to the content of a specific conversation, are constantly exposed to the public. Like a man's facial characteristics, or handwriting, his voice is repeatedly produced for others to hear. No person can have a reasonable expectation that others will not know the sound of his voice, any more than he can reasonably expect that his face will be a mystery to the world. * * *

Since neither the summons to appear before the grand jury, nor its directive to make a voice recording infringed upon any interest protected by the Fourth Amendment, there was no justification for requiring the grand jury to satisfy even the minimal requirement of "reasonableness" imposed by the Court of Appeals. A grand jury has broad investigative powers to determine whether a crime has been committed and who has committed it. The jurors may act on tips, rumors, evidence offered by the prosecutor, or their own personal knowledge. No grand jury witness is "entitled to set limits to the investigation that the grand jury may conduct." And a sufficient basis for an indictment may only emerge at the end of the investigation when all the evidence has been received.

> "It is impossible to conceive that * * * the examination of witnesses must be stopped until a basis is laid by an indictment formally preferred, when the very object of the examination is to ascertain who shall be indicted." Hale v. Henkel, 201 U.S. 43, 65, 26 S.Ct. 370, 375, 50 L.Ed. 652.

Since Dionisio raised no valid Fourth Amendment claim, there is no more reason to require a preliminary showing of reasonableness here than there would be in the case of any witness who, despite the lack of any constitutional or statutory privilege, declined to answer a question or comply with a grand jury request. Neither the Constitution nor our prior cases justify any such interference with grand jury proceedings.[1]

The Fifth Amendment guarantees that no civilian may be brought to trial for an infamous crime "unless on a presentment or indictment of a Grand Jury." This constitutional guarantee presupposes an investigative body "acting independently of either prosecuting attorney or judge," whose mission is to clear the innocent, no less than to bring to trial those who may be guilty. Any holding that would saddle a grand jury with minitrials and preliminary showings would assuredly impede its investigation and frustrate the public's interest in the fair and expeditious administration of the criminal laws. * * * The grand jury may not always serve its historic role as a protective bulwark standing solidly between the ordinary citizen and an overzealous prosecutor, but if it is even to approach the proper performance of its constitutional mission, it must be free to pursue its investigations unhindered by external influence or supervision so long as it does not trench upon the legitimate rights of any witness called before it.

Since the Court of Appeals found an unreasonable search and seizure where none existed, and imposed a preliminary showing of reasonableness where none was required, its judgment is reversed and this case is remanded to that Court for further proceedings consistent with this opinion.

It is so ordered.

United States v. Mara

Supreme Court of the United States, 1973.
410 U.S. 19, 93 S.Ct. 774, 35 L.Ed.2d 99.

■ MR. JUSTICE STEWART delivered the opinion of the Court.

The respondent, Richard J. Mara, was subpoenaed to appear before the September 1971 Grand Jury in the Northern District of Illinois that was investigating thefts of interstate shipments. On two separate occasions he was directed to produce handwriting and printing exemplars to the grand jury's designated agent. Each time he was advised that he was a potential defendant in the matter under investigation. On both occasions he refused to produce the exemplars.

The Government then petitioned the United States District Court to compel Mara to furnish the handwriting and printing exemplars to the grand jury. * * * The District Judge rejected the respondent's contention that the compelled production of such exemplars would constitute an

1. Mr. Justice Marshall in dissent suggests that a preliminary showing of "reasonableness" is required where the grand jury subpoenas a witness to appear and produce handwriting or voice exemplars, but not when it subpoenas him to appear and testify. Such a distinction finds no support in the Constitution. The dissent argues that there is a potential Fourth Amendment violation in the case of a subpoenaed grand jury witness because of the asserted intrusiveness of the initial subpoena to appear—the possible stigma from a grand jury appearance and the inconvenience of the official restraint. But the initial directive to appear is as intrusive if the witness is called simply to testify as it is if he is summoned to produce physical evidence.

unreasonable search and seizure, and he ordered the respondent to provide them. When the witness continued to refuse to do so, he was adjudged to be in civil contempt and was committed to custody until he obeyed the court order or until the expiration of the grand jury term.

The Court of Appeals for the Seventh Circuit reversed. * * *

We have held today in *Dionisio*, that a grand jury subpoena is not a "seizure" within the meaning of the Fourth Amendment, and further, that that Amendment is not violated by a grand jury directive compelling production of "physical characteristics" which are "constantly exposed to the public." Handwriting, like speech, is repeatedly shown to the public, and there is no more expectation of privacy in the physical characteristics of a person's script than there is in the tone of his voice. * * * Consequently the Government was under no obligation here, any more than in *Dionisio*, to make a preliminary showing of "reasonableness."

Indeed, this case lacks even the aspects of an expansive investigation that the Court of Appeals found significant in *Dionisio*. In that case 20 witnesses were summoned to give exemplars; here there was only one. The specific and narrowly drawn directive requiring the witness to furnish a specimen of his handwriting violated no legitimate Fourth Amendment interest. The District Court was correct, therefore, in ordering the respondent to comply with the grand jury's request.

Accordingly, the judgment of the Court of Appeals is reversed, and this case is remanded to that court for further proceedings consistent with this opinion.

It is so ordered.

■ MR. JUSTICE MARSHALL, dissenting [in both *Dionisio* and *Mara*.]

* * *

The Court concludes that the exemplars sought from the respondents are not protected by the Fourth Amendment because respondents have surrendered their expectation of privacy with respect to voice and handwriting by knowingly exposing these to the public. But even accepting this conclusion, it does not follow that the investigatory seizures of respondents, accomplished through the use of subpoenas ordering them to appear before the grand jury—and thereby necessarily interfering with their personal liberty—are outside the protection of the Fourth Amendment. To the majority, though, "[i]t is clear that a subpoena to appear before a grand jury is not a 'seizure' in the Fourth Amendment sense, even though that summons may be inconvenient or burdensome." With due respect, I find nothing "clear" about so sweeping an assertion.

There can be no question that investigatory seizures effected by the police are subject to the constraints of the Fourth and Fourteenth Amendments. * * * [T]he present cases involve official investigatory seizures which interfere with personal liberty. The Court considers dispositive, however, the fact that the seizures were effected by the grand jury, rather than the police. I cannot agree.

* * *

In the present cases * * * it was not testimony that the grand juries sought from respondents, but physical evidence. The Court glosses over this important distinction from its prior decisions, however, by artificially bifurcating its analysis of what is taking place in these cases—that is, by effectively treating what is done with individuals once they are before the grand jury as irrelevant in determining what safeguards are to govern the procedures by which they are initially compelled to appear. Nonetheless, the fact remains that the historic exception to which the Court resorts is not necessarily as broad as the context in which it is now employed. Hence, I believe that the question we must consider is whether an extension of that exception is warranted, and if so, under what conditions.

* * *

The Court seems to reason that the exception to the Fourth Amendment for grand jury subpoenas directed at persons is justified by the relative unintrusiveness of the grand jury process on an individual's liberty. The Court * * * suggests that arrests or even investigatory "stops" are inimical to personal liberty because they may involve the use of force; they may be carried out in demeaning circumstances; and at least an arrest may yield the social stigma of a record. By contrast, we are told, a grand jury subpoena is a simple legal process, which is served in an unoffensive manner; it results in no stigma; and a convenient time for appearance may always be arranged. The Court would have us believe, in short, that, unlike an arrest or an investigatory "stop," a grand jury subpoena entails little more inconvenience than a visit to an old friend. Common sense and practical experience indicate otherwise.

It may be that service of a grand jury subpoena does not involve the same potential for momentary embarrassment as does an arrest or investigatory "stop." But this difference seems inconsequential in comparison to the substantial stigma which—contrary to the Court's assertion—may result from a grand jury appearance as well as from an arrest or investigatory seizure. Public knowledge that a man has been summoned by a federal grand jury investigating, for instance, organized criminal activity can mean loss of friends, irreparable injury to business, and tremendous pressures on one's family life. Whatever nice legal distinctions may be drawn between police and prosecutor, on the one hand, and the grand jury, on the other, the public often treats an appearance before a grand jury as tantamount to a visit to the station house. Indeed, the former is frequently more damaging than the latter, for a grand jury appearance has an air of far greater gravity than a brief visit "downtown" for a "talk." The Fourth Amendment was placed in our Bill of Rights to protect the individual citizen from such potentially disruptive governmental intrusion into his private life unless conducted reasonably and with sufficient cause.

Nor do I believe that the constitutional problems inherent in such governmental interference with an individual's person are substantially alleviated because one may seek to appear at a "convenient time." * * * No matter how considerate a grand jury may be in arranging for an individual's appearance, the basic fact remains that his liberty has been officially restrained for some period of time. In terms of its effect on the individual, this restraint does not differ meaningfully from the restraint imposed on a suspect compelled to visit the police station house. Thus, the nature of the intrusion on personal liberty caused by a grand jury subpoena cannot, without more, be considered sufficient basis for denying respondents the protection of the Fourth Amendment.

* * *

Thus, the Court's decisions today can serve only to encourage prosecutorial exploitation of the grand jury process, at the expense of both individual liberty and the traditional neutrality of the grand jury. Indeed, by holding that the grand jury's power to subpoena these respondents for the purpose of obtaining exemplars is completely outside the purview of the Fourth Amendment, the Court fails to appreciate the essential difference between real and testimonial evidence in the context of these cases, and thereby hastens the reduction of the grand jury into simply another investigative device of law enforcement officials. By contrast, the Court of Appeals, in proper recognition of these dangers, imposed narrow limitations on the subpoena power of the grand jury which are necessary to guard against unreasonable official interference with individual liberty but which would not impair significantly the traditional investigatory powers of that body.

The Court of Appeals in *Mara* did not impose a requirement that the Government establish probable cause to support a grand jury's request for exemplars. It correctly recognized that "examination of witnesses by a grand jury need not be preceded by a formal charge against a particular individual," since the very purpose of the grand jury process is to ascertain probable cause. * * * [I]t ruled only that the request for physical evidence such as exemplars should be subject to a showing of reasonableness. This "reasonableness" requirement has previously been explained by this Court, albeit in a somewhat different context, to require a showing by the Government that: (1) "the investigation is authorized by Congress"; (2) the investigation "is for a purpose Congress can order"; (3) the evidence sought is "relevant"; and (4) the request is "adequate, but not excessive, for the purposes of the relevant inquiry." See Oklahoma Press Publishing Co. v. Walling, 327 U.S. 186, 209, 66 S.Ct. 494, 506, 90 L.Ed. 614 (1946). This was the interpretation of the "reasonableness" requirement properly adopted by the Court of Appeals. And, in elaborating on the requirement that the request not be "excessive," it added that the Government would bear the burden of showing that it was not conducting "a general fishing expedition under grand jury sponsorship."

These are not burdensome limitations to impose on the grand jury when it seeks to secure physical evidence, such as exemplars, that has traditionally been gathered directly by law enforcement officials. The essence of the requirement would be nothing more than a showing that the evidence sought is relevant to the purpose of the investigation and that the particular grand jury is not the subject of prosecutorial abuse—a showing that the Government should have little difficulty making, unless it is in fact acting improperly. Nor would the requirement interfere with the power of the grand jury to call witnesses before it, to take their testimony, and to ascertain their knowledge concerning criminal activity. It would only discourage prosecutorial abuse of the grand jury process. The "reasonableness" requirement would do no more in the context of these cases than the Constitution compels—protect the citizen from unreasonable and arbitrary governmental interference, and ensure that the broad subpoena powers of the grand jury which the Court now recognizes are not turned into a tool of prosecutorial oppression.

I would therefore affirm the Court of Appeals' decisions reversing the judgments of contempt against respondents and order the cases remanded to the District Court to allow the Government an opportunity to make the requisite showing of "reasonableness" in each case. To do less is to invite the very sort of unreasonable governmental intrusion on individual liberty that the Fourth Amendment was intended to prevent.[2]

NOTES

1. **Nonconstitutional Limits on Grand Jury Subpoena Power.** Statutes and court rules provide limitations upon grand juries' ability to exercise the subpoena power, especially with regard the power to compel the production of documents or items.

Under Federal Rule of Criminal Procedure 17(c), a person served with a subpoena commanding the production of papers or other objects (a subpoena *duces tecum*) may move the court to quash or modify the subpoena on the grounds that "compliance would be unreasonable or oppressive." Application of the provision to grand jury subpoenas was addressed in United States v. R. Enterprises, Inc., 498 U.S. 292, 111 S.Ct. 722, 112 L.Ed.2d 795 (1991). A federal grand jury investigating allegations of interstate transportation of obscene materials issued subpoenas to R. Enterprises and two other companies owned by Martin Rothstein; the subpoenas called for production of records. All three companies moved to quash the subpoenas, primarily on the ground they called for material irrelevant to the grand jury's investigation; the district court denied the motions. The Court of Appeals, however, reversed. In United States v. Nixon, 418 U.S. 683, 94 S.Ct. 3090, 41 L.Ed.2d 1039 (1974), the Supreme Court held that a subpoena calling for production of documents before trial is to be enforced only if the party seeking it shows relevancy, admissibility and specificity. The Court of Appeals in R. Enterprises held that these standards were also applicable to grand jury subpoenas *duces tecum* and those issued in the case did not meet the standards.

The Supreme Court reversed. Given the function of the grand jury, Justice O'Connor explained, the *Nixon* standards do not apply to grand jury subpoenas. Rule 17(c) imposes a requirement of "reasonableness" on grand jury subpoenas, she continued, and the Court's task was to fashion a standard for reasonableness in the context of grand jury proceedings:

> [T]he law presumes, absent a strong showing to the contrary, that a grand jury acts within the legitimate scope of its authority. Consequently, a grand jury subpoena issued through normal channels is presumed to be reasonable, and the burden of showing unreasonableness must be on the recipient who seeks to avoid compliance. * * * [W]here, as here, a subpoena is challenged on relevancy

2. * * * [A] requirement that the Government establish the "reasonableness" of the request for an exemplar would hardly be so burdensome as the Court suggests. As matters stand, if the suspect resists the request, the Government must seek a judicial order directing that he comply with the request. Thus, a formal judicial proceeding is already necessary. The question whether the request is "reasonable" would simply be one further matter to consider in such a proceeding.

grounds, the motion to quash must be denied unless the district court determines that there is no reasonable possibility that the category of materials the Government seeks will produce information relevant to the general subject of the grand jury's investigation.

498 U.S. at 300–01, 111 S.Ct. at 728, 112 L.Ed.2d at 807–08. The subpoenas at issue were not challenged as too indefinite or calling for overly burdensome production, and consequently the Court did not consider such claims.

A person served with a subpoena may not know the general subject matter of the grand jury's investigation, the Court noted. Therefore, even if such a person has a valid claim to have the subpoena quashed he may not be able to make the showing necessary under the standard set out by the Court. *R. Enterprises, Inc.* did not resolve this difficulty. The Court suggested, however, that in a case where unreasonableness is alleged, the District Court might be justified in requiring the Government to reveal the general subject matter of the investigation before requiring the challenging party to carry its burden of persuasion. To discourage subpoena challenges as a means of achieving discovery, Justice O'Connor added, such disclosure might be required *in camera*.

Turning to the facts of the case, the Court noted all three companies were owned by one person and did business in the same area. One of the three, further, shipped sexually explicit material into the district of concern to the grand jury. From these undisputed facts the District Court could have properly concluded there was a reasonable possibility the records would produce information relevant to the grand jury's investigation into the interstate transportation of obscene material. Thus the District Court correctly denied the motions to quash the subpoenas.

2. **Use of Subpoena For Intrusive Evidence Gathering.** Despite the principal cases, some federal courts have balked at permitting the use of grand jury subpoenas to compel persons to submit to particularly intrusive procedure for developing evidence. One, for example, held that a grand jury subpoena may not be used to compel a person to produce a sample of blood:

> We hold that the United States' decision to seek T.S.'s blood sample with a grand jury subpoena was not an appropriate use of such a subpoena. To allow the United States to use a Rule 17(c) subpoena for this purpose would abrogate T.S.'s Fourth Amendment rights and, thus, transform the subpoena into an instrument by which an illegal search and seizure is effectuated. This is a result clearly not intended under the Federal Rules of Criminal Procedure, the Fourth Amendment, or applicable Supreme Court precedent.

> Therefore, we conclude that the United States must obtain a warrant before we will compel T.S. to comply with the demand for blood samples. To do so, the United States must establish probable cause that T.S.'s blood samples will yield evidence of a crime.

In Re Grand Jury Proceedings, 816 F.Supp. 1196, 1205–06 (W.D.Ky.1993). Another federal court has relied on the same reasoning to bar the Government from using a subpoena to obtain a saliva sample. United States v. Nicolosi, 885 F.Supp. 50 (E.D.N.Y.1995).

In contrast, the court in In re Grand Jury Proceedings (Vickers), 38 F.Supp.2d 159 (D.N.H.1998), employed a more complex analysis for such problems. Even if a suspect's Fourth Amendment rights are implicated by a grand jury subpoena, the *Vickers* court reasoned, the grand jury's independent investigatory function precludes courts from barring the use of a subpoena and requiring the government or the grand jury to obtain a search warrant. Instead, the district court should entertain a motion to quash the subpoena. In ruling on that motion, the court should subject the grand jury's demand to scrutiny, although of a less rigorous type or degree than it would apply to a search warrant application.

A subpoena may seek evidence that is not within Fourth Amendment protection. This is the case with a subpoena that demands the production of fingerprint or hair samples, *Vickers* reasoned, since persons do not have a constitutionally protected privacy interest in their fingerprints or the characteristics of their hair. In such a case, the court should inquire only whether the subpoena describes the evidence sought with sufficient particularity, that evidence is reasonably related to a legitimate aspect of the grand jury's investigation, and complying with the subpoena would impose an unreasonable or oppressive burden on the suspect.

A subpoena may alternatively seek evidence implicating the suspect's Fourth Amendment interests. This is the case, for example, if the subpoena demands the production of saliva samples, since obtaining such samples involves an intrusion compromising the suspect's Fourth Amendment right to bodily integrity. In a case of this sort, *Vickers* indicated, somewhat more rigorous review of an application is required:

> [T]he relevant inquiry is not whether the subpoena is supported by "probable cause." Instead, the court must simply determine whether the subject matter and scope of the subpoena are reasonable under the circumstances, including consideration of the subpoenaed person's constitutional rights.
>
> The following questions are pertinent to that "reasonableness" assessment: (1) Does the subpoena command the production of things relevant to the investigation being pursued by the grand jury?; (2) Does the subpoena specify with sufficient particularity the things being sought?; (3) Is the subpoena sufficiently narrow in scope to be considered reasonable?; (4) Has the subpoena issued for reasons other than to harass the subject?; and (5) Can the subject provide the requested evidence without unnecessary risk of personal harm (e.g., potentially dangerous invasive surgery) and/or personal humiliation (e.g., unnecessary invasion of bodily integrity or dignitary interests)? In short, the court must determine whether protected constitutional values or rights are likely to be unduly burdened or violated if the subpoena is not quashed.

38 F.Supp.2d at 164.

The subpoenas before the *Vickers* court sought, in part, production of saliva samples for a grand jury investigating pipe bombing incidents in Concord, New Hampshire. It evaluated the subpoenas in light of publicly known information and *in camera* review of certain submissions by the government. The court concluded:

> [T]he government has demonstrated that the evidence sought: (1) is plainly relevant to a legitimate and ongoing investigation being conducted by the grand jury; (2) is described with sufficient particularity to notify respondents of precisely what is sought; (3) is not sought to harass respondents or to impose some burden because of their social or political views; (4) could be probative in identifying or eliminating persons who may have participated in, or may have knowledge of or evidence relating to, the crimes under investigation; (5) can be obtained from respondents with very minimal invasion of their bodily integrity (i.e., by simply swabbing the inside of the mouth); and (6) can be obtained with no risk of physical pain, injury, or embarrassment to respondents, and with the most minimal personal inconvenience.

* * *

On balance, therefore, the court concludes that the grand jury subpoenas at issue are neither "unreasonable" nor otherwise properly subject to an order to quash. The grand jury's justification for issuance and enforcement of those subpoenas is more than adequate to warrant denial of respondents' motion to quash.

38 F.Supp.2d at 167–68.

Some state courts have also developed limits on the grand jury subpoena process, sometimes as a matter of state constitutional law. An Oklahoma court, for example, held that a subpoena for a blood sample should issue only if the grand jury foreman submits to the trial judge an affidavit permitting the judge to find that probable cause exists to believe the sample would result in developing evidence of criminal activity. Woolverton v. Multi–County Grand Jury, 859 P.2d 1112 (Okla. Crim.App.1993). See also, In the Matter of a Grand Jury Investigation, 427 Mass. 221, 692 N.E.2d 56 (1998) (when grand jury subpoena seeks blood sample, Fourth Amendment and state constitution are satisfied if the grand jury is shown to have a reasonable basis for believing resulting tests will significantly aid it in investigating circumstances it has good reason to believe involve crime).

3. **Use of Grand Jury For Trial Preparation.** A few limitations upon the grand jury's investigatory power are widely acknowledged. It is improper for a grand jury to take testimony for purposes of pursuing civil remedies available to the government. United States v. Procter & Gamble Co., 356 U.S. 677, 78 S.Ct. 983, 2 L.Ed.2d 1077 (1958).

Similarly, a grand jury abuses its procedure by using the subpoena power to assist the prosecution in preparing for trial. This was illustrated by State v. Johnson, 287 N.J.Super. 247, 670 A.2d 1100 (1996). Johnson was indicted for murder. In preparing for trial, the prosecutor interviewed Thomas, who acknowledged she had seen Johnson fleeing from the scene of the killing. She added, however, she would not give a sworn statement because she feared retaliation. Soon after, she was brought before a grand jury (other than the indicting one) on a bench warrant and, under oath, she testified she had seen Johnson flee the scene. At trial, she testified she had not seen anyone run from the scene. Her contrary grand jury testimony was then admitted as a prior inconsistent statement. On appeal, Johnson argued the prosecutor had improperly used the grand jury process to prepare for trial:

Defendants do not argue, nor could they, that a prosecutor must cease all investigatory efforts once an indictment is issued. Similarly, defendants do not argue, nor could they, that a grand jury cannot continue an investigation once an indictment has issued, if the purpose of the investigation is to identify further crimes committed by the indictees or to identify unnamed actors. Defendants contend that Thomas' testimony was not obtained in the course of an investigation of further charges against defendants or others. Rather, they contend that her testimony was obtained solely to prepare for the trial of the pending indictment.

* * * Generally, it is considered appropriate for the government to interrogate witnesses on subjects relevant to a continuing grand jury investigation, even when the evidence received may also relate to a pending indictment.

Use of the grand jury, however, * * * solely to prepare and preserve the testimony of a witness for the trial of a pending indictment is an abuse of the grand jury.

* * * On its face, the transcript suggests that the prosecutor was presenting witnesses to the grand jury as part of an investigation regarding additional charges against defendants, such as [tampering with a witness or retaliation against a witness]. This suggestion, however, is belied by the prosecutor's comments in response to a direct question from the trial judge to explain the purpose of the Thomas testimony. She stated:

It's further investigation, Judge,* * * it's in order to have them for a factfinding trial * * *

The inescapable conclusion from this statement is that Thomas was brought before the grand jury solely to preserve her testimony for trial. The second grand jury panel was not conducting a further investigation concerning the * * * murder or any actions by defendants after the shooting. The use to which the prosecutor put this second grand jury was improper * * *.

827 N.J.Super. at 259–61, 670 A.2d at 1105–07.

4. **Subpoena Directives to Cooperate With Police or Prosecutors.** To what extent can a grand jury subpoena direct a witness not to appear or produce items before the grand jury but rather to cooperate with police or prosecutors?

The issue was addressed in In re John Doe Grand Jury Proceedings, 717 A.2d 1129 (R.I.1998). The subpoenas at issue were served by police officers. Each subpoena asserted by its terms that the officer serving the subpoena was an agent of the grand jury and then directed the documents sought "should be given directly to him." When officers obtained possession of the documents, they were permitted to use them without participation by the grand jury and, in fact, subject to no limits at all. Thus, the documents could be used to bring misdemeanor charges not requiring grand jury approval. Holding the practice unauthorized, the court relied to some extent upon the risk that, under this practice, information would be disclosed in a manner violating grand jury secrecy. But its major basis of decision was considerably broader:

> We declare this practice to be well beyond the power of the grand jury and to be potentially abusive to the rights of citizens, resulting in a roving investigating commission that is the very antithesis of the purpose of the grand jury.

* * *

> Of greatest concern * * * is the demonstrated abuse of the grand jury subpoena power and the usurping of that power by the state's prosecutors. At oral argument it was disclosed that the Office of the Attorney General utilizes the grand jury for the issuance of subpoenas to obtain evidence concerning matters that are not before the grand jury and may never come before the grand jury. The prosecutor revealed to this Court that approximately 250 subpoenas were issued by the grand juries in Rhode Island for investigations and cases that are not grand jury matters. The state attempts to justify this practice on the grounds of management problems inherent in a procedure that limits grand jury subpoenas to grand jury matters, stating that this would give rise to the need for additional grand juries and staff to handle the increased volume. This practice, however, is simply unlawful and results in a total eradication of the independence of the grand jury and a merger of the identity of the grand jury with the prosecuting arm of the executive branch of government.

> We remind the state's prosecutors that the General Assembly has not seen fit to authorize the Office of the Attorney General or the state's police departments to issue subpoenas for criminal investigations. * * * [T]he process issued by the grand jury is the process of the court, not the prosecutor.

> Therefore we find ourselves constrained to declare that the grand juries of this state have no authority to appoint agents to recover documents in furtherance of investigations not related to the grand jury. We conclude that the issuance of so-called forthwith subpoenas for the immediate production of documents is more akin to the issuance of a warrant without the intervention of the neutral magistrate and is therefore impermissible. In addition, in

circumstances in which a witness seeks to be excused from appearing before the grand jury and voluntarily surrenders records in lieu of a personal appearance, such materials are to be returned to the grand jury forthwith and a record is to be prepared and signed by the witness memorializing the transaction and the fact that the witness voluntarily waived his or her right to a personal appearance and right to contest the subpoena.

717 A.2d at 1138–39.

5. **Self-Incrimination Privilege to Resist Production of Documents.** Grand jury subpoenas *duces tecum* direct the subpoenaed witness to produce documents or other items. Does the Fifth Amendment privilege against compelled self-incrimination justify such a witness in refusing to produce the described documents or items for the grand jury?

Despite language to the contrary in Boyd v. United States, 116 U.S. 616, 634–35, 6 S.Ct. 524, 534, 29 L.Ed.2d 746, 752 (1886), Fisher v. United States, 425 U.S. 391, 96 S.Ct. 1569, 48 L.Ed.2d 39 (1976), held the Fifth Amendment did not protect *the contents* of a document. Any self-incriminating admissions made by putting them in the document occur before the subpoena. Thus, those admissions cannot be compelled by the subpoena. But, Justice White continued for the Court in *Fisher*, compliance with a summons or subpoena for documents may have incriminating and communicative aspects. Compliance with the subpoena may constitute tacit acknowledgments: (1) that the documents described in the subpoena exist and are in the person's possession; and (2) that the produced documents are the ones described and thus constitute an "implicit authentication" of the documents produced. The acknowledged facts may be incriminating. Further, he observed, the act of complying—or the act of production of the documents—is clearly "compelled." But whether particular tacit acknowledgments are both "testimonial" and "incriminating" are questions without categorical answers. Both matters depend upon the facts and circumstances of particular cases or classes of cases.

The Court then turned to tax cases like the ones before the Court in which subpoenas seek from taxpayers' lawyers work papers of the taxpayers' accountants that might incriminate the taxpayers. Justice White first noted the attorney-client privilege permitted the attorneys to resist production if—but only if—the clients could do so. In these cases, however, the client-taxpayers had no right to resist. The Government will already know of the papers' existence and the subjects' access to them; the act of production's confirmation that the documents exist and that the taxpayers have access to them will not significantly add to what the Government knows. Seeking preparation and delivery of the papers by the accountant is not illegal; any testimonial admission to these facts by the act of production, therefore, poses no realistic threat of incriminating the taxpayer. Tacit acknowledgment of the described documents' existence and their possession will not justify noncompliance.

Turning to the danger of implicit authentication by the act of production, *Fisher* noted the taxpayers lacked firsthand knowledge as to the preparation of the documents, could not vouch for their accuracy, and therefore would not be competent to authenticate them. If the documents were eventually offered as evidence of the taxpayers' guilt in a criminal trial, they would not be admissible without authenticating testimony other than evidence the taxpayer produced them in response to the subpoena. "Without more," Justice White reasoned, "responding to the subpoena in the circumstance before us would not appear to represent a substantial threat of self-incrimination." 425 U.S. at 413, 96 S.Ct. at 1582, 48 L.Ed.2d at 57.

A witness was held entitled to resist production of subpoenaed documents in United States v. Doe, 465 U.S. 605, 104 S.Ct. 1237, 79 L.Ed.2d 552 (1984). Grand jury subpoenas issued directing Doe to produce certain records of his businesses. The government conceded these records were or might be incriminating. The district court quashed the subpoenas and the Supreme Court upheld this action.

The facts made a sufficient showing that under *Fisher* the act of producing the documents would involve testimonial self-incrimination. By the act of producing any described documents he had in his possession, Doe would acknowledge—in a testimonial fashion—such documents did exist and they were in his possession. Further, his acknowledgments might relieve the government of the need for other evidence to authenticate those documents should they be offered against Doe in a criminal prosecution. The Court noted the Government was not foreclosed from rebutting this possibility by producing evidence the existence, possession and authentication of the documents were "foregone conclusion[s]," and therefore Doe's act of production would not significantly add to what the Government already knew and had. But no such evidence was produced. Unlike the situation in *Fisher*, the record in *Doe* failed to establish the act of production would have only minimal testimonial value and would not operate to incriminate. As a result, Doe's acts necessary for production of the subpoenaed documents were privileged by the Fifth Amendment. He could not be compelled to produce them.

The *Doe* majority further commented that production of the documents could be compelled if Doe was granted immunity from the use of evidence which might be created by his acts in producing the documents. Immunity as a means of eliminating the risk of "incrimination" is discussed later in this chapter.

B.   QUESTIONING AND THE PRIVILEGE AGAINST COMPELLED SELF-INCRIMINATION

As the Supreme Court's opinion in *Dionisio* recognized, there is universal agreement that the Fifth Amendment privilege against compelled self-incrimination is available to a witness appearing before a grand jury. There is also agreement a witness can, in reliance upon this privilege, decline to answer specific questions put by the jurors or the prosecutor. The major questions concern the extent to which the privilege or sound policy requires that various procedures be followed to implement the right to remain silent. Miranda v. Arizona, presented in Chapter 7, held a suspect undergoing custodial interrogation by police must be afforded the right to the presence of counsel and warnings designed to assure he is aware of the rights to silence and to counsel. Should Fifth Amendment law impose identical or similar requirements when a suspect is interrogated before a grand jury?

There are also additional questions raised by the grand jury process. One who has been taken into custody and questioned by police generally has notice that he or she is a suspect in the investigation, since police do not do this to persons not a target of their investigation. But the grand jury may subpoena witnesses not suspected of criminal involvement, so a person subpoenaed cannot infer from the subpoena that he is a suspect. In light of this lack of notice, does or should one suspected of involvement—a "target"—have the right to be warned of that fact when called to testify before the grand jury?

United States v. Washington

Supreme Court of the United States, 1977.
431 U.S. 181, 97 S.Ct. 1814, 52 L.Ed.2d 238.

■ MR. CHIEF JUSTICE BURGER delivered the opinion of the Court.

The question presented in this case is whether testimony given by a grand jury witness suspected of wrongdoing may be used against him in a later prosecution for a substantive criminal offense when the witness was not informed in advance of his testimony that he was a potential defendant in danger of indictment.

(1)

The facts are not in dispute. Zimmerman and Woodard were driving respondent's van truck when a Washington, D. C., policeman stopped them for a traffic offense. Seeing a motorcycle in the rear of the van which he identified as stolen, the officer arrested both men and impounded respondent's vehicle. When respondent came to reclaim the van, he told police that Zimmerman and Woodard were friends who were driving the van with his permission.

He explained the presence of the stolen motorcycle by saying that while driving the van himself he had stopped to assist an unknown motorcyclist whose machine had broken down. Respondent then allowed the motorcycle to be placed in his van to take it for repairs. Soon after this the van stalled and he walked to a nearby gasoline station to call Zimmerman and Woodard for help, leaving the van with the unknown motorcyclist. After reaching Zimmerman by phone, respondent waited at the gasoline station for his friends, then returned to the spot he had left the van when they failed to appear; by that time the van had disappeared. Respondent said he was not alarmed, assuming his friends had repaired the van and driven it away. Shortly thereafter, Zimmerman and Woodard were arrested with the stolen motorcycle in the van.

Not surprisingly, the officer to whom respondent related this tale was more than a little skeptical; he told respondent he did not believe his story, and advised him not to repeat it in court, "because you're liable to be in trouble if you [do so]." The officer also declined to release the van. Respondent then repeated this story to an Assistant United States Attorney working on the case. The prosecutor, too, was dubious of the account; nevertheless, he released the van to respondent. At the same time, he served respondent with a subpoena to appear before the grand jury investigating the motorcycle theft.

When respondent appeared before the grand jury, the Assistant United States Attorney in charge had not yet decided whether to seek an indictment against him. The prosecutor was aware of respondent's explanation, and was also aware of the possibility that respondent could be indicted by the grand jury for the theft if his story was not believed.

The prosecutor did not advise respondent before his appearance that he might be indicted on a criminal charge in connection with the stolen motorcycle. But respondent, after reciting the usual oath to tell the truth, was given a series of other warnings, as follows:

"Q. * * *

"You have a right to remain silent. You are not required to say anything to us in this Grand Jury at any time or to answer any question."[3]

"Anything you say can be used against you in Court.

"You have the right to talk to a lawyer for advice before we question you and have him outside the Grand Jury during any questioning.

"If you cannot afford a lawyer and want one a lawyer will be provided for you.

"If you want to answer questions now without a lawyer present you will still have the right to stop answering at any time.

"You also have the right to stop answering at any time until you talk to a lawyer.

"Now, do you understand those rights, sir?

"A. Yes, I do.

"Q. And do you want to answer questions of the Grand Jury in reference to a stolen motorcycle that was found in your truck?

"A. Yes, sir.

"Q. And do you want a lawyer here or outside the Grand Jury room while you answer those questions?

"A. No, I don't think so."

In response to questions, respondent again related his version of how the stolen motorcycle came to be in the rear of his van. Subsequently, the grand jury indicted respondent, Zimmerman, and Woodard for grand larceny and receiving stolen property.

Respondent moved to suppress his testimony and quash the indictment, arguing that it was based on evidence obtained in violation of his Fifth Amendment privilege against compelled self-incrimination. The Superior Court for the District of Columbia suppressed the testimony * * * holding that before the Government could use respondent's grand jury testimony at trial, it had first to demonstrate that respondent had knowingly waived his privilege against compelled self-incrimination. Notwithstanding the comprehensive warnings described earlier, the court found no effective waiver had been made, holding that respondent was not properly advised of his Fifth Amendment rights. The court thought the Constitution required, at a minimum, that

"inquiry be made of the suspect to determine what his educational background is, and what his formal education is and whether or not he understands that this is a constitutional privilege and whether he fully understands the consequences of what might result in the event that

---

3. This was an obvious overstatement of respondent's constitutional rights; the very purpose of the grand jury is to elicit testimony, and it can compel answers, by use of contempt powers, to all except self-incriminating questions.

After the oral warnings, respondent was also handed a card containing all the warnings prescribed by Miranda v. Arizona, 384 U.S. 436, 86 S.Ct. 1602, 16 L.Ed.2d 694 (1966), and a waiver form acknowledging that the witness waived the privilege against compelled self-incrimination. Respondent signed the waiver.

he does waive his constitutional right and in the event that he does make incriminatory statements * * * .''

The court also held that respondent should have been told that his testimony could lead to his indictment by the grand jury before which he was testifying, and could then be used to convict him in a criminal prosecution.

The District of Columbia Court of Appeals affirmed the suppression order. That court also took the position that "the most significant failing of the prosecutor was in not advising [respondent] that he was a potential defendant. Another shortcoming was in the prosecutor's waiting until after administering the oath in the cloister of the grand jury before undertaking to furnish what advice was given."[4]

(2)

The implicit premise of the District of Columbia Court of Appeals' holding is that a grand jury inquiry, like police custodial interrogation, is an "interrogation of persons suspected or accused of crime [that] contains inherently compelling pressures which work to undermine the individual's will to resist and to compel him to speak where he would not otherwise do so freely." Miranda v. Arizona, 384 U.S. 436, 467, 86 S.Ct. 1602, 1624, 16 L.Ed.2d 694 (1966). But this Court has not decided that the grand jury setting presents coercive elements which compel witnesses to incriminate themselves. Nor have we decided whether any Fifth Amendment warnings whatever are constitutionally required for grand jury witnesses; moreover, we have no occasion to decide these matters today, for even assuming that the grand jury setting exerts some pressures on witnesses generally or on those who may later be indicted, the comprehensive warnings respondent received in this case plainly satisfied any possible claim to warnings. Accordingly, respondent's grand jury testimony may properly be used against him in a subsequent trial for theft of the motorcycle.

Although it is well settled that the Fifth Amendment privilege extends to grand jury proceedings, it is also axiomatic that the Amendment does not automatically preclude self-incrimination, whether spontaneous or in response to questions put by government officials. * * * Absent some officially coerced self-accusation, the Fifth Amendment privilege is not violated by even the most damning admissions. Accordingly, unless the record reveals some compulsion, respondent's incriminating testimony cannot conflict with any constitutional guarantees of the privilege.[5]

---

4. Though both courts below found no effective waiver of Fifth Amendment rights, neither court found, and no one suggests here, that respondent's signing of the waiver-of-rights form was involuntary or was made without full appreciation of all the rights of which he was advised. The Government does not challenge, and we do not disturb, the finding that at the time of his grand jury appearance respondent was a potential defendant whose indictment was considered likely by the prosecution.

5. In *Miranda*, the Court saw as inherently coercive any police custodial interrogation conducted by isolating the suspect with police officers; therefore, the Court established a *per se* rule that all incriminating statements made during such interrogation are barred as "compelled." All *Miranda's* safeguards, which are designed to avoid the coercive atmosphere, rest on the overbearing compulsion which the Court thought was

The Constitution does not prohibit every element which influences a criminal suspect to make incriminating admissions. * * * Of course, for many witnesses the grand jury room engenders an atmosphere conducive to truth telling, for it is likely that upon being brought before such a body of neighbors and fellow citizens, and having been placed under a solemn oath to tell the truth, many witnesses will feel obliged to do just that. But it does not offend the guarantees of the Fifth Amendment if in that setting a witness is more likely to tell the truth than in less solemn surroundings. The constitutional guarantee is only that the witness be not *compelled* to give self-incriminating testimony. The test is whether, considering the totality of the circumstances, the free will of the witness was overborne.

(3)

After being sworn, respondent was explicitly advised that he had a right to remain silent and that any statements he did make could be used to convict him of crime. It is inconceivable that such a warning would fail to alert him to his right to refuse to answer any question which might incriminate him. This advice also eliminated any possible compulsion to self-incrimination which might otherwise exist. To suggest otherwise is to ignore the record and reality. Indeed, it seems self-evident that one who is told he is free to refuse to answer questions is in a curious posture to later complain that his answers were compelled. Moreover, any possible coercion or unfairness resulting from a witness' misimpression that he must answer truthfully even questions with incriminatory aspects is completely removed by the warnings given here. Even in the presumed psychologically coercive atmosphere of police custodial interrogation, *Miranda* does not require that any additional warnings be given simply because the suspect is a potential defendant; indeed, such suspects are potential defendants more often than not.

Respondent points out that unlike one subject to custodial interrogation, whose arrest should inform him only too clearly that he is a potential criminal defendant, a grand jury witness may well be unaware that he is targeted for possible prosecution. While this may be so in some situations, it is an overdrawn generalization. In any case, events here clearly put respondent on notice that he was a suspect in the motorcycle theft. He knew that the grand jury was investigating that theft and that his involvement was known to the authorities. Respondent was made abundantly aware that his exculpatory version of events had been disbelieved by the police officer, and that his friends, whose innocence his own story supported, were to be prosecuted for the theft. The interview with the prosecutor put him on additional notice that his implausible story was not accepted as true. The warnings he received in the grand jury room served further to alert him to his own potential criminal liability. In sum, by the time he testified respondent knew better than anyone else of his potential defendant status.

However, all of this is largely irrelevant, since we do not understand what constitutional disadvantage a failure to give potential defendant warnings could possibly inflict on a grand jury witness, whether or not he

caused by isolation of a suspect in police custody. * * *

has received other warnings. It is firmly settled that the prospect of being indicted does not entitle a witness to commit perjury, and witnesses who are not grand jury targets are protected from compulsory self-incrimination to the same extent as those who are. Because target witness status neither enlarges nor diminishes the constitutional protection against compelled self-incrimination, potential-defendant warnings add nothing of value to protection of Fifth Amendment rights.

* * *

(4)

Since warnings were given, we are not called upon to decide whether such warnings were constitutionally required. However, the District of Columbia Court of Appeals held that whatever warnings are required are insufficient if given "in the cloister of the grand jury." That court gave no reason for its view that warnings must be given outside the presence of the jury, but respondent now advances two justifications. First, it could be thought that warnings given to respondent before the grand jury came too late, because of the short time to assimilate their significance, and because of the presence of the grand jurors. But respondent does not contend that he did not understand the warnings given here. In any event, it is purely speculative to attribute any such effects to warnings given in the presence of the jury immediately before taking the stand. If anything, the proximity of the warnings to respondent's testimony and the solemnity of the grand jury setting seem likely to increase their effectiveness.

Second, respondent argues that giving the oath in the presence of the grand jury undermines assertion of the Fifth Amendment privilege by placing the witness in fear that the grand jury will infer guilt from invocation of the privilege. But this argument entirely overlooks that the grand jury's historic role is an investigative body; it is not the final arbiter of guilt or innocence. Moreover, it is well settled that invocation of the Fifth Amendment privilege in a grand jury proceeding is not admissible in a criminal trial, where guilt or innocence is actually at stake.

The judgment of the Court of Appeals is reversed, and the cause is remanded for further proceedings not inconsistent with this opinion.

Reversed and remanded.

■ MR. JUSTICE BRENNAN, with whom MR. JUSTICE MARSHALL joins, dissenting.

* * *

I would hold that a failure to warn the witness that he is a potential defendant is fatal to an indictment of him when it is made unmistakably to appear, as here, that the grand jury inquiry became an investigation directed against the witness and was pursued with the purpose of compelling him to give self-incriminating testimony upon which to indict him. I would further hold that without such prior warning and the witness' subsequent voluntary waiver of his privilege, there is such gross encroachment upon the witness' privilege as to render worthless the values protected by it unless the self-incriminating testimony is unavailable to the

Government for use at any trial brought pursuant to even a valid indictment.

NOTES

1. **Perjury Prosecutions.** Insofar as the Fifth Amendment privilege against compelled self-incrimination applies in grand jury proceedings, it provides no license to commit perjury.

In United States v. Wong, 431 U.S. 174, 97 S.Ct. 1823, 52 L.Ed.2d 231 (1977), the defendant was called before a grand jury investigating police corruption. She was warned of her privilege against self-incrimination and then denied giving money to police officers or discussing gambling activities with them. Subsequently, she was indicted for perjury on the basis of these statements, which were false. At a hearing on her motion to dismiss the indictment, she convinced the District Judge that because of her limited command of English she had not understood the warning concerning the Fifth Amendment privilege and, further, had believed she was required to answer all questions. The district judge suppressed her testimony before the grand jury and the Court of Appeals affirmed. A unanimous Supreme Court reversed:

> [T]he Fifth Amendment privilege does not condone perjury. It grants a privilege to remain silent without risking contempt but it "does not endow the person who testifies with a license to commit perjury." * * * The failure to provide a warning of the privilege, in addition to the oath to tell the truth, does not call for a different result.

431 U.S. at 178, 97 S.Ct. at 1825, 52 L.Ed.2d 235. The Court also rejected the argument that the failure to provide an effective warning violated due process requirements of fundamental fairness: "perjury is not a permissible way of objecting to the Government's [unfair or oppressive] questions."

2. **Statutory Rights of Grand Jury Targets.** There is wide variation concerning the rights, if any, a target of a grand jury investigation has under state case law and legislation concerning testimony before the grand jury. The Indiana Code provides:

§ 35–34–2–5 Subpoenas; contents; failure to obey; contempt

* * *

Sec. 5. (a) A subpoena duces tecum or subpoena ad testificandum summoning a witness to appear before the grand jury * * * must contain a statement of the general nature of the grand jury inquiry.

(b) If the subpoena is issued to a target, the subpoena shall also contain a statement informing the target that:

(1) he is a subject of the grand jury investigation;

(2) he has the right to consult with an attorney and to be assisted by an attorney * * *; and

(3) if he cannot afford an attorney, the court impaneling the grand jury will appoint one for him, upon request.

Utah by statute requires a grand jury witness be notified when he appears that he is a "target" ("a person regarding whom the attorney for the state, the special prosecutor, or the grand jury has substantial evidence that links that person to the commission of a crime and who could be indicted or charged with that crime") or a "subject" ("a person whose conduct is within the scope of the grand jury's investigation, [if] that conduct exposes the person to possible criminal prosecution"). Utah St. §§ 77–10a–1, 77–10a–13.

New Mexico statutes require a person who is a target of a grand jury inquiry be advised of that fact and be given an opportunity to testify. N.M.Stat.Ann. § 31–6–11(B). Further, the target is not to be subpoenaed "except where it is found by the prosecuting attorney to be essential to the investigation." N.M.Stat.Ann. § 31–6–12.

3. **Constitutional Right to Counsel.** Under *Miranda*, a suspect has the right to the presence of counsel during custodial police interrogation. As the Supreme Court suggested in *Washington*, the Court has not extended this right to questioning before the grand jury. In United States v. Mandujano, 425 U.S. 564, 96 S.Ct. 1768, 48 L.Ed.2d 212 (1976), the grand jury witness (and subsequent perjury defendant) was informed that if he desired he could have the assistance of counsel, but his lawyer could not be inside the grand jury room. "[T]hat statement," the Supreme Court commented, "was plainly a correct recital of the law." The Court has subsequently, citing *Mandujana*, explained, "A grand jury witness has no constitutional right to have counsel present during the grand jury proceeding, and no decision of this Court has held that a grand jury witness has a right to have her attorney present outside the jury room." Conn and Najera v. Gabbert, 526 U.S. 286, ___, 119 S.Ct. 1292, 1296, 143 L.Ed.2d 399, 400 (1999). It added that it "need not decide today whether * * * a right [to have an attorney present outside the grand jury room] exists."

4. **Statutory Rights to Counsel.** A number of jurisdictions presently provide for at least some grand jury witnesses to have counsel present during questioning. The Colorado statute providing for representation attempts to address a number of potential problems counsel might create:

> Any witness subpoenaed to appear and testify before a grand jury or to produce books, papers, documents, or other objects before such grand jury shall be entitled to assistance of counsel during any such time that such witness is being questioned in the presence of such grand jury, and counsel may be present in the grand jury room with his client during such questioning. However, counsel for the witness shall be permitted only to counsel the witness and shall not make objections, arguments, or address the grand jury. Such counsel may be retained by the witness or may, for any person financially unable to obtain adequate assistance, be appointed * * * . An attorney present in the grand jury room shall take an oath of secrecy. * * *

Colo.Rev.Stat. § 16–5–204(4)(d). Kansas provides by statute that any grand jury witness is entitled to have counsel present and adds:

> (2) Counsel for any witness may be present while the witness is testifying and may interpose objections on behalf of the witness. He shall not be permitted to examine or cross-examine his client or any other witness before the grand jury.

Kan.Stat.Ann. § 23–3009.

The Massachusetts statute, Mass.Rev.Stat. ch. 277, § 14A, specifies further, "no witness may refuse to appear for reason of unavailability of counsel for that witness."

5. **Immunity.** A witness's Fifth Amendment right to decline to respond to questions in the grand jury context as well as in other situations depends upon the answers' "incriminatory" nature. If no danger of incrimination exists, there is no self-incrimination privilege to refuse an answer. The danger of incrimination can be removed by the expiration of the period of limitations for the offenses at issue, an executive pardon for them or—as is more frequently the case—an effective grant of immunity from prosecution. Brown v. Walker, 161 U.S. 591, 16 S.Ct. 644, 40 L.Ed.

819 (1896). In Ullmann v. United States, 350 U.S. 422, 76 S.Ct. 497, 100 L.Ed. 511 (1956), for example, a grand jury witness asserted testifying would result in loss of his job, expulsion from a labor union, ineligibility for a passport and general public opprobrium. Despite a grant of immunity from prosecution, he urged, he had a right to refuse to provide information to a grand jury. Rejecting the argument, the Court stressed that the Fifth Amendment protects only against criminal liability. For a grant of immunity to be effective, it added, "the immunity granted need only remove those sanctions which generate the fear justifying invocation of the privilege * * *."

The major question presented by grants of immunity is the type of immunity required to render the privilege inapplicable. Specifically, must the immunity be from prosecution for the offenses which the answers concern (so-called "transactional immunity," because the immunity is from criminal prosecution for the transaction concerning which the person is required to testify)? Or, is immunity from the use of the answers (so-called "use immunity") is sufficient? The matter was addressed in Kastigar v. United States, 406 U.S. 441, 92 S.Ct. 1653, 32 L.Ed.2d 212 (1972). Kastigar had been called before a federal grand jury and was granted immunity under 18 U.S.C.A. §§ 6002, 6003. Section 6003 authorizes a federal district judge to issue an order requiring a person to give testimony or provide information if: (a) the person has refused to give testimony or provide information in a proceeding before a court or grand jury of the United States; and (b) the United States attorney requests the order. A person who testifies or provides information under such an order is entitled to certain immunity under Section 6002, which provides as follows:

> Whenever a witness refuses, on the basis of his privilege against self-incrimination, to testify or provide other information in a proceeding before or ancillary to—
>
> (1) a court or grand jury of the United States, * * * .

and the person presiding over the proceeding communicates to the witness an order issued under [Section 6003], the witness may not refuse to comply with the order on the basis of his privilege against self-incrimination; but no testimony or other information compelled under the order (or any information directly or indirectly derived from such testimony or other information) may be used against the witness in any criminal case, except a prosecution for perjury, giving a false statement, or otherwise failing to comply with the order.

Kastigar nevertheless declined to answer the questions and consequently was found in contempt of court. The Supreme Court upheld the contempt citation, concluding the grant of immunity was sufficient and, therefore, Kastigar had no Fifth Amendment basis for refusing to answer:

> The statute's explicit proscription of the use in any criminal case of "testimony or other information compelled under the order (or any information directly or indirectly derived from such testimony or other information)" is consonant with Fifth Amendment standards. We hold that such immunity from use and derivative use is coextensive with the scope of the privilege against self-incrimination, and therefore is sufficient to compel testimony over a claim of the privilege. While a grant of immunity must afford protection commensurate with that afforded by the privilege, it need not be broader. Transactional immunity, which accords full immunity from prosecution for the offense to which the compelled testimony relates, affords the witness considerably broader protection than does the Fifth Amendment privilege. The privilege has never been construed to mean that one who invokes it cannot subsequently be prosecuted. Its sole concern is to afford protection against being "forced to give testimony leading to the infliction of 'penalties affixed to * * * criminal acts.'"

Immunity from the use of compelled testimony, as well as evidence derived directly and indirectly therefrom, affords this protection. It prohibits the prosecutorial authorities from using the compelled testimony in any respect, and it therefore insures that the testimony cannot lead to the infliction of criminal penalties on the witness.

406 U.S. at 453, 92 S.Ct. at 1661, 32 L.Ed.2d at 222.

Kastigar argued that persons compelled to testify who were later prosecuted would experience difficulty in determining whether evidence offered against them was derived from their compelled testimony. In response, the Court held after a grant of use immunity, a prosecuted witness can require the Government to prove its evidence was not derived from compelled testimony. A defendant creates the Government's obligation by demonstrating the prosecution concerns a matter as to which he was compelled to testify under a grant of use immunity. The prosecution then has the burden of showing that its evidence has a legitimate source independent of the compelled testimony and is therefore not tainted by that testimony. Justice Marshall, dissenting, argued the majority's holding fails to sufficiently protect an immunized witness. As a practical matter, a criminal defendant cannot effectively challenge a prosecution claim that evidence offered at trial has a source independent of prior compelled testimony. Only transactional immunity, he concluded, can effectively protect such persons from the use of their testimony and its "fruits."

6. **Immunity and Perjury.** Immunity does not protect against prosecution for or proof of perjury committed during immunized testimony. Applying this position, the Supreme Court has permitted extensive use of compelled testimony in perjury proceedings.

In United States v. Apfelbaum, 445 U.S. 115, 100 S.Ct. 948, 63 L.Ed.2d 250 (1980), Apfelbaum was called before a federal grand jury to testify concerning a suspected robbery and extortion. He invoked his privilege against self-incrimination, was granted immunity under 18 U.S.C.A. § 6002, and testified concerning a number of matters. Subsequently, he was charged with perjury on the basis that during his grand jury testimony he had falsely denied attempting to locate one Harry Brown during December, 1975 and loaning Brown money. At trial, the government introduced over objection portions of Apfelbaum's grand jury testimony other than that charged in the indictment as perjured testimony. This testimony concerned his relationship and discussions with Brown, a trip on another occasion to Florida to visit Brown, and similar matters; the government argued this evidence put the allegedly perjured statements "in context" and proved that Apfelbaum knew they were false. Apfelbaum was convicted. On appeal, he successfully argued the federal statute and the Fifth Amendment prohibited, even in a perjury trial, the use of immunized testimony not specifically the basis for the perjury charge. The Supreme Court reversed the Court of Appeals.

After considering the legislative history of the immunity statute, the Court concluded Congress intended to permit use of both truthful and false statements made during immunized testimony, if use of such statements was permitted by the Fifth Amendment. It then turned to the defendant's argument that the Fifth Amendment prohibited the use of immunized testimony except for the "corpus delicti" or "core" of a perjury charge. The Court of Appeals held that use of defendant's immunized testimony must be limited to that charged as perjury on the following rationale: A grant of immunity must be coextensive with Fifth Amendment protection; this means a defendant must be placed in as near a position as possible to that which he would have occupied had he retained the privilege. The need to prevent perjury requires a narrow exception to this rule permitting the use of perjured testimony in a prosecution for that perjury. But because an immunized witness would not have given the other testimony had he retained the privilege, this other, i.e., nonperjured, testimony must not be used even in a perjury prosecution where it is relevant to guilt. The Supreme Court rejected the Court of Appeals' rationale. It reasoned that for a grant of immunity to provide protection coextensive with that of the privilege, it need not treat the witness as if he had remained silent. As long as the use of immunized testimony is limited to perjury prosecution, the exception is sufficiently narrow. "[W]e hold," the Court concluded, "that neither the statute nor the Fifth Amendment requires that the admissibility of immunized testimony be governed by any different rules than other testimony at a trial for making false statements."

Justices Brennan, Blackmun, and Marshall concurred, preferring to withhold comment on situations not before the Court. Specifically, they expressed reservation concerning the admissibility of immunized testimony in a prosecution for perjury allegedly committed after immunized testimony rather than, as in *Apfelbaum*, during immunized testimony.

CHAPTER 10

EYEWITNESS IDENTIFICATION

Analysis

EDITORS' INTRODUCTION: THE PERSUASIVE POWERS AND RISKS OF EYEWITNESS IDENTIFICATION

Eyewitnesses testifying at trials that they recall the defendants as the perpetrators of the charged crimes may, course, be incorrect. This may be because they are lying or because—despite the confidence with which they testify—they are actually unable to accurately recall what they observed at the crime scene. Criminal trial law has long recognized the risk of inaccurate eyewitness testimony. Nevertheless, traditional criminal procedure trusted triers of fact to evaluate the credibility of eyewitness testimony, using common sense knowledge as to what testimony is worthy of belief and what is not. The risks that eyewitnesses are mistaken and that jurors are ill equipped to evaluate eyewitness testimony's credibility have been the subject of recent scientific study that may helpfully inform the law in this area.

"Scientific psychology was in its infancy when articles about mistaken eyewitness identifications began appearing in the field [in the early 1900s]," Michael R. Leippe, The Case for Expert Testimony About Eyewitness Memory, 1 Psychol. Pub. Pol'y & L. 909 (1995), pointed out. But, he added, "[a] great upsurge in eyewitness memory research began in the early 1970s, and much of this research has revealed a disturbingly high error rate and ever more ways in which eyewitness identifications and recollections are susceptible to error." A leading researcher and author in this area is Elizabeth F. Loftus, Ph.D., a psychologist. See generally, Elizabeth F. Loftus, Eyewitness Testimony (1979); Elizabeth F. Loftus and James M. Doyle, Eyewitness Testimony: Civil and Criminal (3rd ed. 1997).

The Utah Supreme Court in State v. Long, 721 P.2d 483, 488–90 (Utah 1986), summarized the substance of the basic research:

> The literature is replete with empirical studies documenting the unreliability of eyewitness identification. See generally P. Wall, Eyewitness Identification in Criminal Cases (1965); E. Loftus, Eyewitness Testimony (1979). There is no significant division of opinion on the issue. The studies all lead inexorably to the conclusion that human perception is inexact and that human memory is both limited and fallible. * * *

> [T]he process of perceiving events and remembering them is not as simple or as certain as turning on a camera and recording everything the camera sees on tape or film for later replay. What we perceive and remember is the result of a much more complex process, one that does not occur without involving the whole person, and one that is profoundly affected by who we are and what we bring to the event of perception. See R. Buckhout, Eyewitness Testimony, 15 Jurimetrics J. 171, 179 (1975) (reprinted from 231 Scientific American 23 (Dec. 1974)).

> Research on human memory has consistently shown that failures may occur and inaccuracies creep in at any stage of what is broadly referred to as the "memory process." This process includes the acquisition of information, its storage, and its retrieval and communication to others. These stages have all been extensively studied in recent years, and a wide variety of factors influencing each stage have been identified.

> During the first or acquisition stage, a wide array of factors has been found to affect the accuracy of an individual's perception. Some of these are rather obvious. For example, the circumstances of the observation are critical: the distance of the observer from the event, the length of time available to perceive the event, the amount of light available, and the amount of movement involved. However, perhaps the more important factors affecting the accuracy of one's perception are those factors originating within the observer. One such limitation is the individual's physical condition, including both obvious infirmities as well as such factors as fatigue and drug or alcohol use. Another limitation which can affect perception is the emotional state of the observer. Contrary to much accepted lore, when an observer is experiencing a marked degree of stress, perceptual abilities are known to decrease significantly.

> A far less obvious limitation of great importance arises from the fact that the human brain cannot receive and store all the stimuli simultaneously presented to it. This forces people to be selective in what they perceive of any given event. To accomplish this selective perception successfully, over time each person develops unconscious

strategies for determining what elements of an event are important enough to be selected out for perception. The rest of the stimuli created by the event are ignored by the brain. These unconscious strategies of selective perception work quite well in our day-to-day lives to provide us with only the most commonly useful information, but the strategies may result in the exclusion of information that will later prove important in a court proceeding. For example, the significance of the event to the witness at the time of perception is very important. Thus, people usually remember with some detail and clarity their whereabouts at the time they learned of John F. Kennedy's assassination. Those same people, however, are generally less accurate in their descriptions of people, places, and events encountered only recently in the course of their daily routines. For instance, few of us can remember the color or make of the car that was in front of us at the last traffic signal where we waited for the light to turn green. An everyday situation such as this presents an excellent opportunity to observe, and yet, while such information may be a critical element in a criminal trial, our process of selective perception usually screens out such data completely. To the extent that court proceedings may focus on events that were not of particular importance to the observer at the time they occurred, then, the observer may have absolutely no memory of the facts simply because he or she failed to select the critical information for perception.

Another mechanism we all develop to compensate for our inability to perceive all aspects of an event at once is a series of logical inferences: if we see one thing, we assume, based on our past experience, that we also saw another that ordinarily follows. This way we can "perceive" a whole event in our mind's eye when we have actually seen or heard only portions of it. The implications of this memory strategy for court proceedings are similar to those of selective perception.

Other important factors that affect the accuracy of a viewer's perception, and which are unique to each observer, include the expectations, personal experiences, biases, and prejudices brought by any individual to a given situation. A good example of the effect of preconceptions on the accuracy of perception is the well-documented fact that identifications tend to be more accurate where the person observing and the one being observed are of the same race.

The memory process is also subject to distortion in the second or retention stage, when information that may or may not have been accurately perceived is stored in the memory. Research demonstrates that both the length of time between the witness's experience and the recollection of that experience, and the occurrence of other events in the intervening time period, affect the accuracy and completeness of recall. Just as in the perception stage, where the mind infers what occurred from what was selected for perception, in the retention stage people tend to add extraneous details and to fill in memory gaps over time, thereby unconsciously constructing more detailed, logical, and coherent recollections of their actual experiences. Thus, as eyewitnesses wend their way through the criminal justice process, their reports of what was seen and heard tend to become "more accurate, more complete and less ambiguous" in appearance. * * *

Research has also undermined the common notion that the confidence with which an individual makes an identification is a valid indicator of the accuracy of the recollection. K. Deffenbacher, Eyewitness Accuracy and Confidence: Can We Infer Anything About Their Relationship?, 4 Law and Human Behavior 243 (1980). In fact, the accuracy of an identification is, at times, inversely related to the confidence with which it is made.

Finally, the retrieval stage of the memory process—when the observer recalls the event and communicates that recollection to others—is also fraught with potential for distortion. For example, language imposes limits on the observer. Experience suggests that few individuals have such a mastery of language that they will not have some difficulty in communicating the details and nuances of the original event, and the greater the inadequacy, the greater the likelihood of miscommunication. An entirely independent problem arises when one who has accurately communicated his recollection in a narrative form is then asked questions in an attempt to elicit a more complete picture of the event described. Those asking such questions, by using a variety of subtle and perhaps unconscious questioning techniques, can significantly influence what a witness "remembers" in response to questioning. And as the witness is pressed for more details, his responses become increasingly inaccurate. In addition, research has documented an entirely different set of no less significant problems that relate to the suggestiveness of police lineups, showups, and photo arrays.

Among those factors addressed in the research is "weapon focus"—the tendency of a person exposed to a complex scenario involving—among many other aspects—the display of a weapon to concentrate on the weapon. Weapon focus, the research suggests, reduces the person's ability to accurately recall other details of the situation. See Elizabeth F. Loftus and James M. Doyle, Eyewitness Testimony: Civil and Criminal 29–30 (3rd ed. 1997).

Another factor research suggests may influence identification testimony is "transference"—a phenomenon in which a person observed in one situation is inaccurately recalled as a person seen in a second situation. See Elizabeth F. Loftus and James M. Doyle, at 88–90. Thus a witness who saw a robbery and observed X earlier in the day may unconsciously "transfer" the memory of observing X to the context of the robbery and consequently inaccurately recall X as the robber. Loftus and Doyle indicated such unconscious transference "has been documented in empirical studies." "[I]n any given situation," they added "it is nearly impossible to say definitively that an unconscious transference has occurred, only that it may have occurred."

Can the common sense of jurors and the information they bring to trials be relied upon to enable those jurors to properly evaluate eyewitness identification and thus properly discount testimony of doubtful accuracy? As the *Long* court's discussion indicated, evidence suggests not. Jennifer L.

Devenport, Steven D. Penrod, and Brian L. Cutler, Evaluating Common-sense Evaluations, 3 Psychol. Pub. Pol'y & L. 338, 353 (1997), for example, surveyed the research and concluded:

> [R]esearch * * * has consistently revealed that jurors tend to rely on factors that are not diagnostic of eyewitness accuracy, such as an eyewitness's memory for peripheral details and eyewitness confidence, tend to overestimate eyewitness accuracy, and have difficulty applying their commonsense knowledge of lineup suggestiveness to their verdict decisions.

The results of at least one study, they commented, suggest nearly three out of four mistaken identifications presented to juries may be believed.

Recent technology has give rise to a particularly significant reason to doubt existing mechanisms for testing the credibility of eyewitness identification adequately identify testimony of insufficient reliability. A study commissioned by the National Institute of Justice examined 28 cases in which defendants convicted of serious crimes were later found on the basis of DNA analysis improperly convicted. E. Connors, T. Lundregan, N. Miller and T. McEwen, Convicted by Juries, Exonerated by Science: Case Studies of the Use of DNA Evidence to Establish Innocence After Trial (1996). In all but one case the convictions followed jury trials. Identification testimony was frequently used. All of the 22 nonmurder cases involved victim identification both prior to and during trial; even in the murder cases eyewitness testimony often put the accused in the vicinity of the offense. The eyewitness testimony in these cases was wrong, the study noted, and yet the triers of fact failed to recognize this. These inaccurate convictions make clear the need for improved evaluation of the reliability of eyewitness identification.

A major issue in criminal justice administration, then, is whether the law should respond to this research and, if so, how it should do so.

A. CONSTITUTIONAL ISSUES

EDITORS' INTRODUCTION: THE SUPREME COURT'S EYEWITNESS TRILOGY

In 1967, the United States Supreme Court decided a trilogy of eyewitness identification cases designed to deal constitutionally with some risks of eyewitness identification. These decisions, and the constitutional requirements they established, are considered in the present section. The first two cases, United States v. Wade, 388 U.S. 218, 87 S.Ct. 1926, 18 L.Ed.2d 1149 (1967), and Gilbert v. California, 388 U.S. 263, 87 S.Ct. 1951, 18 L.Ed.2d 1178 (1967), dealt with the right to counsel, the subject of the first subsection following. The third case of the trilogy, Stovall v. Denno, 388 U.S. 293, 87 S.Ct. 1967, 18 L.Ed.2d 1199 (1967), indicated a pretrial identification procedure could be so suggestive that using testimony of the witness who participated in the procedure violated due process of law. This is the subject of the second subsection.

Those cases were decided before the "great upsurge in eyewitness memory research" described by Leippe. Thus there may be reason to reconsider—in light of that research—whether the approach taken in them was appropriate or adequate. Legal requirements other than those mandated by the 1967 trilogy have been suggested as appropriate supplements to the demands of the constitutional requirements. Several of these are considered in Part B of this chapter.

1.   Assistance of Counsel

Much as the Supreme Court regarded the right to counsel as the appropriate vehicle for dealing with problems raised by law enforcement interrogation techniques, the Court also called that right into play to combat some difficulties with pretrial identification procedures. Consider what the Court anticipated would be the role of counsel in lineups and similar identification procedures. Does the right to counsel mean the right to have counsel at least heard regarding objections to the manner in which an identification procedure is conducted?

In addition, consider the effect of a violation of the right to counsel at a lineup upon the admissibility of later testimony. Specifically, consider the difference between the effect of a violation on in-court identification testimony by the witness and upon testimony as to an identification made by the witness at the lineup.

United States v. Wade

Supreme Court of the United States, 1967.
388 U.S. 218, 87 S.Ct. 1926, 18 L.Ed.2d 1149.

■ Mr. Justice Brennan delivered the opinion of the Court.

The question here is whether courtroom identifications of an accused at trial are to be excluded from evidence because the accused was exhibited to the witnesses before trial at a postindictment lineup conducted for identification purposes without notice to and in the absence of the accused's appointed counsel.

The federally insured bank in Eustace, Texas, was robbed on September 21, 1964. A man with a small strip of tape on each side of his face entered the bank, pointed a pistol at the female cashier and the vice president, the only persons in the bank at the time, and forced them to fill a pillowcase with the bank's money. The man then drove away with an accomplice who had been waiting in a stolen car outside the bank. On March 23, 1965, an indictment was returned against respondent, Wade, and two others for conspiring to rob the bank, and against Wade and the accomplice for the robbery itself. Wade was arrested on April 2, and counsel was appointed to represent him on April 26. Fifteen days later an FBI agent, without notice to Wade's lawyer, arranged to have the two bank employees observe a lineup made up of Wade and five or six other prisoners and conducted in a courtroom of the local county courthouse. Each person in the line wore strips of tape such as allegedly worn by the robber and upon direction each said something like "put the money in the bag," the words allegedly uttered by the robber. Both bank employees identified Wade in the lineup as the bank robber.

At trial the two employees, when asked on direct examination if the robber was in the courtroom, pointed to Wade. The prior lineup identification was then elicited from both employees on cross-examination. At the close of testimony, Wade's counsel moved for a judgment of acquittal or, alternatively, to strike the bank officials' courtroom identifications on the ground that conduct of the lineup, without notice to and in the absence of his appointed counsel, violated his Fifth Amendment privilege against self-incrimination and his Sixth Amendment right to the assistance of counsel. The motion was denied, and Wade was convicted. The Court of Appeals for the Fifth Circuit reversed the conviction and ordered a new trial at which the in-court identification evidence was to be excluded, holding that, though the lineup * * * held as it was, in the absence of counsel, already chosen to represent appellant, was a violation of his Sixth Amendment rights * * *.

I.

Neither the lineup itself nor anything shown by this record that Wade was required to do in the lineup violated his privilege against self-incrimination. * * * Schmerber v. State of California, 384 U.S. 757, 761, 86 S.Ct. 1826, 1830, 16 L.Ed.2d 908. [This part of the Court's holding is discussed in Chapter 2. Editors.]

* * *

II.

[I]t is urged that the assistance of counsel at the lineup was indispensable to protect Wade's most basic right as a criminal defendant—his right to a fair trial at which the witnesses against him might be meaningfully cross-examined.

The Framers of the Bill of Rights envisaged a broader role for counsel than under the practice then prevailing in England of merely advising his client in "matters of law," and eschewing any responsibility for "matters of fact." * * * This * * * is reflected in the scope given by our decisions to the Sixth Amendment's guarantee to an accused of the assistance of counsel for his defense. When the Bill of Rights was adopted, there were no organized police forces as we know them today. The accused confronted the prosecutor and the witnesses against him, and the evidence was marshaled, largely at the trial itself. In contrast, today's law enforcement machinery involves critical confrontations of the accused by the prosecution at pretrial proceedings where the results might well settle the accused's fate and reduce the trial itself to a mere formality. In recognition of these realities of modern criminal prosecution, our cases have construed the Sixth Amendment guarantee to apply to "critical" stages of the proceedings. The guarantee reads: "In all criminal prosecutions, the accused shall enjoy the right * * * to have the Assistance of Counsel *for his defence.*" (Emphasis supplied.) The plain wording of this guarantee thus encompasses counsel's assistance whenever necessary to assure a meaningful "defence."

[W]e [have] * * * recognized that the period from arraignment to trial was "perhaps the most critical period of the proceedings * * *," during which the accused "requires the guiding hand of counsel * * *," if the guarantee is not to prove an empty right. * * *

* * *

[Our decisions reflect the] principle that in addition to counsel's presence at trial, the accused is guaranteed that he need not stand alone against the State at any stage of the prosecution, formal or informal, in court or out, where counsel's absence might derogate from the accused's right to a fair trial. The security of that right is as much the aim of the right to counsel as it is of the other guarantees of the Sixth Amendment— the right of the accused to a speedy and public trial by an impartial jury, his right to be informed of the nature and cause of the accusation, and his right to be confronted with the witnesses against him and to have compulsory process for obtaining witnesses in his favor. The presence of counsel at such critical confrontations, as at the trial itself, operates to assure that the accused's interests will be protected consistently with our adversary theory of criminal prosecution.

In sum, the principle of [the Sixth Amendment right to counsel] requires that we scrutinize *any* pretrial confrontation of the accused to determine whether the presence of his counsel is necessary to preserve the defendant's basic right to a fair trial as affected by his right meaningfully to cross-examine the witnesses against him and to have effective assistance of counsel at the trial itself. It calls upon us to analyze whether potential substantial prejudice to defendant's rights inheres in the particular confrontation and the ability of counsel to help avoid that prejudice.

III.

The Government characterizes the lineup as a mere preparatory step in the gathering of the prosecution's evidence, not different—for Sixth Amendment purposes—from various other preparatory steps, such as systematized or scientific analyzing of the accused's fingerprints, blood sample, clothing, hair, and the like. We think there are differences which preclude such stages being characterized as critical stages at which the accused has the right to the presence of his counsel. Knowledge of the techniques of science and technology is sufficiently available, and the variables in techniques few enough, that the accused has the opportunity for a meaningful confrontation of the Government's case at trial through the ordinary processes of cross-examination of the Government's expert witnesses and the presentation of the evidence of his own experts. The denial of a right to have his counsel present at such analyses does not therefore violate the Sixth Amendment; they are not critical stages since there is minimal risk that his counsel's absence at such stages might derogate from his right to a fair trial.

IV.

But the confrontation compelled by the State between the accused and the victim or witnesses to a crime to elicit identification evidence is peculiarly riddled with innumerable dangers and variable factors which might seriously, even crucially, derogate from a fair trial. The vagaries of eyewitness identification are well-known; the annals of criminal law are rife with instances of mistaken identification. * * * A major factor contributing to the high incidence of miscarriage of justice from mistaken identification has been the degree of suggestion inherent in the manner in which the prosecution presents the suspect to witnesses for pretrial identification. * * * Suggestion can be created intentionally or unintentionally in many subtle ways. And the dangers for the suspect are particularly grave when the witness' opportunity for observation was insubstantial, and thus his susceptibility to suggestion the greatest.

Moreover, "[i]t is a matter of common experience that, once a witness has picked out the accused at the lineup, he is not likely to go back on his word later on, so that in practice the issue of identity may (in the absence of other relevant evidence) for all practical purposes be determined there and then, before the trial."

The pretrial confrontation for purpose of identification may take the form of a lineup, also known as an "identification parade" or "showup," as in the present case, or presentation of the suspect alone to the witness * * *. It is obvious that risks of suggestion attend either form of confrontation and increase the dangers inhering in eyewitness identification. But as is the case with secret interrogations, there is serious difficulty in depicting what transpires at lineups and other forms of identification confrontations. * * * [T]he defense can seldom reconstruct the manner and mode of lineup identification for judge or jury at trial. Those participating in a lineup with the accused may often be police officers; in any event, the participants' names are rarely recorded or divulged at trial. The impediments to an objective observation are increased when the victim is the witness. Lineups are prevalent in rape and robbery prosecutions and present a particular hazard that a victim's understandable outrage may excite vengeful or spiteful motives. In any event, neither witnesses nor lineup participants are apt to be alert for conditions prejudicial to the suspect. And if they were, it would likely be of scant benefit to the suspect since neither witnesses nor lineup participants are likely to be schooled in the detection of suggestive influences.[1] Improper influences may go undetected by a suspect, guilty or not, who experiences the emotional tension which we might expect in one being confronted with potential accusers. Even when he does observe abuse, if he has a criminal record he may be reluctant to take the stand and open up the admission of prior convictions. Moreover any protestations by the suspect of the fairness of the lineup made at trial are likely to be in vain; the jury's choice is between the accused's unsupported version and that of the police officers present. In short, the accused's inability effectively to reconstruct at trial any unfairness that occurred at the lineup may deprive him of his only opportunity meaningfully to attack the credibility of the witness' courtroom identification.

---

1. An additional impediment to the detection of such influences by participants, including the suspect, is the physical conditions often surrounding the conduct of the lineup. In many, lights shine on the stage in such a way that the suspect cannot see the witness. In some a one-way mirror is used and what is said on the witness' side cannot be heard.

What facts have been disclosed in specific cases about the conduct of pretrial confrontations for identification illustrate both the potential for substantial prejudice to the accused at that stage and the need for its revelation at trial. * * * [S]tate reports, in the course of describing prior identifications admitted as evidence of guilt, reveal numerous instances of suggestive procedures, for example, that all in the lineup but the suspect were known to the identifying witness, that the other participants in a lineup were grossly dissimilar in appearance to the suspect, that only the suspect was required to wear distinctive clothing which the culprit allegedly wore, that the witness is told by the police that they have caught the culprit after which the defendant is brought before the witness alone or is viewed in jail, that the suspect is pointed out before or during a lineup, and that the participants in the lineup are asked to try on an article of clothing which fits only the suspect.

The potential for improper influence is illustrated by the circumstances, insofar as they appear, surrounding the prior identifications in the three cases we decide today. In the present case, [for example,] the testimony of the identifying witnesses elicited on cross-examination revealed that those witnesses were taken to the courthouse and seated in the courtroom to await assembly of the lineup. The courtroom faced on a hallway observable to the witnesses through an open door. The cashier testified that she saw Wade "standing in the hall" within sight of an FBI agent. Five or six other prisoners later appeared in the hall. The vice president testified that he saw a person in the hall in the custody of the agent who "resembled the person that we identified as the one that had entered the bank."

The few cases that have surfaced therefore reveal the existence of a process attended with hazards of serious unfairness to the criminal accused and strongly suggest the plight of the more numerous defendants who are unable to ferret out suggestive influences in the secrecy of the confrontation. We do not assume that these risks are the result of police procedures intentionally designed to prejudice an accused. Rather we assume they derive from the dangers inherent in eyewitness identification and the suggestibility inherent in the context of the pretrial identification. * * *

Insofar as the accused's conviction may rest on a courtroom identification in fact the fruit of a suspect pretrial identification which the accused is helpless to subject to effective scrutiny at trial, the accused is deprived of that right of cross-examination which is an essential safeguard to his right to confront the witnesses against him. And even though cross-examination is a precious safeguard to a fair trial, it cannot be viewed as an absolute assurance of accuracy and reliability. Thus in the present context, where so many variables and pitfalls exist, the first line of defense must be the prevention of unfairness and the lessening of the hazards of eyewitness identification at the lineup itself. The trial which might determine the accused's fate may well not be that in the courtroom but that at the pretrial confrontation, with the State aligned against the accused, the witness the sole jury, and the accused unprotected against the overreaching, intentional or unintentional, and with little or no effective appeal from the judgment there rendered by the witness—"that's the man."

Since it appears that there is grave potential for prejudice, intentional or not, in the pretrial lineup, which may not be capable of reconstruction at trial, and since presence of counsel itself can often avert prejudice and assure a meaningful confrontation at trial, there can be little doubt that for Wade the postindictment lineup was a critical stage of the prosecution at which he was "as much entitled to such aid [of counsel] * * * as at the trial itself." Thus both Wade and his counsel should have been notified of the impending lineup, and counsel's presence should have been a requisite to conduct of the lineup, absent an "intelligent waiver." No substantial countervailing policy considerations have been advanced against the requirement of the presence of counsel. Concern is expressed that the requirement will forestall prompt identifications and result in obstruction of the confrontations. As for the first, we note that in [this] case[ ] * * *, counsel had already been appointed and no argument is made * * * that notice to counsel would have prejudicially delayed the confrontation[ ]. Moreover, we leave open the question whether the presence of substitute counsel might not suffice where notification and presence of the suspect's own counsel would result in prejudicial delay.[2] And to refuse to recognize the right to counsel for fear that counsel will obstruct the course of justice is contrary to the basic assumptions upon which this Court has operated in Sixth Amendment cases. * * * In our view counsel can hardly impede legitimate law enforcement; on the contrary, for the reasons expressed, law enforcement may be assisted by preventing the infiltration of taint in the prosecution's identification evidence.[3] That result cannot help the guilty avoid conviction but can only help assure that the right man has been brought to justice.

Legislative or other regulations, such as those of local police departments, which eliminate the risks of abuse and unintentional suggestion at lineup proceedings and the impediments to meaningful confrontation at trial may also remove the basis for regarding the stage as "critical." But neither Congress nor the federal authorities have seen fit to provide a solution. * * *

V.

We come now to the question whether the denial of Wade's motion to strike the courtroom identification by the bank witnesses at trial because of the absence of his counsel at the lineup required, as the Court of Appeals held, the grant of a new trial at which such evidence is to be excluded. We do not think this disposition can be justified without first giving the Government the opportunity to establish by clear and convincing evidence that the in-court identifications were based upon observations of the suspect other than the lineup identification. Where, as here, the admissibil-

---

2. Although the right to counsel usually means a right to the suspect's own counsel, provision for substitute counsel may be justified on the ground that the substitute counsel's presence may eliminate the hazards which render the lineup a critical stage for the presence of the suspect's *own* counsel.

3. Concern is also expressed that the presence of counsel will force divulgence of the identity of government witnesses whose identity the Government may want to conceal. To the extent that this is a valid or significant state interest there are police practices commonly used to effect concealment, for example, masking the face.

ity of evidence of the lineup identification itself is not involved, a *per se* rule of exclusion of courtroom identification would be unjustified.[4] A rule limited solely to the exclusion of testimony concerning identification at the lineup itself, without regard to admissibility of the courtroom identification, would render the right to counsel an empty one. The lineup is most often used, as in the present case, to crystallize the witnesses' identification of the defendant for future reference. We have already noted that the lineup identification will have that effect. The State may then rest upon the witnesses' unequivocal courtroom identification, and not mention the pretrial identification as part of the State's case at trial. Counsel is then in the predicament in which Wade's counsel found himself—realizing that possible unfairness at the lineup may be the sole means of attack upon the unequivocal courtroom identification, and having to probe in the dark in an attempt to discover and reveal unfairness, while bolstering the government witness' courtroom identification by bringing out and dwelling upon his prior identification. Since counsel's presence at the lineup would equip him to attack not only the lineup identification but the courtroom identification as well, limiting the impact of violation of the right to counsel to exclusion of evidence only of identification at the lineup itself disregards a critical element of that right.

We think it follows that the proper test to be applied in these situations is that quoted in Wong Sun v. United States, 371 U.S. 471, 488, 83 S.Ct. 407, 417, 9 L.Ed.2d 441, " '[W]hether, granting establishment of the primary illegality, the evidence to which instant objection is made has been come at by exploitation of that illegality or instead by means sufficiently distinguishable to be purged of the primary taint.' Maguire, Evidence of Guilt, 221 (1959)." Application of this test in the present context requires consideration of various factors; for example, the prior opportunity to observe the alleged criminal act, the existence of any discrepancy between any prelineup description and the defendant's actual description, any identification prior to lineup of another person, the identification by picture of the defendant prior to the lineup, failure to identify the defendant on a prior occasion, and the lapse of time between the alleged act and the lineup identification. It is also relevant to consider those facts which, despite the absence of counsel, are disclosed concerning the conduct of the lineup.

* * *

On the record now before us we cannot make the determination whether the in-court identifications had an independent origin. This was not an issue at trial, although there is some evidence relevant to a determination. That inquiry is most properly made in the District Court. We therefore think the appropriate procedure to be followed is to vacate the conviction pending a hearing to determine whether the in-court identifications had an independent source, or whether, in any event, the intro-

---

4. We reach a contrary conclusion in Gilbert v. California, [discussed in the notes following this case], as to the admissibility of the witness' testimony that he also identified the accused at the lineup.

duction of the evidence was harmless error, and for the District Court to reinstate the conviction or order a new trial, as may be proper.

The judgment of the Court of Appeals is vacated and the case is remanded to that court with direction to enter a new judgment vacating the conviction and remanding the case to the District Court for further proceedings consistent with this opinion. It is so ordered.

Judgment of Court of Appeals vacated and case remanded with direction.

NOTES

1. In actual fact, no further proceedings took place in the trial court. The case was remanded to the district court which scheduled a hearing. Wade, however, absconded and never appeared. Interview With Weldon Holcomb, Counsel for Wade, May, 1991.

2. **Per Se Rule of Inadmissibility for Testimony Concerning Identification Made at Lineup.** In Gilbert v. California, 388 U.S. 263, 87 S.Ct. 1951, 18 L.Ed.2d 1178 (1967), a companion case to *Wade*, the Court also concluded that a pretrial lineup had been conducted in violation of Gilbert's Sixth Amendment right to counsel. Unlike in *Wade*, however, at trial in *Gilbert* the prosecution solicited from one of the eyewitnesses on direct examination that he had picked Gilbert out of the pretrial lineup. The Supreme Court characterized that testimony as "the direct result of the illegal lineup 'come at by exploitation of [the primary] illegality.' * * *. The State is therefore not entitled to an opportunity to show that testimony had an independent source. Only a *per se* exclusionary rule as to such testimony can be an effective sanction to assure law enforcement authorities will respect the accused's constitutional right to the presence of counsel at the critical lineup."

3. **Attachment of Right to Counsel.** The right to counsel recognized in *Wade* applies only if the identification procedure is conducted after the Sixth Amendment right to counsel attaches. When does this occur?

In Kirby v. Illinois, 406 U.S. 682, 92 S.Ct. 1877, 32 L.Ed.2d 411 (1972), the defendant was arrested and transported to the stationhouse. Shortly thereafter, the robbery victim came to the station where he immediately identified the defendant as one of the men who had robbed him. Kirby was not advised of his right to counsel and no lawyer was present on his behalf. The Supreme Court held the resulting identification evidence was properly admitted because Kirby's right to counsel had not attached:

> The initiation of judicial criminal proceedings is far from a mere formalism. It is the starting point of our whole system of adversary criminal justice. For it is only then that the government has committed itself to prosecute, and only then that the adverse positions of government and defendant have solidified. It is then that a defendant finds himself faced with the prosecutorial forces of organized society, and immersed in the intricacies of substantive and procedural criminal law. It is this point, therefore, that marks the commencement of the "criminal prosecutions" to which alone the explicit guarantees of the Sixth Amendment are applicable.

> * * *

> In this case we are asked to import into a routine police investigation an absolute constitutional guarantee historically and rationally applicable only after the onset of formal prosecutorial proceedings. We decline to do so. * * *

Id. at 689–90, 92 S.Ct. at 1882–83, 32 L.Ed.2d at 418.

Kirby indicated the right to counsel attached at the commencement of judicial criminal proceedings. It failed, however, to identify that point. The lower courts' post-*Wade* assumption that the controlling point was the filing of the formal charge—the indictment or information—was proved erroneous by Moore v. Illinois, 434 U.S. 220, 98 S.Ct. 458, 54 L.Ed.2d 424 (1977). Moore was arrested for a rape. The morning after the arrest, a policeman accompanied the victim to the courtroom where Moore appeared for his preliminary hearing to determine whether there was probable cause to bind him over to the grand jury. At the hearing, Moore was led before the bench and told by the judge he was charged with rape. The judge then called the victim, who had been waiting in the courtroom, to come before the bench. The State's Attorney asked the victim whether she saw her assailant in the courtroom; she pointed at Moore. Moore was not represented by counsel at this appearance and the court did not offer to appoint an attorney. At trial, the victim testified as part of the prosecution's case-in-chief that she had, at the preliminary hearing, identified Moore as the man who raped her and made an in-court identification of Moore as her assailant.

The Supreme Court held that Moore's Sixth Amendment right to counsel applied at the identification made at the hearing. Although the identification confrontation occurred prior to indictment, the Court explained, Moore's Sixth Amendment right to counsel attached because the "prosecution in this case was commenced under Illinois law when the victim's complaint was filed in the court." The State committed itself to prosecute.

Moore also rejected the argument that the right to counsel does not apply to one-on-one identification procedures. Similarly, it refused to exempt from the right to counsel identifications made in the course of judicial proceedings such as the preliminary hearing at issue in the case.

A considerable amount of case law defining the commencement of the prosecution for Sixth Amendment purposes has developed in case law dealing with law enforcement interrogation of suspects. This case law is presented in Section C of Chapter 7. The interrogation case law almost certainly also applies to attachment of the Sixth Amendment for *Wade-Gilbert* purposes.

4. **Photo Showings.** To what extent does the right to counsel apply at investigatory procedures not involving a physical confrontation between the defendant and a potential prosecution witness?

In United States v. Ash, 413 U.S. 300, 93 S.Ct. 2568, 37 L.Ed.2d 619 (1973), the Court held counsel is not required at a photo array showing. Witnesses to a bank robbery were shown five color photographs shortly before trial and long after Ash had been indicted. Finding no violation of the right to counsel, the Court distinguished *Wade* and *Gilbert*. The opportunities for suggestion and the difficulty of reconstructing a suggestive lineup were used in *Wade* only to address whether—assuming a right to counsel at the lineup existed—providing counsel only at trial would be sufficient, the Court explained. Whether the right to counsel attached at the lineup in the first place was determined in *Wade* by the Court's conclusion the lineup constituted a "trial-like confrontation" requiring assistance of counsel to counterbalance any prosecution "overreaching." The critical question, therefore, is whether a photo showing is a "trial-like confrontation" in this sense.

Addressing that question, the Court noted a defendant has no right to be present at the showing of a photo display and most likely will not be present. Thus the showing is not a "trial-like adversary confrontation." There is no possibility that the defendant might be "misled" by his lack of familiarity with the law or overpowered by his professional adversary. Both sides have equal access to witnesses for purposes of showing them photographs. The traditional counterbalance in the American adversary system for the prosecution's ability to interview witnesses and to show them photographs is the equal ability of defense counsel to seek and interview witnesses himself. While counsel's ability to do this does not remove all potential for abuse, "it does remove any inequality in the adversary process itself and thereby fully satisfies the historical spirit of the Sixth Amendment's right to counsel guarantee." The primary safeguard against abuses of pretrial identification, the Court noted, is the ethical responsibility of the prosecutor. "If that safeguard fails, review remains available under the due process standards." The majority then concluded, "We are not persuaded that the risks inherent in the use of photographs are so pernicious that an extraordinary system of safeguards is required."

2.   PROHIBITION AGAINST IMPERMISSIBLY SUGGESTIVE PROCEDURES

EDITORS' INTRODUCTION: THE DUE PROCESS PROHIBITION AGAINST EXCESSIVE SUGGESTIVENESS

The third case of the 1967 identification trilogy, Stovall v. Denno, 388 U.S. 293, 87 S.Ct. 1967, 18 L.Ed.2d 1199 (1967), recognized a due process right to have excluded eyewitness testimony tainted by certain excessively suggestive pretrial procedures.

Stovall involved an attack upon a husband and wife in the kitchen of their home at about midnight, August 23, 1961. The intruder stabbed both; the husband died but the wife, stabbed 11 times, survived. On the basis of evidence found at the scene, Stovall was arrested and arraigned on August 24. The wife underwent surgery on that date for her wounds and there was still substantial question as to whether she would survive. About noon on August 25, Stovall was brought to the wife's hospital room. He was handcuffed to one of five police officers who accompanied him; two prosecutors were also there. Stovall, the only Black in the room, was required to repeat a few words for voice identification; no one could later recall what words he said. After a police officer asked if Stovall "was the man," the wife identified him. At Stovall's later trial, the wife testified that he was the person who assaulted the couple. Stovall was convicted. The Supreme Court held the right to counsel announced in *Wade* and *Gilbert* did not apply retroactively, so the failure to accord Stovall the right to assistance of a lawyer at the confrontation did not entitle him to relief.

Nevertheless, the Court found potential merit in Stovall's alternative claim that "the confrontation conducted in this case was so unnecessarily suggestive and conducive to irreparable mistaken identification that he was denied due process of law." This, the Court commented, "is a recognized ground of attack upon a conviction independent of any right to counsel claim." Whether a violation of due process of law occurred, however, depends upon "the totality of the circumstances" surrounding the confrontation. Stressing the victim's condition made the confrontation "imperative," however, the Court found no due process defect in *Stovall*.

In a number of subsequent cases the Court considered claims that pretrial procedure's suggestiveness rendered witnesses' testimony unavailable to the prosecution as a matter of due process. It has generally found such claims without merit. See Neil v. Biggers, 409 U.S. 188, 93 S.Ct. 375,

34 L.Ed.2d 401 (1972); Coleman v. Alabama, 399 U.S. 1, 90 S.Ct. 1999, 26 L.Ed.2d 387 (1970); Simmons v. United States, 390 U.S. 377, 88 S.Ct. 967, 19 L.Ed.2d 1247 (1968).

Only in Foster v. California, 394 U.S. 440, 89 S.Ct. 1127, 22 L.Ed.2d 402 (1969), did the Court find a violation of the due process standard. Foster was arrested for the late-night robbery of a Western Union office; the only employee present when the two robbers entered was Joseph David, the late-night manager. The following then occurred:

> David was called to the police station to view a lineup. There were three men in the lineup. One was [Foster]. He is a tall man—close to six feet in height. The other men were short—five feet, five or six inches. [Foster] wore a leather jacket which David said was similar to the one he had seen underneath the coveralls worn by the robber. After seeing this lineup, David could not positively identify [Foster] as the robber. He "thought" he was the man, but he was not sure. David then asked to speak to [Foster], and [Foster] was brought into an office and sat across from David at a table. Except for prosecuting officials there was no one else in the room. Even after this one-to-one confrontation David still was uncertain whether [Foster] was one of the robbers: "truthfully—I was not sure," he testified at trial. A week or 10 days later, the police arranged for David to view a second lineup. There were five men in that lineup. [Foster] was the only person in the second lineup who had appeared in the first lineup. This time David was "convinced" [Foster] was the man.

At trial, David identified Foster as one of the robbers and testified to his identification of Foster at the second lineup; Foster was convicted. Finding the suggestive elements in the identification procedure "made it all but inevitable that David would identify [Foster] whether or not he was in fact 'the man,'" the Court concluded the procedure "so undermined the reliability of the eyewitness identification as to violate due process."

Manson v. Brathwaite

Supreme Court of the United States, 1977.
432 U.S. 98, 97 S.Ct. 2243, 53 L.Ed.2d 140.

■ MR. JUSTICE BLACKMUN delivered the opinion of the Court.

This case presents the issue as to whether the Due Process Clause of the Fourteenth Amendment compels the exclusion, in a state criminal trial, apart from any consideration of reliability, of pretrial identification evidence obtained by a police procedure that was both suggestive and unnecessary. This Court's decisions in Stovall v. Denno, 388 U.S. 293, 87 S.Ct. 1967, 18 L.Ed.2d 1199 (1967), and Neil v. Biggers, 409 U.S. 188, 93 S.Ct. 375, 34 L.Ed.2d 401 (1972), are particularly implicated.

I.

Jimmy D. Glover, a fulltime trooper of the Connecticut State Police, in 1970 was assigned to the Narcotics Division in an undercover capacity. On May 5 of that year, about 7:45 p. m., e.d.t., and while there was still daylight, Glover and Henry Alton Brown, an informant, went to an apartment building at 201 Westland, in Hartford, for the purpose of purchasing narcotics from "Dickie Boy" Cicero, a known narcotics dealer. Cicero, it was thought, lived on the third floor of that apartment building. Glover and Brown entered the building, observed by backup Officers D'Onofrio and Gaffey, and proceeded by stairs to the third floor. Glover knocked at the door of one of the two apartments served by the stairway.[5] The area was illuminated by natural light from a window in the third floor hallway. The door was opened 12 to 18 inches in response to the knock. Glover observed a man standing at the door and, behind him, a woman. Brown identified himself. Glover then asked for "two things" of narcotics. The man at the door held out his hand, and Glover gave him two $10 bills. The door closed. Soon the man returned and handed Glover two glassine bags.[6] While the door was open, Glover stood within two feet of the person from whom he made the purchase and observed his face. Five to seven minutes elapsed from the time the door first opened until it closed the second time.

Glover and Brown then left the building. This was about eight minutes after their arrival. Glover drove to headquarters where he described the seller to D'Onofrio and Gaffey. Glover at that time did not know the identity of the seller. He described him as being "a colored man, approximately five feet eleven inches tall, dark complexion, black hair, short Afro style, and having high cheekbones, and of heavy build. He was wearing at the time blue pants and a plaid shirt." D'Onofrio, suspecting from this description that respondent might be the seller, obtained a photograph of respondent from the Records Division of the Hartford Police Department. He left it at Glover's office. D'Onofrio was not acquainted with respondent personally but did know him by sight and had seen him "[s]everal times" prior to May 5. Glover, when alone, viewed the photograph for the first time upon his return to headquarters on May 7; he identified the person shown as the one from whom he had purchased the narcotics.

The toxicological report on the contents of the glassine bags revealed the presence of heroin. The report was dated July 16, 1970.

Respondent was arrested on July 27 while visiting at the apartment of a Mrs. Ramsey on the third floor of 201 Westland. This was the apartment at which the narcotics sale had taken place on May 5.[7]

---

5. It appears that the door on which Glover knocked may not have been that of the Cicero apartment. Petitioner concedes, in any event, that the transaction effected "was with some other person than had been intended."

6. This was Glover's testimony. Brown later was called as a witness for the prosecution. He testified on direct examination that, due to his then use of heroin, he had no clear recollection of the details of the incident. On cross-examination, as in an interview with defense counsel the preceding day, he said that it was a woman who opened the door,

received the money, and thereafter produced the narcotics. On redirect, he acknowledged that he was using heroin daily at the time, that he had had some that day, and that there was "an inability to recall and remember events."

7. Respondent testified: "Lots of times I have been there before in that building." He also testified that Mrs. Ramsey was a friend of his wife, that her apartment was the only one in the building he ever visited, and that he and his family, consisting of his wife and five children, did not live there but at 453 Albany Avenue, Hartford.

Respondent was charged, in a two-count information, with possession and sale of heroin * * *. At his trial in January 1971, the photograph from which Glover had identified respondent was received in evidence without objection on the part of the defense. Glover also testified that, although he had not seen respondent in the eight months that had elapsed since the sale, "there [was] no doubt whatsoever" in his mind that the person shown on the photograph was respondent. Glover also made a positive in-court identification without objection.

No explanation was offered by the prosecution for the failure to utilize a photographic array or to conduct a lineup.

Respondent, who took the stand in his own defense, testified that on May 5, the day in question, he had been ill at his Albany Avenue apartment ("a lot of back pains, muscle spasms * * * a bad heart * * * high blood pressure * * * neuralgia in my face, and sinus,") and that at no time on that particular day had he been at 201 Westland. His wife testified that she recalled, after her husband had refreshed her memory, that he was home all day on May 5. Doctor Wesley M. Vietzke, an internist and assistant professor of medicine at the University of Connecticut, testified that respondent had consulted him on April 15, 1970, and that he took a medical history from him, heard his complaints about his back and facial pain, and discovered that he had high blood pressure. The physician found respondent, subjectively, "in great discomfort." Respondent in fact underwent surgery for a herniated disc at L5 and S1 on August 17.

The jury found respondent guilty on both counts of the information. He received a sentence of not less than six nor more than nine years. His conviction was affirmed *per curiam* by the Supreme Court of Connecticut.

Fourteen months later, respondent filed a petition for habeas corpus in the United States District Court for the District of Connecticut. He alleged that the admission of the identification testimony at his state trial deprived him of due process of law to which he was entitled under the Fourteenth Amendment. The District Court * * * dismissed respondent's petition. On appeal, the United States Court of Appeals for the Second Circuit reversed [and ordered relief granted].

In brief summary, the court felt that evidence as to the photograph should have been excluded, regardless of reliability, because the examination of the single photograph was unnecessary and suggestive. And, in the court's view, the evidence was unreliable in any event. We granted certiorari.

* * *

IV.

Petitioner at the outset acknowledges that "the procedure in the instant case was suggestive [because only one photograph was used] and unnecessary" [because there was no emergency or exigent circumstance]. The respondent, in agreement with the Court of Appeals, proposes a *per se* rule of exclusion that he claims is dictated by the demands of the Fourteenth Amendment's guarantee of due process. He rightly observes that this is the first case in which this Court has had occasion to rule upon strictly post-*Stovall* out-of-court identification evidence of the challenged kind.

[In *Biggers*, the victim had identified the defendant at a one-on-one showup conducted before the Supreme Court's decision in *Stovall*. The "central question," *Biggers* indicated, "was whether under the 'totality of the circumstances' the identification was reliable even though the confrontation procedure was suggestive." Since the testimony presented "no substantial likelihood of misidentification," that testimony was properly admitted into evidence. The question now before the Court is whether a stricter standard should be applied where the identification procedure was conducted after the Court's decision in *Stovall*.]

[T]he Courts of Appeals appear to have developed at least two approaches to such evidence. The first, or *per se* approach, employed by the Second Circuit in the present case, focuses on the procedures employed and requires exclusion of the out-of-court identification evidence, without regard to reliability, whenever it has been obtained through unnecessarily suggest[ive] confrontation procedures.[8] The justifications advanced are the elimination of evidence of uncertain reliability, deterrence of the police and prosecutors, and the stated "fair assurance against the awful risks of misidentification."

The second, or more lenient, approach is one that continues to rely on the totality of the circumstances. It permits the admission of the confrontation evidence if, despite the suggestive aspect, the out-of-court identification possesses certain features of reliability. Its adherents feel that the *per se* approach is not mandated by the Due Process Clause of the Fourteenth Amendment. This second approach, in contrast to the other, is ad hoc and serves to limit the societal costs imposed by a sanction that excludes relevant evidence from consideration and evaluation by the trier of fact.

* * *

The respondent here stresses * * * the need for deterrence of improper identification practice, a factor he regards as preeminent. Photographic identification, it is said, continues to be needlessly employed. He notes that the legislative regulation "the Court had hoped [United States v. Wade, 388 U.S. 218, 239, 87 S.Ct. 1926, 1938–1939, 18 L.Ed.2d 1149 (1967),] would engender," has not been forthcoming. He argues that a totality rule cannot be expected to have a significant deterrent impact; only a strict rule of exclusion will have direct and immediate impact on law enforcement agents. Identification evidence is so convincing to the jury that sweeping exclusionary rules are required. Fairness of the trial is threatened by suggestive confrontation evidence, and thus, it is said, an exclusionary rule has an established constitutional predicate.

---

8. Although the *per se* approach demands the exclusion of testimony concerning unnecessarily suggestive identifications, it does permit the admission of testimony concerning a subsequent identification, including an in-court identification, if the subsequent identification is determined to be reliable. The totality approach, in contrast, is simpler: if the challenged identification is reliable, then testimony as to it and any identification in its wake is admissible.

There are, of course, several interests to be considered and taken into account. The driving force behind United States v. Wade, 388 U.S. 218, 87 S.Ct. 1926, 18 L.Ed.2d 1149 (1967), Gilbert v. California, 388 U.S. 263, 87 S.Ct. 1951, 18 L.Ed.2d 1178 (1967) (right to counsel at a postindictment lineup), and *Stovall*, all decided on the same day, was the Court's concern with the problems of eyewitness identification. Usually the witness must testify about an encounter with a total stranger under circumstances of emergency or emotional stress. The witness' recollection of the stranger can be distorted easily by the circumstances or by later actions of the police. Thus, *Wade* and its companion cases reflect the concern that the jury not hear eyewitness testimony unless that evidence has aspects of reliability. It must be observed that both approaches before us are responsive to this concern. The *per se* rule, however, goes too far since its application automatically and peremptorily, and without consideration of alleviating factors, keeps evidence from the jury that is reliable and relevant.

The second factor is deterrence. Although the *per se* approach has the more significant deterrent effect, the totality approach also has an influence on police behavior. The police will guard against unnecessarily suggestive procedures under the totality rule, as well as the *per se* one, for fear that their actions will lead to the exclusion of identifications as unreliable.

The third factor is the effect on the administration of justice. Here the *per se* approach suffers serious drawbacks. Since it denies the trier reliable evidence, it may result, on occasion, in the guilty going free. Also, because of its rigidity, the *per se* approach may make error by the trial judge more likely than the totality approach. And in those cases in which the admission of identification evidence is error under the *per se* approach but not under the totality approach—cases in which the identification is reliable despite an unnecessarily suggestive identification procedure—reversal is a Draconian sanction.[9] Certainly, inflexible rules of exclusion that may frustrate rather than promote justice have not been viewed recently by this Court with unlimited enthusiasm.

We therefore conclude that reliability is the linchpin in determining the admissibility of identification testimony * * *. The factors to be considered * * * include the opportunity of the witness to view the criminal at the time of the crime, the witness' degree of attention, the accuracy of his prior description of the criminal, the level of certainty demonstrated at the confrontation, and the time between the crime and the confrontation. Against these factors is to be weighed the corrupting effect of the suggestive identification itself.

V.

We turn, then, to the facts of this case and apply the analysis:

9. Unlike a warrantless search, a suggestive preindictment identification procedure does not in itself intrude upon a constitutionally protected interest. Thus, considerations urging the exclusion of evidence deriving from a constitutional violation do not bear on the instant problem.

1.   The opportunity to view. Glover testified that for two to three minutes he stood at the apartment door, within two feet of the respondent. The door opened twice, and each time the man stood at the door. The moments passed, the conversation took place, and payment was made. Glover looked directly at his vendor. It was near sunset, to be sure, but the sun had not yet set, so it was not dark or even dusk or twilight. Natural light from outside entered the hallway through a window. There was natural light, as well, from inside the apartment.

2.   The degree of attention. Glover was not a casual or passing observer, as is so often the case with eyewitness identification. Trooper Glover was a trained police officer on duty—and specialized and dangerous duty—when he called at the third floor of 201 Westland in Hartford on May 5, 1970. Glover himself was a Negro and unlikely to perceive only general features of "hundreds of Hartford black males," as the Court of Appeals stated. It is true that Glover's duty was that of ferreting out narcotics offenders and that he would be expected in his work to produce results. But it is also true that, as a specially trained, assigned, and experienced officer, he could be expected to pay scrupulous attention to detail, for he knew that subsequently he would have to find and arrest his vendor. In addition, he knew that his claimed observations would be subject later to close scrutiny and examination at any trial.

3.   The accuracy of the description. Glover's description was given to D'Onofrio within minutes after the transaction. It included the vendor's race, his height, his build, the color and style of his hair, and the high cheekbone facial feature. It also included clothing the vendor wore. No claim has been made that respondent did not possess the physical characteristics so described. D'Onofrio reacted positively at once. Two days later, when Glover was alone, he viewed the photograph D'Onofrio produced and identified its subject as the narcotics seller.

4.   The witness' level of certainty. There is no dispute that the photograph in question was that of respondent. Glover, in response to a question whether the photograph was that of the person from whom he made the purchase, testified: "There is no question whatsoever." This positive assurance was repeated.

5.   The time between the crime and the confrontation. Glover's description of his vendor was given to D'Onofrio within minutes of the crime. The photographic identification took place only two days later. We do not have here the passage of weeks or months between the crime and the viewing of the photograph.

These indicators of Glover's ability to make an accurate identification are hardly outweighed by the corrupting effect of the challenged identification itself. Although identifications arising from single-photograph displays may be viewed in general with suspicion, we find in the instant case little pressure on the witness to acquiesce in the suggestion that such a display entails. D'Onofrio had left the photograph at Glover's office and was not present when Glover first viewed it two days after the event. There thus was little urgency and Glover could view the photograph at his leisure. And since Glover examined the photograph alone, there was no coercive pressure to make an identification arising from the presence of another. The identification was made in circumstances allowing care and reflection.

Although it plays no part in our analysis, all this assurance as to the reliability of the identification is hardly undermined by the facts that respondent was arrested in the very apartment where the sale had taken place, and that he acknowledged his frequent visits to that apartment.

Surely, we cannot say that under all the circumstances of this case there is "a very substantial likelihood of irreparable misidentification." Short of that point, such evidence is for the jury to weigh. We are content to rely upon the good sense and judgment of American juries, for evidence with some element of untrustworthiness is customary grist for the jury mill. Juries are not so susceptible that they cannot measure intelligently the weight of identification testimony that has some questionable feature.

Of course, it would have been better had D'Onofrio presented Glover with a photographic array including "so far as practicable * * * a reasonable number of persons similar to any person then suspected whose likeness is included in the array." The use of that procedure would have enhanced the force of the identification at trial and would have avoided the risk that the evidence would be excluded as unreliable. But we are not disposed to view D'Onofrio's failure as one of constitutional dimension to be enforced by a rigorous and unbending exclusionary rule. The defect, if there be one, goes to weight and not to substance. * * *

The judgment of the Court of Appeals is reversed.

It is so ordered.

■ MR. JUSTICE MARSHALL, with whom MR. JUSTICE BRENNAN joins, dissenting.

Today's decision can come as no surprise to those who have been watching the Court dismantle the protections against mistaken eyewitness testimony erected a decade ago * * * .

* * *

[I]n determining the admissibility of the * * * identification in this case, the Court considers two alternatives, a *per se* exclusionary rule and a totality-of-the circumstances approach. The Court weighs three factors in deciding that the totality approach * * * should be applied. In my view, the Court wrongly evaluates the impact of these factors.

First, the Court acknowledges that one of the factors, deterrence of police use of unnecessarily suggestive identification procedures, favors the *per se* rule. Indeed, it does so heavily, for such a rule would make it unquestionably clear to the police they must never use a suggestive procedure when a fairer alternative is available. I have no doubt that conduct would quickly conform to the rule.

Second, the Court gives passing consideration to the dangers of eyewitness identification recognized in the *Wade* trilogy. It concludes, however, that the grave risk of error does not justify adoption of the *per se* approach because that would too often result in exclusion of relevant evidence. In my view, this conclusion totally ignores the lessons of *Wade*. The dangers of mistaken identification are, as *Stovall* held, simply too great to permit unnecessarily suggestive identifications. * * * [T]he Court's opinion today points to [no] contrary empirical evidence. Studies since *Wade* have only reinforced the validity of its assessment of the dangers of identification testimony. While the Court is "content to rely on the good sense and judgment of American juries," the impetus for *Stovall* and *Wade* was repeated miscarriages of justice resulting from juries' willingness to credit inaccurate eyewitness testimony.

Finally, the Court errs in its assessment of the relative impact of the two approaches on the administration of justice. The Court relies most heavily on this factor, finding that "reversal is a Draconian sanction" in cases where the identification is reliable despite an unnecessarily suggestive procedure used to obtain it. Relying on little more than a strong distaste for "inflexible rules of exclusion," the Court rejects the *per se* test. * * *

[I]mpermissibly suggestive identifications are not merely worthless law enforcement tools. They pose a grave threat to society at large in a more direct way than most governmental disobedience of the law. For if the police and the public erroneously conclude, on the basis of an unnecessarily suggestive confrontation, that the right man has been caught and convicted, the real outlaw must still remain at large. Law enforcement has failed in its primary function and has left society unprotected from the depredations of an active criminal.

For these reasons, I conclude that adoption of the *per se* rule would enhance, rather than detract from, the effective administration of justice. In my view, the Court's totality test will allow seriously unreliable and misleading evidence to be put before juries. Equally important, it will allow dangerous criminals to remain on the streets while citizens assume that police action has given them protection. According to my calculus, all three of the factors upon which the Court relies point to acceptance of the *per se* approach.

* * *

Since I [believe that a *per se* approach] should govern this case, but that even if it does not, the facts here reveal a substantial likelihood of misidentification in violation of respondent's right to due process of law, I would affirm the grant of habeas corpus relief. Accordingly, I dissent from the Court's reinstatement of respondent's conviction.

NOTE: INDEPENDENT SOURCE

If a witness identifies a defendant at a pretrial procedure found unconstitutionally suggestive, does the independent source analysis used in the right to counsel cases apply? May the prosecution nevertheless introduce in-court identification testimony if it persuades the judge by clear and convincing evidence that this testimony would have an "independent source"—that is, that the testimony would be untainted by the defective procedure? In Foster v. California, 394 U.S. 440, 89 S.Ct. 1127, 22 L.Ed.2d 402 (1969), discussed in the Editors' Introduction to this section, Justice Black, dissenting, found the Court's case law ambiguous on that point.

Arguably the Court's post-*Foster* cases resolve Justice Black's concern indirectly. *Braithwaite* approved *Biggers'* analysis in which testimony concerning an out-of-court identification made at an impermissibly suggestive procedure is admissible if it presents "no substantial likelihood of misidentification." In contrast, where a case involves an in-court identification by a witness who made an identification of the defendant at an impermissibly suggestive pretrial procedure, the testimony is admissible if it presents "no substantial likelihood of *irreparable* misidentification." Simmons v. United States, 390 U.S. 377, 384, 88 S.Ct. 967, 971, 19 L.Ed.2d 1247, 1253 (1968) (emphasis supplied). This focus upon irreparable misidentification arguably leaves open the possibility that events between an inadmissible out-of-court identification and a later in-court identification might so reduce the risk of unreliability as to make the in-court identification testimony admissible although testimony regarding the out-of-court identification remains inadmissible.

Where the prosecution presents in-court identification testimony by a witness who identified the defendant at a unconstitutionally suggestive pretrial procedure, in other words, the issue is not independent source. Rather, it is whether the unnecessarily suggestive pretrial identification procedure gave rise to a substantial likelihood of *irreparable* misidentification.

B. EVIDENTIARY AND PROCEDURAL SAFEGUARDS AGAINST UNRELIABLE EYEWITNESS TESTIMONY

EDITORS' INTRODUCTION: EXPERT TESTIMONY AND JURY INSTRUCTIONS AS SAFEGUARDS AGAINST MISTAKEN EYEWITNESSES

Critics of the law's traditional assumption that jurors are inclined and able to evaluate the credibility of eyewitness identification testimony have proposed two means of encouraging more critical consideration of the weight given such testimony. One is the admission of expert testimony designed to assist jurors in identifying factors suggesting eyewitness testimony in general, or the testimony of a specific eyewitness in particular, is accurate and reliable. A second is a jury instruction on the credibility of eyewitness testimony and perhaps suggesting to the jurors how they might evaluate a testifying eyewitness's credibility.

Expert Testimony

Most and perhaps all jurisdictions now at least *permit* trial judges to admit expert testimony on this subject. In State v. Schutz, 579 N.W.2d 317 (Iowa 1998), the Iowa Supreme Court concluded Iowa was the only jurisdiction with a blanket prohibition against the use of expert testimony relating to the accuracy of eyewitness identification. Convinced its rule was no longer sound, the court embraced the majority position: "The exclusion of expert testimony is a matter committed to the sound discretion of the trial court and we will reverse only for an abuse of that discretion."

Some argue expert testimony is often or perhaps always unnecessary— since it conveys only what jurors already know from common sense—and unhelpful—since explanation of the mechanisms identified by research "may be of academic interest, but it is of little aid to the jury in judging reliability of the particular eye witness identification before them." *Schutz,* 579 N.W.2d at 321 (Carter, J., dissenting). Lichael R. Leippe, The Case for

Expert Testimony About Eyewitness Memory, 1 Psychol. Pub. Pol'y & L. 909, 922 (1995), however, suggested the strongest objection to the use of expert testimony is its potential for being affirmatively harmful. Such testimony "may prejudice jurors against the eyewitness rather than compel them to carefully apply new knowledge in their own evaluation of the eyewitness may be the strongest objection to such testimony."

Under the general discretionary approach adopted in *Schutz*, appellate courts have been reluctant to hold trial judges who excluded expert testimony abused their discretion in doing so. See United States v. Hall, 165 F.3rd 1095, 1104 (7th Cir.1999) (reaffirming rule that trial court has discretion on expert testimony related to eyewitness identification, and finding no error in excluding testimony in case before the court). Perhaps as a result of the lack of appellate reversals trial judges are too quick to reject such testimony. One appellate court observed in an analagous situation:

> [W]e conclude the trial judge did not abuse his discretion in declining to give the * * * identification instruction.
>
> It deserves mention, however, that the judge * * * was quick, once the Commonwealth objected, to place weight on the circumstance that no Massachusetts case had yet required such an instruction. That is so, but * * * such an instruction ought not to be the target for automatic rejection by * * * a trial judge, or, put another way, a judge should consider a request for such an instruction with a measure of favorable inclination to grant it.

Commonwealth v. Jean–Jacques, 47 Mass.App. 909, 910–11, 712 N.E.2d 1150, 1151–52 (1999).

The hostility of some trial judges to such testimony may be due to their perception that the substance of testimony offered in particular cases renders it unhelpful. Some courts, upholding trial judges' exclusion of expert testimony, have expressed frustration at experts' inability or unwillingness to offer well-based testimony regarding the likelihood that specific eyewitness identification testimony is inaccurate. Experts may even be unwilling to offer opinions concerning the specific factors—which *generally* reduce reliability—affecting the testimony in particular cases. In Jordan v. State, 950 S.W.2d 210, 212 (Tex.App.—Fort Worth 1997, pet. ref'd), for example, the expert—a Dr. Finn—offered to testify to a variety of factors research showed reduced the accuracy of eyewitness identification, such as weapon focus, confabulation, and memory hardening. But, the court noted:

> When asked whether he could testify with any reasonable degree of scientific certainty whether [these] factors * * * influence[d] an identification, Dr. Finn responded: "All I can say, as a scientist, or somebody who talks to scientists, these are processes that operate in normal human processes to a greater or lesser degree. How much they operate in this case, I can't say."

In State v. McClendon, 248 Conn. 572, 587, 730 A.2d 1107, 1115 (1999), the expert testified to several areas of scientific inquiry concerning eyewitness identification. Nevertheless, the court complained, he refused to give an opinion regarding what the scientific inquiries suggested about the specific facts of the case to a "reasonable degree of scientific certainty." He admitted, the court noted critically, "that 'we don't always know what factors are influencing' an eyewitness. He conceded that a controversy existed in the area of the statistical probability of false identification, the one kind of information inaccessible to the average juror."

On the other hand, some courts regard as inappropriate expert testimony concerning specific identifications. In Currie v. Commonwealth, 30 Va.App. 58, 63, 515 S.E.2d 335, 338 (1999), for example, the trial judge admitted some testimony by a defense expert but ruled further: "Defendant's expert will not be allowed to testify as to the specific identification in this case as to its reliability nor as to its validity. Such testimony would usurp the function of the jury to determine the credibility of witnesses."

Experts declining to address the factors influencing particular eyewitnesses may be conscientiously respecting the research's results. Elizabeth F. Loftus and James M. Doyle, Eyewitness Testimony: Civil and Criminal 307 (1997), suggested "the inherently probabalistic nature of psychological knowledge" means that it is questionable whether that knowledge can ever be used "in directly assessing an eyewitness account of a specific event."

If the nature of psychological knowledge means that experts cannot scientifically assess the accuracy of a specific eyewitness's account of a particular event, is the research and expert testimony based on it of insufficient assistance to jurors to justify its use in litigation? Perhaps such testimony will not assist jurors in identifying eyewitness testimony that should be disregarded but rather will make jurors so skeptical of *all* eyewitness identification testimony that they will unjustifiably disregard or discount even reliable testimony of this sort. Leippe, at 912. Whether this result is acceptable or not, of course, depends upon whether the dangers of inaccuracy affect most or at least a sufficient proportion of eyewitness identifications. Many courts assume that the research does not cast doubt upon the traditional assumption that most or nearly all eyewitness identification testimony is accurate and reliable. Thus, the law's objective should be to assist jurors in identifying the very few exceptional situations in which this testimony should be discounted or disregarded. If this assumption is still supportable, the law most likely should not permit use of expert testimony encouraging jurors to discredit all or most eyewitness testimony.

Jury Instructions

Another means by which jurors' ability and inclination to identify and discount unreliable eyewitness identification may be stimulated and facilitated is the giving of a cautionary jury instruction. A typical instruction of this sort, based on a model offered in United States v. Telfaire, 469 F.2d 552 (D.C.Cir.1972) (per curiam), was set out in People v. Ochoa, 19 Cal.4th 353, 425 n. 5, 966 P.2d 442, 486 n. 5, 79 Cal.Rptr.4th 408, 452 n. 5 (1998):

> "Eyewitness testimony has been received in this trial for the purpose of identifying the defendant as the perpetrator of the crimes charged. In determining the weight to be given eyewitness identification testimony, you should consider the believability of the eyewitness as well as other factors which bear upon the accuracy of the witness'

identification of the defendant, including, but not limited to, any of the following:

"The opportunity of the witness to observe the alleged criminal act and the perpetrator of the act;

"The stress, if any, to which the witness was subjected at the time of the observation;

"The witness' ability, following the observation, to provide a description of the perpetrator of the act;

"The extent to which the defendant either fits or does not fit the description of the perpetrator previously given by the witness;

"The cross-racial or ethnic nature of the identification;

"The witness' capacity to make an identification;

"Evidence relating to the witness' ability to identify other alleged perpetrators of the criminal act;

"Whether the witness was able to identify the alleged perpetrator in a photographic or physical lineup;

"The period of time between the alleged criminal act and the witness' identification;

"Whether the witness had prior contacts with the alleged perpetrator;

"The extent to which the witness is either certain or uncertain of the identification;

"Whether the witness' identification is in fact the product of his own recollection;

"Any other evidence relating to the witness' ability to make an identification."

At least one court, persuaded by the research discussed earlier in this chapter, disapproved of any suggestion in such an instruction that the degree of the witness's certainty should be considered as bearing upon the reliability of the witness's identification. See Commonwealth v. Santoli, 424 Mass. 837, 841–45, 680 N.E.2d 1116, 1181–21 (1997).

The Maryland court considered a proposed instruction which "sets forth the factors that the jury should consider in evaluating the identification testimony, advises the jury that identification of the defendant by a single eyewitness is sufficient to convict, informs the jury that the State bears the burden of proof, and cautions the jury to 'examine the identification of the defendant with great care.' " It addressed the variety of views courts have taken:

The appropriateness of such an instruction is generally unsettled among the various jurisdictions. * * *

Some courts have suggested that an identification instruction is mandatory if eyewitness testimony is the only evidence of the identity of the criminal actor or if the reliability of the identification testimony is in doubt. The leading case advocating this approach is United States v. Telfaire, 469 F.2d 552 (D.C.Cir.1972) * * *.

* * *

Proponents of the *Telfaire* approach emphasize that eyewitness identifications are perhaps less reliable than the average juror appreciates, and consider a cautionary instruction necessary to minimize the risk of erroneous convictions. * * *

Other jurisdictions have expressly rejected *Telfaire*-like instructions, however, based on the conclusion that eyewitness identification instructions amount to an impermissible judicial comment on the evidence or places an improper emphasis on eyewitness testimony * * *.

We concur with those courts that have declined to adopt either of the rigid rules on the appropriateness of an identification instruction, and have instead held that the decision as to whether to give such an instruction lies within the sound discretion of the trial court.

Gunning v. State, 347 Md. 332, 340–45, 701 A.2d 374, 378–80 (1997). This view—that trial judges have discretion to give or not give such instructions—is probably the majority approach. See State v. Chinn 85 Ohio St.3d 548, 574–75, 709 N.E.2d 1166, 1187 (1999) (whether to give a *Telfaire* instruction "is a matter committed to the sound discretion of the trial court"). Compare, however, State v. Maestas, 984 P.2d 376 (Utah 1999), in which the Utah Supreme Court reaffirmed its holding in State v. Long, 721 P.2d 483, 488–92 (Utah 1986), that, if requested, a trial court *must* give a cautionary eyewitness identification instruction in every case where identification is a central issue.

Generally, jury instructions on matters such as eyewitness testimony are relatively neutral and simply suggest factors that jurors may consider. Judge Frank H. Easterbrook of the United States Court of Appeals for the Seventh Circuit suggested trial judges might make more vigorous and creative use of jury instructions on such matters rather than relying upon potentially conflicting experts on a case-by-case basis:

[A] judge, recognizing the main conclusions of the scholarly study of memory—that "accuracy of recollection decreases at a geometric rather than arithmetic rate (so passage of time has a highly distorting effect on recollection); accuracy of recollection is not highly correlated with the recollector's confidence; and memory is highly suggestible—people are easily 'reminded' of events that never happened, and having been 'reminded' may thereafter hold the false recollection as tenaciously as they would a true one"—could block a lawyer from arguing that a given witness is sure of his recollection, and therefore is more likely to be right. The judge could inform jurors of the rapid decrease of accurate recollection, and the problem of suggestibility, without encountering the delay and pitfalls of expert testimony. Jurors are more likely to accept that information coming from a judge than from a scholar, whose skills do not lie in the ability to persuade lay jurors (and whose fidgeting on the stand, an unusual place for a genuine scholar, is apt to be misunderstood). Altogether it is much better for judges to incorporate scientific knowledge about the trial process into that process, rather than to make the subject a debatable issue in every case.

United States v. Hall, 165 F.3d 1095, 1120 (7th Cir.1999) (Easterbrook, J., concurring).

* * *

The decision following addresses the need for a jury instruction on a subaspect of eyewitness reliability, and the relationship between expert testimony and propriety of a jury instruction concerning it.

State v. Cromedy

Supreme Court of New Jersey, 1999.
158 N.J. 112, 727 A.2d 457.

■ COLEMAN, J.

* * *

The novel issue presented [in this appeal] is whether a cross-racial identification jury instruction should be required in certain cases. * * *

I

On the night of August 28, 1992, D.S., a white female student then enrolled at Rutgers University in New Brunswick, was watching television in her basement apartment. While she was relaxing on the couch, an African–American male entered the brightly-lit apartment and demanded money from D.S., claiming that he was wanted for murder and that he needed funds to get to New York. After D.S. told the intruder that she had no money, he spotted her purse, rifled through it, and removed money and credit cards.

The intruder then placed his hand on D.S.'s leg, demanded that she be quiet and closed the window blinds. He led her by the arm into the brightly-lit kitchen and ordered her to remove her shorts. The intruder then vaginally penetrated D.S. from behind. Throughout the sexual assault, D.S. was facing the kitchen door with her eyes closed and hand over her mouth to avoid crying loudly.

Once the assault was over, D.S. faced her attacker who, after threatening her again, turned around and left the apartment. At the time of the second threat, D.S. was standing approximately two feet away from her assailant. The attacker made no attempt to conceal his face at any time. D.S. immediately called the New Brunswick Police Department after the intruder left the apartment.

The police dusted for fingerprints and took D.S.'s initial statement. D.S. described her assailant as an African–American male in his late 20's to early 30's, full-faced, about five feet five inches tall, with a medium build, mustache, and unkempt hair. She stated that the intruder was wearing a dirty gray button-down short-sleeved shirt, blue warm-up pants with white and red stripes, and a Giants logo on the left leg. D.S. was then taken to Roosevelt Hospital where rape samples were taken.

The next day, D.S. made a formal statement to the police in which she again described the intruder. Three days later, a composite sketch was drawn by an artist with her assistance. The following day at police headquarters, D.S. was shown many slides and photographs, including a photograph of defendant, in an unsuccessful attempt to identify her assailant.

On April 7, 1993, almost eight months after the crimes were committed, D.S. saw an African–American male across the street from her who she thought was her attacker. She spotted the man while she was standing on the corner of a street in New Brunswick waiting for the light to change. As the two passed on the street, D.S. studied the individual's face and gait. Believing that the man was her attacker, D.S. ran home and telephoned the police, giving them a description of the man she had just seen. Defendant was picked up by the New Brunswick police and taken to headquarters almost immediately.

Within fifteen minutes after seeing defendant on the street, D.S. viewed defendant in a "show-up" from behind a one-way mirror and immediately identified him as the man she had just seen on the street and as her attacker. Defendant was then arrested and, with his consent, saliva and blood samples were taken for scientific analysis.

No forensic evidence linking defendant to the offenses was presented during the trial. The police did not lift any fingerprints belonging to defendant from the apartment. D.S.'s Rape Crisis Intervention Kit, processed by the Middlesex County Rape Crisis Center at Roosevelt Hospital, was submitted to the New Jersey State Police Chemistry Biology Laboratory in Sea Girt for analysis. Testing of the victim's blood revealed that she was a secretor, meaning that she falls within the eighty percent of the population that secretes their blood type in all of their bodily fluids. When defendant's blood and saliva were tested by the same laboratory, it was determined that both the victim and defendant have type "A" blood, but defendant was found to be a non-secretor. That meant that although the rape kit revealed the presence of seminal fluid and spermatozoa, the specimens received from defendant could not be compared with the semen and spermatozoa found on the victim. In other words, the genetic markers found in the semen and spermatozoa could not be said to have come from defendant because he is a non-secretor. On the other hand, the genetic markers were consistent with the victim, who is a secretor.

[D]efense counsel sought a cross-racial identification jury charge. The following language was proposed:

> [Y]ou know that the identifying witness is of a different race than the defendant. When a witness who is a member of one race identifies a member who is of another race we say there has been a cross-racial identification. You may consider, if you think it is appropriate to do so, whether the cross-racial nature of the identification has affected the accuracy of the witness's original perception and/or accuracy of a subsequent identification.

In support of that request, defendant cited the June 1992 New Jersey Supreme Court Task Force on Minority Concerns Final Report, 131 N.J.L.J. 1145 (1992) (Task Force Report).

The trial court denied the request * * [and] instead provided the jury with the Model Jury Charge on Identification. The jury convicted defendant * * *. [The conviction was affirmed on appeal to the Appellate Division.]

* * *

II

Defendant argues that the trial court committed reversible error in denying his request for a cross-racial identification charge. He maintains that cross-racial impairment of eyewitnesses "is a scientifically accepted fact," and that the courts of this State can take judicial notice of the fallibility of trans-racial identifications and approve the report of the Task Force that recommended adoption of a cross-racial identification jury charge. Defendant argues that expert testimony is not a necessary factual predicate for such a jury charge. Alternatively, defendant argues that if the Court should require an expert to testify regarding factors that affect the reliability of eyewitness identification, and cross-racial identification specifically, we should remand the case to the trial court to afford him an opportunity to present that evidence.

The State argues that the trial court properly rejected defendant's request for a cross-racial identification charge. The State maintains that there is no consensus within the scientific community that an "own-race" bias exists. The State argues that because some researchers do not know whether cross-racial impairment affects "real life" identifications, and because even some of the scientists who believe that cross-racial impairment does affect identification cannot say what factors influence a person's ability to identify correctly a member of another race, the Court should reject a cross-racial identification charge. Alternatively, the State argues that this Court should not adopt a cross-racial charge until there is general acceptance that cross-racial impairment exists and general agreement on what factors influence a person's ability to correctly identify a member of another race.

A

A cross-racial identification occurs when an eyewitness is asked to identify a person of another race. The reliability of such an identification, though discussed in many cases throughout the country, is an issue of first impression in New Jersey. Because defendant requested a cross-racial identification jury charge, he bore the burden of showing that a reliable basis existed to support the requested charge. Defendant relied on common knowledge, the Task Force Report, and judicial notice to support his request. Rather than calling an expert to testify regarding the factors that may make some cross-racial eyewitness identifications unreliable, defendant maintained that an expert would not aid the jury. In this context, we must decide whether a cross-racial jury instruction should be required where scientific evidence demonstrating the need for a specific instruction has not been presented.

B

For more than forty years, empirical studies concerning the psychological factors affecting eyewitness cross-racial or cross-ethnic identifications have appeared with increasing frequency in professional literature of the behavioral and social sciences. [Some studies] have concluded that eyewitnesses are superior at identifying persons of their own race and have difficulty identifying members of another race. This phenomenon has been dubbed the "own-race" effect or "own-race" bias. Its corollary is that eyewitnesses experience a "cross-racial impairment" when identifying members of another race. Studies have consistently shown that the "own-race effect" is "strongest when white witnesses attempt to recognize black subjects."

Although researchers generally agree that some eyewitnesses exhibit an own-race bias, they disagree about the degree to which own-race bias affects identification. In one study, African–American and white "customers" browsed in a convenience store for a few minutes and then went to the register to pay. Researchers asked the convenience store clerks to identify the "customers" from a photo array. The white clerks were able to identify 53.2% of the white customers but only 40.4% of the African–American subjects. The overall accuracy rate for all participants was only 44.2%. Similar studies have found that own-race bias exists to a lesser degree. A snap-shot of the literature reveals that although many scientists agree that witnesses are better at identifying suspects of their own race, they cannot agree on the extent to which cross-racial impairment affects identification.

* * *

Many studies on cross-racial impairment involve subjects observing photographs for a few seconds. Because the subjects remembered the white faces more often than they recalled the African–American faces, researchers concluded that they were biased towards their own-race. Yet, there is disagreement over whether the results of some of the tests can be generalized to real-world situations in which a victim or witness confronts an assailant face-to-face and experiences the full range of emotions that accompany such a traumatic event.

C

The debate among researchers did not prevent the Supreme Court of the United States, in the famous school desegregation case of Brown v. Board of Education of Topeka, 347 U.S. 483, 494 n. 11, 74 S.Ct. 686, 692 n. 11, 98 L.Ed. 873 (1954), from using behavioral and social sciences to support legal conclusions without requiring that the methodology employed by those scientists have general acceptance in the scientific community. * * * Thus, Brown v. Board of Education is the prototypical example of an appellate court using modern social and behavioral sciences as legislative evidence to support its choice of a rule of law.

In United States v. Telfaire, 469 F.2d 552 (D.C.Cir.1972), Chief Judge Bazelon urged in his concurring opinion that juries be charged on the pitfalls of cross-racial identification. He believed that the cross-racial nature of an identification could affect accuracy in the same way as proximity to the perpetrator and poor lighting conditions. He felt that a meaningful jury instruction would have to apprise jurors of that fact. To achieve that objective, Judge Bazelon proposed the following instruction:

> In this case the identifying witness is of a different race than the defendant. In the experience of many it is more difficult to identify members of a different race than members of one's own. If this is also your own experience, you may consider it in evaluating the witness's testimony. You must also consider, of course, whether there are other factors present in this case which overcome any such difficulty of identification. For example, you may conclude that the witness has had sufficient contacts with members of the defendant's race that he would not have greater difficulty in making a reliable identification.

[Id. at 561 (Bazelon, C.J., concurring).]

Judge Bazelon rejected the notion that instructions on interracial identifications "appeal to racial prejudice." Rather, he believed that an explicit jury instruction would safeguard against improper uses of race by the jury and would delineate the narrow context in which it is appropriate to consider racial differences.

* * *

D

[D]ecisions have been rendered by courts in other jurisdictions. The majority of courts allowing cross-racial identification charges hold that the decision to provide the instruction is a matter within the trial judge's discretion. Omission of such a cautionary instruction has been held to be prejudicial error where identification is the critical or central issue in the case, there is no corroborating evidence, and the circumstances of the case raise doubts concerning the reliability of the identification.

A number of courts have concluded that cross-racial identification simply is not an appropriate topic for jury instruction. Those courts have determined that the cross-racial instruction requires expert guidance, and that cross-examination and summation are adequate safeguards to highlight unreliable identifications.

Other jurisdictions have denied the instruction, finding that the results of empirical studies on cross-racial identification are questionable. See *Telfaire*, supra, 469 F.2d at 561–62 (Leventhal, J., concurring) (rejecting cross-racial instruction because data supporting hypothesis is "meager"). One jurisdiction has even rejected cross-racial identification instructions as improper commentary on "the nature and quality" of the evidence. See State v. Hadrick, 523 A.2d 441, 444 (R.I.1987) (rejecting such instruction in robbery case where victim viewed perpetrator for two to three minutes at close range during robbery and identified him from a line-up).

E

The defense in the present case did not question whether the victim had been sexually assaulted. Rather, the defense asserted that the victim's identification of defendant as the perpetrator was mistaken. It is well-established in this State that when identification is a critical issue in the case, the trial court is obligated to give the jury a discrete and specific instruction that provides appropriate guidelines to focus the jury's attention on how to analyze and consider the trustworthiness of eyewitness identification.

[This]   requires that as a part of an identification charge a trial court inform the jury that the State's case relies on an eyewitness identification of the defendant as the perpetrator, and that in weighing the reliability of that identification the jury should consider, among other things, "the capacity or the ability of the witness to make observations or perceptions . . . at the time and under all of the attendant circumstances for seeing that which he says he saw or that which he says he perceived with regard to his identification." What defendant sought through the requested charge in the present case was an instruction that informed the jury that it could consider the fact that the victim made a cross-racial identification as part of the "attendant circumstances" when evaluating the reliability of the eyewitness identification.

The Court-appointed Task Force discussed and debated the issue of the need for a cross-racial and cross-ethnic identification jury instruction for more than five years. That Task Force was comprised of an appellate judge, trial judges, lawyers representing both the prosecution and defense, social scientists, and ordinary citizens. * * * Task Force sessions were conducted in much the same way as legislative committees conduct hearings on proposed legislation. The Task Force consulted a substantial body of professional literature in the behavioral and social sciences concerning the reliability of cross-racial identifications. Except for the view expressed by a county prosecutor, the Task Force was unanimously convinced that a problem exists respecting cross-racial identifications and that the Court should take corrective action. Ultimately, in 1992 the Task Force submitted its final report to the Court in which it recommended, among other things, that the Court develop a special jury charge regarding the unreliability of cross-racial identifications.

The Court referred that recommendation to the Criminal Practice Committee. The Criminal Practice Committee * * * decided against recommending a charge to the Court. Development of a cross-racial charge was deemed to be premature because the issue of admissibility of evidence to support the charge had not been decided by case law. * * *

F

We reject the State's contention that we should not require a cross-racial identification charge before it has been demonstrated that there is substantial agreement in the relevant scientific community that cross-racial recognition impairment is significant enough to support the need for such a charge. This case does not concern the introduction of scientific evidence to attack the reliability of the eyewitness's identification. Defendant's requested jury instruction was not based upon any "scientific, technical, or other specialized knowledge" to assist the jury. He relied instead on ordinary human experience and the legislative-type findings of the Task Force because the basis for his request did not involve a matter that was beyond the ken of the average juror.

This case requires us to focus on the well-established differences between adjudicative or hard evidence, argument, and jury instructions. The hard evidence revealed a cross-racial identification and the circumstances under which that identification was made. The State argued to the jury that the identification was credible based on the evidence. Counsel for defendant, on the other hand, argued that there was a mistaken identification based on the totality of the circumstances. Defendant requested a cross-racial identification jury instruction that would treat the racial character of the eyewitness identification as one of the factors bearing on its reliability in much the same way as lighting and proximity to the perpetrator at the time of the offense.

A national review of the use of cross-racial identification jury instructions reveals that only a small minority of jurisdictions have declined such an instruction because studies finding unreliability in cross-racial identifications lack general acceptance in the relevant scientific community. The majority of jurisdictions that have rejected the instruction did so based on judicial discretion. Those discretionary rulings were influenced by factors such as the nature and quality of the eyewitness identification, the existence of strong corroborating evidence, the fact that the eyewitness had an adequate opportunity to observe the perpetrator, or a combination of those reasons.

[W]e hold that a cross-racial identification, as a subset of eyewitness identification, requires a special jury instruction in an appropriate case.

Indeed, some courtroom observers have commented that the ordinary person's difficulty of "cross-racial recognition is so commonplace as to be the subject of both cliche and joke: 'they all look alike.'" Although laboratory studies concerning the reliability of cross-racial identifications have not been validated in actual courtroom atmospheres, the results of many of those experiments suggest that "decreased accuracy in the recognition of other-race faces is not within the observer's conscious control, and that seriousness of criminal proceedings would not improve accuracy." Moreover, the stress associated with the courtroom atmosphere, based on human experience, is likely to diminish rather than enhance recognition accuracy.

We embrace [an approach] requiring a cross-racial identification charge under the circumstances of this case despite some differences of opinion among the researchers. Notwithstanding those differences, there is an impressive consistency in results showing that problems exist with cross-racial eyewitness identification. We conclude that the empirical data encapsulate much of the ordinary human experience and provide an appropriate frame of reference for requiring a cross-racial identification jury instruction. Under the jurisprudence of this Court, in a prosecution "in which race by definition is a patent factor[, race] must be taken into account to assure a fair trial." State v. Harris, 156 N.J. 122, 235, 716 A.2d 458 (1998) (Handler, J., dissenting).

At the same time, we recognize that unrestricted use of cross-racial identification instructions could be counter-productive. Consequently, care must be taken to insulate criminal trials from base appeals to racial prejudice. An appropriate jury instruction should carefully delineate the context in which the jury is permitted to consider racial differences. The simple fact pattern of a white victim of a violent crime at the hands of a black assailant would not automatically give rise to the need for a cross-racial identification charge. More is required.

A cross-racial instruction should be given only when, as in the present case, identification is a critical issue in the case, and an eyewitness's cross-racial identification is not corroborated by other evidence giving it independent reliability. Here, the eyewitness identification was critical; yet it was not corroborated by any forensic evidence or other eyewitness account. The circumstances of the case raise some doubt concerning the reliability of the victim's identification in that no positive identification was made for nearly eight months despite attempts within the first five days following the commission of the offenses. Under those circumstances, turning over to the jury the vital question of the reliability of that identification without acquainting the jury with the potential risks associated with such identifications could have affected the jurors' ability to evaluate the reliability of the identification. We conclude, therefore, that it was reversible error not to have given an instruction that informed the jury about the possible significance of the cross-racial identification factor, a factor the jury can observe in many cases with its own eyes, in determining the critical issue—the accuracy of the identification.

For the sake of clarity, we repeat that the purpose of a cross-racial instruction is to alert the jury through a cautionary instruction that it should pay close attention to a possible influence of race. Because of the "widely held commonsense view that members of one race have greater difficulty in accurately identifying members of a different race," *Telfaire*, supra, 469 F.2d at 559 (Bazelon, C.J., concurring), expert testimony on this issue would not assist a jury, and for that reason would be inadmissible. We request the Criminal Practice Committee and the Model Jury Charge Committee to revise the current charge on identification to include an appropriate statement on cross-racial eyewitness identification that is consistent with this opinion.

The judgment of the Appellate Division is reversed. The case is remanded to the Law Division for a new trial.

NOTE

Other courts have looked with more favor on expert testimony concerning cross-racial identifications. In Currie v. Commonwealth, 30 Va.App. 58, 65, 515 S.E.2d 335, 339 (1999), for example, the court noted, with apparent approval, that the trial judge permitted an expert "to testify about the mechanical processes of memory and cross-racial identification because these subjects were not within the common knowledge and experience of the jurors."

*

INDEX

References are to Pages